RUTHERFORD B. HAYES

And His America

RUTHERFORD B. HAYES ABOUT 1845

RUTHERFORD B. HAYES
And His America
by Harry Barnard

NEW YORK / RUSSELL & RUSSELL

Lines on page ix are reprinted from *From Death to Morning* by Thomas Wolfe; used by permission of the publishers, Charles Scribner's Sons.

PRINTED IN THE UNITED STATES OF AMERICA

To Ruth
Wife and Coauthor

"Few are the sons who attain their fathers' stature: and very few surpass them. Most fall short in merit."

—The Odyssey, translated by T. E. Shaw (1932)

"O! Jove! May he be as his father . . . . live a good life and rule powerfully, and some one may say, 'And be better than his father in many things.' "

—The Iliad, translated by R. B. Hayes (1837)

FOREWORD

A short story or piece, very moving, by Thomas Wolfe, included in the volume *From Death to Morning*, is called "The Four Lost Men" —and one of the "lost men" is President Hayes. By "lost" Wolfe meant "forgotten," or possibly "misknown," to use Carlyle's word. An excerpt:

Garfield, Arthur, Harrison, and Hayes, time of my father's time, blood of his blood, life of his life, had been living, real, and actual people in all the passion, power, and feeling of my father's youth. And for me they were the lost Americans: their gravely vacant and bewhiskered faces mixed, melted, swam together in the sea-depths of a past intangible, immeasurable, and unknowable as the buried city of Persepolis. And they were lost. For who was Garfield, martyred man, and who had seen him in the streets of life? Who could believe his footfalls ever sounded on a lonely pavement? Who had heard the casual and familiar tones of Chester Arthur? And where was Harrison? Where was Hayes? Which had the whiskers, which the burnsides: which was which? Were they not lost?

The answer is yes, indeed—and Hayes perhaps most of all, "lost" not only as President but as a man who personified, more than many, his era.

Should Hayes have been forgotten? I do not think so. Of course, as some readers may guess, I have, apparently, a predilection for forgotten figures in American history. This may be a matter of temperament. Or it could be a conviction that frequently more is to be learned, even about supposedly well-known periods in history, from a study of "lost" men (or women) than from a reading and rereading of books, even new ones, about "remembered" figures. Of course, Hayes has not been wholly "lost." But he has been so nearly "lost" that no one would deny that Wolfe was justified in the theme of his story.

A number of questions could be asked as to why Hayes has been so little known, at least until lately. It may be inquired if there has been a carry-over within his own political party, which he helped to found just 100 years ago, of the antagonism that the "stalwarts" of his day felt for him. It is interesting in this connection that as late as 1910, when Boss Platt of New York was feuding with Governor Charles

Evans Hughes because Hughes was somewhat nonpartisan in making appointments, the worst Platt could think of to say about Hughes was that he was "like Hayes." Has Hayes been neglected, or scoffed at, because of a feeling of guilt for much of the doings in the "Gilded Age"? Or have some writers, including Republicans, succumbed to the urge of using RBH as a kind of whipping boy for the purpose of suggesting that, after all, they are "objective"?

Or is it that Hayes has been unfortunate in his biographers? The usual fault, I am sure, has been that too much has been claimed for him or against him. Especially have the admiring biographers claimed too much, both in regard to his personal and his public character, particularly in the matter of ending reconstruction, as it is said. So RBH, the man, has been lost, which seemed to me a pity, since he so strikingly personified the educated, but typical, middle-of-the-road American of his day, the disciple of Webster and Emerson, who thought about and reacted to American problems in pretty much the American way, as boy and man, as soldier in the Civil War, as member of the Reconstruction Congress, as three-time governor of Ohio, as President (after the weirdest election on record), and at the end as a private citizen who championed some social ideas which today might have gotten him denounced as a "dangerous man." In this phase, too, he was typically American, for, though we tend to forget it, the representative American from the beginning always has been considered dangerous by those who fear any kind of change or social progress.

My function has been to try to bring RBH back—to restore him, so to speak, not on a pedestal in some marmoreal pose, nor like the incredible painting of him in the White House, but as he was, a man who, as Wolfe imagined, was "torn, as we have been, by sharp pain and wordless lust, the asp of time, the thorn of spring, the sharp, the tongueless cry," and who sought in his time and in his fashion "new lands, the promise of the war, and glory, joy and triumph, and a shining city." So this is intended not so much as a biography of a President as a biography of a man who happened to become President.

HARRY BARNARD

May 1954

Chicago

CONTENTS

CONTENTS—*Continued*

CHAPTER   PAGE

Book Four
The Young Gentleman

Book Five
The Bachelor of Law

Book Six
Lucy and the Pilgrim's Progress

Book Seven
The "Tall Man"

Book Eight
The Great Lawsuit

CONTENTS—*Continued*

Book Nine
The President

Book Ten
The "Nihilist"

LIST OF ILLUSTRATIONS

BOOK ONE

Sophia and Little Rud's World

"Alas! A widowed life is desolate, cold and cheerless."

—Chloe Smith Hayes in her diary, September 7, 1839

" 'Whom the Lord loveth he chasteneth.' We have more blessings to be thankful for than sorrow to complain of."

—Sophia Hayes to Sardis Birchard, December 4, 1858

CHAPTER I

LONELY LITTLE BOY

1

THE SLENDER little boy with the reddish hair dawdled over his breakfast porridge. For him this was strange. Usually, since the passing of the frailty that had marked his infancy, he was quick and cheerful at meals. Ordinarily, too, the trusting blue eyes were lively, but this morning they were quiet and sad. They saw only a cheerlessness and a barrenness about his house. Everything seemed like a discarded toy—old, shabby and dreary.

His house, of two stories with a brick front, really was a pleasant place. It was not old but new, and better, more genteelly furnished than most of the other dwellings in Delaware, Ohio. It even had— luxury of luxuries in that time—real carpeting, loomed in the East, draperies in the parlor and glass for lights in the windows. It was spacious, with the walls freshly whitewashed just that week end, and pleasantly located on two lots, with an extra lot for a playground.[1]

Warm weather had come abruptly that year. Already the fruit trees in the garden, the peach, the apple, the quince and—in his mother's phrases—the "fine English" cherry, which could be seen through the windows, bloomed "with special exuberance." They made a sight normally pleasing to the boy. But he had no spirit for being delighted. He was not even interested in "poor, affectionate Puss." Sunday morning, May 14, 1826, little Rud Hayes, not yet four, felt lonely.[2]

2

Because it was Sunday, and spring, his mother, Sophia Hayes, planned to take him and his sister Fanny, age six, up to the farm for the hours between services at the Presbyterian meetinghouse. The farm was located several miles north of the town on the east bank of the river. Meandering amiably through the town, not far from Rud's house, this river would be known later as the Olentangy, just as the Indians called it. But at this time it was styled the Whetstone. A few miles south at the new city of Columbus it joined the Scioto River which, further south near Cincinnati, helped to make the Ohio.

Calling it the Whetstone pleased the settlers from Vermont and other parts of New England, who were in the majority in the town. For this reminded them of the stream that flowed into the Connecticut at Brattleboro, Vermont. Especially was the name Whetstone pleasing to Rud's mother, as it had been also to his father, Ruddy Hayes. For that other Whetstone, "the pure stream," as Sophia recalled it, was a nostalgic landmark of their youth. It flowed alongside her husband's family place back in Brattleboro and helped to make it in her memory "O! . . . a sweet spot!" [3]—all the sweeter since Ruddy Hayes was dead. He had died before Rud Hayes was born.

The farm belonged to Sophia—the first purchase of Ohio land made by Ruddy Hayes back in 1817. One of the best fruit-growing places in the whole area, it was now the chief source of her cash income. Several times lately Sophia had turned down good offers for these acres, one for twice what her husband had paid. Everyone agreed she was prudent in not selling this property, though she was thinking just then of disposing of some of her other land holdings, especially "the wild lands" of the Sandusky Plains, up near Bucyrus.[4]

At the farm lived and worked a Pennsylvania Dutch couple, the Van Bremers, with their nine children. They were the Hayes family's tenants. They share-cropped the place, paying as rent one third of all the crops and one half of all the fruit, mainly peaches and apples, these "to be delivered in our barn and house." [5] The Van Bremers each time welcomed Rud, his sister and his mother with warm salutations and much handshaking, followed by happy gossip and jaunts by the youngsters to hunt for quail and turtle eggs, to pick nuts and berries, and to indulge in a dozen other delights.

These expeditions to the farm formed high spots in Rud's life up to then. Especially were they so when made on horseback, instead of in the spring wagon. Sitting on the family mare, with Fanny in front of him and his mother in back of him, Rud felt like some bold warrior described in his best-loved storybooks, those that were filled with tales of knights in armor. A special thrill of the journey itself came from the fording of the river. The splashing sent him and Fanny into squeals of tense laughter each time. "Glorious! glorious!" Except that Rud on that day did not care if he went or not.[6]

3

The trouble was, all the menfolk in Rud's house were gone. Only females were left there with him—his mother, his sister and his

mother's spinster cousin, Arcena Smith, whom he knew as Aunt
Arcena. Of course, he liked them. He liked them a great deal. Most
of the time they were fun.

True, his mother frequently had such a faraway, sad look in her
eyes that even he noticed. Sometimes her hug of him was too hard
and lingering, as if she were reaching for someone else. She was also
overfond of talking to him, in serious tones, of God and heaven and
salvation. He liked better the stories about knights and giants and
cats in boots in his and Fanny's books. When his mother read to him, the
book usually was *Pilgrim's Progress*. Next to the Bible, it was the best
book of all, she assured him, though he could not help but find most
of it dull. But for all that, she was pleasant, even if too watchful over
him, and often they laughed together.[7]

He knew—no boy could have known it more clearly—that he was
loved in his house, by his mother, by Fanny and by Arcena, who "was
always good to sister Fanny and myself . . . so kind." [8] They filled
his world with affection. This love, above everything else, defined his
later character. Though its lavishness would have its perils and its
price, it would give to him the basis for a wonderful inner security
that he finally was to achieve. Even then, as a child, he was grateful
for it. "How I loved them!" he exclaimed as a grownup.[9] But just
then they suffered in his estimation a serious handicap. They wore
petticoats and skirts.

4

There was a time, not so long ago, when he made no distinction of
sex in his feelings about the people in his world. Indeed, he had
identified himself completely with Fanny. He would play at dolls with
her and sit contentedly beside her on his little chair, sewing intently
with thread and needle at a scrap of cloth, while she made a pillow-
case.[10] But this neuter stage in his growth was going. By then he
knew that he was a man-child. He had even become especially conscious of this fact. Instead of playing with dolls, he made a point of
playing at being a soldier. He stuffed his pockets with buckeye nuts,
home-whittled tops, knives and rocks.

He was a friendly person who liked people in general—and always
would be so. There was something appealing and magnetic about his
personality already that attracted people of all kinds, causing women
to wish to mother him and even rough men to pat his head or take

his hand—for example, the boisterous neighbor, Otho Hinton, operator of the Delaware to Columbus stagecoach line.

Nor was this wholly because he was a fatherless boy who made up for being fatherless by being especially friendly toward adults. His marked friendliness was deep in his nature. But it was now mainly directed toward men. He eagerly took in the talk of men. He repeated as well as he could manly stories, and mimicked masculine mannerisms. With no men around that day, and none in prospect, his little world had gone stale.

CHAPTER II

The Endless Search

1

Rud Hayes's life seemed so empty all of a sudden mainly because Sardis Birchard, his uncle, younger brother of his mother and the most important man in his life, was gone. Sardis had ridden off on his mare the previous Wednesday, though yet coughing and "pale and emaciated" from his long siege of illness. Probably he was already riding along the shore of Lake Erie. Unless, that is, he decided after all to sell the horse at Portland (later called Sandusky, Ohio), then take the lake boat to the newly opened Erie Canal for the big part of his trip to Vermont.[1]

Sardis' departure would not have been so crushing for Rud had not the two lodgers also chosen this particular time to be away. Sam Rheem, the honest mason, was on a bricklaying job in a near-by village. He had been a part of the Hayes household even before Rud was born, having been hired by Ruddy Hayes to lay the bricks for the house—then stayed on to live in it. He was as fond of Rud as if he were his own child.[2]

The Welsh lodger, Mr. Wasson—no one called him anything else, not even Arcena, who finally became Mrs. Wasson—also had some business outside of Delaware. He liked to tease Rud by chanting, "Rud! Rud! Look out for the mud!" and Rud enjoyed this and other attempts at humorous play.[3] Neither was half so important to him as Uncle Sardis. But they were men, and his friends, and now they too were gone.

Besides all this, Mr. Hinkle, an itinerant Lutheran preacher, turned out to be a disappointment to Rud. In town to administer the sacrament to other German newcomers, "the Dutch immigrants," as they were called, Mr. Hinkle had arrived on Friday. With very little urging he had stayed overnight at Rud's house, sleeping in one of the absent boarders' beds.[4] Missing the other men, Rud became anxiously attached to Mr. Hinkle. "You must stay here till Uncle Sardis comes back—then you may go home," he told him on Saturday.[5]

Mr. Hinkle would have liked to humor Rud for good reasons of his own. In Delaware Rud's home was a preferred stopping place for unattached preachers of all sects. There they were sure of a cordial welcome, of being listened to attentively and of getting good meals and a bed with a real mattress imported from Vermont. It was better accommodation than at any tavern, and all out of Christian fellowship, at no cost. For Rud's mother liked nothing better than to have long theological discussions with these preachers, who ranged from the "new" Methodist sect to the newer Swedenborgians. Best of all, some were even from New England, as likely as not sent to her house by her own mother's brother, Linus Austin, a Baptist missionary in Vermont.[6] Sophia showed her pleasure over having these visitors by heaping their plates with extra portions of everything, something nearly all, and especially Mr. Hinkle, appreciated. But Mr. Hinkle could not linger.

It was some, but not much, comfort for Rud that another minister, a member of his father's family, the Reverend William Hayes, was expected with his wife that day. For the Reverend Mr. Hayes, a "hardshelled" Presbyterian and chief censor of Granville, Ohio, (which boasted, in this second year of the Presidency of John Quincy Adams, that "the drunkard, the fornicator, the Sabbath-breaker are not to be found here,") reminded Rud of portraits he had seen of angry prophets. He was not at all jolly like Mr. Hinkle.[7] It was no wonder that Rud looked mournfully at the ladies and little girl at the breakfast table, saying, "How can we eat breakfast? All the folks are gone." [8]

2

Predictably his sister Fanny, small for her age, precise and sharp, usually also good-humored but with a sprinkling of spice in her make-up, was derisive. Toward Rud she directed a loud guffaw (something her mother long had been trying to discourage as unladylike). Also she made a grimace calculated to be horrible and terrible to look on, in which department pert little Fanny surpassed any person her little brother knew.[9] Being Fanny, she of course reminded Rud that all the folks were not gone. Even if he did not count their mother and Aunt Arcena, she, Fanny, was there!

To be sure, this Fanny Arabella Hayes was delightful to be with nearly all the time. She thought up wonderful games and other means for entertaining Rud. When Rud remembered the period of his being "a sickly, feeble boy," it was Fanny, more than his mother, who emerged in his mind as his "protector and nurse." Fanny was "loving, kind, and very generous." [10] "Oh, her beautiful character, her winning ways . . . her sweet affections! She loved me as an only sister loves a brother whom she imagines almost perfect, and I loved her as an only brother loves a sister who is perfect." So he later said in summing up his feelings for his sister.[11]

Indeed, in this round and plump little Fanny there then existed the most important single individual in Rud's life ahead. She was a subtle, polarizing force. From her would flow to him many of the strongest of all his impulses and dream materials. She was also a kind of new and refined Chloe Smith Hayes, their father's mother, then still living in Brattleboro, the remarkable woman who, thirty years after her death, captured the imagination of the novelist William D. Howells.[12] Yet Fanny, sparkling and loving as she was, could not then fill in Rud's life the place of a man, especially not the place of Sardis.

Fanny also missed her uncle. But not so much as did Rud. Besides, she had Arcena, with whom she slept and whom she loved dearly. Then, too, at this period Fanny and Sardis did not get along well at all times. She was in a stage when she was "quick tempered and obstinate with grown persons," and especially so with Sardis. Rud remembered: "To tease her, Uncle Sardis would put her on the mantel-piece, and tell her she must stay there until she asked him to take her down. This she would not do, but sitting perfectly upright to avoid falling, her face flushed with anger, she would bid him defiance —and rarely if ever give up." [13] They had had such a set-to just before Sardis left. The incident had upset Rud, exciting incomprehensible uneasiness in him. It distressed him to see Sardis, above everyone, attacked, as he interpreted Fanny's conduct. For his loyalty to Sardis was that of a boy to a father, and this was also why he missed his uncle so greatly.

3

Rud, whether he consciously realized it or not, felt a need for a father. In truth, as a psychological matter, much of his life was to be an endless search—for a father. It would be a search without end until he attained a status whereby, in a manner of speaking, he himself would stand in the image of a towering father figure, surpassing all his father figures. In large part, this search tended to shape him into the friendly, trusting person, who "would willingly hurt the feelings of no one," as he himself was to say.[14] Because he was so, he always would attract many substitute fathers.

But of all these substitutes, warmly human, earthy, lanky Sardis Birchard, now away, was the most satisfying that Rud ever would find in his search. Without Sardis Birchard Rud's life ahead would not have been the same. If not for Sardis, Rud might well have been ruined by Sophia and Fanny, all unknowingly on their part. As it was, Sardis was his balance wheel. Permissive, masculinely affectionate, generous and undemanding, this uncle was destined to shield Rud from perils that he faced in growing up among adoring women. Sardis Birchard clearly was a factor in his achieving a personality that was one of the most level of his time, though not without his undergoing his share of tension, pain and groping.

CHAPTER III

SARDIS

1

IN RUD's view Sardis Birchard, then twenty-five, was nearly perfect. Five feet nine inches tall, with dark-brown hair, thin-slit blue eyes, and a small mouth and small chin to give a puckish look to the narrow Yankee face with the high Birchard forehead and long Birchard nose, Sardis could do anything and everything, as Rud saw things.[1] Nobody could ride a horse more expertly than Sardis, or bag more turkeys, deer and squirrels. Or, with Old Tige, his dog brought from Vermont, worry more the wolves that occasionally came too close to the town.[2]

Nobody could play chess better than Sardis, nor get more amusement from checkmating his adversary. Nobody could spin yarns more successfully, with such dry humor. Some years later, on discovering Tristram Shandy, Rud would say that the amusing "habits" of the Laurence Sterne hero were "like much of Uncle's drollery & whimsical way of arguing for absurdities . . ." which kept him in stitches.[3]

True, a number of people then considered Sardis something less than a good model for a boy of a good Christian home. They spoke sorrowfully of "wild company" he kept, of his penchant for "wild sports," of how he sometimes went hunting just for the fun of it, like some Daniel Boone, when other men, more respectably, worked their fields.[4] They deplored, too, the drinking bats he had gone on before his health broke with other "wild ones," like Ben Powers (later the town's foremost banker), rip-roaring Otho Hinton, or the noisy sons of Sheriff Sidney Moore.

2

One such infrequent, though effective, drinking bat in September 1824 (the year, ironically, the temperance movement really started) was of heroic dimensions. Deciding to look over the little town of Detroit, Sardis, with Ben Powers and a jug of fine brandy, started off through the woods for Lower Sandusky. He had not intended to stop there but to board immediately the boat to cross Lake Erie. However,

27

along the way at various stopovers he and Powers introduced acquaintances to their brandy, and participated in friendly return offerings of local whiskies. By the time Lower Sandusky hove unexpectedly into view, through a fog of one kind or another, they were the signal for the launching of a string of impromptu celebrations that soon set the whole settlement agog.

At home Rud's mother was writing to the folks in New England, telling of Sardis' trip to Detroit. "Bad weather for Sardis on the Lake," she wrote. "I know not but he may now be dashing about upon the angry waves, but I must leave him in the hands of Him that made him." [5]

Sardis was indeed in stormy weather, dashing about—from town to town—guzzling, with his companions in and around Lower Sandusky, enough brandy and whisky to float the boat for Detroit, the *Walk-in-the-Water*, which he missed. By the time he finally did set off for Detroit nearly a week later in another boat, a "fine schooner," even ribald Lower Sandusky had not seen—or heard—the like. [6]

3

Naturally, in view of such lapses by Sardis, Rud's mother at times had qualms about him. How often Sophia Hayes prayed for his salvation, that he would join a church and find a good wife to tame him! [7] Yet she was loyal to him, thanking God a dozen times a day that she had him for a brother, and eager to emphasize his good points. "He goes to meeting every Sunday, which I think is a good omen," she wrote to another brother. [8] In some ways Sardis reminded her not so much of their father as of their revered grandfather, Daniel Austin.

One thing was certain about Sardis. He could be counted on in any emergency not to lose his head and to do the right, common-sense thing. If he said he would do a thing, he did it.

There was, for example, that incident back in the winter of 1817, soon after the family had come to Delaware from Vermont, when Sardis was only seventeen. Word had come of an emergency need for hogs to feed a group of families snowbound at Fort Ball (later Tiffin). This was a settlement on "the wild Sandusky Plains" about sixty miles to the north, beyond the Indian-fabled Tymotchee Creek, near which trail blazer Colonel William Crawford, a friend of George Washington, was betrayed, as was said, by evil Simon Girty and burned to death by the Wyandots. [9]

With some men Sardis was hired to drive a herd of hogs to Fort Ball. The others were really in charge, but they became drunk. "Soon after leaving Delaware, the whole business depended on Birchard. It was in the bitterly cold weather of early winter; the roads and streams were impassable; but with an energy and spirit which delighted his employers, he pushed through to the Tymotchee." [10]

In the late fall of 1824, shortly after his sober return from the visit to Detroit, Sardis had another hog-droving experience that he enjoyed relating to Rud. With Steve Bennett, later a rich commission merchant, he undertook to deliver in Baltimore the largest herd of porkers ever to leave Delaware. The project took them six weeks and involved the hiring of a dozen or so others to assist them, their route taking them through Pennsylvania on the Cumberland Highway, by then completed to Ohio.

There were few fences, so it took all the hands that Sardis and Bennett had hired to keep the wild hogs, 200-pounders with tusks, on the road. "On a soft day," Sardis said, "a day's drive would be ten or fifteen miles. When the roads were frozen hard, two or three miles was all that could be made." The worst hurdle was crossing the Ohio River at Wheeling, where the unfrozen river flowed nearly full. There was then no bridge.

The trick was to persuade the leading hogs to jump into the water and then swim to the opposite shore, causing the others to follow. "The leading hogs missed the landing, and struck the shore where the bank was steep and no hog could get out. For a time, it seemed that all would drown. A few were lost. But finally a leading hog turned down to the right spot, and the drove landed safely." So it all turned out well, Sardis told Rud, and he and his partner netted $500 apiece from the sale of their drove.

Quite as exciting was a certain personage he met on that trip. As the hogs were being pressed along the road in Pennsylvania, filling the highway from edge to edge, a handsome carriage—the handsomest carriage Sardis had ever seen—pulled by four horses and accompanied by two or three well-dressed men on horseback, overtook them. The carriage was lined with morocco leather and curtained with lace, and inside it were two handsomely dressed women, one past middle age, another young and lovely.[11]

It was obvious that Sardis' hogs were impeding the progress of somebody important. To let the carriage pass, the hogs had to be separated, and several started in all directions. The tallest man on horseback, an especially distinguished-looking man with a lean face, high forehead and white hair, helped to straighten them out. The man also stopped long enough to chat pleasantly with Sardis about the market for hogs.

"This gentleman," said Sardis to Rud, "was General Jackson, hero of New Orleans." [12] Indeed, it was Old Hickory himself, that day on his way to Washington shortly after the fiercely fought, mixed-up Presidential election of 1824. Jackson did not yet know whether he or Mr. Adams—though certainly not Mr. Clay—would be chosen President.

Sardis had not voted for Jackson. Henry Clay of Kentucky was his choice. For Mr. Clay was a Western man who stood for "internal improvements," especially in the Ohio country. But Sardis told Rud that he would not be surprised to see General Jackson, who made "a pleasant impression," elected President some time, perhaps even in 1828. It might even be worth it, said Sardis, just so he could say he had been that close—as close as he was then to Rud himself—to one who was on the path to the Presidency! [13]

4

Coming endlessly from Sardis, such stories enhanced the fondness that Rud had for his uncle. Moreover, rough as he liked to imagine himself, both Yankee and by now pure Buckeye to boot, already a true Western man, Sardis reciprocated Rud's adoration. He took seriously the entry that stated officially he was Rud's guardian, as well as Fanny's, even though this was strictly for legal purposes concerning property. He did not forget the debt he owed to his own guardian, Rud's father, and to Rud's mother herself, who had been mother as well as sister to him after he had been orphaned as a boy.[14]

Sardis had become ill in the excessively hot summer of 1825. He had suffered sunstroke, so it was thought, while mowing hay on another bit of Hayes-family land.[15] There followed, paradoxically, a good time for the hero-worshiping Rud, once Sardis began to recover. For then, even though recuperating fairly well under the nursing by Sophia and Arcena, Sardis had to remain "housed up" for weeks. Rud had liked that, for he was able to be with Sardis almost all the time. Rud hung on every word of Sardis', mimicked his every expression, even copied his lingering "very distressing" cough, which led to the fear that Sardis was also "in consumption." [16]

THE DOTING TRIUMVIRATE

Hayes's mother, Sophia, his uncle, Sardis Birchard, and his sister, Fanny Arabella

(Top) THREE SONS OF KENYON COLLEGE, 1842

Sitting, Hayes and Stanley Matthews; standing, Guy M. Bryan

(Bottom) "BILLY" ROGERS AND EBENEZER S. LANE

Respectively Hayes's law partner and his most trusted adviser when he was a young man

This fear made his going away all the more distressing. For when Sardis loped off toward the north, his wild-oats period largely over, sad-eyed though managing a joke as usual, he could not tell Rud when he would be coming back, or if he would ever be back. Like his own father Roger, on that sad trip to Saratogue Springs twenty-one years ago, Sardis was a pilgrim seeking a cure for the consumption. If he found it in Vermont, he might stay back there with his brothers, as he and his sister had agreed. "There is no need for New England people to fill Ohio, for I believe the foreigners will do it," Sophia, referring to the Germans, Irish and Welsh immigrants then beginning to stream in, had quipped about Sardis' going back to Vermont to live. This had been even before he had become ill. She had thought then that it might be better for Sardis' morals·if he lived in New England.[17] And now . . . So there was all the more reason for Rud to feel that truly "all the folks were gone."

CHAPTER IV

THE SCORCHING FIRE

1

RUD's mother, the widow Sophia Hayes, also felt lonely after Sardis went away. On the evening following Rud's sad breakfast she wrote a letter to her brother, Roger Birchard, in Vermont:

Delaware, May 14, 1826.

Dear Brother:
It was indeed a great trial to part with Sardis. His room is now desolate and solitary. I have depended very much upon him—he has been a great help to me. If he had enjoyed good health I could not have consented to his leaving this country, but this is a world of trial. The dearest Friends must part. But, Alas! I have but few left in this Country that will ever cause my heart a sigh, or my eyes a tear. They are mostly torn from me. *Where are they?* . . .

By "they" she meant not only her husband, Ruddy Hayes; she meant also another son, Lorenzo, and another daughter, Sarah Sophia, the two children born in Vermont and brought to Ohio only to die there. Her thoughts often were of those three who lay together in the cemetery in Delaware. She found herself often counting off the names of all the loved ones she had lived to see pass on, though she was not yet thirty-five. It was a long list: her father, her mother, her sister Arabella, her brother Lorenzo, all the cousins of Arcena's family, her own first-born child, as well as Arcena's mother and father, her grandfather Daniel Austin, her grandmother Abigail Austin—all these in addition to her husband, the boy Lorenzo and the girl Sarah Sophia.

2

It was good indeed for her that from her youth Sophia Hayes had been prepared for just such a chain of losses by her reading of *Pilgrim's Progress*, of the Reverend Michael Wigglesworth's poetry and of her Bible. For Sophia, fortunately, was as certain then as she had

32

been when a child that all her dead loved ones were "in the Mansions of the Blessed," "in some humble Mansion of our Saviour's Love," and that one day she would meet them all again, "in that happy world where dear Friends never part." [1]

Without this faith it is doubtful that Sophia could have survived or retained her sanity. It would have been no cause for surprise had she met the fate of her sister Cynthia. From having lost her husband, Cynthia existed back in Vermont "with a dark cloud passed over her that shrouded her intellect in more than midnight darkness." [2] But Sophia managed to do more than to retain her sanity. She exhibited also a hardy vitality that made of her, despite much melancholy-sounding talk, a quite pleasant person. "She is grand company!" once exclaimed a Yankee brother-in-law. "She talks a perfect hailstorm, faster and faster, and never is tired. Oh, it did me good to hear her!" [3]

It helped, of course, that both Rud and Fanny had such sunny dispositions, "happy children," as she liked to note. She frequently remarked that she was "pleasantly situated," that no mother possessed two finer, more regardful, more loving children than the bright boy and the alert girl who were at the breakfast table with her and Arcena Smith. [4] "After you and Fanny became healthy," she once told Rud, "and time had soothed the agony of grief, I felt the duty of submission to the Divine Will and have since been cheerful and happy, never more so than when my time was devoted to the care and education of my children." [5] Sophia Hayes, thanks to her faith, really meant this.

3

The town never knew a more useful, active woman than Rud's mother. She was an organizer of the first Sunday school of the village, herself taught a Bible class in the basement of the Presbyterian meetinghouse. [6] She was the efficient treasurer of the Ladies' Aid Society and an active member of the first Temperance Union. When there was formed a Delaware County Bible Society, with Sam Rheem as its treasurer, the other pious women of the village met in her house to form the Ladies Branch Bible Society, electing her treasurer. Among the Delaware residents, including even roistering, nonbelieving Otho Hinton, there were few not solicited by her for twenty-five and fifty-cent contributions to be used "to encourage a wider circulation of the Holy Scriptures." [7] Like a man, she managed her property, collecting the rents and determining when to sell or not to sell land as shrewdly as a banker.[8]

Sophia Hayes also kept up with the news of the world, becoming happily excited over such events as the recognition by the Congress, at last, of "the late Spanish provinces in America as independent from Catholic Spain," which, her newspapers said, marked "the breaking of shackles of tyranny." [9]

She let herself become absorbed in the controversy over the seating of John Quincy Adams in the Executive Mansion by the House of Representatives, which raged in the papers all through his term until Jackson, aided by "King Mob," as proper New Englanders said, succeeded him in 1828, as Sardis had half predicted. Inasmuch as Mr. Adams was a New Englander, naturally Sophia could never believe the charges that he had become President through "a corrupt bargain," as the Jacksonians alleged—an allegation to be leveled at a later President named Hayes.

All events, big and small, produced a reaction in Sophia. She would mourn when she read in the paper from home the news that Daniel Webster's wife Grace had just died; and that back in Dummerston, Vermont, an old friend of hers, Mrs. Kathan, had fallen down the cellar steps and also died. She would be patriotically thrilled when great personages, like Webster, Henry Clay and Justice Henry Baldwin, visited Delaware to try its sulphur water, as President Monroe had done earlier.[10] She kept up (with an eye to the possible effect on the value of her lands) with the progress of the digging of the new Ohio canal system begun at last in 1825.

She followed the troubles of Dr. Lyman Beecher, soon to be accused of heresy at Cincinnati; volubly deplored with him the "new menace" of Romanism in America; lamented the low order of politicians (mainly Jacksonians in her view); and discussed animatedly with Arcena, Sam Rheem and Mr. Wasson the latest religious cults, as well as the relative merit of colonization of the Blacks in Liberia or over in Cuba as the solution of the Slave Question to be preferred to Abolitionism. She was certain, as Rud was to be impressed, that this "problem of the Blacks" should not be settled by force and that the Abolitionists probably were "wicked." This last was a point on which she differed sharply with Sam Rheem, who was firm in asserting that, despite the recently adopted Missouri Compromise, the Negroes *must* be freed, South as well as North.[11] Sophia, of course, reflected the opinion of "the best people."

4

As a personal matter, Sophia wore her griefs openly. But this did not keep her from spreading cheer to others and imparting it also to her children, no matter how often tears brimmed her eyes, or gloomy quotations from the Bible issued, often torrentially, from her mouth. No one in Delaware prepared more soup for sick neighbors, gave away more fresh fruit, or sat more often with the ill. Such was Rud's widowed mother Sophia—brave for herself, fearful for others; practical in living, yet mystical in thinking; very much of the present, yet living greatly in the past; extravagantly dolorous in her talk and writing (a veritable Mrs. Michael Wigglesworth). But the best and gossipiest companion imaginable on a winter night or at a sewing bee, especially when assuaging the grief of others. She was disdainful of vanity, yet always dressed Rud and Fanny in the finest cloth, buttons and bows.[12] Above all, she was a conformist in all things, reflected always the conventional viewpoint.

She was a widow living far from her native place, and many pitied her for this. But in fact she made for herself, along with Rud and Fanny, a life fuller than most around her had. Yet she had her painfully lonely nights—and Rud's remark that "all the folks are gone" would be such as to help set off one of the most lonely. It would be such a night when, lying awake in bed, she could see plainly in her mind's eye the squat limestone shaft in the Delaware cemetery and read the words about little Rud's father:

Rutherford Hayes

Who Departed This Life

July 20, 1822,

aged 35 years.

Forgive Blest Shade the Tributary Tear
That mourns Thy exit from a world like this.

Forgive the Wish that would have kept Thee here
And Stay Thy Progress to the Seats of Bliss. . . .

Especially at this time of year would her thoughts of her husband's passing be sharp. For the new warm nights served to remind her of the similar weather when Ruddy Hayes fell mortally sick with the very fever that his mother, Chloe Smith Hayes, and all the others back in Vermont had feared when he and his family, with Sardis and Arcena, had left for Ohio. It was the same treacherous fever that in the previous October had carried off pretty little Sarah Sophia, "a darling child," then four.

On this May four years later there would come back to Sophia, as she said, "the horror of those dark and gloomy days when the sun seemed like a scorching fire and the face of nature a scene of desolation."[18] Everyone in the house had been down with the fever, including herself. After Ruddy Hayes died, Sophia suffered more than from the fever a wretched, numbing, ashes-tasting grief that choked and seemed to strangle her. And all the while in her womb was Ruddy's last child.

When this posthumous child, Rud, was born during her continuing grief and her own sickness, "the most sad days of my life," he was so weak and puny that everyone expected him to join his father in a matter of days.[14] Even months later one neighbor, after inspecting Rud, said, "It would be a mercy if the child would die." "He must die; and it is a waste of strength [to try to save him]," said another.[15] But Sophia, though ready, gladly, to die herself, feeling "alone in a strange land," prayed for the boy to live, and saw him through. How she did it, except that God, Arcena and Sardis were with her, she never could tell.[16]

5

Only pleasant thoughts now of the boy and girl in the next room could stop the renewed moistening of her cheeks and help to bring at last a dream-filled sleep. These, with her religious faith, gave her strength to face each new day. She still dreaded, and always would, "the season of the year always sorrowful to me."[17] Yet, being Sophia, she carried on bravely, watching and hovering like a mother eagle over Fanny and Rud, alert to their every peril, physical or moral. In her mind they faced many, though she told herself that she trusted fully the Psalmic promise of "protection by the Father of the widow and of the Fatherless."

She had high hopes especially for her remaining son, though even in this time she often said that "God forbid" Rud should ever be enticed into a political career and thus meet the fate of the Honorable John Noyes of Brattleboro and Putney, Vermont, her husband's brother-in-law, who returned from Washington a victim of alcohol after a term in Congress in Madison's time. She liked to think that Rud's family heritage of itself foreordained for him a more useful life, as good a one (though she hoped more prolonged) as that lived by his father.

BOOK TWO

The Yankee Heritage

CHAPTER V

PROGENITOR

1

RUD HAYES's heritage, distinctly Yankee, properly began, as his mother viewed the story of his people, with Daniel Austin. Known as the Old Captain, though the basis for the title was obscure, he was Sophia's grandfather, and to a large degree he symbolized all Rud's forebears.

Born in 1720 (according to the new calendar), the Old Captain, a wrinkled, somewhat shrunken, but still tall man, was yet living in the time of the Presidency of Thomas Jefferson. He was a revered fixture of his daughter Drusilla's house, the often patched and remodeled homestead of her farmer-merchant spouse, Roger Birchard.

There in the little hill town of Wilmington, Windham County, Vermont, Daniel Austin made his home along with his wife, Grandma Abigail, in these last failing years. He was a relic who sometimes dropped a vague remark, sipped slowly a cup of flip, and liked to pat the heads of his grandchildren, especially the one who doted on him the most—Drusilla's girl, Sophia.

He was a link with a past already as remote as the War of Jenkins' Ear, in which, indeed, he had been a combatant of a sort.[1] Like most of his neighbors in this Green Mountain section, he was a transplanted New Englander, a newcomer from lower down the valley of "the Great River," the Connecticut. Suffield, in seemingly far-off Connecticut, was his real home.[2]

In Vermont the Old Captain was a fugitive from the hard times that had come after the Revolution, and also from the worn-out soil down below, as in truth many of his neighbors had been fugitives— literally—from Massachusetts authorities. Mostly solid citizens, some even judges and sheriffs in Vermont, these, under another captain, had participated in Shays' Rebellion. It had been madness for them to resort to mob action under Captain Daniel Shays to prevent land foreclosures. But one aftermath, their flight, certainly had helped to populate Vermont, itself a child of insurrection.[3]

41

2

Daniel Austin had descended from the very early settlers of New England. Not, to be sure, of the line of bold men who formed companies of "adventurers" and chartered ships. Nor was his line the breed of non-conformist preachers whose goal was to plant new Jerusalems.

Rather, he was of the uprooted agricultural and artisan people of England. These were the social expendables of the Industrial Revolution (as it later came to be known), sucked by disrupting social change out of their native villages, then tossed into the unpremeditated role of transatlantic pioneers. In the main, their spur was a vision of rising to the status of self-sustaining, free owners of land. Each hoped to become in America as independent a British subject as any manorial lord, and most of all, to be saved from the dismal life of a factory hand, the destined fate of so many who remained in England.

In some instances these immigrants made surprisingly swift progress toward their goal of a decent livelihood for their families. For most, however, the progress was slow, even in the second and third generations. Reckoned materially, these in truth were not much better off, though assuredly no worse, in New England than their kind who remained in old England.

Among these humble ones, slow to rise, were the Austins. In time, a hundred and fifty years or so, and after much crossbreeding, they too would produce some figures, lucky, energetic, or both, to emerge above the common level. Among many others these would include Moses Austin, who would own, if only temporarily, half the territory to be called Missouri, and Stephen Austin, his son, the "father" of the Republic of Texas.[4]

For the most part, however, the clan never rose much higher than the status of the Richard Austin, an unemployed tailor in England who came in the great migration of the middle 1630s to start the search for good land which Captain Daniel Austin continued when he moved up from Suffield in Connecticut to Wilmington in Vermont.

This Daniel was the farming son of a farming son of a farming son of the tailor. In his leathery person, topped with the white hair still braided in 1804 in the style of the previous century, he now not only embodied most of the solid traits of his clan but reflected as well the contradictions in many fellow Vermonters. By all accounts he was a strict Congregationalist who had turned Baptist for reasons more related to taxes than to a less rigid doctrine.[5] He was a man of peace who had three times gone to war; a patriot who had been loyal to the British king and also to that "independency of the independency," Ethan Allen's Republic of Vermont; a Federalist who, even so, sympathized with the men of Shays' pitiful uprising.

3

Obviously he had lived long past his allotted span. A man who had heard the preachers Jonathan Edwards, George Whitefield and James Davenport, the elder—who, indeed, had been baptized by the venerable and usually gentle Reverend Ebenezer Devotion—could not help but feel outdated among a people now extravagantly stirred by such modern exhorters as Lorenzo Dow, after whom Drusilla had named her latest boy-child. The hysterical furor in Vermont caused by Jedediah Birchard, a preacher-kin of daughter Drusilla's husband, called a crazy sensualist for inducing his hearers to go into the jerks, or to bark like dogs, was for the Old Captain a twice-told tale.[6]

He could recall the day in 1739, when, along with other youths from Suffield, Hadley and Granby, he was almost sent to Cartagena, where thousands of New Englanders perished in Jenkins' War, but instead found himself landed at Santiago de Cuba. Still lucky, he was captured by the Spaniards before much shooting occurred. But he did not avoid the hardships which made that war a nightmarish thing for all.[7]

Daniel remembered the disastrous, bloody, choleric, sickening failure of the whole expedition, even at Santiago. It would be 160 years before other Americans, including one direct descendant, would take and hold this same Santiago de Cuba,[8] albeit his strongest recollection was of his "embarrassment" over sneaking in and out of the Spanish prison to beg beer from the natives.[9]

When his adventure was over and he had been exchanged for a Spanish prisoner, he settled down in Suffield, became a true "visible saint" of the First Church Society, Congregational, and married. So many Austins in and around Suffield had married Phelpses that it was predictable that the chastened Daniel should do likewise. His bride was Abigail Phelps, of the Suffield family of Timothy Phelps. Her mother had been a Griswold, of another Yankee family of the Connecticut Valley, one that produced not a few governors, judges and university presidents among other dignitaries, as well as many, like Abigail's immediate kin, listed only in the annals of the ordinary. Daniel earned a livelihood for Abigail, his children and himself by working as a carpenter and farmer.[10]

A new English war in Europe, against the French, spread to the New World in the 1750s. Daniel this time successfully resisted the recruiting officers' rum-enforced blandishments. However, for a seventeen-day stretch he found himself in this war, too. For there came the day of a great defeat suffered by the British and colonials near Lake Champlain. Worse yet, the French had allowed their intoxicated Indian allies to slaughter, for booty, captured Connecticut and Massachusetts men.

So, with the rank of "clark," Daniel "went to Fourt Edward in the allarum of August 1757" in Captain Jonathan Pettibone's company of Suffield men. Again he was lucky. There was not much further fighting. But for this service he and other Suffield men were included in an imposing-looking, seal-bedecked charter for 23,040 acres of land in the New Hampshire Grants. His share was 400 acres.[11]

4

He had seen the American Revolution coming long before it happened. When it broke he was in his fifties and more interested in rebuilding his home, which had burned to the ground in May 1774,[12] than in entering this new conflict. A good many of his neighbors were decidedly unsympathetic, deserving the epithet Tory. In fact, among the foremost of those loyal to the king were Phelpses, kin to his wife Abigail Phelps. However, some Phelpses also were Continental patriots, like seventy-six-year-old Dan Phelps of Windsor, Connecticut, who "chased a company of British cavalry through Danbury, riding nearly twenty-four hours, mourning on his return that he did not get a shot at one Britisher." [13]

Daniel was no flaming revolutionist. But neither was he a Tory. And because he had this attitude, when the cry for volunteers, even for men of his age, went up all over Connecticut on two occasions after the British had invaded the colony, Daniel answered both times.[14]

He was never "an officer under General Washington," as it would be said. But he had experienced and witnessed enough so that his "tales of the revolution," told to the grandchild Sophia on his lap, caused her to weep.[15] Then, until the war ended and afterward, he and other New Englanders battled against new enemies: inflation, worthless currency, unheard-of taxes, the threat of losing his farm. On the Massachusetts side of the valley precisely this complex of hardships in dozens of towns like Suffield produced, in the blizzardy winter of 1786, the unpremeditated rebellion, led by that "desperate debtor" Daniel Shays, a hero of the Battle of Bunker Hill.[16]

At Stockbridge, in the Sheffield area, there occurred on February 26, 1787, toward the end of the uprising, the very worst collision between the Commonwealth militia and the Shays men. When it was over two militia members and two rebels had been killed. About fifty Shays men, out of the several hundred who participated, were captured. Many of the captured were from Sheffield, and these included an alleged leader, Nathaniel Austin, nephew of Daniel Austin.[17]

5

This Nathaniel Austin, then so unexpectedly caught in the web of history and almost never referred to on Rud Hayes's family tree, had served the republic well as a soldier, even more lengthily than had Daniel. As a volunteer for liberty, he had been in the battle of Saratoga against "Gentleman Johnny" Burgoyne's forces, in the battle of Stillwater, at Forts George and Ann, and in the Bennington alarm.[18] Now in the following March he found himself on trial for his life before the Supreme Court of Judicature at Great Barrington, along with one Peter Wilcox, Junior. The charge was treason.[19]

A jury of Berkshire County squires found both men guilty and they were sentenced to be "taken . . . to the place of Execution and there be hanged by the neck until . . . dead." The double hanging was set to take place at Great Barrington on May 24, 1787.[20]

Fortunately for Nathaniel and his comrade, as well as for the family escutcheon, there occurred developments which kept the sentence from being carried out. Politically the sentence was not popular. A newly elected governor of Massachusetts, John Hancock, who could not help remembering that he himself in the Revolution had been considered a rebel, issued two reprieves and indicated that he planned a pardon for Nathaniel Austin and Peter Wilcox.[21]

Just before the news of the second reprieve reached the Great Barrington jail, the condemned men were freed by means other than Hancock's mercy. As related in the Massachusetts *Centinel* for June 23, 1787: ". . . Wilcox and Austin, two of the rebels who were to have been executed on Thursday next, made their escape from the gaol in Great-Barrington, in the night of Friday last. The means made use of to effect their escape are somewhat singular; two women, having introduced themselves to the centinel [sic] with a bottle of spirits, soon got him intoxicated therewith, and then found means to liberate the prisoners."

The prisoners never were recaptured. Thus the escutcheon of a future President's family was spared the dark blot of a hanging. But when such shaking occurrences could so closely catch up with sons of the sons of sons of New England founders, regardless of the merits, it seemed a time for many people, the Austins in Suffield too, to be moving on.

6

Then Daniel Austin, nearly seventy, had occasion to remember that royal charter given in 1765 to Suffielders in the New Hampshire Grants, that part then called the Republic of Vermont. Theoretically, at least, he still had title to those 400 acres.

Some of his wife's people, bustling, industrious Phelpses, had long been in the Green Mountain country, for them a new frontier. They appeared to be prospering there, at least enough to become prominent in much of the ruckusing by Ethan Allen's Green Mountain Boys.[22] A number of others from the Suffield area followed them, including Medad Smith, whose son James married Daniel's youngest daughter, Sallena. Soon Sallena and James, who would have a daughter named Arcena, followed Medad.[23] They settled at Fullum, later absorbed into Wilmington, on, so far as anyone could ever know, the very acres intended by King George III for Daniel. And before long Daniel and Abigail, with the remaining daughters and their youngest boy, Linus, also made the move.

By 1804, his last year, this all seemed long ago to Daniel Austin, as far in limbo as nephew Nathaniel's foolhardy flirtation with the gallows. With his own thin-slit blue eyes the Old Captain had seen, even if not with full comprehension, the remnant of originally theocratic New England disappear into a wholly new New World. No longer was New England but a copy of the countryside in old England, as the theocracy had intended. It was already something of a commercial land, like mercantile England. Emerging also were some uncalculated gradations among the people, even in New England. These were reflected in bitterly contesting political parties.

A sign, among others, of the contentious, factious spirit of the times was a still-repeated allegation against Jefferson. This charged that he had gained the Presidency by entering into a corrupt bargain, that the post became his if not through chicanery on his own part, then at least because he was a knowing beneficiary of such guilty practice. This first "disputed election" of 1800 was a passion-inflamed episode. With surprising duplication, down to details, it would all happen at least once again seventy-five years later, and with special implications for a descendant of Daniel Austin.

But the Old Captain, who, of course, could not even have dreamed of the later case, was by the time of this crisis too old to be more than casually interested in the first one. He had lived enough to know that there was a time for dying. In the last week of June 1804, when he was eighty-four, in the shadow cast by Mount Haystack over the rolling green hills and the foliaged ravines which set off clearings he had helped to make, Daniel Austin, great-grandfather of Rutherford B. Hayes—the boy Rud, not yet born—went to his final judgment.

CHAPTER VI

YOUNG SOPHIA

1

THE GIRL Sophia Birchard, then twelve, was one mourner who truly believed the promise of resurrection engraved on Grandpa Daniel Austin's gravestone. Even in this still simple time in Vermont there were those who were skeptical, or who openly scoffed. But Sophia, the second of Roger and Drusilla Birchard's seven children, believed profoundly and all-souledly. The Lord was, in truth, her rock.

Sophia was then a little thing, but with so much obvious nervous and physical energy that her size was not important. She was not a beauty. But she was attractive in a chaste and clean way, with a trim figure, of those nice proportions which "Old Pope" Timothy Dwight, the hawk-nosed president of Yale, found pleasant to gaze on during a trip in the area at just that time.[1] Not even the homemade linsey-woolsey dress, which she wore almost to the ground to conceal her bare feet, could completely hide the graceful lines of her body. She was, indeed, a fine, yet typical, specimen of New England girlhood in that year of 1804.

To be noticed first about her were her cheeks. Even in summer they were so red that strangers once embarrassed her by calling out, "O, see the paint!" Sophia wept that so horrible an accusation, reminiscent to her of the fleshpots of a town called Vanity, could be leveled against her, even in jest.[2]

Slate-blue eyes, like Grandpa Daniel's, softened her long Yankee face. Properly spaced above the well-fashioned nose, they looked out from below her tightly combed butternut-brown hair with a piercing, questioning intentness. They were not brooding eyes. But they were thoughtful, shaded serenely, yet also illuminated by a tremendous truth. This truth was that life on earth, pleasant though it be for a girl of twelve, was but a temporary and futile combination of vanities and pitfalls, that the only real and truly joyous existence was in "the Mansions of the Lord, the Pearly and Golden Mansions not made with Earthly Hands," where Grandpa Austin was. Ever since she remembered knowing anything, Sophia, true child of her time, possessed this philosophy.

2

She already was a kind of theologian. She could not have been otherwise, given her temperament. She was a great reader, reading late at night, "by a bad light," endangering her eyesight,[3] and almost all the printed matter available to her concerned God and religion. Her favorite book, which she read again and again, the one that was "most instructive" to her, was *Pilgrim's Progress*.[4] Its recital of the evils in the town called Vanity, "the lusts, pleasures and delights of all sorts, as harlots . . . and what not," horrified as well as fascinated her. Such things, "all Vanity," were to be shunned, she knew.

In the district school down by Cold Brook near the ancient red bridge, no pupil recited with greater ardor than Sophia the lines from *Dilsworth's Reader* by the Reverend Mr. Michael Wigglesworth:

> Learn what deceitful toys, and empty things,
> This world and all its best enjoyments be;
> Out of the earth no true contentment springs,
> But all things here are vexing vanity. . . .

Likely as not, her exultation over such a recital made her more cheerful than usual when she visited a neighbor, after her own home chores were done, indulging in gay chatter, helping with the neighbor's wash and generally making herself welcome. For despite her preoccupation with the idea of death and the attractions of the afterworld, the neighbors always considered her an entertaining little chatterbox, radiant and lively.[5]

In some fact, as well as in her own childish fantasy, she was the real mother in the family. It was she who saw that Austin washed himself thoroughly; that Roger, Junior, did not stray off into the woods, or fall into Deerfield Creek, or even set fire to the house; it was she who sang to, and otherwise entertained, Arabella; kept the then puny Sardis from tumbling adventurously into the dye tub near the fireplace; changed Lorenzo's diapers at decent intervals. She brought the cups of beer to the two Grandmas, Abigail Austin and Sarah Birchard, setting them down with an efficient aplomb on the round tea table, the prized piece of furniture in the house, which her mother had transported all the way from Suffield in Connecticut.

A thousand other tasks and responsibilities kept her life a busy one. Out of all her busyness and her love, she drew a special kind of happiness and security that bolstered her faith in her God-centered world and prepared her for what still lay ahead there in Vermont and later, beyond the veil, in Ohio.[6]

CHAPTER VII

Young Ruddy and the Clan of Hayes

1

WHILE SOPHIA was maturing in Wilmington, there was growing up fourteen miles down the valley, where the clear-flowing Whetstone met the Connecticut to mark the west end of Brattleboro, the youth Ruddy Hayes. This Rutherford Hayes, Junior (to use his full name), with hair almost as bright red as Sophia's cheeks, was "the flower of the Hayes family," up to then.[1] In his earlier youth he had been accounted frail. But now he was strong-bodied and so active as to suggest that he was making up for the earlier time.[2] In 1804 he was seventeen.

Among testaments to Ruddy Hayes's good mind was a certificate won at the select school at Atkinson, across the river in New Hampshire. "This certifies that Master Rutherford Hays [sic] left off at the head of his class in spelling this 6th day of June, 1800. J. FORBES, Instructor."[3]

That Ruddy had attended the Atkinson select school was also a testament that his family was coming up in the world. For such special schooling was then given only to a few Brattleboro boys. Quite possibly Ruddy owed this to the ideas of his intellectual sister, redheaded Polly, then wife to the Honorable John Noyes, himself an Atkinson product. Noyes had even gone to Dartmouth to study for the ministry, and stayed to tutor, among others, a lad of Ruddy's age named Daniel Webster.[4]

2

Ruddy's father, notable in those days for his neat black wig and his always clean hands, which he washed with a solemn ritual a dozen times a day, was the nominal head of the clan.[5] But the real head was Ruddy's mother, the sharp-eyed, black-haired, stocky Chloe Hayes. She was the real manager of the Hayes Tavern in Brattleboro, which Ruddy's father, then called Rutherford Hayes, Esq., owned in 1804.

She was a Smith, fifth daughter of Israel, of the tribe of Samuel, John, Medad, Chileab, Peletiah, Perez, Ichabod, Zedediah, Preserved, Peregrine, Seth, Richard, Peleg and sundry other Smiths in the Valley of the Connecticut since 1635. Her original ancestor in America,

"Ye Faithful Lieutenant" Samuel Smith of Weathersfield and Hadley, a fellmonger in England, was, in fact, progenitor of perhaps one fourth of all the Smiths in America later.[6]

That Chloe was a dominant woman, much more virile for all her fancy needlework and busy piety than her roly-poly husband, there can be no doubt. She had one goal. This was to see each of Ruddy's six sisters well married.

Ruddy's father also had a goal. Once each year he liked to be able to make the trip down the hills to his native New Haven to get his fill of oysters. When he otherwise acted positively by way of shaping his destiny, his action was likely directed at getting out of the path of trouble. He did not like contention, perhaps in reaction to his own father, Ezekiel, who in 1804 still lived in Branford, in Connecticut, a suburb of New Haven.[7]

3

Ezekiel's great contribution to his progeny resulted from a display of gall. This was to woo Rebecca Russell of Branford shortly after he had left his near-by native village, Salmon Brook, to go to New Haven in search of work as scythemaker. For Rebecca was the daughter of Judge John Russell of Branford, the most distinguished pillar of the community.[8] Her grandfather, the late Reverend Samuel Russell of Branford, had been one of the drafters of the celebrated Saybrook Platform, a milestone document in Congregational church history. He was the first chief executive of Yale College. Indeed, it was in Samuel Russell's house that this great institute of higher learning was born, back in 1701.[9]

There was even more to the pedigree of these Russells. They were, in fact, among the most justly renowned of original New Englanders, a family of that breed of strong men of strong faith in God and themselves who pursued with almost equal fervor the twin Puritan goals— God and fertile land. Back in 1645, when the Reverend Thomas Hooker, "the son of thunder," started a famous ecclesiastical and polit- ical rumpus in the Massachusetts Bay Colony, one that proved to be a forecast of the American Revolution itself, the first John Russell, a glazier, was his stout right hand. He helped to lead Hooker's flock of rebels, with Chloe Smith Hayes's ancestor, Samuel Smith, tagging along, up the Connecticut River Valley to found a new settlement, Wethersfield.[10]

Twenty-five years later, in the New England theological era of "thunderings, lightnings and earthquakes," as Cotton Mather put it, Wethersfield was itself struck by a great schism—half the people moving away to found the town of Hadley in Massachusetts. This same Russell, with his son the Reverend John, just out of Harvard College, was again at the center of the commotion.[11]

In the "terrible years of affliction," 1675-76, when the Indians under King Philip, egged on by the French, went on the warpath to wipe out the English settlers in the valley, the Russell son and father acted most bravely.[12] The Worshipful Major John Pyncheon, heading the militia wanted everyone to retreat and abandon Hadley and the other settlements to the Indians. But the Russells held that God wished the colonists to stay. They had their way.

Nor was this all, or even the best, about the Russells' service to New England. When King Charles II attempted to subvert the charter of Massachusetts Bay, the Reverend Russell, a full century before Jefferson composed the better-known Declaration of Independence, on April 25, 1665, wrote a declaration which bristled with Rights of Man sentiments. "We have the right from God and Man to chuse [sic] our governors and live under our own laws. Our liberty and privileges we prize and hold as our lives; this makes us freemen and not slaves. . . ."[13]

The Reverend Russell also had been a hero in one of New England's proudest pre-Revolution episodes. For it was in his house in Hadley that for twelve years the two regicides, Edward Whalley, cousin to Oliver Cromwell, and William Goffe, a general in Cromwell's army, were concealed from agents of the British Crown. Whalley and Goffe had been members of the Rump Parliament that decreed the beheading of Charles I.

Never once, apparently, did the Reverend Russell flinch in protecting the two regicides, not even when edicts came from the Crown threatening death to anyone who concealed the pair. He kept them in his house until both died, then buried them in the walls of his cellar, where their bones fell out when the house was remodeled—about the time Ruddy Hayes, up the valley, was nine or ten.[14]

4

So there was grandeur in the Russell line, including a family connection with Cromwell. Yet there was Zeke Hayes, a mere scythe-

maker, paying court to Judge Russell's daughter as confidently as if
he had been a Yale College student himself. A fellow worker asked
Ezekiel how he justified his wooing Rebecca Russell, who lived in the
biggest house on Branford's best tree-lined street. "I always reach for the
highest twig!" Ezekiel replied.[15] He attained it, too. Rebecca became
his bride in 1749, the same year that Daniel Austin, over in Suffield,
married Abigail Phelps. Not only was this bride a Russell, but her
mother was a Trowbridge, a family of large interests. Moreover, one
of her grandmothers was a Rutherford, with the Cromwellian connections, this last explaining the fulsome first name, Rutherford.[16]

Whatever else he may have inherited from the Russells, or from his
father, the first Rutherford Hayes did not inherit their aggressiveness
or their belligerence. In truth, Ruddy's father was a man of peace and
wanted no part of heroics.

In 1778, the year he became twenty-one, he was working in New
Haven as a blacksmith. That was a crucial time of the Revolutionary
War and Connecticut had adopted a conscription act applying to men
twenty-one and over. His family, to be sure, was on the side of independence. His father was a captain of the Branford militia and a collector of provisions for the colonial troops.[17] His mother's kin, the
Trowbridges and Rutherfords, were high up in the ranks of Connecticut regiments. But Rutherford Hayes, the first, unlike a later Rutherford Hayes, simply had no desire to be a soldier.

So just in time to avoid the attack on New Haven that brought
Sophia Birchard's Grandpa Daniel running as a ten-day volunteer,
Blacksmith Rutherford Hayes, carrying his worldly goods in a "hair-
covered trunk," departed for Vermont, to get away, as his wife Chloe
phrased it, "from the din of war."[18] Vermont, playing an individualistic
role in the Revolution, had no conscription act.

Ironically he did not find complete peace in Vermont after all. He
found instead that when he married into the Smith family, he had
married into a separate war, of a sort. For the Smiths in Brattleboro
were leading Yorkers, partisans of the claim that most of Vermont,
especially in the area of Brattleboro, really belonged to New York.

This was a potentially dangerous allegiance, so long as Ethan Allen
and his Green Mountain Boys were in the vicinity to make good their
counterclaims against the New York monopolizers. Moreover, Rutherford Hayes's father-in-law, Israel Smith, was a lieutenant in a New
York militia regiment, the South Company of "the County of Cumberland, New York," as Yorkers called Brattleboro. This regiment had

been specifically formed by Governor George Clinton of New York to oppose the Green Mountain Boys.

Naturally when young Rutherford Hayes from New Haven married Israel Smith's daughter Chloe, he was expected to join the Yorker militia too. He reluctantly did, holding the rank of ensign.[19] Fortunately, from his point of view, the South Company was called on to do little physical fighting against Ethan Allen's boys. But of alarms and of verbal clashes there were plenty.

There were frequent declarations from the Green Mountain Boys that threatened to "make a Sodom and Gomorrah" out of Brattleboro and "to cut off the ears of anyone who served Governor Clinton." One of Rutherford Hayes's friends on the Allen side is duly recorded in New York archives as commenting on a Clinton proclamation: "It is a Damn thing and the Governor may stick it in his ARS. . . ." [20] But mainly, to young Hayes's relief, this verbal ferocity was not translated into any exchange of shots.

5

Long after the Revolutionary fighting had ceased, the Yorkers and Ethan Allen's boys were glaring and cursing at one another around Brattleboro. Uncle Seth Smith was indicted by the Allen regime in the Windham County court (which Brattleboro did not recognize) in January 1784 "for conspiring and attempting an invasion, insurrection and public rebellion against Vermont." So Seth "felt obliged to depart and seek shelter in New York state under the wings of Governor Clinton." [21] When this occurred the remaining Yorkers drafted a petition of peace directed to the Republic of Vermont. This document prayed for an end to hostilities, "for a general pacification, and an amicable settlement of past misunderstandings." Not surprisingly (and perhaps prophetically for another time of conflict between people of various states on the American mainland) one of the sixteen names attached to this plea of conciliation was that of Rutherford Hayes.[22]

It was easy to see that from his father Ruddy Hayes had received a love of fun and of peace; from his mother, a desire to get up in the world, even to be rich, in accord with the village standards. Given a good horse to ride through the woods, preferably along a new trail every day; some hale-boy companions to exchange earthy jokes with; the dreams he dreamed of one day running a mercantile establishment like that of the Honorable Noyes, who had recently hired him as a clerk in the firm of Noyes & Mann, and he was in 1804 the happiest youth in the valley, "a pleasant lad . . . the glory & pride of our family," as his mother Chloe said.[28] He was so when the girl Sophia Birchard first came to know him.

CHAPTER VIII

THE CONNECTICUT YANKEE

1

ROGER BIRCHARD, the father of the girl Sophia, coughed his insides apart all during the winter after the Old Captain died. Spring found him not much better. It was plain that already the hand of death was stretching toward him, although tight-lipped Roger was then only forty-nine. His wife Drusilla knew; his older children, including Sophia, knew. He himself knew.

Several times after his consumption first came on him, Roger had gone over the Green Mountains into New York to take the water cure at Saratogue Springs. In the past these visits had been refreshing. At the end of that spring, though it was a bad time to be absent from his farms and store, he decided he had better try the water cure again.

Around the fifth of June 1805 Roger set off on horseback for Saratogue. Twenty-three years had passed since he had first settled in Wilmington, coming up from Connecticut on foot in 1782. With his lean frame, his sharp blue eyes, his long nose and his taut, careful manner, he was still the perfect Connecticut Yankee. Then in 1805, however, he was going downhill, instead of up.

2

Like the Austins, the Russells, the Hayeses and the Smiths, Roger Birchard, father of Sophia, Sardis and the others, was a product of the early people of the Connecticut's valley. True, the first Birchard in America had lived for a long time off the Massachusetts coast, at Edgartown, on Martha's Vineyard. But even this stout patriarch (who was listed among the passengers on the *Truelove* from England in 1635 as "Thomas Burchard, labourer, 40") finally moved into the valley, for at Martha's Vineyard he had become involved in a rebellion against the authorities, probably one concerning distribution of land. This was about the time the Russells, Austins and Smiths were having their Indian troubles along the Connecticut. So he left Edgartown by request.[1]

Roger Birchard was born on a not now discoverable day—it could have been Christmas—in December 1757 in Pleasant Valley, near the Willimantic River between Mansfield Centre and Windham, Connecticut. His father, Elias, had settled there just the year before. From Samuel Storrs, Esq., the leading landowner of Mansfield, Elias acquired seventy-eight acres on Pudding Lane, "westerly of the new dwelling house of Joseph Jacobs Jr." [2] This geographic description was important. For Joseph Jacobs, Jr., Squire Storrs's son-in-law, had several marriageable daughters, including Sarah Jacobs. "Elias would very naturally fall in company with Sarah," commented the leading Mansfield Centre historian. Indeed, this happened so promptly that there is evidence that Roger came into the world even before Elias and Sarah went through the formality of their marriage. [3]

Years later this haste caused a good deal of genealogical trouble to a son of Roger's daughter. For when Rutherford B. Hayes tried to fix Roger's exact birthdate, he ran into trouble. "Keep pumping. You'll get something after awhile," he urged a helper. [4]

What was turned up was slightly unexpected, although circumstantial. However, such matters, even in a family that also produced the eminent Congregationalist preacher, Richard Salter Storrs, were not really important in that time. Bundling was a universal and encouraged custom, especially among the farmers of the Connecticut Valley settlements, as, it was said, "a matter of convenience and necessity." [5] There was certainly nothing irregular in the marriage that Elias and Sarah established. In a respectable domestic environment on Elias' farm, they reared Roger and six other children.

3

Never could it be said that Roger—like the whole Birchard family —did not participate patriotically in the Revolutionary cause. Not only he and his father Elias but two younger brothers as well had shouldered muskets in Mansfield Centre regiments. [6] In 1774 they had been among the Mansfield Centre folk who applauded at a town meeting a "draft of a declaration of freedom," written in the main by the young and dashing Mr. Experience Storrs, Roger's cousin. [7]

Despite a certain frailty, Roger marched off in June 1775 with his cousin Experience, a captain and regimental leader, to render aid to besieged Boston. Thus, as a private in the Connecticut Third Regiment under "Old Put" himself (Major General Israel Putnam), Roger was a participant in the Battle of Breed's Hill, later styled Bunker

Hill, along with Daniel Shays.[8] So he had done his part, and could not be blamed if, in the spring of 1782, he headed for quieter Vermont, like Ruddy Hayes's father.[9]

After a few years in Vermont he became owner of several farms, and he had also made himself a country retail merchant, the first in Wilmington, specializing in importing notions and wet goods, notably Jamaica rum, from Connecticut.[10] In 1778 or 1789 he began courting Drusilla Austin, one of the Old Captain's daughters. At first she found him to be yokelish. But they were married in December 1790. He then moved his store and house to a site in Wilmington, on the newly built pike to Brattleboro. There, in 1791, their first child, Cynthia, was born. On April 5, 1792, the year Vermont entered the union, Sophia arrived. At evenly spaced intervals, a third daughter and the three boys, including Sardis, were born.[11]

4

Roger Birchard never returned from that visit to Saratogue. His first letter to Drusilla and the children was full of the consumptive's optimism. But his next communication, in July 1805, a note scrawled in a weak hand, said: "Dear Wife: I shall not Return home as soon as I expeckted when I wrote Before, for I get better But slowly." A short time later Drusilla received a more woeful message, not from Roger but from a casual friend at Saratogue, one which sent her flying off to him, Sophia's brother Austin sitting behind her on the horse. She and the boy arrived in Saratogue only to bury Roger there on August 22, 1805.[12]

CHAPTER IX

LOVE IN THE GREEN MOUNTAINS

1

So ONCE again the girl Sophia experienced the sorrow of death. More troubles lay ahead for her, too. These began when, in February 1809, her mother took a new husband, a certain Major Lewis Joy, keeper of a tavern on the western outskirts of Wilmington.[1]

In part, the impulsive Drusilla was motivated to marry again by economic reasons tied in with needs of her brood. As attested by bankruptcy notices published in all the Windham County papers, Roger Birchard's land acquisitions had in truth, as Sophia had dimly feared from her reading of Bunyan, turned out to be "vanity, all vanity." With all her father's industriousness and apparent prosperity while he was living, his estate was adjudged "insufficient to pay all debts."[2]

Drusilla felt the need of a man's help in providing for the children. It was also evident that she had succumbed wholly to the manly charms of Major Joy. But Drusilla's second marriage, always referred to in the family as "unfortunate," lasted little more than a year.[3] Then Sophia, as well as the others, had to adjust to another shock, an event akin to disgrace—her mother's divorce in April 1810.

2

Fortunately Ruddy Hayes, then twenty-two, at just this time came into eighteen-year-old Sophia's life, thanks to a program of expansion on the part of the Brattleboro firm of Noyes & Mann. Deciding to operate a chain of stores, Ruddy's brother-in-law, the Honorable John Noyes, and his partner, General Mann, first opened another store at Putney and then one in Wilmington. To Sophia's town, as "managing clerk," Ruddy was sent.

Many were the Wilmington maids, and their mothers, who were aflutter over Ruddy Hayes's presence in the town. They enthusiastically endorsed the statement, "Mr. Hayes, being a young man of good character and position, was a very desirable escort for the ladies."[4]

His name was often mentioned teasingly to Sophia. "I will never marry a redhead!" she exclaimed.[5]

But this was before their first real exchange of glances and conversation on the day she mounted the family work horse and rode down to the new Noyes & Mann store to sell a bag of rags to young Mr. Hayes. The spectacle of Sophia that day—the nearly matured, flaming-cheeked, bright-eyed young lady, so slender, lugging into the store with aggressive, though completely feminine, independence a heavy sack of rags—made an instantaneous impression on Ruddy. As nearly as any storybook tale ever had it, the result was love at first sight, and they soon were betrothed.[6]

In 1810 he was transferred back to Brattleboro to be in the main Noyes & Mann store. Sophia and he saw each other then only on week ends when he would come riding up to her through the hills from Brattleboro, or when she visited down there with a friend. But the letters that they exchanged, written by candlelight and posted with friends or even strangers who went between the towns, kept the flame burning. One of his said:

My dear—— I am not fond of far-fetched sentiment. But do not think I mean to throw all Ceremony out of the Question and by a careless indifference alienate your affections and weaken the bonds of friendship. No, rather than be accused of that, I would search the tales of romance . . . and the Dictionary should be robbed of all the long words I can find. . . . I suppose you can guess by this time who this is from. But that you may be certain it is from a real friend, I subscribe in full truth the name of—   RUTHERFORD HAYES, JR.
P. S. Pardon me, I love you, Sophia.[7]

A normally happier time Sophia never was to know.

3

Nor soon, save for one ahead, an unhappier period. For there came then, in 1810 and 1811, to the Green Mountain hill towns and farms the milksick and the spotted fever. While the doctors argued among themselves, literally over the bodies of their patients, on how to treat their cases, scarcely a home escaped death.

Up in Wilmington the plague was devastating. Out of the family of Sophia's Aunt Sallena, only her favorite cousin, Arcena, was spared. All the other Smiths of this Austin connection—Sallena and James

Smith and eight grandchildren of Captain Austin—were carried away. In August 1811 Sophia's littlest brother, Lorenzo, took the fever and died. In the following month Arabella, the younger of her sisters, also died of it. Arcena Smith of course went to live with the Birchards.[8]

Sophia, for all her faith, fell into deepest melancholy. Ruddy was her lifesaver. He rode his brindled horse up to Wilmington more often. He wrote oftener.

Soon Sophia became her old self again. She even attended a dance or two in Wilmington with young men not named Ruddy Hayes, girlishly testing him. He passed the test. "No, Sophia, [he wrote] the lass with the roseate cheeks shall not long be forgotten by the lad with the rubicand hair."[9]

In March 1813 Sophia suffered another blow. Her mother one day found, lying in the road, "a soldier sick with spotted fever." She took the youth in the house to nurse him. "The disease was very contagious. She took it and died within three days." So then, with Ruddy Hayes beside her, Sophia buried her last parent and became, because of her responsibility for the three brothers, a woman.[10]

4

Ruddy Hayes was by then managing a store in near-by Dummerston. Indeed, in this store he had an interest, the new establishment being officially called "Noyes, Mann & Hayes." Thanks to the Honorable Noyes, his dream of getting on in the world was coming true. He decided that the time had come for him and Sophia to wed.

Sophia's brother Austin had been sent to live with an uncle in Paris, New York; her brother Roger to live with Cynthia, by then married to the doctor son of the Reverend Hezekiah Taylor in Newfane. This left the boy Sardis, then twelve. Sophia wished him to stay with her. There was also her cousin Arcena Smith.

Well, said Ruddy, Arcena and Sardis could live right with him and Sophia, once they were married. Indeed, he would adopt Sardis as his own, and put him to work in the Dummerston store.

On September 13, 1813, in the tavern home that had belonged to Drusilla's vanished major, Sophia and Ruddy were married. There was some dancing to the music of a fiddle, and some tinkling of glasses. Then the "lad with the rubicand hair" and his bride, "the lass with the roseate cheeks," went to live in bustling Dummerston township.[11]

CHAPTER X

War and Peace

1

"The Times! The Times!" Ruddy Hayes had written to Sophia a few weeks before, out of concern over business ups and downs, high prices for manufactured articles, low ones on produce and outrageous government regulations. His customers wanted English products. But these were forbidden by law. "This is very disgusting to our customers and 'tis impossible to please them at present. In truth, I cannot please myself very well," Ruddy said.[1]

In truth, the times were out of joint. For since June 18, 1812, the nation had been officially at war again with England.

Fortunately, despite Ruddy's affiliation with the Dummerston militia as a captain, entitled to wear "a red-sashed uniform with a flashing sword and nodding plume," [2] the danger of his having to go off to fight was slight. If it were a question of demonstrable patriotism, Ruddy would no doubt have gone. But in New England "Mr. Madison's War" was considered anything but patriotic by the people of Ruddy's station, in particular by merchants.

Indeed, in view of the strong position on the matter taken by his hero and patron, the Honorable John Noyes, it would have been surprising had Ruddy been anything but a peace-party man. For in the fall of 1812 Sister Polly's husband was the Federalist candidate on a "peace" ticket for Congress from the Brattleboro district. Like all Federalists, he declaimed that President Madison had plunged the United States into a needless war in order to assure for himself a second term as President.[3]

Noyes was defeated then but pursued the interest in politics, which explained in part his decision to make Ruddy his junior partner in the Noyes & Mann store in Dummerston.

Moreover, the Honorable Noyes and the Honorable Samuel Elliot, a lawyer soon to be the second husband of Ruddy's widowed sister, Linda, were the leaders of the Brattleboro branch of the Washington Benevolent Society, a secret political society of Federalists. This society, which the Jeffersonians called "seditious," had its regular Brattleboro meeting place in the Hayes tavern. Ruddy's father and brother,

Russell, were full-fledged members and Ruddy himself would have been were he not then living in Dummerston.[4]

Ostensibly formed to do charity and perpetuate the memory of George Washington, its real purpose was to oppose the war.[5]

Sophia Hayes was uneasy about this agitation against the constituted government at Washington. It all seemed contrary to her Christian principles. But she was certainly pleased that Ruddy's peace views kept him from dashing off to join the war. Indeed, save for the shadow of the war and the bad times, Sophia felt that her cup of joy really was running over. For she had her loving and beloved Ruddy. "He did not let me know if he saw my imperfections. He was always cheerful and kind," she said.[6]

2

Yet Sophia's lot did not permit happiness to be long unaccompanied by some sorrow. In August 1814, in the month British troops burned the Presidential Mansion in Washington, her first child was born. It was a boy, and with red hair like Ruddy's. It was to be called Rutherford Birchard Hayes—so it had been decided.

But this child was born dead—"never had the breath of life" in him. Then it was Ruddy Hayes who went into melancholy. "He would cry out loud, seemed to have no command over his feelings." [7]

And this time Sophia proved to be the lifesaver. "Did you ever observe this singular trait in her of being rather disposed to look on the dark side when others are joyous, & rising as others are depressed . . . thus preserving the equilibrium in our family?" one of her children asked later.[8] Then she displayed this quality clearly. She soothed, and chattered, and loved Ruddy's depression away.[9]

3

After that there occurred a chain of events that lifted everyone's spirits. In the fall the Honorable John Noyes ran again for Congress, and this time he was elected.[10] Later his election to Congress was not considered good. He himself said, "It is a dog's life—and worse!" [11] But what troubled his family most was that in Washington John Noyes acquired, or finally yielded to, his "most saddening vice," an "overweening taste" for alcohol.[12] However, in November 1814 Noyes's election triumph was counted a matter for rejoicing. Besides,

Ruddy profited. General Jonas Mann, disapproving of Noyes's politics, withdrew from Noyes & Mann. Thus Ruddy became a full partner in the Dummerston store, henceforth called Noyes & Hayes.[13]

In the following June there was cause for even greater joy in the Dummerston household of Ruddy and Sophia Hayes. On June 9, 1815, Sophia gave birth to another son, a healthy child, also a redhead. He was called Lorenzo. A month earlier the war was ended by a treaty signed in Russia, just in time to prevent adoption of a conscription law that might have caught Ruddy, if it did not first split the Union. A rousing celebration was held in the Hayes Tavern. Ruddy and Sophia helped to serve the drinks and joined in the toasts that gave thanks to God and to Federalists.[14]

CHAPTER XI

To the Far-Distant Land

1

But peace brought a bewildering consequence. As in Daniel Austin's time, economic depression struck the New England states. With the need for supplying the army and navy gone, farm-produce prices went into a sharp decline. Restored trade with England brought a glut also in manufactured items.[1]

Moreover, much of the land in Vermont, used too prodigally, seemed just then to have given out all of a sudden. This time there was no Shays' Rebellion. The stricken common folk had a better outlet for their discouragement: "the western fever." Family after family in Vermont especially set out for western New York and Ohio.

Each family gone from Dummerston meant, of course, one less customer at Ruddy Hayes's store, and he became restless. He wished to yield to the urge to move on. Already dozens, even hundreds, of his and Sophia's kin had yielded to that same urge. Austins, Smiths, Hayeses, Birchards, Phelpses and members of various families into which they had married—Kilbourns, Fields, Pettibones, Bigelows, Cooks, Tafts, Grants, Shermans, Chandlers, Moodys—swarmed out of the Connecticut River Valley to settle in the West, though some also went to the South. They spilled over the land, as far as California.[2]

Great numbers of the kin of course remained in the old Valley of the Connecticut, like one cousin of Ruddy's mother, Sophia Smith, who was to establish Smith College at Northampton, and another cousin who was to establish Mount Holyoke College at South Hadley. Some came back from the West, like Seth Smith, no longer dashing, who returned from western New York to die at last in old Granby, a widower of two wives.[3]

But so many had joined the new migration that all the other valleys of America were being populated by them. By 1815 it was plain that Ruddy Hayes of Dummerston was destined to join in the exodus, with his eye especially on the Ohio country.

2

This was contrary to Sophia Hayes's deepest desire. She did not wish to leave Vermont, ever. The only move willingly contemplated by her was one of fifteen miles—from Dummerston to Brattleboro. But Ohio! The tales of fortunes to be made out there did not inspire her. Instead, they reminded her of the warnings in Bunyan's Vanity Fair.

Sophia's desires might have prevailed except for nature's taking a hand in the year 1816, called "the year 1800-and-froze-to-death." In the town of Peacham, Vermont, a farmer lost a toe as a result of frostbite in June. Even in August there was frost. Corn was so scarce that one ear alone cost twenty-five cents. Ministers said this was a visitation from the Lord, punishment for war and other sinning.[4]

But the western fever became an epidemic even so. "A sort of stampede took place from cold, desolate, worn-out New England," as Peter Parley said.[5] A constant stream of emigrants clattered past the Hayes Tavern in Brattleboro. Among Dummerston families to depart were Ruddy's close friends the Millers, with whom he had boarded before he married Sophia, now in Newark, Ohio. Already in Delaware, Ohio, was Sidney Moore, comrade of Ruddy in the Dummerston militia.[6]

3

In 1816 Sidney Moore, then a clerk in the Government Land Office at Delaware, returned to Dummerston for a visit. He gave Ruddy specific information about the Ohio country. "He pictured the golden opportunities for business in Ohio and remonstrated with him for proposing to spend his life where there was no propect of increasing business or of social advancement for his family." [7]

As it happened at just this time, on finishing his term in Congress, John Noyes decided to retire from business as well as politics and to sell his interest in the stores. Instead of buying out the Noyes interest in the Dummerston store, Ruddy decided to sell out too.[8] On March 20, 1817, he placed in the Brattleboro *Reporter* a notice that the firm of Noyes & Hayes was to be "dissolved" by April 15, next. That meant that Ruddy had determined on the western venture.

Unlike others, Ruddy did not intend to go out to Ohio with his family without first prudently inspecting the situation there himself. Besides, Sophia was again big with a new child. The Noyeses, having moved temporarily to Dummerston while a new home for them was being readied in Putney, took Sophia and Lorenzo in with them, so that she would be properly cared for if the baby should come before Ruddy's return.[9] With Sardis, now fifteen, and Arcena Smith to help at the store, which was not yet sold, Ruddy, on the seventeenth day of June, 1817, rode off, a young Yankee Ulysses, to inspect the beckoning West.[10]

4

He had no specific destination in mind as he and his horse joggled up and down the often steep westward trail, a route later called U. S. 20. Cleaveland, in Ohio, at first interested him most.[11] He found this new village of Cleaveland then in a state of both "boom and bust." True, there was talk of digging a canal from the village to the central part of the state, which would eventually connect Cleaveland with Cincinnati on the Ohio River. Cleaveland's boosters insisted this would make it a great metropolis—if the Erie canal were completed. But Ruddy was skeptical. It would take a long time to cut a canal. Work had been projected on the Erie to connect Albany with Buffalo since 1812. That ditch was not yet finished.[12]

Eighty miles to the west there was a settlement called Lower Sandusky. Land there could be obtained cheaply enough, especially as much of the area was black swamp. And it was a good location for a business because of the port facilities and an Indian reserve.

But Ruddy learned that Lower Sandusky, settled then mostly by ex-soldiers from Kentucky and by French Canadians, was a rowdy place. It had no church, and the place wanted none—then.[13] Even fifteen years later a Presbyterian missionary just out of Princeton described Lower Sandusky as "this *seat of Satan*, this *Canton* of his western Empire . . . famous for vice and Infidelity, a resort for Counterfeiters, horse thieves, highway robbers &c &c." [14] Ruddy knew that Sophia could never be happy in such an ungodly spot—never.

5

Following a stagecoach route through the dense forests, he came at last to Delaware, town of his friend, Sidney Moore. There, in a popu-

lation of 400, Ruddy found so many Vermonters and other New Englanders that it was like being in Brattleboro again.[15] In Delaware there
were already well-settled churches, including one established by John
Noyes's Dartmouth classmate, young Philander Chase, later to be
famous as the Episcopal bishop of Ohio and founder of Kenyon College.
This, he knew, would please Sophia, as indeed it pleased him.

Ruddy looked over some of the choice farm land. On July 21,
1817, he selected a tract about a mile and half north of Delaware,
alongside the Whetstone. His tract comprised "by estimation, 124
acres and sixty-four perches," for which Ruddy agreed to pay $2,888.[16]
He also inspected some city lots, on which to build a home.[17]

He rented from Colonel Moses Byxbe, originally of Granville, Massachusetts, a frame house, one of some thirty houses in the town, on a
path called William Street not far from the river. Then, filled with
elation, Ruddy Hayes started for home to "see properly," as he phrased
it, Sophia and their boy, Lorenzo. He arrived back in Vermont at the
end of July for joyous embraces and reunions and to prepare for the
removal of his family to Delaware. His return was made even happier
by the presence of his second child, Sarah Sophia, who had been born
July 10, 1817.

6

By the following September all was ready for Ruddy to go back to
Ohio with Sophia, with the boy Lorenzo, then two, with the infant
girl, and with Arcena Smith and Sardis. Ruddy had made his preliminary trip by horseback, but this time he provided two covered
wagons and a spring wagon.[18]

On Sunday, September 9, 1817, the day before their departure, the
travelers visited with Ruddy's parents in Brattleboro. They attended
services in the Congregational meetinghouse, located on land which
Chloe's father, Israel Smith (now dead in New York State), had do-
nated. To the parents, as to Sophia, going to Ohio was like going to
a foreign country—like China. Ohio to them was, as said by Chloe,
"a far distant land." [19]

In her diary, the very day of their departure, Chloe wrote:

Sept. 10, 1817. With tender emotions and feelings which cannot
be erased from my mind I will reckon the transactions of this day—
a day long to be remembered by me. Can a mother forget her darling
child, one who has rendered himself more dear by all that we call

lovely—by all the ties of nature and mutual friendship? The tenderest sympathy subsisted between us—not a frown in his looks or an angry word ever escaped his lips—was always obedient to his Father and me. Can I forget such a son—can I think of him at such a distance as he now will be placed without tears in my eyes and my heart ready to break? . . . I hope a kind Providence will protect them thru all the dangers they may have to pass. They have left their native land and gone to land of strangers. . . .

7

Everybody assembled there at the Hayes Tavern that fall day seemed to sense, with trembling hearts, that a portentous new chapter now was opening for the family of the Russells, Smiths, Austins, Birchards and Hayeses in America. Like Ruddy, Sophia, Lorenzo, Sarah Sophia, Arcena and Sardis, America itself was moving westward.

The Victorian Age, as Anglo-Saxons called it, was dawning, though for Americans it almost as justifiably could be called the Hayesian Age.

And Ruddy and Sophia were setting out to help in its birth, or at least to play the part that God in His Infinite Wisdom apparently had willed for them, as Sophia would say. On the spring wagon next to Ruddy, with tiny Sarah Sophia at her breast, she took last long sorrowful looks at the mountains above Brattleboro.[20] Yet she managed to smile through tears. The Lord was still her rock.

8

Ruddy Hayes lost no time and shirked no activity in pursuing his goal of making a fortune. As soon as he had settled his family and himself in Delaware, after the journey of forty days, mainly over the Cumberland Road, he was, as Sophia wrote, "always busy." [21]

Not only did he invest in other plots of some of the best land in and around Delaware; in addition, he dealt in imported merchandise and also, in partnership with a physician, Dr. Reuben Lamb, ventured into what seemed to be the safest and most lucrative of all endeavors, whisky distilling. Judging from the number of kettles and other apparatus that Ruddy owned, his distillery was one of the best in all Ohio.[22] Located "on the run in the [later] grounds of the Wesleyan University near the Sulphur Spring," [23] it alone should have poured a fortune into Ruddy's lap.

But despite all his industry and his daring, the fortune he had so confidently expected eluded him. For all his natural optimism, he found himself feeling defeated. In truth, lacking Sophia's faith and ability to adjust to misfortune, and grieving that he had probably erred in having brought Sophia to Ohio, he had a broken heart.[24]

9

Sophia always believed that Ruddy's dismal situation resulted from his yielding to "a spirit of speculation," that, in defiance of the warnings in *Pilgrim's Progress* against the enticements of "the place called Vanity," he had invested too extensively, bought too much land— just as had happened to her father in Wilmington.[25] But Ruddy's real mistake was in having let himself be the embodiment of the general western, rosy-hued optimism of the time. He was an original believer in the American idea of Manifest Destiny. His belief was well founded, but his timing turned out to be wrong. For no sooner had he got started than the western boom suffered an excruciating collapse.

The heartbreaking turn in Ruddy's material fortunes had one good result from Sophia's viewpoint. Up to then Ruddy had shunned affiliation with any church.[26] But the depression, coming on the heels of little Sarah Sophia's death, put him into a chastened mood. On June 6, 1822, he was admitted on examination to the communion of the Presbyterian Church.[27] Thus, so Sophia later felt, his "disappointment was no doubt the greatest blessing that Providence could send, and led him to place his affections on things above." [28]

Just thirty-nine days after joining the church Ruddy was stricken with "the fever" while working in his fields in the Sandusky Plains near Bucyrus. He was dead three days later. And so his new child, the boy Rud, was destined to be, like President Andrew Jackson, a posthumous son.

BOOK THREE

Fanny and the Buckeye Youth

"I love you like my own life."

—Fanny Arabella Hayes to
RBH, April 3, 1847

"Oh, what a blessed sister she was!"

—RBH in his diary, December
28, 1856

CHAPTER XII

THE MOTHER'S BOY

1

THE BOY Rud, product of all that heritage, of all the mixture of adventuring and stolid living, of rebellion and conformity, of heroism and humbleness, was born October 4, 1822. This was two months and two weeks after his father died. "It was a gloomy night . . . in the west room of the old house which stands on William street. I went for Dr. Lamb. Dr. Hills was your mother's regular physician, but Dr. Lamb was most convenient to find. Arcena was sick. It was about nine or ten o'clock in the evening. It was rather cool for the season. I built a fire. Mrs. Smith, a most excellent nurse, attended your mother. I paid Dr. Lamb $3.50 for his job."

So his uncle Sardis Birchard, then "the man of the house," later told Rud the details of his birth. [1] The full name given to him, Rutherford Birchard Hayes, was first officially set down in June 1823 when his mother carried him, a mewling, "feeble and fatherless child," to the Presbyterian meetinghouse in Delaware to be baptized. At the same time she herself, up to then a Baptist like her immediate kin in Vermont, became a Presbyterian, thus conforming to the trend of New Englanders in Ohio. [2]

From his birth and all through childhood, Rud was reared as an extraordinarily sheltered boy. In large part this was because of his early feebleness. Even after he was a year old, his body was so emaciated that Sardis feared he would always be an invalid. Outspoken Sam Rheem, the mason with an eye for proportion, joked wryly, "In a year or two, he will be all head!" though he added cheerfully, "Stick to him! I shouldn't wonder if he should really come to something yet!" "For two years," Sophia recalled, "I had little hope of his life." [3]

Until he was seven he was not allowed to play much with other children. His sister, Fanny, was almost his only child companion. In that period Sophia "kept him in the house a good deal" and never willingly let him out of her sight unless some member of the household was with him. [4] He was nine before he was permitted to engage in sports with other boys. [5] All the while he was shielded from the

73

slightest manual labor, not even being allowed to chop sticks for the family fireplaces or to help carry from the barn pails filled with milk.

He wanted to do all these things and more. But Sophia would not have it, except for some emergency.[6] The most that he was permitted was to accompany his sister down the street to an abandoned tanyard for filling a little basket with kindling.[7]

Not trusting even to send him to the little district school in the village until long after he was ready, Sophia herself taught him to read, spell and write. It was for her that he copied over and over moralistic sentiments from his dead brother Lorenzo's schoolbooks: "If in our breast we pine at the rich, we commit the sins of greed and envy. . . . Sullenness or obstinacy is perhaps a worse fault of temper than the other two. . . . Ten years I will allot to the attainment of knowledge and ten I will pass in foreign travel." And it was to Sophia that Rud spelled out from the *Dilworth Reader* such reading exercises as:

> No man may put off the Law of God.
> The way of God is no ill way.
> My joy is in God all the day.
> A bad man is a foe to God.[8]

2

It was no wonder that neighbors in this period considered him as "timid as a girl." [9] He would be called "a boy who was never known to crawl under the shady side of a circus tent, who never got behind a fence and drank up half the milk his mother sent him for; never dug out half the inside of a warm loaf of bread on his way home from the baker's; in fact—never did anything but be good." This was nearly true. But it was clearly not his fault. Not even forty years later, when others would acclaim him for his manliness, could his mother really see him as other than a boy in need of sheltering.

Sophia might have treated him otherwise, in spite of the early ill-health, which disappeared anyway before he was four, if not for certain special circumstances. Undoubtedly her brother Sardis would have seen to a different upbringing for Rud had he returned to live in Rud's house after his going away that sad day in May 1826. But this was not to be.

True, after reaching Vermont Sardis had found that he was too much of a Buckeye to be able to live comfortably again in New England. Even if they gave him the whole of the Green Mountains, he simply could not abide the Vermont ways of that period.[10] New England narrowness, as he saw it, especially the New England pre-occupation with worn-out religious questions and the petty ways of doing business, were enough to make of him a Jackson man in politics —almost.

Still seeking relief from his cough, but not caring to find it there, Sardis set off in less than a month for New York City. There he introduced himself to the delights of the theater and "fancy" parties. He bought himself a handsome suit of clothes and discovered also "some beautiful girls." Then he sailed in a cargo-laden windjammer for Georgia, and remained in the South for months.[11]

All the while Rud, in Delaware, "looked forward anxiously" to Sardis' return to the room that was still kept made up for him. "Fanny and I followed him in his travels by tracing his route from his letters on the map," he recalled. "We talked of him constantly. His absence of perhaps ten or fifteen months seemed like an age." [12]

In the end Sardis did decide to stay in the West after all, to enjoy its free ways and opportunities—even if its climate were to kill him. On his return from the South he bought some merchandise in New York on credit for $2,000, and returned to Ohio to enter business, cough and all. But to Rud's dismay he decided not to live again in Rud's house, nor even in Delaware.[13] Instead, he went up into the northern part of Ohio to live and to engage in trade.

Perhaps Sardis really forsook Delaware because he, too, found living with so many womenfolk tiresome. Perhaps his decision was concerned with Arcena, who by then was obviously seeking a husband and becoming, as Sophia once suggested, quite coy for "an old maid." [14] Whatever his real reason, when he did get back to Delaware it was to stay at Rud's house only one day.

Then he was off again, to peddle a pack of notions he had arranged to have sent from New York City to Portland on Lake Erie.[15] Fort Ball was Sardis' first selection as his base. There, on the west bank of the Sandusky River, he opened a store and hoped to do better than he had done as sutler to the canal diggers near Cleaveland while on his way to Delaware.

But he remained in Fort Ball only a few months. The trouble was, to prosper there he had to cheat the Indians, first selling them enough liquor to get them drunk, and this Sardis refused to do. So he moved his store up the river to the bigger settlement of Lower Sandusky, the place Rud's father had passed up because of its morals, and the scene of his own great binge with Ben Powers.

Lower Sandusky was then becoming a busy river port, linking the West with Buffalo, New York, to which wheat from the Sandusky plains was being shipped. There Sardis remained, boarding at "a Respectable French Lady's house," and slowly—at first—working up a trade. Soon he was prospering, for the word spread quickly that "S. Birchard, merchant," was a man to be trusted.[16]

After this, high points in Rud's life were Sardis' visits to Delaware.[17] Sardis usually brought fine gifts. For Rud and Fanny he came with books that became their favorites—*The Lady of the Lake, Lalla Rookh, The Last Dying Speech and Confession of Poor Puss, Tit for Tat,* and some poems mainly glorifying heroes of the Revolution. For Sophia he brought some Bibles, printed in Brattleboro. Best of all, in Rud's view, he brought also a fund of new stories. But he never lived at Rud's house again.

3

Things also would have been different for Rud had his mother remarried. The opportunity came to her several times, as attested by a number of visits made to Rud's house during his childhood by men who were not visiting clergymen. Usually accompanied by women, out of deference to Sophia's sense of propriety, these men often made ingratiating eyes at Rud, or fondled him unctuously, he thought, as they talked in the parlor to his mother.

Sophia, in truth, welcomed some of these visitors, so long as their talk remained on matters religious or political. But she soon cut them off if the conversation turned to anything romantic, as happened more than once.[18]

One man in particular wooed her. A widower, he wrote to Sophia that he had hesitated long before broaching "the tender subject" because he was not certain about the effect on his own children. But he now had arranged for his children, he said, to accept "a new mother," and as for Rud and Fanny, "your dear little ones, *I could, I can, I do love them.*"[19] A "Christian brother," as he described himself, he apparently was well liked by Sophia. But her response to his letter was decidedly negative.

Later, after he had proposed verbally, she sent him a stern refusal.

Sir: I have reflected seriously upon the course I now take. My resolution is not to be shaken. I have often told you that I could not accede to your proposals, however honorable I consider them. My only wish is that the remembrance of them may be buried in oblivion. Justice to myself and Family require me to make one serious request. That is, that you never again visit my house while you remain a *Widower*. After what I have written I should consider a visit from you an intrusion upon the comeliness of my situation, and I should bear it with an ill grace. This scrawl, plain as it is, requires no answer.[20]

Other men made similar proposals, but Sophia's reaction was the same. It did not matter to her that her close friend the Widow Hughes, once wife of the first minister in Delaware, also with a baby posthumously born, had just remarried, going off to the town of Bellepoint, which her new husband, Warden James Kooken of the State Penitentiary, had founded.[21] Bishop Chase also had recently remarried. Her brother Austin, whose own first wife, Roxanna, had died within a year after their marriage in 1819, hinted that she should remarry, as he had done.[22] Even Rud's grandfather, the first Rutherford Hayes in Brattleboro, wrote such hints to Sophia. He told her how happy his brother, Ezekiel, Junior, was in New Haven with his new third wife, "a very agreeable woman," after he had "buried two wives." [23]

But Sophia could never forget the pain caused by the unfortunate remarriage of her mother, Drusilla. More important, she could never see herself as bride to anyone but Rud's father. She was sure that Ruddy Hayes lived on, "in Heaven, not among the goats, but at the right hand of the Judge." [24]

He certainly lived on in her heart and mind. On one "dark, raining, lonely evening," she wrote to a brother-in-law, "Should I ever be so unfortunate as to change my mind (which Heaven forbid) . . . you shall have the earliest confirmation respecting it. Nothing is more calculated to make me sensible of the loneliness of my situation than to have that subject intruded upon me." [25]

She never changed her mind. So Rud was deprived of a stepfather and all that that could have meant for him, for better or for worse. Indubitably this decision by Sophia had a major, even a decisive, influence on Rud's whole life ahead. An immediate result was the centering of almost all her attention on him and bringing him up as an oversheltered boy.

4

It was the same with another decision she made when Rud was
still quite small. Had she picked up her children and returned to
Vermont after Ruddy Hayes died, which would have been natural,
his childhood, to be lived among many kinfolk, including many little
cousins, instead of in "lonely Ohio," then would have been another
matter. But that was not to be either. Not even though Sophia,
while her husband still lived, had always dreamed of the day when
they all would return to Vermont. After Ruddy died the pull toward
her native place became all the stronger. Moreover, on his deathbed
Rud's father had said that she should sell their property in and around
Delaware and "go back home." [26]

For many months Sophia was acutely undecided about this. Friends
and relatives, both in Delaware and back in Vermont, said she should
go; others advised that she stay. The practical ones advised staying.
They pointed out that to sell the new brick house and the farm
lands, as well as other holdings Ruddy had purchased, at the depths
of the depression then prevailing would mean a gigantic loss.[27] If
Sophia were to go back in such circumstances, they said, she would
be a widow with almost no income property, certainly without enough
to sustain herself and the children. Among others, she asked advice
by mail from Dyar Bancroft, husband to Ruddy's sister Sally and a
shrewd lawyer in Chesterfield, New Hampshire. In the spring of
1823 Lawyer Bancroft answered her:

Dear Sister: . . . Many are the pensive hours spent in melancholy
contemplation of [you], our Sister Sophia. . . . We all wish to have
you return. But whether it would be best for you and the children, is
the question; and it really is a question of some difficulty. If, however,
I were satisfied that the climate of your *country* was unhealthy, and I
were afraid that the health and lives of yourself and children would
be jeoparded by staying there, I should by all means advise you to
return. . . . But if not, then arises the consideration of the sacrifice
of property contrasted with the nearer and more immediate enjoyment
of the society of your family & friends, and you can much more easily
determine this point than I can.

This lawyerlike communication did not really help. To resolve
her problem, Sophia decided to make a visit to Vermont. Fortunately
Rud's health took a turn for the better in the summer of 1824. So,
leaving him and Fanny in the care of Arcena and Sardis, Sophia

made the "hazardous and tedious" month-long journey to Vermont, to talk with her advisers and also to test her affection for her native surroundings.

It proved pleasant to be in Vermont again. Yet it left on her much the same impression it had on Sardis. The little Green Mountain towns, so glorious in her memory, could not but appear to her as narrow and drab in reality. For the expansiveness and energy of the West had got into Sophia's blood too. The fact was, Sophia had grown away—and up—from her old environment.

After her return to Ohio she wrote Lawyer Bancroft her decision. "I reflect with much pleasure upon the very agreeable visits I had with my N. [ew] E. [ngland] friends. The thought that I shall meet them no more is painful indeed. . . . Our climate is impregnated with disease and death. *But here our lot is cast.*" [28]

5

So it was determined that Rud would be reared as a Buckeye in Ohio. It was a fateful decision for his future, for otherwise the world might never have heard much about Rutherford Birchard Hayes. But the decision also made it necessary, Sophia felt, that she be especially careful about him as a child.

Topping all these reasons for Rud's being so sheltered was the fact that his older brother, Lorenzo, had followed his father in death. The boy Lorenzo was still alive when Sophia made the decision to remain in Ohio. Indeed, she had taken him along with her on the trip to Vermont, a secondary reason for the journey having been to show him off to the kinfolk there.

Nearly nine when Rud was not quite two, Lorenzo, in Sophia's eyes, was well worth displaying. For presenting him to the relatives, who had not seen him since he was two, Sophia dressed him, as if to make up for his western ways, "in a pale blue mixed satinett round-about . . . & pantaloons," as his grandmother, Chloe, noted. Thus got up, he did indeed make a good impression. All the relatives exclaimed how like Ruddy Hayes he was.[29] And so in that regard, when Sophia returned to Delaware in the late fall of 1824 with Lorenzo, she counted her trip to Vermont a great success.

But only a few months afterward, in January 1825, occurred Lorenzo's tragic death. He had gone skating on a frozen millpond near the Whetstone. Suddenly there was a treacherous crackling sound. The boy had fallen through the ice. Soon his lifeless body was carried to Sophia.

In Brattleboro as in Delaware the "unspeakable anguish of that dreadful day," as Sophia recalled it, caused much grieving.[30] In her diary Grandmother Chloe wrote: "Our dear Lorenzo is drowned. It happened on the twentieth of January, just two years and a half after the death of his beloved father. Dear Sophia, my heart aches for you! You have sorrow upon sorrow. I hope you have support that the World cannot give. Alas! How every earthly comfort is taken away from you."

6

The boy Rud could not then know the meaning of the sudden stillness of his home, of the new tears that washed away Sophia's remaining youth, of the fact that he had lost his only brother, while Fanny had lost her "earliest protector." He scarcely remembered his brother, but he was to feel immediately, as well as for long afterward, the effect of Lorenzo's death; and the first consequence was Sophia's double resolution to protect him from perils, real or fancied. She kept up the excessive sheltering long after her professed excuse, his poor health, had ceased to have any validity. For, in fact, he had become quite sturdy, with "a great appetite for food," especially "mince pies and fattening sweets of all kinds." [31]

In Sophia's defense it should be said that this was not merely feminine folly on her part. There were realistic reasons enough, or so she reasonably could have believed, to set her on a course that might have ruined her one remaining son. For it was a time of general peril for all children. Aside from the dangers of such accidents as that which befell Lorenzo, youngsters also fell in wells and cisterns and drowned, as proved later to be the fate of a son of Arcena. The doctors then had made but little progress toward analyzing, let alone curing, children's diseases. Just the fall before Lorenzo was drowned there occurred in Granville, Ohio, then considered a very healthy place, an epidemic of the fever, in which forty children died within days.

"They are taken on the right hand and on the left. The Voice to us is 'be ye also ready,' " Sophia wrote. "My dear children are perfectly well, but I am filled with fear for them." [32] She determined fiercely that Rud should survive. Most of her mistakes stemmed from this single, understandable, rigid resolve. Inevitably, if temporarily, he became a mother's boy, especially as Sardis remained at Lower Sandusky and only occasionally visited Delaware.

CHAPTER XIII

LEGACIES

1

FORTUNATELY there were other influences which operated on Rud Hayes as he was growing up, including some that stemmed from Lorenzo's death, that set up in him a defensive, countering trend toward manliness. For one thing, there was his reaction to all the talk he had to hear during his childhood about Lorenzo's handsomeness, Lorenzo's courage, Lorenzo's generosity and Lorenzo's brilliant mind. He was never permitted to forget how fine a brother had been lost, how "kind and good-natured, prompt, energetic and courageous" Lorenzo had been.[1]

To this was added the effect of his having heard almost as much about his own shortcomings as a baby, in contrast to Lorenzo, "of those weeks of crying and nursing which Mr. Rheem narrates so often." [2] It all created in him a desire to emulate, even surpass, his dead brother, a desire that never ceased and which caused him to set for himself a goal for achievement higher than he would have had otherwise.

To be a "good boy" like Lorenzo, and thus to be loved and admired as Lorenzo had been, became his great aim. So "the fair Lorenzo" had not lived in vain. Rather, the dead boy's contribution to the living Rud was both good and bad, and in an important sense Lorenzo became, after his death, part of the life of the younger brother who survived.

It was so also concerning his father. Ruddy Hayes, too, left in death an influential legacy to his posthumous son. For so long as Sophia Hayes lived, she impressed on Rud that it was a double pity that he had not known even the touch of his father. Not only did Sophia constantly lament that Rud could not personally appreciate his father's qualities; she also felt that he would have had a better chance to become something important in life if only Ruddy Hayes had lived to help guide and rear him.[3]

In his grown-up years Rud told Sophia that he did not think he had suffered much, if any, from his father's absence.[4] She knew better, of course. "If you had known *your* Father, you would not

81

think children as well cared for as those with a *good* Father," she firmly replied.[5]

But if Rud was not convinced of this, he nonetheless was greatly inspired by the knowledge that he had derived from a father whom everybody recalled with esteem.[6] Indeed, from the way Ruddy Hayes was remembered in Delaware, Rud felt at times that he was more favored with his dead father than his fellows with their live fathers.

There were those who spoke of Ruddy Hayes's good looks and strength of body. Others recalled his good humor in time of trouble, except toward the end. Still others spoke of his industry and integrity. Some, like Sam Rheem, recalled Ruddy Hayes as one who charitably minded his own business, who did not judge others harshly, as illustrated by his refusal in 1820 to participate in an attempted lynching in Delaware of a handsome young physician who had been accused of "lewdness" with a woman in the town.[7]

Some mentioned Ruddy Hayes's liberality and tolerance of opinion. He had contributed indiscriminately to the support of several of the new Delaware churches, buying an Episcopal pew when St. Peter's Church was being erected by the rugged Bishop Chase, and contributing seventeen gallons of his best grade whisky to the steeple raising of the Methodist Church—this at a time when he himself had not yet felt the need to join a church. He gladly listened to all preachers, even German ones.[8] This fact about his father later pleased Rud, who was to emulate him in that respect.

2

Young Rutherford Birchard Hayes never for a moment considered that his father had in any way been a failure. Sardis had told him, "Your father was the best businessman I ever knew." At the time that Sardis said this, the comment was high praise indeed.[9]

In truth, his father became for Rud a grand dream figure, a godlike man. When he had an occasion to set down a description of him, he wrote enthusiastically: "My father was straight, slender, healthy and active, full of energy and life—a witty, social, popular man who made warm friends and few enemies. Could do a great deal of labor and do it well. . . . "[10]

Like his own father, Rutherford Hayes, Senior, the amiable tavernkeeper in Brattleboro, Ruddy Hayes had been a man of peace. Yet his son, Rud Hayes, came to picture his father as a soldier hero.

It is clear that the image in Rud's mind of Ruddy Hayes was a fusion of many childhood heroes, real and imaginary—of George Washington, of Captain Daniel Austin, about whose service in the Revolution his mother had told him, of the gallant knights who saved lovely maidens from danger in the stories of chivalry he and Fanny read, of General Jackson at New Orleans, of General Harrison at Tippecanoe, of his uncle Sardis Birchard and even of the broad-backed Lorenzo.

To be like his father—to be to Sophia and to Fanny what his father had been—for him meant becoming all those figures in one, and that, in fantasy, was his own image of himself. So the mother's boy became, in fact, a lad who, as he himself recalled, "was always ambitious, dreaming of future glory, of performing some virtuous or patriotic action," especially "of military fame, of the laurels which adorn the victor's brow, the pride, pomp and circumstances of glorious war." [11]

Situated as he was, this was largely to the good. But the exaggerated ideas and fancies about his father also exacted a price. For although they filled him with pride and the desire of emulation, they also were responsible for much anxiety.

It was clear that he often suffered from feelings of falling short of his father, from too much fear of failure which, in turn, excited even more ambition in him. His anxiety was betrayed by his over-readiness as a boy to laugh and poke fun at all things. Indeed, because of this means of concealing his disturbance, he swung so far from earlier timidity by the time he was twelve as to be considered a kind of "harum-scarum boy" and "giddy from fun-loving" to the point of irresponsibility. Hearing him get off puns and quips, some perilously close to making fun even of God, was enough to cause Sophia many a sleepless night.

3

However, the great and most lasting effect on Rud of his father's death was that it made him "the man of the house." As it turned out, this prepared him for leadership, for a certain self-reliance, even a pronounced kind of self-assurance, despite the underlying anxiety in his nature.

It also had a significant result with regard to his mother. As his childhood receded, there developed between him and Sophia a changed relationship, one that was a part of growth, but which was also a sign of more than ordinary maturity. This change was due in large part to his precocity. But there was something else.

He became not so much a son to Sophia as a kind of brother, or even a father, and she seemed to accommodate her own attitudes, except for matters quite realistic, to this new psychological role of his. In point was the occasion when, at sixteen, in a letter to Sophia he signed himself, "Affectionately, your Brother," a slip that his sister Fanny caught instantly, making a huge joke of it. "Really," Fanny shot back, "you have established a double relationship—pray what is your authority? Ha! Ha! Ha! F. H."

Rud laughed too. "My authority for signing brother is a certain Indian Chief who lived in the time of Caesar & ruled in Denmark, by name, Mr. Col. Wyconneechechochuckekirmunpananathenother." [12]

It was a great joke—but it was also a true and revealing slip. Fact was, if Rud then had a mother at all, psychologically his true "mother" was not Sophia but sparkling, aggressive Fanny Hayes, his sister. Thus, the mother's boy changed, as he moved into adolescence, to the "sister's man," an easier, though still anxiety-laden role. Thus, too, the influence of Fanny Hayes became in turn the basic key to the temperament and even the career that finally was his.

CHAPTER XIV

The Beloved Sister

1

FROM DEEP motivations and psychological problems of her own, petite Fanny Hayes encouraged the somewhat odd triangular pattern into which Rud's family life shaped itself. She was glad to play the role of mother to her brother, even insisted on it.

Nor did Rud usually object. Looking up to Fanny, as well as adoring her, he nearly always followed her lead. In all that he did or thought, even long after she was gone, Fanny was the dominant, guiding image in his mind, the truly dynamic source of all his ambition, of all his feelings of exultation—and of guilt.

To him lovely, lively Fanny was, as he once Byronically said in a Byronic age, "the dear one," the "beloved sister," his inspiration "to be just and truthful, wise, and pure and good." [1] As such, she was also the source of trouble, of emotional disturbance to be overcome before he could fully mature.

Because Fanny was so agreeable to him, and also so resourceful, he really did not miss having other companions in the period during which he was kept so isolated by his mother. Fanny made up for a dozen playmates, boy or girl. When they both were small, it was she who invented the games they played, she who pulled him on his sled, hopped and skipped with him, taught him poetry and told him stories from her own books, and made up little dramas—one from Scott's *Lady of the Lake*—in which they acted, she the director as well as leading lady. She was never at a loss for thinking up some pleasant excitement, be it reciting a poem, creating a doll, or painting—"daubing," she called it. [2]

It was the same when they grew older. For all her daintiness, Fanny was as competent as any boy in sports and other boy activities. Indeed, as Rud fondly recalled, she "shocked the refinement of Delaware" by her tomboyishness. "She was the best rifle shot of any lady I ever knew. She could even beat Uncle Sardis in playing chess and shooting a rifle at a mark." [3] Rud loved that.

85

2

Yet they did not always get along well, despite the mutual adoration. "We loved each other dearly," he once recalled, "and yet behaved often as if we were hateful enough."

Fanny, who had objected so strongly to Sardis' teasing, was frequently a tease herself, with Rud her victim. This led even to violent fisticuffing. "To her ridicule," he said, "I could only oppose my superior strength. . . . We had many little quarrels, she always having the better with her tongue and I with my fists." [4]

He recognized this exceptionally violent reaction on his part to Fanny's ridicule as a "singular fact." [5] Yet he never fully recognized that this singular fact reflected an inner turbulence that Fanny—and Fanny alone—was able to evoke in him, a mixture of love and something else, and to be speculated about. He had to have Fanny's approval, compulsively so. Yet deep within him he also resented and feared this need. "I remember," he once said, "how I feared her ridicule." [6]

3

Outwardly quite feminine, daintily and charmingly so, a lover of beauty in art and nature, seemingly "a retiring, quiet, modest little girl even so as to be a favorite with those whose sense of propriety swallows up every other virtue," [Rud's words], Fanny Hayes nevertheless was a victim of strong masculine urges. She "longed to be a boy," with all that this meant. All her life she would try to resolve this desire through an almost complete identification with her brother, attempting to live his life as though she were he and he were she. [7] This led her to try repeatedly to dominate him, often subtly and affectionately, but surely and relentlessly, even so.

In Fanny's mind there obviously burned ambitions greater than any Rud himself voluntarily had. Quite early Fanny sensed that because she was a girl she would be forced to attain her own aims through her brother. Though here and there a few women were launching on careers, forerunners of a woman's-rights movement soon to begin, it was then definitely a man's world, and Fanny knew it.

Thus, from childhood she began a campaign (as it turned out to be) of pressuring Rud, out of love for him as well as out of self-love, to become "somebody important," which was what she wanted for herself. Unless he did become important, her desire, more even than his own, would give him no rest—ever.[8]

He did not wholly submit to her domination. Had he done so, he might have become a mere shadow of his sister, a kind of willowy puppet, in effect the passive complement to Fanny's underlying strength. Thus, Fanny's hopes for him and herself would have been defeated. As it was, his own inner strength saved him. Yet the drive to yield to Fanny was still so deep that much painful tension inside him was inevitable.

4

On the whole, so far as either realized, their relationship then and later had an idyllic quality that was the basis for the excruciatingly beautiful love that developed between them. He had only the happiest memories of their childhood together.

With Fanny it was the same, even more markedly so. She never ceased to enjoy conjuring from her memories pleasant word pictures of their life together in their native village, pictures always of her and Rud, Rud and her, seldom of Sophia except as some shadowy, though loved, person who was there, but only as background for the memories of her and her brother.[9]

Fanny once wrote to Rud after they were grown:

As I recall our early days, they were all long merry ones, when we laughed & laughed, if it were only at the sound of each other's voices. Those weekly walks to the farm are only remembered as rambles in the shade when, sitting down, we bathed our feet in the brook & watched the minnows, or gathered pebbles. Our toiling along the dusty road the *long* mile that seemed so weary is almost always forgotten. How many Saturday afternoons at this season of the year we have wandered through the woods after nuts, making all the noise we could rustling through the fallen leaves—in Winter how many times in the early morning we have scampered off to the "run," to slide until breakfast time. . . . Can we ever enjoy anything with such zest again?[10]

Two "half sad, half agreeable" memories in particular gave her great pleasure. One was of herself and Rud, "two simple-hearted children . . . [who] come out & lie down in the shade of the great cherry trees, with their books—the books lie closed on the grass, while they curl dandelion stems & hang them on their ears, string Four O'clocks on long straws of timothy, or dig mimic wells & fill them with water." [11] The other concerned their playing in the little cemetery near the low mound under which were buried their father, the little sister and the brother.

Not far from the cemetery mound, below what seemed to Rud and Fanny a steep cliff, there ran through foliage a narrow brook. Fanny remembered with pleasant nostalgia the wonder of the day she found "that lonely brook with its overhanging banks." Excitedly she called it to the attention of little Rud. Something about the brook, perhaps its sunny contrast to the quiet of the burial grounds, its promise of merriment and motion despite the quietude all around, induced in both a mood of sudden, uninhibited exultation. They spent all the rest of the day climbing up and down the "cliff" near the chattering, lively stream, shouting merrily, "High banks! High banks!" [12]

5

This idyllic companionship with Fanny had its compensations, of course. It gave to Rud's youth a poetic quality which helped to shape in him a rosily optimistic frame of mind, so in keeping with a basic spirit of his era. But it had for him its perils also. Indeed, in view of Fanny's influence and the high-tension love between them, together with his mother's sheltering of him and the strongly feminine atmosphere of his home, it was something of a miracle that he did not become permanently marked as excessively feminine.

This did not happen to him. Instead, the pulls in him toward manliness—toward what Sardis and his image of his father represented—triumphed. Rather than the seemingly inevitable sissy, he became an almost typical Buckeye boy, "full of life and fun." [13] After Sophia let the bars down, he had many boy friends, even though Fanny, being possessive, did not like that.

But he never grew away from Fanny. She would have been able to see that he did not, even had he wished to, which he didn't. But after he was nine, she did have to share him with boys, with whom he engaged with special gusto in all manly sports, "hunting, fishing, rowing, sailing, swimming, skating, riding and the like," and in which he became "an expert." [14]

Moreover, contrary to the impression he made by his neat appearance, the reddish curly locks, the innocent blue eyes, he became a boy who, like most real boys, had to be cajoled, scolded and threatened with the direst of punishments, both by his mother and his sister, to oil his shoes, clean his nails, brush his clothes and submit to a hair trim.[15]

He was not so wholly masculine as his father had been, nor so sturdy and intrepid as Lorenzo. Nor was he nearly so completely western as Sardis. But despite the certain wistful, moony manner and the youthful face as finely shaped as a lovely girl's when he was in his teens, he was manly and Buckeye, nevertheless.

CHAPTER XV

The Secret Burden

1

Indeed, he was a belligerently loyal Buckeye. He made a special point of showing devotion to western ways and ideas, which, to him, represented rugged manliness. He professed only contempt for what struck him as soft eastern effeteness. "As you know, I have an aversion to Yankees," he told Sardis when he was fifteen. In imitation of Yankee talk, he added, "I hate to find one that there a'nt some fault peculiar to them where I cannot have an excuse for. . . ." [1]

His mother worried that he had become too Buckeye. In her opinion much of his language was shocking. She found his voice to be "too loud," his manners "unpolished," and complained about this to Sardis, though in these very things Rud was modeling himself, he thought, after no one so much as Sardis. [2]

But Rud vowed that no one would make of him anything but a western man. Inspired by his reading of Walter Scott, he drew a heraldic crest for himself. It turned out to be a circle in which he sketched a scythe, a rake, a pitchfork crossed, a haycock (for Hayes), and beneath it all, in bold letters, the motto:

R. B. H.
BUCKEYE

In later years he chose for a formal motto the word "*Recte!*" But as a youth he would have scoffed uproariously at any such mark of "eastern gentility" as that. [3] Buckeye was what he intended to remain.

2

Outwardly he became a boy with pronounced self-assurance. So, at least, most persons viewed him, especially friends who were impressed by his ability and willingness to deliver memorized orations on patriotic themes with very little or no coaxing. These he got off with such vigorous aplomb that admiring young auditors were often convinced they were indeed listening to Patrick Henry, Henry Clay, or Daniel

Webster, especially the last, whose "Reply to Hayne" was and remained his favorite recitation.[4]

Fanny in particular was delighted, and her encouragement, even permission, was important to him, deeply so, then as in after years. One of her specific dreams for Rud was that he should be another Daniel Webster, her patriotic hero.

A young cousin who heard Rud "give a specimen of his oratory and strength of lungs on top of a hill" was so impressed that she was sure then that young Rutherford Birchard Hayes, "so clever and learned," as she considered him, a boy "with the biggest head I ever saw, would one day be the President of the United States." [5]

He liked the center of the stage but did not insist on it. He encouraged others to "orate" also. He was "remarkable for self-esteem," as he himself once quipped.[6] But he was loyal to his friends. He was still the friendly fellow, practicing instinctively the art of give and take in human relationships, and continuing to build the group of well-wishers that started collecting around him when he was just a little boy.

It was easy to see that, being the beneficiary of so much love in his family, he was able to have an attitude of good will toward almost everyone. He knew that he did not have to be miserly with love but could dispense it freely. Thus, as was the case with his father in the Connecticut River Valley, he was liked and admired by everyone. He was, as they said, "solid," and "a right fellow," a kind of tower of strength in his circle.

3

' However, inside him stirred confusing, turbulent emotions. He was anxiously conscious throughout his youth of a great feeling of nervousness, of deep, incomprehensible tension. Indeed, all unknown to anyone else (though Fanny and also Sardis learned later to suspect it) there was such turmoil in him that, as he himself confessed, he at times felt "nervous to the verge of disaster." He "went to pieces on the slightest provocation," he said.[7]

Oddly he ascribed this nervousness to a fear that there was a streak of insanity in his family, expressing the opinion that this fear had come from awareness "of a number of near relatives on both my mother's and father's side of the house having become insane." [8] He came to believe, curiously, that the source of that supposed tendency was none other than the proudest branch of his ancestral tree, the Russell clan.[9]

But this was rationalization. While apparently satisfying him, it missed the real cause of his disturbance. It was to be found not in his inheritance, nor in any realistic fear of that inheritance, but in the effect of his immediate environment, in his home, in the subtle and also not so subtle pressures on him from Fanny, from his mother, from his having to grow up as a posthumous son in a home dominated, except for his uncle, by women.

If he owed anything to his inheritance, he owed not his nervousness, but a strength that permitted him in the end to overcome that nervousness.

A major cause of his disturbing tension was obvious. It was the ineffably close relationship, so tender, so beautiful, so satisfying, so important, so constructive and yet so destructive, that flowered between himself and the beloved and loving sister, Fanny.

4

Fanny was his girl, his mother, his comrade (as much a boy as girl in this instance), all in one. When they were apart the letters that she wrote to him were the letters of a sweetheart. "Dear brother Rud," she began one letter to him. "Must we wait till Winter before we see you? . . . Oh, it makes my heart ache to think that our affection may be chilled by absence! . . . Sometimes [I] awake in the night & feel I must go to you & see if you are indeed safe. You are daily the object of my waking thoughts & almost nightly of my dreams. Dear brother, be careful of yourself I entreat you, for *our* sakes if not for your own. . . . Write, do write dear brother, Adieu, FANNY." [10]

A little later, though more subtly, she wrote him in a way that told much: "I am reading between daylight & dark 'House of Seven Gables.' Poor old Hepzibah is the only novel heroine I should never think of emulating, but if I had been an old maid & you Clifford— no, just yourself with Clifford's griefs—I should have gloried in being Hepzibah. . . ." [11]

At the time Fanny thus unburdened herself, she had long been securely married, and happily so, as far as she knew.[12] She was also the mother of several children. But in fact as well as fantasy, Rud remained her one true love, as she was his, with tension inevitable. Yet he dissembled his anxiety so well that only rarely would anyone have guessed, from observing him, that he did carry this hidden burden. He labored valiantly at steadying his nerves. It would turn out that he would be magnificently victorious in this struggle, though not without setbacks. Actually, because of the struggle that it meant for him, his secret burden played a greatly constructive part in his whole life. For his overcoming of the burden proved to be a major step toward the maturity he slowly attained.

CHAPTER XVI

The Ancestral Valley Beckons

1

IN THE SUMMER of 1836, when he was nearly fourteen, he went off to a boys' academy at Norwalk in the upper part of the state, and thus was separated for the first time, physically at least, from his tension-charged home. Not that this was his own wish or plan, however. Rather, it was the idea of his uncle, Sardis Birchard.

Up at Lower Sandusky Sardis Birchard had found by then, if not robust health, the road to considerable wealth. For reasons related mainly to timing and to luck the same gods that had frowned so sternly on Ruddy Hayes had smiled on Sardis. In 1836 he was the leading man of Lower Sandusky, his position symbolized by the fringe beard that now genteelly framed his face.

In part, Sardis' comfortable financial position had come from his partnership in R. Dickinson & Co., acclaimed as the largest and best-stocked merchandising house west of Cleveland. Previously Sardis had done very well at Lower Sandusky with his own business, which had included shipping wheat, pork, timber, staves and barreled fish to Buffalo, New York, and at times even to Europe.

Moreover, he had an especially good thing in being exclusive provisioner to the reservation for Seneca Indians in the vicinity. This franchise came to him after the Senecas had had a sad experience with their leader, Chief Hard Hickory, whose duty it was to go to Albany, New York, to collect an annual payment owing to them in gold from the State of New York for their having moved out to Ohio. One year soon after Sardis settled in Lower Sandusky, Hard Hickory, instead of returning promptly with the money he had collected as usual, went on a binge and returned empty-handed, telling his people that the payment was delayed.

At a solemn council trial in the village, Hard Hickory was sentenced to be killed—and after that Sardis, as an "honest pale-face," was appointed as the person to collect the annual payment for the tribe. The arrangement was for Sardis to keep the money "on deposit," the Indians to receive the equivalent in merchandise from his store.[1] So he often prospered when other merchants did not, this to a degree that by 1832 he had decided to retire from trade and divide his time between taking trips—still for his health, one of which took him to South America—and merely watching his investments in land.

2

At just this time Rudolphus Dickinson, Jr., a young, shrewd and aggressive lawyer from Whateley, Massachusetts, whose kin included the less worldly poet Emily Dickinson, came to Sardis with a sure-fire business proposal. A Jacksonian Democrat with Whiggish views, just as Sardis was a Henry Clay Whig often with Jacksonian views, Lawyer Dickinson, a Williams College graduate, had become a political power in the State of Ohio as a result of the "Jacksonian Revolution." Specifically he became a member of the State Board of Public Improvements, which had jurisdiction over road building and state canal projects. Just then a new macadamized road, the Western Indiana and Maumee, was being constructed, with a large labor camp at Maumee, not far from Lower Sandusky. The contractors needed to buy great amounts of provisions for their hundreds of laborers. It was Dickinson's idea to sell these provisions, but he needed a store for that purpose and someone to direct it. Obviously since he controlled the road-building contracts, the contractors would see the point of dealing where he suggested.

So R. Dickinson & Co. was formed, with Sardis a silent partner in it. The firm prospered immediately. Moreover, when business became slack, Dickinson had a ready remedy. He simply went to the state legislature at Columbus and lobbied through some new road or canal project, which guaranteed additional business for the firm, to the profit of himself, of Sardis and two other partners.

What made this political aspect of the business run so smoothly was an interesting fact: While Dickinson (who later was elected to Congress) was able to win the favor of Democrats in the legislature, Sardis, who in 1832 became a founder of the Whig Party in Sandusky County, was able to do the same with the Whig members.[2]

3

However, it was still another arrangement, a veritable fairy-tale stroke of fortune, that formed the basis for the considerable wealth that Sardis in the end was to amass—with consequent important results for the career of Rud Hayes. This windfall, as it turned out to be, really had its beginning that gloomy year in Rud's life when Sardis left the home in Delaware.

On his visit to New York City that year of 1826, in search of some merchant there who might sell him goods on credit, Sardis attracted the attention of William P. Dixon, a partner in the wholesale dry-goods firm of Amos Palmer & Company. Dixon took an instantaneous liking to Sardis as they talked in front of the store on Maiden Lane, and one upshot was that Amos Palmer & Company staked Sardis to the merchandise with which he had begun business first at Fort Ball and then at Lower Sandusky.[3]

Even more fruitful was a second upshot of the continuing friendship between Sardis and Dixon. In 1835, as during the time when Ruddy Hayes had been enticed from Vermont to Ohio, a new boom in western land developed. Whole towns in the West, like Chicago, Milwaukee and Toledo, seemed to grow overnight after sleeping as mere settlements for years.

Dixon became tremendously interested in taking fliers in western speculation, and Sardis looked to him like a good agent. After making a killing selling gunpowder and similar war matériel to France in connection with Emperor Louis Philippe's invasion of Africa, Dixon made a proposal to Sardis. He would put up $10,000 for purchasing western land. Sardis was to do the selecting and the buying. Profits would be split equally; loss would be absorbed by Dixon.[4]

Sardis thus had the use of what then represented a large sum of money. He bought prudently, yet boldly. Dixon put up another $10,000, and another, and still others, and urged Sardis to buy more than he would have on his own hunches. "Do not be afraid!" Dixon exclaimed. "I look forward to the time when this investment will make us both rich. With your good judgment, industry & with me to furnish the money, we shall do well. We must keep operating & when a good opportunity offers for selling out at a good profit, then sell and invest again, thus keeping things moving."[5]

Before long both Sardis and Dixon had acquired a profit several times the size of the original $10,000. In one deal alone Sardis bought $15,000 worth of property in the vicinity of Maumee and Toledo. "I have made you rich, Sardis! I will now make you very rich!" Dixon said—and the prophecy came true.

But in the end Dixon had to pull out. A money crisis in 1837-39, the so-called Jackson panic, forced him to sell most of his own holdings at reduced prices in an effort to stave off the threatened bankruptcy of his firm. "We are all fools together & have all been deranged. We have all sold too many goods . . . imported too much . . . bought too much land & we must all come back to first principles. We have all been Jack Asses," he told Sardis. In October 1837, when nearly all banks in the United States suspended payments, Dixon moaned: "The Whole Country gone to Hell." By 1839 he was asking Sardis for help, even had to sell his holdings.

But because he was on the ground, Sardis managed to hold on to many of his own best buys. When the economic sun shone again, he was independently wealthy for life, no matter what new depressions might come.[6] The Seneca Indians gave him a special name: An-Se-Queg, the Man Who Owns Most of the Land.[7]

4

Sardis' relative affluence was accompanied by his development of one of the widest circles of influential acquaintances in Ohio. For business reasons, or to enjoy his stories and the fine brandies and whiskies that he always had on hand, the leading men of Ohio and also men destined to be leaders beat a path to his door. In particular these included Mr. Justice Ebenezer Lane of the Ohio Supreme Court, who then lived at Norwalk, and a young lawyer, Morrison R. (Mott) Waite, then of near-by Maumee, a future Chief Justice of the United States.

These friendships, and other connections of Sardis', would be important in the future for Rud Hayes, already known in Lower Sandusky as Sardis Birchard's nephew. He would never be able to travel very far in Ohio without meeting someone who knew his uncle and was eager to do some favor for him because of a debt, pecuniary or social, owed to Sardis. They were also important at this time for Rud. For Sardis, though almost without any formal schooling of his own, developed from such friends as Judge Lane and Lawyer Waite a great admiration for college-bred ways—at least for Rud. He took a strong stand that Rud should be a college man also.

By then Sardis doubtless suspected that, despite some romantic efforts which had come to nothing, he would always remain a bachelor. Thus Rud would be his heir and the equivalent of his own son. In truth, that was how Sardis increasingly considered Rud. And his position was that, though he still preferred the rougher ways for him-

self, Rud must grow up as a gentleman like "Mott" Waite and especially Judge Lane, who, a transplanted New Englander too, was then
one of the most urbane men in northern Ohio.[8]

5

Rud himself wanted nothing of the kind. It was true that at the
little private grade school in Delaware, operated by Dr. Hill's daughter
Mrs. Murray, he was chosen as the outstanding boy scholar. Like his
father, he had won certificates as a champion speller. "Not one in a
thousand could spell me down!" he once boasted.

But he showed his real attitude toward the scholarly life then,
when, given his choice for an award in Mrs. Murray's school between
a book and a jew's-harp, he unhesitatingly chose the jew's-harp, much
to Fanny's dismay and Sardis' amusement—at the time.[9]

At any rate, after he finished with the grade school he scoffed at the
idea of preparing for a college career. He intended to be a self-made,
outdoor man—like Sardis. So while Sardis was thinking and writing
to his mother about a collegiate career for him, he was "splendifer-
ously happy" in Delaware whitewashing the walls of his house, clean-
ing out the old cistern and putting in a new one, proud of his skill
and of his mother's gratitude for his helpfulness around the house.
"Rutherford is a good boy," Sophia wrote to Sardis. But she agreed
"he should be at something of more importance." [10]

Rud also agreed. But he still dreamed of soldierly fame, and what
had that to do with college?

This attitude would not do, Sardis said. Rud had to become a
young gentleman. That meant going away to school, first to an academy and then to a college, preferably in the East.

At first, Sophia tended to be on Rud's side, but only because she
shuddered to think of Rud leaving her, even for the further education
she too felt he ought to have. With Fanny (who sided with Sardis)
also desiring to go away to school, at least for one year, Sophia told
Sardis that she could not "think of being separated from both my children." [11] However, Sophia also was still worried over Rud's "unpolished manners." She knew that he needed the discipline of more
school.

Sophia had hoped that Rud could get this schooling right there in
Delaware. She was elated when some Delaware leaders began organizing a boys' academy. But this plan came to nothing. Then Sophia

engaged Sherman Finch, a Delaware lawyer who had been a Yale tutor, to act as private tutor to Rud. But Finch was often away on law business. When this happened Rud did no studying. "You must not expect to see Rutherford much improved in manners—neither does he study. . . . Mr. Finch heard him recite, but started suddenly for New York and Rud had no person to hear him recite, and you know he never would study without a teacher. I cannot blame him much." So Sophia wrote to Fanny, then at the Female Seminary at Putnam, Ohio.[12]

6

In the end Sophia agreed that Rud should attend the Norwalk Academy, a Methodist boarding school highly recommended by Judge Lane, who had placed his own son Will there, and whose house was next door to it.[13] So to Norwalk Academy Rud was sent. Though objecting at first, he soon became "anxious to go." [14]

He liked it at once. "Dear Uncle—I do not think I shall have to go home because I am homesick. . . . The object of my letter is to have you send me—if you can get—my shoes. I want them very much." [15]

"I am doing very well in my studies," he wrote to Sophia on October 13, 1836. "Wednesday was composition day. I wrote one about Liberty. A week ago Wednesday was speaking day. I spoke an eulogy on Lord Chatham. I got along tolerably well, considering. I was not scared, as much as the most of the boys are the first time they speak. Write soon. Tell who is elected to the offices of the county. Ask Mr. Wasson about it."

With Norwalk only sixteen miles from Lower Sandusky, Sardis went over several times to see how Rud was doing and to pay for his board, $1.75 a week.[16] "I am glad to hear you say Rd^s [sic] morals will not be corrupted," Sophia wrote in response to a report on Rud's progress.[17] Later she herself happily reported to Sardis: "He seems to think he is getting along bravely—says he is through Virgil." [18]

But the next summer Rud liked vacation so well that he said he did not wish to continue going to school. Among others Fanny scolded him, gave him quite a lecture. Sophia then thought of entering Rud at Kenyon College in Gambier, Ohio, the institution founded by Bishop Chase. "It will be better than the Norwalk school for him at this time," she told Sardis.[19]

His morals were what concerned Sophia most. She was certain

that any college established by Bishop Chase (though he had departed for Illinois following a schism) would be good for Rud in that respect. However, Sardis again intervened—or (it may be said) there then came a beckoning call to Rud from the ancestral valley of the Connecticut River, which was not to be denied. For when Judge Lane sent his son to Isaac Webb's Preparatory School at Middletown, Connecticut, on the banks of "ye Great River," Sardis succeeded in seeing that Rud went to Isaac Webb's too.

7

There in 1837, in the area settled by so many of his ancestors, in the environment of his heritage, he grew (as he wrote to Sardis) "very tall." Also he received instruction designed, as promised by the school catalogue, to emphasize that "truth, justice, honor, and religion [are] to be regarded as the cardinal points of character," all for $250 a year, board and room.[20]

As at the Norwalk Academy, Rud got along splendidly at Isaac Webb's (later absorbed into Wesleyan University). He found himself keeping up easily with students who had entered six months earlier. This was "rather curious," he told Sardis.[21] He soaked up much Latin and Greek, winning first prize in both, and was especially enthusiastic about translating the *Iliad*.

With gusto he set down in big script one Homeric excerpt in particular: "O! Jove! May he be as his father . . . live a good life and rule powerfully, and some one may say, 'And be better than his father in many things.'" [22]

He enjoyed his life on the banks of the Connecticut. "There are divers things in this blue country I like better than Ohio, for example, Thanksgiving dinner, or even a fast, for we had one the 22d, and if that is a Yankee fast, I move I should like to see a feast!" [23] He was a leader in "The Cobwebbs," a secret society with passwords, pass signs and queer names, most taken out of *Oliver Twist*, then Rud's favorite book. D. Converse Stoddard from Zanesville, Ohio, was Bill Sikes; Tom Hogg of Raleigh, North Carolina, was Fat Jack of the Bone House; Rud was Tin Shins, Earthquake, Rum, but most often Charley Bates, the lad in *Oliver Twist* who was always laughing.

"The Cobwebbs" went off on hunting expeditions, gave parties, consumed liquor and generally made a great noise. They indulged in much collective complaining about the headmaster. As one of Rud's chums said, "Old Webb is getting real sneaking now-a-days. We have not had fresh meat for so long we are all as salty as brine. I believe the beans have begun to shout in me." It was all good fun.[24]

After a year in Connecticut a decision had to be made whether Rud was to stay on in the East. At first he thought he would like to stay at Isaac Webb's for another term and then go to Yale, for that was Judge Lane's program for Will Lane, and it was expected of an Isaac Webb pupil. Rud said he did not want to leave Will Lane, whom he described as "a splendiferous chap, a very odd chap [who] will make, if nothing happens, a very smart man, as smart as his father."[25] He liked the idea then of becoming a Yale man. But he also found that he wished to be in Ohio with Fanny, Sophia and Sardis, especially Fanny.

There burned in him too an intuitive resistance to New England— to Yankees—to the old valley itself. Here was a kind of crisis. Like some lotus land, the old valley would keep beckoning to young Rutherford B. Hayes, as if claiming its own. The old valley had won when he entered Isaac Webb's. Now in the form of Yale, in the establishment of which his ancestor, the grandfather of Rebecca Hayes of Branford, had played a role, it was pulling at him again. Rud was uncertain.

8

Sardis sided with the old valley and Yale. But Sophia did not. She no longer wanted Rud so far away. She insisted that Ohio had just as good colleges as any in New England, especially in Kenyon College. Besides, she decided that Rud, after all, was too young to be so far from home. "He may be led into vice," she told Sardis. "There are so many bad boys sent away to school, [and] he is naturally so full of mirth that he will be more exposed than a more sober boy."[26]

Every time Sophia read in her newspaper about some scandal involving young people, and this was often, she felt renewed alarm about Rud's being in an eastern college. Fortunately she did not yet suspect what lurid sexual scrapes Rud's first cousin, redheaded young John Humphrey Noyes, son of the Honorable John Noyes and Polly Hayes Noyes, would get into after attending Yale—scrapes that proved forerunners of his founding of Bible communism and also of a community at Oneida, New York, which would be accused of standing for free love.[27]

But it was bad enough in her eyes that young Roswell M. Field (destined to be the father of Poet Eugene Field), another of Rud's cousins, had become involved in an open scandal of such proportions that the whole Green Mountain area was shocked. Even Sardis, on one of his trips, heard about it down in Alabama. "In travelling some days ago I stept into a bar room, took up a paper and saw that R. M. Field was married to another man's wife." [28] This was not quite accurate. But the facts were shocking enough to cause more worry for Sophia over Rud's fate, if such things could occur right in his own family.[29]

To Sardis Sophia wrote:

I told Ruth[d] [sic] that I thought he had better return; Fanny is so anxious to see him that she cannot think of his staying. I should consent to his staying if I thought it best, but I think it would be just as well for him to go to college here the next two or three years, then his mind will be more mature, and if we think best he can spend his last year in an eastern College.[30]

Sardis tried to get Sophia to change her mind. But it was no use. She decided, after Judge Lane again was consulted, that Rud should continue his education in the following fall at near-by Kenyon College. She settled things with finality by writing a letter to Isaac Webb that withdrew Rud from the Connecticut school.[31]

9

The disappointment Rud had felt disappeared as soon as he found himself in Delaware again with his sister. Years later he recalled that reunion. "We had been separated a whole year. The stage coach drove up to the door of our old home in Delaware. Fanny, her face so beautiful and joyous, ran out to meet me." He would never, he said, "forget the happiness" that he felt.[32] Fanny felt the same, all the more because it was true that her "man" had become "very tall," precisely the same height as his father.

Sophia, of course, was overjoyed. Yet she could not help but feel a certain disappointment in her teen-age Rud. "I presume," she reported to Sardis, "that he has acquired considerable book knowledge, but he is just as unpolished as ever. I see no great improvement in his manners." [33]

Rud's own appraisal of the year in the old valley was set down by him in a notebook entry.

Entrance in October,	$125.00
Entrance in June,	$125.00
Needfuls in summer term,	$25.00
Needfuls in winter term,	$30.00
	$305.00

Present worth of what I've learned,	$500
Cost	$300
Profit in one year	$200

WERRY GOOD THAT! HAH! HAH! [34]

Obviously at sixteen he had not yet become the young gentleman that Sardis wanted him to be. Yet despite Sophia's misgivings, the process in fact was at work.

BOOK FOUR

The Young Gentleman

CHAPTER XVII

SON OF KENYON

1

KENYON COLLEGE for boys at Gambier, Ohio, which he entered in
the fall of 1838, was fine for pouring into young men a knowledge
of the classics, Christian ethics, theology and all other subjects considered proper for the cultivation of a gentleman in the genteel tradition of culture of the era. Indeed, probably no college in the nation
then was better suited for that, not even Yale or Harvard.

Oddly Rud's mother was for a long time unhappy over what she
considered Kenyon's failure to do better for him in the very field in
which it excelled—to turn out young gentlemen. She feared that it
would be no more successful than Isaac Webb's school had been.

Sophia even considered in the first year taking him out of Kenyon
in order to send him to a "sound" Presbyterian school, like Hudson
College near Cleveland, or Marietta College at Marietta, Ohio. "I
am told the society [at Marietta] is very good—and if you had gone there
perhaps you might have escaped picking up some of the vulgarisms
that you find in Kenyon. I never heard you say 'by George' till the
last time you were at home, nor speak any other such low language!" [1]

Sophia was needlessly worried about Kenyon, as was so often the
case with her in other matters. True, this Episcopalian school failed to
make Rud a professed Christian. It tried, especially during a revival
held at the end of his first year at Gambier. "There are now but ten
in the whole college who are not changed," he reported to Sophia in
August 1839. "*I am among the ten as yet.* . . . Every single one of
my best friends are 'gone,' as it is called. I attend the meetings and
read all the books that my friends request me to, but I find it is the
loss of my friends which affects me more than anything else. I have
but little hope I shall be among them."

It would always be the same with him. Though he considered himself a Christian, something in his make-up would keep him from professing Christ, no matter how heroically the Kenyon faculty and
others later labored with him and prayed for him. But otherwise Kenyon would do for him superlatively what Sophia wanted done in the

way of refining him—though, fortunately, not so completely as she thought she wanted.

2

For a time he himself had seemed willing to leave Kenyon, though for reasons opposite to Sophia's. He objected as fiercely as any student there to the rigid discipline which the Kenyon faculty then attempted. " 'Resist tyranny in every shape,' is my motto, 'but in none is it so dangerous as when exercised by a number of tyrants.' This latter clause suits the faculty of Kenyon College," he told Fanny in February 1839.

"They give a student a fair trial, they say, but do not allow him to say a thing for himself. This is a 'fair trial' truly! Mother wants me to like my teachers. Well, I do like them—a great ways off. She says I must not think my teachers are partial. Well, I don't think they are. I know so."

When Fanny also suggested that he like his teachers, he replied with scorn even to her. "So F. A. Hayes wishes R. B. Hayes to like his teachers. You better get Uncle, Mr. Wasson and all the others concerned to write me to like my teachers." [2]

He talked again of going to Yale—"I suppose on account of the honor of graduating from there," Fanny told Sardis. [3]

But this rebel spirit did not last long. Besides, life at Kenyon was not at all so bad as the rebellious students made out in their letters home, especially during the regime of the Reverend Dr. William Sparrow. [4] For all the discipline, the compulsory chapel attendance, the rigid checking-in and checking-out, Rud and the others got away with much mischievous fun.

Though hunting was forbidden, they hunted often in the woods along Owl Creek, Rud in particular. "We were forbidden to have any guns. I always had two," he once recalled. "There were also strict rules against cooking in the rooms, but we cooked and I had considerable of a reputation as a cook. . . . Dr. Sparrow had a bigger nose than mine. He used it, for he could smell a cooking rabbit further than any mortal. . . ."

Quite possibly Rud was the culprit in the incident that caused Dr. Sparrow to deliver a fire-and-brimstone sermon in chapel one morning "after the discovery of a turkey roast in one of the rooms by a tutor, Ufford." The tutor, one to whom Rud was assigned as a student, had broken down the door and caught the "rascals" in the very act, "all dripping, as the Doctor said, with sweat and gravy and thoughts intent on clandestine enjoyment." [5]

Moreover, in young Hayes's Kenyon account book there was at least one shocking item: "1 pint of alcohol & sasarty . . . 25 cents."

3

Some of the lads—though not Rud—even managed to acquire some extracurricular education of a nonliterary sort by sneaking off to near-by villages, such as Mount Vernon, where they partook experimentally in delights offered freely, or for pay, by certain attractive maidens partial to well-dressed young college boys. Of course, Rud knew all about these exploits, and joined in the palaver about them. "Tell me how A. Picket flourishes with the gals. Tell him I flourish like a green bay-tree," he once wrote a chum.[6]

But this was boastful persiflage. At this stage, though he talked about girls, he would not be caught within ten yards of one if there was danger of anything but talk.

Naturally this was so. His heart still belonged, whether he fully realized it or not, to his sister Fanny. She maintained her hold on him through bright letters, in which she excelled, letters that entertained him and made verbal love to him, and most of all, pressed on him her old ideal of achievement.

In one letter Fanny wrote:

Oh, how I wish you were at home now! We have got plenty to read, & plenty to eat, nothing to do—& as happy as clams, but we want you to scold at. You know it won't do very well for me to scold Mother & if she scolds me, why, you see, I get mad, so we are obliged to let our talents in that line lie dormant, which is a great pity. . . . I have just got "Nicholas Nickleby." Have not read it yet, but the illustrations are *grinable*. Forget whether [or not] I told you in my last [letter that] R. Moody sent me "Oliver Twist." I read all the papers I get. . . . *Be a good boy. Be first in your class.* Keep your teeth clean. Nails ditto. . . .[7]

In another letter she wrote: "Do not waste your time in school as so many do. My aspirations for you are high. Do not disappoint them." [8]

And along the same line: "I have been reading the last week Lockhart's 'Life of Walter Scott' & have made a wonderful discovery. Scott was one of our 'kinsfolks'. Scott's mother was a Rutherford. Now, as we never heard of any other family by that name, what is more rational than to conclude that our ancestors are the same? To prove it, you *must* turn out a genius." [9]

He loved Fanny's letters, saved them all as treasures in his student's trunk, and was not at all prepared when, in the summer of 1839, he received from Sophia some jolting news. Fanny, his "girl," was to be married!

July 20, 1839

DEAR RUTHERFORD:
". . . Seventeen years this day since your dear Father left this world of pain and sorrow. . . . I fear that [another] sad change is coming over my prospects of happiness. You must be away till your education is finished. Your Uncle's health I fear will never be restored and what will be still more strange, Fanny intends to leave her Mother's house and go to Columbus. What do you think of that? If you are angry about it, you must reconcile yourself to it before you come home. You will then see Mr. Platt and *try to like him well enough for a brother*. He is as much undersized as Fanny and of course a pretty good match. For further particulars, I refer you to herself. Get pantaloons if you need them. . . .

4

Two days later, from Fanny herself, he received confirmation of her betrothal. She started her letter with some merry satire of Sophia's sermons, meant to put him in good humor. Then:

Well, verily, Mother has told a doleful tale of my intentions—trust you will bend the sympathising ear & enter fully into the sad horrors of the case. The base ingratitude of a daughter leaving her mother's house—a proper brick one, too—& going to that vicious place, Columbus, than which Sodom & Gomorrah would be more tolerable!

Now you perceive that the sin lieth in leaving the *house,* for the Mother has agreed to go with the daughter withersoever she goeth. And now comes the exhortation—when your anger waxeth hot & burneth, as in all reason it will—you must restrain it—you must chain your hands that in your rage you may do no violence to yourself nor to others & bridle your tongue lest you speak evil words with it. After your anger is a little abated, then try to acquire a spirit of resignation, for many things will you be compelled to suffer when you reach home —therefore come armed with fortitude and forbearance. . . .

You will be required to *"try to like him well enough for a brother"* —mark the expression and draw consolation from it—your conscience may be quieted by *trying* to like him—only think how much more dreadful the requirement would have been if that one little word "try" had been omitted! Fancy one "as much undersized" as the writer, who cannot be compared to the pyramids of Egypt, nor the cedars of Lebanon, nor the tower of Babel. . . .[10]

5

Always so ready to laugh, Rud read Fanny's hilarious announcement without laughing. It was funny, as witty as only a letter from Fanny could be. And yet . . . and yet . . .

Somehow his feelings were quite like those he had back in 1826—so many years ago!—when Sardis went away. A Kenyon lad did not weep, was supposed to grin and say "No odds!" Yet this Kenyon lad, the merriest who ever fished in the Kokosing Creek, or imprudently roasted a rabbit in Old Main, wept.

It took him a full ten days to adjust to the news. When he did adjust he manfully got off a letter to her that was also designed to be hilarious. But between its lines were unmistakable signs of his shock over the realization that a new and disturbing factor had entered into his relations with the beloved sister. Significantly he could not use the words "married" and "husband" in relation to Fanny. He used dashes instead.[11]

Nor could he bring himself to attend the ceremony when Fanny and William Augustus Platt of Columbus were married September 2, 1839.

6

From then on, he gradually became a more serious young man than before. Previously he had not made a real effort to lead his class in scholarship. Rather, he had had a reputation for being more interested in politics and reading newspapers.[12] Now he was different, so much so that Sardis, who had worried that Rud was not taking college seriously enough, was to urge that he should "not study too hard." [13]

Until then he had no clear idea of why he was studying so diligently, or of what career he proposed to follow. "I would like to be a farmer," he once told his mother prior to going to Kenyon.[14] Another time he considered becoming a physician—"a disciple of Esculapius," as Fanny put it.[15] He soon decided that "cutting up people" was not for him, especially since the sight of blood affected him greatly.[16] Besides, Fanny did not think he would make a good physician.

Sophia thought she would like Rud to become a businessman, like his father, like Sardis. Otherwise she preferred that he be a minister, like so many of her kin. For a time, even Rud seriously considered the career of clergyman. "Don't congratulate yourself too much about my making short sermons when I am a preacher. If you had seen some documents that proceeded from my pen, you'd be congratulating yourself on the idea of what a long time you'd have to sleep in my sermons," he quipped to Fanny.[17]

He ended in laughing at the idea, especially as, no matter how hard he tried to provoke it, the necessary urge to accept God and Church still did not come to him completely. Fanny laughed at the idea that he could ever be a businessman. "The thought that Rud could ever make enough money to support himself excited the risibles," she said.[18]

Before long Rud himself decided that he would be a lawyer. Fanny was exultant. For this was her own real goal for him. She envisioned Rud, the lawyer, making some great oration someday, which, like Daniel Webster's great speeches, would thrill and move the world. He himself had this same vision. At Kenyon he excelled in declamations and was fond of participating in debate tournaments. He liked particularly the applause that always followed his stirring recitation of Webster's "Reply to Hayne." "Liberty AND Union, now and for ever, one and inseparable!" [19]

He could speak those phrases in his sleep. He identified himself with them and with Webster. He was eager, with Fanny, for the day when he should say something equally moving, and at Kenyon he studied mainly with this goal in mind.

CHAPTER XVIII

YOUNG WHIG

1

THE FOUR Kenyon years turned out to be among the sunniest of his whole life. In the main, this was because at Gambier he made so many friendships, most with older youths, which were satisfying on their own account and also contributed to his sense of security in his manliness.[1] His little room on the attic floor of Old Kenyon became the "hangout" for a large group of his most personable fellow students. This acceptance by manly youths was especially pleasant for him.

Yet, over him, over Kenyon, over the whole land in these 1840s, there was the shadow—the issue of slavery, which, despite or because of the politicians, ministers, businessmen and other leaders, produced underlying tension everywhere. Not even in the tranquil hills of Gambier could the shadow be avoided, not even by young men there from the North and from the South who were pledged to be bosom friends throughout life.

In the main, the Kenyon faculty tried to ignore this subject. They saw what happened to the Lane Seminary down at Cincinnati. When heated controversy over slavery developed there, the trustees finally forbade discussion of the subject even in private. Lane Seminary was pretty nearly wrecked. Almost half the faculty and students, in 1833, finally broke away—these, of course, being Abolitionists. They went into the woods in the general direction of Cleveland to found the "radical" Oberlin Collegiate Institute, some of whose leaders were influenced by none other than Rud's first cousin, John Humphrey Noyes, who, along with his unorthodox ideas on Christian "perfectionism," became an early crusader for Abolitionism. Indeed, this first cousin of Rutherford B. Hayes was credited with giving to William Lloyd Garrison the concept for the inflammatory slogan that the Constitution of the United States, because it then did not outlaw slavery, was a "compact with the Devil." [2]

Down at Ohio University at Athens, Ohio, there was an ugly eruption. William Gilmore, a student from Chillicothe, Ohio, cousin of a girl named Lucy Webb, was assailed by Southern students in 1839 as a "damned Abolitionist," forced to "eat dirt or fight," and, fighting, had his arm broken.³ About the same time the Ohio legislature threatened to expel State Representative Joshua R. Giddings of Cleveland, because he had presented petitions for helping a school that admitted Negroes.

2

At Kenyon, when Rud was a student there, an extraordinarily large number of the faculty members, including President Sparrow, were Southerners committed to defending slavery. It was the same with the student body, and especially with Rud's close friends, notably his most intimate chum, a handsome lad from Texas whose family owned many slaves. This was Guy Bryan, a descendant of Stephen Austin, "father" of Texas, hence a kin of Rud's through Daniel Austin.⁴

In the main, these likable Southerners at Kenyon, well-to-do youths who were so studiedly chivalrous, so sporting, so courageous and so given to living by a Sir Walter Scott's code of honor, did more to indoctrinate their Northern friends at Kenyon than the other way around.⁵ Sophia, with her remarkable prescience, sensed this more than anyone else, and was uneasy. As she told Sardis, "I hope he will do well there, but I am afraid there are too many Southern scholars. . . . I hope Judge Lane is not deceived in the character of the school." ⁶

True, Sophia was still not for Abolitionism. As for Sardis, who in 1839 ran for election as a Whig for State Senator (much to Sophia's dismay) and was defeated, largely because he declined to take a strong stand against slavery, he expressed his views when he wrote to his brother Austin: "I despise our Abolitionists." ⁷

3

Rud naturally shared Sardis' Whiggish attitude. Indeed, while he was an Isaac Webb student, Rud's conservatism on this subject made him something of a disappointment to the Noyeses and others of his kin in Vermont, when he visited them during a recess at the Connecticut school. As he wrote then to Sardis: "Uncle Noyes' folks tried to make an Abolitionist of me, but that would not work. They all thought Mr. Webb's would be a good place for George

[Noyes], but when I told them there was not an Abolitionist in the school, oh! horrible! They'd as soon send him to a lion's den!" [8]

From a Northerner's viewpoint, there was some justification for Sophia's fears about the Kenyon influence on Rud on the slavery issue, even though she herself deplored "excessive" agitation of the subject by either side. For as a Northerner, Rud, though eschewing Abolitionism, was supposed at least to frown on the institution of slavery as a matter of morals, if not of economics. This he did in a conformist way.

Yet it was scarcely possible for him then to see even a slight connection between, for example, the gentle, generous, high-minded young slaveowner Guy Bryan and the picture of a typical Southern slave master.[9] Forty-five years later, at a crucial time in his career in which the Southern problem was paramount, he was to say that while he found "the Southern character" at times "over-bearing," it was to him also admirable—"brave, courageous, hospitable to a fault, generous." [10] He had in mind, of course, his fellow sons of Kenyon, as he knew them. So he tended then to gloss over the slavery issue.

He considered himself an intense young American patriot. Yet at this time he carried his toleration for the views of his Southern friends so far as to agree even that, if worst came to worst, it might be better if the Southern slave states withdrew from the Union and formed their own independent nation.

In a debate in the Philomathesian Society, in which group he was a leader, he very easily expounded the affirmative of the question, "Was South Carolina Justified in Attempting to Secede from the Union?" [11] This was a strange position for a declaimer of the famous Websterian peroration. But at this time he was seeing things as his friends saw them—and eager to avoid offense to them.

There was no doubt that he, like Webster, was for the Union, indivisible and forever, as an underlying principle. In a little essay that he wrote at Kenyon on the American Revolution, he closed by observing that the Revolution succeeded because the states, North and South, stuck together,

no sectional jealousies to divide their councils and weaken their exertions . . . no envious distinctions between the rich and poor. . . . The bonds of *Union* then formed were . . . sealed by the life's blood of some of the purest patriots who ever lived. And if we would guard that "sacred Seal," inviolate the *Union* must be preserved. It was that which enabled oppressed people to "startle the tyrant in his dreams of power." It was *Union* that reared the majestic columns of *our* Nation's glory, and *that* alone can prevent *it* from *crumbling into ashes.*[12]

This boyish essay expressed his true feelings. He would never really change. But at times on this question he drifted, like America itself in the 1840s and 1850s.

4

Much of his drifting on the North-South issue was a matter of his personality, of the instinct to get along with others, of shying away from trouble—like the two other Rutherford Hayeses. But much of it also was because he was so naturally in his politics a pronounced young Whig. He had gone to Kenyon knowing that he was a Whig. Sardis was one, and most of the men whom he admired, including Webster, were Whigs.

The four Kenyon years confirmed him in his Whiggery, for the whole outlook on life and the world that the Kenyon curriculum tended to produce was definitely of a Whiggish cast. In fact, Kenyon then was as much Whig as it was Episcopalian. It was frankly so, perhaps because Henry Clay, the Whig Party founder, had been greatly instrumental in helping Bishop Chase to get English funds to establish Kenyon. Also because Whigs, North and South, were, generally speaking, those who sent their sons to college.

Their Whiggish orientation did not mean that Rud and the other Kenyon lads were urged to place practical matters frankly above the idealistic. On the contrary, they were given indoctrination in highly romantic notions about government and politics. But it was a characteristic of Whiggery that practical things, like high tariffs and internal improvements—like the road building which helped to make Sardis rich—were championed because they were in accord, the Whigs believed, with idealistic, moral and highly patriotic objectives, as any Websterian speech attested.

Moreover, the political roots of Whiggery were intertwined with the concept of what a gentleman then was supposed to think, do and not do. At Kenyon Rud did not receive much perceptive instruction in realistic history or social thought. But he did get much about the code of a gentleman.

Indeed, in the education of Rutherford B. Hayes, this gentleman's code was basic. To be honorable. To be just. To be generous and chivalrous. To be responsible. To speak well of everyone, except on justified provocation. To place honor and loyalty above all else. To seek success in life. To be restrained in emotion and speech. To see the other fellow's viewpoint. To be charitable toward the moral lapses of the other man, while striving for excellence in one's self.

These formed the code, the code of "the model *brave bourgeois,*" as Rutherford B. Hayes would be called. This was all carefully formulated and drilled into him at Kenyon through liberal dosages especially of writings like those of the philosopher-theologian Paley.

5

Gentlemen perforce were Whigs. They believed in building up the wealth of the nation by honorable means and also by the most direct and efficient means—for the benefit, of course, of all, even Democrats. They believed, above all, in stability, considered maintenance of the *status quo* as a supreme virtue—so there would be room for gentlemen.

True, even gentlemen were thrilled by innovations in industry which were bound to disturb stability; by explorations, notably of John C. Frémont, in the far American West, Colorado, Nevada, California and Oregon; by political eruptions in Europe, Latin America and the Orient. But they favored stability nevertheless.

Rud Hayes was destined to be a perfect example of this educational process, even if in the end he would revolt, though prudently, against much of it, including its inevitable lukewarm attitude toward the great moral problem of the day—slavery.

CHAPTER XIX

"Statesman of Reunion"

1

Yet not even Kenyon could escape flaring tempers and collisions over the North-South issue. Young Hayes found himself involved, especially in connection with the Philomathesian Society, though, as befitted so stanch a Whig and so fervent an admirer of Henry Clay and Daniel Webster, his involvement was in the role of soother and compromiser, the very role for which his temperament always so perfectly suited him.

The Philomathesian Society was originally the only society there. But back in 1832, during the excitement about the South Carolina threat to secede over President Jackson's antinullification stand, the Southern lads withdrew. They formed Nu Pi Kappa, which adopted a resolution saying: "Agreeable to the wishes of the Philomathesian Society, we elect members hereafter only from the slave-holding states."

For the most part, after this, the two groups were fairly friendly, if exclusive. But shortly before Rud arrived at Kenyon, intense hostility over the slave issue again flared. It was so strong that "members upon both sides carried arms, ready for attack or defense." [1] And while Rud was there, the tension again grew to the point where it looked, one July Fourth, as though a "collision," probably with gunfire, would result. [2]

2

Rud did more than anyone else to allay this tension and bring about peace. He was particularly cut out for that role, especially as the Southern lads liked him. Guy Bryan, for one, paid him the supreme compliment to come from a Southerner: "I do not exactly know why, but there is, Hayes, something in your offhanded and independent manner in doing everything which makes me often think you were born under a Southern sun." [3]

Then, too, he had the reputation for possessing "the levelest head in the college." [4] Even boys much older came to him for advice—

and, more significantly, accepted it. It was because of Rud's counsel that young Bryan gave up the idea of going back to Texas to take part in the Republic of Texas war against Mexico. "You, Rud," wrote Guy, are "a *friend,* a *true friend,* one on whose judgment I rely with the utmost confidence & one who would give advice with the intention only of subserving my *true interests. . . . You,* Rud, I will remember with love & gratitude—till the heart stands still forever." [5]

Similarly, another Kenyon student, young Stanley Matthews (destined to be a Justice of the Supreme Court of the United States—with the help of his friend Hayes) had reason to appreciate the soundness of Rud Hayes's counsel. Matthews, a Kentucky youth, had become involved with other seniors in a row with the faculty. He was faced with the choice of apologizing or being expelled. Other hotheads urged Matthews to stand on his honor. But Rud persuaded Matthews to make the apology and thus get his college degree. "I would do it, if I were in your place," he said. "It is right. . . . Think of your family." [6] Matthews accepted this advice and was grateful ever afterward for it.

3

By the time he was a junior and nineteen, young Hayes had the reputation of a student whose opinions in any kind of conflict were worth heeding by other students. It was he who saved the day for Nu Pi Kappa, when that society of Southern youths faced extinction in 1840 because in that particular year only a few new students from the South came to Kenyon. Rud made a proposal to his Philomathesian brothers. Some of them, chosen by lot, should join Nu Pi Kappa. It should be done, he urged, to maintain "good relations" between the sections, if for no other reasons. Some hotheaded Northerners were opposed. But Rud's motion was adopted, and Nu Pi Kappa was saved. [7]

On another occasion he took an even clearer stand for settling the North-South antagonism. It had been proposed that the old custom of limiting Philomathesian membership to Northerners be abolished. Rud favored letting down the bars and taking in Southern lads. He said:

It is admitted by all that we are forming opinions & habits of thinking which will remain with us through life. We should form no opinions or prejudices which would be injurious to the country if held by all. . . . The dislike of the North on the part of the NPK can be no less than ours toward them & if such hatred against each other prevailed throughout the whole country of the North & South, the Union would be dissolved at once & thus this republic, the first which ever existed, would fall.

Lovers of liberty in all countries would give up the belief that man was capable of self-government & thus would the whole civilized world be injured. . . . Already has this ill feeling been carried too far. Let us not labor to keep it up, but treat the Southerners at least as fellow countrymen & do unto them as they would do unto us, if we were in their situation. . . .[8]

Rutherford B. Hayes, "statesman of reunion," as he would be called, was emerging.

4

When graduation time in 1842 neared, peacemaker Rud Hayes, the perfect young Whig, was easily the most popular student at Kenyon, a "first-rate fellow," as one classmate, Lorin Andrews, later president of the college, called him.[9] Indeed, he had won the same kind of popularity as had been his father's back in the old valley.

He was also at the head of his class scholastically, and was designated valedictorian. The college sent to his mother a communication that satisfied even her.

March 15, 1842

In his studies he has evinced the possession of intellectual powers of a superior order. For strength of mind, clearness of perception, soundness of judgment, he is surpassed by none among us. In all his studies, he has attained the highest grade. His delinquencies are as follows: 0, 0, 0. . . . His conduct has been most gentlemanly and exemplary. In the opinion of all who know him, he bids fair to become a bright ornament to society.

5

By later standards, if not those of his own era, this "ornament to society" lacked a good deal, despite the fulsome praise given him by Kenyon. He was not in fact equipped very well to face the real world. Many of his concepts about life were decidedly foggy. For a youth prepared, as the Kenyon faculty hoped, for leadership, he had only the vaguest notions about the real forces that were then shaping his world. The new industrial classes, the masses of the people, might just as well not have existed. In his education no attention was paid to them or their condition.

But he did have as good a general education as any young man to come out of any college in this time, indeed better than most. He did have, and would retain, a lively intellectual curiosity about all things, even of the scientific, which was to serve him in good stead through life. It was something extraordinary then to be a college graduate at all, and young Rutherford B. Hayes neared the end of college buoyed by a sense of achievement. He faced his future with eagerness.

Yet his graduation period, climax of four happy years of "feasts, studies, good times together," as he recalled them to Guy Bryan,[10] was marred for him by still another shadow. This was not a political shadow like the slavery issue. It was a personal one, a baffling illness that suddenly struck the beloved sister.

CHAPTER XX

FANNY, ALAS!

1

FANNY, everyone agreed, had made a brilliant marriage. Her husband was an up-and-coming man, one exactly in tune with the commercial spirit that increasingly marked the period. In the beginning he operated a jewelry store in Columbus. At the end he headed the Columbus gas company, the Columbus Door, Sash and Lumber Company, the Columbus cemetery, owned at least forty houses and various land companies and became a director of banks and railroads, and he had a publicly estimated worth of more than a half million dollars.[1] He was eager to provide Fanny with everything she desired in the way of comfort and luxury, and he did. He adored Fanny and respected her refulgent intellect.

On her part, Fanny admired Will Platt. She achieved with him a pleasant domestic establishment. But from her view, if not his, there obviously was something missing in their marriage. This, clearly, was the element of romance which permeated so many of the books that Fanny, still the avid reader, absorbed. In truth, there was much about Fanny suggestive of her fictional contemporary, the tragic Emma of Flaubert's *Madame Bovary*, a classic victim of too much romantic reading. As Fanny herself once observed, "My thinking always runs to sentimental musings." [2]

She was not content with the domesticated life that went with the role of wife to staid, sober, successful William Augustus Platt, though she made the best of it and outwardly seemed happy. Had she her mother's faith in the old religion, or even a fraction of it, Fanny might have been better off—as Sophia lost no opportunity to remind her. But Fanny was too modern in spirit to accept Sophia's Presbyterianism. Like her brother, she never experienced conversion.

But while her brother tended to be a serene pragmatist on religion, Fanny worried. Significantly after going from Presbyterianism to Episcopalianism and investigating Methodism, she was most attracted by mystical Swedenborgianism, then becoming a vogue in fashionable circles. Had she lacked her sense of humor, she might have joined her redheaded cousin John Humphrey Noyes in his peculiar cultism.

122

For, as could have been predicted from her childhood, Fanny obviously was seeking something in life beyond her own personality.[3]

2

The truth is, Fanny had been reluctant to get married at all. Though she surrendered to her fate and consented to be the bride of solid Will Platt, with his egg-shaped head, long nose and sharp, honest eyes, she never yielded up the interests that were really important to her—a love of music, of art, or literature, and the romantic dreams, most of which centered around not her husband, but her brother.[4]

After her marriage she even started to write an "epic poem," called "The Indian Maid."[5] She was obsessed, she once told her brother, "with a kind of bibliomania—all my air castles lined with books."[6] She still also felt the old longing to be a man.

She resented, though often with humorous resignation, the concept that woman's place is in the home. She represented, in truth, an early case of the emancipated woman. Declining to leave politics to the menfolk, she was as emotionally involved in politics as her brother, indeed more so. As she wrote to Sardis during the boisterous "Tippecanoe and Tyler too" campaign of 1840, when she was an excited partisan of General Harrison, the first successful Whig Presidential candidate, whom Sardis had the honor of escorting through part of the state, "Uncle, do not be afraid to write me about politics—I am as warm on the subject as anyone. F."[7]

3

Indeed, Fanny was "warm" on politics. Also on all other subjects, intellectual, social or theological, which in that day and age were usually reserved for the menfolk. When the glamorous Louis Kossuth made his tour of America to seek aid for the liberation of Hungary, including Columbus, Ohio, in his itinerary, Fanny was one of his most enthusiastic hero-worshipers and had his framed picture in her house.[8] The appearance of Jenny Lind about the same time sent her into almost a delirium of excitement.

But she was still "warmest" of all on the subject of her brother's potential career. She envisioned him as another Webster or even a Harrison. For she still identified her own ego with his, as in the old days when she and he played on the high banks of the little creek in the Delaware cemetery near the graves of their glorified father and older brother.

Will Platt did not object to Fanny's interests. But neither did he share them all by any means. "I make quite a martyr of my husband dragging him about to lectures & concerts, but he still bears it with Christian fortitude," Fanny once quipped to her brother.[9] It was, of course, inevitable that Fanny should turn to Rud to share her most intense interests, whether in literature or politics, and that the bond between them thus became strengthened rather than lessened, even after she began a family of her own. Besides, Fanny was often dismayed, even while professing to be only amused, over Will Platt's preoccupation with financial success and his excessive care about business and personal affairs.[10]

She frankly confided to her brother that she hoped he at least would never become so absorbed in business interests. She told him in the third year of her marriage:

I do hope that you will "make a living" easily, & more than that I trust you will not desire. Stronger & stronger is my faith in the proverb, "Money is the root of all evil." I will not deny that I should like as well as anyone to have all the luxuries that money will buy, but if you have not a fortune to begin with, you may toil away the days for enjoying it & when you are old look aghast at your gold—& die! . . . [This is] suggested by my husband's present close confinement to business.[11]

4

However, Fanny's heaviest burden was to become something else. "Melancholy never lasts long with me," she had written to Sardis concerning her momentary emotion of sadness at leaving the old home in Delaware.[12]

But after she married, it was discovered that she was destined to be a special victim of the most intense kind of melancholy. For Fanny turned out to be one of those women so delicately balanced that, for whatever reason, physical or temperamental, childbirth often resulted in their minds blacking out.

In the first year after her marriage this happened to Fanny on the birth of her first child, Sarah Sophia. Her illness then was of short duration, her recovery coming so quickly that Rud, at Kenyon, was

not even told about it. "Fanny is perfectly restored," Sophia reported
to Sardis. "She is clothed in her right mind. The prayers of her
Friends have been heard." [13]

In June 1841 another blow fell. The little girl died. This grief,
however, Fanny bore with almost Sophia-like fortitude.

> My *dear* Brother: And my *good* brother, too, for writing so often.
> I knew you must feel our loss as you said you did, for I thought you
> loved our bright, beautiful child. Time is all that can heal such a
> wound, yet I feel calm & cheerful. . . . At first, I could have sat
> & wept the livelong day, but I resolved to seek employment & interest
> myself about something—writing I found easier than anything—read-
> ing poetry & making some rhymes of my own. . . . I cannot tell
> you how much I long to have you with us—your careless laugh, if
> anything, would make me happy again.[14]

5

In April 1842, after Fanny gave birth to another girl, Laura, the
hardest blow of all fell. Rud was visiting in Columbus when this
baby was born but returned to Kenyon feeling that all was well.

Shortly after, however, he received from Will Platt a letter that
made his head swim from a sense of ineffable disaster. For Platt
wrote that Fanny had been "mentally deranged since the night
following your departure." She had become so violent that she had
had to be tied to her bed.[15]

A few days later Platt sent even more distressing news. "We have
just passed a sad & silent Sabbath. . . . Fanny is now.in the Lunatic
Asylum. This will startle you, my dear brother, & pierce your soul,
but severe as it is, you must know the truth." [16]

From Sophia Rud received an even more pitiful letter.

> To think that our lovely and amiable Fanny should be the compan-
> ion of lunatics—alas, and one herself—is heartrending. She has been
> too much our Idol and the Lord has seen fit to deprive us of her. Let
> us bow in humble submission to His will and pray that this sore afflic-
> tion may be removed from us, and that our darling may be restored
> to us. . . .
> The first days after you left, she enquired after you continually—
> would not believe you were gone. . . . When speaking of you one
> day, she said, 'You know I have always thought Rutherford was almost
> perfection, and I must see him.' [17]

6

Rud was so stricken that he could not go to see Fanny. He wanted to. But he simply could not. It was impossible for him. Then, in truth, occurred the most intense experience Rutherford B. Hayes ever would be called on to endure—a supreme, well-nigh crucifying, test of his whole personality and character. Another youth, as sensitive as he, as entwined by love and the most profound other personal associations with his sister, might have been shattered completely.

He was in danger of this, but was saved by the protective instincts which kept him from witnessing Fanny's condition, and by his own strength. But the blow left its impact on him forever.

To Will Platt he managed to write: "If her state were different, I would wish to be with her. As it is, I could not bear to see her. I have now no desire to come home on her account. How does mother support this calamity?" [18]

As it happened, Sophia "supported" it better than anyone else. She efficiently took care of the little girl, of Will Platt, kept everyone informed, and never gave up hope that Fanny would recover.

Fanny, in fact, did recover. Her mind was restored, as bright and alert as if the black-out had never occurred, all her old interests intact, indeed even enhanced. In the following fall she and her husband took a second honeymoon trip to the East, which both hugely enjoyed, and she returned her old vivacious self.

"Fanny came home exceedingly fat," Rud joked to Sardis. "It appears to be the object now with fashionable ladies to bring their forms as near as possible to that of a soap tub. In the accomplishment of this, Fanny succeeds admirably, for between the flesh and the padding, she has rendered herself considerable broader *one* way than another." [19]

But she had not recovered in time to be present—was still a patient in the hospital—when Rud received his diploma at Kenyon.

7

Sophia and Sardis were there, of course. At first Sophia had hesitated about leaving Fanny's infant, even for Rud's graduation. But Sardis overruled her.[20] Spruced up in a new suit, he journeyed down from Lower Sandusky to Columbus to accompany her.

Both then were somewhat bowed, Sophia from her years—she was fifty then, with traces of gray in her thinning brown hair, and her formerly slim figure growing fleshy—and Sardis from his continuing poor health. But together, their hearts overflowing, they made the hot, sun-baked trip in a borrowed carriage, over the bumpy, dusty, winding roads, up and down the hills, to the lovely village of Gambier to see Rud graduate.

That glorious, blue-skied morning of Wednesday, the fifth of August, 1842, young Rutherford B. Hayes was easily the star of the commencement exercises. As he strode with a quick step across the platform to the lectern in Rosse Chapel, his generous shock of auburn hair parted liberally toward the left, then trimmed neatly enough to suit even Sophia, his body straight, his stride true, his blue eyes forthrightly open and unafraid, he looked, at least to Sophia, like a very godlike man, like another Ruddy Hayes. It was so despite the outlandish getup that his class had selected for the commencement— a blue coat of Kentucky jean, with velvet collar, white waistcoat and white linen trousers.[21]

His voice was clear, bell-like, already mannish, his diction and pronunciation distinct and faultless. He looked frankly at his listeners, an earnest smile now and then playing on his well-shaped lips. Seemingly perfectly at ease, he talked too long, especially as ten other speeches and poems had been delivered before his. But his talk was not too long for his mother or his uncle.

Even Sophia Hayes then could not help but realize, if only momentarily, that her boy was no longer the "feeble and fatherless child" in need of her sheltering. Only a short time before Sardis had made an appraisal of him that was worth even more than Kenyon's encomiums. "He has got good hard Horse Sense," Sardis had written to his brother, "and I think he is much like his Father." [22]

Except for the ache over Fanny, this was the happiest day Sophia had known—would ever know again—since the time Ruddy Hayes first came riding up on his sorrel mare through the Green Mountains from Brattleboro to Wilmington to tell her that he loved her. In fact, Sophia could not have been happier, even were her son Rutherford that moment chosen to be President of all the United States.

CHAPTER XXI

HAPPY INTERLUDE

1

FOLLOWING his graduation, feeling "much as if a load were off my stomach," young Rutherford Hayes went to Columbus to make his home with Fanny at her house on High Street near Spring.

The Delaware period for himself and the others was over. The house in Delaware had been sold, and it was understood that his residence then would be with Fanny and Will Platt in Columbus, as was the case with his mother. There, after Fanny returned from the hospital completely well, he began one of his happiest, most carefree periods. He gadded about, as he phrased it. Between times he read law in preparation for his professional career. And, most pleasant of all, he was with Fanny.

He liked being a citizen of Columbus, as he now considered himself. In contrast to Delaware, Columbus seemed to him a metropolis, filled with educated persons like himself.

Actually it was nothing of the kind. It was still but a village, scarcely more populous than Delaware, and just as dusty in summer and as muddy in spring. Pigs roamed the streets freely. It was not at all uncommon for customers of Will Platt's jewelry store on High Street to have to thread their way through a herd of porkers in order to inspect his line of diamond-studded bracelets, enormous gold watches and heavy tableware.

Still, Columbus already had some attractions quite metropolitan—bookstores, in which he liked to browse; Peter Ambos' confectionery, where he indulged his sweet tooth with ice creams and other dainties "unsurpassed in any part of the United States"; the Buckeye Coffee Shop ("turtle soups on Tuesdays and Thursdays"); the Tontine Coffee Shop, where he could enjoy a lemonade or some oysters; the Neil House; the American Hotel; the Commercial House, where he could pick up newspapers from Cincinnati, New York and London.[1]

Especially did he enjoy Columbus when the politicians were in town for the legislature sessions. Or when famous lawyers—Justice John R. McLean of the United States Supreme Court, Senator Tom Corwin, Senator William Allen, Salmon P. Chase, H. H. Stanberry, Josh Giddings, or Edwin P. Stanton, and Sardis' special friend Judge Lane—were there to argue cases.

(Top, left) Lucy W. Webb at 16; (right) After Marriage, about 1856

(Bottom) The Newly Married R. B. Hayeses, December 1852

(Top) Boyhood Home in Delaware, Ohio
(Bottom) Rutherford B. Hayes's Home in Cincinnati, 1855-1867

The posturings, the boasting and the obvious finagling of the politicians fascinated him. "Rutherford has gathered many choice bits of fun at political meetings and corners of the streets here," Sophia told Sardis. "William said it was quite a saving of time to him—he could stay at home and Rutherford could bring him all the news at supper." [2]

Fanny was most pleased of all. "Our family is quite completed now," she told Sardis. "Rutherford is good to laugh with, Mother to save odds & ends, William to make money, & myself to spend it, not forgetting the baby." [3]

2

In those congenial surroundings, with even Sophia beaming with contentment (her only worry at the time was the stubborn resistance of various Irish-Catholic maids to conversion to Presbyterianism), Rud got in a monumental amount of studying along with his gadding. He took seriously the learning of law. At the same time he began studying German and also French, the latter so as to keep up with Fanny.

He valiantly set for himself a rigid regime. "My rules for the month," he noted in his diary, "are: First, Read no newspapers. Second, Rise at seven and retire at ten. Third, Study law six hours, German two, Chillingworth two. Fourth, In reading Blackstone's 'Commentaries,' to record my difficulties." [4]

It was his original thought to become a lawyer simply by studying in the law office, above White and Huntington's bookstore, of Thomas Sparrow, a brother of Dr. Sparrow of Kenyon. Fanny and Sophia encouraged him in this, for they did not wish him to go away again.

He himself, for a time, was satisfied. "[Mr. Sparrow] is not so learned or experienced as many others, but he gives me more instructions than law students usually receive," he told Sardis. "My legal tuition costs me nothing; my German, twelve dollars per quarter. The first I consider cheap." [5]

3

Soon, however, he found that this "cheap" legal training was not really what he wanted. Will Lane was studying law at Yale, and Rud figured that if he wished to keep up with such friends, he ought to go to a professional school also. Would it be Yale for him too? At first he thought so.

But once again Yale—and the ghost of the Reverend Samuel Russell—lost him. For he finally decided that if he went to any law school, it would be the Harvard Law School at Cambridge, in Massachusetts. He was satisfied that Harvard possessed, in the persons of two outstanding instructors—Simon Greenleaf and Joseph Story, a Justice of the Supreme Court of the United States—an advantage over Yale. He was especially impressed by the fact that Justice Story tried many real Supreme Court cases before his Harvard students.

There were many family conferences on this. Sophia was naturally heartsick over the idea that he might go east again, thus bringing to an end this period of happiness for her. Fanny also was disturbed, though she saw her brother's points about Harvard.

Sardis was all for his having at least one year of study at a real law school. He offered to pay for it, though at this time, owing, he felt, to Democratic policies, even *he* was pressed for ready cash. "Hard times in our state," he told Brother Austin. "I have lost enough money the last six years to make a man rich."

But Sardis said he would gladly scrape up the money for his nephew to study at the Harvard Law School. "The money will be well paid out," he said. "Rutherford is a sound boy and has got good hard sense, like a Horse." [6]

4

In the end Rud had the approval, though reluctantly, of Sophia, and, with even some enthusiasm, of Fanny, who later wrote to him: "I looked forward to your year at Cambridge, in the intellectual atmosphere of Boston, with as pleasant anticipations as you could have had, for although I knew the parting would be painful, I thought you would there have better opportunities for becoming more & more what I desire my dear, my adored, brother to be." [7]

So, carrying a letter from Thomas Sparrow which affirmed that he was "a young man of good character," he set off from Columbus in August 1843 for Harvard. There he was to sit spiritually at the feet of Justice Story and Professor Greenleaf, two conservatives of the conservatives. And there he was to allow the "intellectual atmosphere of Boston," as Fanny, Sophia, Sardis and he himself hoped, to do the work of completing the process of his becoming "in manners, morals, and feelings, a true gentleman." [8]

CHAPTER XXII

SON OF HARVARD

1

AT CAMBRIDGE, MASSACHUSETTS, where he learned much, including much that had to be unlearned, he found at once acquaintances "who treated [him] like a gentleman." He "got a room and boarding place to suit, was introduced to the professors, with whom [he was] much pleased, and was duly registered as a law student." The boarding place was Mrs. Ford's, located not far from the small, oblong-shaped Grecian building called the Dane Law School, where his classrooms were.[1]

Mrs. Ford's new boarder was then almost twenty-one. For the first time a reddish fuzz was showing up on his long, forthright face. He was well-built, broad-shouldered, intent-looking. Pantalooned, waistcoated and cravated in the most modish, Websterian manner, he appeared outwardly as proper a Bostonian as any there.

On August 22, 1843, when he registered as a member of the "middle class" in law at Harvard, the act completed some full circles of family history. Just two hundred years before the Reverend John Russell, protector of the regicides, had departed as a graduate from this same institution of learning to become settled as minister at old Wethersfield and then at old Hadley. Just one hundred years before Daniel Austin had marched off from this same Connecticut River Valley to join in the War of Jenkins' Ear. Precisely sixty-eight years before Roger Birchard, Sophia's father, had gone with the Mansfield Centre regiment under his cousin, Experience Storrs, to fight at Bunker Hill in the American Revolution.

Now, by the way of the Valley of the Ohio, their descendant, Rutherford B. Hayes, was back once more among the Yankees he thought he still despised, not guessing how really like them he was becoming himself, for all the Buckeye in his make-up.

2

One of the first things he did after settling himself at Cambridge was to visit at Bunker Hill. Seemingly an ordinary tourist at the battlefield, he then symbolized, in the spectacular difference between himself, a gentleman of Harvard, and the humble Daniel Austin and Roger Birchard, realization of the original American dream. That there was such a difference seemed proof that the dream of all the Birchards and Austins and Hayeses of the old valley as to the opportunities in America had been no illusion, despite the vicissitudes. In large part, the central theme of their dream up to then had been that simple folk of rude beginnings could produce gentlemen. There, in the summer of 1843, in the person of the new Harvard student was the living, optimistic evidence.

He was aware of this. He felt elevated by the idea that such things could be and always would be, if his countrymen would but cling to the principles that had made it all possible. He would be true, he was sure. He longed, as he wrote in his diary, for the opportunity to demonstrate this, and pursued his studies then with that as a major goal.

Fame was what he frankly sought. In his diary a short time later he would hedge and write, "Fame, I care *nothing* for—positively nothing." [2] The truth, however, was otherwise. It was so because he was driven to meet the expectations of Fanny, Sardis and all the others, especially of Fanny, who wrote after he had become well launched on his Harvard routine: "I suspect that I am more ambitious for you than you are for yourself. But if love & ambition keep pace with each other in my feeling for you, it is your own fault. . . . Your success thus far has given impulse to ambition & once aroused, 'tis a passion difficult to restrain." [3]

One might say, "Poor, favored, beloved Rutherford B. Hayes, so lucky, so unlucky, to have a loving, prodding sister like Fanny Hayes!" He wished to have, he had to have, her esteem. He had to strive to be her image of him. "How my heart swells with pride when I anticipate the possibility of your swaying the multitude with your eloquence!" she wrote following a murder trial in Columbus in which some of Ohio's most prominent lawyers had performed.[4] So, to live up to her image of him, he stuffed his mind at Harvard, often cruelly, frequently to the point of painful exhaustion.

3

"Oh, how little I have done! How little I have learned!" he once mourned. Yet all the while, until "wearied out from study," even begrudging himself a game of baseball, he pumped into his head great quantities of Aristotle's *Ethics,* more of Paley's natural philosophy, Beattie's psychology, Hoffman's logic, Locke's *Essays,* all the "great orations" he could find, took French lessons and was tutored in German, looked into Greek, kept up with his Latin. This on top of studying his law texts, to master the mysteries of bailments, evidence, pleadings, the common law, real property, equity, contracts and the higher constitutional theories. No wonder he once concluded, "I am now as dull and stupid as an ass!" [5]

But he plowed on. He was sure that this regime was necessary for attaining the twin goals of becoming famous, or at least being worthy of fame, and a gentleman. "I must try to acquire greater mildness of temper and affability of manners," he would say. "The rudeness of the student must be put off. . . . Trifling remarks, boyish conduct, are my crying sins. Mend! Mend!"

This was rather sad, for he did not have to strain so. He merely thought he did, trying to keep up with classmates who bore such proud names as Saltonstall, Lowell, Coolidge, Hoar, Cabot, Dana, Adams, Forbes, Thayer and Peabody, of the great Boston families, which, if he had only stopped to realize it, actually were the descendants of forebears like his own.[6]

4

During a recess he went dutifully to see the relatives in Vermont again, especially Chloe Hayes. "How I dread that visit!" he said, before going.[7] But he was pleasantly surprised. He learned that Grandmother Chloe was keeping a diary, setting down in it her recollections of her family, which was also his, the story of the Smiths, Hayeses, Chandlers, Hales, Noyeses and all the rest.

Perhaps it was the Boston influence that excited it, but whatever it was, Chloe's journal aroused in him an interest in his forebears that he had never felt before. It was more than genealogical, rather, a new form of his old search for his father. It was also a seeking, in the lives of those who had produced him, an answer to the numerous problems of his nature, queer fears, sexual urges, repressions, unformed hopes and ambitions, ambivalences and aggressions, all of which disturbed him, despite his apparently calm Harvard exterior.

Chloe wrote Sophia:

Your only Dear Son is here examining some of my old manuscripts, with as much intenseness as he would Cicero or his text law books. What a silly boy for that! What a treasure he is to you. His countenance is somewhat changed. He appears like a noble youth now. . . . But, oh, remember he is but an Earthen Vessel. The bell has been tolling. An old man has died this morning or last night. Every such death seems to be a knock at my door and says, "Be ready, your turn will soon come." . . . I cannot be here much longer.[8]

Grandmother Chloe was right. Her time was nearly up. Rutherford B. Hayes, the one grandchild to carry on the Hayes name, was much in her thoughts toward the end. "Oh, warn him to flee from every vice, from intemperance, Profanity, and Sabbath-breaking," she urged Sophia.[9] She also told Sophia, "The important thing for him now to attend to is to get a good principled wife." [10] Not long after so writing, in her eighty-fifth year, she joined Grandpa Austin and Rud's other forebears.

4

Gone then was a link with the time of the great Russells of the regicides, of Ethan Allen, of the American Revolution, Shays' Rebellion, the Washington Benevolent Society, the endless controversies over religious doctrines. Chloe Hayes's passing emphasized that her grandson was about to begin his career in the time of Modern Industrial America. Between Chloe Hayes's youth in old Hadley and his own, the face of the land had changed, and more than its face.

Already the telegraph was being used. New modes of living were being followed, some quite astonishing even to his immediate forebears. "Almost every family has a bathroom in Vermont now," Sophia incredulously reported to Sardis after another visit there. "It is considered important to the well and the sick to wash and rub themselves all over thoroughly every day." [11]

Equally a cause for amazement to Sophia, iron rails for steam locomotive trains were being laid in her beloved Green Mountains. Soon such trains would be moving on journeys to the West, supplanting the covered wagons, in time reaching even the Pacific, California, the Oregon country (then disputed with England) and even Russian America, areas already being explored and mapped in these 1840s by a new set of Ruddy Hayeses, exponents of still another westward movement.

5

Young R. B. Hayes, Harvard law student, was in tune with the changes. The Buckeye in him was now definitely becoming subordinated. In its place was the spirit of a Middle American, an Ohio Valley man, part Buckeye but also part Yankee, a nice fusion, in which model New Englanders—the Reverend William Ellery Channing, Justice Joseph Story, the Reverend Ralph Waldo Emerson, Professor Louis Agassiz, Professor Henry Wadsworth Longfellow and Professor Simon Greenleaf—now became hero figures, along with Sardis, Judge Ebenezer Lane, General William Henry Harrison, Henry Clay and, of course, Daniel Webster.

This amalgam that he symbolized was the typical upper-middle-class American. Yet, thanks to Fanny, to Sardis, to Kenyon and now to Harvard, he was not really the perfect son of his own age at all. Rather, he was now becoming a son of the age to come, a link between two eras, the dying era of Jonathan Edwards and the coming era of Darwin and Emerson.

Naturally he was full of contradictions. In Boston he attended every Sunday some church or another—now Dr. James Walker's, now Theodore Parker's, now Dr. Kirk's, now a Unitarian meeting, which he found "conducted a good deal like Methodist classmeetings." [12] Yet he was also still a skeptic. Thus he was drawn almost against his will toward the liberalism, even unitarianism, of Channing and Emerson, rejecting the ideas of Hell and Original Sin long before the Reverend Henry Ward Beecher. "The gloomy theology of the orthodox —the Calvinists—I do not, I cannot believe. Many of the notions— nay, most of the notions—which orthodox people have of the divinity of the Bible, I disbelieve," he wrote in a diary entry that would have shocked Chloe Hayes and his mother.[13] But he also considered himself a Christian believer just the same.

6

He was a devotee of liberty, intensely republican—"Resistance to Tyranny" still being his motto. But, largely influenced by Sardis and now also by his favorite Harvard professor, the witty but moss-covered ex-Democratic Justice Story, he was also convinced that the Jacksonian "masses," if not their leaders, somehow endangered the Republic unless led by safe men, meaning Whigs.[14]

He considered "the most eloquent lecture" he ever heard one made by Justice Story, which was "particularly directed at the Abolitionists." The judge said that it was un-American to oppose the Constitutional provision which

[gave the] slaveholder the right of reclaiming a fugitive slave from the free States. . . . If one part of the country may disregard one part of the Constitution, another section may refuse to obey that part which seems to bear hard upon its interests. Thus the Union will become a mere "rope of sand," the Constitution worse than a dead letter, an apple of discord in our midst, a fruitful source of reproach, bitterness, and hatred, and in the end, discord and civil war; till exhausted, wasted, embittered, and deadly foes have severed this Union into four, six, or eight little confederacies, or the whole shall crouch under the iron hand of a single despot.[15]

At this time Hayes was sure that Justice Story was correct. It was wrong, he felt, to deny the South its legal, constitutional due. Yet, characteristically, he had doubts too. For he also admired John Quincy Adams, who held an opposite view.

7

It was painful for so conscientious a young man to recognize that the deplorable agitation over escaped slaves would not stop, that even Harvard men, like Kenyon youths, lost their tempers in the controversy. In his diary he recorded an incident that reminded him of the ugly clashes at Gambier: "May 18, 1844.—We have had a little excitement here for a few days, occasioned by a skirmish between some of the Southern law students and the members of the senior class in college. It has resulted in a few slight bruises, the loss of a few soaplocks, and the expulsion of one or two from each department. 'Sic transit, etc.' "

So even in genteel Boston tempers caused violence over this issue of slavery! Even at Harvard, despite Justice Story, there were those who insisted on applying Biblical, rather than legalistic, tests to the peculiar Southern institution! This was disturbing, indeed, to one who felt, or wanted to feel, that gentility and patriotism, as well as common sense, required that this problem be ignored or permitted to work itself out.

One future day this Rutherford B. Hayes would have to face up to this problem in accord with his true moral nature. He would be forced to apply to it the tests of the Protestant Christian ethics that had been drilled into him by his mother and which were so much a part of his heritage, just as the Methodist Church in its General Conference held in New York that same May of 1844 finally faced up to it and voted a Southern bishop out of the episcopacy because he admittedly owned slaves.[16]

To an objective onlooker, it would have been obvious that Rutherford B. Hayes would be forced to decide eventually against Justice Story—against even his beloved Guy Bryan and other Southern friends, like Jabez LaFayette Monroe Curry of Talledaga County, Alabama, a fellow boarder at Mrs. Ford's.

This was foreordained by his heritage. It was foreordained by the fact that he was a Buckeye, by the fact that he was his mother's son and the son of those who had helped to establish this valley. But he did not know this in the pleasant New England summer and fall of 1843, as he listened reverently to Justice Story, chatted amiably with the other young Harvard gentlemen, or walked along the tree-lined banks of the River Charles, admiring the fine Boston mansions erected out of profits derived largely from manufacturing, which in itself was to doom slavery as effectively as would the old Biblical concepts.

Luckily for his temporary peace of mind on the slavery question, even in New England, at this time, unquestioned moralists, notably Dr. Channing, surely a safe interpreter of the Christian position, were also uncommitted. In fact, such moralists were critical of the "ultras" on both sides of this disturbing matter, as was Hayes.

What young Hayes represented in all his attitudes then jelling, in politics, religion, sex and all else, was then and later the middle ground. This position was his true and even inevitable nature. It was no accidental whim that in trying to master Aristotle's *Ethics* he was most impressed by the argument for balance in all matters. "The work treats of virtue and vice," he wrote in his diary. "Virtue is defined to be *mediocrity*, of which either extreme is vice." [17] He definitely agreed.

8

Originally the plan was for him to stay at Harvard for only two terms of twenty weeks each, then return home. But because he feared not having the best possible law education, he determined to remain for three terms, and thus win the Bachelor of Laws degree. At first Fanny objected but finally was won over. He was really continuing for her, for her dreams. "If it is to add one *mite* to your intellectual strength, I will bide the time patiently," she wrote.[18]

Sardis also objected at first, thinking two terms were enough, but Fanny made him see the light. As for Sophia, she was so much concerned then because Fanny was again pregnant—soon to give birth to a boy to be named William Rutherford, after her husband and brother—that she neglected to have any opinion.

So he stayed on, compromising with a month's vacation in Ohio, of which in his diary he recorded: "I spent my vacation very pleasantly in Columbus. I did not fall in love nor meet with any uncommon accidents." [19]

On January 17, 1845, the Harvard Law School awarded its Bachelor of Laws degree to Rutherford Birchard Hayes, Esq. "Now I shall begin to *live!*" he told himself as he packed to return home.

In young Harvard graduate Hayes's mind then were thoughts not unlike those his father had back in 1817—concerned with the future, a desire to leave a mark, a world of some kind to conquer. But one big difference there was between Rutherford Hayes, the father, and Rutherford B. Hayes, the son. The father had few, if any, doubts about the purpose of his life. His was to build a better home than his own father's, and to prosper for the sake of his wife and children.

The son, then twenty-two, was troubled by many doubts. Many questions, some philosophical, some theological, some professional, some highly personal, most of which never occurred to his father, perplexed him. In his diary he wrote during a last week at Harvard: "I believe I know what true gentility, genuine good breeding, is. Let me but live out what is within and I am vain enough to think that little of what is important would be found wanting." [20] But the doubts persisted as he went home to display to Sophia, to Sardis and especially to Fanny, his trophy, the Harvard Law School degree.

BOOK FIVE

The Bachelor of Law

CHAPTER XXIII

FALSE START

1

THE RETURN of R. B. Hayes, Esq., LL.B., Harvard, '45, Attorney at Law and Solicitor in Chancery, to Ohio was not so happy as everyone concerned had anticipated. His sister Fanny found it heartbreakingly sad. Sophia found it greatly disturbing. Young Hayes himself found it quite painful. And all this because, after the first loving embraces, he announced that he would not practice law in Columbus.[1]

For Fanny especially this was earth-shaking. "I love you like my own life," she would tell him now.[2] She had thought she had everything perfectly planned for her brother. Back in his Kenyon days she had written to him about the obvious advantages of Columbus as the site for launching his career as lawyer. She had said:

Try to locate yourself in a place where you will have an opportunity to see legal procedures conducted in the largest scale. Now where, my dearest brother, could you find these things as in *Columbus,* the capital of the state!—where are gathered together for a great part of the winter all the chief lawyers & judges from all the country roundabout, where the United States court & Supreme court hold their sessions? Yes, here is the place for you. . . . Oh, I will not believe that we are always to live apart! In all my future plans you fill a large corner & just think, Rud, how happy we shall be—you shall have a snug room in our house, with places enough for your gun, mechanical tools, &c, &c. . . .[3]

Fanny was correct about the advantages of Columbus. But he passed them all by. He had to. The very attraction of Columbus which appealed to him most—being with Fanny—also now repelled him. There was still too much tension in their relationship. He sensed instinctively that he could not grow properly in the shade—or light—of Fanny's superstrong affection and leadership.

2

He had to have a life of his own. To attain that goal, it would have been better had he decided at this time to settle in the biggest city in

141

Ohio, Cincinnati, or in up-and-coming Cleveland, or, if not in Ohio, Boston. Certainly his education fitted him for practice in a metropolis. He knew this, and he did have his eye on Cincinnati.[4]

But he was not yet ready. To have settled there then, in 1845, when he was not yet twenty-three, would have meant a clean break from his childhood associations, from the fixations in which Fanny and Sardis were the chief figures. It would have meant a firm step into manhood. He was still unprepared for that. Instead, he compromised. In a kind of panic, leaving before dawn so as not to have to say good-by to Fanny and Sophia, he went to start his law practice in Lower Sandusky, Sardis' little "shanty town," as he called it, where, in a cubicle of a building owned by Sardis, "a little tenement about 15 ft. sq.," he set out his lawyer's shingle on April 12, 1845.[5]

This move was not at all a good compromise. Being with Sardis at this time was not much different for him psychologically from being with Fanny. It was a retreat back to the security of his childhood, when Sardis was the all-knowing, all-doing, affectionate protector of the adoring little boy Rud. That kind of security was not good for R. B. Hayes, Esq., pleasant and wholesome as it had been for the little Rud Hayes. He still had to learn that his only real security had to come from standing by himself.

But this spring of 1845, when he was outwardly a strong young man, good to look on, well groomed, his auburn hair and blue eyes exuding health and determination and sound character, he was not wholly ready for that.

3

He did not, however, have his living quarters with Sardis. By then a confirmed bachelor, his uncle lived with a farm couple, James and Maria Vallette. In fact the Vallette residence, about a mile and a half from the village proper, was Sardis' home. Hayes took up residence at a little hotel, the Thompson House, sharing a room with a cousin, John Rutherford Pease, whose father, first husband of a sister of Hayes's father, had died in the milksick of 1811.

Pease was a "character," a plain man who would just as soon have gone about the village in his bare feet, even after he became well-to-do in the stove business and the town mayor. He styled himself a Jackson Democrat, and scoffed at Hayes's and his uncle's Whig views, though he too appreciated the value to his business of Whig policies about internal improvements and banking.

Pease and R. B. Hayes, Esq., made an odd pair as roommates—the backwoodslike transplanted Yankee from Brattleboro, who "could not write or speak grammatically," and the Harvard collegian.[6] But they got along quite well.

Joking over Pease's "eccentric" politics helped to relieve the tedium of the village life. "If he once stops, a forty-horse-power can't start him again; and if he starts in a certain direction you can't turn him [with] a locomotive," Hayes related.[7] To Fanny he reported that he and Pease "have fine times. We sleep in the same room, have got up a good 'washing machine' in which we take a shower bath every morning as soon as we get out of bed. Quite as good as a pill-box for health." [8]

He lived for close to five years at the Thompson House, paying two dollars a week for board, plus "washing at .50 per doz.," calling the period his "pilgrimage." They were mainly "doleful years," as he himself would say.[9] True, it was wonderful to be close to Sardis. But he suffered, among other things, the realization that the law business that was his in the "shanty town" was not law business at all, certainly not the kind for which he believed his training at Harvard had prepared him. He longed to show his mastery of profound legal principles. Yet all that he had to do mainly, even with most of the matters that Sardis referred to him, was to look up the title of some cow patch, draw a testament disposing of a plow, a bed and some dishes, prepare a divorce petition in a highly unromantic domestic situation, or usually just sit idle in his rude office.

4

During all the years in the village he was stimulated by only two law cases, both handed to him by Sardis. One grew out of Sardis' effort to establish title to most of the land occupied by Lower Sandusky on the basis of purchases he had made back in the days when he was secret partner to William P. Dixon. The other was a plea for an injunction against a railroad using a bridge over Sandusky Bay—this an effort to stifle a company that was competing with a railroad that Sardis was promoting from Toledo to Cleveland via Lower Sandusky.

These matters, at least, involved constitutional questions. Both were appealed to the Supreme Court of the United States, and although outside lawyers were retained by Sardis, Hayes did most of the work. But the excitement over these turned sour in the end, for both cases were lost.[10]

It was disillusioning for him that the railroad case went against Sardis after Judge Lane, formerly associated with Sardis' project, had gone over to the other side, joining certain New York capitalists. But this, as he was to learn, was business, as even honest men practiced it then. Judge Lane was merely being shrewd and watching the main chance. The upshot was that Sardis sold out, thus losing a chance to be a founder of what later became the New York Central System, and Judge Lane emerged, some time later, as managing director of the Illinois Central System in Chicago, employing among other lawyers one Abraham Lincoln.[11]

About the most exciting case Rud had was one that involved himself. This was prosecution of a fellow boarder at the Thompson House, who broke into his room and stole his gold watch, as well as Pease's wallet, causing Sophia, when she heard about it, to explode, "*That* is the *good society* Rud is in [at Lower Sandusky]—thieves sitting at the same table with him!" [12]

It was "sport," he told Fanny, to handle the divorce case of "our late Presbyterian minister's lady against her lord. Extreme cruelty was alleged, but the real difficulty was that Mrs. Backus had some property which the Rev. Mr. B. was resolved to get. . . . Finally her 'sistern' in the church persuaded her to apply for a divorce and trumped up for causes a dispute about peas, a chicken, some rain water—a quarrel in which the word 'old hag' was used, &c, &c." [13]

Such matters were amusing, but only temporarily. Clearly they were not "the law" as he had envisioned it while sitting at the feet of Justice Story in the Dane Law School Building at Cambridge. There was bitterness, as well as attempted humor, in him when he commented to Fanny, "I assisted in pettifogging a case last week, and have hopes of becoming quite a pettifogger in time." [14] And to Sophia: "I have hopes of living to see the place at least half-civilized one of these afternoons." [15]

The truth was, he felt cheated—by himself. Quite clearly he had made a false start.

5

Thanks to Sardis' intervention and good intentions, he became, technically, a partner of the leading lawyer in the community, R. P. Buckland, who had handled much of Sardis' local legal work. The local Whig paper carried a card:

BUCKLAND & HAYES
Attorneys at Law

Will attend to the Business of Their
Profession in Sandusky and Adjoining
counties. Offices on the Second Story
of M. and J. S. Tyler's building.[16]

But this association with industrious Lawyer Buckland was really
worse for Hayes than if he had stayed on his own. Ten years older,
a big, humorless man, not brilliant, yet sharp enough to have edited
the Toledo *Blade* for a stretch, mainly self-made, Buckland took a
rather patronizing attitude toward his Harvard associate, even referring to him still as a student.

Hayes admired Buckland for his "strict integrity." [17] But he did not
really like him. However, his main objection to the partnership of
Buckland & Hayes was that there was much more Buckland than
Hayes to it. He was not functioning on his own, which was what he
needed most.

He made valiant efforts to become an accepted citizen of the village
life. He went out of his way to be friendly with the German immigrants then coming into this part of Ohio, amusing them by trying out
his German on them. He attended church regularly, usually the Episcopalian, expecting, as he told Will Lane, to be "as good an Episcopalian as any." [18] He joined a new fraternal order, the Odd Fellows.
He joined the new Sons of Temperance Society, making speeches, as
did Lincoln in Illinois, against the evils of alcohol, to Sophia's great
delight (though he himself did not really believe much in the evil
then).[19]

When he attended country dances, it was often he who saw to it
that the fiddler was paid, thus presumably ingratiating himself with
the other citizens. When village leaders, spurred by Sardis and Pease,
launched a movement to get a telegraph office in the town, "so we
shall be within speaking distance of the great world," he was as enthusiastic as any native, collecting pledges and contributing ten dollars
to the common fund.[20]

Though he was still a friendly person, he was never really accepted
in the village. He was too much different, in clothes, in manners, in
outlook, in his interests. Kenyon and Harvard had done that to him,
and the virtues of his college training were now handicaps. The fact
that he read books regularly, especially such ones as Gibbon's *Decline*

and Fall of the Roman Empire and Schiller's *Poetry,* made him an object of suspicion. There was always a barrier.[21]

When Henry Howe, the peripatetic Connecticut historian, wandered into Lower Sandusky in 1846 to gather material for his Ohio Historical Collections, he spotted young Lawyer Hayes instantly as a kind of sport among more rugged plants. Jocosely referring to Howe as "a second Herodotus," Hayes spent hour on hour with him, not only because he was interested in Howe's project, but because he was starved for intellectual talk.[22] As he wrote to Fanny, "I have dabbled a little in law, a little in politics, and a little in temperance reform. Yet with all these matters, I have had to fall back on Shakespeare and miscellaneous readings to get happily rid of these long days." [23]

Had he not been Sardis' nephew, he probably would have been completely isolated, even ostracized, except for one or two of the other lawyers in Lower Sandusky. It did not even help him much that he began to dress like the other villagers, discarding most, though not all, of his city clothes and customs. "I don't care anything about shirt-bosoms or patterns as long as I stay in Lower Sandusky," he told Sophia. "Nobody here knows anything about shirt-bosoms!" [24]

6

He did a great deal of "sparking," starting numerous "incipient courtships, smitten, but not in love." [25] One evening, to pass the time with a certain village lass, he climbed the fence of a Catholic convent near the village to be with her.[26] This interest in sparking the village girls, really nothing more than passing time, caused Fanny some alarm. She urged:

Do *not* fall in love with any of the Sandusky beauties. Perhaps I am prejudiced, but I wish you to take into consideration that you will not always live in Sandusky. So do not marry a wife you will blush for anywhere. Do forgive me, brother, if I am meddling; if you do not like such interference, say so, & I shall forbear in the future.[27]

He did not mind Fanny's "meddling" at all. He agreed too readily that most of the girls in the area were, by Fanny's standards, hayseeds, about as characterless in his educated view as the houses of the village, "built not merely without good taste," as he told Fanny, "but with apparent disregard of all taste and comfort." [28] Of one choice made for him by Sardis and Pease he told Sophia, "There are many points about their selection which would please you, some that please me, but a *very few* that Fanny would like. As I must suit you all, our Sandusky girl will hardly catch me at present." [29]

The truth was, he was not yet ready for a wife. He did a lot of talking about girls—and with girls. A good many fell for him, like Julia Buttles of Columbus, who, Fanny reported, "turned sick at hearing your name" because he did not court her.[30]

He often insisted in his diary that he wanted "a wifey," and perhaps he did.[31] But he certainly was not ready to do anything about it. Besides other impediments, he had an image of "a wifey" that was hard to realize—a girl that always looked like his sister Fanny, an image that presented psychological perils and problems.

7

He tried to persuade himself that he was making progress, by way of preparing for the time when he would leave Lower Sandusky. He still thought a good deal about Cincinnati, though not, to Fanny's dismay, of Columbus.[32] But the months stretched on and he remained in the village, still wifeless and practically briefless, known more as Sardis Birchard's nephew than as R. B. Hayes, Esq. He could not hide from himself a fact: Many of his Kenyon and Harvard classmates were making markedly more progress than he.

Down in Brazoria County, Republic of Texas, Guy Bryan, with whom he kept up a cordial, chatty correspondence, was running his family's imperial plantation and was engrossed in high Texan politics soon to erupt in annexation of his republic to the United States. In Cincinnati Stanley Matthews, after editing an antislavery paper in Kentucky, was practicing law without even having attended law school, and doing so well that Salmon P. Chase, one of the town's great lawyers, would soon take him into his law firm. Back in Massachusetts young Ephraim Bond, a special Harvard friend, had more major law business, he told Rud, than he could handle, was a candidate for selectman of the city of Springfield, and on his way to becoming a Whig leader and president of the Massachusetts Mutual Life Insurance Company, as well as director of the Pynchon Bank.[33] Down in Mississippi Will Hedges was also in banking, with a lovely wife to boot, and finding both banking and marriage glorious occupations, the latter especially "the real poetry of life." [34] Over in Sandusky Will Lane was appearing in important law cases and also getting ready to take a "grand tour" of Europe.[35]

8

Yet there in a kind of mud puddle was R. B. Hayes, going nowhere, going backward, going stale. . . . At times he tried to buoy his ego by telling himself philosophically that he really did not want success and fame after all, that it was more important that he be simply respectable and happy. Even Fanny, when she sensed that he was worrying, professed to agree. "Your feelings with regard to the future —your *modest confidence* & your freedom from selfish ambition accord with my *present* views entirely," she now said.[36] But neither he nor Fanny really believed what they were telling each other.

Their childhood dreams—mainly her dreams—of his some day placing at her feet a wonderful laurel wreath of glory still persisted. He was tormented by what seemed to him the lack of even a slim chance of realizing them. It had been clear to him in the first "doleful year" in Lower Sandusky that he had made a mistake in going there. He ought to have left then. "Oh, the waste of those five precious years!" he later exclaimed.[37]

CHAPTER XXIV

FIRST LOVE

1

ALONG WITH his boredom and disappointment with life in Lower Sandusky, there was an additional sad situation that accented in him an uncharacteristic tendency toward gloominess. It was a bad time just then to be a Whig, especially one so sentimentally loyal as he.

The Whig Party, to which he was so devoted, seemed extraordinarily inept after it had elected General Harrison. It seemed symbolic that the 1840 triumph was short-lived, that Harrison should die within a month after his inauguration, to be succeeded by Vice-President John Tyler, really a Democrat. Then in 1844 the Whigs lost the Presidency to an avowed Democrat, Polk.

Hayes had to admit that his party seemed to lack a positive policy, at least one that was inspiring to him. All that his party seemed to do was nag at President Polk. His Whigs, as he especially would have occasion to recall ruefully, even stooped to criticism of Mrs. Polk for being "too devout a Presbyterian," and for eliminating parties at which wine flowed freely.[1]

The one inspiring political development of this time was the raising of the cry, "Fifty-four forty or fight!"—a slogan credited to United States Senator William Allen.[2] True, Allen, from Chillicothe, Ohio, was a Buckeye. But he was a Democrat. As a Whig, young Hayes was supposed to be opposed to Allen's challenge to Great Britain in the dispute over the boundary of the Oregon territory. In fact, he was sympathetic, for the Democrats obviously were expressing in the most direct way the doctrine of Manifest Destiny. He believed in this fervently.

He did not at all agree with his mother, the perfect Whig, who said, "If the time that has been wasted talking about Oregon had been spent in educating the ignorant or in improving the moral condition of the youth of this land, instead of inflaming their minds about 'War & Honor,' it would be better." [3]

2

Young Hayes wanted to be inflamed about "War & Honor." Indeed, in one of his papers at Kenyon College, he had extolled the idea

149

of war's being a good thing, especially for a republic, in that it "united the people" and prevented "decadence." [4]

Simultaneously with the Oregon matter, trouble over Mexico exploded. President Polk dispatched troops. Soon there was a war, one that the Whig Party opposed. The Whig State Central Committee of Ohio declared: "Our beloved country is imbroiled in a most unnatural, ruinous and unnecessary war with a sister Republic, which war has been produced by the imbecile and wicked councils that have prevailed in the administration of our federal government" [5]—the same kind of objections that Federalists in the Washington Benevolent Society in Brattleboro had raised against "Mr. Madison's War" back in 1812-14.

Hayes also spoke disparagingly, after the manner of the leading Whigs, of the Mexican War as nothing more than an effort of slaveholders to enhance their territory and their political power. "It is now getting to be a great hoax, though to be sure rather too serious for a joke," he wrote to Will Lane. He pretended to be scornful of youths who talked of volunteering. With amusement he quoted one youth as telling a group of girls, "I long for the time I shall *ravish* in the Halls of the Montezumas!" adding, "Every low blackguard talks that way." [6]

Later he was to conclude that the Whigs had "misunderstood" the Mexican War, that in reality "the hand of God was in the work of adding a number of grand, rich states to our country, with every acre of American soil better as a result." [7] But at the time he dutifully approved the antiwar views openly expressed by Whig Congressman Abraham Lincoln of Illinois and in particular the Whig Senator from Ohio Tom Corwin, who won fame with an eloquent speech against "Mr. Polk's War," in which he used the sentences: "If I were a Mexican, I would tell you, 'Have you not room in your own country to bury your dead men? If you come into mine, we will greet you with bloody hands and welcome you to hospitable graves!'"

Young Hayes approved such an attitude toward the war as a matter of political orthodoxy. But emotionally he was really all for the war. From his office window he watched the drilling of Lower Sandusky volunteers, farm lads in jeans who used pitchforks and sticks for guns. Though he professed to scoff, he really felt envious—and cheated.

Among his law books, or lying awake nights on his cot in the Thompson House, he pictured himself at the head of some regiment, plunging into battle at some place with a romantic Spanish name. His reason suppressed these urges, but he was unhappy about it. His life in Lower Sandusky seemed duller than ever.

Moods of depression gripped him.[8] He made valiant efforts to shake off his complex of blues. He stepped up the amount of reading he indulged in. The more moody he became, the more he turned to his books. But this proved no cure. From too much reading, of Byron especially, he became more introspective than ever. He desperately longed for romance, of the Walter Scott type at least. He longed for excitement, for a sense of achievement, for being in the main current of things. In a word, he longed for *living*.[9]

3

So far as his nature and the ties with Fanny let him, he tried love.

Back in June 1846 Judge Lane had told him that a pretty young niece of Mrs. Lane's, a girl from New London, Connecticut, would be visiting the Lanes in Sandusky City. The judge recommended that he look in on the young lady. At first Hayes was only casually interested, being under the impression that the girl was a cousin whom Will Lane himself was wooing. "I have a great respect for prior acquired rights in these things and shall do nothing in the premises until I find out the truth of the matter," he hastened to write to Will.[10]

Before going over to Sandusky City to investigate the girl's charms for himself, he cautiously waited until he received from Europe Will Lane's assurance that it was all right for him to woo the girl, that Will's own sweetheart was another cousin. By then it was September. Going to Sandusky City, he found that the girl, blue-eyed and twenty-one, did come up to her advance billing. But alas! she was already surrounded and pursued by a number of eligible young men, including especially a Harvard student, J. A. Camp, who gave the vague impression that he and the young lady were engaged.[11]

Consulting his code of a gentleman, Hayes decided that it required that he go slow or even withdraw. He wrote a full report to Will Lane.

I *did* see your pretty Coz, and *was* pleased with her—an exact fulfillment of your hope. I spent a few hours with her as pleasantly as I ever did with any one; and thought I learned to know her very well. . . . As soon as I saw her I resolved to see her again and as often as possible, and, as you intimate, "who knows but what?" Then I learned what you speak of, that friend Camp, very foolishly, as I thought for one in his situation, was in love with her, though one could hardly blame him. He "being in," I drew off, not wishing, of course, to appear under such circumstances in the attitude of a rival. . . . As it is, Camp has the course to himself. . . .[12]

His last statement was not precisely accurate. He had no intention of withdrawing completely from the chase. In his diary, as an entry marking his twenty-fourth birthday, he cautiously wrote: "A year ago I expected to be married before this time. I wish I were now a married man. I have had no loves as yet. Before another birthday I am resolved at least to make a choice. I've said enough to show what is now uppermost in my thoughts." Then he added that he knew of two girls, "either of whom" he "might love." These, he noted, were a Columbus lass, one picked by his mother and sister, and "F. G. P.— who is engaged already to another, I fear." [13] F. G. P. was the Lanes' house guest and, obviously, his first choice.

4

Her name was Fanny Griswold Perkins. But this was not to be learned from Hayes, then or later. He made many mentions of her in his diary and in letters, but always merely by her initials. In particular he kept her identity from his sister. Indeed, he carefully tried to make sure that nobody would learn who his "lady love" in this period was.[14]

Fanny tried to draw him out: "I am quite in love with *the lady*," she said. "My imagination has been on the full canter conjuring 'things to come.'" But when she asked him to tell her who she was, his response was: "The young lady's name is Fanny—a well sounding name in my ear; but not Fanny Hayes and probably never will be. The other name might be Smith or Snooks, you would be none the wiser if I were to tell it to you." He apparently never did, not even after he no longer disguised the fact that he really wished to marry this Fanny Perkins.[15]

At last, he thought, he had met a girl who suited even his sister's requirements. For his sister he set down—still withholding her name —a description of the other Fanny's qualities.

She is a homebody. She is pious (very) after the Puritanical School —N.B. suits mother—a little, perhaps a good deal—aristocratic (N.B.

suits you)—a mixed disposition, half frolicksome, half poetical (N.B. suits me)—a decided taste for reading, and music, and I think perfectly sincere. Taken all together, that's as good character as could be desired. What think ye? [16]

Not even his sister, in her status as Mrs. William Augustus Platt, could have asked for better family connections. On the Griswold side of Fanny Perkins' family there were at least twelve governors, thirty-six high judges and many other eminent men, including a later president of Yale University, the same Griswold clan, incidentally, with which Hayes was connected through his great-grandmother, Abigail Austin, whose mother had been a Griswold.

The Perkinses themselves were almost equally distinguished in the New London area. Her father, Thomas Shaw Perkins, was a Yale graduate, prominent as a lawyer and as a judge and a man with enough capital to permit him to be an investor in the Bank of Norwalk, Ohio, along with Judge Lane and Sardis Birchard. By the marriages of various kin, Fanny Perkins was related to, among others, Peter Lorillard, the tobacco magnate, to Edward Everett Hale, the orator and author of *The Man without a Country*, and to Harriet Beecher Stowe.[17]

5

This "noble-hearted F—," as he referred to her in his diary, quite clearly returned Hayes's interest. For even though she appeared to be Camp's girl, she permitted Hayes to play the game of love with her throughout her stay in Ohio. But no resolution was reached. Just before she returned to Connecticut, Hayes tried to pin her down, though in a bantering way, as to whether or not there would be a chance for him. She was evasive.

After she had gone, he turned to his sister for counsel. He sent along to her a letter from Miss Perkins which, he said, puzzled him. He wrote Fanny:

I don't know precisely what to think of her letter. I wrote her a very droll one, never so much as intimating that I cared a straw for her (of course, she might infer *that* from the fact of my writing). My excuse for writing was: She & I made a wager of 12 pr. gloves that she would be *engaged* before she reached home. She was to let Mrs. Lane know by some byword & through her, me, whether I lost or won. This she failed to do, I having been at the Judge's a dozen times (more or less) and hearing nothing of it. So I wrote her, "How about those gloves" &c. Of course, I wasn't stupid enough to talk as if I *needed an excuse,* but this was in fact the ground work & from that I talked off as merrily & sillily (an 'orrid adverb) as could be. Her letter is throughout, as lawyers say, "responsive" to mine; that is, she alludes only to things alluded to by me. You see she winds up by telling me *not to write any more.*

Possibly my girl means "aye" when she says "no", but that's the question. Now I wouldn't tease her with any more letters . . . only my judgment is in her favor and I have a sort of presentiment that she is probably *the one.* . . . I have a good excuse to write again in an indifferent sort of way, but that I shall not do. If it is deemed advisable to run the risk, I mean to "blab it out," not bluntly to be sure, but "in a foxy style" that will take with her, if she is ready to be taken, but "that's the question" once more. You have the lights. What think ye? . . . I'll follow your advice in the premises *or not,* just as the wind takes me. "Now to it." [18]

Of course, he really knew what to do without being told by his sister—if he wanted Fanny Perkins he should have set boldly out to get her. His sister told him precisely that. He should write not "foxily" but romantically, and to go to see the young lady in Connecticut —if he wanted her. He did write, sending the letter first to his sister for her "approval." [19] But he could not bring himself—yet—to go and get her.

He was stumbling all over himself, uncertain, indecisive, wishing one thing, doing another, making excuses that really were nothing more than excuses. Such as assuring himself, as he later told both his sister and Will Lane, that, as a gentleman, he had no right to be desiring Fanny Perkins so long as "friend Camp had got his foot in." [20]

6

He recognized that he was merely making excuses for failing to act the part of a mature man—and this recognition began to trouble him. The truth was, he had scored a personal failure and sustained a blow to his ego, already much deflated by his unhappiness in Lower Sandusky. In his diary at a later time he wrote that he was "reluctant" to set down much about his love affairs. He was "afraid of profane eyes and, with shame be it said, that one day I might myself blush to see it; not the love, but the *repulse.*" He added: "Success, success even in affairs of the heart, is the thing which crowns and enobles." [21]

This lack of success with F. G. P. more than anything else disturbed him.

He tried to laugh it off. He set out to court other girls. He wrote glibly to his sister that perhaps he would be satisfied, after all, with "Miss W—" in Columbus, who, he then decided, was "quite like my Yankee girl" anyway.[22] But he did not believe this. He wanted the Yankee girl. Deeper depression from this new frustration gripped him.

He fell into a state of general mental and emotional confusion. There is a hectic entry in his diary:

December 23, 1846.— . . . What a world of time and brains are wasted in idle daydreams, castle-building, visions of happiness too rapturous for reality. Am I in love, that it grows on me, or is it habit rioting unchecked? . . . If in love, where's the sweetheart? Is it the noble-hearted F—? . . . The settled object is wanting. It is useless to attempt to cast myself free from the cords which a too warm imagination throws about me. The only cure is marriage. If that is not the specific, I may as well despair of ever making even a respectable figure in life; for now in spite of all my advantages—a happy disposition, fair abilities, and good principles—I am almost wholly worthless. . . . I feel as if something was approaching in the future which is to determine my fortunes hereafter, and over which I have no control. . . .

R. B. Hayes was in a bad way.

CHAPTER XXV

Confusion and Decision

1

Something, indeed, was "approaching in the future"—a nervous breakdown, or very close to it. Physical symptoms included bloodshot eyes and a curiously chronic cough, with which he brought up blood. He was unable to concentrate. He was not interested in anything. The old nervousness returned with a vengeance. As he walked desolately about the village, he had spells of weeping.[1] He began to fear that he was going crazy. Recalling Fanny's illness, he was haunted by the idea that he too might land in a "lunatic asylum."[2]

Punished and pummeled by the demands made on him by Fanny, by Sardis' faith in him, by his own expectations of what a college-bred youth should achieve, his ego had gone into a state of almost complete collapse. Moreover, he could not unburden himself to those who were closest to him, to Fanny, Sardis, or his mother, because they were part of his problem. Significantly it was to Judge Lane that he finally described his plight, writing him of his feelings of "prostrated mental energy" and utter hopelessness.

2

When he consulted doctors in the village about his cough, they were puzzled. His symptoms suggested tuberculosis, but it was plain that he did not have it. They decided that his life was too sedentary, that he had to give up his studying, that he needed a change to an outdoor existence.[3] He clutched at this advice and translated it to mean that he should volunteer for service in the war against Mexico.

Once he had decided this, the old dreams of glory reawakened. He began to show some interest in life. He pulled the proper strings to secure the proper letters to politicians in an effort to get for himself a commission—"a good appointment"—if possible.[4]

He recognized that his volunteering for the war meant turning his back on his professed political principles, but he rationalized that.[5]

He recognized frankly, too, that the desire to plunge into the war was related somehow with his sex life, or lack of it. At a later time, in discussing the occupation of the soldier, he made the observation, "A favorite—the final test—most admired and best loved always by good women—is the truly ideal soldier." [6]

But there was also a less romantic factor. "I must," he said, "sow my wild oats, according to the vulgarism on this subject. Had I married, as I wish I had, a year ago, I am persuaded this would not have occurred. My health might have been safe and myself a well-behaved civilian, instead of a rough volunteer. But as it is, so is it. . . . I shall remain as pure as need be." [7]

3

Fanny became nearly hysterical over the idea that he intended to go off to war.[8] But he proceeded with his plan nevertheless, and even showed up at the volunteers' center in Cincinnati, Camp Washington, without waiting for word about a commission. He worked himself into a regiment, commanded by Colonel John Brough, later "war" governor of Ohio, drilled with enlisted men, slept outdoors in a tent, even in rain, heedless of the effect on his throat, assuming all the while that he really was going off to fight.[9] But he reckoned without knowledge of what his uncle was up to.

Sardis had enough insight not to oppose Hayes's plan directly. He understood that something more than whim was moving his nephew. Sardis went down to Columbus to urge that Fanny not press her objections, letting her know for the first time how distraught her brother had been. Fanny yielded, conscience-stricken when her intuition warned how responsible she was. She wrote to Hayes, "My ambition that you should excel in mental acquirements was too great." Then she professed to give her assent to his idea of going to war.[10]

Sardis also professed to agree. But he shrewdly extracted from Hayes a promise which in the end resulted in the regiment to which he had been tentatively attached going off to Monterey (and disaster) without him. The promise bound him to consult two Cincinnati physicians, Drs. Dresbach and Mussey, and abide by their verdict as to whether going off to Mexico would be good for him.

Both physicians firmly told him that he should not go. The southern climate was precisely the *worst thing* for him. What he really needed was some bleeding, a careful diet including cod-liver oil and snakeroot, and, most of all, *northern climate*.

So he withdrew from the volunteers. He had promised, and he kept his promise.[11] What he did not know was that Sardis, abetted by Fanny and Sophia, and aided by Will Platt, had reached both physicians and convinced them that it was to Hayes's benefit, regardless of his physical condition, that they advise him to abandon the war plan. Everybody but Hayes was delighted. "We are rejoicing," Sophia told Sardis. "Fanny was growing so pale and poor that I had some fears for her if he had gone." [12]

Meanwhile Sardis had become satisfied that Hayes should not return immediately to Lower Sandusky. As the Drs. Dresbach and Mussey had recommended some loafing in a northern climate, Sardis now urged that Hayes take a trip to the East, that he visit Harvard, chum with Ephraim Bond and other college friends, take in New York and other places, and not come back until he felt like it.[13] Hayes fell in with this proposal. He gave the impression that his purpose in going east was merely to take things easy, "to live the life of a gentleman with becoming composure," as Fanny now urged. But he had something more specific in mind. If he couldn't be a war hero, perhaps, after all, he could attain—he thought, he hoped—the other requisite, a wife.

For Fanny Perkins was still in his thoughts. He determined to see if he could not retrieve defeat in that quarter. So, after arriving in the East, and as soon as he could do so "without exciting any comment," he "got clear of Ephraim Bond," and "pushed hot foot" for New London, Connecticut.[14]

4

In her home surroundings he found Miss Perkins as attractive as in Sandusky City; more so, in fact. Also, he liked what he saw of her family life. Best of all, he discovered that while J. A. Camp was still somewhere in the picture, Miss Perkins did not reject his attentions at all. She clearly did not consider herself engaged to Camp. Or, if she was, she showed that she might be willing to break any such alliance and become engaged to young Mr. Hayes, whom she introduced happily to all her friends and relatives, including her minister.

This time Rud did not let any scruples about Camp keep him from pressing his case. With a show of aggressiveness that surprised himself, he frankly discussed marriage with Fanny. But the courtship took an odd turn. Miss Perkins emphasized that her mother would be "much put out" if she were to marry an Ohio man and leave New

England. She made this seem a great impediment. Would Mr. Hayes consent to live in Connecticut? [15]

Here once more was a call to young Rutherford B. Hayes from the old valley, in its most seductive form. Not only did it offer him his first real love, but secure social status and undoubtedly professional success also, in view of the Griswold-Perkins connections. He would have fitted very well into the society of New London, Connecticut. Before long he doubtless could have seemed like a native there. He could have taken pride in that this very New London had been founded, in a sense, by his great-great-grandfather, John Birchard, its first town clerk, that old Grandpa Daniel Austin had been one of its saviors during the Revolution.

5

But again, and this time with finality, he turned a deaf ear. Like his own mother years before, he cast his lot with Ohio. He told Miss Perkins that if they were wed, their home would have to be in the West.

They had some emotional and, on the girl's part, some tearful discussion on this point, she insisting that she could not leave her mother. Quite possibly the young lady was testing him, wishing him to show he would make some great sacrifice to get her. Undoubtedly he could have won her over to going to Ohio—had he really tried. (Subsequently she did live in Ohio—as Mrs. J. A. Camp.)

But he did not really try. He merely stated his position, leaving the girl to give in, which she did not do. She could not think of leaving her mother, she said. It was the same when they saw each other again after he took a trip up to Cambridge, Brattleboro and other points in upper New England, accompanied, oddly enough, by his rival, Camp. [16]

Of his second discussion with Fanny Perkins, he wrote to his sister:

I found things as I had left them, only worse. I accordingly told F— that if her mother's consent could be granted to a removal to Ohio, I should be glad, otherwise I had nothing to say on the subject. This was the substance. We talked it over deliberately and frankly, at least on my part & I think on hers—and the result was that I could not get her without more feeling & trouble than was to my taste, and that if I should get her it would be under such circumstances that the after consequences might be still more unpleasant. I told her so.

With this understanding, we both soon became satisfied and joked & laughed as usual. There was of course a little feeling at first & I told her I hoped she would select the best of the five or six that her mother & sister had chosen for her & I would call & see her someday, & she said she would be glad to pay her respects to Mrs. Hayes when I came East on my wedding trip! & so we parted. Queer, wasn't it?

6

So ended his "first love affair," as he himself called it. He was not happy about the result, though to Fanny, who agreed that "it was queer" and said both he and the girl had acted "rather unloverlike," he claimed that he was not really affected, "except perhaps to make me a little more difficult to suit." [17]

However, the episode, despite the failure it represented, did have a significantly constructive result. By having proposed to Fanny Perkins, having at last made the manly effort, he had learned to take an adult step toward shaping his own destiny, instead of merely drifting or letting his sister, his mother, or Sardis make such decisions for him. Having learned this, he won a security within that he had lacked before.

By then it was probably plain even to him that his physical illness had been what later doctors called psychosomatic, for the symptoms, including those that suggested consumption, disappeared as soon as he came out of his bad emotional state. Quite offhandedly he reported to his sister, "I forgot to say my health is perfectly good . . . have not thought about before in a fortnight. The only part of Dr. Mussey's prescription that I stick to is cold water and bathing." [18]

7

One more decision remained to be made: to leave the village of Lower Sandusky and strike out, against real competition, on his own. When he returned to Ohio he was almost ready for this decision too. With his new sense of security he announced that he was thinking of setting himself up as a lawyer in a larger community, preferably Cincinnati. "I'd like to live in Cincinnati, if I could get a fair start," he seemingly casually said to his sister, knowing that she would still wish him to select Columbus.

He made plans to visit Cincinnati again, to satisfy himself that "an attorney of [my] years and calibre would get business enough to

BATTLE OF SOUTH MOUNTAIN

Inset left, Colonel R. B. Hayes
Inset right, Sergeant William McKinley

A PREDICTION THAT CAME TRUE

Two months before the Republican convention the *Daily Graphic* of New York featured this illustration. The sun of Hayes was rising. The comets were Benjamin Bristow, on Murat Halstead's back (upper left); Carl Schurz and Horace White, piloted by "the Great Unknown" (upper right); Samuel Tilden, riding the back of "Marse" Henry Watterson (middle left); Charles Francis Adams, on the back of Samuel Bowles (middle right); and James G. Blaine, on the back of Whitelaw Reid.

pay office rent." [19] As an interim matter, however, Sardis had an idea. About a year before Guy Bryan had invited Hayes down to his Texas plantation. Hayes had not seriously considered accepting. But now Sardis suggested that he make the trip. Better yet, Sardis said he would go along with him.

After seeing their 1848 Whig candidate for President, General Zachary Taylor, safely elected, both of them working like troopers for Old Zack, they set off for Texas. As Sardis had anticipated, this interlude of three months was better for Hayes than any regime any doctor could have prescribed. The best part of it was that on this trip he established a new relationship with his uncle, that of man to man. When they returned to Ohio in March 1849 he was full of hope for the future—and able to make his next, necessary decision. This he did—to wind up his affairs in Lower Sandusky and start fresh where he should have started in the first place, five years before —in the Queen City of the Ohio, Cincinnati.

8

Again he met opposition from Fanny—and Sophia. Once more Fanny recited the advantages of Columbus: These were even greater now than in 1845, for the capital city had grown much since then. Will Platt's connections alone would assure him a good law practice. "Oh, why did he have to choose some city away from her!" [20]

Sophia's objections concerned Cincinnati itself. She was sure that it was a wicked city, like the city of Vanity in *Pilgrim's Progress,* which she was rereading "with even greater pleasure." The picture she had of Cincinnati was that of a city of corrupt politicians, of wicked women lying in wait for innocent men, to take from them virtue and fortune, of violent crimes. She would not have been more disturbed had he announced the intention of going to California to dig for gold, as many were doing that year, including a brother-in-law of Platt's. "If only he had his father to guide him!" [21]

Sardis again took a hand. Going down to Columbus, he told Sophia and Fanny that they must cease their objections. They would have to sacrifice their personal desires for Hayes's sake, just as Sardis himself was prepared to do. For Sardis had hoped that Hayes would stay with him. He still expected to put over his railroad scheme, despite the apparent duplicity of Judge Lane and the eastern capitalists. He was also planning to establish in Lower Sandusky a bank, inasmuch as most of the merchants looked to him for financing anyway. He wanted Hayes in it with him, especially as his idea was that the bank and all his enterprises would go to Hayes in the end.

But Sardis knew that his nephew was right in deciding to be on his own, and Cincinnati was the place for him if he preferred it. It would be the making of him, Sardis said. Fanny and Sophia finally understood—at least they understood that it was no use to oppose Hayes's plan.[22]

At a gathering in Fanny's home in May 1849 the cord that bound him to both his sister and mother was loosened at last when he made it plain that he would go to Cincinnati. Sophia took it better than Fanny. "I should like to have you go to Cincinnati if you think best," she wrote without qualification, after he had returned to Lower Sandusky following the family discussion.[23]

Fanny also wrote him to show that she too had yielded. But she could not hide her real feelings. "I had a most romantic feeling of loneliness after you went away this time. I went about putting away the battledores & backgammon board with a sad feeling like taking leave of pleasure. . . . I am blue." [24] Hayes, for a time, was blue too. But his determination remained fixed.

9

His going to Cincinnati was delayed until winter because of an outbreak of cholera that brought to a halt almost all travel in Ohio for months. In the meantime he did one thing of lasting import in Lower Sandusky, participating in its change from status of village to that of town, in the process of which the name Lower Sandusky disappeared. For the new town decided to have a new name, what with the existence of Sandusky City to the north, Upper Sandusky some forty miles to the south, and also settlements called Little Sandusky and Middle Sandusky. Hayes was designated by the town council to head a committee for selecting a new name, finally hitting on Fremont, to honor the explorations of Colonel John C. Frémont. In August 1849 he presented a court petition by which Lower Sandusky, Ohio, became Fremont, Ohio.[25]

In the following days he passed some time by promoting a Sons of Temperance meeting in Fremont. An effort was made to get the Honorable Samuel F. Carey, Ohio's leading temperance orator, to come. Unfortunately the Honorable Mr. Carey had to decline. "I have been afflicted all summer with derangement of the bowels and although recovering, I find that my public efforts bring back upon me the difficulty," he wrote to "Worthy Brother R. B. Hayes." So this final activity in Sardis' town fell through.[26] In November Hayes left Fremont—forever, he thought.

He spent a month at Columbus with Sophia and Fanny. Then on the evening of Christmas 1849, "a cold, clear night," precisely at 9:30 o'clock, carrying his personal belongings in a green carpetbag, he showed up at the Pearl Street House in Cincinnati. As he put it, he was "a stranger seeking room." He felt quite like an ancient pilgrim, somewhat uncertain, yet determined.[27] At twenty-seven he was beginning, at last, his real career.

BOOK SIX

Lucy and the Pilgrim's Progress

"You are Sister Fanny to me now."

—RBH to Lucy Webb Hayes,
February 14, 1862

CHAPTER XXVI

Cincinnati Lawyer

1

On the basis of advance arrangements made by Judge Lane, he had expected to begin law practice in Cincinnati in association with an established lawyer there, a Swedish Frenchman named James Florant Meline. But Meline, who dabbled in poetry and music, later giving up law altogether, had made other arrangements by the time Hayes arrived.[1]

This was really a boon, for it forced him to set up on his own. He promptly did so, renting for ten dollars a month use of one half of an office in the new Law Building on Third Street, between Main and Sycamore, the very heart of the business area, a short distance from the Ohio River.

The other tenant in the office was John W. Herron, a sociable fellow of his own age, lately from Chillicothe, Ohio, who was just starting out in law, and was to become financially successful as well as the father-in-law of President William Howard Taft. Herron and Hayes immediately struck it off splendidly.

They never became, as was sometimes said, partners, but they formed at once a friendship that lasted throughout their lives. Both unashamedly used their twelve-foot-square office for living quarters too. "We sleep on little hard mattresses in a little room cooped off from one end of our office. Quite like living my college life over again," Hayes said.[2] He thriftily took his meals at a boardinghouse "three squares off," at Fourth and Vine streets, operated by a Mrs. Fulton whom he described as "a very excellent widow lady—a Presbyterian after Mother's own heart—who has the reputation, like General Taylor, of never deserting her sick and wounded."[3]

Room No. 6, his office on the third floor of the Law Building, reached by a circular staircase, was "one of the best, if not the best in the building," he assured Sardis.[4] All around him in the Law Building were other lawyers, about eighteen in number, including some of the more prominent in the city as well as other unknowns like himself.

Down the street in Chase's Building was the office of his old

Kenyon friend, Stanley Matthews. Also in Chase's Building was young Manning Force, son of Peter Force, the collector of items on American history, whom Hayes had known at Harvard and with whom he now began a lasting friendship. Another Harvard friend (though in the end an enemy) was then in Hayes's Law Building— George Hoadly, destined to become governor of Ohio and United States Senator and to play a role of special significance in Hayes's career.

It was like a reunion for Hayes to be so close to these and other acquaintances of his college days.

2

His day began at five in the morning, when "an Irishman, who is not a Son of Temperance, comes in and builds a fire and sweeps out the office." At seven a newsboy arrived with the morning paper, the Cincinnati *Gazette,* of course, since it was Whig.

We get up, scratch open our eyes, read the news and go to breakfast. . . . After breakfast, I read law, student-fashion, until noon, when one of us goes to the postoffice and then read news and letters, if there are any, until dinner. Every few days a forenoon is spent in court, if anything interesting is going on. Dinner at one o'clock. Remain in the office until near four, when we sally out to call on friends or ladies—in short, in search of *prey.* About half-past five, I go to the gymnasium.[5]

For the rest in his first weeks, he sat at his table in the office, often even at night after supper, and waited for clients. "All who stay and are found in their offices ready to do business, do get it," he advised Sardis, echoing what he had been told by the other lawyers. It so turned out for him. After he had waited about three weeks, "a substantial coal dealer accidentally stumbled in and gave me a five-dollar retainer to defend a suit for which I shall charge him twenty-five dollars when finished." [6] Thus his Cincinnati practice began.

More important, however, than this early start in practice was the wholesome effect on his general mental attitude just from being in the busy city. He fell in love with the bustle of the Queen City of the West, the Cincinnati which then was enjoying its Golden Age commercially and culturally, a metropolis in 1850 more than twice the size of Cleveland and five times as big as Chicago.

Just walking through its streets was stimulating to him. Fanny especially noted this salutary effect on him when she and Will Platt came down the following March for the opening of the first railroad line from Columbus to Cincinnati. He was so "redolent with health & hope" that almost against her will she at last became reconciled wholeheartedly to his being there instead of in Columbus.[7] In Cincinnati he had found his element.

3

Very quickly he caught on that he had to make "some kind of a noise"—get his name known—or be lost. He noted that in Cincinnati, for a lawyer to succeed, it was necessary for him to "Push, Labor, Shove."[8] Such behavior was really alien to him; it certainly did not fit in with the concept of law practice that he had formed at Harvard. But he forced himself to "Push, Labor, Shove" with the others—to the extent that he was able.

He observed in particular that one especially successful lawyer, burly and tall Alphonso Taft of the firm of Taft, Key and Mallon, often got his name in the papers for speeches at public gatherings, mainly on his hobby—building railroads.[9] Alphonso Taft's way of attracting attention struck Hayes as worth emulating, which it was.

As a step in this direction Hayes became an avowed joiner. He promptly joined the Cincinnati Odd Fellows (Eagle Lodge, No. 100) and the Sons of Temperance, as he had in Fremont. He became a member of the Young Men's Mercantile Library Association, where he showed himself at all its lyceum lectures which, for two dollars a season, brought to town Ralph Waldo Emerson, Park Benjamin, Horace Mann and Theodore Parker in one course alone.[10] Through Manning Force he joined the Ohio Historical and Philosophical Society, which met every Monday evening in the old City Clerk's office to discuss—already—the history of Cincinnati.[11] He made it a point to appear on alternate Sundays at two leading churches, the Episcopalian and the Presbyterian, though he did this, quite frankly, as much to show himself to the "right people" as in compliance with his mother's hope that he go to some church regularly even if he still was not a professed converted Christian.

For publicity he sought opportunities to make speeches. Despite, or perhaps because of, the large wine and beer-drinking German population in the area called "over the Rhine," the city then was dotted with temperance society lodges—Cadets of Temperance, Sons of Temperance, Daughters of Temperance, with units and degrees as numerous as the Masonic order.[12] These lodges were constantly in search of speakers. Even P. T. Barnum, master showman of them all, went in for talks on temperance, notably in Cincinnati.[13]

Because Hayes was a lawyer, bids to make such speeches soon came to him, and most of these he accepted. He was still not so sold on temperance as, say, the Honorable Samuel Carey. "I am a sincere, but not an extreme or violent friend of the temperance cause," he carefully stated.[14] Moreover, like wealthy, eccentric Nicholas Longworth, whose hobby was raising Catawba grapes and who complained publicly that "there is so much temperance abroad in these days that I dare not send even the pure juice of the grape to public exhibition," he felt that the movement could go too far—like the *"ultras"* of antislavery.

Then, as later, he opposed the idea of prohibiting by law the sale of liquors, a movement which was starting in the State of Maine and which Sam Carey was promoting in Ohio. Interestingly enough, in view of allegations that he was a Puritan bluenose on the subject of controlling the drinking habits of others, one of his cases with a partner, after he had been in Cincinnati several years, placed on him the duty to upset an Ohio variation of the Maine law. He argued:

When once a man imbibes the principle that government was instituted to regulate all things, social and domestic, as well as political, it is the most natural error in the world that he should not stop where he began. He wants to apply it to every imaginable case of wrong. . . . This spirit, which induced the passage of this law . . . if fostered, will go on until there will be no personal rights left to the people.[15]

Thus Rutherford B. Hayes in 1854, temperance orator though he was, and he never changed. He also opposed then, as later, conversion of temperance sentiment into a political party. As he noted in his diary in August 1851, he "tried his powers as a talker in a little speech in the County Temperance Convention. The question was on organizing a temperance party. I earnestly opposed it." But if it were necessary at this time to seem to be somewhat extreme, he quite frankly contrived to appear to fill the bill without actually doing so, and made the speech that was wanted.[16]

It was good business, he felt. He counted every newspaper mention of his name in connection with these speeches as all to his advantage, in line, as he put it, with "my recently adopted policy of blowing my own trumpet"—even though his first mention in a Cincinnati paper appeared as "Brother R. H. Hays" and other times he showed up in the press as "R. G. Hays." [17]

He also made the circuit of all the Odd Fellows lodges in the area, making talks on such subjects as "Happiness," and "Benjamin Franklin," that were innocuous and dull. But they did extend his acquaintance and helped to get his name bruited about until, at last, a good portion of Cincinnati became aware that R. B. Hayes—not "R. H." nor "R. G." and not the misspelled "Hays"—was a new resident there.

4

He joined a newly formed group called the Literary Club of Cincinnati, which held its first meetings in the basement of the Presbyterian Church on Fourth Street. Culturally, and later politically, one of his most important steps, as matters turned out, was his affiliation at this time with this club, "a delightful little club," as he referred to it to Sardis; "a group of gentlemen of education and taste," as the Cincinnati *Enquirer* described it on its formation.[18] Through it Hayes came into association with a wide circle of influential merchants, newspaper editors and writers, public functionaries and other lawyers he would not have met so soon or so congenially.

Mainly Whiggish, the Literary Club seemingly was but an innocent collection of young men who liked to orate—as well as to consume huge quantities of oysters, ham sandwiches and sour wine— in respectable surroundings. In fact, it was the incubator of ideas which ultraconservatives were to recognize as dangerous. For this group was composed of most of the young intellectuals of Cincinnati. Some of its members, like the English emigrant Henry B. Blackwell, who later married Lucy Stone, the bloomer-girl suffragette and Abolitionist crusader, were indeed quite radical, a few as freethinking, almost, as Hayes's cousin, John Humphrey Noyes. In its debates and in papers, the club acted like yeast on the thinking city.

In the end it would be clear that this club was a major factor in hastening the death of the Whig Party in Cincinnati, hence in Ohio generally, particularly because of the issue of slavery. Hayes himself considered his membership in this club the "most educational adventure" of his life.[19]

Before long young R. B. Hayes became known as one of the liveliest members of the Literary Club. Temperance orator though he was, he held his own with any in the consumption of wine. When properly mellowed, he rendered on the slightest or no provocation a stirring recitation of "Webster's Reply to Hayne," which inevitably called for more toasts and made him the life of the meetings.[20]

"What good times we had! Wit, anecdote, song, feast, wine and good fellowship—gentlemen and scholars!" [21] So he recalled the Literary Club. And all the while he received, particularly from members like Henry Blackwell, soon to be called Mr. Lucy Stone and to be prosecuted for singlehandedly rescuing a fugitive slave from a pursuing slave master, fresher ideas than he had before on such Literary Club debate topics as "Abolition," "Manifest Destiny," "Shall the Suffrage Be Given to Women?" and "The Railroads."

He blossomed in other ways, too. To Fanny he wrote:

I have got me a sign, newer, larger, showier and more richly gilt than any other on the front of the Law Building, albeit its face was adorned before with more numerous and gaudy shingles than any other in the city. Whether the staring gold capitals on a field of lemon will draw more flies into my web than are wont to stray in thither, Time can alone discover. . . . I am of the impression that gaseous bodies do better. Don't be alarmed . . . lest you shall hear that I am blown up in an explosion, or gone off in a vapor. No, I mean to begin with creeping and ascend gradually to the enviable height of a decided "blow." [22]

Even if he meant only half of this, here indeed was a changed, or changing, Hayes. The show of attempted aggression paid off, too. He had been in Cincinnati scarcely more than three months before he had more cases than he had customarily handled in a year up in Fremont.

5

Indeed, he was soon so busy that, after John Herron moved from Room No. 6 to join some better-settled lawyers as a junior partner, he invited another young lawyer, William K. Rogers, also a Kenyon graduate, to move in with him on the understanding that Rogers would function as a kind of assistant in addition to office mate.

Billy Rogers looked up to him as if he were an older brother. For all practical purposes their association was a partnership—with Hayes the senior member. Rogers was so passive that Hayes, in association with him, seemed more aggressive, much more the leader, than he really intended to be. They became the closest friends. But more important than this new friendship was the effect on Hayes of the hero worship that Rogers bestowed on him. For without knowing it, Rogers contrived to bring out the strongest drives in Hayes, subtly encouraging him to be the leader, to make the important decisions for both of them. It was a case of two young men psychologically right for each other, having met at the proper time. Rogers was "too guileless for practical life." Hayes once said.[23] The contrast with himself made Hayes seem the very model of a practical man—all to the good for his professional standing.

Some of the business that came to him was from strangers who happened to knock on his door. Some came from acquaintances struck up at the Literary Club, the Odd Fellows and the Sons of Temperance. He obtained business also because he spoke German.[24] He obtained some clients, including on one occasion even Nicholas Longworth, because of Sardis Birchard's influence.

But much of his business, after he had been in Cincinnati about a year, came from other lawyers. His Harvard training, such a handicap in Fremont, now stood him in good stead. The older Cincinnati lawyers came to recognize that if they wanted an associate who could get up a truly learned, exhaustive, up-to-the-minute brief on a knotty subject of law, Cincinnati's new young lawyer Hayes was just the man.

Especially did they like to call him in because of the respectful attitude he had for older men, vestige of his old search for a father, which showed up notably in his penchant for being a good listener when older lawyers were speaking.

Before long he was being called in regularly on cases that required careful research, and getting for himself a reputation as a "lawyer's lawyer." [25] By June 1852 he was already so well thought of in the profession that he was chosen to examine graduates of the Cincinnati College of Law for admission to the bar at exercises in Smith & Nixon's Hall, sharing the honor with Flamen Ball, Salmon P. Chase's partner.[26]

CHAPTER XXVII

LAURELS FOR FANNY

1

His reputation in particular was that of a lawyer who was reliable and, despite the somewhat ribald Saturday nights at the Literary Club, always sober. This was not a common legal reputation. It was a fashion for lawyers then, especially those who appeared often before juries, to assure themselves that they were the better pleaders if they fortified themselves with alcoholic refreshment. In some cases this worked; in others it did not, as for example in the case of the city attorney who was discharged about this time for drunkenness.[1]

Hayes, at least, never tried mixing law with alcohol. Precisely because other lawyers of his acquaintance did, he found himself—at least temporarily—one of the most prominent criminal lawyers in the city in the second year of his practice there. It happened as a result of his being in court one day in October 1851 to prosecute a merchant named Cunningham, from Kentucky, on a technical charge of grand larceny.[2]

On that same day a hearing was being held in the case of a girl, a servant, Nancy Farrer, accused of poisoning to death four persons in two families that had employed her. Her lawyer, appointed by the court, clearly was in his cups. Judge R. B. Warden, noting this, and also observing how efficiently Hayes handled his grand-larceny case, dismissed the girl's counsel and appointed Hayes in his place.[3]

While he was preparing for this case, former Judge N. C. Read asked his help in still another homicide case, that of a river-boat captain, James Summons, also accused of murder by poison. Summons' case was probably the most prominent of the era in Ohio. Because of the number of times it had been tried—four before Hayes became involved—it became a *cause célèbre*. Just to be associated with it was a feather in Hayes's cap.

Fortunately for Hayes, Read was a member of the alcoholic school of lawyers. As Hayes told Sardis, "James Summons was again convicted, as he ought to have been. Thereupon, his counsel, Read, got too drunk . . . so I got up the bill of exceptions, argued the motion for a new trial, etc., etc." He won the motion, too. The upshot was that Read withdrew entirely—later left Cincinnati for "the shores of the Pacific"—and Hayes was in full charge of the sensational case.[4]

Almost immediately still another highly publicized murder case came to him. A laborer, Henry LeCount, in a fit of drunken anger had thrown a boulder at another workingman, William Klink, on a downtown street not far from Hayes's office. Then he beat his victim to death with a dray pin, all the while shouting that Klink had been responsible for his having been placed in the penitentiary for a previous crime. Obviously LeCount needed expert defense, so friends picked as his lawyer the one man then most prominent in the criminal courts—R. B. Hayes.[5]

On June 11, 1852, the Cincinnati *Gazette* carried an interesting legal news item. "There are three persons in our County Jail under sentence of death, viz: James Summons, Nancy Farrer and Henry LeCount." All were clients of Lawyer Hayes, a fact that gave him a publicity importance in the city unequaled then by any other member of the bar.

2

Unfortunately all these figures were guilty, a sad fact for a defense lawyer who wished to make a record. LeCount had no defense. A dozen persons saw him attack Klink. Captain Summons unquestionably had purchased from a pharmacist the arsenic by which his sister had died, though he had cleverly, and almost successfully, blamed her death on the cholera outbreak of 1849.[6] As for Nancy Farrer, "the ugliest girl ever known in Cincinnati," daughter of a Mormon "prophetess" who claimed to be "the bride of Jesus," the best that anyone had said in her defense was that she was half-witted.

Yet none of these defendants had cause to complain of Hayes's efforts—not even Henry LeCount, who was hanged "near the Court House" on November 26, 1852, an event which Hayes forced himself to witness, feeling it his "duty," though it made him ill.[7]

He did not free his other clients, but he did save both from being executed—the captain's sentence finally was commuted to life and Nancy Farrer committed to an insane asylum. In view of the evidence against both, these results were startling victories, tributes to the zeal and ability with which he handled them. The fact was, from Hayes's way of handling the Summons and Farrer cases, following through every technicality, going sleepless many nights from his planning, it was clear that James Summons and Nancy Farrer were no more on trial than was Hayes himself—as a lawyer.

He became emotionally involved especially in the effort to save the girl from the gallows. He resolved that he, who had been brought up by women, would not be responsible for a woman's being hanged, especially as it was so plain to him that Nancy Farrer was insane.[8] His sister's illness was on his mind as he tensely delivered one speech in Nancy's behalf:

The calamity of insanity is one which may touch very nearly the happiness of the best of our citizens. We all know that in some of its thousands forms it has carried grief and agony unspeakable into many a happy home. We must all wish to see such rules in regard to it established as would satisfy an intelligent man if, instead of this friendless girl, his own sister or his own daughter were on trial.

Nancy's predicament was his "pet case," he himself said. At the very outset he vowed in his diary to make her defense "the best effort" of his life and to save her from death.[9] Save her he did, as much from emotional drive, which influenced both judges and juries, as from all the complicated legal maneuverings he had mastered in her behalf.[10]

3

In so doing he won also his own "trial." After his appearances before the Ohio Supreme Court in connection with these cases, there was no doubt that he was worthy of his profession. The newspapers carried flattering references to his "able presentations." His arguments in the Nancy Farrer case especially were cited and discussed for years afterward in legal decisions and also in medical and psychological journals, the case recognized as a landmark in jurisprudence concerning insanity and criminal responsibility.[11]

During a Summons case hearing before the Supreme Court at Columbus some of the most important lawyers in the state spontaneously came up to congratulate him for the effort he had made. Thomas Ewing, the leading lawyer in Ohio, exclaimed, "Are you listening to that argument! That young man will make his mark in the state!" [12] Hayes pretended to be nonchalant about this praise. Going to Fanny's house to tell her of the day's events, he only casually mentioned the "golden opinions from his legal brethren." But suddenly, on noting "the glow of pleasure" on his sister's face, he broke down and wept like a child.[13]

CHAPTER XXVIII

At Last, A Wife

1

ALL THESE years he and Fanny had dreamed of the laurels he would win. Now he had won them, and like a knight in a story by Walter Scott, still the favorite author of them both, he had laid them at her feet. From then on, he was almost an emancipated man, as if some mortgage on his life suddenly had been lifted.

In one phase of his pilgrimage toward maturity, however, he still stumbled all over himself. For further growth he obviously needed to enter into a satisfactory marriage. Yet in this he remained so clumsy and indecisive that it looked as if he might stay a bachelor, like his uncle. But he was not the carefree, contented type of bachelor. Rather, he fretted constantly over being wifeless.

He was troubled more than ever by physical desires. On a night when he attended a lecture by Professor Agassiz at the Young Men's Mercantile Library Association, he was driven to a curious act for him. He found himself so attracted by the pretty face of a girl sitting near him that after the lecture he followed her in the rain through the downtown streets to her home near the river. He would have tried to strike up an acquaintance with her except that he was offended by the shabbiness of the house into which she disappeared.

He dutifully recorded the matter in his diary, obviously sure that the girl was a prostitute. He retreated to his bachelor room, confused, ashamed and troubled more than ever that he was not securely and comfortably married.[1]

Yet precisely then he was assuring himself that he was in love again—at least "probably" so—with two desirable young ladies. His problem, he supposed, was to choose between them. One was a friend of Fanny's, Helen Kelley of Columbus, daughter of Alfred Kelley, the cofounder of Cleveland in the time of Ruddy Hayes, who became a wealthy Columbus figure of importance and a railroad magnate.[2] The other girl, a choice of Sophia's, was Lucy Ware Webb of Chillicothe, then living in Cincinnati.

2

These two were as different as any girls could be—as different, indeed, as Fanny was from Sophia. Helen Kelley was a sophisticate, "a gay figure in the world of fashion," a coquette, surrounded always by a number of suitors, some of rather "fast" reputations.[3] Lucy Webb, a graduate of the Wesleyan Female College in Cincinnati, was the very opposite. Everyone referred to her as a sweet girl and commented on her pleasant disposition. Even Hayes's sister, though at the time not partial to Lucy as a choice for her brother, said, "She has the very finest disposition, with a perhaps few exceptions, that woman was ever blessed with—so frank, so joyous, her spirit sheds sunlight all about her." [4]

Lucy had suitors, too. But no one would have accused her of playing the kind of coquettish game that Helen Kelley enjoyed. No one would have considered Lucy capable of entering on such a game. In all her relations with, and attitudes toward, men—and sex—she was the very essence of the Victorian propriety of her time. Her suitors, significantly, included some Methodist ministers, who were attracted by her devotion to the Methodist faith.[5]

Helen Kelley was "smart looking," always fashionably garbed and scented. Lucy—"tolerably good looking," in Fanny's phrase—was noteworthy for a pair of bright black eyes that gave her a special attractiveness, particularly for young R. B. Hayes. He found them "simply perfect." Her demure face seemed to him to denote "soulfulness." [6] Helen Kelley was exciting to Hayes, sexually attractive in obvious ways. Though just as feminine, probably more so, Lucy exuded serenity. Helen's eyes promised passion—perhaps. Lucy's promised peace and tenderness. The one set young Mr. Hayes aflame; the other soothed him, or at least permitted his temperature to stay about normal.

It was plain that Lucy, not greatly different from Fanny Perkins, really was the girl for him. The more glamorous Miss Kelley frightened him as much as she attracted him. With Lucy Webb he was as completely at ease as he was with his mother. Probably this was the decisive factor in Lucy's favor. She was more like Sophia than Sister Fanny, whereas it was the reverse with Helen. Fanny remained his dream type. But psychologically it was impossible for him to choose for a mate a girl who resembled so closely Fanny's shining and aggressive personality, as Helen Kelley did.

Shortly after he moved to Cincinnati he had called on Lucy, then still a student at the woman's college. He spent a pleasant evening with her, and returned many times.[7] When Lucy was graduated from the college, he attended the exercises in Wesley Chapel, and complimented her for her speech, "The Influence of Christianity on National Prosperity." [8] More and more mentions of her showed up in his diary. He commented frequently about her "beautiful, dreamy, tender" eyes, her "soft" voice, her "quiet" ways. It was clear that Lucy with her seemingly passive manner, unlike Helen Kelley, made him feel all the more manly, which was what he really sought, really needed, from a woman.

3

To be sure, Lucy Webb was not quite so passive as she seemed. Beneath her soft exterior there was much strength. Indeed, while appearing to be only following, she had a subtle way of leading. She had her firm ideas—for example, on the subject of slavery, which she had been trained from childhood to abhor. Her father's and mother's people were Southerners and slaveholders in Virginia and Kentucky. But at least her father's family, the Webbs of Louisville, were among those Southern Methodists who turned against slavery on religious grounds and freed the Negroes in their possession.

Lucy was proud of this. Unlike Hayes, she knew precisely where she stood on this question of the day. Also, Lucy had what almost amounted to an inbred allegiance to the temperance cause, not a casual one like young Hayes's, but a firm and uncompromising one. This was perhaps inherited from Judge Isaac Cook of Chillicothe, Ohio, her grandfather, one of Ohio's earliest advocates of the temperance movement, who pledged all his family, including Lucy, to undying, aggressive support of it.[9] In any event Lucy was strong on these questions. But she produced the illusion of being always wholly submissive, agreeable and amenable—especially where Rutherford B. Hayes was concerned.

There can be no doubt that Lucy was willing all along, even eager, to have him. From the time she was fourteen she heard often that young Hayes was her "man of destiny." This began when she and her mother, Maria Cook Webb, a physician's widow, went to live in Delaware while her two brothers, Joseph and James, studied at the new Methodist university there in preparation for becoming physicians in Cincinnati. Mrs. Webb became friendly with Mrs. Lamb, widow of the distillery partner of Hayes's father. Through Mrs. Lamb she met Sophia, who visited with Arcena in Delaware. The three widows soon decided that Mrs. Hayes's son and Mrs. Webb's daughter "would make a fine match," though Hayes then was twenty-five while Lucy was only fourteen.[10]

Sophia especially liked Lucy for her strong devotion to religion, whereas the world, Sophia feared, already was "getting away from God." She also liked Lucy for another and more personal reason. "I am thankful," Sophia later observed, "that Lucy knows how to treat old people . . . a rare and excellent trait of character which I would not give for all the discussions we have on literary people and favorite authors." [11]

In those days Hayes paid very little attention to Lucy Webb. He was amused that his mother had selected "a mere child . . . a clever school girl" for him, though he conceded that Lucy's youth was "a defect that she is fast getting away from and may perhaps be entirely rid of before I shall want her." [12] But by 1850, when she was eighteen and a college graduate, living with her mother and her brothers in a modest home at No. 141 West Sixth Street, Cincinnati, Lucy had largely overcome the "defect." Moreover, if the truth were known, bachelor R. B. Hayes then "wanted" her very much indeed.

She certainly was often in his mind. Indeed, only five days after he had followed the girl at the Agassiz lecture, he wrote of Lucy in his diary: "Her low sweet voice is very winning, her soft rich eyes not often equalled, a heart as true as steel, I know. . . . Intellect she has too, a quick, sprightly one, rather than a reflective, profound one. She is a genuine woman. . . . It is no use doubting or rolling it over in my thoughts. By George! I am in love with her!" [13]

4

But he could not get the fascinating Helen Kelley out of his mind. Some of her attraction undoubtedly lay in the fact that she was his sister's choice. One reason for that was her membership in a well-to-do family, whereas Lucy Webb, though connected by blood and through the marriages of kin with several first families of Virginia,

Kentucky and Ohio, and with Edward Tiffin, Ohio's first civilian governor, was then but the daughter of "a widowed mother, in narrowed circumstances." [14] In preferring the Kelley girl, Fanny was being practical—the trait she so often deplored in Will Platt. But in her mind also was an old desire—that Hayes would settle at last in Columbus, and this, she felt, would happen if he married Helen Kelley.

Fanny's preference aside, Hayes was drawn to the Kelley girl by attractions more pertinent to romance, the qualities that made her so successful as a charmer of men. She certainly used her arts of coquetry on him, playing him off against other suitors, now holding him away, now drawing him to her, now professing to love him, now expressing doubt, and keeping him generally in a stew.

He obviously obtained a kind of masochistic pleasure from this treatment, recording it all faithfully in his diary, including this on March 17, 1850:

She has been at times "coy and hard to please" and again yielding and kind, smiling sweetly upon my protestations of affections. . . . I now fear she is thinking of another. She asks for *her* letters, but wishes to keep *mine!* To free herself and to keep me in chains. As long as there is a hope, my love is so blindly strong I must cling to it, though my pride prompts decision. When a straw indicating a favorable "air from heaven" is seen, I am happy as the angels. . . . When she frowns, the world is drear and desolate. It is as a "blast from hell." I am more infirm of purpose than a child, weaker than an infant. Shall I say to her "now or never"? This suspense must have an end!

However, he took a long time to end it. He gave her up. He went back to her. He gave her up again, and again returned to her. He vowed "to visit her, flirt with her, and talk love with her, as long as it is agreeable, as it now appears to be, to her and to myself," but to put "all thoughts of real love" for her out of his mind. Yet no sooner was this resolve recorded than he confessed that merely looking at a letter from her sent his blood "leaping hotly." [15]

After this ambivalent affair had been going on for a year and a half, he did bring matters with Helen Kelley to an end in January 1851.

What a scene was *that one* of last night! The more I think of it the sadder I feel. . . . I had come to consider her as unfitted by temper and disposition for my bosom companion. . . . We talked over our whole past intercourse. Everything was called up, errors and misconstructions corrected, apologies, confessions and repentances exchanged, until all was clear again. I was told with the emphasis of both hands clasped warmly over mine, and a tearful eye and husky voice, again and again, that no other man was or could be so esteemed—so *liked* as I still was. It only was no longer love. I heard it with a smile, not of a triumph, but of sympathy and happiness that "the affair" could end so happily. . . .[16]

5

Lucy Webb meantime waited patiently. In the following June he did get up enough courage to ask her to be his wife.

On a sudden the impulse seized me. I grasped her hand hastily in my own and with a smile, but earnestly and in quick accents said, "I love you." She did not comprehend it; *really* no sham. . . . I *knew* it was as I wished, but I waited . . . repeated my declaration again, until she said, "I must confess, I like you very well." A queer, soft, lovely tone, it stole to the very heart, and I, without loosing her hand, took a seat by her side, and—and the faith was plighted for life![17]

He told himself that he was as happy as a king. However, he had not yet resolved his indecision about marriage. While there was no realistic reason for not setting an early date for their wedding, it was indefinitely delayed, more on his account than hers. Indeed, he and Lucy played a kind of game with friends and relatives about whether or not they really were betrothed. It took him six months before he actually confirmed the fact to Sophia, to Sardis and to Fanny.[18]

In August 1852, by which time they had been betrothed more than a year, Sardis blurted out in Hayes's hearing to Mrs. Vallette, "Why doesn't the young fool marry her? I don't believe she'll have him. If she will, and he doesn't marry her pretty soon, I'll get mad and marry some old maid myself!"[19]

That gave him a needed push. Finally on December 30, 1852, the wedding took place in the Webb home in Cincinnati. Oddly, though Sardis and Fanny were there, his mother was not. Sophia had made the excuse that it was necessary that she stay in Columbus with Fanny's children. Fanny's presence, and Sophia's absence, underlined, of course, a psychological fact. In taking a wife Hayes had cut, though not completely through yet, the silver cord. But it was one that had bound him not to his mother, but to his sister.

CHAPTER XXIX

The Contented Man

1

THE RESULTS showed up almost immediately in the emergence of a stronger Rutherford B. Hayes. He was no longer so plagued by introspection, by vague doubts and subterranean conflicts that had made of him, despite the outward calm and friendly good humor, a bundle of insecurity. He began to walk with a firmer step and to talk with a surer tone before judges and juries as well as at the Literary Club. Instead of being a kind of spectator of the Cincinnati scene, he became a settled part of it, a man giving every indication of belonging there as definitely as the Longworths and the Tafts. Hayes, the pilgrim "seeking room," was disappearing, being replaced by the citizen of Cincinnati.

He made a decided improvement in his way of practicing law. Except for his informal association with Billy Rogers and a similarly vague arrangement with W. C. McDowell, a Literary Club fellow, he had been practicing in the old-fashioned solitary manner. But following his marriage, he watched for an opportunity to place his practice on the more businesslike basis of a law firm, to earn more money. The chance came when the firm of Smith, Corwine and Holt began dissolving.

This firm was among the most active in the city, thanks largely to Caleb B. Smith, formerly a Whig member of Congress from Indiana (later Secretary of the Interior in President Lincoln's cabinet), an attorney who knew how to convert political connections into law fees.[1] Chosen president of the Cincinnati & Chicago Railroad, Smith was moving to Indianapolis, R. S. Holt was going to Tennessee, leaving Richard M. Corwine with the business of the firm and open for a new partner.

"Corwine, you know, may not be the right sort of person for me," Hayes admitted to Sardis shortly after negotiations were opened between himself and Corwine.[2] Corwine was a showy fellow. He was constantly seeking election to some office, hoping for a sinecure. While liking him, Hayes naturally had reservations about him. But the amount of business that was to remain with his firm, even after Caleb Smith was gone, was undeniably attractive, certainly worth the

$1,200 that Hayes was asked to put up for a one-third interest. So Hayes decided to take the chance, persuading Billy Rogers also to join him in the venture. Formation of the law firm of Corwine, Hayes & Rogers was announced in December 1853.[3]

2

There were disadvantages enough. Corwine, the perfect politician type, was never so scrupulous in choice of clients as Hayes. He turned out to be lazy, "an easy, clever fellow," as Hayes described him to Guy Bryan.[4] But having discounted these things in advance, Hayes managed in the main to circumvent them, and saw the number of his clients and his income rise. He moved with his partners into more comfortable quarters in Suite A of the Selves' Building at No. 17 West Third Street, between Main and Walnut.[5] "I like my new arrangements very much," he told Sardis. "I see no reason to regard them as otherwise than fortunate."

He liked especially the fact that he did not have to hustle for business. He was the real lawyer of the firm, the man who researched the precedents, wrote the briefs and appeared in court. "Once in a while there is a pretty tough day's work, but in the main we get along with it very comfortably." [6] He had, in fact, arrived professionally.

Corwine, Hayes & Rogers never received the cream of the law business in Cincinnati, the new railroad corporations, for example, passing it by for Alphonso Taft and others. Still, no reckoning of the bar of the city could leave out the firm in which Hayes was the main element —this after he had been there only three years, a fact that caused people already to speak of something called "the Hayes luck."

3

Within six years, starting in 1853, Lucy presented him with three sons, with other children to come. The first son was called Sardis Birchard, though later renamed Birchard Austin. The second was called James Webb, though later renamed Webb Cook; and the third, Rutherford Platt. From the beginning, too, Lucy's mother was a part of the household. For a time, also, one of her brothers, Dr. Joseph T. Webb, made his home with them. Just like his father before him in the little house in Dummerston, Hayes found marriage a bridge from the status of bachelor to that of the head of a teeming household.

He was delighted that the lives of so many persons revolved around him, and took special satisfaction in the fact that he had started another generation to carry on the line of the Austins, Birchards, Russells, the Hayeses and all the others.[7]

At first he and Lucy had made their home at Mrs. Webb's house. But after his first son arrived, he purchased a larger home two blocks away, at No. 383 Sixth Street. This was a three-story, narrow red brick residence with all the marks of middle-class respectability, suggestive then of R. B. Hayes himself, who had begun wearing a neatly trimmed fringe beard under his chin, like his uncle.

To a cousin in New England he wrote in 1855, "I am moving along quietly and happily, not much disturbed by the anxious cares of so many. My wife and boy, (a bright, healthy little fellow of two years,) are my treasures, and are quite as satisfying as any blessing which I ever expect to find." [8] In his diary he exclaimed: "These ties, these affections—nothing in life to equal them!" [9]

4

He meant all this. The old and disturbing desires for important achievement, for the fame he had jawed about with his Kenyon mates and toward which Fanny had pressed him, seemed pushed aside forever by an immense contentment with his status as it was. He gave the impression that he did not even recall the younger Hayes who had dreamed of being like Webster, of going to Congress, of being a hero in some war. His sole objective, at the moment, seemed to be to make a good living for his family.

Shortly after he came to Cincinnati, he had invested as a flier in some "waste land" in the western part of Virginia, land that contained coal beds. He increased his holdings there, the cost being low —starting at sixteen cents an acre. After Billy Rogers went to Minnesota Territory to find a cure for chronic dysentery and at the same time to get a fortune out of speculating in the cheap land there, Hayes caused Rogers to buy some Minnesota land for him also. To try to get rich, or at least comfortably secure, from investing in this new western land which one day might rise sharply in value—that seemed to be the thing. In short, he was planning to emulate exactly his father and Sardis.[10]

He dabbled in politics (as a Whig, of course), but only as a lawyer normally would, in a casual sort of way. But that was all. Politics, he then said, was for him just a side show, an amusement. Fanny, whom he visited fairly often, set down a faithful word portrait of him two years after his marriage. "He is in fine health & spirits—romps with his boy & turns the whole of life into a joke." [11] He became that rarity, a contented man.

CHAPTER XXX

On Freedom's Road

1

YET the impression he gave of one so preoccupied with a happy and tranquil personal existence as scarcely to notice developments in the world around him was appearance only.

Much, indeed, was going on in this notably uneasy decade of the 1850s in America.

There was a stirring that was prelude to what everyone of perception undoubtedly sensed was coming, collision between North and South in a civil war, but which most, like optimistic Hayes, naïvely hoped could be avoided. Rather than being oblivious to the signs of crisis, he perceived the trend more clearly and with sharper concern than he let on. Also, he became involved sooner, and more deeply, than he really intended.

One evening in October 1854 an occurrence at his new home, though quite incidental, proved symbolic of his personal involvement. On the front steps he was startled to find "a bandbox with a Negro infant child, naked. . . . After a deal of trouble, got the little thing into the Negro Orphans' Asylum," he recorded as the solution of that particular problem.[1]

But he could not escape the implication that the general unsolved problem of Negro slavery in America had been placed, so to speak, right on his doorstep. There, in fact, it was to be found again and again, politically and otherwise, no matter how much he might try to avoid facing up to it.

He did try, as befitted a Whig, to avoid taking a committed stand, like nearly all who still remained Whigs, including the lawyer in Illinois, Lincoln. For a variety of reasons, some personal and some impersonal, this evasion was not possible for Hayes. Indeed, he found himself taking his stand at last even before many more prominent Whigs, and aggressively on the side of antislavery.

2

One influential reason was none other than Lucy, his wife.
As Lucy Webb Hayes's husband, he sensed that he was expected to

187

stand clearly against slavery, as a moral if not a political matter, assuming the two aspects could be separated. For Lucy's Methodism decreed that the "peculiar institution" of the South was a sin against the laws of God. On this subject, religiously sure of her ground, Lucy could be decidedly un-Lucylike in firmness.

She was fond of pointedly telling how her mother, having come into ownership of some slaves in Kentucky on the death of her husband's people, had refused to sell the Negroes but granted them freedom instead. She would rather "take in washing" than profit from such traffic.[2] As Hayes was in harmony with Lucy in most things, achieving a special oneness in their marriage, he soon harmonized with her in this also. Probably both would have been astonished had they fully realized that Lucy was such an influence on his political thinking.

Lucy's influence aside, however, and because he was a decent man, proud of possessing decent, genteel principles, he was bound to react positively against slavery in view of events right there in Cincinnati. On the border between slave and free territory, Cincinnati was the frequent scene of one ugly aspect of slavery. This involved the often brutal methods by which slaveowners, their agents and government officials returned to slavery Negroes who crossed the river into Ohio to attain freedom—the "Uncle Tom" story repeated many times in real life.

Federal laws as well as the Constitution were on the side of the slave catchers, as Justice Story had emphasized in his Harvard lectures to Hayes and his other students. In 1850 a stronger fugitive-slave law had been passed, as a sop to the South and with Whig connivance. This law not only made it legal to seize and take back to the South slaves who had escaped to free territory, but it made it a crime, in effect, if Northern citizens failed to co-operate in the process.

3

Hayes discovered that it was one thing to defend this kind of law as an academic matter in the calm atmosphere of Harvard Law School and quite another to witness its actual enforcement on the streets and in the courts of Cincinnati. To see with his own eyes helpless, frightened black men, and sometimes women with babies, pursued like animals, beaten and dragged through the streets, their only crime their search for freedom, was something more than most decent Northern men could witness and easily accept.

Such occurrences certainly placed a different face on slavery from what he had seen on Guy Bryan's pleasant plantation in Texas, and revealed a different aspect of Southern chivalry from what he had known at Kenyon.

Some respectable men, members of his circle, could see these things enacted before their eyes, express displeasure, yet excuse it all by saying that it was in accord with the law. After all, the law decreed that these slaves were property.

Hayes's friend Stanley Matthews, a little later as Assistant United States Attorney in Cincinnati in the Buchanan Democratic administration, would be found actually prosecuting a newspaper writer, a fellow Mason even, for having allowed a fugitive slave to hide in his room for a few hours. Matthews was to regret this act, but could justify it by holding it was in the line of his duty.[3] However, Hayes, as a private citizen, was not able to react so coldly.

4

In 1853 one Cincinnati incident in particular showed Hayes how the brutality implicit in slave catching could spread until white men as well as blacks would be the victims. This involved a fellow member of the Cincinnati bar, John Jolliffe. Jolliffe was then the official attorney for the Underground Railroad. When a slave was trapped and held by government officials, the U.G.R.R. would try to get him his freedom through legal means, usually on the plea that once on free soil, not even a black man could be considered a slave. If this plea could not be sustained—and usually it could not without a sympathetic judge—an effort would be made to show that the Negro was on free soil by voluntary act of his master. This, it was argued, amounted to granting him freedom, and, if proved, the argument worked.

Not often were good cases made for freedom—not even though Salmon P. Chase himself, with all his prestige as a corporation attorney and United States Senator, made this argument in so many cases that he became known as "Attorney General for the Fugitive Slaves." But Jolliffe did his best. He was, indeed, the chief support of Levi Coffin, the Cincinnati Quaker, who was president of the U.G.R.R.[4]

In August 1853 the mild-mannered Jolliffe appeared in the court of Judge Jacob Flinn on behalf of a family of fugitive slaves. An uncouth political type, Judge Flinn made such short and ugly work of sending the family back to slavery that antislavery groups in the city were particularly outraged. They called a mass meeting to protest, and a movement to have Judge Flinn impeached was launched. Several days later, when Jolliffe was taking a stroll with his small daughter, Judge Flinn came up to him on the street and caned him brutally.[5]

This outrage aroused Hayes's decent, humane instincts and made him act. He decided then he had to dissent from Justice Story, concluding that "a law making the escape from bondage a crime, and compelling citizens under rigorous penalties to aid in the capture of slaves was suited to barbarians, not to Christian people." [6]

A few days after the caning incident he went to John Jolliffe and offered his services, "freely," as a lawyer, for defending fugitive slaves.[7] He had come to a fork in the road on the slavery issue. Like his Russell ancestors, like his Austin and Birchard and other ancestors in the time of the American Revolution, he chose to travel on freedom's road.

5

From then on Hayes was on call at all hours, when a quick writ of habeas corpus, or similar legal action, was needed for some trapped slave, or to give the time needed for the U.G.R.R. to spirit the Negro away—to Delaware, for example, where Sam Rheem helped to operate a "station of freedom." [8] "There was a period when I never went to bed without expecting to be called out by Levi Coffin," he recalled.[9]

How many fugitive slaves he defended or counseled cannot be stated. For, unlike his desire for publicity on his temperance talks and in the Summons and Farrer murder trials, he did not welcome notoriety over his participation in the defense of the slaves; rather, he tried to avoid it. This was prudent, professional caution, as well as a certain lingering hesitancy about being on freedom's road.

Publicity in such matters would not have helped the business of the firm of Corwine, Hayes & Rogers, the temper of the business community in Cincinnati being then what it was. For Cincinnati then was almost as much a Southern as a Northern city. Its commercial houses did much business with the South. The city was divided, with the majority seemingly on the side of the South. Hayes, as well as other lawyers, had to take this climate into account. The safer course for a lawyer still seeking economic security was to avoid taking sides openly until it became clear which way matters were going, to stay clear of early actions that committed and labeled.[10]

6

Yet in at least two of the most noted legal battles to outmaneuver the slave-catching fraternity, both *causes célèbres* in the literature of antislavery, Hayes was boldly at the very center of the struggle on the side of freedom. These were the cases of a boy slave called Louis, and of a girl slave called Rosetta, who was once the property of former President John Tyler's family.

He helped win freedom for both of these Negroes. The girl's battle was won because, as in the case of Nancy Farrer, he used every possible legal technicality and all the considerable acumen that he possessed. Senator Salmon P. Chase was also in this case. But everyone conceded that it was Hayes who mapped and carried out the successful maneuvers in state and federal courts. As Fanny, who followed it all closely in the papers, wrote to Sardis: "You may be proud of 'your boy'—Rutherford has made the best speech in the 'Rosetta case' —won Laurels from his legal brethren & everyone who heard him." [11]

Louis obtained his freedom in the end by simply walking out of the courtroom while Hayes and the other lawyers were wrangling— as uch to Hayes's astonishment, perhaps, as anyone else's. As an officer of the court, he had to profess to be sorry. But he was not.[12] The getaway of Louis made it a great day for freedom in Cincinnati, and Hayes enjoyed the victory as much as any of the antislavery folk. He had become a "co-laborer in a field where none but men went to battle," as Levi Coffin's son reminded him years later.[13]

CHAPTER XXXI

The New Republican

1

HE STILL had a painful and fateful political decision to make. Because of the continued festering of the North-South issues, the old parties were being splintered. By 1854, the year of the revival in Wisconsin and Michigan of an old political name, Republican, his beloved Whig Party was most affected. Not even the eloquence of Clay and Webster, who had placed their prestige behind desperate compromises on the slavery question, had been able to save it. The death of both men in the 1850s merely hastened its demise.

The Whigs were a national party, strong in the South as well as in the North, a fact that Hayes, exactly a dozen years hence, was to have important reason to recall. But after Whig General Winfield Scott (for whom Hayes's uncle was an Ohio elector) lost the 1852 Presidential election to Franklin Pierce, numerous Whigs in the North abandoned it forthwith, many because of its compromises in behalf of slavery.

In the South Whigs in droves departed also because they feared it was against slavery. In the North many Whigs joined the new Free-Soil Party, a few switched over to the heretofore despised Democratic Party, and many others helped to form the new American Party, commonly designated as the Know-Nothing Party. In the South many of the discontented Whigs entered the Democratic ranks, having been shown the way earlier by John C. Calhoun.

On general economic questions most of these Southern Whigs remained Whiggish. In particular, they liked the Whig policy of having the national government underwrite internal improvements, if in the South, being not at all advocates of State rights in that regard. Especially, too, they were interested in having the national government supply funds for a railroad to the Pacific that would run through the South, this, indeed, being an underlying and major, though not often openly discussed, bone of contention between the North and the South.

But Northern antagonism toward the South on the slavery issue, which while economic was only partly so, and fear of Northern supremacy commercially, in which the Pacific railroad dream was one factor, were enough to persuade them to make common cause with the Democratic Party, even with its State rights slogan and opposition to internal improvements—before they in fact took it over in the South.

2

In the North, too, there was a great shaking up among the Democrats. Numerous Northern Democratic leaders, including notably Salmon P. Chase in Hayes's Cincinnati, came out firmly against slavery, as well as for civil rights for Negroes, making curious alliances with the Free-Soilers and also with dissident Whigs. Indeed, party affiliations became so blurred that only zealots or opportunists, for the most part, knew for a certainty where they stood by 1854, or when they would be forced to choose new political havens.

Though, as would be expected, he clung to the Whig Party so long as it lasted, Hayes was among those who were confused—and disturbed. To Guy Bryan, who was among Southern Whigs to join the Democrats, Hayes even suggested that he might follow suit, which, indeed, confirmed his political confusion. He felt like "a waif on the political sea," he told Guy.[1]

What made the political sea exceptionally stormy, beginning that year of 1854, was certain legislation enacted in Congress. This developed under the leadership of forceful Senator Stephen A. Douglas of Illinois, champion of a doctrine called popular sovereignty. A new compromise on the slavery issue, this legislation negated the Missouri Compromise of 1820. It permitted slavery to be established in the new territories of Kansas and Nebraska if slaveholders settled there and were able to muster a majority vote. Bloody fighting between proslavery and antislavery settlers broke out in these new territories as a result.

Men usually calm became excited, not only from the shedding of blood but by the extremes in suppressing civil liberties to which the proslavery regime in Kansas went. It made it unlawful, for example, for anyone in Kansas even to speak or write against slavery. "It is in truth something to stir one's blood!" wrote the usually composed Judge Lane to Hayes's uncle.[2]

On both sides the uncompromising spirit of a crusade developed.

Out of all this agitation there boiled up, especially in the West, a new political grouping called the Anti-Nebraska Party, one that elected governors, representatives in Congress and also United States Senators, notably Lyman Trumbull of Illinois, who had been a Democrat. But its name doomed it to a short life, as was the fate of the Anti-Masonic Party, also once powerful. The Anti-Nebraska components survived, however, by moving, in 1856, into a coalition party under the name Republican, once identified with Jefferson. Whigs of the North also entered the coalition. So, too, Free-Soilers, and likewise Northern Democrats, such as Chase in Ohio, who could not stomach slavery. Indeed, in the formation of this new, sectional Republican Party, which for a hundred years was to be the main antagonist of the Democratic Party, Democrats were as prominent as Whigs, perhaps more so.

3

Confusion from all this shifting was all the greater because of considerable, if temporary, strength shown by the Know-Nothings. The Know-Nothing Party attempted to win political power—and did in numerous local and state elections—by closing its eyes for the most part to the North-South controversy in general. It sought to make a basic political issue out of the immigrants streaming in from Europe. It wanted these people to be considered as second-class citizens, to be barred from holding offices or voting, despite the Constitution, alleging that they would Europeanize America.

In particular, the Know-Nothings raised the issue of Roman Catholicism, emphasizing that many of the immigrants were Irish or German Catholics and warning native Protestants to be on guard against the papal power. So successful were these appeals, especially with descendants of the Protestant New England founding families, that for a time it appeared that out of the splintering of the old parties the basic issue in American politics would become native Americanism against "the foreigners."

In the end it became clear that the North-South question could not be sidetracked. For it involved not merely moral and emotional issues, but basic economic issues and the real power bases of politics. It was the old sectional power struggle, the old game of maneuvering manifest in the days of the first Rutherford Hayes, when Alexander Hamilton, to get two additional Northern senators, finally persuaded New York to end its fight against Ethan Allen's Vermont. The Southern political leaders were fighting to hold the dominant, or at least equal, power in the country they had before the West was opened.

They were fighting also to prevent the increasing industrialization of the North, with its natural kinship with the West. This industrialization, they saw, would make of the feudal South a mere minority section, a development Southern leaders strove anxiously to prevent. In a broad sense the South, to defend its way of life, was attempting to halt the material progress of the nation, trying to stop the Industrial Age on the American continent.[3] With the stakes so basic, with the economic interests of each section so greatly involved and with the formulation of public opinion so uncompromising, all sure that "morality" was on their side, war probably was inevitable.

4

By his heritage, his education, his friendships—with Guy Bryan, for one—his instinct for conciliating opponents, Hayes was pulled this way and that. His partner Corwine became a Know-Nothing. So also did his friend Stanley Matthews, before going over to the Democrats, finally to settle among the Republicans.[4] Members of his Literary Club went in all directions, some Whigs becoming Democrats, others Know-Nothings, Anti-Nebraskans and (in 1856) Republicans, some going over to the "ultra" side with the Abolitionists.

Reflecting the tension in Cincinnati over the slavery question, the Literary Club, incidentally, nearly became a casualty of all this upheaval. Discussions became so heated that the heretofore so-agreeable group had to adopt a rule which for a time prohibited any mention of slavery.[5]

Unquestionably Hayes was tempted for a while to take the safe middle road and, like Corwine and Matthews, join the Know-Nothings. In the 1850s, and for some decades, to oppose and fear Catholic power were accepted and dominant American attitudes. Hayes did share some of the Know-Nothing views on Catholics, if not on the foreigners. But he did not become a Know-Nothing, though at a crucial time later the allegation that he had been one would be made against him. He opposed Catholic power in American politics. But he did not believe that Catholics should be proscribed as citizens and he firmly opposed barring immigrants from citizenship.

He was saved from going to the Know-Nothing extremes by his

friendly nature and a deep sense of justice. On one occasion, in the spring of 1854, at a political meeting of which he was named chairman because of his acknowledged fairness, he co-operated with leaders of the German elements in preventing Know-Nothing leaders from taking over the district Whig organization. The Germans did not forget this. Nor did a young newspaperman named William Henry Smith, who saw clearly the dangers of the Know-Nothing movement, and who was destined to be important to Hayes.[6] Thus, though not actively antagonistic toward it, Hayes remained out of the Know-Nothing movement. Its narrowness did not square with his nature.[7]

5

His inevitable choice, in view of his stand on the fugitive-slave question and also in view of his temperament—and Lucy's—was the new Republican Party. That he no longer could tolerate the complete neutralism on slavery of either the Whig Party or the Know-Nothings was shown publicly by him for the first time in March 1854. A call was issued for a meeting of Cincinnati citizens to protest against the "Kansas-Nebraska surrender," the formal statement calling Senator Douglas' proposal a "threatened outrage." Hayes's name was signed to the call along with even acknowledged Abolitionists.[8]

By no means did this mean that he was then becoming "ultra," as he would word it. It was not in him to be one of the growing number of Northerners who developed a hatred for the South or Southerners. In a letter to Sardis in June 1854, he expressed his displeasure over the Kansas-Nebraska legislation, calling it "a deed that promises no end of evil to the country." But his strongest criticism he reserved for Northerners who had co-operated in it. "The Southern people have been educated to believe in the superiority of their social system; in the primacy of the State; in an undefined obligation of the Constitution to protect their peculiar property everywhere," he said. He could not blame the South for its point of view, for pressing every advantage.[9]

He had in mind, largely, his friend Guy Bryan, who now brought and sold slaves in his own right and who, in 1859, would be a member of Congress from Texas fighting for the Southern position and, incidentally, for national support of a Texas railroad to the Pacific. He did not hesitate to tell Guy frankly how he himself stood, even writing him that he had tendencies "towards Black Republicanism." [10] But while using a label so hateful to a Southern slaveowner, he also was sure that he and Guy and other Southerners could remain friends. This was a conviction on Hayes's part to be remembered.

6

In the political complex that was shaping up, the year 1856 was one of decision. Then the new Republican Party, a patchwork of many parts, entered on the national stage with the glamorous John C. Frémont as its candidate for President. Hayes had played a role in this, for he was delegate to the first local Republican conventions of Ohio and, as such, a founder of the new party. He "supported Frémont in 1856 zealously, ardently, joyously." [11] True, the new party lost in 1856 to the Democrats under James Buchanan. But the die was cast. Ironically, in view of his own special role in history, the new Republican Party that he so "joyously" supported was to fix for nearly a half century the North-South conflict as a basic division in the land.

CHAPTER XXXII

Sorrow and Advance

1

By UNHAPPY coincidence 1856 was also a year of crisis for Hayes in his intimate life. He was called on then to endure the most shaking event that would happen to him ever. Once again it was the beloved sister—his "other love," as he referred to Fanny then apropos of Lucy[1]—who was involved.

For that June 1856 poignantly disturbing news came from Columbus. Then thirty-six, Fanny had given birth to twin girls, both of whom died immediately, the delivery leaving her in a seriously injured state. Infection and other complications developed. Also, she tended to drift into the same mental condition that overcame her in 1842, though not so acutely.

This time Hayes was able to be with her at her bedside, and even face the intermittent periods when Fanny's mind strayed.[2] They had nostalgic talks when her mind was clear, about their childhood, conversations that were tragic for Hayes, for Fanny's manner indicated that she knew that she was dying.[3] Though her doctors had given her up, she rallied for a time, so remarkably that Hayes felt it safe to return home. To Sardis he wrote: "Her fine, elastic constitution is all that can save her. God grant it may do it. I can't write about it. It is too dreadful to think of. I have not given up hope and shall not while she still lives."[4]

But soon after he left her she took a turn for the worse. On July 16, 1856, within four days of the anniversary of the death of their father, in the season that still shadowed the heart of their mother, there came to him from Sardis the final, telegraphed message: FANNY IS GONE. COME UP BY FIRST TRAIN.

2

"Oh, what a blow it is! During all my life she has been the dear one. . . . All plans for the future, all visions of success, have embraced her as essential to complete them. . . . My heart bleeds and the tears flow as I write." So Hayes poured out his grief to Guy Bryan.[5]

He had then to reorganize the whole emotional side of his life. Lucy's love was a help to him. But it really was not enough—not yet. Indeed, Lucy's love served to remind him only the more sharply of the love object that was gone. Lucy was not, could not be, the same as Fanny—not yet, though when, and if, she would be, Hayes would at last attain his full maturity and security.

He turned in various directions for support; curiously not much toward his mother, then sixty-four, who offered the ancient solace, her own old faith, that one day they would all join Fanny and "the others" in heaven, and who accepted Fanny's death with greater composure than any of the family because she was "needed" to look after Fanny's children.[6] For a time, he went to be with Sardis in Fremont. They took a trip together, as during his depressed period when he was living in Lower Sandusky, this time going to look over Chicago.[7]

Most of all, significantly, he turned to Billy Rogers. Something in the relationship with Rogers made his law partner the strongest comfort that he had. He wrote to Rogers:

I wish you were my brother, so I should have a *claim* upon your thoughts and your affection. When I am alone and have leisure I constantly find myself full of sadness thinking of Fanny. I think of others that are left and whom I love, and wish to be with them. . . . I feel well disposed to many—have a favorable opinion of many—and there are many with whom I could form close friendships if circumstances threw us together—but one, two, three is the limit of the chosen circle with whom the intimacy can actually exist. . . . I feel lonesome and lost without you. So now be a good brother to me, write often.[8]

This was a revealing letter, shedding much light on the basic nature of his relationship to the beloved sister.

He even entertained the idea of moving to Minnesota to be with Rogers, if his partner were forced to stay there permanently. "I feel almost as if I would have to follow you," he said.[9]

3

This was only passing desperation. With his ability to master his feelings he threw himself into the 1856 Presidential campaign for

Frémont, with its appealing, though unsuccessful, slogan, "Free Soil, Free Men—and Frémont!" "I am very glad of this excitement. I could not have endured this last month without it," he told Rogers.[10]

The vital fact was that, despite all that Fanny had meant to him, he did not break. He came out of the experience whole. Indeed, for all the sadness of his sister's passing, for all the love between them, Fanny's death helped his further maturing.

She had made possible the idyllic childhood and stimulated him toward achievement. But she had also helped produce the traits and the tension that had made him so much the victim of indecision, tension bound to remain so long as she continued to live. It is clear that this tension shadowed his marriage, happy as it was. Lucy could not help but sense it, even if Hayes himself did not do so acutely. It was a divisive element in their life pattern. With it gone Hayes and Lucy, as man and wife, were the better for its absence.

True, Fanny continued to exert an influence over him, still representing a super-conscience for him, imposing ideals toward which to strive. "May her precious memory serve to make me better, purer, truer, in every relation of life—a better husband, father, friend and citizen," he wrote in his diary.[11]

But the strain was gone after she had gone.

4

From then on he moved ahead with still surer drive. Within a month or so after Fanny's death he considered becoming the Republican candidate for Congress in his district. He began pulling some strings tentatively.[12] For him this was something new. When friends several times in the past had urged that he stand for some elective office, such as prosecuting attorney or judge, he had begged off.[13] Now he was ready for a more active public life.

He did not get the nomination for Congress then, owing in part to some peculiar maneuverings of his partner Corwine. Instead, he was slated for judge of the Common Pleas Court of Hamilton County. This he finally declined, deciding that "the small salary" and also an uncertain chance of victory because of a local situation and some ill-humored jockeying between the Know-Nothings and Republicans, did not make it worth while for him to enter the race.[14]

He began to learn and properly evaluate some lessons about the ways of politics—the deals, the trades and all the rest, not included in his courses at Kenyon or Harvard. Politics was recognized by him as not quite the romantic activity he had envisioned it in his youth. "I am amused at the doings of the convention," he wrote to Sardis. "Contrary to the natural order, the Congressmen were nominated after the judges, so that I was got out of the way by nomination to a judgeship before congressmen came up—a good dodge which would of course have been seen to if it had been known that I wanted the nomination for Congress." [15]

But it all showed that he had become a man to be reckoned with in the whirl of Cincinnati politics. He had a following, people who looked on him as stable and trustworthy. He demonstrated a capacity for looking before he leaped in politics, a kind of savvy that Sardis had. In the scrimmaging for position and control of the new Republican Party that went on among the Know-Nothings, the Anti-Slavery Democrats led by Salmon P. Chase, and the old Whigs, he kept his head. He refrained from the name calling that went on, also from aggressively seeking office, consequently making fewer enemies than probably anyone else in the political arena of Cincinnati. Hayes, the public man, with support from various, even opposing, groups, was emerging.

When candidates for office were considered his name kept popping up, right along with the names of veterans like Judge Alphonso Taft, Judge George Hoadly and Caleb Smith, Corwine's former partner, who by then had returned to the city. Hayes was mentioned again in the summer of 1858 as a possible Republican candidate for Congress. When he did not get the nomination the *Enquirer*, leading Democratic organ, expressed relief. "We were apprehensive for awhile that Mr. Hayes would be the candidate," it said. [16]

About the same time almost all of the leading lawyers of the city, representing all political shades, signed petitions urging that Salmon P. Chase, then governor, appoint him judge of the Common Pleas Court to fill a vacancy. [17] He still was not eager to be a judge. But he was tempted because he was dissatisfied with Corwine as a partner, particularly as Billy Rogers was out of the firm, having decided that his health required that he stay in Minnesota. The judgeship would have provided a graceful way out. [18] The judicial appointment did not materialize. But his prominence in the maneuverings connected with the filling of the post was another straw in the wind.

5

In December 1858 S. M. Hart, the city solicitor of Cincinnati, was struck by a Little Miami Railroad locomotive and killed. In Hayes's description the suddenly vacant office was "the best lawyer's office in Cincinnati at the time," which explained the subsequent scramble for it.[19]

Among a dozen, Caleb Smith actively sought it and was considered the leading contender. The power of appointment was with the City Council, the thirty-six members of which were about equally divided among Republicans, Know-Nothings and Democrats. It was obvious that the winning candidate would have to be someone who could get support outside his own party. Smith seemed to fit the bill, as he was expected to have strong Know-Nothing as well as Republican support.

But an almost forgotten event rose to plague Smith. In 1853 Cardinal Bedini, a papal nuncio, had visited the United States and his visit occasioned violent anti-Catholic demonstrations, engineered particularly by radical Germans, fugitives from the 1848 revolutions in Europe, who denounced him for alleged cruelty toward Italian revolutionists.[20] On Christmas Eve 1853 a parade against him was organized in Cincinnati. Reporting that the marchers planned to attack St. Peter's Cathedral, where the cardinal was a guest of Cincinnati's Archbishop Purcell, the city police broke up the parade. In the fracas the police killed one marcher.

A number of the demonstrators were arrested, including a leading German editor, Friedrich Hassaurek, known then as the most radical of the German "forty-eighters" in Cincinnati.[21] The demonstrators brought countercharges against the police, asserting that the police had violated their civil rights in breaking up the parade. In this litigation, which aroused the city along pro-Catholic and anti-Catholic lines, Smith had volunteered his services in defense of the police, and he vigorously denounced the demonstrators, especially Hassaurek, as perpetrators of "mob rule." [22]

By 1858 Hassaurek was a much subdued man. Indeed, he was then a leading Republican, one of the many German forty-eighters who saw a relationship between opposition to slavery in the United States and the old 1848 revolutionary ideals in Europe. As such, he was a political ally of Caleb Smith. However the 1853 matter still was held against Smith by Hassaurek followers. The German members of the City Council, and certain of the Know-Nothings, felt that Smith's role in the Bedini incident showed too much sympathy for Catholics. They declined to support him for city solicitor.

6

Hayes benefited indirectly from this. He also benefited from a friendship between Corwine and R. M. Bishop, the Democratic president of the council, afterward governor of Ohio. Corwine persuaded Bishop that Hayes "would make a good solicitor." [23] More than twenty ballots were taken. With the votes of Republicans, of Know-Nothings and one vote steered to him by Bishop from the Democratic faction, Hayes won the office—by one vote.

The taste of this political victory was "sweet in the mouth," he said. [24] The Republican *Commercial* referred to him as "one of the most honest and capable young lawyers of the city," adding, "It would have been very difficult to have made any other selection of a solicitor equally excellent." Even the Democratic *Enquirer* praised him. He was elated over this, quoting the newspapers to his mother and Sardis.

Characteristically Sophia did not share his and Lucy's elation. She still remembered the Honorable John Noyes's fate. "If you wish to be happy, never aspire to political honors. They are nothing but vanity and vexation of spirit," she told Hayes. But Sardis was proud. To his brother in Vermont he wrote: "The position is one that is generally filled by the best talent of the city—*so far so good.*"

CHAPTER XXXIII

Lawyer for Cincinnati

1

His personal world just then seemed especially roseate and stable. True, another depression had gripped the land, the new attack of hard times starting right in Cincinnati with the 1857 failure of the big Ohio Life Insurance Company.

Yet so far as Hayes was concerned personally, this depression was not worrisome, thanks to the "good berth," as he called it to Sardis, of the city-solicitor post. His $3,500 annual salary, a comfortable sum then, was as good as his net income from the Corwine partnership, though their books showed a larger income.[1] Moreover, at the election in 1859, a few months after the appointment by the council, he led his ticket and won the office for another two years. So he had no cause for concern about income until 1861.

Then, too, there was a sudden diminution of the agitation over the slavery issue, the calm before a storm, as it turned out. In large part this was political. When Buchanan, Northern Democrat with neither pronounced antagonism toward the South nor a bent for action, took office as President in March 1857, everyone seemed to relax, if only from emotional exhaustion. Had Frémont been elected, there would have been a crisis.

But as it was, even firebrands on the Great Issue, excepting some persistent politicians and also some men like William Lloyd Garrison, Wendell Phillips and John Brown, and some women, like the wife of Hayes's Literary Club comrade, Lucy Stone, tended to embrace other interests—the feminist movement, the new psychology, animal magnetism, phrenology, free love, Bible communism (after Hayes's cousin Noyes), and the supposed socializing effects of octagonal houses.

There was increased interest also in old, as well as new, religious doctrines, with a young Brooklyn, New York, preacher named Henry Ward Beecher suddenly in the limelight. Businessmen sponsored revival meetings—modern "stirs." At one of these in Cincinnati, Stanley Matthews, then Assistant United States Attorney, became converted in public to Presbyterianism. Intellectuals heatedly discussed, on the platform and in print, the claim that Shakespeare's plays were written by Francis Bacon.

2

Of course, in 1857 there was the Dred Scott decision by the Supreme Court. It had resulted from a slave case initiated in St. Louis by none other than R. M. Field, Smith-line cousin of Hayes, who obviously had recovered from the shocking love affair of the 1840s.[2] This decision said the North could do nothing about slavery, even on its own territory, and produced new resentment there.

There was also John Brown's wild raid in Virginia to free slaves and, perhaps, set off servile revolution, his brash act followed by his execution. This, too, stirred the old agitation. Ahead was the political campaign of 1860, when more and more Southern leaders would threaten secession, if, as they said, the "radical" new Republican Party were successful in its second effort to win the Presidency.

But in the meantime it was a relatively relaxed time. So often in tune with the general climate of the land, Hayes seemed most relaxed of all. Though never a faddist, he, too, went in for some of the current escapism, read up especially on animal magnetism and phrenology, took a cautious, though mostly amused, interest in Cousin John Noyes's sexual eccentricities, and encouraged Sardis' conversion to the Presbyterian faith, though still on the side lines religiously himself.[3]

"You ask what I am doing," he wrote to Sardis in February 1860. "Not working hard—not working much. I earn my salary, I am sure, and am therefore conscience clear. . . . I never enjoyed life better." He took Lucy on a second honeymoon. He enlarged his house to be able to house guests more comfortably, especially Sardis and Sophia.[4] He did much reading for pleasure, continued to romp with his three sons—Birch, Webby and Little Ruddy—and moved leisurely with Lucy among a pleasant group of friends.

His family, rather than public affairs, formed his chief interest. "I am in the boy business chiefly these days," he wrote to eighteen-year-old Laura Platt, Fanny's eldest child and then his favorite kin. "Playing with the boys, scolding the boys, telling the boys how it used to be when I was a little boy. . . . Lucy is in a different line of boy business, washing the hands of the boys, the faces of the boys, the feet of the boys, making boys' pants, jackets and shirts; mending ditto,

ditto, ditto." [5] Thus City Solicitor R. B. Hayes in 1860, the year before the storm.

3

To be sure, he did not neglect his duties as city solicitor. Rather, from his first day, December 9, 1858, in his first public office, he started a record fully justifying the reference to him by the Mayor of Cincinnati as "our very competent Solicitor." [6] He demonstrated a capacity for being businesslike and wrote crisp and to the point opinions on the large variety of subjects that came to him from the other city departments.[7]

At the very outset he prepared a communication high-lighting an unshakable personal determination—that he, at least, would be one official beyond suspicion of profiting improperly, let alone illegally, from public office. His law firm held a contract with the city to collect certain claims, the agreement being with Corwine and himself personally. There was no legal, or even ethical, bar, by common understanding, against his continued participation in this arrangement. But he scrupulously informed the City Council: "Having accepted the office of City Solicitor it will be improper for me to receive any compensation from the City for professional services rendered under said contract. . . . Any share of what may be earned under the contract while I am City Solicitor will belong to the City and be paid into the City treasury." [8]

4

The city solicitorship was usually looked on by lawyers as a stepping stone to a more lucrative private law practice. There was a tendency for its occupants to curry favor with "important interests," at times adversely to the city. But Hayes betrayed none of this opportunism. The city was his client, and he watched its interests alertly.

When "important interests" tried, for example, to establish the principle that a horse-drawn streetcar system could use the city streets without paying compensation to the city, he staged a vigorous fight, winning a landmark decision in municipal law that demanded that compensation—about $3,000 a month—had to be paid.[9] In one court hearing in this litigation, mild-mannered as he usually was, he did not hesitate to bring to light the apparently ugly fact that the judge owned stock in one of the streetcar corporations.

His general conduct of the office revealed an interesting personal pattern. It would be expected that in a political office, at the very heart of city hall, he would display a keener interest than ever in the political game. But he studiedly gave the impression of being less political than ever. Not that Frémont's defeat had diminished his partisan zeal for the Republican cause. He said in 1856 that he was "enlisted" for the final triumph of the new party, and he meant it.[10] But he was strongly conscious, as city solicitor, of being employed by the people of Cincinnati, regardless of partisan divisions, and he strove to conduct himself as nonpartisanly as possible, even going out of his way to show regard for Democrats in patronage and policies. True, he was still no crusader. But he hewed to the nonpartisan, honest line—the perhaps naïve gentleman's notion of political conduct —and did his job according to his conscience, the strict one that Fanny and Sophia had helped to develop in him.

CHAPTER XXXIV

Lincoln—and the Storm

1

In May 1860 there was held in Chicago the second Republican national convention, the one which nominated Lincoln for President. Undoubtedly, had he wished it, Hayes could have been a delegate, just as his friend Congressman Guy Bryan was delegate and chairman of the Texas contingent to the Democratic national convention that nominated the other Illinoisan, Stephen A. Douglas. His former partner Corwine was a delegate. So also was Hassaurek. Likewise, although again rated as an Indiana resident, Caleb Smith. But Hayes remained at home.[1]

Steeped in his nonpartisan job, as he saw it, he seemed almost disinterested in whom the Republicans would nominate for President in fateful 1860. Dick Corwine, as always the beaverlike politician, had some preconvention correspondence with Lincoln.[2] But not City Solicitor Hayes.

He really had no firm choice for the nomination. Ohio had several favorite sons, including Governor Chase and Senator Wade. Prominent in the running too, was another Ohioan, John McLean, of Lebanon, Justice of the Supreme Court of the United States since 1830, by appointment of Jackson. If pressed, Hayes probably would have preferred the seventy-five-year-old Justice McLean. In refutation of a supposed tradition that Supreme Court justices do not become involved in politics, Justice McLean, well known by Sardis, had been seeking some Presidential nomination since the 1840s, came close to getting the Republican nomination in 1856 and won renewed "availability," it was thought, for the 1860 nomination by a strong antislavery dissent in the Dred Scott case.[3] But any of these would do, Hayes indicated to Sardis.[4]

As for Lincoln, Hayes did not mention him at all, being only vaguely aware, before the nomination, of Lincoln's existence. Even after the nomination he did not have any great enthusiasm for Lincoln. His attitude was that Lincoln would do, and that was about all. To Sardis, just after the nomination, he wrote: "Lincoln you are, of course, pleased with. He takes well here." But this was perfunctory, party-loyalty comment. He showed more excitement over the visit of the Prince of Wales, later England's King Edward VII, to Cincinnati that fall than he did over Lincoln. "I cannot get up much interest in the contest," he told Sardis as late as September 1860. [5]

2

Of course, as a loyal Republican, he favored Lincoln's election. He served on a Wide-Awake Committee for distributing Republican literature in his ward, the Fifteenth.[6] He volunteered some sound advice on strategy, urging, for example, that at least in Cincinnati, where the Republicans were cautiously known as "the Opposition Party," Lincoln should be warned not to emphasize in a speech there that he was a Republican. This might "displease the American (i.e. Know Nothing) element of our organization," he wrote,[7] showing that for all his idealism about his own conduct in holding political office, he could still be the practical politician where winning office was concerned, as practical as Lincoln.

After Lincoln's election, though pleased, Hayes still betrayed no elation. Later the name Lincoln would be exciting in itself, the man becoming a demigod for Hayes, as for others, a greater one than even Webster or Clay. But just then Lincoln to him was simply another political figure. In February 1861, when Lincoln was on his way east from Springfield, Illinois, to be inaugurated, Hayes, taking Lucy along, was among Cincinnati dignitaries to meet him at Indianapolis to escort him to Cincinnati. He was quite casual about talking with him, and did not even bother to tell about it in his diary.[8]

To Laura Platt he did write an interesting letter about having gone "to see 'Ole Abe' at Indianapolis," and also of the subsequent reception for Lincoln in Cincinnati. "We had a party of nice people with us and enjoyed it much," he wrote. "Lincoln is sound. He makes good speeches. He has health enough as well as other qualities. . . . Homely as L. is, if you can get a good view of him by *day light*, when he is talking, he is by no means ill-looking."

Then, recalling that Laura had told him that their cousin Elinor Mead (later Mrs. William Dean Howells), a granddaughter of Polly Hayes Noyes, was adept at making sketches and was visiting her in Columbus, Hayes continued, concerning Lincoln's stopover in Columbus: "Don't let Elinor fail to catch Lincoln's awkward look when he bows. It can't be caricatured. It is beyond compare—exceeds caricature. His chin rises, his body breaks in two at the hips—there is a bend of the knees at a queer angle. It's good." [9]

3

By then several Southern states had left the Union, or, as others put it, rebelled against the United States. The South was making good the threat of its leaders that Republican victory would mean secession.

High excitement or deep gloom marked most politically minded Americans as the announcements of secession came. And Hayes? He maintained a calm, almost casual, attitude, similar to his reaction to Lincoln and Lincoln's election. He, who had been always so vocal about the necessity for preserving the Union, demonstrated an odd objectivity about the breakup. To Sardis, on January 12, 1861, he commented:

I rather enjoy the excitement, and am fond of speculating about it. We are in a revolution; the natural result is to divide us into two nations, one composed of free states, the other of slave states. What we shall pass through before we reach this inevitable result is matter for conjecture. While I am in favor of the Government promptly enforcing the laws for the *present*, defending the forts and collecting the revenue, I am not in favor of a war policy with a view to the conquest of any of the slave states; except such as are needed to give us a good boundary. . . . A war of conquest we do not want. It would leave us loaded with debt and would certainly fail of its object. The sooner we get into the struggle and out of it, the better.

Two weeks later, in his diary:

Six states have "seceded." *Let them go.* If the Union is now dissolved, it does not prove that the experiment of popular government is a failure. . . . But the experiment of uniting free states and slave-holding states in one nation is, perhaps, a failure. . . . There probably is an "irrepressible conflict" between freedom and slavery. It may as well be admitted, and our new relations may as well be formed with that as an *admitted* fact.[10]

Strange sentiments, these, to be expressed by Rutherford B. Hayes, when measured with later actions and attitudes, though, of course, they were in line with his Whiggish upbringing and education, as well as his bent for conciliation in any controversy, such as he had shown at Kenyon. The time was to come when it would puzzle him that he could have said so calmly, "Let them go." True, he was not alone in expressing confused and contradictory opinions, or seeming to take a stand in opposition to his true beliefs. Editor Horace Greeley, the great Whig, and then Republican, also said in effect, "Let them go." Even Seward, who had coined the phrase, "the irrepressible conflict," now talked of compromise. So also did an Illinois Congressman, William Kellogg, known to be a spokesman for Lincoln.[11]

4

In Hayes's case—perhaps also with most Americans then—the main reason for the confused thinking was the impossibility of digesting immediately a momentous fact. A new situation had arisen in America which was bound to cause his heretofore serene private world to disappear. It had seemed to him that the kind of life he had led up to 1861 was the kind he would always lead. It was hard to grasp the idea that happenings of the kind that one read about in history books, or that were told of with reference to his ancestors, had the power to impinge on his life as city solicitor, as husband to Lucy, as father to his boys.

However, even before the event that was to bring nearly everyone of Hayes's status and sympathies out of confused general thinking, when the issue became starkly the Union, rather than slavery, he was given a realistic personal jolt.

On April 1, 1861, the month following Lincoln's inaugural, a municipal election was held in Cincinnati. He was up for re-election as city solicitor. Ordinarily he could have expected to win. But, because of the national crisis, a panicky reaction against the Republican Party developed in Cincinnati. A new, temporary Union Party was organized by the Democrats with the Know-Nothings, under the slogan, "Save the Union!" It denounced all Republicans as being responsible for the secession movement in the South and the frightening crisis as a whole.

The strategy proved effective against the whole Republican municipal ticket. All its candidates, Hayes included, became in effect the first, but not the last, casualties to result from storm produced by Lincoln's victory. As Hayes afterward told Sardis, "The Union-saving avalanche has overtaken us. . . . My little potato patch went down with the rest."[12]

CHAPTER XXXV

AT LAST, A SOLDIER

1

HE ACTED promptly to get back into private law practice. A few years before Friederich Hassaurek had gone into the law as partner to Leopold Markbreit, a half brother, and developed a good German practice. As a reward for helping swing the German workingmen's vote to Lincoln, Lincoln appointed this ex-revolutionary as U. S. Minister to Ecuador, Hassaurek thus getting, as Hayes quipped, "the highest office, viz., nine thousand feet above the sea at Quito." Hayes took over Hassaurek's vacated law office and began a kind of partnership with Markbreit. "I feel free and jolly," he told Sardis.[1]

Actually he was in a mood for something different from private law practice. His interest in the law profession was waning. A feeling that the practitioners had to be too subservient to clients and judges disturbed him. "As a lawyer, a man sacrifices independence to ambition, which is a bad bargain at best." So he told another lawyer, William McKinley, a few years later.[2]

Quite possibly he would soon have joined Sardis in his bank, or in a railroad enterprise. Sardis had recently completed building a fairly large brick home in a pleasant grove up in Fremont, purchased so cheaply by him back in the panic of 1839, which, he now said, he intended as a summer place for Hayes. Actually this was his uncle's bait to get Hayes to go back to Fremont, this time as an associate in preparation for taking over his enterprises.

But before Hayes had been in his new law office a week, there occurred the Fort Sumter incident. The long-gathering storm, seen coming even in the days of Daniel Austin, had broken. The North and the South were at war.

2

On the instant he learned of the shooting, his attitude of "Let them go" fell away. It had been a denial, anyway, of the Hayes who had made the Websterian phrases, "Liberty and Union, Now and Forever, one and inseparable!" so much a part of his subconscious being.

Then, too, there were his childhood dreams of winning glory on a battlefield. An observer, seeing only the staid, fringe-bearded citizen and lawyer, the settled family man, would not have suspected that in his so-sober and commonsensical head there still whirled the old fantasies of great and romantic deeds. But they were still there, as strong as during the Mexican War fifteen years back. This time the dreams were not to be put aside. Not even though in 1861 he was nearly forty and the father of three children, facts which made it quite reasonable for him to leave fighting to youths without family responsibilities. Not even though Sardis and others close to him would try to intervene again.

Sardis, in fact, did hope that Hayes would refrain from getting into actual combat service. As a practical man, Sardis believed that Hayes's proper role, like his own as a banker in Fremont, was at home.

At first Hayes gave Sardis to understand that this view was his also, though at the outset he did advise Sardis, concerning Lucy and himself, "We are all for the war."

During the excitement over Lincoln's first call for volunteers, he wrote to his uncle, "At the first, I put down my foot that I would not think of going into this first movement." [3] This did not rule out later movements. Three weeks after the Fort Sumter incident, in one of his last letters for a long time to Guy Bryan, who, as an admitted original secessionist was an early volunteer on the Confederate side, Hayes still wrote in the same vein. "I shall not take an active part, probably, unless Kentucky goes out," he wrote Bryan. "We shall, of course, not agree about the war. We shall, I am sure, remain friends." He signed himself, "As ever, R. B. Hayes." [4]

3

Yet, four days later he was writing Sardis, "I may be carried off by the war fever, and would like to hear from you on it." [5] Actually he was already "carried off." A month before he had been the leader in organizing about half the members of the Literary Club into a drilling company called Burnet's Rifles, after a former army officer who was persuaded to drill it. Hayes was the captain.[6] Ostensibly this was just a home guard. But for Hayes, as well as for other members, it was really preparation for military service.

He went through a struggle about getting into the war. But this was a short one. Without waiting for any discussions with anyone, especially Sardis, he made up his mind. It was impossible for him not to be a soldier.

When she heard of this decision later, Sophia suddenly regretted having emphasized to him, in her stories of his heritage, the military service of some of his ancestors in the American Revolution, without having brought out that others did not fight.[7] For he later told Sardis, "In this war, I could not feel contented if I were not in some way taking part in it. I should feel about myself as I do about people who lived through the Revolution, seeing their neighbors leaving home, but doing nothing themselves—a position not pleasant to occupy."[8]

Sardis, as well as Sophia, could have told him of those members of his family, including the first Rutherford Hayes, who felt otherwise. But he did not give either Sardis or Sophia the chance.

He did have a talk with Stanley Matthews. Matthews already regretted his earlier prosecution of fugitive-slave cases, and was considering fighting for the Union. After this talk, Hayes wrote in his diary:

May 15, 1861.—Judge Matthews and I have agreed to go into the service for the war,—if possible into the same regiment. I spoke my feelings to him, which he said were his also, viz., that this was a just and necessary war and that it demanded the whole power of the country; *that I would prefer to go into it if I knew I was to die, or be killed in the course of it, than to live through and after it without taking any part in it.*

4

The next day he wrote to Sardis again. "You say nothing about my going into the war. I have been fishing for your opinion in several of my late letters. Unless you speak soon, you may be too late."[9] Of course, it was already too late. The fact is, he really had known what he would do even before he talked with Matthews.

Lucy presented no problem. As he had said, she too was all for the war. Indeed, the seemingly gentle Lucy herself wanted to strike personal blows against "the slave power." Hayes told much about her in describing to Sardis the reactions of the women in his household when the first call for volunteers came. Sophia, then visiting him, took to her Bible and "read vigorously." Mrs. Webb "quietly grieved." But Lucy "enjoys it and wishes she had been in Fort Sumter with a garrison of women."[10]

5

He was a soldier in the Union Army for the next four years, mainly in Virginia, in the Kanawha River Valley. Names more militarily famous than his emerged from the conflict. But it may be set down as fact that there was no more soldierly man on either side than Rutherford B. Hayes.

At the start he was Major Hayes of the Twenty-third Ohio Volunteers Infantry. As such, in his first months he served mainly as adjutant general, prosecuting or judging discipline cases. This he did not like. "I am practicing law," he complained. Even before he was ready for it, he wanted to be a fighting man.[11] He got his wish, by asking for a fighting assignment. It was not long before he became Lieutenant Colonel Hayes, and then Colonel Hayes, a fighting commander.

"Colonel" was the title that he liked best of all—"It is the best sounding title I know," he once said [12]—until, that is, at the end, when he was brevetted a brigadier general on the battlefield for gallantry and courage. He finally came out of the war experience as Major General R. B. Hayes. Later he possessed an even more imposing title—indeed, the very highest—one that America bestows on few of its sons.

But "General" was the title he most warmly responded to, what he liked to be called at the end of his life. It was a title earned by him as it was by few men, certainly by few in this Civil War, when so many generalships were passed out for political reasons. It symbolized for him the four best years of his life, more enjoyable, he said, than even the four Kenyon years, an appraisal which was indeed superlative, coming from him.

A good many other men in blue or gray who fought in that war—perhaps most of them—would not have so characterized their experience at the time. For example, Dr. Joseph Webb, Lucy's brother, who served with Hayes in the Twenty-third as a surgeon, did not share Hayes's view. He also had done his part. He had volunteered in the first call, and participated bravely in many of Hayes's adventures. But after the war, when he was asked to attend a reunion of the Twenty-third Regiment, Dr. Webb wrote: "You ask if I shall attend the reunion. . . . I shall not. Its memories and associations are not pleasant; it was the mistake of my life in joining the Reg^t [sic]. I sacrificed *my business*, and all for what?" [13]

For Hayes to entertain an idea about the war even remotely like his brother-in-law's would have been impossible. He suffered monumental hardships—intense cold, intense heat, torrential rains in tents that leaked, or without tents, marches that were endless, up and down mountain ranges, often without food. All this aside from the physical danger in actual battle and the sight of comrades wounded or killed. He was wounded by bullets five times, once seriously. Four horses were shot from under him during battle.[14] Yet it was all "enjoyable" to him.

6

In one of his early war letters to Lucy, written when he was in a training camp near Columbus, he said: "You know how I love you; how I love the family, all; but Lucy, I am much happier in this business than I could be fretting away in the old law office near the courthouse. It is *living*." [15] And a little later: "We have been busy as bees a large part of the time in scorching sun; but so far it is great fun. I enjoy it as much as a boy does a Fourth of July." [16]

The weather along the Kanawha at times turned so cold that his men feared freezing to death. Colonel Hayes's attitude was "It is healthy." Often his clothes were rain-soaked to the skin, or he had to sleep in mud, conditions that caused Dr. Webb to prepare for an epidemic of pneumonia. Hayes spoke of the predicament as "jolly." In western Virginia, on being ordered into an area in which, for the first time, attacks by guerrillas, or bushwhackers, were to be expected, he felt no concern at all for the danger around him and ahead. He was delighted.

"I really feel badly when I think of several of my intimate friends who are compelled to stay at home," he wrote to Lucy. "These marches and campaigns in the hills of western Virginia will always be among the pleasantest things I can remember. The feeling that I am where I ought to be is a full compensation for all that is sinister, leaving me free to enjoy it as if on a pleasure tour." [17]

The pleasure tour soon included, in September 1861, at a point close by the Gauley River, near the towns of Summersville and Sutton, a skirmish with the enemy. He was given the order to lead a platoon to hold a point on a hillside. It was to prove his first test under fire. Bullets and cannon balls whined all around him.

It was still all enjoyable. Like most new soldiers, he was anxious to know how he would react under fire. Would he be tempted to run? Not Colonel Hayes. He was "nervous," yes. But his nervousness was no more than what "I have often felt before beginning an important lawsuit." [18]

"You need have no fear of my behavior in fight," he wrote to Lucy. "I don't know what effect new dangers might have on my nerves, but the other day I was several minutes under sharp guerrilla fire—aimed particularly at Captain Drake and myself (being on horseback), so I know somewhat of my capacity. *It is all right.*" [19]

7

Nothing was so satisfactory to him as this knowledge. In a personal sense it was really the important thing to him, more important, in a way, than winning the war, even though he considered it "the divinest war ever waged." [20] Later, under fire, he would not even feel nervous any more. In view of his jittery temperament as a child and youth, this, in his own estimation, was probably his greatest personal triumph during the war.

He was proud of the fact that he could even catch up on sleep practically in the midst of battle.

When the battle of Winchester was on, my command was seventeen miles away when Sheridan ordered that headlong rush to the front. We reached the verge of battle badly blown, and were halted for twenty minutes rest before going on. The thunder, and blaze, and smoke of the great fight filled the air, but I knew what I needed, of all things, just then was sleep. And so I threw my bridle to an orderly, wrapped my gloves together for a pillow, threw myself on the ground, and slept for twenty minutes, as peaceful as a child. . . .[21]

To Lucy he wrote: "The echoes of . . . cannon and bursting shells through the mountain defiles were wonderful." [22]

He had become, at last, R. B. Hayes, Hero.

CHAPTER XXXVI

Search's End

1

"I shall come safely out of this war," he had told Lucy when he first put on his uniform and bade her and their boys good-by.[1] Through all the four years he conducted himself as if he truly believed some charm assured that he would be safe.

In view of reckless chances that he took, always insisting on getting out in front during any charge, never thinking twice about dashing into the thickest of gunfire, many of his men came to believe too that he did indeed lead a charmed life. "It was my fortune to be near him a good many times when it seemed that only an Unseen Hand was his shield," one of his subordinates recalled.[2] It was marveled that, while he was standing with a group in a wet field, a bolt of lightning struck him—and no harm done.[3] Later a Minié ball hit him full in the head but simply bounced off, leaving him to joke that the bullet probably had spent itself going "through somebody else."[4]

In a diary one soldier, just after an engagement with the Confederates in May 1862, near Princeton in western Virginia, set down a word picture of him.

Some of our boys think we are in a tight place and will be marching to Richmond as prisoners. We are trotting like deer to get back. We see that our modest Lieutenant Colonel Hayes is a lion of a leader. . . . We see Colonel Hayes come riding at a gallop the whole length of the line, waving his sword, the grand anger of battle flashing in his eyes. . . . It puts fight in us to see Colonel Hayes riding at full gallop towards the rebel battery. . . . *Who could not follow him in battle. . . .*[5]

2

To those who knew him as the quiet, gentlemanly lawyer, or as the amiable Literary Club fellow, he seemed indeed a different man. In truth, he was—with much of the difference to remain with him henceforth. He did not lose his old friendliness. But the war experiences did bring out conduct and capacities that changed him, making

218

of him a man who could be aggressive in the extreme when the occasion suited.

He who only a few years back became ill from witnessing the hanging of a client, LeCount, now was able to announce calmly, "If any of my men kill prisoners, I'll kill them!" [6] And he who was always so congenial was able now to draw a pistol on a man in his command who showed signs of running away from the enemy before a skirmish and tell him to go in and fight, or he would kill him on the spot. The soldier fought and lost his life, after which Hayes said that he had given the man a hero's death instead of a coward's, and what could be better than that? [7]

On his staff was a sergeant named William McKinley, who also would have a niche in history. McKinley especially noted a different Hayes. "His whole nature seemed to change when in battle. From the sunny, agreeable, the kind, the generous, the gentle gentleman . . . he was, when the battle was once on . . . intense and ferocious." [8]

3

He was even able to talk back to a commanding officer of the rank of general—something quite unexpected in him. This he proved to Major General Jesse Lee Reno, his corps leader in General Burnside's Army in 1862.

His regiment was resting near Leesboro in Maryland, in the area of South Mountain, in the tense time when Union forces under General George B. McClellan and Confederate armies under General Robert E. Lee were massing and maneuvering for crucial battles near the Potomac River, with the fate of Washington, D. C., seemingly at stake. Some of his men had borrowed stacks of straw and wheat from a farm on which to lie. Technically this was against the rules, "pilfering the countryside," which the federal War Department was trying to stamp out then because of the propaganda use the Confederacy was making out of charges that Union troops were conducting themselves in an "outrageous manner against civilians." In particular, the War Department was anxious to avoid incidents that would offend the citizens of Maryland.

With this in mind General Reno, on riding up to the resting men, went into a "passion." He called Hayes's men "You damned black sons of bitches," and heatedly ordered them to return the "plunder." [9]

Then Reno called for their officer in charge to denounce him for not having imposed proper discipline. The officer, of course, was Hayes, who, incidentally, had been more scrupulous than many Union officers, perhaps more than most, in preventing pilfering of even Confederate possessions.

"I presented myself and assumed the responsibility, defending the men," Hayes said. "I talked respectfully but firmly. . . . Gradually he softened down." But when Reno made some remark about his "determination" to have no "pilfering" by soldiers under his command, Hayes found himself looking the general in the eye and saying pointedly, in the hearing of his men: "Well, I trust our generals will exhibit the same energy in dealing with our foes that they do in the treatment of their friends." [10] Hayes's remark had reference to reports just then that a number of Union generals were sending back to slavery, under Union Army escorts, black men who had escaped from the South to seek freedom behind the Union lines.

Reno was "offended," how strongly was suggested by Hayes's notation in his diary the next day: "It is said that when talking with me, he put his hand on his pistol; that many standing by began to handle their arms also!" Reno demanded to know what Hayes meant. "Nothing—at least I meant nothing disrespectful to you," Hayes said.

But Hayes's manner showed that he stood by his men—and up to the general. Reno rode off scowling, "cut to the quick," and all the more angered because the soldiers all around cheered Hayes. Reno still talked the next day of "putting colonels in irons if their men pilfered." He continued for several days to be "quite bitter" about Hayes's remark. There was discussion of transfering Hayes's regiment from Reno's corps.[11]

Indeed, the matter attained national attention as word of the encounter spread through the army and articles appeared in the civilian press. These mostly favored Hayes.

Quite possibly the Reno incident could have resulted in court-martial proceedings against Hayes. But a week later, September 14, 1862, events occurred which put an end to the court-martial possibility. These included the battle of South Mountain, prelude to Antietam, during which General Reno was killed.

4

Hayes himself was close to being killed at the same time. For it was at South Mountain that he received what he fiercely wished for, a serious wound, one suffered in the heat of conspicuously gallant action.

He and his men had been given the assignment of going up a mountain path, in full view of the enemy, to take a battery supposed to consist of two guns. "If I find six guns and strong support?" he asked. "Take them anyhow," he was told. That was what he wished to hear.[12] A Confederate force a good deal stronger than had been expected was, in fact, waiting for him.

He set down some of the details that stood out of the confusion. "Soon saw from the opposite hill a strong force coming down towards us . . . soon received a heavy volley, wounding and killing some. I feared confusion; exhorted, swore, and threatened."[13] He yelled, "Give them hell! Give the sons of bitches hell!" though this he did not put in the diary. Probably he did not wish to shock Sophia, should she read his diary—she who had objected so to his having used the phrase "By George!" at Kenyon. He later admitted to her, when the news of his "ferocity" reached her, that his "speech at South Mountain was not religious."[14]

His men proceeded to give the enemy hell. "Our men halted at a fence and kept up a brisk fire upon the enemy, who were sheltering themselves behind stone walls and fences near the top of the hill, beyond a cornfield in front of our position." He gave the command to charge and led the way. But the enemy was not inactive. It was then that he obtained "the red badge of courage" that he so obviously was seeking.

A musket ball struck his left arm just above the elbow. It was a "stunning blow," one that fractured bones and set his blood flowing. He felt weak, faint and nauseated. For all he knew, an artery had been cut. He asked a soldier to tie a handkerchief around his arm. In spite of his faintness, he got up on his feet and "began to give directions about things," though shortly he had to lie down again.

As he lay there, the battle raged on. "Balls passed near my face and hit the ground all around me," he recalled. Then for a time there was a lull. He thought he was abandoned. "Hallo, Twenty-third men! Are you going to leave your colonel here for the enemy!" A half-dozen Twenty-third men showed up instantly, apparently coming from nowhere, to carry him "wherever you want us to." But just then enemy guns blazed again. Hayes ordered his rescuers back to cover.

They obeyed, leaving him exposed. "While I was lying down [he later wrote], I had considerable talk with a wounded [Confederate] soldier near me. I gave him messages for my wife and friends in case I should not get up. We were right jolly and friendly; it was by no means an unpleasant experience." Shortly he was taken out of range of fire, and had the satisfaction of knowing that his mission had been successful.[15]

His wound was extremely painful for many days. But this did not seem important to him at all. His great concern was that when McClellan's and Lee's forces met along Antietam Creek on September 16, 1862, inaugurating two days of some of the bloodiest fighting of the entire war—the Battle of Antietam, as it was called—with 12,000 Union men killed or wounded and nearly as many Confederates also casualties, he was forced to miss the show.

His injury at South Mountain kept him out of action two months. Sardis, among others, urged that he ought to be satisfied and take the occasion to return to civilian life.[16] Stanley Matthews had left the service before the war was over, getting himself elected a judge again in Cincinnati. So did many others, notably "political" officers. But Hayes insisted on staying on until the very end.

5

Nor was he more cautious than before. Indeed, after the South Mountain experience he was even less cautious. He now undertook ventures that were outside his duty—such as volunteering to dash behind Confederate lines to rescue Union men held prisoners, and joining, also voluntarily, in the pursuit of Morgan's Raiders, Confederate commandos (as they would have been called at a later time) who terrorized Union communities just north of the Ohio River in 1863.[17]

In view of the exhilaration of it all, it was no wonder that something happened to Rutherford B. Hayes philosophically. The war did for him what his mother and Kenyon College had tried but failed to do for him. He came to admit for the first time a belief in God. In the midst of the war he wrote in his diary: "But will I not take refuge in the faith of my fathers at last? Are we not all impelled to this? The great abyss, the unknown future—are we not happier if we give ourselves up to some settled faith? . . . Am I not more and more carried along, drifted, towards surrendering to the best religion the world has yet produced? It seems so. . . . " [18]

He did not realize the full meaning of what he had said. But it is obvious that here was a record of further psychological growth. Without going through the kind of emotional experience he had been unable to achieve at Kenyon, he had finally accepted God, but in his own way, one in which God became a part of himself. Because of these new feelings of strength that surged through him, because, in the war excitement, he felt as good as any man, stronger indeed than most, even godlike, he had become his own father symbol.

So ended, at last, his old search for the missing father. He himself had become, in his mind's eye, what he believed his father had been, what Sardis had been to him in his childhood, what he and his sister Fanny wished always for him to be—a hero figure, a godlike man, in a good cause.

CHAPTER XXXVII

REWARDS

1

SUCH martial gallantry, of which the citizens of Cincinnati were kept well informed, thanks to newspaper correspondents who had a special liking for him, naturally called for a special reward. This came to him in the fall of 1864 when the Republican Party, then prudently styling itself temporarily the Union Party, nominated him for Congressman from the Second (Cincinnati) District.

In large part this was the work of William Henry Smith, the newspaperman who had been so impressed by Hayes back in the 1850s because of his resistance to the maneuverings of the Know-Nothings. Smith then was a power in state Republican circles and a candidate himself for Ohio Secretary of State. He urged that party leaders select Hayes for Congress as a tribute to his war gallantry.

But aside from that, Smith was motivated by a practical political situation. As of the early months of 1864 his party was in a predicament, especially in Ohio. The war was not going well from the standpoint of the North. There was much pessimism among civilians who remembered the promises made back in 1861 that six months, a year at the most, would be sufficient to bring the seceding states to their senses. In 1862, on the basis of the gloom, the Democrats carried the Ohio Congressional elections. In 1864 they expected confidently to win the nation as well as the state. They said that the war was a failure, that Lincoln was weak, incompetent and also a failure. Ironically many important Republican leaders agreed with the Democrats in this estimate of Lincoln.

More dangerous to Republican prospects for victory was a line taken by the Democrats to the effect that the war could and should be ended by a compromise with the South. A slogan was coined: "The Union As It Was—the Constitution As It Is." This meant peace and reunion with slavery intact in the South. It was only necessary in this view that the Southern states give up their claimed right to secede. Only this point—the matter of secession—was worth fighting about, the Democrats said. Until the climactic victories of the Union forces under General Grant, there can be no doubt that a great portion of the people in the North tended to accept this Democratic thesis.

With its background of commercial and social ties with the South Cincinnati was a stronghold of the so-called "peace Democrats," a fact that caused Hayes to tell his uncle at the time of Morgan's raids that "it might be good" if Morgan's men sent some shells into Cincinnati to "wake up" the home folk. In this mood Hayes was against any compromise whatever. He was sure then that the rebellion and its leaders had to be "crushed," certain, without any qualification, that slavery was "the crime of the centuries." [1]

Such views by Hayes, if broadcast, would not by themselves have helped to make him look like a winning candidate for Congress in Cincinnati, not even to his devoted admirer Smith. However, as a keen appraiser of public opinion, Smith felt that Hayes's reputation as a soldier of extraordinary courage did make him look like a winner. Even voters afflicted with the poison of peace propaganda could not help but be impressed by Hayes's gallantry, Smith reasoned. They would vote for a hero even if they did not accept his politics, he felt, and so persuaded other Republican leaders. So, while Hayes in 1864 was in the Shenandoah Valley with General Phil Sheridan's army, adding to his stature as hero with new acts of courage, or recklessness, a movement to draft him for the nomination was launched.

2

He did not seem much interested when the possibility of the nomination was first mentioned to him. To go to Congress was still one of his ambitions, but his "soldiering," he said, had to come first. He considered sending Smith a formal declination, one that could be published to make the refusal final. But "it was merely easier to let the thing take its own course than to get up a letter declining to run and then to explain it to everybody who might choose to bore me about it," he later told Sardis.[2] So he didn't do that. But when some of the men in the Twenty-third organized a "Hayes for Congress" movement as a spontaneous tribute to their "lion of a leader," he stopped it. He would have no mixing of soldiery and politics where he was concerned, he said.[3]

After the nomination by a district convention was made, with much fanfare about his war record, he accepted it with the firm stipulation that he would not, like many other soldier candidates in both leading parties, and as Smith had suggested in his case, take a furlough from the army to conduct a campaign.

To Smith he sent a forceful rejection of any such idea. "Friend Smith. . . . Your suggestion about getting a furlough to take the stump was certainly made without reflection. An officer fit for duty who at this crisis would abandon his post to electioneer for a seat in Congress ought to be scalped. You may feel perfectly sure I shall do no such thing. . . ." [4]

Nor did he. When the election was held in October 1864 he was with his troops in the Shenandoah Valley, and there received the result. He was elected by a handsome majority, news, incidentally, that pleased not only him but also President Lincoln, who, on hearing of Hayes's victory, considered it a sign pointing to his own re-election in the following November.[5]

To Lucy, Hayes wrote a few days later: "I suppose you are pleased with the result of the election. Of course, I am on *general* reasons. My *particular* gratification is much less than it would be, if I were not so much gratified by my good luck in winning 'golden opinions' in the more stirring scenes around here." [6]

3

The "stirring scenes" concerned the battle of Cedar Creek, memorialized by Thomas Buchanan Read's celebrated poem, "Sheridan's Ride." [7] Of this battle, also known as Winchester, the new Congressman-elect left a good record of his own:

Wednesday, October 19, 1864.—Before daylight under cover of a heavy fog, Rebels attacked the left. Colonel Thoburn's First Division was overwhelmed. His adjutant . . . brought me the word. We hurried up, loaded our baggage, and got into line. Nineteenth Corps went into the woods on right. General Sheridan was absent. General Wright, in command, directed my division to close up on the Nineteenth. Too late; the fugitives of the First Division and the Nineteenth's brigade came back on us. The Rebels broke on us in the fog and the whole line broke back. The Rebels did not push with energy. We held squads of men up to the fight all along. My horse was killed instantly. . . . We fell back—the whole army—in a good deal of confusion, but without panic. Artillery (twenty-five pieces) fell into Rebel hands and much camp equipage. About two and one-half miles back, we formed a line. Rebels failed to push on fast enough.

P.M. General Sheridan appeared; greeted with cheering all along

the line. His enthusiasm magnetic and contagious. He brought up
the stragglers. "We'll whip 'em yet like hell," he says. General
Crook's men on left of pike. Line goes ahead. A fine view of the
battle. Rebels fight poorly. Awfully whipped—Cannons and spoils
now on our side.

To which account, possibly the clearest of many about this often-
storied battle, he added a characteristic Hayesian word: "Glorious!" [8]
And in connection with that battle another reward came to him—his
citation on the field as a general.

4

And Lucy? And Sophia? And Sardis? For them the four years of
war had not been at all glorious. For them, the only truly bright time
of the war was its ending. True, like many another businessman,
Sardis prospered in a financial way, one sign being that his former
small private bank had become the thriving First National Bank of
Fremont, the fifth such chartered by the federal government. But he
was filled with anxiety over his nephew.

True, too, Sophia had finally become reconciled to the necessity
of crushing "the vile rebellion." The fighting was "wicked," but she
had come to see rebellion against the federal government as "more
wicked." By 1863 she wrote to Hayes, "If I had ten sons, I would
rather they were all with you than to have one Friend among the op-
posers of our Government." [9] But she was "sure" that she would never
again see her son, and called the war period "the worst years" of her
life.[10]

True, Lucy never wavered in her zeal for the Union and antislavery causes. Yet, though both later referred to this period as "our
golden age," Hayes expressed well the ordeal she endured when he
recalled: "Every horror of that awful time struck sledgehammer blows
on her very heart." [11]

5

By his letters, which always contained affirmations of his love for
her, Hayes did much to lighten Lucy's burden. Often he wrote daily.
After engagements which he knew would be reported in the papers,
he telegraphed, when possible, to let her know that he was safe.

After his incapacitation at South Mountain he sent for her, and she remained at his side until his arm was well again, nursing him as well as other soldiers. In the quiet period of his service, when he was near the Ohio River, he went home on short furloughs. On at least three occasions he had her and their children with him at his camp, once for as long as three months. Indeed, from these reunions two more sons were born to them during the war, though in the end the fate of both these boys was part of the sadder phase of the war period, especially for Lucy.

The first of these was born early in the war, in December 1861. If it had been a girl, Hayes intended to name her Fanny Lucy or Lucy Fanny, thus "linking together the names of the two dear ones, wife and sister." [12] As it was, Lucy selected the name, calling the boy Joseph.

Little Jody, as he was referred to, brought much pleasure to Lucy. "Oh, how dear he is to me—he is now asleep—is so lively and happy and grows very fast," she wrote to Hayes in one of her letters shortly after his birth. He was, she later wrote, more like his father in appearance than the other boys—"a miniature likeness of Lt. Col. R. B. H. . . . a laughing, joyous little fellow whenever he has a chance." [13]

In June 1863, during a lull in fighting when Hayes was camped along the Kanawha River in what was then called the new state of West Virginia, he had Lucy come for a visit with all the boys. All looked forward to a happy time.

At first it was a happy time. But ten days later Little Jody died in the camp. "Teething, dysentery, and brain affected, the diseases," Hayes noted in his diary. For Hayes, Little Jody's death was not a devastating blow, for he had not been with "the sweet bright boy" enough to get to know him. But Lucy was a long time recovering from this grief.

She gave birth to the second war child during the tense period just before the battle of Cedar Creek. Reports and rumors of disaster were numerous then, making it an especially anxious time for her. Indeed, just after this birth the papers reported that Hayes had been killed. A reporter had seen Hayes thrown from his horse at Cedar Creek and assumed this was the end of him. Fortunately the Cincinnati newspaper that carried "the complimentary obituary notice," as Hayes phrased it later, was kept from Lucy until one of Hayes's captains had sent off a telegram, "The report that your husband was killed this morning is untrue." [14]

Little George Crook Hayes, named after Hayes's favorite commander, also was a "sweet, bright boy," but in the first year following the war he also died. So both little boys became symbols of the war suffering that Lucy had to bear.

All in all, except for the pride that she felt in her heroic husband—"You are constantly in my heart, filling it with love and pride in the one so dear to me," she wrote to him in a typical letter[15]—there was little in the war to give Lucy any of the constant sense of elation that Hayes felt. Like him, she too moved about much during the war. But not on exciting marches, accompanied by band music and with flags flying.

She had her marches. But these, with her children, were a constant round of visits, now with Sardis, now with Sophia, now with her own relatives in Chillicothe and in Lexington, Kentucky—seeking not glory but the comfort of family and friends to help her endure the slow-moving, anxious days, months and years.

6

Yet Lucy had her reward also. It lay in the fact that Hayes came back more completely hers than he would have been without the war experience. The proof was in a letter. He sent it to her from his home town of Delaware, after he had gone there during one of his furloughs to spend some time with Sophia, then on one of her visits with Arcena.

Dearest Lucy:
I reached here last night. . . . *Old* Delaware is gone. . . . Old times come up to me—Sister Fanny and I trudging down to the tan-yard with our little basket after kindling. All strange; *you are Sister Fanny to me now, dearest.* . . .[16]

BOOK SEVEN

The "Tall Man"

"You have been a good boy."
—Sardis Birchard to RBH, 1873

CHAPTER XXXVIII

"Capitalist," Perhaps

1

In 1875 a stockily built, blue-eyed, reddish-haired man in his early fifties lived in the large, red brick house set pleasantly in a Buckeye grove on the outskirts of Fremont, Ohio. Though a benign person, of obvious good humor, he carried himself in the erect manner and with the quick step of a soldier. A full beard, mahogany in shade with traces of gray, emphasized his dignified bearing. He exuded success. Though not at all ostentatious, his home, with its fifty acres of grounds, testified that its owner was a person of wealth and status.

He was, in fact, the leading citizen of Fremont, a community proud of its recent designation as a city. Fremont was not yet a city of the "first class," as census officials reckoned matters. Its population was approximately 7,500. But it was a city nonetheless. For Fremont, the earlier Lower Sandusky in what, by 1875, seemed almost a prehistoric era, had grown along with America, thanks to its share of the new industrialization that now marked the land, even in the South.

Fremont's leading citizen, the man with the beard, was often referred to as "Governor," though it pleased him more to be addressed as "General." The master of the house in the grove was Rutherford B. Hayes, ten years after the Civil War.

2

There at his estate, Spiegel Grove, as it was called, in the place so much associated with his uncle, Sardis Birchard, whom he had succeeded as the first man of the community, Hayes expected in this year 1875 to live henceforth as a private citizen, in a state of retirement from public affairs. So at least he said.

This meant occupying himself mainly with plans for building up his wealth—and eschewing any further political activity. He did not mean that he considered himself old, which, of course, he was not. On his fifty-first birthday, October 4, 1873, he had noted in his diary certain "symptoms of old age." But, he added, "on the other hand, a youthful and elastic spirit; fondness for all young people and their employments and amusements . . . fresh, ruddy complexion and considerable physical strength and activity almost persuade me that I am still in my youth." [1] The fact was, he and Lucy had been producing more offspring up to 1873.

His family, then complete, seemed to be one of two generations besides his and Lucy's. The three sons who were born in the first years of his marriage were then in college, Birchard and Webb at Cornell, with Birchard set to enter Harvard Law School, while young Rutherford was at the University of Michigan. (It was interesting that none of the sons was sent to Kenyon, that in this "new age" of the 1870s Hayes felt that a religion-dominated school was not desirable, as nostalgic as he himself still felt over the "glorious" college days at Gambier.)

The other generation consisted of a girl, Fanny, then seven, and a boy, Scott Russell, then four. There had been still another son born in 1873 and called Manning Force, after Hayes's Cincinnati friend, but he had joined the "war babies" in death, dying at Spiegel Grove when only a year old.

In view of the existence of little Fanny and little Scott, both sparkling youngsters, Hayes had little chance, as a personal matter, to sink into the frame of mind that his retirement to Spiegel Grove meant he was on the downhill of life. The activity in his household, as much as his own real feelings, suggested that, while the career already behind him had been a crowded one, much more was still ahead for him—though how much he did not guess.

3

He no longer considered himself to be a lawyer. He listed himself in the city directory as "Capitalist." This was a designation, though hardly suited to Hayes, quite in tune with the new America that had emerged from the war, especially in this era—the Gilded Age, as Mark Twain called it.

It pleased Hayes then to think that, like many another, even he might become a millionaire, mainly out of his own and Sardis' investments in land. Though the nation was again in a depression, one that dated from the failure in 1873 of the Philadelphia banking house of Jay Cooke, formerly of Sandusky, Hayes, with his usual optimism, was confident that he would become wealthy from a rise in the values of land he owned, especially in near-by Toledo and in the new city of Duluth.[2]

Clearly there was self-deception in the concept that on his return to Fremont in May 1873 he was done with public life as a career, a man interested only in building a private fortune. Yet that was his expressly stated idea. His uncle was still alive then, though he died on January 21, 1874, passing away while Hayes held his hand. "You have been a good boy," Sardis had told him not long before he died, and Hayes liked to recall these words of his uncle's.[3]

He had indeed been a "good boy," not only by Sardis Birchard's practical hopes of success for him, but also by the moralistic standards of his mother. She had died in October 1866 in her seventy-fourth year, while he was out in the Nebraska territory as a member of Congress attending a ceremony for the linking of the Union Pacific and the Central Pacific railroads—the transcontinental railroad at last.

True, Sophia to the end had worried because he still had not joined a church—not even under Lucy's influence. She also remained fearful of what would happen to him as a Congressman. "I trust that he will be preserved from the vile and frivolous company that surrounds Washington," she wrote.[4] But from his tender attentions to her, his "clean" look, his contentment with Lucy, the fact that his name was never connected with any scandalous political allegations in the papers she carefully read—at a time when scandals filled the press—she knew of a certainty that he, indeed, had been "preserved."

As for Sardis, he died with the gratifying knowledge that his "boy" already had scored achievements beyond those of most men. And Hayes had done so on his own, really. The property that Sardis left to him was merely an extra matter, though substantial.

The very fact that he was able to return to Sardis' town, scene of his early false starts and failure, was a reflection of the personal success and security that he had achieved. He could not have come back there to live had he not been so successful. As he himself wrote: "I left Fremont for Cincinnati in 1849 and now come back, having achieved as much as I expected, or even hoped, by my life in Cincinnati, with kindly feelings towards all the world, to spend the closing years in the home of my youth, and the favorite resort of my childhood."[5] Overlooked or forgotten was the "doleful" character of the "wasted" years that he had spent in Fremont as a young lawyer.

4

Had he been less ambitious, less susceptible to the old lure of fame, there would have been some basis for his apparent contentment with the idea that his public career was all in the past. Starting with the appointment to the Cincinnati city solicitorship before the war, his list of public honors already was long enough for an ordinary, or even extraordinary, full life.

After his election to Congress in 1864, he had been re-elected in 1866. Then, when he had only just begun his second term in the House of Representatives, influential Republican leaders, with William Henry Smith again prominent among them, secured his nomination for governor of Ohio.[6]

To have won the election as governor in 1867 was something of a political miracle. The Democrats had put up an especially strong man in Judge Allan G. Thurman, later to be known as "the Old Roman" of the United States Senate, several times considered for Democratic candidate for the Presidency, a figure then much more widely known than Hayes. Moreover, the Ohio Republicans in 1867 were seriously divided on a major issue, that of granting the right to vote to Negroes in the state, this before the Fifteenth Amendment to the federal Constitution.

Though favoring Negro suffrage in the South, in accord with the Fourteenth Amendment, a good many Republicans, and not just in Ohio, were against it for their own states in the North.[7] Others did not favor Negro suffrage then at all, North or South, and these included the incumbent Republican governor, General Jacob D. Cox. It was Cox's surprise position, incidentally, that opened the way for Hayes's nomination. For when the dominant party leaders put through a platform favoring Negro suffrage, Cox declined to stand for re-election.[8]

Hayes was firmly for granting the Negroes the right to vote, in Ohio as well as in every other state. "It is right," he said.[9] To be sure, he was aware of the political as well as moral reasons for granting suffrage to the freedmen. But his moral stand was consistent with all that he had stood for after he had finally made up his mind on the slavery issue, consistent with his defense of fugitive slaves in Cincinnati and with his war service.

5

It was also consistent with his voting record as a Representative in the Thirty-ninth and Fortieth Congresses. These, of course, were the Reconstruction Congresses after the assassination of Lincoln, during which the so-called "Black," or "Radical," Republican leadership under Representative Thaddeus Stevens of Pennsylvania—"Thad Stevens, grim-looking, cool," as Hayes described him, admiringly[10]— challenged the authority of President Andrew Johnson, rejected his more or less lenient program for the South, and began pushing through its own plans for the reconstructed states that had seceded.

On every crucial vote in this contest between the President and the Congress while he was in Congress, Hayes allied himself with the Black Republican leadership. In his very first week he voted for establishment of the Joint Committee of Fifteen, of which Stevens was to be the leader, for setting the conditions under which "the states which formed the so-called Confederate States of America" were to be declared again in the Union. Not even all loyal Republicans went along with that "revolution" against Johnson and the Presidential power. For example, Congressman James Garfield of Ohio did not. But Hayes followed the Stevens lead.[11]

He was recorded with the ayes on the proposals that became the Fourteenth Amendment, the so-called "harsh" provisions of which the former Confederate states were forced to ratify as a condition of readmission.[12] He frankly favored the "radical" Congressional plan for keeping the Southern states under military control until they had accepted reconstruction, and so told even Guy Bryan, with whom he had resumed the old friendship, urging him to accept it also. The Thad Stevens program for the South was "righteousness," he said.[13]

In January 1867 his Ohio colleague, Congressman James Ashley of Toledo, rose in the House to intone a resolution which accused President Johnson, because of his opposition to the Black Republican program, of acts "designed or calculated to overthrow, subvert, or corrupt the government of the United States." Ashley called for an inquiry as to whether or not Johnson should be impeached. Hayes voted for the Ashley resolution. In so doing he proved more loyal to the radical cause than even a certain New York colleague, Roscoe Conkling, a name to be remembered.[14]

6

In July 1867 Johnson vetoed the Congressional program for military control of the Southern states, mainly on the ground that it placed army officers above the authority of civilian officials. In the debate on sustaining or overriding the President's veto, new demands for impeachment were voiced, in particular by Congressman Benjamin F. Butler of Massachusetts. At a later time Hayes was to hear this same Ben Butler call for the impeachment of still another President, a President named Hayes, in a controversy related to and not unlike the one involving Johnson, the power struggle between the Presidency and Congress, and Southern policy. Then Hayes would have a different view of Johnson, of the Presidential powers, of proper policy for the South and of Butler. But in 1867 he voted along with Butler for overriding the Johnson veto.[15] So also did he later with respect to Johnson's veto of a Tenure of Office Act, by which Congress restricted the President's authority to remove officials under his jurisdiction, defiance of which by Johnson finally did lead to his impeachment.[16]

True, even in 1867, despite the carry-over of the war spirit, Hayes had certain mental reservations about some of the harsher aspects of the Black Republican program. At times Lucy chided him for expressing privately some misgivings, for suggesting that the North might better be less harsh on the South. "My wife says she is glad you have sound views on the treatment of Rebels. She doubts her husband," Hayes himself wrote to an army friend who was for "thorough reconstruction." [17]

Then, too, at a caucus of Republican Congressmen, he urged that there be an educational qualification to apply to citizens of all races in the matter of conferring voting rights in state or federal elections. But when this proposal by him was rejected—one much more in keeping with his true ideas than the Black Republican program—he did not withhold his support of the accepted provision, which later became a part of the Fourteenth Amendment.[18] In short, he had conformed wholly to the radical line. Thus he was altogether available as the "Radical Republican" candidate for governor of Ohio against Judge Thurman.

7

In view of the division in the party and the obvious unpopularity of Negro suffrage in the state, especially in the southern tier of counties, political prudence indicated that Hayes in the campaign might have been well advised to pussyfoot on the radical program. But this he did not do. Instead, he vigorously championed radicalism.[19]

This forthrightness nearly cost him the election. For, as the later voting revealed, the antiradical position of Governor Cox was actually more in line with the sentiment of most Ohioans than was the stand advocated by Hayes. The state actually went Democratic. Surprisingly Hayes's own Cincinnati district elected a Democrat to succeed him in Congress, the victor turning out to be the Honorable Sam Carey, the temperance lecturer of the 1840s, who in 1867 was preaching not liquor but monetary reform.[20] A majority of the winners for the legislature were Democrats, and they promptly proceeded to elect Judge Thurman to the United States Senate, replacing Republican Ben Wade.

The proposed state constitutional amendment to permit Negroes to vote was snowed under. Not even vigorous support of it by church groups, notably Methodist and Presbyterian, could save it.[21] For several days after the election Hayes thought that he also was defeated—a situation he was destined to endure again. "You need not be told how much the result of the election disappoints me. You know I will bear it cheerfully and philosophically," he wrote to Sardis. However, it was finally found that he had won by about 3,000 votes.[22]

The appeal of his personality and the many friends that he made, especially in Cincinnati, the real battleground, together with the influence of his uncle with his many friends in northern Ohio, explained why Hayes was almost alone among Republicans in surviving the Democratic sweep.

8

In 1869, standing for a second term as governor, he again faced a star vote getter of the Democratic Party, indeed, a national figure. This was Congressman George Pendleton of Cincinnati, who in 1864 had been the Democratic candidate for Vice-President. Pendleton, later U. S. Senator, a strikingly handsome man with a glistening black beard, then was being groomed for the Presidential nomination in 1872 against General Grant who, in 1868, had succeeded Johnson as President. "Handsome George" Pendleton's entry in the Ohio gubernational race was a trial run for the Presidency on an issue destined to emerge again just then as a leading factor in American politics for the next generation and beyond.

This was the revival of the demand for "soft money," one heard periodically in America since the Shays' Rebellion time and revived as "the Ohio idea." Basically inflationary, the Ohio idea called for the federal treasury to redeem bonds sold during the war with greenbacks, rather than with gold. Pendleton argued that the bonds had been purchased largely with greenbacks, and that to pay them off in gold amounted to granting the bondholders a manifold bonus, which, in fact, was true. But the main argument, with the widest popular appeal, was that the Ohio idea would increase the money supply of the nation, thus bring down interest rates, relieve debtors and boost wages.

In the broad view the Ohio idea was deemed a tenet then of the Democratic Party. But it really cut across party lines. Republican leaders known to be otherwise sound flirted with the idea and even espoused it. Even John Sherman, the Senator from Ohio, later considered an apostle of "hard money" doctrine, was among these; likewise Senator Oliver P. Morton of Indiana, whom Hayes called "the great statesman" of the party.[23]

Hayes, however, stood against the greenback movement. He considered paying the bondholders in greenbacks as repudiation. His Whig background, his association with Sardis, his own experiences as a boy with "shinplaster" money, his concept of public honor, made him temperamentally, if not intellectually, a "hard money" man. His position, of course, was approved by conservatives. But, as was the case with his advocacy of Negro suffrage in 1867, he was clearly not on the popular side. So his chances of victory again did not seem bright.

9

Moreover, in a new form the issue of Negro suffrage was up again, this time as ratification of a new reconstruction amendment to the federal Constitution—the Fifteenth. This new amendment was designed to close a loophole in Negro rights left by the Fourteenth Amendment, which had merely provided a penalty—reduction in representation in Congress and in the electoral college—if a state denied Negroes the right to vote. It did not flatly require Negro suffrage. However, the proposed Fifteenth Amendment flatly stated: "The right of citizens of the United States shall not be denied or abridged by the United States or by any State on account of race, color, or previous condition of servitude." It also provided that "Congress shall have the power to enforce this article by appropriate legislation."

In the last analysis this amendment was the great political result of reconstruction. It not only removed (subject to judicial interpretation and also subterfuges) color and race as bars to suffrage but it struck down State rights in this field and, in addition, gave to the Republican Party potentially some 4,000,000 Negro adherents in the Southern states.

This last factor in particular made the issue of ratification a crucial one between the Republican and Democratic parties, a factor that overshadowed the moral issue of Negro suffrage and also the near-revolution in American political theory that the amendment represented. The sponsors of the amendment counted on the moral issue, if nothing else, to win ratification of it in the North. But in Ohio especially opposition was rampant.

If anything, with the war now four years ended, there was less sympathy in Northern states like Ohio for Negro rights than before, a fact which the Republican national platform in 1868 had recognized with the assertion that while equal suffrage was necessary in the South, the question in the "loyal states" was to be decided as they wished.[24] But Hayes stood for the amendment and pledged his influence as governor to have the Ohio legislature ratify it. So in this, too, he was on the unpopular side. Yet when the returns were in he had defeated Pendleton by more than twice the majority he had won over Thurman, winning by 7,500 votes.[25] His re-election was another personal triumph that he especially appreciated. He considered it a fitting climax to his public career and right then began thinking of retiring from politics while he was on top.

CHAPTER XXXIX

The Good Governor

1

"I AM enjoying the new office," he wrote to his uncle soon after he had begun the four years, 1868 through 1871, of residing again in Columbus, this time as governor. "It strikes me as the pleasantest I have ever had. Not too much hard work, plenty of time to read, good society, etc." He might have mentioned much more significantly that what he enjoyed most was the authoritative role he then was playing. This indeed, by itself, made the governorship greatly preferable for him to his Congressional service.

He had, in fact, scarcely enjoyed being a Congressman at all. For one thing, it had meant separation for long stretches from Lucy, still the beloved wife, still as lovely in his eyes as ever, though, as he would set down in his diary these days, she had grown "heavier," as he had himself.[1]

"My life with you has been so happy—so successful—so beyond reasonable anticipations, that I think of you with a loving gratitude that I do not know how to express," he wrote to her on his forty-eighth birthday.[2] That is the way he always felt, and the absences from her while he was in Washington had been painful experiences for both.

Moreover, the reality of Congress had not come up to the romantic expectations he still possessed. Instead of being a Webster, he felt generally like a mere clerk. Instead of delivering stirring orations on "The Indivisible Union" or on "Manifest Destiny," he found himself rising mainly to present such petty matters as: "By Mr. Hayes—The Petition of Ernest F. Kleinschmidt, of Hamilton County, Ohio, for the return of $12.50 paid to the Collector of the Second District of Ohio at a tax sale made without authority of law."[3]

The only debate he engaged in concerned a resolution by him to have the House appropriate $2,000 as a down payment to an Ohio artist, William H. Powell, for a $25,000 painting depicting "some naval victory" to be hung in the Capitol.[4] To be sure, there were occasions enough for him to have participated in debate over reconstruction. But he refrained. Perhaps he was overawed by elder statesmen such as Thad Stevens. Perhaps, despite his radical votes, he was being prudent. In any event he made no effort to live up to his earlier vision of himself as an eloquent statesman.

2

This, he discovered, did not disappoint at all important constituents. The Ohio Wool Growers' Association expected him to support without question its lobby for higher and higher tariffs. It did not wish him to be a statesman but expected him merely to act as its lobbyist. When he failed to react mechanically to its demands he found himself bitterly, and unfairly, he felt, attacked for using his own judgment.[5]

With such incidents in mind he described himself to Lucy as "errand boy to one hundred fifty thousand people." [6] To Murat Halstead, a fellow member of the old Literary Club in Cincinnati, now beginning his climb to fame as one of Ohio's great journalists, he got off a quip that told his general reaction to being in Congress. "Do you want any books, apple seeds, or oats? I am in that trade now." [7]

True, he accomplished one thing of which he was proud. As chairman of the Joint Committee on the Library, he caused Congress to approve merger of the Smithsonian Institution library with the Library of Congress, won approval of purchase for the Library of Congress of the large collection of Americana owned by Peter Force, father of his friend Manning Force, and also of authorization for the Library of Congress, until then a mere adjunct of Congress, to serve other departments of the government and the general public as well. Thus he helped to start the Library of Congress on the path to becoming one of the great general libraries of the world.[8] But on the whole, his service in Congress was a colossal disappointment to him, and he was glad to be done with it.[9]

Besides, he did not like the "smell" of much that many Congressmen did or were suspected of doing in the way of extracting profit for themselves or others from various transactions at the expense of the public treasury. The smell was especially strong then. For this was the time of "the Great Barbecue," as Vernon Parrington phrased it, of many small and also large legislative swindles, including the scandalous Crédit Mobilier affair involving the Union Pacific Railroad.

A number of colleagues whom he admired, Hayes learned later, were in that mess. Of course, he was not. But he had not been a Congressman long when he wrote to Lucy that there often ran through his mind the phrase, "Politics is a bad trade," adding, "Guess we'll quit." [10]

3

As governor, however, he blossomed because of the deference that was paid to him. He relished the power that went with the office, limited as it was then, when the governor of Ohio lacked even the right to veto legislative acts. He was particularly pleased by the special satisfaction that Lucy took from being "the governor's lady."

He did not overdo the authoritative role. On the contrary, he was quite modest in using his power, though on something which he felt strongly about he showed that he could be quite stubborn. For example, when there was presented to him the case of a Mrs. Victor, a Cleveland woman convicted of murder, he promptly commuted her death sentence to life imprisonment without regard to the legal arguments or the facts. Showing that he was still the same Rutherford B. Hayes who had defended Nancy Farrer, still revealing the effects of having been brought up by women, he said: "So long as I am Governor of Ohio, no woman will be hanged in this state!" [11]

He was not a "great" governor. But the word "great" was rarely used then concerning any governor. Governors were mainly figureheads, useful for speeches, mere dispensers of patronage to party workers, men soon forgotten unless they became Senators, Chief Justices, or Presidents.

True, just after Hayes returned to Fremont, the governor of New York, Samuel J. Tilden, won national attention for action against the "Boss" Tweed ring. But the sensation caused by Governor Tilden was in large part due to astonishment that a governor could so act. Though Hayes in Ohio had asked the legislature for authority to expose corruption in Ohio cities even before Tilden's rise to fame on that issue, he had no such sensational opportunity as the Tweed ring presented to attain greatness. [12]

But he was a good governor, exceptionally so. That he should be rated as such was obviously his conscious goal. He conducted himself almost always in accord with an idealistic concept of what a good governor should be, the concept of the genteel, educated man in politics, dignified, calm, a man willing to listen to all viewpoints, benevolent even toward political opponents. Because he was so, even Democratic newspapers found it possible to praise him.

This was an unusual thing at a time when the bitterest partisanship was the hallmark of the press. But the Democratic editors could not fail to be impressed that, as governor, as formerly when city solicitor, he showed his interesting capacity to be quite nonpartisan, not always, but often, once he was in office.

This is not to say that he held himself wholly aloof from partisan activity. Like any other loyal party man, he let partisan considerations influence certain of his actions. An example was his conduct in connection with a contested Congressional election in the fall of 1870. The incumbent, General R. C. Schenck, Republican, was declared defeated by a Democrat, former Congressman L. D. Campbell, but by a small majority. Schenck contested Campbell's victory. Before the issue was decided President Grant appointed Schenck U. S. Minister to England (with disastrous results later for the reputations of both), whereupon Schenck resigned from Congress.

The Democrats insisted that under the law Hayes had to order a special election immediately to fill the Schenck vacancy. Probably correctly they reasoned that Campbell would easily win. But Hayes took the position that there was not enough time for "a fair election" to be held before the Schenck term would expire, and he declined to issue the proclamation. His decision obviously served the interests of his party. He deserved the criticism that the Democrats heaped on him.[13]

But by and large he consciously sought to administer his office so that Democrats would recognize that he was governor of Ohio, not a Republican governor. Thus, in his first term, in making appointments to various state boards, he insisted that some of the men appointed should be Democrats. This was a new departure for governors. "I was assailed as untrue to my party," he later recalled, "but the advantages of minority representation were soon apparent, and the experiment became successful."[14]

By itself this was an innovation that made him outstanding among governors from the beginning. Moreover, though he made some mistakes, his partisan appointments were notably above the average. As a friend said, "Hayes attracted good men, freezing the bad."[15]

4

Generally he gave the impression of being most interested in standing for conservative financial and tax policies, content to be known as a safe and sound official. But he showed also a capacity to strike out in some new directions, at least in the field of reform. Thus, he recommended, when this was almost pioneering, that voters be registered as a means of preventing election frauds.

Even more radical in the eyes of stanch partisans was his recommendation for a state civil-service system. Noting that even President Grant had cautiously gone on record for federal civil-service reform in the national government, Hayes called for placing a guarantee in the Ohio constitution that merit qualifications should determine the tenure of wardens of the penitentiaries and the superintendents of asylums and reformatories, as well as their assistants.[16] Of course, the party bosses were incensed at such "naïveté."

He called, too, for firm regulation of the railroads by the state. That the state should inject itself aggressively into this field was then considered radicalism, a yielding to the "unreasonable" demands of farmers' Grange organizations. Yet Hayes, the conservative, was as insistent as any Grange leader that the railroads should be rigidly supervised by the state. The roads operated on the basis of state charters and so "it is not to be doubted that they can be controlled by the state," he said.[17]

He was not an advanced thinker on government. After his public career was all over, he would surprise observers—and also himself—by flirting with the American socialistic doctrines of the 1880s and 1890s.[18] But during the years he was in office he held, as was expectable from his education, the orthodox nineteenth-century view of *laissez faire*—the less government the better.

5

He was aware of the so-called "plutocracy" of the Gilded Age. In a notable speech in 1871 he stood out among Republicans by referring to "the colossal fortunes which, under the sanction of law, are already consolidating into the hands of a few men—not always the best men— powers which threaten alike good government and our liberties." But the solution, he said, was "in the home, the school, the platform, the pulpit, and the press," in education, with "all good men and women . . . the educators," every place, that is, except in government action.[19]

Yet when he saw concrete situations of corruption, injustice or inefficiency, he urged enactment of laws in advance of the common thinking. He supported enactment of the state's first code of safety in coal mining, again entering a field which had been considered in the accepted thought of the period as secure from government intervention.[20]

His great interest was in the humanitarian responsibility of the state. He devoted much attention to the prisons, the correctional institutions for girls and boys, and the hospitals for the mentally ill. Accompanied usually by Lucy, he visited these institutions more than any other previous governor, talking to the inmates as well as to the superintendents. Once he even considered entering one of the prisons himself as a pretended convict in order to see precisely what treatment the prisoners received.[21]

He made it a point to obtain advice on the correctional institutions from professional experts in the field, starting then the interest in prison reform to which he became devoted later. Offshoots of this interest were his trail-blazing recommendations, some adopted while he was governor, others effected later, for separating hardened criminals from first offenders, for giving indeterminate sentences and for the building of reform schools on the plan of cottages rather than the forbidding bastille type of structure.[22] He was, in short, except for his "radical" support of Negro rights, a perfect model of the conservative gentleman in politics—never doctrinaire, never extreme right or left.

6

Though neither he nor anyone else recognized it then, his most important single achievement related to establishment of Ohio's largest modern university. Under the federal Morrill Act the state was entitled to a fairly large sum of money. Hayes urged that the legislature enact the necessary legislation for obtaining this fund. However, nine existing colleges in Ohio brought pressure to have the fund distributed among them. This appealed to legislative leaders, but Hayes saw that this meant spreading the fund so thin as to bring no lasting benefits. He called in the leaders and argued for using the entire fund for a new state university. By "working hard" at it, as he later said, he won his way, and the money was used to purchase a large tract of land on the outskirts of Columbus. There was established the Ohio Agricultural and Medical College, which in 1878 became Ohio State University.[23] As would be said later, Hayes "shaped the necessary legislation, procured its passage, and appointed the board of trustees which located the university, prescribed its general courses of study and elected its faculty." [24]

He, however, believed at the time that his great achievement was getting the Ohio legislature to ratify the Fifteenth Amendment.[25] Even with a Republican majority, it was by no means certain that this amendment would be adopted when Hayes recommended its approval. Several Republicans from Cincinnati, styling themselves "reformers," announced that they intended to vote with the Democrats against it. Indeed, Hayes faced a major test of his strength as a political leader, a test with national implications, for the amendment was having hard sledding in the nation as a whole.

"Vast interests are depending upon the vote of Ohio," Senator Morton, in charge of a national campaign for ratification, advised Hayes.[26] Justice Noah H. Swayne of the U. S. Supreme Court wrote: "It is very important that Ohio should ratify." [27]

7

Indeed, it was. As national Republican leaders viewed the crisis, the fate of the national Republican Party, not to mention the incidental factor of Negro suffrage, was at stake.

In the end, through shrewd use of state as well as federal patronage, the ratification resolution was adopted in Ohio—by one vote in the senate and two votes in the house.[28] In Washington there was jubilation among the Republican leaders. A scroll of appreciation was sent to Hayes, one signed by almost the entire Republican membership of the House and Senate.

As political matters looked then, Hayes had saved the Republican Party and Northern dominance of the nation. For the Fifteenth Amendment was deemed essential to preventing a revival of Southern —and Democratic—ascendancy. Obviously this was a service which called for a national reward. The national reward was to come, too, prefaced by the placing, for the first time, of the national spotlight on him. Politically Hayes had begun to arrive.

CHAPTER XL

"NO MORE AMBITION"

1

YET AT this time, at the start of his second term as governor, he stated his decision to retire from politics. "I . . . mean to be out of politics," he wrote to a friend. "The ratification of the Fifteenth Amendment gives me the boon of equality before the law, terminates my enlistment, and discharges me cured." [1] To one of Lucy's brothers in June 1870 he said, "The cause I enlisted for is completely mastered, and the new questions do not interest me. There is no feeling or interest in political matters." [2]

In the following year he made a similar statement to Charles Nordhoff, the influential New York newspaper editor. Formerly a Cincinnatian, Nordhoff had come to know Hayes through his marriage to one of Lucy's schoolmates. He had high admiration for Hayes and, privately as well as in print, urged that he stay in politics, with a national role in view.

Nordhoff was among a growing group of Republicans who already were turning away from President Grant. In Nordhoff's opinion Hayes, as a symbol of integrity, was needed to offset "Grantism." But to Nordhoff Hayes said, "I go out of politics with the end of this term. The old questions interested me so much that the new ones seem small." [3]

About this time he was being mentioned for the U. S. Senate in place of John Sherman, whose term was expiring. But in his diary he wrote:

The senatorship to be decided this year in Ohio seems to be as likely to fall to me, if I enter the struggle for it, as to any other Republican. . . . I cannot consent, after having borne my part in the glorious struggle against slavery during the last seventeen years, now to endure the anxiety belonging to political life for the sake of the honors of office merely. . . . I do not expect or desire to withdraw from all interest and participation in passing events. It is simply, I am out of the race for promotion. I am not a candidate, and shall avoid being made one, for the senatorship or for any other high office. [4]

It is interesting that he emphasized that he would not seek "promotion." This did not rule out a lesser position. Indeed, he deliberately said that he might accept a lesser role. To an Ohio editor he stated: "I shall, of course, not cease to take an interest in politics, and am very likely to be a candidate for subordinate positions." [5]

He emphasized this attitude in a letter to one of his war comrades. "I am looking forward to a release from public life and to freedom as hopefully as a schoolboy to his coming vacation. . . . I retire absolutely. I shall make no attempt to go higher. If I ever accept public employment again, it will be incidental and for special reasons, not as falling within the line of my life as now chosen." [6]

2

There is a psychological puzzle here. One key to the puzzle may be that Hayes suddenly had suffered, if only temporarily, a kind of guilt over success, that he began to fear going higher in politics. Or, perhaps in that period, when the reputations of so many men high in politics were becoming tarnished, including that of President Grant himself, he decided that he ought to be content with two terms as governor and not take chances on his own reputation's becoming soiled.

His mention in his diary of the "anxiety belonging to political life" and also a letter to Sardis, written the day after he retired as governor, seem to support this. He wrote to his uncle:

I feel foolishly happy this, my first day of freedom. For a week or two past, there has been a feeling with me that something might happen to cast a shadow on the four years of good fortune in the governor's office. . . . It looks as if I might have been Senator. My refusal gives me position, and, true or not, the common remark is that I am the most esteemed of the governors within the memory of people living. But enough of this vanity. . . . [7]

To be sure, there was a certain realism in his fear that some shadow might be cast over his record. No governor, or any other government executive, may be certain that some subordinate might not be found to be faithless, with consequent reflection on the man who appointed him. Then, too, Hayes may have been worried over possible misinterpretation of his investments in Duluth land. [8]

Duluth was largely a development of the financier Jay Cooke as part of the promotion of the Northern Pacific Railroad. Cooke had let Hayes, along with Billy Rogers and Manning Force, make the Duluth investment, which for Hayes amounted to $8,000, "at a bargain," as

Cooke pointedly emphasized to Hayes.[9] This transaction would be cited against Hayes, with the innuendo that it involved him in some of the spoils alliances of the day. It in fact was quite innocent of any such connotation. Cooke was anxious to sell the Duluth land to raise funds for building his railroad. Hayes paid for it in cash, and he felt not the slightest obligation to the financier, other than that of a friendship which had existed before.

3

Yet it was a mistake for Hayes to have dealt with Cooke, who, on encountering trouble in selling Northern Pacific bonds, did ask him, as governor, to recommend that the Ohio legislature grant tax exemption to his bonds. Cooke argued that building the railroad was a public service, and hence Northern Pacific bonds should be treated on a par with government bonds.[10]

Hayes made no such recommendation. He avoided Cooke's trap. But that Cooke would make such a suggestion to him undoubtedly forced him to realize that in making the Duluth investment, he had skirted what to him would be a supreme disaster—impeachment of his integrity. So the Duluth matter may have been a shadow deep in his mind, a cause of anxiety which he probably could not have named.

Then, too, he may have been involved in some conflicting attitudes toward his party, in particular toward Grant. He was not so naïve that he could not see, as clearly as Nordhoff, that Grant, manipulated by spoilsmen, was not only turning from the best elements of the party, but actually was antagonistic toward them. This troubled him—as would come out more clearly later. But he wished to be loyal to Grant. After all, Grant was the "great commander" during the "divine" war. If Hayes became Senator, as was being urged, he would either have to be associated with the Grant administration and support it, or take a place with the "bolters," with men like Senator Charles Sumner of Massachusetts or Senator Carl Schurz of Missouri, whom he also admired. He did not wish to make any such decision —yet.

4

So there were political as well as personal factors in his ambivalence toward going higher in politics That he was in doubt over his decision to retire is indicated by a constant need he showed for assuring himself, in his diary and letters, that the decision was correct, that he meant it. An example was a letter he wrote to Lucy in May 1871, when he was in Washington on state business. "I see no reason here to regret *our* choice and decision. We are quite sound on the matter. Out of public life is independence. There may be times of loneliness and lack of excitement, but the general result must be good." [11]

To Guy Bryan he wrote in the same vein. "I long for freedom and independence. My family and private affairs will be my care hereafter. . . . No more ambition." [12]

Realistically, however, nothing was further from the truth, as time was to show.

CHAPTER XLI

RENUNCIATIONS

1

EVEN so, at the very end of his second term as governor, he certainly conducted himself as if, indeed, he had "no more ambition." First, there was the matter of the Senatorship. It was one thing to say that he did not wish to be a United States Senator before the offer of a nomination was made, and another thing to reject the idea if election were in his grasp. Yet he did precisely that.

The election of a Senator by the Ohio legislature was set for January 1872. Influential elements in the Republican Party were opposed to Senator Sherman being re-elected. Some charged that Sherman was a "corruptionist," that he had grown wealthy in office. E. L. Godkin's *The Nation* magazine, then the organ of purists in politics, referred to Sherman as a "base politician." Others opposed him because he tended to flirt with the greenback movement and other monetary proposals held "unsound," in his capacity as chairman of the Senate Finance Committee.[1]

Sherman's opponents in the Republican Party assured Hayes that he could win the party's endorsement. They also indicated that he could expect support from Democrats, enough to guarantee that he would defeat Sherman. But Hayes firmly renounced this opportunity. He would not permit his name to be used.[2]

In his diary he said, "Now, of course, I would like to be a senator, notwithstanding the solid reasons there are why I should quit this sort of life. But I do not care enough for it to go into a struggle for it. And so I told my friends to look elsewhere for a candidate and they have formed other alliances."[3]

Then, about the same time, he was also urged to stand for a third term as governor. This was an honor that truly appealed to him. Only once before, many years back, had there been paid to any man the honor of three consecutive elections as governor of Ohio. Moreover, Hayes could have had the third nomination from his party without any fight, and this time with assurance of victory. But this he also renounced.

"If my name is offered as a candidate, it will be withdrawn," he

253

said.[4] To Nordhoff he gave the excuse that "usage and personal inclination" were against a third-term nomination.[5] To cinch matters, he threw his support for the Republican nomination behind a Cincinnati friend, Edward Follansbee Noyes, a member of the same Noyes clan that included the Honorable John Noyes, the partner of Hayes's father back in Vermont. Noyes was nominated and elected—and Hayes professed to be pleased.[6]

2

Just before Hayes surrendered the office to Noyes, the Senatorship matter came up again. This time he was given even more positive assurances that the Democrats in the legislature, with few exceptions, would vote for him and that enough Republicans, who were in the majority, would absent themselves to elect him. Only his passive consent was needed.

"It is rather pleasant to be so endorsed by one's opponents," he told Sardis.[7] But as he stated in his diary, he "squarely and steadfastly" refused his consent. For all his supposed desire to retire, however, he did confide to his diary: "Yet, I suppose, if the majority of the Republicans should wish it, that I would consent. But of that there is no probability, unless I become actively a candidate, and *that* I shall not do." [8]

The Republican caucus voted to support Sherman. Hayes then considered that it was regarded as final that Sherman would be chosen and that he could put aside the matter.

But he was still not let alone. On the evening of January 9, 1872, with the legislature to pick the Senator the next morning, he was presented with the Senatorial question again in a dramatic manner. For no sooner had he turned out the lights in his Columbus residence to go to bed, than the front doorbell rang. A Republican state senator and a Republican representative were waiting to see him.

"Well, I come to business at once," the state senator began. "We want to make you Senator." Eight Republicans were prepared to desert Sherman, he said, adding, "The man now elected Senator over the caucus will be the next President of the United States."

This, of course, was an interesting, attractive and even realistic suggestion, tying in with the growing opposition within the party to Grant and a trend of dissident Republicans to form a coalition with Democrats. But Hayes did not reach for that bait. "I urged the importance of not splitting the Republican party; of electing a Republican President once more at least; that the defeat of Grant now was to give the Government to the enemies of recent amendments and to unsettle all." [9]

He talked to his callers also of his sense of duty and honor. The Republicans in the legislature had pledged themselves to Sherman. In effect, this was also a pledge to the Republican voters. Repudiation of the pledge would be morally wrong. He could not be a party to it, nor did he think his visitors should be. He could not possibly enter into a deal with Democrats to knife a fellow Republican.

"Well, if we vote for you, and elect you, will you not accept?" he was asked.

No, he would not fall in with that procedure either. He "would not be used for the purpose . . . in any way, or under any circumstances."

It was no use, his callers then saw. "It is strange," said the state senator, departing, "to see a man throw away the senatorship," with the Presidency in prospect.[10]

3

Nor was that the end of the pressure on him. That same night, after those callers departed, he received another visitor. As he wrote in his diary: "I went to bed after telling it to Lucy, who laughed and said she would not sleep now for fear of some Democrat slipping in. I soon fell into a sound sleep; was aroused by repeated ringing of my door-bell. Went down in my night shirt. In came my friend, John G. Deshler." [11]

Deshler, a member of Columbus' leading banking family, represented elements of the highest respectability and influence—and he, too, had come to offer the Senatorship to Hayes. A "party" had been meeting at his house for a week. "They are now there, have been all evening, and they can elect you and have decided to do it, if you will consent. You must consent," said Deshler. Coming from a man of Deshler's standing, this could have been construed by Hayes as a call of duty. Moreover, Deshler's assurances that he could be elected were ironclad.

Again Hayes did not change his mind. "I can't honorably do it, and there is no use talking," he said. "It is settled and has been for weeks."

Deshler said, "Well, if you say *that*, I must give it up."

Sherman was re-elected Senator the next day, and with gratitude for Hayes's renunciation, a gratitude that was destined to return to Hayes a political dividend of crucial importance after his mood of retirement had passed.

SAMUEL J. TILDEN

Drawing, based on a photograph, in *Frank Leslie's Illustrated Newspaper,*
November 11, 1876

CHAPTER XLII

PIQUED "STALWART"

1

IN JANUARY 1872, after Noyes took over as his successor as governor, Hayes went back to Cincinnati with Lucy, little Fanny and little Scott. So far as anyone knew, he contentedly planned to resume residence permanently there. The old house on Sixth Street had been sold. So while he and Lucy looked for a new residence, they had temporary lodgings in the Carlisle House, "at fifty dollars a week." He began to conduct himself as if he had gone back to the law and took space in the law office of a casual friend.

Actually the law office was just a base for his own business affairs, though he did study some law pertaining to railroading, for he already had in mind the Toledo-to-Columbus project.[1] He also became interested in a proposed railroad line into Cincinnati as part of the Atlantic and Great Western system.[2] Politics? That was all past, he said. Yet within six months he was engrossed in politics again.

2

That was the year of the "Liberal Republican" revolt against "Grantism," when the Republican Party split down the middle. In the light of political principles later identified with him Hayes was a natural for participation in a Liberal Republican movement. Basically this movement stood for ending the radical program in the South— for reconciliation instead of more reconstruction—and for reform in appointments and legislation. Its leaders, nationally and locally, though including opportunists, were in the main Hayes's kind, the genteel, educated, so-called "silk-stocking" elements of the party—Carl Schurz, Charles Francis Adams, Samuel Bowles, of the Springfield (Massachusetts) *Republican*, Joseph Medill, of the Chicago *Tribune*, and Whitelaw Reid, of the New York *Tribune*, associate of Horace Greeley. Locally they included Hayes's own Cincinnati friends, Murat Halstead, John Herron and Stanley Matthews. In fact, Matthews was temporary chairman of the Liberal Republican convention when it was opened in Cincinnati.[3]

257

William Henry Smith, the general agent of the Associated Press in Chicago, also joined the movement.[4] From the time Smith suggested Hayes for Congress during the war their political thinking had been almost identical. To be sure, Smith's political switch in 1872 could be discounted by the fact that most of the publishers who controlled the Associated Press then were in the Liberal Republican movement. Nonetheless, it was extraordinary for Smith, whom Hayes called his most trusted political counselor, to be on the opposite side.

3

Naturally, in view of his reform record, Hayes had been invited to join in the revolt, which culminated in the nomination of Horace Greeley as Liberal Republican candidate for President, with the Democrats also naming him as their candidate. Back in 1870 Nordhoff began this solicitation, urging Hayes to join in a third-party movement with Schurz, Adams and others in the Liberal revolt.

But Hayes wrote to Nordhoff:

I read the future this way: the two old parties will be *the* parties until after the next Presidential election. Whatever shortcomings belong to the record of the Republican party, it is greatly to be preferred at the next election to any party led and ruled, as the Democratic party is, by New York City plunderers. All sorts of reforms are desirable in our tax and revenue laws. A Republican will prefer to fight for them inside of the Republican party. I therefore would advise against attempting to organize a new party. . . .[5]

To another Easterner who broached the same subject to him, he was even more emphatic. "I wrote Nordhoff that I wanted no new party and would have nothing to do with organizing a new one."[6]

4

He not only held aloof from the Liberal Republicans but accepted election as an Ohio delegate to the regular Republican national convention in Philadelphia, at which it was a foregone conclusion that Grant would be drafted to succeed himself, and that the Liberal Republicans would be denounced as traitors. He was made a delegate "against my protest," he told Sardis, but felt it "smoother to go than, by resigning, to get ranked with the Greeley men."[7]

He obviously enjoyed the regular party convention activity and was in the thick of much of it.[8] He supported Grant's renomination enthusiastically. Moreover, as a member of the Committee on Resolutions, he played a major role in drafting the platform on which Grant based his bid for re-election.[9]

Hayes had occasion later to view his role as an author of the 1872 Grant platform as a strange thing. He then would see that the platform which most closely incorporated the principles for which he was to stand in history was not the one he helped to write. It was the 1872 Liberal Republican platform, with its advocacy of a new departure in Southern policy, its stress on reform and its stand for limiting Presidential service to one term.[10] With all these policies Hayes would be identified more precisely than any other American, particularly with the one-term proposal. That was a direct attack on Grant. But in 1872 he was still on the "stalwart" side.

5

For a man who kept insisting that he was out of politics, he certainly behaved even more oddly after the 1872 Presidential campaign was under way. Indeed, his participation in the renomination of Grant aside, his retirement was altogether curious. After his renunciation of the Senatorship and a third term as governor, despite all his statements publicly and privately made that he was out of public life, when election time rolled around, none other than Hayes was a candidate for Congress—of all offices—from the Second Cincinnati district. He permitted himself to be seduced by the appeal that his candidacy was necessary to save Ohio from being carried for Greeley, whom he called "laughable."

"The Greeley strength is in my district," he later wrote.[11] Grant strategists feared that the result in Ohio might be so close that the vote in the upper-middle-class Second District alone might be decisive, especially as the Liberals and Democrats had put up for Congress a good man, Henry B. Banning, also a Kenyon graduate. Not only did Banning have an excellent war record, but he also had been a regular Republican.

The party leaders asserted that no one but Hayes could be expected to defeat Banning. At first he replied that for him to be a candidate was "out of the question." [12] He had the press announce specifically: "Ex-Governor R. B. Hayes has refused to become a candidate." [13] But the party leaders, as well as some of his personal friends, including Manning Force and Richard Smith, publisher of the Cincinnati *Gazette,* kept pressing him. They assumed that he was not really so firm in his resolve to retire from politics as he professed. They knew, too, of the interesting qualification he had made about his retirement while he was still governor—that he would not seek promotion, but might accept a lesser office.

6

Had his friends seen certain entries in his diary, they would have been even more sure. On July 25, 1872, with the nominating convention scheduled for August 6, he wrote:

I do not want to return to Congress and, of course, do not wish to be nominated. Having said to several gentlemen who were named as probable candidates that I did not mean to run, I cannot consent under any circumstances to allow my name to be used against them. [But] if it is the general wish of the Republicans, also of the candidates themselves that I should be nominated, I cannot refuse my assent. I greatly prefer that some other citizen be made the candidate. This is the true state of the case, but I must not say so. I have not said so because the consent, conditional though it is, would be used to force other candidates out of the way.

Among these candidates was William E. Davis, a friend. To make certain that Hayes's refusal would be placed before the convention, Davis asked him for a blunt statement to that effect to be sent to him, so that he could get it to the delegates. Hayes complied with Davis' request.[14]

But the convention nominated him anyway. He kept the political leaders in suspense for several days. However, to Manning Force he wrote: "I am now placed in a position where to withdraw might be injurious to the cause. I shall probably stand."[15] And stand he did —only to be defeated by a Greeley sweep of his district, though Grant, of course, defeated Greeley in the nation.

This defeat, his first since the anti-Lincoln sweep in 1860 cost him his post as city solicitor, did not set well with him. Later, this "sacrifice," like that of his refusal to oppose Senator Sherman, would pay a dividend. It would be cited as a sign of his party loyalty that entitled him to party trust—and reward. But at the time it left him in a state of pique. One solace he had. In his district he had run ahead of Grant. "It is well to beat somebody!" he exclaimed to his son Webb.[16]

7

It was just after this that he made the decision to move to Fremont.[17] Before this move President Grant gave him another chance to reconsider his decision to go into retirement. There had been talk that Grant would offer Hayes a cabinet post, perhaps that of Secretary of the Interior, which ex-Governor Cox had held but resigned.[18] Perhaps he would have accepted. But Grant, without consulting him, sent his name to the Senate for Assistant Secretary of the Treasury in charge of the Cincinnati district. This inferior appointment Hayes declined.

He was piqued by this, too, and also by the way the appointment was canceled after he had refused it. The proper procedure was for the President to withdraw it. Instead, it went to a vote and was "rejected." Oddly Senator Sherman participated in that clumsy move— to "expedite" matters, he explained:

To Sherman, Hayes, in a mood reminiscent of his altercation with General Reno, sent a letter expressing his resentment. "The action taken was calculated, although not so intended, to injure me and wound my feelings, and frankness requires that I should say that I think you were in error. . . ." [19] It was one of the few angry letters he ever permitted himself to write.

When he recorded the matter for his diary he still could not disguise his pique. "I am glad General Grant appointed me," he wrote. "It enables me to decline an office of profit just as I leave Cincinnati, and so to leave with a well-rounded political record. But the office I would not take except as a means of keeping hunger from the door. After what I have been and had and done, it would be small potatoes to grasp this crumb. Thanks be given, I am independent of office for my daily bread!"

In that frame of mind he went back to Fremont in May 1873, finished with politics, "definitely, absolutely, positively." So he said and perhaps really believed.

CHAPTER XLIII

Farewell to "Stalwartism"

1

By accident, if not shrewd intuition and the Hayes luck, he had picked a good political time for retirement. For it coincided with lean days for Republicanism. True, the Liberal Republican revolt, as such, had been crushed. Most of its chastened leaders, including Stanley Matthews and even Carl Schurz, had returned to the fold. Yet "Grantism" and "stalwartism" apparently took nose dives in popular esteem almost as soon as the regular Republicans had finished celebrating Grant's second inauguration.

A major cause was the panic of 1873. But there was also marked dissatisfaction with Republican conduct generally. Outbreaks of violence in the South between Ku Klux Klansmen, or "White Leaguers," and carpetbaggers and the Negro freedmen, especially in Louisiana, over reconstruction—despite Grant's campaign utterance, "Let there be peace"—fanned the new storm. So also did outbreaks of scandals touching Grant's own personal and official families.

So strong was the popular dissatisfaction that even Grant, though late and clumsily, began to veer toward a new course, if only to woo the former Liberal Republicans and to ease the tension in the South. Indeed, it was then, in 1873, under Grant rather than in 1877 as usually is said, that reconstruction came to an end. What remained was a mopping-up operation and the official obsequies.

That same year, 1873, in the first fall of Hayes's return to Fremont, Noyes, his friend and successor as governor, was defeated for re-election, unseated by a seventy-year-old Democrat, William Allen of Chillicothe. Now called "Rise Up Allen," so quiet for years that many believed him dead, this was the same Allen who, as U. S. Senator, had thrilled even Whiggish young Hayes back in the 1840s with the slogan, "Fifty-four forty or fight!" in the almost-forgotten Oregon boundary issue.[1]

2

That Allen's victory was no aberration became clear in the 1874 Congressional elections, when the Democrats won in a majority of

Ohio districts. The debacle in Ohio was in line with a general trend, for the Democrats obtained control of the national House of Representatives. Worse yet from the Republican "stalwart" view, all but three of the former Confederate states had been redeemed, that is, they had voted out the carpetbag or scalawag governments and were then Democratic, or the equivalent by other names. Thus, it seemed altogether probable that Hayes's party was in for a long, even a permanent, national eclipse, and that the "party of treason," as many Republicans then called the Democratic Party, was on its way back.[2]

With Democracy again in the saddle in most of the South, and now with even Northern states deserting "the party of Lincoln," a good many Republicans felt that Republican ascendancy had joined slavery as a lost cause. The most stalwart among them were prepared even for more bloodletting, if necessary, identifying their party's fate with freedom, at least in public utterances. And these, to be sure, had their counterparts in the South, though the majority of Americans were clearly for peace, at almost any price short of another breaking up of the Union.

3

Engrossed, as he seemed, in private business affairs, or in local civic activity in Fremont—such as the launching there of a free public library, to be called the Birchard Library (funds for which Sardis had provided before his death)—Hayes was still political enough in his retirement to ponder much about the new political scene. In his pondering he took a new—and more objective—look at his old war hero Grant. He never ceased to admire Grant as a man. But this was mainly sentiment related to his own war service. To turn on Grant personally would seem to deprecate the "glorious" war itself, as well as to reject one of his father images. But he was able now to make a distinction in his mind between Grant the general and Grant the President.

As part of his reappraisal of Grant, he took a new look also at the reconstruction policies of his party. Despite his basic instinct for conciliation, none of his public utterances made while he was in politics to date permitted the impression that he had had any doubts about the reconstruction program. As governor in 1868, when he was asked to advise the Ohio caucus in Congress on how to vote on the guilt of President Johnson, he telegraphed: CONVICTION.[3]

He still believed in the stated moral objectives of reconstruction. But the measures taken in the South—the use of federal troops, suspension of habeas corpus, the so-called "force bills,"—now evoked typical genteel qualms. Like the editors of *Harper's Weekly* and *The Nation*, who by 1875 also were taking new looks at reconstruction and changing their minds, Hayes had no doubt that the Negroes should be supported, at least in principle, in their new rights as citizens, or that terrorism by such organizations as the Ku Klux Klan should be suppressed. But doubts arose when evidence mounted—some of the most impressive published in 1875 in a book, *The Cotton States in the Spring and Summer of 1875,* by Hayes's friend, Charles Nordhoff—that in too many cases unscrupulous men were using reconstruction for their own private and political ends. Also, that Negro officeholders, who caught on quickly to the acquisitive ways of politics, for the most part were proving, quite like white officeholders, something less than paragons of virtue.[4]

To be sure, to blame the atmosphere of corruption in the carpetbag and Negro regimes of the South wholly on reconstruction was unrealistic. For corruption had existed in the South before, as it would again, and conditions North were not much different. To Guy Bryan, Hayes pointed this out. But in so doing, in January 1875, he also made some comments showing that he was no longer so pronounced a radical as he had been, though he was not antiradical either.

He told Bryan:

I recognize fully the evil of rule by ignorance. I see enough of it under my own eyes. You are not so much worse off in this respect than New York, Chicago, and other cities having a large uneducated population. But the remedy is not, I am sure, to be found in the abandonment of the American principle that all must share in government. The Whites of the South must do as we do, *forget to drive and learn to lead* the ignorant masses around them. . . . But I will not argue. You and I are now nearer together than we have been since our boyhood. We shall probably soon vote the same ticket. But not if you continue to indulge a hope that slavery is in some form to be restored. That is surely not to be.[5]

The fact was, however, restoring slavery in some form—that is, restricting the Negroes to second-class citizenship—was the aim of dominant white elements in the South. That was what they meant by putting the Negro in his place, by their so-called "Black Codes."[6] As he indicated to Bryan, Hayes could not endorse any such program.

But he also had lost much of his faith in his party's program. *"I doubt the ultra measures relating to the South,"* he wrote in his diary on March 28, 1875. In short, he was getting back to the conciliatory viewpoint he had held before the war, nearly back to the Whiggish attitude of his youth.

4

In common with most Northerners, he was moving inevitably toward a compromise, seeking a bridge between "ultraism" and the white-supremacy doctrines of Southern leadership, a position that could satisfy neither the full implications of the reconstruction amendments nor the Southern position. This resulted from a dilemma in which nearly all decent, yet pragmatic Americans such as he were placed by the Southern problem.

By law and by the results of the war the Negroes were entitled to full rights. However, because of the obdurate stand of the most articulate of Southern whites, nothing but "ultra measures" could have secured these rights for the Negroes, at least not until both Negroes and whites had been educated for the new legal situation. But education was a long process. Not even genteel Southerners, like Guy Bryan, intended to do the right thing, as that would be defined by Hayes, unless coerced. So, if the Negroes in the 1870s were to have their rights, the program of reconstruction was the only way, apparently. But reconstruction by 1875 was largely a discredited program.

Rightly or wrongly, the general public, North and South, judged it from the viewpoint of Claude G. Bowers' later phrase, "The Tragic Era." For the most part only "stalwart" Republicans, seeing in it a means of keeping their wing of the Republican Party in power, North and South, professed to see complete good in it. Even many Negroes were disillusioned, as well as bewildered.

Perhaps, though this is doubtful, a better or wiser man than Grant in the Presidency then would have caused a less tragic story of the reconstruction era to be compiled. But Grant was President. Contrary to hopes, his administration in his second term was worse than in his first term. "Grantism" became an epithet standing for wholesale corruption. Then, too, when it appeared that Grant was not averse to seeking even a third term, something no President up to then presumably had ever considered, another epithet became current: "Caesarism." [7]

Grant discredited reconstruction even more than was necessary by his support of strong-handed methods, in Louisiana in particular where beneficiaries of Grant's zeal included James F. Casey, his brother-in-law.[8] Thus Grant laid himself open to the charge that he used federal troops to keep in power a Republican regime because of a personal family interest. No wonder Hayes doubted, for all his personal loyalty to Grant the man, and despite his own former status as a Radical Republican, the Grant program toward the South.

But his disillusionment with Grant as President was not confined to the Southern question. "I do not sympathize with a large share of the party leaders," he wrote in his diary in March 1875. He "hated the corruptionists" around Grant, of whom, he said, Ben Butler was the leader. He was "opposed to the course of General Grant on the third term, the civil service, and the appointment of unfit men on partisan or personal grounds." [9]

Less than three years before, in a speech during his ill-fated Congressional race, he had said, "Grant has begun the work of reconstruction in a masterful way and with marked success." [10] He had also written, though at the start of Grant's first term, "If anybody could overthrow the spoils doctrine and practice, Grant is the man. It has been thought impossible hitherto, but I hope with some confidence that he will win." [11]

5

The contrast between these comments and his 1875 diary entries was, of course, remarkable. No Democrat, let alone a Liberal Republican, could have set down a much stronger indictment of Grant's administration in 1875. Had Hayes publicly voiced his new views at this time, his retirement probably would have been permanent. The Grant administration would have marked him for liquidation. As it was, Grant leaders could only suspect, on the basis of his guarded remarks to friends, that he had begun to stray from the path of "stalwartism" but had not deserted altogether.

The contrast was a measure, of course, not only of what had happened to Grant but also to Hayes. It is worth noting here that the change in Hayes dated from 1875, not 1877 as usually would be stated.

It measured also confusion over reconstruction that years of study, "revisionist" or other, by historians North and South, probably never will dispel. Reconstruction was too much involved in emotion and in personalities, too mixed in good and bad motives, too political for clear assessment. As one historian commented, "In the welter of confused charge and countercharge . . . even an honest and merciful man might well become bewildered." [12]

Besides, the only effective way the South could have been made to accept reconstruction was through a military occupation over a long period and a ruthless purge of leading elements, after the manner of later totalitarian dictatorships. Not even Grant, nor most of the men around him, would have stood for any such course. In this view the real tragedy of reconstruction, from the standpoint of those who had wished it to succeed for honest and idealistic reasons, was that its full aims were impossible of achievement by any means consonant with American standards—official recognition of which fact it remained for Hayes to implement.

6

Reconstruction was not the complete failure or total evil it generally has been portrayed, not even for the white South.[13] Nor was the South prostrated or ruined by it, as so many accounts put it. It did better economically during and after reconstruction than before, thanks mainly to Northern capital, supposedly despised, and to carpetbagger enterprise and leadership, supposedly all wicked. It owed its public educational system to reconstruction, for one thing. Atlanta was a mere village, Birmingham nonexistent, before the war.

The fact was, of the three carpetbagger Republican regimes that still remained in the South in 1875 two had broad support from native white elements of top social status. These were the governments of South Carolina and of Florida. Even by Southern white standards these two Republican state administrations conducted reasonably honest, fair and efficient governments; their records were as good, on balance, as those of the white Democratic regimes in the "redeemed" states, if not in fact better. Except at electiontime the native whites had little to complain concerning Governor Daniel Chamberlain of South Carolina or Governor Marcellus Stearns of Florida, though both were carpetbaggers.

Clearly, at electiontime, the cries of "carpetbagger villainy" in South Carolina and Florida were palpably Democratic Party propaganda in the main, propaganda designed more to promote the cause of the party than the cause of white supremacy as such.

In Louisiana the situation was different. There the Republican regime was shamefully corrupt. But even in Louisiana more native whites were a part of the Republican organization than usually is suggested by the conventional accounts of reconstruction.

So behind the revolt on the part of most of the Southern whites against reconstruction, though the revolt was real enough, there was as much sheer partisanship as Southern principle. Reconstruction was disliked. But a major aim of many Southern leaders, who most busily, and successfully, stirred up emotional resentment against reconstruction, was the acquisition of political place and power, though these leaders talked chiefly about Southern "freedom."

Moreover, not all carpetbaggers were hated. Some, notably certain ones from Ohio, such as Judge William B. Woods of Newark, later of Georgia and Alabama (whom Hayes was to place on the U. S. Supreme Court), became more Southern than the native Bourbon colonels, while some of the native colonels engaged in more rascality of a carpetbagger nature than any of the Northern invaders.

Then, too, there was as much politics in the conventional Southern hatred for reconstruction as there was in the orthodox Republican advocacy of its virtues. Hypocrisy and falsehood were about evenly distributed, and persisted in history books long after the history was made.

7

The aims of reconstruction were logical results of the war. They were also consistent with the American idea. But with people, including politicians, being what they are, these were largely doomed to be, at least for two generations, as much a lost cause as the rebellion itself had been.

So Hayes, in cooling off on reconstruction, was in tune with American thought generally, as so often was the case with him, even when his views were romantically naïve. He was also in step with the realistic march of American history. When the march was swift toward freedom he stepped valiantly along with it—as when he had defended Rosetta, Louis and other fugitive slaves, opposed the slaveowners' designs on Kansas and Nebraska, and acted the hero in the "divine war." These services in freedom's cause could never be taken from him, though historians and others, including politicians who had never marched at all, would tend to gloss them over. But when the march slowed for consolidation of gains, he slowed also.

In effect, by doubting the "ultraism" toward the South and by opposing the main features of "Grantism," he was saying farewell to his "stalwartism." The "stalwart" label never had fitted him anyway. Returning was Hayes, the Kenyon- and Harvard-bred gentleman—in political terms the benign conciliator, the advocate of moderation, of respectability, of decency and of the practical. In short, the Websterian Whig, with modifications suited to the new times and issues.

CHAPTER XLIV

Third-term Feather

1

In the spring of 1875 a new movement by party leaders to end his retirement was the spur that caused him to put into words, though privately at this time, his indictment of Grant's administration and policies.

It was 1872 for him all over again. But this time, for the sake of the party, he was asked to stand again for governor. Governor Allen had made a good record, despite the infirmities of his years, which included hands so shaky that the legislature passed a special bill to let him use a rubber stamp for signing official documents.[1] Republican leaders were desperate for a strong vote getter to run against him. A caucus in Columbus concluded that Hayes was their man.[2] As Congressman Garfield said, "We must put forward an unexceptionable man for governor. I think we must take Hayes." [3]

"I am kept for an hour or two daily replying to letters importuning me to run for governor," Hayes told son Webb. "The Republican nomination is at my refusal. But I say 'no,' with the assent of all our household." [4]

But his "no" was really not very firm. "The independence of all political and other bother is a happiness," he wrote earlier in his diary. But the two years of his happiness had not dimmed the old urge for political distinction. Indeed, for all his protestations they had increased it. There was the fact, too, as his sister had suggested years before, that he was really not cut out to be a businessman. Nothing concrete came from his railroad projects. The rise in value of his land was still in the future. A reckoning of his two years' activity found him, despite the inheritance from Sardis, close to being land-poor and in debt. An arrangement he felt compelled to make with Oberlin College, to which Sardis had left a bequest of $5,000, told the story. Instead of making the payment, as administrator, he "borrowed" the sum from Oberlin at seven per cent.[5]

2

A return to politics began to seem good to him, even necessary to his ego—provided it were made successfully. To himself he admitted this. There was now no more self-deception. "A third term would be a distinction—a feather I would like to wear," he confessed in his diary.[6]

The only serious obstacle to his acceptance of the nomination concerned Judge Alphonso Taft of Cincinnati. Before the movement to draft Hayes was begun, it was understood that Taft would be the party's choice. Influential Republican newspapers throughout the state had been booming Taft. The largest party organization in Ohio, that of Cincinnati, was behind Taft.

Moreover, Taft was a Grant man—soon he was to be in Grant's cabinet as Secretary of War and then Attorney General—and the administration bloc in the state supported him. As a founder of the Republican Party, more important than Hayes in that respect, and a party wheel horse ever since, Taft undoubtedly had claims for support that were considerable. After Hayes's earlier declination was made public, Taft became an avowed candidate.[7]

This confronted Hayes with a delicate situation. Should he agree after all to be a candidate, this would raise the political danger of a violent split in the party ranks on the issue of "Grantism." For "Grantism" was the basis of much opposition to Taft—and of clamor for Hayes. To become involved in an open clash on this issue, Hayes saw, could create wounds that might be fatal in the election. To alienate Taft personally could have the same result.

3

So he emphasized that he would not accept a nomination obtained in opposition to Taft. "If Judge Taft and others should withdraw, and the convention generally should insist on my candidacy, I shall not refuse. This is not likely to happen," he wrote in his diary several days before the nominating convention met in Columbus. "If the friends of Taft or of other candidates still present their names, I will under no circumstances be a candidate against them. In that event, my name must be unqualifiedly withdrawn." [8]

Taft's name was presented, although Hayes, in the first ballots, led him by a comfortable margin. "Never did I witness such enthusiasm for a leader as burst forth for you," William McKinley, the delegate from Canton, told him.[9] One advantage he held over Taft resulted from his removal to Fremont. Northern Ohioans, jealous of Cincinnati dominance in party affairs, now considered Hayes one of them, though he still also had much Cincinnati support—the Hayes luck once more. However, standing by his expressed position, Hayes sent to a Taft leader a telegram: I CANNOT ALLOW MY NAME TO BE USED IN OPPOSITION TO JUDGE TAFT. HE BECAME A CANDIDATE AFTER I DECLINED. HE IS AN ABLE AND PURE MAN AND A SOUND REPUBLICAN. I WOULD NOT ACCEPT A NOMINATION OBTAINED BY A CONTEST WITH HIM.[10]

His supporters then resorted to a drastic tactic. They raised an issue against Taft which the practical leaders had hoped to soft-pedal so long as there was the chance he might be their candidate. This was the so-called Catholic issue. For some time it had been plain that Republican Party strategists, to offset the decline in appeal of the old Civil War issues, planned to make much of a charge that the Democratic Party was part of a conspiracy to destroy the public-school system and also "to take over America for the Pope."

This was the period just after the Vatican Council in Rome had proclaimed the doctrine of papal "infallibility," and Pius IX had become highly articulate against modernism and political liberalism. These positions set off, especially in England and America, a wave of renewed Protestant antagonism toward Romanism and so-called "ultramontanism," pictured, outstandingly by England's William Gladstone, as a conspiracy for world domination by Catholicism. In America there was no doubt but that Catholics were mainly in the Democratic Party.[11]

4

In Ohio the Catholic issue was considered an especially powerful one. The Democratic state legislature had passed a bill which provided that every inmate of state prisons and hospitals should be permitted to have the kind of religious instruction he desired and that "ample and equal facilities" for religious ministrations should be furnished to all.[12] Its purpose was to open the door to appointment of Catholic priests as chaplains. State chaplains up to then had been exclusively Protestant.

This Geghan Bill, so-called after its author, a Roman Catholic, was quite innocuous, certainly by later standards. But it produced excitement of surprising intensity, especially as tactless statements had been made by its author. In a letter to the Cincinnati *Enquirer*, Geghan said he expected the Democrats in the legislature to pass his bill because his church had "a prior claim" on the Democratic Party, in that "most Catholics were Democratic voters in Ohio." Unfortunately, too, the *Catholic Telegraph,* organ of Archbishop Purcell of Cincinnati, followed a similar line, saying, "The Democratic party is now on trial." [13] After the bill was passed the *Telegraph* said, "The unbroken solid vote of the Catholic citizens of Ohio will be given to the Democrats at the Fall elections."

Also Archbishop Purcell and Bishop Richard Gilmour of Cleveland had been aggressively calling for a share of public-school funds for their parochial schools. In a pastoral letter in 1873 Bishop Gilmour said: "Were Catholics alive and united on the school question; were they to demand from every man who asks their vote a pledge that he would vote for our just share of the school fund, legislatures would learn to respect the Catholic vote, and give us our just rights." [14] Such was the temper of the times that utterances like these were considered by Protestants as treasonous.

So conspicuous did this issue become, with the Republicans certain of its potency as a vote getter, that President Grant, in his 1875 annual message to Congress, urged that the federal Constitution be amended to prohibit states or municipalities to use any funds for religious schools.[15] Such an amendment, designed to be the Sixteenth, was in fact introduced in the House of Representatives by the Republican floor leader and former Speaker, James G. Blaine, who hoped to be the Republican candidate for President in 1876.

This proposal lost, but all Republicans present in both houses voted for it, while every Democrat present voted against it, leaving no doubt as to how the parties stood on the issue. Nor was there any doubt that the Republicans intended to use this issue in the coming elections. "You are to be slaughtered [on it] and with you the Democratic party of Ohio," Governor Allen was told.[16]

5

Unfortunately for Judge Taft, there was in his record an episode which, while it won for him, a Unitarian, a reputation for tolerance on religious questions, was deemed fatal to his ambition to be the candidate for governor in 1875, if brought up against him. This was an 1870 decision by him in a lawsuit involving the use of the Bible in the public schools of Cincinnati. Catholics had persuaded the City Board of Education to stop the use of the King James Bible. The matter was fought out before a three-man court, the lawsuit creating so much heat

that Stanley Matthews felt impelled to resign as elder of his Presbyterian church because he had appeared as attorney for the school board.
The Catholics lost the case, but Taft wrote an opinion upholding the
right of the school board to ban the Bible. His opinion also contained
some statements indicating that he sympathized with, if he did not
support, Catholic complaints that they were taxed to support the public schools.[17]

In the hope of countering use of this against him Taft sent a letter
to Charles Foster of Fostoria, Congressman from Hayes's home district.
In it Taft said he opposed any division of the public-school funds. But
when Foster, later a governor of Ohio and also Secretary of the Treasury under President Harrison, read this letter to the convention it produced a result contrary to what Taft expected, causing comment later
that Foster, who had solicited the letter, had intended this.[18] As a result
of bringing this issue out in the open "apprehension of the delegates was
aroused." [19] In the next balloting the vote stood: Hayes, 396, Taft 151.

Charles P. Taft, son of the judge, then decided that his father could
not win, withdrew his father's name and moved the nomination of
Hayes by acclamation, which was given. In Fremont Hayes took this
to mean that his requirement had been met, and he accepted the
nomination.[20]

6

In the campaign Hayes did not hesitate to use the Catholic issue.
He would have been a peculiar Republican then had he refrained
from using it.[21] Indeed, he pressed it immediately. "I think the interesting point is to rebuke the Democracy by a defeat for subserviency
to Roman Catholic demands." [22] In this he was encouraged by such
other leaders as Garfield. "It is evident," said Garfield, "that the
Catholic Church is moving along the whole line of its front against
modern civilization and our fight in Ohio is only a small portion of
the battlefield." [23]

Before the campaign was over, however, another issue became even
more important, certainly with respect to Hayes's future. This was
the monetary question, "the great greenback theory," which Hayes
thought had been buried when he defeated Pendleton for governor.[24]
For Allen emerged as a vigorous exponent of financial policies more
inflationary than the Ohio idea of Pendleton's. He stood not only
basically against "resumption"—that is, placing the currency on a spe-

cie basis—but also for the issuance of even more paper money not necessarily redeemable in coin.

In stressing this issue, which had nothing to do with state affairs but much to do with the depression still on, Governor Allen, like Pendleton in 1869, quite obviously was making a bid for the Presidency in 1876. Indeed, because of his "soft-money" stand he was already being boomed for the Presidential nomination by John R. McLean, owner of the Cincinnati *Enquirer*.[25]

7

As in 1869, Hayes championed "hard money," this time even more vigorously. Soon the conviction was held generally that the Ohio campaign really involved high national policy. If Hayes now won, the Republican Party nationally might become a "sound-money" party, though Grant had come close to embracing Allen's "rag-baby" proposal.[26] Perhaps the Democratic Party also would stand for sound money. If Allen won, the opposite result would follow. So political analysts reasoned.

Toward its end the campaign seemed like a Presidential election, with leaders of national repute from outside the state coming to take sides on the monetary issue mainly. Especially prominent was Carl Schurz, who took the occasion to make an uneasy peace with the regular Republicans for his role as leader of the Liberal Republican revolt. Certain Democrats, who stood against inflation, assisted Hayes, making contributions to the Republican campaign organization. According to some accounts, these included, oddly enough, even Governor Tilden of New York.[27]

Throughout the canvass Hayes held to two main themes in his own speeches: "Our motto is honest money for all and free schools for all. There should be no inflation which will destroy the one, and no sectarian interference which will destroy the other."[28] He won, though the result was close: Hayes, 297,817; Allen, 292,273.

Even so close a victory had far-reaching results. Schurz called it "that famous campaign for 'sound money,'" which caused key Republicans generally to cease "dangerous" wavering on the monetary question, with sound money becoming, almost, a tenet of official Republican doctrine.[29] Sectarian control of the public schools emerged from local, subterranean discussion into a major national issue.

As for Hayes, the victory determined that he would be considered with the greatest seriousness as a Presidential possibility. It was not lost on the "kingmakers" that in his three campaigns for governor he had defeated, one after another, three men groomed as Democratic candidates for President. Also, he had demonstrated that he could unite Grant and anti-Grant elements, and bring back into the party fold the former Liberal Republicans, notably Schurz.

Moreover, reform was in the air. Even James G. Blaine professed to be for reform. If the party, in 1876, intended to present a man for President who met the requirements of reform, it could not overlook Hayes, "a proved winner." [30]

"If victorious, I am likely to be pushed for the Republican nomination for President," he himself, while waiting for the returns at Spiegel Grove, wrote in his diary.[31] Perhaps he recalled then a prediction that one of his mother's brothers had made about him to his sister in 1839. "That boy will make a *tall* man, a very *tall* man in every sense of the word." [32] It was so. In 1875 he was plainly one of the "tallest" men on the American scene.

CHAPTER XLV

THE "PASSIVE" RUNNER

1

In the following June 1876, when he was approaching fifty-four, prophecy that the victory over Allen would project him prominently into the Presidential sweepstakes came true. It was the fashion then, as later, to adopt the line that this was altogether accidental and unexpected. Almost invariably, at times rather contemptuously, he was described as a dark horse. The implication was that he was not seriously considered by the party leaders for the great political prize until the last moment, that his name came up as a last resort and only to break a deadlock not foreseen.

But a review of the true political situation affirms that the leading avowed candidates for the Republican Presidential nomination that year could not have won the prize. Months before the convention it was apparent that Hayes was a logical nominee.

Moreover, destiny seemingly was at work for him once more, as if in support of the idea that one with his heritage—encompassing so much of the history of the nation—should naturally be in line for the office that symbolized that nation. This was the centennial year of America as an independent nation. It was also the bicentennial of the heroic role of his Russell ancestors in saving, in 1676, the original Connecticut River Valley settlements from destruction by the Indians. It was fitting that in 1876 the Russell-Austin-Birchard-Smith-Hayes clan should come into its own.

2

That he assisted destiny was undeniable. He desired the nomination, and sought it. In 1876 he showed little of the indecisiveness that had marked him during his period of retirement from politics. Forgotten was the declaration, "No more ambition." To McKinley he later wrote, "Men in political life must be ambitious." [1]

In earlier years he had felt it necessary to cover up this fact from himself, after the mode of copybook maxims. Now he faced it. After it became clear that the Ohio Republicans, in a state convention, would officially proclaim him as Ohio's choice for President—with no attempt by him to hinder the action—he wrote:

I feel less diffidence in thinking of this subject than, perhaps, I ought. It seems to me that good purposes and the judgment, experience, and firmness I possess, would enable me to execute the duties of the office well. I do not feel the least fear that I should fail. This all looks egotistical, but it is sincere.[2]

Obviously these were the words of a man who was receptive to the idea of running for President—and more than receptive. Such was the case despite later assertions by him in his diary that he had "discountenanced all efforts at organization or management in my interest," and that he had "discouraged rather than encouraged 'the Hayes movement.' "[3] Actually he had no intention of calling off "the Hayes movement."

Son Webb, now out of college and functioning as a secretary to his father, supplied some evidence of Hayes's true feelings in a letter to his brother Birch, then still in law school. He expected to get permission for a trip to the East, Webb wrote, because "His Excellency is *slightly* talked of as a candidate for President and consequently is . . . *quite amiable.*"[4]

3

In 1875, on the day after Hayes had been elected governor for the third time, Manning Force, then a judge in Cincinnati, sent him an interesting letter.

When I wrote last, I said Judge Taft would not be nominated and that you would be nominated . . . and now for the after fruits. It is natural that you should now be spoken of for the presidency. . . . In this matter, you, of course, must be passive. The rule is almost without exception that one who seeks the presidency never gets it. Morton, Conkling, Blaine, who might as a means of defeating each other in the end unite on you, would fight against you, if you should become too prominent before the convention meets.[5]

Hayes liked Force's word "passive" to describe his course. To William Henry Smith, already using his influence in Chicago as general manager of the Western Associated Press to boost him for President, he wrote: "It seems to me so entirely the thing on all accounts to be

passive that I am under no temptation to meddle." [6] And to Guy
Bryan again: "In any event, I must be passive." [7]

Passive he was—outwardly. But he answered every letter bearing on
his chances with great care, invariably coupling his disavowal of any
desire for the nomination with statements that kept the pot boiling in
his favor.

4

The avowed candidates were those mentioned by Force: Blaine of
Maine, Morton of Indiana, Conkling of New York. There was also
one other, Benjamin H. Bristow of Kentucky. Blaine was easily foremost. Bristow was next. As Secretary of the Treasury in Grant's cabinet, he was then prosecuting the notorious whisky-tax frauds. This
skyrocketed him to prominence as a reformer. He was especially
the favorite of most of the leaders of the old Liberal Republican
movement.

Conkling, supposedly, was Grant's choice and, aside from this, a
strong factor in his own right as favorite son of New York, the state
with the largest number of delegates and electoral votes.[8] Morton was
the strongest among the Southern delegations. Because of the vigor
and intelligence with which he consistently defended in the Senate
all reconstruction measures, this Hoosier was then, if anybody was, the
"Mr. Republican" of orthodox party views on the Southern question.

However, the supposed strong points of the other leading contenders,
each personally more brilliant, more glamorous, than Hayes, proved to
be also their weaknesses.

Conkling's intimacy with Grant, and his open, even defiant advocacy of spoils, were enough to ruin him with the former Liberal
Republicans, whose support was deemed essential to one more Republican victory. One certain way to provoke another Liberal split was to
nominate Conkling.

Morton's uncompromising support of reconstruction worked against
him because of fear that his nomination would assure a solid Democratic
South. Moreover, his special appeal to the West, as an inflationist, made
him *persona non grata* in the extreme to the sound-money champions.
Against Morton, too, was the fact that his legs were paralyzed.

As for Blaine, he was subject from the start to having all the others
unite against him because he was in the lead. Besides, Blaine was
vulnerable on the score of alleged scandalous financial transactions

while he was Speaker of the House—a blot on his record that would be made public, with Hayes supporters helping, in due time.

Bristow's weakness was obvious. The plaudits of reformers had won him the enmity, secret if not open, of the Grant administration. Many of the convention delegates were bound to be Grant appointees. If he were nominated, Grant might well take the stump against him.[9]

Yet, next to Hayes, Bristow came the closest to being considered in early reckonings as a winner. None other than Sardis Birchard's old friend, "Mott" Waite of Toledo, then Chief Justice of the United States, in a special position to get accurate soundings, wrote in November 1875: "No human being can now give even an intelligent guess as to who will be the man. Hayes is kindly spoken of by all. If I should indulge in a guess, it would be that he and Bristow just now are on the upper rounds of the ladder." [10] The Chief Justice, incidentally, was also in a position to put in good words in the proper places for Birchard's nephew, and did—as did another influential friend of Sardis', Clark Waggoner, editor of the Toledo *Blade*.

In the spring of 1876 Hayes himself made statements indicating that he favored Bristow—if the prize were not to be his. "His war on the whiskey thieves gives him prestige as the representative of reform. I am not sure but he would be the best candidate we could nominate. I am sure I prefer him to any other man," he wrote in his diary.[11]

That March he received a letter from an almost-forgotten fellow student at Isaac Webb's—"Fat Jack of the Bone House," Dr. Thomas D. Hogg of Raleigh, North Carolina—who suggested Chief Justice Waite as a candidate. After telling Dr. Hogg that Waite had taken himself out of the field with the declaration that no one holding the position of Chief Justice should be considered for President, Hayes said: "Bristow is a good man, and growing in public favor. Why not take him?" [12]

5

So flat a declaration for Bristow suggested that Hayes meant his disavowals of his own candidacy. But by getting on record as a supporter of Bristow he was actually boosting his own chances. His friend and fellow Literary Club member Halstead, then a Bristow supporter, saw this. "General Hayes was wise enough to see that the chances were very much against the nomination of Bristow, but that the Bristow movement was a diversion from Blaine and might easily be for the

Governor of Ohio. He treated my antagonism with hilarity, saying I could not possibly be doing as much for him if I was supporting him directly; and so it turned out." [13]

The fact was that of all those considered by the "kingmakers," Hayes not only was the one man who could command the support of the natural Bristow supporters, but also the one man who could expect support from the followers of Blaine, Conkling and Morton as well. John M. Harlan, Bristow's campaign manager and law partner, wrote to Bristow: "Blaine cannot be nominated—nor can Conkling—nor can Morton. I am sure that neither of them could be elected. The choice will be between yourself . . . and Hayes." [14]

Even Conkling, who hated Blaine (as later he came to hate Hayes), already was on record as saying that if he did not win the nomination, New York would be for Hayes.[15] Despite Hayes's new lukewarmness on reconstruction, Morton was friendly, this dating from Hayes's aid in the adoption of the Fifteenth Amendment. Blaine supporters who professed to be for reform could find no flaw in Hayes's record in that respect.

6

Then, too, the highest political strategists of the party were convinced that the party should select a Western man, that winning the West was essential. Thanks to Sophia's decision back in the 1820s to remain in Ohio after the death of Ruddy Hayes, Hayes fitted that bill. The politicians wanted also a man deemed certain to carry doubtful Ohio, as Hayes had done against Thurman, Pendleton and Allen, three top Democrats.

Also, to please the highest financial interests, they wanted a man unquestionably sound on the monetary question. They understood the need for a candidate not identified with the Grant regime, yet not so antagonistic to Grant as to offend the administration. They wanted a man whose character and record would appeal to the reformers without, however, being so objectionable to "stalwarts" as to cause them to sulk or deal with the Democracy.[16]

None of the "big four" met these requirements so completely as Hayes. Nor did any of the other favorite sons, such as former Governor Marshall Jewell of Connecticut and Governor John F. Hartranft of Pennsylvania. Especially was Hartranft's hope deemed a lost cause. He had pardoned Charles T. Yerkes, the later Chicago traction

baron, after Yerkes had been imprisoned in connection with a Philadelphia financial scandal, with charges of "irregularity" resulting
against Hartranft.[17]

On May 13, 1876, a month before the convention, Chief Justice
Waite wrote another letter on the political outlook.

Hayes's chances are now decidedly the best of any in the field, I
think. I have information that it is quite possible that New York will
be for him, if it is compelled to leave Conkling. I think you may assume, also, a strong possibility that New York and Pennsylvania will
go together. I saw at Philadelphia, the Governor of North Carolina,
who told me that Hayes stood well there. He is behaving himself with
his usual discretion, and the most scrutinizing detective will not be
able to find a "hole in his skimmer." [18]

7

In January 1876 Senator Sherman, who might have sought the
nomination himself, went into action for Hayes. He had widely published a long letter in which he called on all Ohio Republicans to rally
behind "their governor" and said, ". . . considering all things, I
believe the nomination of Governor Hayes would give us the more
strength, taking the whole country at large, than any other man." [19]

In itself this was a potent stimulant to the Hayes movement. It was
recognized as such by Blaine, who bitterly resented it as a blow at
him.[20] For Sherman's open support gave to the movement the practical standing that it had lacked. Then, too, the Senator went to work
to line up support for Hayes, not only in Ohio, but in the nation and
among the higher echelon "kingmakers" who counted most, not only
politicians but also financiers who influenced politicians, particularly
in the East.

Thus did Hayes collect his handsome dividend for having declined
to run for Senator against Sherman in 1872. As he later observed:
"I declined the bird in hand and it gave me the higher place." [21]

Sherman's endorsement was coupled with publication of approval
from a related source even more influential in certain quarters, among
Union war veterans especially. This was from the Senator's brother,
General William Tecumseh Sherman, Commander of the Army. As
far back as 1871 General Sherman, impressed by a speech Hayes had
made at a soldier's gathering, had said that the country needed for
President a man "so level-headed." [22]

Then another war hero, General Phil Sheridan, came out for Hayes, endorsing Senator Sherman's letter.[23] At the same time "Private" J. M. Dalzell, an Ohioan, the most active leader of the largest war veterans' organization, the Grand Army of the Republic, became indefatigably energetic in promoting Hayes among the ex-soldiers.[24]

8

Among intellectuals and key moulders of public opinion, especially in the East, an attractive and influential literary figure also was busily spreading the word that Hayes was no ordinary politician but an educated man of exceptional integrity, whose former "stalwartism" should not be held against him, that he was the opposite of Grant. This was William Dean Howells, editor and novelist, first biographer of Abraham Lincoln, who, from his marriage to Hayes's cousin, Elinor Mead, had come to know Hayes well, developing a deep admiration for him. "The man fascinates me!" Howells, while writing a campaign biography of Hayes, exclaimed to Charles Dudley Warner, coauthor with Mark Twain of The Gilded Age.[25] Mark Twain, Bret Harte, Joaquin Miller, among others, were soon boosting Hayes.

Other relatives by blood or marriage, some in potent positions, such as editors of newspapers all over the land, also began promoting a Hayes movement. Here in itself was a group not to be ignored. By then the clan was so large it could almost be concluded that just the Smiths, Birchards, Austins, Noyeses, Russells, Hayeses and all the rest constituted a balance of political power in the land, if joined together behind their kinsman, as they apparently were. So, while Hayes himself seemed occupied only with being governor and prudently maintained the demeanor of the passive onlooker, the Hayes pot boiled in crucial areas.

He was not only in the Presidential running. He was running hard—and fast.

CHAPTER XLVI

Secret Maneuvering

1

In the meantime there was brewing, undercover at first, a development which was to prove more important for Hayes than any other single prenomination occurrence. At its very center, operating with his usual political skill and loyalty, was Hayes's friend, William Henry Smith. Certain dealings of James G. Blaine formed the specific subject matter.

Early in April 1876 a newspaper published an article asserting that Senator-elect Blaine had been party to peculiar financial dealings with various railroads, including the Union Pacific. The story was that Blaine had owned bonds of the Little Rock & Fort Smith Railroad with a face value of $75,000, that this road had gone into bankruptcy, yet the Union Pacific had taken the practically worthless bonds off Blaine's hands, advancing him $64,000 for them. The implications, of course, were plain. As Speaker of the House at the time, Blaine was in a position to further legislative interests of the Union Pacific, still under the shadow of the Crédit Mobilier scandal.

Although, as it later developed, the newspaper published this article on the basis of information given to it by a director of the Union Pacific, one appointed by the government, it did not back up its story with factual material. This left the matter in the form of rumors and insinuations. Blaine took the floor of the House with a speech that branded the story as false. Even political enemies felt that he had vindicated himself. His manliness and boldness seemed to have increased, rather than lowered, his stature as candidate for President.

However, by the time Blaine appeared to have cleared himself completely Hayes's friend Smith in Chicago had learned of a collection of letters which seemingly corroborated the newspaper story. These later were styled the "Mulligan letters," so-called because they were held by one James Mulligan, who had been a partner in a Boston brokerage house in which Blaine was a silent partner. The letters were written by and to Blaine and had been taken from the firm's files by Mulligan.

About the same time General H. V. Boynton, Washington correspondent for the Cincinnati *Commercial*, also had caught wind of the

Mulligan letters and was working on the story. Boynton naturally informed his employers, Richard "The Deacon" Smith, publisher, and Editor Murat Halstead.

In the meantime William Henry Smith had advised Joseph Medill, editor of the Chicago *Tribune,* of his information, revealing that his personal source was W. R. Holloway of Indianapolis, brother-in-law and political associate of Senator Morton. As men in control of the Western Associated Press, the two Smiths, Halstead and Medill were, at least temporarily, in a position to determine whether a new and more powerful case should be published against Blaine. They held a number of conferences and exchanged many letters before making a decision.

2

They were all Republicans. If they accomplished the ruin of Blaine, as it appeared to them they could with the Mulligan letters, would they not at the same time ruin the party's chances for victory in the coming election? This was one problem. Another concerned Blaine's possible reaction. As noted, the Cincinnati *Commercial* was supporting Bristow for President, although "Deacon" Smith, and Halstead especially, were accounted personal friends of Hayes.[1] Medill's *Tribune* also was a Bristow supporter, although, as William Henry Smith later told Hayes as part of the "inside history" of the 1876 campaign, Medill was party to a secret arrangement to try to get the nomination for Elihu Washburne of Illinois, close friend of Grant and then U. S. minister to France.[2]

The Bristow supporters in this group wanted the story broken on the theory that this would help their candidate, but they did not wish Blaine to be able to put the blame on Bristow. Holloway had kept the Mulligan story out of the Indianapolis papers because he did not wish Blaine to blame Morton. On the other hand, Boynton, an intimate of Bristow's, was desirous of having Blaine believe Morton responsible. Such were some of the maneuverings within the maneuverings.

3

The story was broken toward the end of May 1876, the convention a month away. To throw Blaine off the track as to how the letters became public, the first publication was in Charles A. Dana's New York

Sun. Mulligan was summoned by a Congressional investigating committee, and Blaine faced his greatest political crisis. Once more, nine days before the opening of the Republican national convention, Blaine took the floor of the House. By an emotional appeal in which he spoke of the possibility of suicide unless he was able to clear himself, he had persuaded Mulligan to let him have the letters. Then he announced that he himself would read them aloud to prove that he was innocent of wrongdoing.

"I am not afraid to show them. Thank God Almighty I am not ashamed to show them!" he said, displaying to his colleagues in the House the package that Mulligan had lent to him. "With a sense of outrage which I think any man in my position would feel, I invite the confidence of 44,000,000 of my countrymen while I read those letters from this desk."

Later it developed that Blaine did not read in full all the letters. But this new audacity, together with shrewd handling of himself at a House investigating committee hearing, won for him so much applause that his supporters believed, or professed to believe, that his chances to win the nomination had not been injured. "He has not been greatly damaged by the investigations," even Hayes said,[3] and this seemed true.

But there can be no doubt that the Mulligan letters episode did injure Blaine. Moreover, if nothing else, it accentuated the hostility of Blaine men toward Bristow, for they did blame Bristow and went to the convention in a frame of mind determined that, if Blaine did not gain the nomination, neither should Bristow. So bitter was the feeling that when Bristow went to pay a call of respect on Blaine, who had collapsed from illness, Mrs. Blaine ordered him from the house.[4] Hayes was to be the beneficiary.

Few persons knew that William Henry Smith, working for Hayes, had played an important, perhaps crucial role in Hayes's behalf in this matter. Perhaps not even Hayes knew, for on April 23, 1876, he had written to Smith that he was "glad that no man who is taking an interest in the Hayes movement has had a hand" in developing the Blaine scandal. Smith did not tell him of the role he had played—at least not then.[5]

4

Almost five weeks before the convention, even before the Mulligan letters came to light,' Dana's New York *Sun* carried a significant editorial. It was not intended especially to boost Hayes. On the contrary, it rather depreciated him, for the *Sun* was not for him. But it reflected inside political opinion.

All signs continue to point to the nomination of Governor Hayes as the Republican candidate for President. . . . He will be nominated, if such be his fate, as Lincoln was nominated in 1860. . . . He is that kind of a neutral man who is always taken when the powerful chiefs can only succeed in foiling each other. . . . He is a man of talent; he is a gentleman; he is rich and independent; he served with credit as a soldier in the war, and his record as Governor of Ohio is without flaw or spot; he would make a very fair President for ordinary times. Those who intend to vote the Republican ticket under any circumstances may about as well make up their minds that Rutherford B. Hayes is the man who will receive their suffrages.[6]

Of course, there still was work to be done. Certain leaders still had to be convinced, men like Governor S. J. Kirkwood of Iowa, a Blaine man, who wrote with some perturbation to Iowa's Senator William D. Allison:

Will Blaine come out of the fire unscorched? . . . If Blaine shall turn out to be unavailable, I can't see any hope except in Bristow and some of our folks say he can't be relied upon as a Republican. . . . We *must* have a clean handed man. No charge of personal crookedness has been made against Morton or Conkling, but they are generally set down as "administration men." Hayes of Ohio would do, but nobody out of Ohio knows anything about him and we want a man with more than a state reputation.[7]

But two days before the convention was to meet William Henry Smith, fortified by confidential reports from all over the nation, party to high-echelon thinking, including that of important contributors of campaign funds, sure of Blaine's and Bristow's final fate because of the Mulligan letters, sent Hayes a telegram: AT THIS HOUR I CAN SAFELY PREDICT THAT OHIO WILL WIN.[8]

CHAPTER XLVII

"Hour of Triumph"

1

ONLY the public was to be surprised. The convention, which opened June 14, 1876, was really a kind of stage play, if not puppet show, full of suspense for the audience and even excitement for players not fully acquainted with the plot. But the plot was all set down and fixed, as William Henry Smith knew.

Even the location was a part of the working of destiny for Hayes. For Cincinnati's Exposition Hall was the scene. Bristow and Morton men had insisted on Cincinnati, as it was close to their home states of Kentucky and Indiana and therefore assured that many of their claquers would be present.[1] But this worked most in Hayes's favor.

In no other city of America would there be so many people who knew Hayes, who favored Hayes, who would conduct themselves so as to impress the delegates that Hayes was the people's choice. Hayes himself remained in Columbus, apparently attending to his duties as governor as usual. "I have kept cool and unconcerned to a degree that surprises me," he wrote in his diary.[2]

If so, this was not true of his supporters, who succeeded in making their supposedly "second-choice" candidate first in all the convention noise. Hayes buttons, Hayes placards, Hayes broadsides, Hayes badges were everywhere.

2

The fact was, he was not so cool and unconcerned as he professed to be—nor so inactive. He made certain that he was well represented at the convention. He spent hours with his old Lower Sandusky law partner, now known as General Buckland, a delegate from the Fremont district, so he could give to Buckland his innermost views. He made doubly sure that Senator Sherman would be at the convention to play the role of Warwick.

To Sherman, a month before, he had sent an interesting note.

It would specially gratify me if you would attend the Cincinnati convention. I do not mean to depart from the position I have taken—

THE PRESIDENT AND HIS CHILDREN

(Top, left) Webb C. Hayes I, the President, and Birchard Austin Hayes; (right) Scott Hayes and Fanny Hayes; (below) Rutherford Platt Hayes

CABINET MEETING IN 1877

Hayes at left, and (clockwise) Secretary of the Treasury John Sherman, Secretary of the Navy Richard
W. Thompson, Attorney General Charles Devens, Secretary of the Interior Carl Schurz, Postmaster General
David M. Key, Secretary of War George W. McCrary and Secretary of State William Marcy Evarts

to remain perfectly passive on the nomination. But it is fair to assume that the time may come when I ought to be withdrawn. To be able to act on this and other possible questions, it is important for me that I have friends of experience and sound judgment on the ground, by whom I can be advised of the exact condition of things and of the proper course to be taken.[3]

This was a communication to be read for what it said and did not say. There was always the danger that some Hayes delegates might be tempted to make arrangements for their own benefit and urge a switch to another candidate on the rationalization that Hayes could not win, but before this was a fact. Sherman would know how to deal with such possibilities.

There was the question of the Vice-Presidency. To head off Hayes, and to win his support, all of the other candidates had indicated they would like him as a running mate. A vaudeville troop from New York scored a hit with a song:

> "Conkling and Hayes
> Is the ticket that pays." [4]

A boom was getting under way, supposedly even with President Grant's support, to make Hamilton Fish, Grant's Secretary of State, the nominee for President. *Harper's Weekly*, backing the idea with a full-page Thomas Nast cartoon, suggested Hayes as an ideal running mate with Fish.[5] If he could not get the first place, Hayes was receptive to the Vice-Presidency, except in the case of Blaine. But an acceptance of second place could be made too soon—and cost him the first place, in case the set "plot" was suddenly changed. A man of Sherman's political astuteness was needed to help assess the real situation for him.

3

Hayes was not at all passive with regard to being second man on a Blaine ticket. He did not desire to be associated with scandal—nor risk apparently certain defeat. When Blaine fell ill he wrote him: "My eyes are almost blinded with tears as I write. . . . This affects me as did the death of Lincoln." [6]

But to Buckland two days later, on the day the convention assembled, he wrote of Blaine in a different vein:

The indications, as I now read them, point to the nomination of Blaine on the first or some early ballot. My sympathies have been very greatly excited by his recent misfortune, and by his pluck in the fearful contest he has gone through. But I feel that his nomination would be fatal to the cause. I do not see how we can get through in Ohio with him at the head of our ticket. It is proposed to put me in second place. . . . I have the greatest aversion to being a candidate on the ticket with a man whose record as an upright public man is to be in question—to be defended from the beginning to the end. . . . All this you fully understand. I therefore have sent you a letter directed to the chairman of the delegation, Governor Noyes, to be delivered to him in the event of the nomination of Blaine, authorizing and requesting him to withdraw my name, if it is proposed, in connection with the Vice-Presidency. Of course, I do not wish to injure Blaine by making any personal allusion to him. . . .

P. S. Make no allusion to this note and what is said of Blaine, even to Noyes, or to any other intimate friend.[7]

There was Hayes, the full-blown politician, whom other politicians, naïvely, would consider—"naïve."

4

It was part of the stage play—and also a reflection of the political morals of this Gilded Age—that, despite the never fully explained charges against him, Blaine should seem at the beginning the winner. In large part this was due to the famous "plumed-knight" nominating speech made for him by Colonel Robert G. Ingersoll of Illinois, then, perhaps, the nation's foremost orator. As one writer commented, in Blaine's behalf Ingersoll made "a virtue of vice."

As a matter of fact, the dazzling Ingersoll had no real interest in Blaine, as he later confessed. His main desire was to defeat Bristow; his real personal choice was Morton.[8] But in the speech Ingersoll had in fact contrived to have the charges of scandal against Blaine seem to be in his favor. "Like an armed warrior, like a plumed knight, James G. Blaine marched down the halls of the American Congress and threw his shining lance full and fair against the brazen forehead of the defamers of his country and maligners of his honor." [9] The convention hall went wild. Blaine's supporters insisted afterward that if the balloting could have been started that same evening, Blaine would have won.

But the real leaders of the convention had remained calm. They had determined beforehand against Blaine for the very practical reason of "unavailability," and the word was given that the balloting be postponed until the next day.[10] That meant that Blaine was not to be the candidate, that Hayes would be. Just before this the New York *Times* had quoted "a distinguished gentleman": "If Blaine is nominated, let us find some handy potter's field to bury the Republican party with such honors as we can." And in the same issue, this headline: HAYES CHANCES IMPROVING.[11]

5

What the dominant party leaders kept firmly in mind was the danger of another split in the party, like the Liberal Republican revolt of 1872, if Blaine were nominated. This danger was real. In May outstanding leaders of the dormant Liberal Republican movement, including Schurz and William Cullen Bryant, editor of the New York *Post*, had met in New York to put the party on notice. They would again bolt unless a candidate was chosen "whose very name is . . . conclusive evidence of the most uncompromising determination of the American people to make this a pure government once more."

It was understood—some members of the gathering made it explicit —that this statement meant Bristow. But with Bristow's nomination obviously impossible in view of Blaine and Grant opposition, the statement logically meant Hayes, who also possessed the kind of mind and character the independents considered were required to keep the party intact.[12]

6

From his "unofficial secretary," his son Webb, full of a nineteen-year-oldster's enthusiasm, Hayes received the most dependable reports of what was happening in Cincinnati. Two days before the convention opened Webb dispatched:

Dear Father:

. . . At a meeting this p.m., all the [Ohio] delegates were enthusiastic for you, except Mr. Carhart of Medina in the 14th Cong. Dist., who read a little speech in favor of Bristow. But he is all right and only wanted to state his position provided Hayes was out. . . . Chas. Nordhoff was there & read a dispatch from some one in Washington saying if Blaine doesn't die, he will lose his mind or his eyesight. In the hotels, however, dispatches are posted to Hon. E. Hale saying [Blaine] is much better and will be all right in a few days. Hum-hum.

Nordhoff & others are much afraid of Conkling. Greatest good feeling prevails towards you on all sides. If you are not nom. for Pres., you will surely be for V.P. The Ohio men are jubilant and willing to sleep with any of the other delegates. All friends—no enemies. . . . Bristow is petering out rapidly. . . . Penna. say they'll go for you next to Hartranft. . . .

Webb wrote after the first session:

6:30 P.M.

Dear Father:

The Blaine men are confident and working hard, but still it is not certain that B. will be nominated. Conkling stock is declining. . . . If Blaine is nominated, you are sure to be the candidate for V.P., *if you do not decline.* I write this to inform you of the above fact so that you may decide what to do. If Blaine is not nominated by the 4th ballot your nomination is considered to be certain. A hard fight is now going on for & against Blaine. A drunken Bristow man expresses himself thus: "Why, I'll vote for Blaine before I will vote for a Democrat, but I hate like hell to vote for a man whose shirt tail is covered with s——. Vulgar but expressive. . . . Noyes made a strong, good speech for you.

7

Blaine started the balloting with what appeared to be an unbeatable lead. The result of the first ballot was:

Blaine, 285
Morton, 125
Bristow, 113
Conkling, 99
Hayes, 61
Hartranft, 58
Jewell, 11

But the night before this Hayes received from Webb a telegram that helped him to continue calm: GOVERNOR NOYES INSTRUCTS ME TO SAY THAT THE COMBINATIONS ARE VERY FAVORABLE.

The fourth ballot, as Webb had learned, was crucial. Blaine still was leader, with 292 votes. But 378 were needed to win. On the fifth ballot the dominant leaders began showing their hand. Ostensibly pledged to Blaine, the big Michigan delegation switched its twenty-two votes to Hayes. This meant that former Senator Zachariah Chandler, then Secretary of the Interior in Grant's cabinet, was for Hayes —and Chandler represented the inner circle of the party leadership. This was the signal.

On the sixth ballot, though Blaine received 308 votes and Hayes only 113, Indiana withdrew Morton's name in favor of Hayes. Thus another party chieftain—Senator Morton—was behind Hayes. Thus also did Morton compensate Hayes for his aid in getting the Fifteenth Amendment ratified.

Bristow's name was withdrawn by his partner, John Harlan, who read a telegram, prepared beforehand by Bristow, releasing his delegation in favor of Hayes. Later Bristow complained that this was done too soon. But Harlan insisted that he was only conforming to the inevitable, as indeed he was.[13]

Promptly New York and Pennsylvania joined the Hayes movement. The leaders had acted. With 384 votes Hayes won the big prize on the seventh ballot. For Vice-President the convention chose—for geographical reasons—Congressman William A. Wheeler of New York. Precisely six months before the knowing William Henry Smith had made a prediction. "This ticket would do it: Hayes and Wheeler." [14] And so it had come to pass.

8

So, too, the stage play had ended as directed in the script—an "hour of triumph" for Hayes, as Smith wrote him. "Private" Dalzell of the Grand Army of the Republic cried: "God is Mighty—Almighty —Give Him all the praise!"

Thoughts akin to these ran through Hayes's mind also. For he was still Sophia's son, and so naturally wrote in his diary just before the news came: "I shall try to do in all things more than ever before, if nominated, precisely the thing that is right, to be natural, discreet, wise, moderate, and as firm in the right as it is possible for me to be." [15]

After the nomination his "deepest emotions," he wrote, followed receipt of a message of congratulation from Blaine. "It for a few moments quite unmanned me." He, the once lonely little Rud Hayes, the "feeble, fatherless child," awed by what he had been told of his father and the brother Lorenzo, had surpassed the biggest figure in American politics, as nearly everyone reckoned such things.

If only his mother had lived for this moment, but more especially Fanny, and Sardis! One of Sardis' friends sent a message expressing precisely that thought. Again, Hayes was "unmanned," and tears blurred the blue eyes.[16] But happily he had had the foresight to send for Billy Rogers to be with him, and even more to the point for easing anxiety in the "hour of triumph," he had Lucy, who then symbolized all the others.

A committee of dignitaries arrived at his office in the Statehouse in Columbus to give him the official notification. He ordered that they wait. First, he had to send for Lucy. The ceremony was delayed until she stood at his side, beaming with pride.[17] "Rutherford B. Hayes, President of the United States" . . . if . . . if . . .

BOOK EIGHT

The Great Lawsuit

CHAPTER XLVIII

"Too Good A Man"

1

Up at Delaware Sam Rheem was still alive. A wrinkled old man now in 1876, the boarder in Hayes's childhood home remembered having sized up the widow Sophia's newborn baby back in 1822, remarking that maybe "it would amount to something yet." But in 1876, a more or less retired contractor rather than a wage-earning bricklayer, Sam was not happy over Hayes's nomination for the Presidency, for a reason that Sophia at least would have understood. He shocked everyone by saying that he wouldn't vote for Sophia's son. "Rutherford is too good a man," he said. "They will murder him. I won't vote his life away." [1]

Sam Rheem, to be sure, was in the minority among Hayes's friends and associates, just as he had been in acting as "conductor" in Delaware for the Underground Railroad. In the minority among them too was Guy Bryan in Texas. Guy was "glad" that Hayes was nominated so that he "might be distinguished." He told other Southerners that Hayes was "the best man *in his party* . . . patriotic, chivalrous, noble & good." But while true to "our friendship, till the heart stands still," as he had pledged at Kenyon to be, Guy said he also had to be "true to my section." This meant he had to vote for the Democratic nominee. [2] However, most of Hayes's many friends and associates were elated and became his ardent supporters. Not a few already began choosing some fine federal positions, a judgeship or a foreign mission, to which they might expect appointment.

So letters of congratulations poured in on him at Columbus, many recalling milestones in his life. "If you live until the next 4th of March, the defender of Nancy Farrer will be President of the United States," wrote the judge who had appointed him on that case, who by 1876 was himself but an obscure federal employee in Washington. [3] Numerous friends of Sardis wrote. Classmates at the old Norwalk Academy, at Isaac Webb's, at Kenyon and at Harvard—including J. A. Camp, who had married the girl F. G. P., only to have her die in 1855 and be buried, along with two small children, at Sandusky— wrote to say that they "always" knew he would be President. In the case of one Kenyon classmate, Dr. John A. Little of Delaware, this had been a fact. For back in 1848, on a visit to Washington, D. C., young Little had wandered into the Executive Mansion on Pennsylvania Avenue, picked up a sheet of Presidential writing paper and on impulse wrote a letter to his friend Hayes, dating it from "President's House," and beginning, "I don't know why, Rud, but I thought of *you* as soon as I arrived *here*." [4]

From Chesterfield, New Hampshire, across "the Great River," came a letter written in the shaky hand of his father's youngest sister, then ninety. Not only was Sally Hayes Bancroft happy that the son of her brother Ruddy had been so honored; it delighted her to think that, if she lived another few months, she could say that she had known all the American Presidents from George Washington—to her own nephew. This pleased Hayes almost as much as congratulations from William Cullen Bryant, James Russell Lowell and Richard Henry Dana, Jr., all so admired by him during the Harvard days.

Their letters, together with some from other primates of American respectability, including George William Curtis, editor of *Harper's Weekly*—the "Journal of Civilization" and "Bible" of the genteel class in America—drew from him some expressions of vanity. "The best people, many of them heretofore dissatisfied with the Republican party, are especially hearty in my support," he wrote. [5] To have the "best people" for him was, indeed, almost his supreme satisfaction. It meant he could feel that the old goal he had set for himself when he went to Harvard—that of being recognized as an American gentleman—had been attained in a positive, "official" way. And to be President, too—!

2

But he was not yet President. He was only the nominee of a party which many felt was doomed to defeat. The acute depression, new scandals smearing the Grant regime, with a member of Grant's cabinet, Secretary of War Belknap, at that very moment facing impeachment on admitted graft charges, the almost complete restoration of the Democratic Party in the South—these were factors that made the outlook for a Hayes victory dim. [6]

He was well aware of this after his early feelings of exultation gave way to sober appraisal of his chances. "The contest will be severe and critical," he wrote to William E. Chandler, retiring secretary of the Republican National Committee, party boss of New Hampshire (later

U. S. Senator), and a figure to be remembered. This was on June 30, 1876, even before the Democrats selected Governor Samuel J. Tilden of New York, around whom much national sentiment for reform centered, as their candidate.

3

Tilden was hardly the wholly pure figure pictured by many of his advocates, contemporary and historical, any more than Hayes was the "plaster saint" of some of his advocates, or the "inflated bladder," as a Democratic relative of Mark Twain put it,[7] of his contemptuous critics. True, Tilden had smashed, or so it was thought, the Boss Tweed-Tammany Society machine in New York City, and also the so-called "canal ring" in New York State. But for years Tilden himself had been an important "wheel" in the Tammany machine. He was a canny political manipulator, though, like Hayes, a man of genteel manners and tastes.

Like Hayes, too, Tilden was a lawyer. But his had not been the run-of-the-mine practice that generally had marked Hayes's legal career, nor one that allied him with any causes other than the strictly political. Tilden's law practice was of the cream financially. Indeed, while Hayes was serving as a soldier and in Congress, Tilden was amassing from fees and investments a huge fortune, one reckoned in the millions, mainly through handling corporation matters, in particular the dealings of railroad corporations and railroad "pools." A bachelor who lived in an elaborate New York City mansion, a man with a scholarly mind, somewhat ascetic except for a penchant for giving expensive gifts to women (though with no "scandal" in that regard touching him), Tilden had the reputation of leading legal intellect in the nation for reorganizing bankrupt railroad lines and creating "systems." Beneficiaries of his talents called him a remarkable businessman, even a genius. But others considered him sharp and ruthless.[8]

In a private talk with Hayes, Chief Justice Waite referred to Tilden as "a miser." Waite cited a personal encounter, which Hayes recorded:

He [Waite] was foreclosing a mortgage on a railroad (perhaps Atlantic and Great Western). Tilden represented the first-mortgage bondholders. Waite, on behalf of his clients, was very anxious to enter a decree. It was also in the interest of Tilden's clients. But it couldn't be done without Tilden's consent. Time was of such importance that Waite spent several hours trying to get Tilden's consent. Tilden had no right to ask any money for his consent. Neither the interests of his clients required it, nor had he rendered any services that entitled him to it. But he had the power. "To get his consent I had to pay him thirty thousand dollars. He probably divided with others. But that is Tilden." [9]

4

This, of course, was not an unbiased view of Tilden. But this view, with certain facts of his career, may properly be used to dilute the picture of Tilden presented during the campaign. Yet Tilden neatly did wear the mantle of reform in 1876, whether completely deserved or not, and as such was a formidable opponent. He shrewdly based almost his whole campaign on one theme, "Throw the Rascals Out," at a time when the American public, even much of the Republican portion, was disgusted with rascality in government. "Tilden and Reform" became the potent Democratic slogan.

Moreover, Tilden in New York had the same vote-getting ability that Hayes had shown in Ohio. Of course, the Democratic leaders had this in mind, in addition to Tilden's popularity in near-by states. "The nomination of Tilden makes doubtful the states of New York, New Jersey and Connecticut," Hayes conceded.[10] If this were true, Hayes and his party were indeed in trouble, especially if Democratic hopes for a solid South came true. For, as Hayes also had noted in his diary, if the Democrats carried *all* the Southern states, as well as New York, New Jersey and Connecticut, Republican defeat was a certainty. Moreover, like the Republicans who had named Wheeler of New York for Vice-President, the Democrats had shrewdly balanced their ticket geographically. They selected for Vice-President a popular Hoosier, Senator Thomas A. Hendricks, a choice designed to counter Hayes sentiment in the West, with the special factor that Hendricks was acceptable to "soft-money" advocates, though Tilden, like Hayes, was a "hard-money" man.

This constituted a straddle on the money issue, and would be denounced as such by the Republicans. But the Republicans were not at all sure, in view of the depression, that the straddle was not superior politics. They had reason to be glad when a third party emerged on that issue, the National Independent Party, commonly called the Greenback Party, with aged Peter Cooper, wealthy iron manufacturer, its candidate for President and, of all people, the Honorable Sam Carey, the temperance man, for Vice-President. Republicans hoped this ticket would drain votes away from the Democrats, thus help Hayes.[11] They surreptitiously fostered it.

5

Indeed, to help matters along, Senator Morton, the party boss in Indiana, gave a curious assignment to John W. Foster (later a Secretary of State under Harrison and grandfather of another Secretary of State, John Foster Dulles). This was to raise some $35,000 to be used secretly to "finance"—a euphemism—a Greenback newspaper for persuading soft-money Democrats in Indiana to desert Tilden and vote for Peter Cooper.[12]

That was but one, and a lesser one, of many undercover maneuverings on both sides which marked a generally weird election, one that came pretty close to supporting Sam Rheem's fears about it for Hayes. For if the Presidential election of 1876 was not the dirtiest, most marked by undercover chicanery and secret or exposed treachery, fraud and violence in the national history up to then, it was certainly the one most clearly and thoroughly revealed in that character. The machines of both leading parties were desperate—the Republicans, in the face of the general dissatisfaction against "Grantism," in their desire not to lose; the Democrats, especially in the South, in a determination again to attain power by overthrowing the last vestiges of so-called carpetbagger and "Negro rule." Nothing by way of crime against laws or morals was omitted by the partisans and henchmen of both sides—bribery, falsification, ballot stuffing, vote repeating, intimidation, perjury, kidnaping, mayhem and murder.[13]

None of this was really new in the election process since the time of Washington. But in 1876 election crime was conducted with more system, more organization and more unconcealed intent, than probably had been the case before. To politicians the aim, normally, of a political campaign is to win. In 1876 there was no doubt that many of them did not disdain any means, though curiously the aim of some on both sides was not to win for their party but for special reasons to lose for it, either for immediate or future gain to themselves as individuals.[14] In the work of winning, or losing, principles were secondary, or by and large left to Tilden and Hayes.

Usually this dismal story is told in terms of the South. But in New York, Chicago and in other Northern cities election crimes, never a novelty, as Hayes observed ᴛᴏ ᴄ᷉ ᴾ⁻ ᴮᵘᵗ there is no doubt that the guilt was most flagrant in the South, and especially in Louisiana, where the perpetrators openly boasted of their deeds, sure that the cause of white supremacy justified anything.

Ever since 1872 Southern leaders had determined to flout the Constitution with regard to Negro suffrage. Under the so-called "Mississippi Plan" the Negroes were to be frightened back "into their places," given to understand that for them, or their white leaders and associates, to try to vote, or to vote Republican, meant inviting action by the Klan, the White League, the Red Shirts and similar groups of white-supremacy vigilantes.

Some of the more circumspect leaders denied this. A few, backed by facts in some instances, insisted that Negroes were not intimidated but willingly abstained from voting or, just as willingly, voted for white-supremacy Democratic candidates. More candid was Robert Toombs, the Georgia Confederate leader.

We got a good many honest fellows into the legislature, but I will tell you how we got them there. I will tell the truth. The newspapers won't tell it to you. We got them there by carrying the black vote by intimidation and bribery, and I helped to do it. I would have scorned the people if they had not done it. . . . These miserable wretches, the Yankees, have injected five millions of savages into the stomach of our body politic, and the man who says he accepts Negro suffrage, I say, accursed be he! [15]

In 1890 a judge in Mississippi boasted: "It is no secret that there has not been a full vote and a fair count in Mississippi since 1875— that we have been preserving the ascendancy of the white people by revolutionary methods. In plain words, we have been stuffing ballot-boxes, committing perjury and here and there in the State carrying elections by fraud and violence . . . " [16]

6

Reconstruction, as the Southerners professed to view it, was revolution. The Mississippi Plan was counterrevolution. By 1876 it was also largely successful. By then, despite "Grantism," only Louisiana, South Carolina and Florida still "suffered" from Republican state regimes. All the other ex-rebel states were under Democratic control.

Moreover, contrary to a cleverly produced propaganda picture which portrayed most of the South still under the heel of the federal army, only in one state, Louisiana, was the army exerting any direct influence over local government. Army intervention in Louisiana was perfectly legal in form. It was in accord with the Constitutional provision that "the United States shall guarantee to every State in this Union a Republican form of government"—"republican" with a small "r."

The background was this: In 1872 the Republicans in Louisiana claimed that William P. Kellogg, a carpetbagger from Illinois, who had been chief justice of the Nebraska territory by appointment of Lincoln, had been elected governor. But the Democrats claimed fraud. They set up their own man, John McEnery, as governor. So there were two governors and two legislatures in New Orleans.

Kellogg ordered the head of his state militia, none other than the Confederate hero General James Longstreet, to disperse the McEnery legislature. In the ensuing conflicts, during which many lives were lost, Kellogg called on Grant to assist him with federal troops, in accord with the Constitutional provision. This was tantamount to asking recognition of the Kellogg regime. Grant gave that recognition, and on the basis of it ordered federal troops to protect the Kellogg setup. To Grant and his supporters this was maintaining law and order in Louisiana. To Democrats and moderate Republicans this was dictatorship, and the improper use of federal troops for fastening an unwanted Republican regime on Louisiana.[17] The troops remained four years—and more.

7

In 1876 Louisiana was to hold another election for governor. The candidates then were S. B. Packard, federal marshal at New Orleans and actual head of the so-called "Kellogg-Packard" Republican machine, and Francis P. Nicholls, Democrat. To make sure this time that there would be no doubt as to which party won, the Louisiana Democrats prepared to put into effect the Mississippi Plan. If Negroes and carpetbaggers were scared away from the polls, or intimidated or otherwise seduced into voting Democratic, there would then be no doubt that the Democrats would carry the election. Then there would be no Republican regime for the federal government to recognize. Hence Louisiana also would be "redeemed."

Such, admittedly, was the plan. Except for one weapon the Louisiana Republicans under Kellogg and Packard had little reason to hope they could offset it. Their weapon was control over the election machinery, in particular the so-called state "returning board." It had authority to throw out *all* the votes in any given election district if there was evidence of *any* fraud or intimidation.

The Democrats feared this power. It had been used in 1872. So the situation in Louisiana then boiled down to this: The Democrats intended to win by flouting the laws and the Constitution concerning Negro suffrage. The Republicans intended, if necessary, to win by using—or abusing—the law on rejecting votes. In this the Republicans expected protection from federal troops, federal marshals and federal judges.

It all had very little to do directly with Hayes or Tilden. But indirectly it had much to do with both.

8

That there would be cheating, brought to its highest art, in Louisiana by both sides went without saying. Perhaps most interesting was the fact that honorable men on both sides condoned the cheating, if they did not participate in it. It remained for Ben Butler, no innocent in political connivance, to describe the situation most pithily. "It is noteworthy that each party justified itself in what it was doing by the claimed acts of the other. The Democracy seemed to insist upon some supposed right to keep the Negro away from the polls because the Republicans were cheating in the returns, and the Republicans claimed the right to cheat in the returns because the Democrats were intimidating voters." [18]

This was true. No political leader could have been so naïve as not to be aware of what was going on. This applied to Tilden and to Hayes, though both called for honest elections. It was a situation made to order for every kind of rogue to operate in.

There was not only skullduggery practiced against each other by the opposing party machines. There was also skullduggery within each party machine. Democrats double-crossed Democrats. Republicans double-crossed Republicans. Party leaders and party henchmen, high ones and petty ones, U. S. Senators, or government clerks, sold out to one another, or offered to sell, with Democrats betraying Tilden and Republicans betraying Hayes. Adventurers, opportunists, gamblers, plain crooks, unscrupulous men—and women—of every shade and variety operated at every level, particularly in Louisiana. Nor were these by any means merely the despised carpetbaggers. Many also were Bourbon colonels.

9

Typical in many ways was a young carpetbagger from Philadelphia, James E. Anderson, a clerk in the customhouse in New Orleans, a scheming, clever, altogether conscienceless rascal, properly, if moderately, called "the Scamp Anderson" by Hayes. As a Republican election supervisor of East Feliciana parish in New Orleans, he conspired with and against Republicans and Democrats. He lied to everyone, committed perjury in affidavits and before investigations, double-crossed friends as well as enemies, engaged in blackmail and, by himself, was responsible for enough finagling in the Louisiana election to effect substantially the end result.

"Scamp" Anderson spewed poison in all directions, some of which splattered Senator Sherman and Stanley Matthews especially, and before he was exposed, Hayes himself—from whom he asked an appointment for "services to the cause." Yet his fantastic maneuverings, powerful enough to help provoke a Congressional investigation into the Hayes-Tilden election, were undertaken not for or against Hayes but to assist a Congressman to get counted in, and also, more specifically, in furtherance of his own ambition to be appointed naval officer of the customhouse in New Orleans, without regard to who was elected President.[19]

It was so also in the case of many of the other participants in the election in Louisiana and elsewhere. In New York, for example, Senator Conkling appeared more interested in preserving his personal hold on the New York Republican machine than in whether or not the state went for Hayes. Some evidence supported a conclusion that in fact Conkling had entered into a deal in behalf of Tilden.

It was a situation and a spectacle in which almost none of the actors escaped being tarred with what Sophia Hayes would have called "the vile" pitch. Not even Hayes escaped, despite all his affirmations of abiding by his code of gentlemen and his determination to conduct himself in accord with a vow he made at Kenyon: "Let me triumph as a man or not at all. Defeat without disgrace can be borne, but laurels which are not deserved sit like a crown of thorns on the head of their possessor." [20] Though he tried earnestly, or thought he did, he could not wholly escape because he was involved, as every Presidential candidate has been, in the process by which Presidents are elected.

10

Even so Hayes was personally less directly involved in the seamy side of the 1876 election than any other leading figure. Actually both he and Tilden were really but figureheads, almost puppets, the fate of each controlled by his party and its activities. Their moral helplessness was implicit in their relationship to the political process. For the contest was not between them as individuals. It was between them as representatives of their parties.

Both Hayes and Tilden wished to come out of the campaign and its aftermath unsullied by improper conduct charges, either their own or their partisans.

Unfortunately neither did, especially not Tilden, though he lost.[21]

Hayes learned, however, what all Presidential candidates, winners or losers, come to learn. With the stakes of a national election being what they are—in power, in offices, in monetary considerations—even good men will participate in or condone rascality. In the midst of the campaign, before he could know the result or aftermath, he set down in his diary a revealing entry. "On personal grounds, I find many reasons for thinking defeat a blessing. . . . I do not fear my pluck or constancy a particle. But to be deceived by the rogues, to find many a trusted reformer no better than he should be—here would be humiliations and troubles without end." [22]

However, having sought and accepted the nomination, he was committed to the process. There was no escape from the penalties save by withdrawal. Of course, this was ruled out as an impossibility by political considerations above and beyond his personal desires and by his own ambitions. There was no turning back, even had he wished it. All he could hope for was that his own skirts would be clean. Politics was still "a bad trade," as he had written to Lucy ten years before when he was in Congress.

CHAPTER XLIX

THE SUPPOSED DEFEAT

1

IT IS CERTAIN that Hayes received much less pleasure from this canvass than from any other. For one thing he, as well as Tilden, adhered to the custom of Presidential candidates making no speeches. All that was left to others. As strategy, he approved. "He is not going to talk himself out of the Presidency," said the New York *Times*.[1] But this policy deprived him of most of the fun. It also left him feeling frustrated.

For another thing, he could not help but feel that the management of the campaign by the Republican National Committee was often inefficient, lethargic and even strangely bungling. On this he had reason to recall a warning by Stanley Matthews.

After wandering among the Liberal Republicans, Matthews was then back in the regular Republican fold. In a sense he was also then a member of Hayes's family, his sister having married Lucy's brother, Dr. Joe Webb. From his former Democratic connections, his kinship by marriage to Editor "Marse" Henry Watterson, close associate of Tilden, and also his clientele (including Jay Gould), Matthews was in a position to obtain "inside" information. Just after the nomination he advised Hayes: "You must insist on naming the Chairman of the National Executive Committee & be sure of your man. *Beware of Chandler.* There is a plot to manage the campaign in the interest of your adversary."[2] The Chandler to whom Matthews referred was Zachariah Chandler, then Secretary of the Interior in Grant's cabinet, who was in fact elected as chairman of the National Committee.

From still another source, a Pennsylvania Republican, Hayes received a similar communication. "The evil . . . in the organization of the Nat. Com. has been done, and your election is a secondary matter with the combination which succeeded."[3] But Hayes had decided to keep hands off the selection of the chairman. The party then was really an oligarchy—and the oligarchs probably would have ignored Hayes's wishes. They did not intend that he should be anything more than candidate—and a figurehead.

2

That Zach Chandler was party to a plot to defeat Hayes is not backed by available documentary evidence. But he certainly conducted himself at times as if in corroboration of Matthews' warning. Not enough money for normal campaign activities was raised or properly distributed by the National Committee, and this appears to have been because of inaction rather than because of any real difficulty in getting funds. At one time the campaign was practically halted because, it was said, the committee was $10,000 in debt.[4] There was no co-ordination of campaign strategy among various areas. Almost no liaison existed between the committee and Hayes. Suggestions from him were usually ignored, at times contemptuously.[5]

Quite early it was clear—with Tilden likely to carry New York and Indiana, and possibly New Jersey and Connecticut, and with even Hayes's own state in the balance—the Republican Party desperately needed to carry at least some of the Southern states. "Our adversaries reckon on a *united South*. This is their hope. We must meet them on this," wrote Hayes on July 8.[6] In at least Louisiana, South Carolina and Florida, where the party still had footholds in the state regimes, this meant every effort should have been made to carry those states, and by majorities that could not be challenged as obtained by fraud.

True, it was the view of many key Republicans, probably the majority, that the only effective campaign in these states was use of federal troops in sufficient numbers to cause the white-supremacy Democrats to abandon their Mississippi Plan. However, President Grant did not wish to resort to this, except on the clearest showing of necessity. He had taken enough criticism on this score.[7] Besides, Grant did not especially care whether Hayes won or lost.

In October 1876 Grant did dispatch troops to South Carolina on the appeal of Governor D. H. Chamberlain, Republican, after race riots occurred during July and September in which perhaps 200 Negroes were killed. In effect, this meant a partial restoration of "bayonet rule" in that state, as Democrats under Wade Hampton, candidate for governor against Chamberlain, charged. But Grant's orders were that the troops do no more than maintain order, and presumably this was his wish also in Louisiana.

It was a mistake to assume that normal campaigning in Louisiana, South Carolina and Florida would not have been effective, that at least one more election could not have been clearly won in all these states and as honestly as anywhere else. Yet "the National Committee was disposed to abandon the South, and did, in fact, virtually abandon it. . . . The National Committee turned away from Louisiana; it attempted nothing for South Carolina, and nothing for Florida." So a seasoned newspaper writer later recalled.[8]

The same observer also gave this account of Zach Chandler's general policy:

The National Committee failed signally in its plan of campaign. It concentrated its main energies on New York and Indiana, and reasoned that with these fifty electoral votes the Solid South might be abandoned to Tilden, with Connecticut and even Ohio thrown in. "I will elect Hayes without Ohio," said Mr. Chandler to [Ohio] Lieutenant Governor [Thomas L.] Young. . . . "We will elect Hayes without Connecticut," was the reply to an appeal for moderate help from men in high position who knew that state and had good grounds for confidence that the little they asked . . . would turn the scale. . . .[9]

If nothing else, this was overconfidence carried to an extreme—and hard to reconcile with Zach Chandler's known political shrewdness.

3

Hayes himself made the most effective single contribution to the campaign. This was through a public letter formally accepting the nomination, a document, incidentally, that most members of the National Committee resented. His "Letter of Acceptance" was chiefly important for its statement of his personal views on reform of the civil service. The party platform had pledged such reform but in general terms. Hayes was specific. He pledged that he would ignore the custom whereby government employees obtained and held their positions solely with the approval of members of Congress or other party leaders. In short, he would end the spoils system by doing away with its basis, the system of patronage.[10]

This was a bold, even revolutionary, stand for the times, more forthright even than the stand taken by Tilden. Moreover, it was a courageous defiance of the very men—the Blaines, Conklings, Mortons, Chandlers, Camerons and all the rest of the political leaders of Hayes's own party—on whom the success of his election campaign mainly depended, if he was in earnest.

That he was in earnest seemed implicit in another pledge. "Believing that the restoration of the civil service to the system established by Washington . . . can be best accomplished by an Executive who is under no temptation to use the patronage of his office to promote his own re-election, I desire to perform what I regard as a duty in now stating my inflexible purpose, if elected, not to be a candidate for election to a second term."

There, clearly, Hayes showed his independence of "Grantism." It was so interpreted—and by Grant. "I have excellent reason for believing that the President has been on a prolonged spree and that [Secretary] Fish took him to Deer Park to cool him down in this sense, as well as politically. He is very mad over Hayes's letter." So Boynton, the newspaper correspondent, advised his friend Bristow.[11] Moreover, Boss T. C. Platt of New York told Hayes that Grant, if not driven to drink by the letter, was deeply offended by it. Personally as well as for political reasons this troubled Hayes. He did not back down, though he did send to Grant an adroitly worded "explanation."[12]

But Hayes had no cause to regret his pledges. He had taken his chances on the reaction of Grant and the politicos in general, and was satisfied. As Carl Schurz related, Hayes had been warned by a friend to whom he had read the Letter of Acceptance before releasing it that it would "displease some very powerful men in your own party." His response was, "Yes, that may be so, but it is right."[13]

4

Even the politicos had to admit that the Letter of Acceptance, no matter how distasteful to them, undoubtedly served a strategic political purpose. It made it possible for independent Republicans to stay in the party, some even with enthusiasm, rather than to fall in with a plan already being hatched for another bolt, as in 1872.[14] The letter made certain that the leading former Liberal Republicans, for the most part, would support Hayes.[15] Schurz, their natural leader, had been wavering. Knowing this, Hayes went out of his way to consult with Schurz about the Letter of Acceptance before releasing it. After the letter Schurz's support was secure. In the end, due in large part to such support, Hayes had as much reform sentiment behind him as Tilden.

To Howells, then editor of the *Atlantic Monthly*, the letter was "the manliest thing since the Declaration, on which it's an improvement in some respects." [16] To Professor Francis A. Walker of Yale, later president of the Massachusetts Institute of Technology, it was a document that "would create life under the ribs of death." Indeed, with its references to reform, as well as to Hayes's approach to the Southern problem (of which more later), it was the great document of the campaign.

However, all of even the legitimate side of the campaign was not conducted on the high plane of that letter, not by Hayes, not by his party in general, nor by Tilden and his party. In keeping with his new views on reconstruction, Hayes's letter had emphasized a desire for harmony between North and South. But he did not hesitate to urge a campaign in the North based on hatred of "the rebels"—the waving of the "bloody shirt." To Blaine he wrote: "Our strong ground is the dread of a solid South, rebel rule, etc., etc. I hope you will make these topics prominent in your speeches. It leads people away from 'hard times,' which is our deadliest foe." [17]

He also encouraged the use of the Catholic issue against the Democrats, although the Democratic platform was as strong as the Republican platform in pledging opposition to use of public-school funds for religious schools. But Governor Tilden was as vulnerable on that issue as Governor Allen had been. For in 1875 Tilden had signed a bill, the "Gray Nuns Act," which authorized a Catholic educational institution to issue certificates of qualification as public-school teachers, though he later signed a bill repealing the act. [18]

5

As is normally the case in American politics, save in periods of extreme crisis, there was no substantial difference between the parties or between Hayes and Tilden on any real issue. But this did not mean a quiet campaign. On the contrary, it was noisy and noisome, all the more so because of the lack of difference on issues.

Both parties were guilty equally of demagoguery, of appeals to race and religious prejudice, and of using false or immaterial allegations. Hayes, for example, was accused of having embezzled money placed in his charge by a soldier under his command during the war. He was also accused of having made off with another soldier's watches.

Tilden was accused of having not fully reported his income for a tax return, an accusation that became for a time nearly the main issue until Hayes, to his embarrassment, discovered that he had overlooked filing any income-tax return during his first term as governor.[19]

To offset the Republican charge that Tilden was "subservient to the priests," the Democrats issued a letter signed "R. B. Hayes," to the effect that he had joined a secret organization known as "The Order of the American Alliance," which not only opposed Catholic "interference in politics" but favored depriving foreign-born citizens of the right to vote or to hold office. This letter was a forgery.[20] Unfortunately the "Alliance" *had* endorsed Hayes. Still more unfortunately Hayes's secretary had acknowledged the endorsement with a letter stating that "Governor Hayes . . . is deeply gratified by this expression of confidence."

In areas with large foreign-born populations Hayes's supporters were thrown into a panic, one not wholly allayed by the explanation that the secretary had written a routine acknowledgment without Hayes knowing about the matter.[21]

William Henry Smith wrote from Chicago to Hayes:

I have had a siege with our Republican friends here yesterday and today about Colonel Lee's letter to the American Alliance. A panic has prevailed and there is a good deal of feeling. . . . Mr. Medill is quite put out—well, downright mad. . . . I hope your wisdom will suggest something to aid us with the great foreign population of the Northwest. It is absolutely necessary to offset the extensive and insidious work of the enemy in Chicago and Wisconsin especially.[22]

Hayes professed to believe that the matter was not important.[23] But this was whistling in the dark. The forgery cost him many votes, especially in New York.

6

There were other headaches. He had to maintain good relations with the "stalwart" party leaders and the independents without offending either group. Blaine especially had to be humored. Conkling of New York was a special problem. Was he really ill? Or did he call off his speaking program in doubtful New York as part of a plan, as later Hayes believed, to throw the election to Tilden?[24]

Schurz was often unhappy. On one occasion this was because he learned that the Republican National Committee was assessing government workers for campaign funds. On another it was because it was reported that the National Committee did not want Schurz making speeches.[25] There was always the danger that Schurz would bolt, something that Hayes, if not the National Committee, would have considered a disaster.

There was the problem of financing the campaign. Hayes had not anticipated that he, as the nominee, would be concerned with finances. Yet Senator Morton insisted on meeting with him to advise that unless Hayes helped collect some $100,000 to be spent in Indiana, the Democrats would carry that state in the October gubernatorial election. This, Morton said, would spread discouragement in other states and cause the loss of the Presidency in November.[26]

Hayes did not wish to be involved in soliciting funds, the surest way of creating obligations embarrassing later. In the end he felt forced to do it, sending Rogers to Boston to see capitalist J. M. Forbes for exactly that purpose. But Rogers was not too successful. Indiana was lost in October, Benjamin Harrison losing the governorship to Representative James "Blue Jeans" Williams, who had won fame for a speech complaining that "hundreds of towels were being used daily by members of Congress, at public expense, while at his home, on his farm, one towel lasted a week, with eleven in the family." [27] Later it came out that Tilden had sent $60,000 to Indiana, part of this a $10,000 contribution in $500 bills from August Belmont.[28]

That same October elections were also held in Ohio. In the state as a whole the Republicans won, the Congressional victors including Hayes's wartime protégé, William McKinley. But there were some disquieting results. The Democrats carried Hamilton County, including Cincinnati. Worse yet, two of Hayes's most intimate friends, Matthews and Manning Force, were defeated for Congress. In the case of Matthews, who lost in Hayes's own former district, an excuse was that the Democrats had used against him the fact that he had prosecuted a befriender of a fugitive slave in 1858. But there was no such explanation for Force's defeat.

A conclusion was inevitable: Hayes might not be able to carry even Ohio in the Presidential contest.

7

It was no wonder that he, usually the optimist, prepared himself for defeat. He also foresaw that he might become involved in a disputed election. On October 22, 1876, in his diary he wrote: "The huge registration in New York City looks sinister. It seems to look to our

defeat in that state. Another danger is imminent: *A contested result.*
And we have no such means for its decision as ought to be provided
by law. This must be attended to hereafter."

He was not alone in seeing before election day the possibility of a
contested election. In a speech at Cooper Institute Murat Halstead
said: "A disputed presidential election would Mexicanize us. There
is incalculable ruin in it. If the New York electoral vote is given the
Democratic candidate, we are imminently threatened with this degra-
dation. If New York is Republican, the danger is over." [29] Halstead's
fear, like Hayes's in this regard, was to be remembered.

Toward the end of the campaign Hayes attended the Centennial
Exposition in Philadelphia, almost the whole family and also a number of friends and relatives going along, including Will Platt. It was
"a happy journey" from a personal standpoint. But his private conferences with political leaders there caused Hayes to write in his diary on
returning to Columbus: "October 29. I return feeling that with the
probabilities of fraud and violence—fraud, North; violence, South—
the chances are that we shall lose the election." On November 1 he
felt the same way. "The contest is close and yet doubtful, with the
chances, as I see them, rather against us."

On November 5, two days before the election, he thought his
chances were "improving." But when he tallied up states considered
as certain, he could get a total of only 144 electoral votes. He needed
185 to win. Among doubtful states he placed New York—and South
Carolina, Florida and Louisiana.

On election day, Tuesday, November 7, he wrote:

Dies irae! . . . I still think Democratic chances the best. But it is
not possible to form a confident opinion. If we lose, the South will be
the greatest sufferer. Their misfortune will be greater than ours. I do
not think a revival of business will be greatly postponed by Tilden's
election. Business prosperity does not, in my judgment, depend on
government so much as men commonly think. But we shall have no
improvement in civil service—deterioration rather, and the South will
drift towards chaos again.

8

On election night he received the returns in the parlor of his residence, a house rented from a Dr. Hawkes, 60 East Broad Street, across
the street from the State house in Columbus. With him and Lucy
were a few friends, including Rogers.

Almost from the beginning of the evening there was bad news. "Ohio was not doing as well as we had hoped," Hayes commented. In the end Ohio was placed in his column, but the close race there suggested trouble elsewhere. "The effect was depressing," he said. Indeed, so much so that Lucy excused herself from the gathering and went to bed with a headache.

Then came reports indicating that Tilden had carried New York City with so large a majority that the state had to be counted for him. "We all felt," said Hayes, "that the State of New York would decide the contest." It was soon found that, with New York, the Democrats also had carried New Jersey and Connecticut. Then came another bad blow. Indiana was lost.

Of course, that night, as for some time afterward, all returns were unofficial. Several states had not been heard from at all. But on the assumption that the South was "solid" for the Democrats, or nearly so, and on the basis of the inroads the Democrats had made in the North, practically everybody decided that Tilden had been elected.

In Washington Garfield was among these. "It now appears," he wrote on November 9, "that we were defeated by the combined power of rebellion, Catholicism and whiskey." [30]

In Boston Richard Henry Dana, Jr., also sure that Tilden had won, wrote a consoling letter to Hayes in a shaky hand. "Do not permit a misgiving to cross your mind that the defeat can be attributed to anything in yourself or your action. On the contrary, the last month of the campaign all we had left was your character and conduct, and your perfect letter—except the bad record of the Democratic party." [31]

9

Hayes was among those who felt he had lost. He had gone to bed after midnight on election night feeling certain of it. His main reaction appeared to be a resolve not to show disappointment and to comfort Lucy. He "talked with Lucy, consoling her with such topics as readily occurred of a nature to make us feel satisfied on merely personal grounds with the result." He and Lucy "soon fell into a refreshing sleep" and for them, he later said, "the affair seemed over." [32]

But the affair was not over. It had really only begun. Ahead for Hayes, Tilden and the nation was the situation that he and Murat Halstead, as well as others, had feared might develop, a contested election, one as "contentious" as Thomas Jefferson's in Daniel Austin's time.

CHAPTER L

The Claim of Victory

1

ON THE afternoon of the day after the election Zach Chandler suddenly displayed more interest in the results than many persons thought he had shown all during the election campaign. From his suite in the Fifth Avenue Hotel, New York, a statement was issued destined to win him more fame (or, as Democrats professed to view it, infamy) than he had attained by anything else in his long political career. It said: "Hayes has 185 electoral votes and is elected."

That night Zach Chandler's claim was elaborated into a statement issued by the Republican National Committee. "Dispatches received at these headquarters report that Louisiana, Florida, South Carolina, Wisconsin, Oregon, Nevada and California have given Republican majorities. There is no reason to doubt the correctness of these reports and if confirmed the election of Hayes is assured by a majority of one in the Electoral College." [1]

Except on the basis of a technicality in the case of Oregon, there was no challenge by the Democrats of this summary of results save for Louisiana, Florida and South Carolina. So these states became the crux of controversy that quickly developed over the claim of victory.

Immediately, to the accompaniment of a chorus of charges and countercharges in the press across the land, leaders of both parties went into action—the Republicans to support Chandler's claim, the Democrats to discredit it.

As was clear later, both sides had agents or allies who, as before the election, were not weighed down by scruples in what they did or attempted to do. Several thousand pages of testimony taken by a half-dozen or more Congressional investigating committees, some dominated by Republicans, others by Democrats, reveal this conclusively.

In terms of the desires of the qualified voters in the election, the truth never was and never will be told. It never would be known how many ballots were fraudulently cast or fraudulently counted.

The "official" count was to show that Tilden received a plurality. But this count did not include, as it could not have included, votes *not* cast, because many qualified voters—mainly Negroes—were scared

316

off from attempting to vote. This was the nub of the situation from the Republican standpoint. This was the case they proceeded to make out to support the claim of victory.

2

The procedure was to have the Republican returning boards in Louisiana, Florida and South Carolina throw out the returns from those districts in which there had been fraud or intimidation, or both, by the Democrats—as the law in each state provided could be done. As these districts were Democratic strongholds, the discarding of those returns in enough districts could change a Democratic victory total into a Republican victory total. Everyone knew that this could be done, that such would be the strategy in case of a close result in any of those states.

Ever since 1872, when this strategy was used in Louisiana to "count in" the Kellogg regime, the Democrats knew that the legal basis for it firmly existed. But they had failed to do anything to change the laws as far as they might concern a Presidential election, though Republicans had been willing to go along with a change. A conclusion was that the Democrats did not want the laws changed, intending to benefit by them themselves when they came into power.

Whether or not this strategy could be executed depended on how much power both parties could exert. Mathematics was not to decide this election. It could not, if the issue turned on votes that were *not* counted. But *power* could decide, naked power, political, economic and social, and—in the last analysis—physical and military.

So this was the true nature of the struggle, in which neither Hayes nor Tilden played more than nominal roles. The victory, it was soon clear, was to go to the party that mustered the most power. In short, after the election contest the Republican and Democratic parties began another contest, a test of strength by other means. This was the meaning of the 1876 Hayes-Tilden election dispute.

3

In depreciation of Zach Chandler's bold claim, much would be said of circumstances suggesting that he would not have made it except for certain incidental happenings. These chiefly concerned goings-on in the offices of the New York *Times*, then Republican; and the doings of another Chandler—William E., of New Hampshire. From the usual accounts the inference is that except for them Tilden's election would have been conceded by the Republican Party, and there would have been no claim of victory by Zach Chandler.

This story begins election night in the office of the *Times*. The first edition of the newspaper was already off the press. It carried a summary of the election which left the national result in doubt but gave, if read carefully, an over-all impression that Tilden probably would win. The New York *Tribune*, also Republican, had already appeared with a story which virtually conceded that Tilden had won. Though the *Tribune* story did indicate that the Republicans might have won South Carolina and Louisiana, its headline went stronger than its story: TILDEN ELECTED.

The *Times* editors considered whether or not to follow suit in a subsequent edition. While they were debating the matter, two inquiries came in. One was from D. A. Magone, chairman of the Democratic committee for New York State, who asked for *Times* figures on the election generally. The other was from Senator William Barnum of Connecticut, a member of the Democratic National Committee, asking in particular for the results from Florida, Louisiana and South Carolina.

These inquiries convinced the editors that the Democratic high command itself was not at all sure of victory, that it was in doubt particularly about the three Southern states.

Why, then, concede victory to Tilden? Thus, the *Times's* 6:30 edition carried the headline: RESULTS STILL UNCERTAIN.

Giving Louisiana and South Carolina to Hayes, its story said that Tilden had 184 electoral votes, Hayes, 181. It concluded that if Hayes carried Florida, he would have 185 and be elected by one vote. The *Times* did not then flatly claim Florida for Hayes. But an editorial pointedly observed that the Republicans did claim it.[2]

4

After this story and editorial had been prepared one of the editors, John Reid, rushed to the Republican national headquarters. While looking for Zach Chandler's room, he encountered slim, energetic William E. Chandler, just in from New Hampshire. The New Hampshire Chandler at once saw the desirability of claiming the doubtful Southern states, and also of making sure that the party leaders in those states would not concede defeat and would be on the alert, as he later emphasized, against fraud by Democrats.

He and Reid aroused Zach Chandler. Being too sleepy, or perhaps too alcoholized, to grasp immediately the situation, he told the other Chandler to do what he considered necessary. William E. Chandler then dispatched telegrams to various states.

To Chamberlain, the Republican governor of South Carolina: HAYES IS ELECTED IF WE HAVE CARRIED SOUTH CAROLINA, FLORIDA, AND LOUISIANA. CAN YOU HOLD YOUR STATE? ANSWER IMMEDIATELY.

To U. S. Senator S. B. Conover in Florida: THE PRESIDENTIAL ELECTION DEPENDS ON THE VOTE OF FLORIDA, AND THE DEMOCRATS WILL TRY TO WREST IT FROM US. WATCH IT AND HASTEN RETURNS. ANSWER IMMEDIATELY. HAYES DEFEATED WITHOUT FLORIDA. DO NOT BE CHEATED IN RETURNS. ANSWER WHEN SURE.

To Packard, the Republican candidate for governor in Louisiana: THE PRESIDENTIAL ELECTION DEPENDS ON THE VOTE OF LOUISIANA, AND THE DEMOCRATS WILL TRY AND WREST IT FROM YOU.

Similar messages went to Oregon and Nevada.

Then William E. Chandler took a train for Florida. His purpose, he said, was to help the local Republicans make sure that the state would not be lost through Democratic fraud. In the meantime answers to his telegrams had come in. These asserted that the states in question had been carried for Hayes.[3] On the basis of them Zach Chandler made his claim. The *Times* the next day carried the headlines:

THE BATTLE WON
A REPUBLICAN VICTORY IN THE NATION

Other Republican journals, including the *Tribune,* also then claimed a Republican victory. On November 10 the *Times* asserted there was "no doubt" that Hayes was elected. It reported that the Republicans had carried Florida by 2,000, Louisiana by 8,000 and South Carolina by 8,000.

5

In substance, all of the foregoing undoubtedly occurred.[4] On his way to Florida William E. Chandler stopped at Lynchburg, Virginia.

From there he wrote a letter to Hayes which confirms, substantially, this account and adds some details, especially concerning the "technical" situation in Oregon. There it had been discovered that one of three Republican electors held a small postmastership, hence was supposedly disqualified under the federal Constitution. Though the Republicans maintained that this defect could be cured by having the elector resign the postmastership before the electoral college was to meet, it was reported that the Democratic governor planned to throw out all of Oregon's three votes, or appoint one Democratic elector in the Republican's place. Either of these actions, if sustained, would give Tilden a majority.

To Hayes, Chandler wrote:

Lynchburg, Va., Novr 9, 1876

My dear Sir:
Yesterday A.M. at daylight I arrived at 5th Av. Hotel from N. H. & found all had gone to bed an hour before, exhausted and convinced of Tilden's election. Just then in rushed J. C. Reed [sic], News Editor Times, with news up to 6 A.M.—he had Florida reported for us & Oregon also by Asso. Press Despatches. I immediately telegraphed to Florida, Louisiana, S. Car., Nevada & Oregon that all depended on them and that with them we were safe, to look out for Demo. frauds & to telegraph us when sure—also telegraphed to Gorham about Oregon & Nevada. My dispatches got off at 6½ ahead of similar demo. dispatches, Reed [sic] & I believed.
Very soon I began to get answers and when our people came around in this morning it seemed as if the dead had been raised. Last night we discovered that the demos were desperate, and that we must prepare for any & every possible emergency; and so I am here en route for S. C., Florida, & for Louisiana if necessary to aid if I may in preventing our being defrauded out of what we have fairly won. One majority is as good as twenty if we hold it but we are more liable to be cheated out of it. Vacancies I suppose can be filled by remaining electors; bribery of one is to be guarded against; also keeping back or falsifying returns. I fear Govr Grover of Oregon who is demo. may be pressed to keep back electoral certificates. If so, as we have Gov^v N. C., he ought to keep back N. C. certificates. Every possible device will be resorted to to hold back Oregon; but we have fortified in every possible way by telegraphs.
Govr Stearns of Florida is I think a true & vigilant and firm man, and I shall confer directly with him. But there are some feuds there that may endanger us. I will do the best I can. I send cypher in another letter. I will sign "Everett Chase." M. A. Clancy will receive dispatches at 5th Av Hotel & has cypher. Sens. G. F. Edmunds &

Z. C. will remain there. The Negroes here are timidly anxious that the one maj.[ority] may save us.

Yrs. Truly,
C.[5]

6

In view of this letter there can be no doubt as to the basic accuracy of the story about the activity of the two Chandlers and the *Times* editors. Even so, too much emphasis on the importance of this activity is naïve. The claim of Democratic victory would have been challenged anyway, if the results were at all close. Back in September Alphonso Taft, then Attorney General and at the center of Republican campaign management, had written to Hayes: "It is a fixed and desperate purpose of the Democratic party in the South that the Negroes shall not vote, and murder is a common means of intimidation to prevent them. In South Carolina, in Florida and in Louisiana, and in North Carolina, we shall try to protect the Negroes. What success we shall have I cannot tell." So the Republicans, before the election, were watching closely the very states with the electoral votes to decide the contest.

Of course, they were aware of the legal power to change the reported results if there was intimidation. Two days before the election Governor Kellogg of Louisiana had sent to Zach Chandler the following:

Dispatches from Ouchita and Morehouse parishes near the Arkansas line, and West Feliciana, near the Mississippi line, report that those parishes are now patrolled by the White League, re-inforced by armed bodies from Arkansas and Mississippi. Most of the Republican leaders have been driven away or murdered.

Under the State law voters are entitled to vote at any poll in the parish in which they reside. The colored people generally are attempting to reach the parish seats of these parishes in order to vote under the protection of the authorities. Numbers of them have been intercepted by the White League pickets and their registration-papers destroyed. In some instances they have been terribly beaten. Some six hundred colored men who have managed to avoid these pickets and reach the town of Monroe, Ouchita Parish, have been ordered by the Democratic mayor to leave town immediately.

In West Feliciana several colored men have come in in like manner to Bayou Sara, the parish seat. The White League of that parish, aided by armed bodies from the adjoining counties in Mississippi, have picketed the approaches to the town to prevent others coming in.

These parishes are largely Republican, but in spite of the intimidation thus practiced, I believe there is no doubt that the overwhelming Republican majorities in other parishes will give us the State.

WILLIAM P. KELLOGG.[6]

To Democrats this was a self-serving document prepared by one of the heads of a carpetbag regime, indeed, the very governor who held his office since 1872 solely by protection of "federal bayonets." But Kellogg did name specific places. The burden of proof that he had lied would be on the Democrats. The fact was, the Republicans had prepared a case for the charge of fraud even before Zach Chandler made his claim of victory.

So what was set in motion was a series of proceedings that would have been started in any event by the local Republicans in the states involved, without prompting from New York. For their regimes also were at stake.

7

Significantly, while individual Democratic leaders in various states and Democratic newspapers heatedly challenged Zach Chandler's claim immediately after it was made, his counterpart in the Democratic Party, Abram S. Hewitt, close friend of Tilden, member of Congress, wealthy iron manufacturer, son-in-law of Peter Cooper, and chairman of the Democratic National Committee, did not issue a rejoinder immediately. A month later Hewitt did prepare a bristling statement claiming that Tilden was elected. But Tilden himself asked that it not be issued.[7]

What Chairman Hewitt did at the time of Chandler's claim was to ask leading Democrats to go to Louisiana to "observe" canvassing of the votes by the returning board in New Orleans. His request, which brought twenty-two "visiting statesmen" to New Orleans, was curiously mild. It merely said that "citizens of New Orleans urgently request that a delegation of prominent gentlemen come there at once to counsel peace and a fair and honest return." [8] A fair conclusion appears to be that the Democratic high command was not so certain as Democratic newspapers maintained that the claim of a Tilden victory was on any more solid ground than the claim of a Hayes victory.

Chairman Hewitt also took some steps with regard to Oregon. He did not deny that Hayes had fairly won Oregon. But he urged that

Hayes be deprived of at least one of Oregon's three electoral votes because of the assumed disqualification of the Republican elector who was a postmaster. On the basis of a legal opinion, worked out mainly by none other than Hayes's Harvard classmate and former friend George Hoadly, Hewitt asked the Democratic governor of Oregon to issue a certificate of appointment to the candidate for elector "receiving the next highest number of votes," a Democrat.[9]

Later Hewitt denied that this was a trick, or device, to win the Presidency for Tilden on a technicality. Rather, Hewitt said, it was to lay the ground for forcing the Republicans to ask Congress to go behind certificates of appointments issued to electors, to get at the actual votes cast, in case the returning boards decided in favor of the Republican electors.[10]

In particular, Hewitt had in mind Louisiana. He was not at all certain that Florida and South Carolina, despite intimidation of Negroes, had not in fact gone for Hayes. In both states there were apparently many white citizens who, though favoring Democratic governors, were not averse to a Republican national regime. In South Carolina, indeed, Tilden had given offense personally to Wade Hampton, the Democratic candidate for governor. In some areas of South Carolina the white-supremacy ticket was "Hampton and Hayes."

So Hewitt and other Democrats were prepared to concede South Carolina and Florida to Hayes.[11]

But Louisiana was different, they felt. If Louisiana could be saved for Tilden, Hayes could not win. Tilden would be President.

CHAPTER LI

SERENE MAN

1

HAYES, in Columbus, had felt all along that intimidation of the Negroes, and also more direct violations of the Fourteenth and Fifteenth Amendments in the South, might influence the result against him. Six days before election day he wrote in his diary, "We shall be beaten, if at all, by crime—by bribery and repeating North, and violence and intimidation in the South."

Also, long before Zach Chandler's claim he had conceived it possible for the Republicans to win some of the Southern states. Those that he named were North and South Carolina, Florida, Mississippi and Louisiana. Of these, Mississippi and North Carolina were conceded to the Democrats, leaving precisely the three states that were disputed. So he could not have been surprised when a claim for them was made by the Republican National Committee.[1]

Yet it was several days before he took the claim seriously. "At this time the Republicans are claiming the election by one electoral vote," he wrote in his diary as late as November 11, with a seeming casualness suggesting more the attitude of an objective reporter than that of one of the two men most concerned in the controversy which already was hot all over the land. "This," he went on, "creates great uneasiness"—a comment in marked contrast to a statement published that same day right in Columbus by the chairman of the Democratic state executive committee of Ohio. To that leader the Republican claim was "anarchy," "revolution" and "a conspiracy to usurp the government."[2]

True, on the day after election Hayes had also written: "It dawned on us that with a few Republican states in the South, to which we were fairly entitled, we would yet be the victors." But he still did not appear to think that the claim by the Republicans could be made good.

Sunday, November 12, he was more certain that he was "fairly entitled" to the three disputed Southern states, and others in addition. He wrote then:

324

In the old slave states, if the recent Amendments were cheerfully obeyed, if there had been neither violence nor intimidation nor other improper interference with the rights of the colored people, we should have carried enough Southern states to have held the country and to have secured a decided popular majority. A fair election in the South would undoubtedly have given us a large majority of the electoral votes, and a decided preponderance of the popular vote.

However, after also writing that "history will show that the Republicans were by fraud, violence, and intimidation, by a nullification of the Fifteenth Amendment, deprived of the victory which they fairly won," he observed: "But we must, I now think, prepare ourselves to accept the inevitable." That is, defeat.

2

That same Sunday, "after church and dinner," he went for a ride with John G. Mitchell, husband of his sister's daughter, Laura. The main topic of conversation, of course, was the election. But, said Hayes, "We talked of the Presidential question as settled and found it in all respects as well for me personally that I was not elected."

On stopping at Mitchell's home he found his son Webb excited over a telegram.

Washington, D. C., November 12, 1876.
TO GOVERNOR R. B. HAYES. YOU ARE UNDOUBTEDLY ELECTED NEXT PRESIDENT OF THE UNITED STATES. DESPERATE ATTEMPTS ARE BEING MADE TO DEFEAT YOU IN LOUISIANA, SOUTH CAROLINA, AND FLORIDA, BUT THEY WILL NOT SUCCEED.   W. DENNISON[3]

3

Hayes had known this Dennison since the 1840s, having met him in Columbus when he was studying law there before going to Harvard. At the outbreak of the war, William Dennison was governor of Ohio. He had helped Hayes to get his commission with the Twenty-third Regiment. He later was in Lincoln's cabinet. As Hayes commented in his diary concerning the telegram, Dennison was " a prudent and cautious gentleman."

If Dennison felt so certain of his election, Hayes decided that the

Presidential question was not settled after all. Dennison's message alone "seem[ed] to open it all up again." [4]

Then, in the next day's mail he received a letter, written November 10, from Schurz. "Today there seems to be good grounds for hope again for sufficient legitimate majorities in Florida, South Carolina, Louisiana, and thus of your election. If this turns out to be the result, accept my congratulations in advance. Your satisfaction can scarcely be greater than mine. . . ." [5] If a figure like Schurz, foremost among anticorruptionists, who had denounced carpetbag corruption as vigorously as any Democrat, felt so about the outcome, this was further potent reason for Hayes to shed still more of the attitude that he was defeated.

True, Schurz also wrote, "I am sure, you are as anxious as I am, and as every patriotic citizen must be, that such a result should not be tainted by any suspicion of unfair dealing. I think the idea put forth in several quarters that some men of high character should go to New Orleans to watch the proceedings of the Returning Board, is a very good one. The Democrats are already sending some of their prominent men, and it ought to be done on our side."

4

With Schurz's desire for honesty Hayes, of course, agreed. Independently of Schurz's suggestion, Grant, by the time Hayes received Schurz's letter, had already decided to ask outstanding Republican leaders, including Senator Sherman, Congressman Garfield and William M. Evarts, who had defended President Johnson in the impeachment case and also denounced carpetbag outrages in Louisiana, to go to New Orleans.

Unfortunately Grant failed to include Democrats in his list of men invited to watch the Louisiana situation, his excuse being that Hewitt's representatives would fill that requirement. Even so, it would not have occurred to Hayes that men of the stature of Sherman and Garfield, let alone Evarts, would participate in or condone alleged dishonesty. Naturally he would gather that they would act as partisans, thus press every advantage in favor of a Republican result. Indeed, that was their duty, as it was also the duty of the Democratic leaders to press every Democratic advantage.

But the lengths to which politicians of both parties actually did go were well indicated by General Lew Wallace, author of *Ben Hur*. He was in Louisiana as a Republican visiting statesman and later went to Florida. From there he wrote his wife:

". . . It is terrible to see the extent to which all classes go in their determination to win. Conscience offers no restraint. Nothing is so common as the resort to perjury. . . . Money and intimidation can obtain the oath of white men as well as black to any required statement. A ton of affidavits could be carted into the state house tomorrow and not a word of truth in them, except the names of the parties swearing and their ages and places of residence. Now what can come of such a state of things?

If we win, our methods are subject to impeachment for possible fraud. If the enemy win, it is the same thing—doubt, suspicion, irritation go with the consequence whatever it may be.[6]

5

Hayes could not have escaped at least suspecting that such was the picture. But he felt secure in the confidence that he could trust the men who went to Louisiana at Grant's request, if only because they could be expected not to risk their own careers by participating in fraud to make him President. Besides, his mind was conditioned now to thinking mainly, if not wholly, about fraud on the part of the Democrats—before, during and after the election.

In particular, he was thinking of the intimidation of the Negroes. Even if forced to worry about charges of unfair dealing in connection with the returning boards, this intimidation naturally struck him as the overriding issue. On this, he later quoted comment by Washington McLean, who succeeded his father as publisher of the Cincinnati *Enquirer*, one of the Democratic papers most vociferous in alleging fraud by the Republicans.

"Oh," said McLean, "we all agree that if the Fifteenth Amendment is to be regarded, you were clearly entitled to the place. No man of sense can deny that we nullified that in the election. The negroes were kept from the polls by our people deliberately, and we in the North looked on with approval." [7]

Clearly the Democrats were on thin ice in crying "Fraud!" concerning the Republican-dominated returning boards, if they themselves were guilty of violating the Constitution, not to mention committing deeds of violence or threatened violence charged to them, or attempted bribery. This was basic to the attitude of Hayes, who by

November 13 was writing to William Henry Smith: "I am in the habit, for a day or two past, of saying: *'undoubtedly,* a fair election in the South would have given the Republicans a large majority of the Electors, and also of the popular vote of the Nation; and I think that a fair canvass of the result will still give us the 185 votes required to elect'."

6

Usually calm men gave in to nerves. "I seemed all day to walk through the valley of the shadow of death," Matthews wrote to Hayes just before going to New Orleans to be a key visiting statesman. There and in Washington Matthews played a role that more than repaid the favor Hayes did for him in the Kenyon days in persuading him not to ruin his college career.[8] Another close friend, "Dick" Anderson in Dayton, wrote: "I do not think I could stand such excitement for another week without going crazy." [9] A few weeks later this friend dropped dead.

Hayes, who used to "go to pieces on the slightest provocation," maintained, however, his usual apparent serenity. He did not make any public claim of victory. Newspaper reporters tried to draw him out. He put them off with pleasantries, or suggestions that everyone be calm. In so conducting himself, he was demonstrating possession of what Sardis Birchard proudly said he had, "good sense, like a Horse."

One false move by him then might have turned the scales against himself, or, in the excited idea of some, "unleashed the dogs of war." He made no such move.

Through the whole ordeal he remained, outwardly at least, the serene man.

CHAPTER LII

"I Have No Doubt"

1

OF COURSE, prior to the final decisions of the returning boards, there was no basis for anyone to make a positive claim one way or another.

These decisions were due by December 6, the date set by federal statute for the electoral college to meet. The South Carolina decision came early, November 22. The Florida decision was delayed until December 5. The Louisiana decision did not arrive until the very last minute, on December 6.

All three were for Hayes. If these decisions, forwarded by the governors of the respective states to the office of the presiding officer of the U. S. Senate in proper legal form, as far as anyone knew, had been accepted as conclusive, this would have ended the matter. Hayes would have been elected by one vote.

But this was not to be. The returning-board decisions did not end the suspense, or the crisis. The crisis had only begun.

2

The Democrats announced immediately that all of the returning-board decisions would be challenged. Double sets of electoral votes were sent to Congress from these states for the final counting, with Oregon, as expected, presenting an additional complication. In Oregon Governor Lafayette F. Grover, Democrat, refused to recognize John W. Watts, the Republican postmaster (who by then had resigned his federal position) as having been chosen an elector.

Grover issued a certificate to E. A. Cronin, Democrat. The Republican electors refused to concede the validity of the governor's action and cast three votes for Hayes, in accord with the conceded election results in the state. Cronin then "appointed" two other men to act with him as Oregon's electoral college, and this trio cast two votes for Hayes and one for Tilden.

So two sets of returns were due from Oregon also, with the one Tilden vote, if held valid, enough to decide the election, regardless of the votes from the Southern states. For the Democrats, who sought to induce the country to believe that they were pure and the Republicans were villainous, this Oregon byplay was a costly boomerang. For evidence later showed that Democratic money was used to achieve the Oregon result, that bribery of a Republican elector was attempted. Moreover, this evidence pointed to none other than Colonel W. T. Pelton, nephew of Tilden, who lived at Tilden's home at No. 15 Gramercy Park, New York, and was secretary of the Democratic National Committee.[1]

3

The seamy story of the Oregon situation began when Dr. George L. Miller of Omaha, member of the Democratic National Committee and then editor of the Omaha *Herald,* was asked by the committee to help arrange for the one Democratic electoral vote. He sent to Oregon one J. N. H. Patrick, described later as a shadowy mine-stock operator.[2] How Patrick, as well as others, looked on his mission is illustrated by a series of telegrams he sent in cipher. In translation one read:

Portland, Nov. 28th, 1876.

TO W. T. PELTON,
NO. 15 GRAMERCY PARK, NEW YORK.
CERTIFICATE WILL BE ISSUED TO ONE DEMOCRAT; MUST PURCHASE REPUBLICAN ELECTOR TO RECOGNIZE AND ACT WITH DEMOCRAT AND SECURE VOTE AND PREVENT TROUBLE. DEPOSIT TEN THOUSAND DOLLARS MY CREDIT KOUNTZE BROTHER, 12 WALL STREET. ANSWER.

J. N. H. PATRICK.[3]

As it happened, a Republican elector was not "purchased." But some $15,000 was provided for Patrick's use through Colonel Pelton, $3,000 of which was known to have been given to a law firm, and another $3,000 to the Democratic elector, Cronin, who insisted he had to have such a sum or he could not deliver his vote in Washington.[4] Colonel Pelton denied "remembrance" of the Patrick message. He asserted that "there was not any attempt to purchase a Republican elector. . . . But even if Mr. Patrick did suggest that, it does not prove anything." [5]

Inferences, however, were inevitable. If "corruption was in the air," in Henry Watterson's phrase, on behalf of the Republicans, the situation was no different, indeed more specific, concerning the Democrats in Oregon. Worse still for the Democrats, other evidence was brought out at the time that Democratic agents were also intent on bribing Republican electors in South Carolina and Florida, matters that further involved Tilden's nephew.[6]

In St. Louis W. G. Eliot, grandfather of T. S. Eliot, the poet, reflected the view of earnest Republicans. The Oregon manipulations, he exclaimed, were "outrageously villainous." [7] The revelations of Democratic perfidy were considered by many sufficient answer to reports of highhandedness, disregard of the law and also of alleged solicitation of bribes on the part of the Republicans that soon came from Louisiana.

4

Of the truth of most of these Louisiana reports there could be little doubt. Certainly there was no doubt in the minds of those aware that the Louisiana returning board was headed by J. Madison Wells, a principal cog in the Kellogg-Packard carpetbagger machine. In 1867 Wells had been removed as provisional governor of Louisiana by none other than General Phil Sheridan, who said he was "a political trickster and a dishonest man." [8] Much testimony would be given later to show that Wells had not reformed. There was some indication that he, or men claiming to represent him, made overtures to both Republicans and Democrats to be paid for "delivering" the returning board.

Hewitt, apparently, was convinced that Wells offered to sell him the decision of the board for Tilden for $1,000,000. Details of this incident added up to a fantastic story—a story suggesting, however, that this alleged "offer" was taken too seriously by Hewitt, that adventurers were operating beyond the real intention of Wells. By the time this supposed offer reached Hewitt it came from one man, who said he represented another man, who had carried a letter from Wells to United States Senator J. R. West of Louisiana, a Republican, all of which could be interpreted in various ways.[9]

Wells may even have desired to give the impression to Republicans that he *might* sell out to the Democrats in order that the decisions he intended to make all along for the Republican cause would be more "appreciated." [10] An associate said Wells "was bulldozing around" to get the Republicans to pay him for doing what he intended to do anyway.[11]

Later Hewitt would say that he was told that Wells and the Louisiana board could be purchased as a whole for $200,000.[12] At another time the figure was set at $30,000. Finally it was said that Wells did persuade some unnamed Republicans to pay him $2,800 for some state warrants worth substantially less.[13]

All of this admittedly was gossip and rumor, or based on testimony of men with reputations no better than that of Wells. The inference would be that if Wells, or persons supposedly acting for him, offered to sell out to the Democrats, and the Democrats declined to buy, the Republicans did enter into such a deal. But this was only inference.

Undoubtedly promises were made to Wells and his associates that they would be "taken care of" in case of Republican victory. They were given jobs later. Democrats pointed to this as proof of bribery. The Republican retort was that, naturally, "faithful" Republicans would be taken care of, that justice required they should not be "abandoned."

Whatever the truth, J. Madison Wells certainly personified the atmosphere that prevailed in New Orleans. Not only did Republicans suspect Democrats, and vice versa, of wrongdoing. Republicans also suspected other Republicans, Democrats mistrusted other Democrats, and numerous key figures changed their stories so many times that the truth about almost any particular matter could never be had.[14] Senator Sherman wrote to his wife: "I have got an insight into the history & conduct of politics here that alarms me for the Peace of the whole country. The spirit of politics is so different [in Louisiana] than with us that we cannot judge of things here by which we see in Ohio."[15] It may be that Sherman was "educated." If so, it was a case of an expert being taught by experts.

5

That the Louisiana board under Wells acted in a highhanded manner during its hearings is unquestionable. In particular, this was true in the throwing out of the votes of various parishes, enough to establish a Republican majority in the state, on the basis of affidavits concerning intimidation.

The law under which the board acted provided that such affidavits, corroborated by at least three persons in addition to the local election supervisors, should be attached to the election returns and mailed to the returning board immediately after the election. In numerous cases this was not done. Some of the affidavits on their face were obviously prepared several days later; some even during the returning-board proceedings. But the returning boards accepted such affidavits.

To be kept in mind is the fact that not all, or even much, of this was done by the Republicans of Louisiana for the national ticket. Rather, their main interest was in keeping control of the state regime in Louisiana, the state ticket presumably rising or falling with the national ticket. Likewise, what the Democrats did was mainly for their state ticket, not for Tilden. If any Louisiana politician really was concerned about either Hayes or Tilden, that was something purely coincidental. But both sides used the national situation for their local purposes, a situation in which both national parties found themselves forced to co-operate.

The Democrats insisted that the admitted failure to prepare many affidavits at the specified time invalidated them, and also was tantamount to proof that there was no intimidation. In general, the Republican defense was that the supervisors did not dare make out the affidavits on the scene for fear of violence against them. It was safe for them to do so only after they had arrived in New Orleans, where they would be protected by federal troops. The Wells returning board said that this danger did in fact justify "technical" violations of the law, in order to get at "the equities." In this, it was supported by the Republican visiting statesmen, including Sherman, Garfield and Matthews.

Counteraffidavits were submitted by the Democrats which refuted the Republican evidence as to intimidation. But these received scant attention from the Wells returning board. Here the board followed the letter of the law, which required it to consider only affidavits of the election supervisors. Later some of the supervisors admitted they committed perjury in the affidavits, at least in details. In at least one case, forgery would be proved in court. "I have no doubt I run the risk of being called a partisan in the position I shall take," Garfield wrote to his wife about his part in helping to prepare some of the affidavits.[16] Of course he was called that. For he was that, as was everyone involved from both parties.

However, the Republican visiting statesmen put forth what they considered an ironclad moral defense of the actions of the returning board. This was the theory that Louisiana would have gone for the Republicans if the Negroes had not been intimidated and that this justified the acceptance of affidavits supporting the fact (as they viewed it) of intimidation, even those sworn to by obvious political rascals. To Hayes on November 23, Senator Sherman wrote from New Orleans:

> We are now collecting the testimony as to the bulldozed parishes. It seems more like the history of hell than of civilized communities. The means adopted are almost incredible, but were fearfully effective upon an ignorant and superstitious people. That you would have received at a fair election a large majority in Louisiana, no honest man can question; that you did not receive a majority is equally clear. But that intimidation of the very kind and nature provided against by the Louisiana law did enter into and control the election, in more election polls than would change the result and give you the vote, I believe as firmly as I write this. The difficulty of gathering this testimony and putting it in the legal form has been very great, but I believe has been fully met.
>
> The whole case rests upon the action of the returning board. I have carefully observed them, and have formed a high opinion of Governor Wells and Colonel T. C. Anderson. They are firm, judicious, and, as far as I can judge, thoroughly honest and conscientious.[17]

Sherman went ridiculously far there in praise of J. Madison Wells. Even Garfield conceded this.[18] But Garfield, too, was convinced of the "hellish" nature of the Democratic tactics. Probably the most candid assessment of the situation was made by another of the Republican visiting statesmen, Congressman William "Pig Iron" Kelley of Pennsylvania, who, on the floor of Congress, later said: "If I should be driven to the alternative of choosing between results of an election attained by peaceful methods of fraud and results obtained by the perpetration of such terrible violence and outrage as I was convinced had been used in Louisiana, I would prefer to rebuke the violence and protect the weak by accepting the results of peaceful fraud." [19]

Still later Kelley said that he "had no doubt that there had been fraud practiced on both sides." [20] He thus voiced the final historical judgment. The decisive factor, at this stage, was that the Republicans had the power, in the returning-board laws, to decide between frauds.

6

This, however, was not the position of Hayes, as he stated it in answering Sherman. "A fair election would have given us about forty electoral votes at the South—at least that many," he wrote. "But we are not to allow our friends to defeat one outrage and fraud by another. There must be nothing crooked on our part. Let Mr. Tilden have the place by violence, intimidation and fraud, rather than undertake to prevent it by means that will not bear the severest scrutiny." [21] So he had to be satisfied fully that what was done in Louisiana to give him its nine electoral votes was justified morally, as well as legally and politically. His conscience would not permit him to adopt easily the Kelley view that one type of fraud justified another.

Associates like Sherman and Garfield knew this. After they had finished their work in New Orleans, they made a point of stopping at Columbus to report to Hayes in person before going on to Washington. Their purpose was to convince him that he need feel no qualms about a favorable Louisiana decision.

"They spread before me very fully the condition of things in Louisiana, and the action of the returning board," Hayes related at the time. "They emphatically endorsed the general fairness and honesty of the board's conduct. They said it was the opinion of all of the Republicans who went down to New Orleans that the Republican ticket was lawfully and honestly entitled to be declared elected."

He also put each "statesman" through cross-examination. "All concurred in saying in the strongest terms that the evidence and the law entitled the Republican ticket to the certificate of election." [22]

Hayes was aware of information that pictured the Louisiana Republican leaders as carpetbaggers guilty of low-order politics, of the type he could not possibly condone. But the men who gave him a different picture were of such stature that, granting he was believing what he wanted to believe, he felt justified in telling Schurz on December 6: "I have no doubt that we are justly and legally entitled to the Presidency. My conversations with Sherman, Garfield . . . and others settled the question in my mind as to Louisiana."

CHAPTER LIII

IMPASSE

1

By THEN the main stage was Washington. The ultimate decision was up to Congress. Endless controversy would ensue over the honesty of the returning boards, as well as over the action in Oregon.

As a practical matter at the time, this controversy was meaningless. The practical questions were: How was the dispute to be settled? Where was the power in law to decide between double sets of electoral votes?

Ordinary citizens assumed the answers could be had readily from a reading of the Constitution. But this was not so. The Constitution provided that the electors in each state shall send the certificates of their decisions "to the seat of the Government of the United States, directed to the President of the Senate," and that "the President of the Senate shall, in the presence of the Senate and House of Representatives, open all the certificates and the votes shall then be counted." Did this mean that the president of the Senate had the power to count the votes? Did counting include "deciding" which votes shall be counted? The language of the Constitution did not permit a definitive answer.

The Constitution was clear as to the procedure in case no candidate for President had a majority of the electoral votes. Then "the House of Representatives shall choose immediately, by ballot, the President." But so long as majorities were claimed for both Hayes and Tilden, this provision did not apply. The Constitution was also clear as to consequences if the House of Representatives did not choose a President before March 4. "Then the Vice-President shall act as President." But on the immediate issue it was silent.

2

By general agreement Congress was assumed to possess the power to clear up the confusion by legislation. It had done so in the past. Between 1865 and 1876 the two houses of Congress had in effect Joint Rule Twenty-two, which provided: If either house rejects the electoral

336

vote of a state, the vote is disregarded. If then no candidate has a majority, the election is to be thrown into the House of Representatives.

But Joint Rule Twenty-two was not readopted by the Congress that convened in January 1876. The reason for this "oversight" was obvious. The House was dominated by Democrats. Leaders of the Republican Senate, notably Senator Morton, saw that to readopt this rule would give the Democratic majority in the House the power to choose the next President in case of a contest.

In 1875 Senator Morton did urge that Congress adopt legislation to provide for a substitute method of deciding between two sets of electoral votes from a state, for this same issue had come up in connection with Louisiana, as well as Georgia, in the 1872 election. But then the dispute was not critical. For Grant had a clear majority over Greeley, without the votes of those states, which were rejected under the joint rule. So Congress delayed passing any legislation. Neither house wanted to do anything affirmative that might give the other an advantage.

3

A good many persons had answers. Guy Bryan thought that Hayes and Tilden should meet as gentlemen, face to face, secretly, and decide between themselves who should have the office.[1] But that kind of solution, like many another, was sophomoric, as also was Guy's intimation that Hayes consider withdrawing "& put away the crown . . . from love of country & love of truth."[2] The office of President of the United States was not to be filled as if it were the same as choosing the head of the Nu Pi Kappa at old Kenyon.

Hayes had one answer. He firmly championed the view that the Constitution should be interpreted so as to give the president of the Senate the power to decide, there then being no Vice-President because of the death of Henry Wilson. Linked to this was the point—indeed, the basic point—that the president of the Senate would accept as valid those certificates which met the legal requirements on their face. That is, he should accept those sent in from the state officials authorized to issue them, and who attested that electors entitled to act as such, by canvassed results of the election, had met and cast their votes at the time prescribed by law.

Hayes, of course, felt that these requirements were met by the certificates issued for him in the three disputed Southern states. For in those states the returning boards had the legal power to declare who had been elected, and the certificates for his election were issued by recognized governors. To be sure, this left a complication with regard to Oregon. But Hayes confidently believed that a second certificate issued by the Oregon secretary of state, giving the state's three votes to him, would be held valid.

Later Hayes modified his position importantly with the idea that once the president of the Senate had decided, a *quo warranto* action should be filed and the proceeding taken to the Supreme Court. In effect, this would give the final decision to the highest court of the land, and the matter would be disposed of like any lawsuit.[3]

Tilden had another answer. He just as firmly held that the president of the Senate should not decide. He maintained that the power of decision was in the two houses of Congress and that the president of the Senate merely had the authority to *open* the certificates. Under his theory Congress had the right to go behind the certificates of the electoral votes to determine if they were based on a valid canvass, and the vote of no state could be counted against the judgment of either house.[4]

In effect, this called for a revival of Joint Rule Twenty-two. The inevitable result, in the Republican view, was that the Democratic House would reject the official certificate of at least one of the disputed states. Thus neither claimant would have a majority. Then the Democratic House would choose the President. This, of course, was what the Tilden Democrats intended. For then the House would elect Tilden.

Interesting was the fact that in the debate that followed Republicans and Democrats changed traditional positions. For Hayes Republicans now stoutly maintained that it was an unconstitutional invasion of a state's rights for Congress to go behind a certificate of electoral votes sent to Congress in proper form. This, they argued, would give Congress, rather than the states, the ultimate power in the election of Presidents. Just as stoutly Democrats rang the rafters with arguments that the only proper procedure was for Congress to go behind the action of the state officials. As often, State rights was a flexible doctrine.

4

With his provision for a final decision by the Supreme Court, the procedure offered by Hayes was clearly the most clean-cut, expeditious and satisfactory from the standpoint of legalistic procedure. A Supreme Court decision would have satisfied all reasonable demands —certainly in theory—that whoever was chosen President would hold the office through established juridical procedure. Republican leaders close to Hayes, notably Sherman and Morton in the Senate and Garfield in the House, supported Hayes's views.

But it was obvious from the beginning that the Democratic House would never consent, and with good reason. The President of the Senate—T. W. Ferry of Michigan—was a "stalwart" Republican. A majority of the members of the Supreme Court were Republicans. The Chief Justice, "Mott" Waite, not only was a Republican but an Ohioan and a friend of Hayes, also a man who apparently hated Tilden.

Such was the partisan spirit of the day that it was assumed openly that Senator Ferry would decide as a Republican. It was also assumed, only slightly less openly, that the Republican members of the Supreme Court would do likewise. It was considered equally obvious that the Senate, being Republican, would not agree to Tilden's solution. No one questioned the assumption that the House, with its Democratic majority, would, if it had the choice, choose Tilden as President because he was the Democrat.

So there was an impasse.

5

Curiously both Hayes and Tilden displayed more aggressiveness in defending their respective views on how the dispute should be settled than in any other aspect of the whole affair. "My judgment is that neither House of Congress, nor both combined, have any right to interfere in the count. It is for the Vice-President [or the President of the Senate] to do it all. His action is final. There should be no compromise of our constitutional rights. We should firmly insist upon them." So Hayes expressed himself.[5]

Tilden was equally obdurate. When a compromise began to be discussed Hayes and Tilden reacted similarly. Each was sure that treachery was being engaged in by his followers. Hayes was most suspicious of Senator Conkling. Tilden was most suspicious of Senators Thurman and Thomas F. Bayard, both of whom had been contenders for the Presidential nomination that Tilden received. Before the issue was ended Tilden seemed suspicious of the loyalty to him of nearly all Democrats, including Chairman Hewitt, and especially of most Southern Democrats—this last with considerable basis. But Hayes also had reasons to wonder about many of his party leaders besides Conkling. On both sides, for various reasons, there were those who stood to profit more from their candidate *losing* than from his winning. This was a phase about the whole situation that could not be overlooked.

CHAPTER LIV

Danger

1

Out in California Henry George analyzed the impasse as a situation "both scandalous and dangerous." It was scandalous, he said, because the uncertainty implied a doubt as to "the efficacy of the law." It was dangerous because "when law fails, force is the necessary resort."[1]

There was, in fact, a good deal of talk, perhaps more than talk, to the effect that the Democrats intended a *coup d'état*, certainly if the president of the Senate should declare Hayes to be elected against the wishes of the House, and perhaps in support of an effort to have the House declare Tilden to be President regardless of the Senate. Likewise, there was much talk, some apparently of an informed nature, that Hayes would be inaugurated with the support of the army under Grant—in short by a kind of military dictatorship.

How much of the strident language heard in and out of Congress, adding up to a threatened armed uprising, most of this Democratic, was bluff could never be known. But even a future Chief Justice, Melville W. Fuller, then a Democratic Party wheel horse in Chicago, made utterances as if he approved an uprising, if Hayes was installed.

"Tilden or Blood" and "Tilden or War" were slogans often uttered. On January 8, 1877, in connection with traditional Democratic celebrations of Andy Jackson Day, meetings were held in many cities throughout the nation at which such utterances were common. The most famous were those of Editor Watterson, then a Democratic Congressman. Speaking in Ford's Theater in Washington, he urged that 100,000 Democrats assemble in the capital to call for the inauguration of Tilden. Watterson included the qualifications that the 100,000 should be "unarmed" and "peaceful," and that their purpose should be merely to exercise their right to petition.[2] But in the excitement of the time these qualifications were generally lost sight of.

2

Other Jackson Day speakers were not so careful. On the steps of the federal courthouse in Toledo, James Steadman, a Civil War gen-

341

eral, offered to lead 100,000 men to Washington, presumably armed. In Columbus another ex-general, Thomas Ewing, Jr., son of the great lawyer who had so fulsomely praised Hayes in the Summons murder case, spoke pointedly of "resistance to tyranny" at a meeting which adopted a resolution declaring that if the president of the Senate tried to count Hayes in as President, the action should be "resisted by the people to the last extremity, even if that extremity be an appeal to arms."

In Indianapolis George W. Julian, a founder of the Republican Party, but then a Democrat, vowed that if the "will of the people," by which he meant Tilden's election, was defied "by overt acts," those who did so "shall receive the same treatment which the nation awarded to the men who appealed from the ballot to the bayonet in 1861." Joseph Pulitzer spoke of a willingness "to bare his breast to the bullets of the tyrant and rush headlong upon his glittering steel." [3]

Reports were widely circulated that actual plans for an uprising had been formulated. The gist of one was that former General John M. Corse in Chicago had organized Democratic war veterans for an "army," with the idea of seizing arms from federal arsenals. A Senate investigation produced some lurid telegrams from General Corse, who was chairman of the Democratic campaign committee in Chicago. To Tilden's nephew, Colonel Pelton, one telegram, sent on December 6, said: GLORY TO GOD. HOLD ON TO THE ONE ELECTORAL VOTE IN OREGON. I HAVE 100,000 MEN TO BACK IT UP.[4]

Earlier Corse sent to a Congressman from Chicago, in connection with the Louisiana situation, the following:

November 15, 1876.

PERRY H. SMITH, SAINT CHARLES HOTEL, NEW ORLEANS, LA. IF LOUISIANA ELECTORAL VOTE IS STOLEN FROM US, WE WILL GET CALIFORNIA AND OREGON. WE HAVE ONE HUNDRED AND SIXTY THOUSAND EX-SOLDIERS NOW EN-ROLLED. VAST NUMBER OF REPUBLICANS WITH US. STAND FIRM.

CORSE.[5]

3

Hayes was told that Tilden himself discussed a *coup d'état*, this on the authority of Murat Halstead.

At the time the southern members of Congress paid a visit to Gramercy Park, when the question of "Tilden or War" was heard throughout the land, Tilden drew from a pigeon hole the details for a war, which showed that he had thoroughly canvassed the subject and meant mischief. He said that Ferry would count you in and that you would be inaugurated at Washn. while he would be inaugurated at New York. He showed them that the Governor of New York [Tilden] would call out the militia, which he thought would amount to 22,000 men; that he could get two regiments from Connecticut; two from New Jersey; two from Delaware, and almost any number from Maryland.

"But," said Lamar, "such an army cannot be supported without money." Said Tilden, "There are $14,000,000 in the sub-treasury at New York, which will be seized at the start. Under this plan, we shall have a complete line from Connecticut to Washington, and back of Washington, we have Virginia and the South." His plan contemplated the leaving of the regiments of Connecticut in Connecticut, to protect himself from New England.

Halstead says that not a line of this has ever been published, but that it is true he has no doubt in the world.[6]

If any such conversation occurred at Tilden's home, it is to be doubted that Tilden seriously considered this plan. Indeed, a complaint of Democratic leaders against Tilden was that he showed little spirit for any kind of fight. There is no reason to disbelieve statements that Tilden made clear his position to Thurman, who had said that the alternatives were: fight, back down, or arbitrate. According to Abram Hewitt, Tilden's reply was: "It will not do to fight. We have just emerged from one civil war, and it will never do to engage in another civil war; it would end in the destruction of free government. We cannot back down. We can, therefore, only arbitrate."[7]

4

But the question remained whether Tilden could control his partisans. Responsible men believed there was a possibility of war, even though Watterson said later, "Truth to say, both sides were playing something of a 'bluff.'"[8] John Tyler, Jr., son of the Whig President, wrote to Attorney General Taft, "Let others cry peace—peace—and it is to be fervently hoped that the peace of the Nation will not be broken, but it seems to me that the practical presumption on the part of our present national authorities should be that there is to be no peace."

He foresaw a situation which would end with either Tilden or Hayes hanged as "a traitor." [9]

Joseph Medill wrote to William Henry Smith that he believed Tilden "plans a coup d'état." He hoped, but pessimistically, that Hayes would be "safely in without war, bloodshed and civil commotion." [10]

General Orville Babcock, Grant's secretary, received a warning that Missouri Democrats were plotting to seize 700 cannon and "fixed ammunition, enough to supply an·army of sixty thousand men," from the St. Louis federal arsenal, with the aid of Democratic officers. [11]

Nor was all this bellicosity on the Democratic side alone, though the Republican line was to make it appear so. "You ask as to the temper of the people on general questions," the chairman of the Iowa Republicans wrote to Senator Allison. "If the Senate believes Hayes elected, and so declares him, Iowa will back it up with 100,000 men, if necessary." [12] And General Sherman, on his own account as well as on instructions from Grant, made conspicuous preparations to place the federal army in an emergency posture in Washington and elsewhere. [13]

5

Tilden, or his associates, it seems clear, were prepared for some kind of drastic action, a kind that obviously could have set off commotion. On December 15, 1876, Stanley Matthews had a highly confidential talk in New York City with David Dudley Field, lawyer and then in Congress, considered Tilden's "next friend." On the basis of this talk, Matthews advised Hayes:

Mr. D. D. F. stated emphatically his present conviction that Tilden has been elected but says he is open to more light and better information. . . . He hopes that the two Houses will agree upon some result, or upon some principles that will decide it. If they do not, he predicts that the Senate will arrive at and declare one result, and the House, another; that you will be inaugurated through the overpowering influence of Grant & the Army & will be recognized as such by the House; but that the latter will concur in making, with the Senate, all necessary appropriations for the support of the Government except the salaries of the Pres^t, Cabinet & Foreign Ministers, including the pay of officers of the Army, but not for the rank & file, the object being to disband it; & that this state of things would continue until the next Congressional election. I pointed out that this was merely anarchy & civil war; but he did not seem to see it; saying, however, that if it should appear necessary for the preservation of the public peace, he would keep up the Army but under stringent provisions of law, forbidding its abuse.[14]

There was more to this important letter, as will be brought out later. But this much suggests that an unprecedented extralegal step was being considered, one amounting to a suspension of the Presidency.

CHAPTER LV

"Fishing"

1

IN SUCH troubled waters there is likely always to be fishing. The fishing is done by men who see an opportunity to use a general situation for achieving particular goals, some relevant, some irrelevant. It was so then. A number of separate crews of fishermen were operating, in both parties and regardless of party. Certain Republicans saw an opportunity to get future political advantage from Hayes by withholding support from him until he had promised certain offices. Certain Democrats followed the same procedure concerning offices—and other matters.

Others had other fish to catch and fry. Some of these efforts were definitely crooked, including attempted "deals," or attempted personal or political blackmail, with financial considerations attached. Others were for reputable ends but to be served by undercover means.

Some had to do with pressure to resolve incidental election disputes, such as the right of Governor Kellogg of Louisiana to be seated as a U. S. Senator by election of the Packard legislature, which the Democrats insisted was no legislature at all. Others were wholly honest and even probably for the good of the nation. In the immense machinery set in motion, there were wheels within wheels.

2

Soon three major efforts along this line emerged. One was an attempt by Southern Democrats to use the crisis as a means of bringing reconstruction to a final, official end. This meant the seeking of an advance agreement that, if they permitted Hayes to be inaugurated peacefully, his administration would withdraw troops from Louisiana, as well as Florida and South Carolina, where they had been sent during and after the election, thus permitting the last three Republican regimes to fall to the Democrats, something, incidentally, which Hayes clearly intended anyway.

Another was an effort by a small coterie to get Hayes to agree to approve a federal subsidy for financing the Texas and Pacific Railroad to the Pacific Ocean, thus achieving the old dream of Southerners of a rail route through the South to the Pacific—in exchange for which interested Southern Democrats would desert Tilden.[1]

A third effort, approved by Hayes himself, spurred by Matthews among others, was a plan by Republicans to place the Republican Party in a new position in the South. Basically this plan was to revive the dead Whig Party but under the Republican name, an object that especially appealed to Hayes, still essentially a Whig, he thought.

This last endeavor called for an alliance of moderate Northern Republicans with the former Whigs who had become Democrats in the South. They, rather than the carpetbaggers, were to be recognized as the leaders of the party in the Southern states, and with them as a nucleus there was to be built a new, national Republican Party, one that could stand for an end to sectionalism.

The considerations here were to include giving to the former Whigs places and posts in the Hayes administration, including even cabinet posts. Also, as a further inducement, the Hayes administration would approve proposals for building up the South economically, for healing the scars of the war, including a generous attitude toward internal improvements (the ancient Whig doctrine) and, possibly, toward the railroad to the Pacific. This Whiggish hope, a grandiose one, was for nothing short of a realignment of politics in America, a going back to the alignment that preceded the war.

At the important meeting that Stanley Matthews, "next friend" of Hayes, held with David Dudley Field, "next friend" of Tilden, attended also by capitalist Cyrus Field, this plan was first broached by Matthews. To Hayes, Matthews reported: "I have suggested to Mr. Cyrus Field, who deprecates very strongly the possible success of Democratic schemes, to find means of influencing leading representatives & Senators from Southern States to offer their alliance to the Republican party, as the most wholesome measure for the cure of the evils peculiar to their section and giving the most satisfaction to the whole country."

Significantly Cyrus Field, brother of David Dudley, was participant that night at a meeting in New York "of a dozen or more of the wealthiest men in this city, equally divided as to politics, for the purpose of consulting as to what course ought to be or could be taken, to bring about . . . a settlement."[2] Thus Matthews had the ears of men with the power, perhaps, to carry out the plan.

Before the crisis was ended, all these efforts were, to an extent, interlocked. The Texas and Pacific subsidy plan and the plan for the

Whig revival were in fact two strings on one fiddle. All played a role in the final result, though not in all cases as the promoters intended. Moreover, in the end only one of the major efforts, the first, was successful, it being in the cards anyway. But the maneuvering in each case bore some fruit, if not precisely the kind wanted.

3

It was the intention of the promoters of the Texas and Pacific matter, as well as the participants in the proposal to revive Whiggery in the South, these last including Hayes, that their efforts should result in adoption by Congress of the Hayes view that the president of the Senate should decide who was elected.

Both groups moved toward that end. It may be that they would have been successful had the Republicans in Congress maintained a solid front. Then, with the support of some Southern Democrats, the Hayes plan could have been put over. But the Republicans were not united.

In Senator Conkling of New York open hostility was met. Conkling, leading a group of Senators, not only challenged sharply the right of the president of the Senate to make the decision, but would be quoted as saying privately that he believed Tilden was the true winner. None other than M. S. Quay, the Pennsylvania political boss wrote to Hayes: "Conkling is undoubtedly faithless and Col. McClure of Philade[lphia] assures me he is in correspondence with Tilden."

Conkling's attitude was ascribed to his ambitious personality marked, Hayes would say later, by a desire to rule or ruin. It was also said that he was motivated by the idea that, if there occurred a complete stalemate, he might emerge as Acting President by being elected president of the Senate.[4] A more basic explanation for Conkling's "treachery," as his conduct was viewed by the Hayes leaders, as well as by Hayes himself, probably was that Conkling represented the hard core of "Grantism" in the party. To this element Hayes's reformist tendencies were anathema. Conkling may well have preferred a Democratic administration to one headed by Hayes.

An effort was made to win Conkling over. Senator Sherman arranged for a meeting between Hayes and a friend of Conkling. Conkling's friend affirmed that the Senator believed Hayes was "in the hands of the reform element." He suggested that Conkling be offered the post of Secretary of State. Hayes would only say on this that he would "try to give just consideration to the claims of all sections of the party."[6] While Conkling's friend professed to be "pleased" with the interview, it brought no results. The split in the party continued.[7]

4

To offset this split, the Hayes Republicans intensified efforts to win over Democrats in the Senate and House to their view for permitting the president of the Senate to decide. There was hope in this strategy, for the Democrats also were divided.

Few Southern Democrats had taken part in the talk about using force to inaugurate Tilden. Watterson was almost a solitary exception. Soon even Watterson dropped his attitude of presumed belligerence, with some evidence existing that he was cooled off measurably by expected or actual benefits from the Texas and Pacific plan.

The great truth that emerged was this: The South wanted no more war. Its real leaders did not believe that the seating of Tilden, even if they felt he was fairly elected, justified a resort to any activity that might lead to armed conflict.

Governor John M. Palmer of Illinois perceived this from the start while in Louisiana as a Democratic visiting statesman. "There is less excitement here than in Illinois," he wrote to his wife on November 19 from New Orleans. "One thing is certain that if there shall be convulsions . . . they will not commence in the South."[8] To the chagrin of Northern Democrats, the dominant leaders of the South, such as Congressman Lucius Q. C. Lamar, later Senator and still later on the Supreme Court, were more interested in freeing the South from "bayonet rule," as they put it.

At a caucus of Democratic Congressmen held in Washington on December 8, Southerners led in emphasizing that their aim was "to secure the peaceful inauguration of Tilden and Hendricks," but with accent on the term "peaceful."[9]

A few days later Garfield became aware that not only were Southerners much less belligerent than Northerners, but some seemed in a mood to desert Tilden altogether. In his diary Garfield noted that Congressman Casey Young of Tennessee had indicated to him "that if we could give such men as he good ground to stand on, fifty Democratic congressmen would stand by Hayes."[10] That was the tip-off.

5

On December 12 Garfield wrote a significant letter to Hayes.

. . . Two forces are at work. The Democratic business men of the country are more anxious for quiet than for Tilden, and the leading Southern Democrats in Congress, especially those who were old Whigs, are saying that they have seen war enough and don't care to follow their Northern associates. . . . Just what sort of assurances the Southern members want is not quite so clear. . . . Let me say I don't think anybody should be the custodian of your policy, or have any power to commit or embarrass you in any way, but it would be a great help if, in some discreet way, those Southern men who are dissatisfied with Tilden and his violent followers could know that the South was going to be treated with kind consideration by you. Several Southern men have said within a week that in the matter of internal improvements they had been much better treated by Republicans than they were likely to be by the Democrats—and they talk a great deal about the old Whigs having been forced, unwillingly, into the Democratic party.[11]

Hayes also received from Congressman John A. Kasson of Iowa an equally significant letter.

. . . I cannot, in a letter, explain to you the situation as I comprehend it. I think, however, that two premises may be assumed: 1st. That 185 votes will be ascertained and counted by the Senate for you, followed by the declaration of your election as President. 2d. That our security against the subsequent election of Tilden by the House is to be found in a division of sentiment in the Democracy, led by Southern Representatives.
The basis of this division exists in the indisposition of a large part of the South to become again embroiled in national disorder, and in their wish to recover intelligent white rule in the South. To give them this need not involve the sacrifice of the constitutional rights of the Negro, nor should it. Nor will they demand it. They perceive an opportunity to establish a cordial union with the North, which is Republican, and end forever the old strife.[12]

6

Later, historians generally described what followed exclusively in terms of a bargain. It was said that Southern Congressmen agreed to back Hayes in exchange for a pledge by his representatives that he would end the use of federal troops in support of the last of the carpet-bag regimes. That, and no more. But this interpretation did not get at the heart of what the negotiators were attempting to achieve. The specific matter of removing troops was but incidental to the broader program. That was going to happen anyway, though the Southerners hoped to get it in writing.

The broader program concerned the new political realignment, which Garfield touched on with his reference to the "old Whigs" and which Kasson also referred to in the phrase, "a cordial union with the North."

The starting-off point was related to Garfield's observation that leading Southern Democrats were old Whigs who had joined the Democratic Party *unwillingly*. By economic philosophy, the normal basis for political affiliation, they naturally belonged with the former Whigs of the North.

The former Whigs of the North—of whom Hayes was an example—in 1876 seemed destined to be the dominant leaders of the Republican Party in its national aspect, insofar as the Republican Party was national. So it was believed that there was a natural basis for the Southern ex-Whigs to become allied with the Republicans, if certain arrangements could be made.

The former Southern Whigs would get representation in the Hayes cabinet—if there were a Hayes cabinet. The former Southern Whigs would absent themselves from the House of Representatives at organization time, thus permit a technical Republican majority. This would let the Republicans organize the House. They would also help assure Republican control of the Senate, then by no means certain. Thus the Republicans would have control of both houses of Congress as well as of the executive branch. Doubtless there was an exchange of views as to future appointments to the Supreme Court. Such were practical, political aspects of the plan.

A logical next step would be disowning of the carpetbaggers. They were to disappear from the political scene as separate entities. With them would disappear also—such was the theory—the Negro issue as a major political question. For a new Republican Party in the South, based on the former Whig leadership, while accepting the new Constitutional rights of the Negroes, would stand for "intelligent white rule," in Congressman Kasson's phrase. The Negroes were to be accorded the same subordinate political status as the white laboring classes of the North.

This was not considered a betrayal of the Negroes. It would be considered a realistic handling of the Negro political problem, based not on racial discrimination but on the theory that political influence should be exercised in relation to economic and social status. Leaders of both parties believed that this idea was realistically, if not legally, in accord with the basic American idea of politics. On this "realistic" theory the Republicans were prepared to admit that the effort to elevate uneducated and propertyless Negroes to political power immediately was a mistake. Of course, this was all expedient rationalization, but it was of a kind nearly all Americans then probably wanted to accept.

7

This new Republican rationalization was sufficiently close to the views of the more intelligent, dominant white elements in the South to permit, perhaps, the ending of division between Democrats and Republicans, and between North and South, over the color line. Also, the new rationalization satisfied the consciences, so to speak, of the Republicans, in that it did not call for considering the Negroes as "subhuman." Nor did it accept the white-supremacy view that Abolition was wrong. But it postponed, for future realization, the social status for the Negroes which idealists had expected would accompany the political status given them by the Constitution. Forcing the whites of the South to accept the Negroes as full citizens was to be abandoned for a policy of letting time take its course.

Hayes could agree to all this because, as a careful reading would show, he had in effect said as much in his Letter of Acceptance concerning harmony and local government in the South. Moreover, in one letter to Guy Bryan, in October 1876, he had said on the Southern question that he believed *"time, time* is the great cure-all," and in another letter, back in 1865, "As to Southern affairs, 'the let alone policy' seems now to be the true course." [18]

Such comments he authorized Bryan to circulate industriously in the South, which Bryan did. This concept was calculated to satisfy the practical-minded Southerners and permit both parties to develop in the South from then on, on the basis of division on governmental questions not related to the racial issue. Such was the long-run political goal of the negotiators.

The Republicans, of course, stood to gain the most, if such an alliance as was hoped for was worked out. They would gain the ending of the election dispute in favor of Hayes. They would gain control of the House of Representatives, thus assuring Congressional support for the Hayes administration program. They would gain a more secure standing in the South than the carpetbag system had made possible.

8

But certain Southerners clearly were not willing to desert Tilden for political reasons alone, certainly not for the mere sentimental motive of old Whig uniting with old Whig. If they entered into an alliance so helpful to the Republican Party, they expected in return more than just cabinet representation and similar political rewards. They expected some concrete and substantial material benefits for the South, for their respective localities and, in the case of some, for themselves.

Nor was this to be dismissed wholly as venality. If they were to make a common cause with the political "enemy," even for high national considerations, they felt they had to be able to show their constituents some practical benefits for their districts. It was in this respect that they were interested, as Garfield suggested, in internal improvements, in federal aid for Southern harbors, highways, bridges, and river dredging, levees and flood control in general, especially in connection with the Lower Mississippi River.

It was in this respect also that the promoters of the Texas and Pacific saw their opportunity—they thought—but without full regard for the scruples that Hayes had concerning any project that smacked of a "subsidy grab," as will appear.

CHAPTER LVI

The Unwanted Compromise

1

IRONICALLY it was a Northern Republican, Thomas A. Scott, the financial and political genius of the Pennsylvania Railroad, who in 1876 was trying to build the Texas and Pacific. On the basis of generous federal land grants in the Indian territories of New Mexico and Oklahoma and equally generous Texas land grants, Scott attempted to go forward with the project under the pressure of being required to complete a given number of miles in a given time or lose the state land subsidies. Financing was to be through the sale of bonds secured by these land grants. His goal was to complete what John C. Frémont had started but failed to achieve before the war. And for a time Scott seemed on the way to success.

But Scott encountered double trouble. One source of trouble was the 1873 depression. Another was opposition from C. P. Huntington, a California railroad magnate who did not wish the Texas and Pacific to compete with his Southern Pacific.

The depression destroyed Scott's prospects of selling bonds in the normal way. As a way out, Congress was asked to pass legislation which, in effect, would place the credit of the federal government behind $90,000,000 worth of fifty-year Texas and Pacific bonds.[1] With interest, that meant about $200,000,000.

Scott was considered the most powerful lobbyist in the country, supposedly controlling numerous Congressmen in the North as well as the South, and, it would be said, twenty state legislatures.[2] A large group of Southern Democratic Congressmen, notably from Tennessee, Arkansas, Kentucky, Texas, Louisiana and Mississippi, supported the Texas and Pacific bill. The most powerful Democratic newspapers in the South were for the bill, making of it a "Southern project."

Yet neither the Democratic House nor the Republican Senate would take favorable action. This opposition mainly was attributed to a general disinclination of Congressmen, regardless of region or party, to support such legislation because of the bad odor of railroad subsidies as a result of the Crédit Mobilier scandal—in which Scott, incidentally, had been involved.[3] In particular was this the official Republican policy, enunciated in the party platform. But the most active opposition came from a rival lobby, that of Huntington, who talked of building a line connecting Texas and California without federal aid.

What vexed the Southern supporters of the bill most was that Northern Democratic Congressmen were no more friendly toward the legislation than Republicans, and in certain cases less so. Indeed, just before the 1876 election a Northern Democrat was responsible for a resolution putting the Democratic House on record against any and all railroad-subsidy legislation. Tilden was reported behind this move, supposedly urging it as evidence that his party really believed in reform.[4] Thus, the legislation continued to be blocked, even though Scott and Huntington had formed a truce by 1876, and both railroad lobbies then backed the Texas and Pacific bill, along with a similar bill for Huntington's Southern Pacific.

2

If the Republicans adopted the Texas and Pacific subsidy as a party measure, that would be reason enough for certain Democrats in Congress to swing their support from Tilden to Hayes, especially if the Republicans controlled the House along with the Senate, under the political deal being discussed. For Tilden, even if he did not still oppose the subsidy, would face a hostile Senate. Only with Hayes in office, and behind the bill, could it pass. So, at least, the argument ran.[5]

That was a persuasive argument. But the question was: How to get it over to enough Southerners, with the understanding that the Republican Party—and Hayes—would support the Texas and Pacific without a public explosion resulting.

Few Republican Congressmen, least of all Garfield, who still winced from the recollection of having been singed in the Crédit Mobilier scandal, wished to be found initiating co-operation with "subsidy grabbers," to win Democratic support for Hayes, regardless of the merits of the Texas and Pacific proposal. That was too dangerous politically.

It was obvious, too, that Hayes would be reluctant to put himself in such a position, even if he were satisfied that the South, as a matter of justice, was entitled to a transcontinental railroad system. When Hayes did feel that he might urge in his inaugural message—if he were to make one—general approval of such a project, he received from Schurz a reaction that showed why the matter was so delicate.

Said Schurz: "Remember the Credit Mobilier, the Blaine letters, etc." [6]

3

Even without such advice, Hayes had already made it plain that he would not enter directly into the Texas and Pacific, or the other, negotiations. Try as they might later, even with the aid of so astute a prober as Ben Butler, and other Republicans, the Democrats could not link Hayes directly with any of the wooing of the Democrats. This was for good reason. For he was not involved by any affirmative action of his own. He remained mainly passive, as during the period before the 1876 nomination. "Your views are so nearly the same as mine that I need not say a word," he told Garfield. But he added, "I am wholly uncommitted on persons and policies, except as my published letters and other public utterances show. There is nothing private." [7]

He intended to remain in that position. Senator Sherman suggested that he come to Washington "in an informal way with a view of conferences as to some important points." Hayes vetoed the idea. [8] To Sherman, however, on Christmas Day, 1876, he significantly wrote:

You know my general course of conduct. It has always seemed to me wise in case of decided antagonisms among friends not to take sides—to heal by compromise, not to aggravate, etc., etc. I wish *you* to feel authorized to speak in pretty decided terms for me whenever it seems advisable—to do this, not by reason of specific authority to do it, but from your knowledge of my general methods of action.

This, of course, went pretty far, but did leave him an out for anything he really disapproved. Hayes also declined requests that he designate someone to act as his official representative. "An authorized representative could remove some troubles . . . but think of yet greater troubles he might create," he told Congressman Kasson. [9]

General James M. Comly, editor of the *Ohio State Journal* in Columbus and a friend, finally did go to Washington. This was at Sherman's request, for the express purpose of assuring Grant that Hayes had no intention of appointing Bristow as a cabinet member, if he were declared elected. [10] Comly remained for a number of conferences with the negotiators, "speaking" for Hayes up to a point.

Moreover, Stanley Matthews was never far out of reach, having been now in Washington with the negotiators, as well as in New York, and now in Columbus with Hayes. Probably more than anyone this former Kenyon classmate was able to speak for Hayes, and often did. The full story undoubtedly would reveal Matthews to have been a key man, if not *the* key man, in association with Sherman and Comly.

4

Comly was able to "speak confidently" in particular about Hayes's reaction to the political aspect of the negotiations to win Southern support. In Comly's home, on December 1, Hayes had a confidential talk with an emissary of the Louisiana Democrats, Colonel William H. Roberts, associate editor of the New Orleans *Times*. Encouraged by Matthews, Roberts had come up to Columbus before the Louisiana returning-board decision—certain what it would be, he would say—to learn Hayes's attitude on the South in case he should become President. He specifically asked Hayes: "What do you propose to do about the respective state governments of Louisiana?" [11]

This was about a month before the white elements behind Nicholls, the Democratic-Conservative contender for governor in the election just held, turned out in armed force, seized the Louisiana Supreme Court chambers, and set up their own state "government" in opposition to that of Packard, who had been declared elected by the returning board along with the Hayes electors. But it was already plain at the time of the Roberts interview that this "revolution" in Louisiana would be attempted—just as it was plain that Wade Hampton in South Carolina would set up a similar dual government in opposition to Governor Chamberlain, also despite the adverse returning-board decision. In both cases it was clear that only federal recognition backed by federal troops could save either Packard's or Chamberlain's regime in case of a showdown. Roberts wished to find out whether Hayes would use the federal power on the side of the Republicans.

Speaking for Nicholls, and also indirectly for Hampton and other Southern leaders, Roberts gave Hayes to understand that his principals were more interested in the "redemption" of Louisiana and South Carolina than in Tilden, if a choice had to be made. [12] "If we felt that you were friendly to us, we would not make that desperate personal fight to keep you out that we certainly will make if you are not friendly," he said.[13] For the first time so far as there was a record, this comment raised the possibility of the later much publicized "bargain" concerning Louisiana and South Carolina.

But Hayes made no definite commitment. He spoke in generalities. He referred Roberts to the comments in his Letter of Acceptance concerning the South, saying, "It meant all it said and all that it implied." [14] The letter had expressed his sympathy for the "efforts" of the people of the Southern states to obtain "the blessings of honest and capable local government."

This could have been interpreted as sympathy for the white-supremacy movement against the carpetbag regimes. True, he had accompanied such expressions with the observations that the rights of all, Negroes and whites, must be respected, and that "all parts of the Constitution are sacred . . . the parts that are new no less than the parts that are old." These comments could be interpreted—though not necessarily so—as being against the white-supremacy movement. So the letter in this respect was purposely vague, though on balance favorable to the white South.

5

However, he made one comment to which no one could take exception, a seemingly platitudinous comment which nevertheless satisfied Roberts that Hayes intended to be "fair" toward the South, as Roberts interpreted "fairness." This was: "I believe, and I have always believed, that the intelligence of any country ought to govern it." [15]

Roberts' interpretation was correct. Hayes was still basically the Whig that he had been in his youth, the idolizer of Clay and Webster. Thus he was completely in sympathy with the political negotiations being worked out by his friends and the Southern former Whigs. In being able to convey assurance of this fact, Comly in Washington cited the Roberts interview and backed it up with his knowledge of Hayes's temperament from their long-standing friendship.

However, in the Texas and Pacific matter Comly could not commit Hayes. Indeed, in this phase of the negotiations Comly's role was to try to convince Hayes that it would be good politics for him to agree to the railroad subsidy. In a report to Hayes concerning a conversation with Garfield and Congressman Charles Foster, Comly pointedly observed that they had expressed "regret" that the Republican Party was on record against such subsidies. "They thought a large following might be gained for the Republican party in the South by favoring this road, and both asserted that Texas might be made a Republican state by advocating the road." [16] But they wanted Hayes personally to take the lead in openly favoring the Texas and Pacific subsidy, so as to protect them against allegations that they had become linked with the Scott railroad lobby.

This Hayes declined to do.

6

By then a separate process of negotiation was going on. The leading figures in this included, among others, most of the same men involved in the exposure of Blaine's railroad dealings before the convention— that is, William Henry Smith, Boynton, Halstead and "Dick" Smith of the Cincinnati *Commercial*, plus, tangentially, Medill, though Medill, as a Chicagoan, was almost necessarily opposed to the Texas and Pacific because of its probable adverse effect on Chicago's hopes to be a dominant railroad center.

The newspaperman Boynton had started things off early in December. He told William Henry Smith that he believed Southern support for Hayes could be obtained if the South could be offered something it wanted. He professed not to know what the South wanted. He later specifically said he "never had the least relations with the Texas & Pacific lobby." [17] But this was not at all accurate.

Actually Boynton had had dealings with the lobby through General Grenville M. Dodge of Council Bluffs, Iowa, chief engineer of the Union Pacific Railroad, who in 1876 held the same post with the Texas and Pacific.[18] Next to Scott himself, Dodge was the most influential individual member of the Scott lobby. He also represented Jay Gould in governmental matters and Dodge's influence extended to Grant himself.[19] So Boynton undoubtedly had the Texas and Pacific matter in mind all along.

After a conference in Cincinnati with the two Smiths, and probably also Halstead, Boynton was soon urging that the way to get the Southern Democratic votes was to get the Scott lobby behind the Hayes position that the president of the Senate should decide the election dispute. Also, that the way to enlist the Scott lobby was to advise Scott that Hayes favored the Texas and Pacific subsidy. To William Henry Smith, Boynton wrote: "What we want for practical success is **thirty or thirty-six votes. West** Tennessee, Arkansas, a large Kentucky element, Louisiana, Texas, Mississippi, and Tom Scott want help for the Texas & Pacific Road." He listed "strong arguments" for making that project an exception to the Republican policy of opposition to subsidies, these of a nature designed to impress Hayes. Then Boynton added:

If such arguments and views commend themselves to Governor Hayes, and [if] Tom Scott, and the prominent representatives of the states I have named could know this, Scott with his whole force would come here, and get those votes in spite of all human power, and all the howlings which blusterers North and South could put up. . . . If Governor H. feels disposed towards this enterprise as many of the best and most honest men in the Republican party do—there would certainly be no impropriety for some recognized friend of his giving Scott to understand it. He would go to work without any suggestion whatever.[20]

Smith was favorably impressed. He sent Boynton's letters to Hayes, hoping that Hayes also would be favorably disposed. He also sent to Hayes some letters from Colonel A. J. Kellar of the Memphis *Avalanche,* who was working with Boynton at Smith's suggestion, Kellar acting as a go-between on the project with Southern Congressmen. Kellar was an enthusiast for the Texas and Pacific project. He also favored a political alliance of former Southern Whigs, as well as industry-minded Democrats of the South, with the Republicans. He hated Northern Democrats. He considered Tilden "the most contemptible and dangerous politician this country has ever seen." [21] So Kellar went at the task of wooing Southern Congressmen for Hayes with gusto. As Boynton reported to Smith, Kellar "was able to do that part of the work which was most difficult for us, namely sounding certain Southern men." [22]

But Hayes returned to Smith the Boynton and Kellar letters with the comment, " I do not wish to be committed to details." He had given "a good deal of thought" to the problem of "peace and prosperity" for the South. "The two things I would be exceptionally liberal about are education and internal improvements of a national character." [23] But whether or not the Texas and Pacific would be included in such internal improvements he left open.

He invited Smith to meet him for a talk. He remained uncommitted. Later he wrote to Smith: "I am not a believer in the trustworthiness of the forces you hope to rally. After we are in, I believe a wise and liberal policy can accomplish a great deal. But we must rely on our own strength to secure our rights. With firmness, it can be done." [24]

7

Was this a complete turndown? Smith did not think so, and told Hayes that he would "pursue" the matter on his "own responsibility." [25] Hayes did not stop him. So Smith assured Boynton that it was apparently safe to let Tom Scott feel that Hayes's sympathy for internal improvements might include support for the Texas and Pacific.

Through General Dodge, Boynton so advised Tom Scott. He soon forwarded an optimistic report to Smith. "From today there will be no lack of help, for Scott's whole powerful machinery will be set in motion at once." Scott believed, Boynton added, that the president of the Senate should decide the election dispute "without flinching" and that he had "the very highest confidence" that he could influence the Southerners toward the goal. "I feel quite confident now of the result," Boynton concluded. [26]

But Boynton and Tom Scott were overoptimistic. Their negotiations were to have some later influence. But on the specific purpose for which they were started—to have the Democratic House agree to let the election dispute be settled by the president of the Senate—they failed.

An even more powerful lobby was behind a solution which rejected both the Hayes and the Tilden positions. This lobby was the combined opinion of the nation's businessmen, as expressed mainly by their chambers of commerce, that Congress should adopt a compromise which would give *both* houses a voice in the decision. Democratic as well as Republican business leaders demanded such a solution. The bickering, which at times seemed to threaten a new war, and the uncertainty were paralyzing the nation's commerce. Congressmen were hearing from the businessmen that a practical end to the controversy was wanted, no matter who became President.

Pertinent to this was an observation made years later by Abram Hewitt. "Senator Conkling and I, as representatives of the great commercial interests of the State of New York, agreed from the beginning that we would perfect a measure. . . ." [27] Besides, Hewitt himself had vast business interests, being, he would say later, "probably the largest owner of iron mines and miner of iron ores in the United States." [28]

Also pertinent to all this, perhaps the most pertinent single event of all, was the meeting of the businessmen of both parties that Matthews had reported on to Hayes on December 15, 1876. Those men exerted power far beyond New York, their holdings reaching into every section of the nation, including the South. And they wished a settlement that would end all danger of a new civil war, or of any commotions whatsoever. Moreover, not even the Democratic members of that meeting were averse to Hayes becoming President, especially in view of his special soundness on the money question. So, regardless of Hayes, regardless also of Tilden, a compromise was reached, with leaders of both parties joining in the move.

8

The compromise finally enacted in the last week of January 1877 provided for the establishment by the two houses of Congress of a unique commission, to be styled "the electoral commission." It was to consist of fifteen members—five from the Senate, five from the House, and five Associate Justices of the Supreme Court. To this tribunal, challenged electoral certificates were to be submitted, and it would sit as a court on them. The commission's decision, by a majority vote, would be final, unless *both* houses of Congress rejected it.

This last was the key feature, for at least one of the houses would, in all likelihood, accept each decision by a strict party vote. Thus it was reasoned that there was bound to be a final result, unless there occurred a filibuster to prevent the completion of the process before March 4 without a President being chosen. What the situation then would be nobody knew for a certainty.

Tilden was opposed to this compromise, but finally sent a message interpreted, probably correctly despite some controversy on the point, as giving his reluctant approval.[29]

Hayes and close associates, however, opposed the plan to the last. Senator Sherman called it "a clumsily constructed machine to allow timid or treacherous men to defeat your election." Hayes agreed. Garfield could not "find words strong enough to describe" his "indignation." [30] Senator Morton vigorously opposed the compromise because it was a compromise. He argued that it was a surrender to "intimidation." Hayes had been elected President "under the forms of law and according to law and . . . if he shall be counted in, as eighteen Presidents were successively counted in from the beginning of this government, he will be inaugurated, and there will be no violence and no revolution." [31]

9

But other Republican leaders favored it. Behind these, significantly, was President Grant. Probably influenced by businessmen with whom he was intimate, he summoned Senator Conkling in particular to tell him that he wished the compromise adopted. Thus was revealed a cleavage in the Republican Party of major proportions—the outgoing President standing in opposition to the man chosen by his party for his successor.[32]

Such was the pressure for the compromise, called "a peace plan," that some members of Congress who were considered spokesmen for Hayes cast their votes for it, including Charles Foster, who, to cover his embarrassment and also to soften the "defeat" for Hayes, announced that he believed Hayes was "really" for the proposal.[33] Foster said he supported the plan not only because it would "give to the occupant of the presidential chair the best possible title," but because "the great business interests of the country will hail it as a measure of peace, safety, and relief. It will unlock capital, it will permit business energy to exercise its functions freely and unrestrained." [34]

As a future touch of irony, there were many more Democratic votes than Republican votes cast for the electoral-commission proposal. In the House 159 Democrats voted for it and only eighteen against, whereas only thirty-two Republicans voted for it, with sixty-eight against. So the compromise to a large extent was a Democratic device, unwanted by Hayes.

CHAPTER LVII

THE "FIFTH JUSTICE"

1

ALL DURING the drafting of the electoral-commission act, a major problem was the finding of a formula. The formula sought was one that would result in a tribunal that everyone could consider to be unbiased.

It had been agreed that the five Senators and five Representatives would be equally divided as to party affiliation, making five Republicans and five Democrats. How the five Supreme Court Justices were to be selected thus became the main issue. Only two of the nine Justices on the bench were Democrats. All of the others were Republicans when appointed. Thus with the two Democratic Justices on the commission, Nathan Clifford and Henry Field—and it was agreed they would be—there was no way to establish a commission which did not consist nominally of eight Republicans and seven Democrats. So the goal of the formula sought was really impossible.

All accounts agree that the conferees considered one solution presumably satisfactory—as satisfactory as possible. This was to assure that Justice David Davis of Illinois would be one of the five Justices. For while Justice Davis had been a founder of the Republican Party and had been appointed to the court by Lincoln, his personal politics had been uncertain for a long period.

Davis was by no means nonpolitical, although a Supreme Court Justice. Agreeably to him, he was often mentioned as a candidate for President. In 1872 he would have liked the Liberal Republican nomination, and he received a substantial number of votes at the Liberal Republican convention. That same year a National Labor Reform Party did nominate him for President. He declined this nomination, but in a way indicating that he was satisfied to be considered an independent.

In 1876 Davis was mentioned both for the Republican and the Democratic Presidential nominations, but most prominently for the Democratic. When it became known that he might be chosen for the electoral commission the Chicago *Tribune,* of his own state, grumbled, "If the fifth judge should be Davis, the Democratic ascendancy on the commission would be complete." But a short time later the *Tribune* asserted that he was not a Democrat.[1] All this uncertainty about Davis lent support to a general feeling that if he were on the commission with seven known Democrats and seven known Republicans, he *might* be considered a fifteenth member who was neutral.

2

But Justice Davis was not the fifth Justice. After the Senate passed the electoral-commission bill, and while it was being taken up by the House, Davis was elected by the Illinois legislature as a United States Senator over the Republican incumbent, General John A. Logan. Democrats and a small group of Granger independents threw their support to him to break a long deadlock. The Justice promptly announced that he would not be available for the electoral commission.

Afterward, as with so many aspects of the whole matter, a legend developed that Justice Davis' election to the Senate was somehow "engineered" by Republicans as part of a "plot" to keep him off the commission because they feared he would side with Tilden.[2] It was said that Senator Morton had been in the Illinois capital for that purpose. But this was mere rumor. William Henry Smith, who was at Springfield, advised Hayes that the Democrats in the Illinois legislature voted for Davis "because Tilden commanded them to do so." [3] But this made little sense in view of the belief of Tilden's associates, notably Hewitt, that Davis' exclusion was a blow to Tilden's cause.[4]

The fact appears to be that Governor Palmer of Illinois, without reference to the Hayes-Tilden dispute, had caused his Democratic followers in the legislature to vote for Davis. Moreover, the choice of Davis for Senator was considered possible before he was mentioned as a member of the electoral commission.[5] Then, too, Davis probably would have refused to serve on the commission anyway. According to an associate, he so advised Justice Clifford before his election to the Senate. He "distrusted the experiment . . . and was unwilling to assume a responsibility which . . . [would] subject him to misrepresentation in history by the defeated party." [6] So the Davis matter apparently had relevance only for showing that consideration was given to establishing a commission not clearly weighted politically in favor of either Hayes or Tilden, and that the Republicans were willing to take a chance that Davis might be the "odd man."

With Davis out, the Justice selected in his place by four Associate

Justices was Joseph P. Bradley of New Jersey, a Republican appointed to the court by Grant. So the commission in the end was one of eight known Republicans and seven known Democrats.

All members of the commission took an oath pledging that they would act impartially. But in the realistic view the political composition of the commission was seen as an advantage for Hayes. For the realistic view held that the political affiliations of the members could not help but be an influence.

Moreover, both parties, as expected, made sure that the Senators and Representatives chosen for the commission were men who could be counted on to stand by their parties, if at all possible. Thus the Democrats selected from the Senate Thurman and Bayard, both so identified with the Democratic Party that it would have been incredible had they acted counter to it despite Tilden's suspicions. The Republican Senators on tne commission were Morton, Frederick Frelinghuysen of New Jersey and George F. Edmunds of Vermont, all on record with vigorous claims that Hayes was entitled to the election. "Both Edmunds and Frelinghuysen . . . are deeply interested in that result," Senator Sherman wrote to Hayes.[7] He did not have to make any comment about Morton.

To represent the House, the Republicans selected none other than Garfield and George F. Hoar of Massachusetts, the latter as certain as Garfield that Hayes was the winner. The Democrats of the House selected Henry Payne of Ohio, Eppa Hunton of Virginia and Josiah G. Abbott of Massachusetts, all firmly committed to Tilden.

3

In Columbus Hayes reflected a general, if not unanimous Republican view of the make-up of the commission. "The commission seems to be a good one. At 2 P.M., Webb announced, 'The judge—it is Bradley. In Washington, the bets are five to one that the next [President] will be Hayes.' "[8] Earlier General Boynton had written to Comly that "if we could get Bradley all would go right I believe."[9]

Yet the Democrats also—at the time—were satisfied with the selection of Bradley. Hewitt recalled:

I had personally known [Justice Bradley] for many years in New Jersey as a very able lawyer and a man of the highest integrity. The confidence which I felt in him was shared by Mr. Tilden, but in order to make assurance doubly sure I requested a mutual friend . . . John G. Stevens, of Trenton, N. J., to confer with Judge Bradley and to ascertain whether he felt that he could decide the questions which would come before the commission without prejudice or party feeling. The report of Mr. Stevens was entirely satisfactory. Judge Bradley was therefore selected with the distinct approval of the Democratic representatives, reinforced by the favorable judgment of Judge Clifford and Judge Field [the two Democratic Justices] who assured me that absolute reliance could be placed upon the judicial fairness of Judge Bradley.[10]

A New York newspaper editor told Blaine: "The Democrats here are jubilant, while the Republicans wear long faces." Moreover, while eight Republicans on the commission presented the possibility of a threat to the Democrats, for all their confidence in Justice Bradley, the Tilden supporters felt this was outweighed considerably by a basic fact that seemed to make Tilden's chances of final victory far better than those of Hayes. This was that Tilden needed to win a favorable decision in only one case.

Tilden could lose the decisions in all of the three disputed Southern states and still win the election, if the commission did no more than uphold the governor of Oregon in the matter of the one Tilden elector of that state. On the other hand, Hayes to win had to get every basic decision and could lose none in the "great lawsuit," as he, Schurz and others called the proceedings that began on February 1, 1877.

CHAPTER LVIII

DECISION

1

FOR THE COUNTING of the electoral votes, including deciding between disputed votes under the terms of the electoral-commission act, the Senate and the House assembled in joint session in the House of Representatives chambers.

The first disputed case, that of Florida, was reached on the first day, by alphabetical order. Three separate sets of returns from Florida, rather than just the expected two, were handed to President of the Senate Ferry.

One was from the Hayes electors, accompanied, as directed by federal statute, by certification of the governor. The governor who signed the certificate, Marcellus L. Stearns, Republican, no longer held the office. For the Florida Democrats had succeeded in making good their claim to victory for state offices. Stearns had been replaced by George Drew. But Stearns had been in office on December 6, the date the electoral colleges were required to meet and vote for President—a crucial point.

A second certificate from Florida came from the Tilden electors—with a certificate from Governor Drew. His certificate recited that the courts of Florida and the Democratic legislature had ordered a recanvass and that this had found that the Tilden electors had won. Although the Tilden electors in Florida had also met as a college on December 6, Governor Drew's certificate showed that the authority claimed for them was the recanvass held on January 19, 1877, weeks after the electoral colleges had been required by law to meet.

A third certificate was from the Democratic Florida attorney general, who had been a member of the state returning board. He had disagreed with the Republican majority on the board, and his paper recited that "the authentic returns" showed the election of the Tilden electors. His statement also said that Florida law did not provide for the result of the returning-board canvass being "certified to the executive"—this to offset the certification of the Hayes electors by Stearns.[1]

At the same time an objection was filed by the Democrats to the counting, in any event, of the vote of one of the Hayes electors, F. C.

Humphreys, on the allegation that he held the office of federal shipping commissioner at Pensacola, and hence was disqualified under the Constitution. This and the three certificates were referred by Ferry to the electoral commission, which sat in the Supreme Court room. So "the great lawsuit" was on.

The proceedings were, in fact, conducted like those of a lawsuit. Elaborate briefs were filed. Both sides were represented by distinguished lawyers. The Republican lawyers were headed by William M. Evarts of New York, the Attorney General in President Johnson's cabinet. His defense of Johnson in the impeachment trial and also of Henry Ward Beecher, accused of seduction, had made him the best-known Republican lawyer of the nation. The Democrats' legal staff was headed by Charles O'Conor, considered at the top of the New York bar among Democratic lawyers. It also included Jeremiah S. Black of Pennsylvania, Attorney General in the Buchanan cabinet. Of special interest personally for Hayes were two other lawyers—Stanley Matthews and George Hoadly, the former on Hayes's side, the latter on Tilden's, both former schoolmates of Hayes.

2

The Florida case was argued mainly on this basic issue: Should the commission go behind a certificate which on its face met all legal requirements? The Republican certificate obviously met such requirements. On its face it showed that the Hayes electors had been declared the winners by a state agency empowered to so declare, that they had voted, and that the governor had attested to these facts. The Republican argument was: For the commission to go behind such a certificate amounted to giving Congress, whose agent it was, the right of veto over the choice of a state for President. This, it was asserted, was contrary to the Constitutional principle by which Presidents were to be selected.

The Republicans also argued that after legally authorized electors had cast their votes on the date set by law, the action became final. To permit the setting aside of the election afterward was to open the door to a situation that could prevent any President being chosen. They argued too that the commission was not a court. So it could not constitutionally act as one, thus did not possess judicial powers to receive and consider evidence as to whether or not the election results justified the state returning board in declaring that one rather than another set of candidates had been chosen as electors. As a practical matter, they said, this would make it impossible for the counting of the votes to be completed by March 4. Any such investigation would have to be thorough. Once the door was opened the commission could not stop with investigating charges of fraud by one side. It would have to investigate those by the other side. Soon it would find itself in the position of having to decide how every citizen had voted. Matthews said:

It was the policy of our fathers, it is the policy of the Constitution, to provide a machinery which, let it work as it will, must nevertheless, by the 4th of March after the election, necessarily work out the result of having *some* President and some Vice President. It was of far more consequence, and was so esteemed by the framers of the Constitution, as by every lover of law and order, that we should have some constituted authority; far more important that the line of continuous authority should be preserved, than that either A or B should hold the place and receive the power and the emoluments of the office.
    . . . The State may provide as it pleases any mode by which the appointment may be made, and by which the fact of appointment may be verified, so as to furnish such machinery and mode of proof as it may choose to verify its own appointment. Yet, nevertheless, it must take effect, if it have any power whatever, prior to the time when, by the Constitution of the United States, those who have the *indicia* of office and the color of office are called upon, as the appointed electors of a particular state, to discharge the constitutional duty of depositing their vote for President and Vice President; so that when the person appointed, or who appears to have been appointed, having in his possession formal evidence of his appointment, in fact exercises the authority conferred upon him under the Constitution of the United States, actually discharges the duty of casting the vote which it is his business to deliver, the transaction to which he has been a party has passed beyond the control of State power and authority.

With the Oregon case in mind, Matthews carefully conceded that "the mere certifying act is not conclusive. It may be dispensed with. Congress, who provided it, furnished it, made it a part of the transaction, may disregard it. . . . But they have directed this commission to receive only that which is competent and pertinent by existing law, and the existing law makes the governor's certificate pertinent and competent and sufficient." [2]

3

The Democratic lawyers, of course, argued in behalf of precisely opposite theories. In the words of one of the Democratic counsel:

. . . If the power does not exist in the two Houses of Congress as a primary and original power . . . to take testimony going behind the certificate, then it must exist in the State to correct its own certificate or impeach it for fraud or falsehood; else we may be irrevocably tied to an accident or mistake, and a presidential election may turn upon a certificate which is known to all the world to be an accident, a falsehood, or a fraud which can neither be impeached by the State that gave it . . . nor interfered with in any way by the Federal government to which it is addressed.[3]

There were arguments over Florida for nearly a week. Then the commission approved a preliminary order: "That no evidence will be received or considered by the Commission which was not submitted to the joint convention of the two Houses by the President of the Senate with the different certificates, except such as relates to the eligibility of F. C. Humphreys, one of the electors." [4]

This was a victory for the Republicans. It was not conclusive—the final decision on Florida's vote still had to be made—but it was a straw in the wind. "The general situation is now regarded as much more favorable to us, and now our friends are very confident of success," Hayes commented in his diary. However, he was forced to take notice of a circumstance concerning this first decision which was unfortunate. ". . . The decision is by a strictly party vote—eight Republicans against seven Democrats! It shows the strength of party ties." [5]

4

This aspect was more than unfortunate; it was a tragedy in American political history, in keeping with much that went on during the whole episode, all the more so in view of the fact that the commission decisions, contrary to general impression, were, in truth, backed up by substantial legal reasoning and precedents. They were certainly not completely arbitrary, as a string of eight-to-seven decisions caused many persons to believe. But there was no avoiding that tragedy apparently. The seven Democrats were as responsible for it as the eight Republicans.

Democratic reaction to the strictly party vote was, of course, much stronger than Hayes's, most of it concerned with Justice Bradley. If Bradley's first vote meant that he, with the seven other Republicans, formed an unwavering Republican majority of eight, then the Democrats saw that they might as well give up then. However, in connection with another decision on the same day, which committed the commission to receiving evidence concerning the eligibility of Humphreys, Bradley voted with the seven Democrats.[6] So the Democrats still had some slight confidence that he might be counted on to prevent the election from being determined in accord with the political affiliations of the commission members. This slight confidence was soon shaken. For in the final decision on Florida the vote was again eight to seven in favor of the Hayes certificate, all of the eight being Republican votes, including Bradley's.

From then on Bradley was the subject of some whispered, then published allegations. On the final decision concerning Florida these stated that he had at first made up his mind to decide for Tilden electors but yielded to "pressure" to change his opinion. Hewitt apparently was the original source of these allegations. He based his charges on what he was told by John Stevens, his and Bradley's mutual friend, who had previously assured Hewitt that Bradley would be "fair."

On the night of February 8 Stevens, a guest at Hewitt's residence in Washington, went to Justice Bradley's home. Around midnight, as later related by Hewitt, Stevens returned to Hewitt to report "that he had just left Judge Bradley after reading his opinion in favor of counting the vote of the Democratic electors of the state of Florida." On the basis of this Hewitt said he attended the session of the commission the next day, confident that Justice Bradley would so decide, only to learn that Bradley had in the end sided with the other Republicans on the final Florida decision. "The change was made between midnight and sunrise," asserted Hewitt. "Mr. Stevens afterward informed me that it was due to a visit to Judge Bradley by Senator Frelinghuysen and Secretary Robeson [Grant's Secretary of the Navy], made after his departure. Their appeals to Judge Bradley were said to have been reinforced by the persuasion of Mrs. Bradley."[7]

5

Later, insinuations of the most serious kind would be printed concerning Justice Bradley. It was implied that he had been bribed.[8] It was also alleged that the Texas and Pacific railroad lobby brought pressure on Bradley, that he was a "creature" of that lobby—this based on a decision he had rendered years before on a railroad receivership case in the South which was favorable to what later became the Texas and Pacific project.[9]

Bradley issued a denial of some of the insinuations. He conceded that he had written an opinion that favored the Democratic side—the one apparently undisputed statement in all the gossip. But he said this was in accord with his custom of writing down preliminary decisions on both sides of a question to see which appeared to be the sounder.[10] He implied that Hewitt's friend could have read an opinion by Bradley, without its having been his final decision. Nothing was ever proved, one way or another.

On the controversy over the vote of Humphreys, Justice Bradley also held with his seven Republican colleagues that the Humphreys vote should be counted. Humphreys, it was shown, had sent his resignation as shipping commissioner to Circuit Judge Woods before the election. The Democrats maintained that the resignation was not valid. The commission did not meet this factor head on, nor decide "the question of the effectiveness of the vote of an ineligible elector." It merely ruled that "the evidence does not show that he held the office of shipping commissioner on the day when the electors were appointed."

So all four of the Hayes votes from Florida were ordered to be counted. The Democratic House voted against this decision. But the Republican Senate voted to accept it. Thus the decision stood, since the act provided that a decision should stand unless overruled by both houses.[11]

The reaction of many Tilden supporters to this first decision was one of gloom and bitterness. "God damn them, they will beat us and elect Hayes, but we shall give them all the trouble we can!" Jeremiah Black said.[12]

6

Louisiana was next. In the Louisiana case the Democrats argued that extensive irregularity, if not downright fraud and bribery, marked the conduct of the returning board. The certification of the Hayes vote by Governor Kellogg was worthless, they said. Kellogg was a usurper, they claimed, one whose government was maintained only by federal troops. In contradiction to this argument they insisted also that Kellogg, because he *was* governor, could not also have served legally as an elector under Louisiana law, which barred double officeholding by state officers. Hence at least his vote for Hayes should be discarded. Also, Louisiana did not have a "republican form of government," because federal troops had to preserve order; hence none of its votes should be counted in the election. They pointed to the fact that the Louisiana votes in the 1872 election were not accepted because of disorder and fraud. As the situation in 1877 was unchanged, the commission should follow the 1872 precedent, they said.

In support of all this the Democrats put up a strong case. But their case mainly required that the commission consider evidence beyond and behind the certificates, "aliunde," as the lawyers phrased it. This the commission majority, following the Florida decision, declined to do.

Senator T. O. Howe of Wisconsin made a retort that epitomized the Republican position on the Louisiana fraud issue: *Perhaps* there was fraud. But he said: "There is more than one foul stream to be found in the state of Louisiana. That to which you have pointed may be dirty. Coming right from that state, I know of other and larger streams which are not merely dirty, but are very bloody. . . . I want your streams all purified as soon as it can be done. If you can aid in that direction, cleanse the *bloody* before you attempt the muddy streams." [13]

In the main the Republicans confined themselves to arguments supporting the authority of the returning board and of Governor Kellogg. Legally there was no question about their authority. In this the Republicans were sustained by the Republican majority of the commission. Its ruling was:

. . . The Commission has by a majority of votes decided . . . that it is not competent, under the Constitution and the law as it existed at the date of the passage of [the electoral-commission act] to go into evidence *aliunde* the papers opened by the President of the Senate . . . to prove . . . that the determination of the said returning officers was not in accordance with the truth and the fact, the Commission, by a majority of votes, being of the opinion that it is not within the jurisdiction of the two Houses of Congress . . . to enter upon a trial of such a question. [14]

So Louisiana was given to Hayes.

7

Then came South Carolina.

Privately the Democrats were prepared to admit that South Carolina had been won by Hayes. They made no effort to sustain the certificate presented by Tilden electors from South Carolina. On its face this Tilden certificate was faulty. No state executive had attested to it, for Wade Hampton, while claiming to be governor, did not associate himself with the Tilden case, thus lending significance to a message he had sent to Hayes back in December indicating "friendship." [15] On the other hand, the Republican certificate from South Carolina was certified to in "regular form" by Governor Chamberlain and the Secretary of State.

The strategy of the Democrats thus was to get the Republican certificate rejected without having the Democratic one accepted, thus voiding South Carolina's Presidential election entirely. The Democratic theory was that the South Carolina election was invalid, as it applied to Presidential electors. This followed, they said, because the legislature had not provided for registration of voters as "required by the state constitution," and because "there was not existing in the State of South Carolina . . . a republican form of government such as is guaranteed by the Constitution to every State of the Union." In support of the second contention they cited the presence of federal troops, holding that a free election could not occur in such circumstances, that a free election was essential to a "republican form of government." [16]

To bolster this argument, one Democratic spokesman, interestingly enough, conceded that the Republicans were right in declaring that Negro voters had been intimidated by Democrats. "We propose to show that rifle clubs were organized which were not disbanded in accordance with the proclamation of the President of the United States, and that under the effect of these rifle clubs and of the intimidation that was practiced in that method, large numbers of Negroes, who otherwise would have voted the Republican ticket, voted the Democratic ticket." [17]

In short, out of desperation the Democrats in the South Carolina case confessed to the truth of the principal allegation on which the Republicans had made a moral, as well as legal, claim to victory in all the disputed Southern states.

8

Just before this, in the Oregon case, the Democrats had done something similar. Mainly through George Hoadly, they had professed to accept the reasoning of the majority of the commission in the Florida and Louisiana decisions, that there should be no going behind the certificate of the governor of the state.[18] Of the governor's certificate Hoadly said: "This is the voice of Oregon, according to the judgment of this Commission in the cases of Florida and Louisiana. Its truthfulness has been impeached; but one thing I am certain I may say in this presence: it is as true as the certificates which have received the approval of this Commission coming from Florida and Louisiana." [19]

This was ingenious argument by Hoadly. But Matthews, who had anticipated it, pointed out that the Republican position was not that a governor's certificate was to be accepted without question. Rather, the Republican position was that the commission should not go behind information contained in the various certificates. It should determine if a governor had certified to facts "which by law constitute a part of the record in the public offices and archives of the State, and of which, being governor for the time being, he has official knowledge." [20] He then showed that the public record in Oregon, as shown by the canvass by the secretary of state, revealed that Cronin was not elected.

After this argument was sustained, the issue became whether or not the vote of Watts should be counted. It was shown that before the electoral college met, Watts had resigned as postmaster and elector. When the other two Hayes electors convened on December 6 they declared that a vacancy existed. Having the authority to fill the vacancy, they then appointed Watts himself to act with them. It was in that capacity—filling his own vacancy—that Republican Watts cast his vote for Hayes. Before ruling on the validity of Watts's vote, the commission decided that the Cronin certificate did "not contain . . . the constitutional votes" to which Oregon was entitled.

This decision on Cronin's certificate was unanimous, none of the Democrats on the commission dissenting, a fact often overlooked.[21] At least on this major point there was not the refrain "eight to seven," so embarrassing to the Republicans. "Poor Hoadly!" Hayes exclaimed some years later when his former friend slurred him as "the Usurper." "He can't get that awful snub of the Electoral Commission, 'Aye, none; Nay, 15' on his Oregon rascality, out of his memory." [22]

But on the decision concerning Watts's vote the commission reverted to the eight-to-seven division. The Republicans upheld Watts, the Democrats voted against him. It was so also on the final decision. So Hayes was awarded all three of Oregon's votes.[23]

9

In the South Carolina case the commission was again unanimous in a preliminary ruling. It held that the Tilden certificate did not represent the vote of the state. Then the issue became whether or not evidence should be received on the allegation that a free election was not held. The commission ruled, eight to seven, that it would not receive such evidence. Then came a final decision on South Carolina.

By the same division, eight to seven, the commission rejected *in toto* the technical objections of the Democrats. On the matter of troops the commission held that these were placed there "at the request of the proper authorities of the State." Their presence did not invalidate the election. The seven votes of South Carolina went to Hayes.[24] Thus the Republicans had won the votes of all the disputed Southern states.

This did not automatically mean, however, that Hayes would be declared elected. The counting of the vote, down to the last of the states, still had to be completed. If enough of its members chose to do it, the Democratic House had the power to prevent the completion. Their weapon was a filibuster.

CHAPTER LIX

FILIBUSTER

1

AFTER THE decision on Louisiana a group of House Democrats, mainly from the North and West, had in fact determined to conduct a filibuster, doubtless in accord with Jeremiah Black's threat. Instead of voting on the Louisiana decision when it was communicated to the House on Saturday, February 17, 1877, they succeeded in getting the House to take a recess until the following Monday, thereby delaying the whole proceedings. They asserted then that the electoral-commission proceedings had turned out to be a fraud.

On the evening of February 17 a Democratic caucus was held. During it the advocates of a filibuster urged that it be "the policy of the Democratic majority in the House" to defeat the count by "all possible dilatory measures . . . and thereby defeating the inauguration of the usurper." [1]

2

The caucus, however, rejected this proposal. Instead, a resolution was adopted pledging the Democratic majority to allow the count to proceed, and thus keep faith with the electoral-commission law. The vote on this resolution revealed that two groups of Democrats were firm for going through with the count—a Southern bloc and a bloc of Northern business-minded Congressmen, exemplified by Hewitt, who wanted an end to the crisis, regardless of the result. In the main, the Southerners were those with whom the negotiations for a coalition with Hayes Republicans had been going on. So these negotiations, though they had failed to block the electoral-commission bill, still were bearing fruit. [2]

The caucus decision did not, however, end the threat of a filibuster. More House Democrats had stayed away from the caucus than had attended it, hence did not consider themselves bound by its decision. Also, Louisiana Democrats wanted the threat of a filibuster held over the heads of the Republicans. They wished to make certain, first, that Grant would not side with Republican Packard in the tug of war with

Democrat Nicholls, and second, that they could get ironclad assurances that Hayes would permit the Nicholls regime to take over in Louisiana. Recognition of Wade Hampton as governor in South Carolina also was a corollary objective of this pressure.

3

Principal agent for Louisiana in Washington was Major E. A. Burke of New Orleans. Immediately after the caucus Burke sought out Hewitt. He denounced Hewitt for causing the "national Democratic party to abandon Louisiana." Hewitt confirmed that he was for letting the electoral-commission proceedings go on to the end. "Mr. Burke," Hewitt said, "the Democratic party cannot afford to take the responsibility of plunging this country into anarchy and strife, upsetting values and disturbing trade. We have determined to put the responsibility of this great fraud fairly and squarely upon the shoulders of the Republican party and go before the people *four years hence.*" [3]

But Burke insisted that Hewitt tell his "associates" that "with the same consistency that they voted for the electoral bill, to preserve the country from anarchy and strife . . . they make the condition that the bayonets are to be taken away from Louisiana and South Carolina, or the conditions of anarchy and strife that they have discouraged will truly follow." [4]

To "Governor" Nicholls, Burke telegraphed: NOW WILL SAVE OURSELVES.[5]

4

Actually by this time, from a conversation the evening before with Stanley Matthews, Burke was satisfied in his own mind that Hayes favored letting the Packard regime fall. Burke also had had some private meetings with Grant. These led him to believe that Grant might even withdraw the troops from the Packard Statehouse in New Orleans as soon as the electoral count was completed, though Grant made it plain that if the Nicholls forces resorted to violence beforehand, he probably would intervene on the side of Packard.[6]

By then, too, Burke's discussions with Matthews and other Republican leaders mainly concerned a concession that the Nicholls regime was asked to make in return for recognition. This did not concern, as often is implied, the filibuster against Hayes directly. Rather, it concerned the two Louisiana seats in the United States Senate. If Nicholls' legislature was recognized as the lawful Louisiana legislature, it would have the power to elect two Senators, presumably Democrats. Presumably, also, the Nicholls legislature would void the previous election by the Packard legislature of Governor Kellogg as United States Senator.

Indeed, here was a collateral matter of extraordinary importance at the time, one, as noted, which did not directly concern the Presidency but which had much more importance in the settlement of the dispute than usually is accorded it. It involved whether or not the Republicans could control the Senate. For on paper the Republicans had only a bare majority of three or four, in the U. S. Senate, and some of these were doubtful. Election of two Democratic Senators from Louisiana, in place of two Republicans, threatened Republican control.

What worried Republicans in this situation, aside from the loss of committee chairmanships, was this: If the Republicans lost control of the Senate, the Democrats were in a position to paralyze a Hayes administration at the start, even if Hayes was inaugurated, by withholding confirmation of a cabinet. Then, politically, anything could happen.

5

When William E. Chandler, for one, learned that Matthews was urging recognition of the Nicholls and Hampton regimes in Louisiana and South Carolina, he protested to Matthews on precisely this danger. He quoted Matthews as having said that the problem had been "arranged," or would be. "By agreement, or concession, or understanding . . . the administration was not to lose the senators, but they were to be Republican." [7] Chandler learned in that connection that Matthews, as well as Secretary of War J. Donald Cameron, had asked Burke to agree that if the Nicholls regime was recognized, its legislature would select not two Democrats for the Senate but two Republicans. Presumably this also involved a way of "rewarding"—or "taking care of"—Kellogg.[8] If anything, this was the real "bargain," so-called, that Matthews and others were then seeking to make over Louisiana. In short, not Hayes's fate but Kellogg's, and also the Republican Senatorial power, were the heart of the negotiations then going on.

Burke did not wish to agree to this. So he was interested in continuing the threat of the filibuster as a weapon for causing the demand for the Senators to be dropped by the Republicans. Besides, as he pointed out to Matthews in a later conference, before agreeing to anything the Louisiana Democrats wished to commit more firmly key Republican leaders to the assumed Hayes policy on Louisiana. Burke later testified:

I said to Mr. Matthews that, while we were inclined to believe the assurances which he and others of Mr. Hayes's friends were giving as to Mr. Hayes's intended policy toward Louisiana, yet we felt that Mr. Hayes would be unable to inaugurate and carry out such a policy if he were opposed by the strong leaders of the Republican party, and that we feared more the strong Republican leaders like Sherman, Garfield, Morton and others than we did Mr. Hayes. We felt that if Mr. Hayes was inclined to carry out such a policy, he would be unable to do so in face of the opposition of the united Republican party, and therefore that the guarantees and assurances which we required should come from the party leaders. . . . Mr. Matthews stated that he could not speak for those people.
We then told him that we would place them in a position where they should speak for themselves, and that he could say to his party associates that we should seek to put their party in peril.
Q. Meaning what?
A. Meaning to jeopardize their Presidential candidate.
Q. In short, to prevent the electoral count?
A. Yes, to prevent the count. . . . We said that. . . . We should advise our friends to join the filibustering movement and swell it to such proportions as to force the Republican leaders to agree to the yielding up of Louisiana and South Carolina.[9]

6

Independently Speaker Samuel J. Randall, ordinarily as conservative as Hewitt and a leader who later won a reputation for being against the dilatory tactics on the electoral count, unexpectedly at a second Democratic caucus called for preventing completion of the count. Probably his real motive was to prevent coalition between the Southern Democrats and the Hayes Republicans. In any event he made what was described to Hayes as "a violent speech," one directed at the Southerners, charging a "bargain" with Hayes.[10] He declared that the Southerners were in the politically foolish position of delivering their part without any positive assurance that Hayes would "deliver."
Randall cited in particular the "understanding," by then widely

reported in the press, that Hayes would not support the carpetbag regimes. Hayes, he said, would not carry out any such policy. He would revive "bayonet rule," the result of which would be "to overwhelm any Southern man in view who aided in carrying out their agreement in good faith." [11]

The Southerners did not go along with Randall. But they were disturbed. They appealed to Congressman Foster, as the Congressman from Hayes's home district and one of the several negotiators, to "say something" that could be interpreted as coming from Hayes. As Foster later told Hayes, "the Southern people who had agreed to stand by us were seized with a fright, if not a panic." [12] Therefore he agreed to make a talk that, by implication, would show that bayonet rule would be dropped by Hayes. With that understanding from Foster the Southerners helped to defeat a motion for another recess of the House which would have postponed House action on the electoral-commission decision on Louisiana.

7

Foster made the promised speech. As a man close to Hayes, he could assure his Southern colleagues, he said, that a Hayes administration "will be wise, patriotic and just," especially toward the South. "The flag will float over States, not provinces; over free men, and not subjects. All necessity or excuse for the formation of parties on a sectional basis and all traces of party color lines" will be "wiped away," he added.

Foster also said: "It has been said sneeringly, and for the purpose of stirring the wild passions of the hour . . . that the South, under President Hayes, must submit to unconditional surrender to the Republican party. No, sir; no such demand will be made. . . ."

But Burke, unlike other Southerners, still was not satisfied. He wanted more than words before he would call off his campaign of encouraging further filibustering. He wanted action. He specifically wanted to get Senator Sherman committed to dropping the Packard regime.

By then it was known that Sherman would be in the Hayes cabinet, as the political leader of the Hayes administration. Sherman had been the chairman of the Republican visiting statesmen in Louisiana and a consistently vigorous defender of Packard, in and out of the Senate. If Sherman could be induced to make a turnabout, then Burke would feel safe. But unlike Matthews, Foster and Dennison, Sherman had held aloof from Burke.

8

Then there occurred a journalistic accident. In the *Ohio State Journal* of February 22, 1877, there appeared a long article, "Why Don't the Republican Majority Govern Louisiana?" The article defended the carpetbaggers in Louisiana. It criticized the Democrats, referring to them as loafers and drunkards. It praised the Negroes, and defended the use of federal troops. It closed with the suggestion that President Grant should "quiet the situation with the forces at his command."

This article was circulated promptly and widely by the filibustering Democrats among Southerners with the observation that it reflected Hayes's "real" views. They backed this assertion with a powerful fact. The editor of the *Journal* was none other than General Comly, Hayes's friend and comrade in the Ohio Twenty-third Regiment, who, everyone "knew," had lately been in Washington in Hayes's behalf. The *Journal* was "a Hayes organ," they said.

Effect of this was like that of a lightning bolt. Southerners who previously had refused to join in the filibuster now threatened to join it. Some did.

In several key quarters there was panic. Suppose the count were not completed before March 4, a Sunday? What then? Would Grant continue as President? Would he be a "dictator"? True, Grant had assured Hewitt that he would not use the army against either candidate.[13] But could he resist supposed marplots around him? Would the president of the Senate become President? Would it be Conkling? Or Morton? From whom would the army take orders if trouble occurred? Even the cool agent of the Louisiana Democrats, Major Burke, became alarmed.

Likewise alarm gripped Senator Sherman, up to then still aloof.

CHAPTER LX

RE-ENTER GRANT—RE-ENTER SHERMAN, FINIS FILIBUSTER

1

IRONICALLY just then, when the filibuster unexpectedly began getting new adherents, Major Burke wished to have its strength held down. He feared that the goal of some of the filibusterers, as shown by various resolutions they were readying, was to hold another election the following November. He learned that certain Republicans in the Senate were secretly supporting such a move, with the idea of installing either Conkling or Morton as Acting President, by choosing one of them as president of the Senate.[1]

Burke reasoned that both Conkling and Morton would be disposed to maintain the carpetbaggers and would make that the issue in any new election. Thus the chances of a new policy under Hayes would be lost entirely, he saw. Louisiana, he telegraphed to Nicholls, would then be "again football of national party."[2]

Along with other Louisiana representatives, Burke preferred to take his chances with Hayes, especially after new evidence developed to show that, though Hayes still would make no explicit statement, he would carry out the views expressed by Foster and Matthews. For on the same day that the *Journal* article reached Washington, Congressman Foster received and showed to Burke a letter from Hayes. It stated that he approved of the speech that Foster had made in the House.[3] Also on that same day Burke himself received a message from Columbus concerning an interview with Hayes by Bishop J. P. B. Wilmer of the Episcopal Diocese of New Orleans. This he interpreted as meaning that Hayes would be "right," from his standpoint, on the Louisiana question.

' The bishop, who was on record publicly as favoring the Nicholls regime, had gone to see Hayes at the suggestion of President Grant, and telegraphed to Burke: PEACE NOT TO BE DISTURBED IN LOUISIANA.[4] It was understood that this meant if the Nicholls regime took over, as it was gradually doing, there would be no armed intervention by the federal government under Hayes.

Moreover, in a roundabout manner Burke had been satisfied that the *Journal* article did not represent Comly's views, let alone Hayes's

DIARY ENTRIES IN 1877

President Hayes sets down two rules on patronage and appointments. The last entry, on withdrawal of troops from the South, reads, "The result of my plans is to get from those States by their Governors, Legislatures, Press and people pledges."

"Injured Innocence"

"Did you ever try to buy a returning board? Never! *What!! Never???* W-e-l-
hardly ever! *Chorus:* And so say his nephews and his partners and his friends!"
This cartoon of Tilden wearing cipher dispatches ran in the *Daily Graphic*
in February 1879.

A friend of Burke's had reported on the effect of the article to Hayes's lieutenant governor, Thomas L. Young. This was a discreet way of communicating with Hayes himself. Back from Columbus came a reassuring message: "Governor Hayes never inspired and never saw the article you refer to until attention was called to it this evening. General Comly, editor of Journal, sick at his home for some days. Hayes too prudent to foreshadow any policy until he has a right to speak." [5] Soon, too, newspaper reports came from Columbus confirming that the article had been run by mistake, as a filler.

2

But the intensification of the filibuster threat which this mistake produced resulted in a series of important conferences. One of these was with President Grant.

For some weeks most of his cabinet had been urging that Grant intervene in behalf of Packard.[6] But Grant refused. He apparently wished to go out of office with the impression corrected that he was a "Caesar," especially with regard to the South. Perhaps, as some observers felt, Grant wanted for himself, rather than for Hayes, the credit for a new Southern policy of conciliation, having in mind a third-term election in 1880.

At any rate Grant had been holding a number of cordial interviews with Burke and several Louisiana Democratic Congressmen. These were so cordial that Congressman E. J. Ellis later said they showed "the gradual process of 'thawing out' by the grim, silent man, whom we had supposed to be opposed *in toto* to the accession of the Nicholls government . . . [to] his ultimate transition into, I will not say exactly our friend, but our adviser and suggester, at times, as to the means by which the accession of Nicholls could be most readily accomplished." [7]

Grant's chief advice had been that the Nicholls government should scrupulously avoid any violence. Thus he would not be subjected to increased pressure to have federal troops go into action, which was what the Packard regime wished. For, as Grant had pointed out in early talks, he was committed, as a Republican, to supporting Packard, if a choice had to be made, until the electoral matter was settled. But he gave approval to a tactic of the Nicholls government which ultimately would starve out the Packard regime. This was to set about collecting state taxes, the principal taxpayers being white property owners who were willing thus to co-operate with the Nicholls regime.[8] Grant, of course, was aware that without tax revenues and without affirmative federal support, the Packard government could not long survive. If Nicholls got the taxes, Packard would be starved out.

3

Grant had wanted his changed attitude kept a secret up to then. But on February 26 he authorized Burke to make public that he had practically deserted Packard. To Nicholls, Burke telegraphed:

Wash'n, Feb. 26, 1877.

I have just had a long and satisfactory interview with the President [Grant]. He says unequivocally that he is satisfied that the Nicholls government is the government which should stand in Louisiana, and that he believes it will stand, because it is sustained by the most influential elements of the State, and that the Packard government cannot exist without the support of troops; that the sentiment of the country is clearly opposed to the further use of troops in upholding a State government.

He repeated his kindly opinion of you, and confidence in your determination to secure a good government and enforce law; that in his opinion there would be no interference with the Nicholls government unless, carried away by possession of power, violent excesses were committed. The President said he had avoided action because he did not wish to inaugurate a policy that might embarrass his successor. You may use this, as the President said he desired his views to be known. . . .[9]

That Grant was willing to let these views be made known caused Burke to have a great hope. By playing his cards right he might get Grant to end military protection of the Packard regime *before* Grant went out of office. Thus the Nicholls regime would not have to take its chances on Hayes being unable to fulfill the assurances given by Stanley Matthews. Also, a commitment on election of the United States Senators could be avoided. Burke felt that his opportunity for all this was at hand when Senator Sherman at last asked for a meeting.

4

At this meeting with Sherman, Matthews and Dennison among those present, Burke said that if the Hayes representatives were sincere in their assurances as to what Hayes's policy would be, they would go to Grant and ask him to order immediate withdrawal of federal troops from New Orleans.

"My God!" exclaimed Sherman, according to Burke. "There's no use talking about Grant; he is surrounded by such people, by such influences, that we cannot hope to accomplish anything with him." [10]

Perhaps Sherman was sincere. Perhaps he was bluffing. Whichever was the case, he had to change his tune. For Burke showed him his message to Nicholls, pointing out that Grant had authorized it. Sherman then was forced to promise that Grant would be told the following morning that withdrawal of protection of Packard by troops would not embarrass the Hayes administration. But Burke at the same time was asked to pledge that the Nicholls forces would not resort to the use of force to get rid of the Packard regime and to agree to wait for gradual processes to operate. He was also asked to agree that the Nicholls legislature would not elect any Senators until after the Hayes cabinet had been confirmed.

Burke saw the desirability of having a Hayes cabinet confirmed. He agreed to recommend to Nicholls that the Democratic legislature refrain from electing anyone, at least to the seat claimed by Kellogg, until after the Hayes administration was safely launched. He also accepted the idea of having the Nicholls government take over gradually.

Burke also agreed that once the Democratic regime was in power in Louisiana, there would be "no persecution for past political conduct," although, he specified, immunity for crime could not be promised. He agreed further, as he had at earlier conferences with Matthews, that the Nicholls government would promise that the new Constitutional rights of the Negroes would be respected, that all citizens would be protected from violence—this being for the benefit of carpetbaggers who might choose to remain in the state—and that the State of Louisiana would provide white and black children with equal education.

So it was then and there, on the afternoon of February 26, in the rooms of the Finance Committee of the Senate, used as an office by Sherman, that the negotiations concerning Louisiana were made definite, along with important pledges from the South to be remembered.

5

Later that night, in the rooms of Evarts in Wormley's Hotel, Washington, D. C., there was held another and larger conference.

Burke suggested that this conference be held so that "there should be no misunderstanding of the views that existed or had been expressed." [11] In short, he wanted as many of Hayes's representatives committed as possible, and also to have as witnesses a comparable number of Southern Democrats. Among the witnesses was Henry Watterson, ostensibly invited to represent South Carolina, though actually there as a newspaperman and ardent Tilden supporter.

Sherman, Foster, Matthews and Dennison were the active Republican participants at this night conference. Garfield also was there. This placed him, a member of the electoral commission, in an awkward position. Garfield recognized this, and in his diary set down comments to indicate that he was an unwilling participant at the instigation of Matthews.

Indeed, at this meeting Garfield put himself on record as opposing any "bargain," as being "neither honorable nor wise." "These Southern Democrats," he said, "who are resisting filibustering, are doing so on the ground of high public duty and honor; and any bargain would make their motives far lower." He "had no doubt that the new administration would deal justly and generously with the South, and the whole nation would honor those Southern men who are resisting anarchy and preventing civil war; but neither they nor we could afford to do anything that would be or appear to be a political bargain." He thought Matthews did not like his remarks, but he made them "so as to prevent any misunderstanding so far as I was concerned and left at eleven, not caring to be present longer." [12] But Garfield's remarks, however sincere, did not change anything.

The fact was that Garfield had stayed at the meeting for two hours and learned all that was decided. This satisfied Burke. Sherman was committed. So was Garfield. These were two of the men destined to be administration leaders under Hayes. It seemed but a detail to Burke that all the Hayes men emphasized that they were not authorized to speak for Hayes, but were acting solely on the basis of what they believed, from their "perfect familiarity with him," would be his policy. [13]

Also satisfied were two leading Louisiana Congressmen, Ellis and William M. Levy. This was sufficient for the Nicholls legislature caucus in New Orleans to adopt, at Burke's urgent request, an important resolution the next day. This resolution ratified the pledges by Burke on fair treatment of the colored population and carpetbaggers, on observance of the freedom amendments, on maintenance of order and peace, on political persecution and on delay in choosing Senators.[14] These pledges should be emphasized and remembered.

6

Matthews the next day kept the part of the agreement about seeing Grant. At least he kept it to the letter, if not the spirit. Matthews did not really wish Grant to get the credit for withdrawing the troops. He wanted that credit for Hayes, in line with the program of getting the Southern former Whigs to work with the Hayes administration and later form the nucleus of a new Republican Party in the South.[15] But to Congressmen Burke and Ellis, Matthews gave a statement:

February 27, 1877.

In an interview with the President this morning, he stated to me that as soon as the Presidential count was finished, and the result officially declared, it was his intention to notify General Augur, by telegraph, that existing military orders issued for the purpose of preserving the *status in quo* of the political situation were rescinded, except so far as simply to require the use of troops when necessary to the preservation of the public peace. He authorized me to communicate this declaration to Mr. Ellis, of the Louisiana delegation.

STANLEY MATTHEWS.

Obviously that did not mean withdrawal of the troops. But the Matthews statement was accepted by the Louisianians as meaning that a Hayes representative had informed Grant, as Burke had wished, that Grant's new attitude would not embarrass Hayes, and that Hayes's representatives were acting in good faith.

Even more to the point was a letter that Matthews wrote on the same day to Packard. Alarmed over "leaked" reports concerning the negotiations, Packard had appealed to Matthews for support. Matthews was blunt.

Without reference to the rightfulness of the origin of your title as governor, I am of the opinion that the circumstances are such that it will be out of the question for a Republican administration to maintain it, as it must necessarily be, by force of Federal arms. As soon as existing military orders are withdrawn, the Nicholls government will become the only existing government, and will have to be recognized as such. In the mean time, it will be the duty of the administration to take care that the result shall not imperil the rights and equality of the colored people of Louisiana, so far as it has lawful power to prevent, and also to take care that staunch Republicans, like yourself, against whom nothing disreputable can be alleged, should not suffer, and should receive consideration and position in some appropriate way. . . .[16]

The Louisiana Democrats could have asked nothing more. So Burke and his colleagues were then ready to use their influence against filibustering.

7

In the meantime a new complication arose from conduct of another Democratic group. Congressman John Young Brown, Democrat of Kentucky, had asked Congressman Foster for a written statement of Hayes's intentions concerning Louisiana and South Carolina. Brown asked that the document be addressed to himself and to Senator John B. Gordon of Georgia.[17]

Actually Brown and Gordon were leaders against the filibuster. They were among the Southerners reached by the Texas and Pacific lobby, and were going to vote for Hayes, no matter what. They needed no assurances. But apparently they wanted to be able to prove to their constituents that they were for permitting Hayes to be President because of "higher ground." On the twenty-sixth Congressman Foster gave a statement to Brown:

Gentlemen: Referring to the conversation had with you on yesterday, in which Gov. Hayes' policy as to the status of certain Southern states was discussed, we desire to say, in reply, that we can assure you in the strongest possible manner of our great desire to have him adopt such a policy as will give to the people of the States of South Carolina and Louisiana the right to control their own affairs in their own way, and to say further that we feel authorized, from our acquaintance with and knowledge of Gov. Hayes and his views on this question, to pledge ourselves to you for him, and that such will be his policy.[18]

This statement was cautiously revised the next day by Matthews to include the qualification that the two states would be given the right to manage their own affairs "subject only to the Constitution of the United States and the laws made in pursuance thereof." Then Matthews as well as Foster signed the revision.[19] This statement would later be publicized—and accepted as such by most historians— as the *sole* basis for the ending of the filibuster. Actually it was of small significance. Nothing would have been changed had it not been prepared.

The same was true of the much discussed Wormley's Hotel conference. The meetings there had merely let others know what the real leaders had decided elsewhere, with the main features omitted. Historically, the Wormley happenings were a blind, which screened the real bargains made and attempted.

It would be said later that none of these negotiations concerning Louisiana had to be entered into by Hayes's friends. General Dodge professed this position, holding that the filibuster threat could have been checked through the Scott influence alone.[20] But this was a self-serving attitude. It was in the interest of the Scott lobby that Hayes be so persuaded that the great factor was the Texas and Pacific matter.

It may be, too, that filibustering would have been halted even by the hotheads, regardless of any negotiations. Burke said later that he was playing a "bluff game."[21] Indeed, on February 28 he advised Nicholls that the filibuster movement "cannot be held together to defeat count."[22] But no one could have been sure at the time, especially as on February 28 the joint session of Congress became involved in an unexpected controversy over, of all states, the State of Vermont, which no one could have suspected of being for anyone except Hayes.

8

President Ferry had submitted only one set of returns from Vermont —votes for the Republican ticket. So it was not expected that an effort would be made to have the electoral commission involved. But an Ohio Congressman, Earle Poppleton, one of the filibusterers, rose to inquire if another set of returns had not been submitted on behalf of Vermont. Ferry said, "There have been none received except the one submitted." Then Abram Hewitt rose to contradict Ferry. He announced that he held in his hand "a package which purports to contain electoral votes from the State of Vermont." The package contained a "certificate" from a Democratic candidate for elector who had been defeated, but who claimed to have been elected because one of the Vermont Republican electors had been a postmaster—the Oregon case over again, in part. Hewitt insisted that Ferry receive the return from the floor. Ferry again refused, pointing out that the law required that returns be filed by the first Thursday of February.[23]

Hewitt knew that Ferry's ruling was correct but continued to challenge it, thus precipitating a stormy debate and giving the appearance that he had joined the filibusters. In a "secret history," published years later, Hewitt would write that he had had no intention of blocking completion of the count. He merely sought to "gain time . . . to avoid completion of the count until an agreement had been reached . . . as to the recognition of the Democratic administration in Louisiana." Speaker Randall, he said, knew of this purpose and they were agreed that "in the last event, filibustering should be suppressed even though no understanding was reached in regard to the Louisiana case." [24] So Hewitt was also playing a bluff game, apparently in the belief that immediate withdrawal of the troops in Louisiana could be won.[25]

But this was beyond the understanding reached with Burke. The result of Hewitt's conduct was to cause the House to separate from the joint session without taking action on Vermont and voting to adjourn until the following day, March 1—a victory for the filibusters.

9

Time was running out. Another stormy session occurred on March 1 in the House. In the meantime Louisiana's Democratic Congressmen were meeting with Grant. They tried to convince Grant that he should act on the troops matter before the electoral count was completed. Grant would not go that far. But he did agree to advise Packard that he could not expect further military support, thus supporting Matthews' message. Taking advantage of a new appeal by Packard for recognition, Grant, to make this declaration, told his secretary to send the following:

> Executive Mansion,
> Washington, D. C., March 1, 1877.

To Gov. S. B. Packard,
New Orleans, La.

In answer to your dispatch of this date, the President directs me to say that he feels it his duty to state frankly that he does not believe public opinion will longer support the maintenance of the State government in Louisiana by the use of the military, and that he must concur in this manifest feeling. The troops will hereafter, as in the past, protect life and property from mob violence when the State authorities fail, but during the remaining days of his official life they will not be used to establish or pull down either claimant for control of the State. It is not his purpose to recognize either claimant.

> C. C. SNIFFEN, Secretary.[26]

That message, Grant said, served to warn Packard not to attempt to use force to maintain himself as governor. Grant also gave Louisianans to understand that *as soon as the count was completed,* he would send orders to General C. C. Augur, in command at New Orleans, even ending the *status quo* arrangements. Then, he indicated, the Nicholls government could take over.

In accord with this understanding, Burke sent a telegram to Nicholls: THE PRESIDENT SAID TODAY IF COUNT FINISHED TONIGHT HAD NO DOUBT WE WOULD BE IN PEACEFUL POSSESSION TOMORROW.[27] That is, on March 2. This plan, if carried out, would have left little for Hayes to do in the way of ending reconstruction in Louisiana or any place else.

In the same message Burke referred to the filibuster in the House as "aimless." He wanted the filibuster ended—at once.

10

Then Congressman Levy hurried from the Executive Mansion to the House to carry out an important assignment. This was to make a speech directed at those members who, sincerely or not, were justifying their delaying tactics by citing the continued presence of federal troops in Louisiana and South Carolina.

The people of Louisiana have solemn, earnest, and, I believe, truthful assurances from prominent members of the Republican party, high in the confidence of Mr. Hayes, that in the event of his election to the Presidency he will be guided by a policy of conciliation toward the Southern states; that he will not use the federal authority or the Army to force upon those States governments not of their choice, but in the case of these States will leave their own people to settle the matter peaceably of themselves. This, too, is the opinion of President Grant, which he freely expresses, and which I am satisfied he will carry out and adhere to.

Thus Congress was advised, with no objections from the Republicans, of the negotiations on Southern policy which heretofore had been publicized only in unofficial newspaper articles. Levy went on:

Actuated by a sense of duty to Louisiana, I shall throw no obstacle, by any action or vote of mine, in the way of completion of the electoral count; but relying upon the good faith, the integrity, and truthfulness of the gentlemen who have given those assurances, and having faith in their individual personal honor, I shall unhesitatingly discharge this duty, and call upon those of my fellow members who have been influenced in their action on this question by a desire to protect Louisiana and South Carolina, to join me in the course which I feel called upon and justified in pursuing.[28]

That speech was accepted as the signal for ending the stalemate on Vermont. A resolution stating that "the House will not be ready to meet the Senate to proceed with the count" until Ferry submitted the second Vermont certificate to the electoral commission was rejected, 148 to 116.[29]

Further delaying motions were made, but none that received the support of as many as 116 votes. So it became apparent that the filibuster was over. Its back had been broken. The right commands had been given.

In the end there were not more than sixty or so House Democrats, die-hards, who still acted as if they seriously intended to block the count, and Randall demonstrated that this number could be controlled.

11

The breaking up of the filibuster did not mean that the Democrats in the House yielded at once to the inevitable. A motion rejecting the vote of the Vermont postmaster was passed, though this was of no effect, as the Senate did not concur. By then it was after ten o'clock at night, March 1.

When the last of the thirty-eight states, Wisconsin, was reached, an elaborate objection was filed against one of the Hayes electors, a Dr. Downs. It was alleged that he too was disqualified, because he served as an examiner for the federal government in pension cases. The two houses separated to vote on this objection. By 11:30 the Senate acted in favor of Mr. Downs. But it was 3:38 A.M., Friday, March 2, before the House finished its vote, rejecting, though futilely, the Downs vote.

To the end of this session, which had lasted eighteen hours, there were disorder and expressed bitterness in the House. A Democratic Kentucky Congressman, Blackburn, declared: "Today is Friday. Upon that day the Saviour of the world suffered crucifixion between two thieves. On this Friday constitutional government, justice, honesty, fair dealing, manhood and decency suffer crucifixion amid a number of thieves."

In one form or another, that would be the public line to be followed by many Democrats. But this was mainly in preparation, as Hewitt told Burke, for the next election. For the Democrats were aware that a political issue had been settled by political means which they also would have used. The whole matter, seen in perspective, was really an extension of the election campaign.

The Republican Party had the greater power—and it had used it, as the Democratic Party also would have done. In private, Democratic leaders admitted this. Indeed, leaders of both parties, who in public glared so fiercely at one another, exchanging most vile public insults, got along very nicely in private. For example, at the height of assumed bitterness Garfield and Halstead chummily dined together with Thurman and Watterson.[30]

12

There was no attempt, as some had predicted, to prevent a final declaration after the Senate had returned to the House chambers about 4:00 A.M., March 2. Besides, Tilden had acquiesced. He sent a message to Speaker Randall that suggested the filibustering be ended.[31] Then, too, even those who cried loudest about fraud knew that the proceedings had been lawful, that to advocate rebellion against the result meant, in effect, to advocate revolution, as Republican organs were quick to point out. Democratic leaders did not intend that.

So at ten minutes after four, on the morning of March 2, 1877, Senator Ferry, as president of the Senate, announced that Hayes and Wheeler had received 185 votes, Tilden and Hendricks, 184. "Wherefore, I do declare that Rutherford B. Hayes of Ohio, having received a majority of the whole number of votes is duly elected President of the United States for four years commencing on the 4th day of March, 1877." [32]

13

The great lawsuit was over just in time. In the result, aside from the victory itself, and the settlement without bloodshed or other commotion, there were three special satisfactions for Hayes. His legal title to the office, for all the cries of fraud, was perfect. There could be no question on that. For, in addition to the authority of the electoral commission, it derived from the Congress, as the Constitution provided. In the negotiations he, of all the leading actors, had played a lesser role than anyone else, almost none, actually. And on the Southern question—on which history was to hold him most accountable, as he knew—he had obtained through Matthews and Sherman and Burke pledges from the South concerning Negro rights and the general welfare of the freedmen superior to any that Grant had obtained, or that Tilden probably would have tried to get, or would have been able to get, pledges of justice for the Negroes, indeed, that satisfied all except "ultras" in the North—if kept.

BOOK NINE

The President

"... He serves his party best who serves his country best."

—RBH in Inaugural Address,
March 5, 1877

CHAPTER LXI

NUMBER NINETEEN

1

MARCH 5, 1877, was cool and cloudy in Washington, D. C. On that day the great-grandson of Daniel Austin, the Old Captain, became the nineteenth President of the United States. Thus the story of the family, whose own settlement and growth and movement from the old Valley of the Connecticut River into all other valleys of the land had typified the settlement and growth of the nation, reached a logical climax. In this perspective, it was plain, indeed, that in Hayes's accession to the Presidency there was a logic that cut through all the political turmoil and controversy that went with the event.

For in his heritage, in the living and striving of his lineal and collateral ancestors, lay the American Story. It was all there—the humble and heroic conduct; the godly and blasphemous conduct; the acts of cupidity, on small or large scale, and the acts of altruism; the participation in all the major migrations; the devotees of, and fighters for, liberty and independence; the defenders of the *status quo,* pacifists and Tories; the champions of law and order, the participants in Shays' Rebellion; the Federalists and anti-Federalists; the land speculators and the land developers; the rich, the poor and, in greater proportion, as befit the special character of America, the neither-poor-neither-rich of the middle class; the Abolitionists, the colonizers, the proslaveryites and the neutrals; the orthodox church folk and the leaders and followers of the new, liberal and even eccentric creeds.

On March 5, 1877, Rutherford B. Hayes stood as an American who, in a special sense, came out of that story. His own life was an integral part of it. Moreover, by virtue of his own career, as well as his heritage he, beard and all, was the personal embodiment of the America of his own era.

2

Perhaps it was this consciousness that enabled him to seem so at ease during the inaugural ceremony—despite all the controversy that still went on, perhaps never to end, about his "right" to be President.

Of all the throng gathered on and around the platform on the east portico of the Capitol that noon, he seemed the least tense. "His step was firm and his eyes were bright." [1] When he delivered a short inaugural address and recited the oath his voice was strong and clear, as during the commencement exercises at Kenyon thirty-four years before. "It was a better spoken and better heard inaugural than any of late years," recalled Ben: Perley Poore, the newspaper writer and friend of Grant.[2]

His demeanor certainly was in contrast to the general nervousness in Washington that day. Lincoln's fate was still freshly remembered. Alongside the carriage, drawn by four horses, which carried Hayes and Grant to the Capitol, walked six secret-service men. Their duty was "to keep a sharp lookout for assassins who were intending, it was said, to prepare the way for the accession of Mr. Tilden to the Presidency." [3]

Hayes had received many threatening letters. A few weeks before, according to Webb Hayes, a bullet was fired through a window in his Columbus residence while he and his family were at dinner, piercing the wall of the library. Whether this actually constituted an attempt on his life, or was just a stray shot in some other connection, would never be known. But the incident, kept secret from the public on Hayes's orders, seemed one that underscored warnings by friends that he should exercise extreme care to escape assassination.[4] In November, in a letter to Bristow, Halstead had been curiously flippant about these fears. "I do not think he [Hayes] will be president. If he is counted in, he will be voted out by some peacemaker in some corner of the country." [5]

Just after the Louisiana decision *The Capital*, a weekly newspaper in Washington, appeared with an editorial which seemed to be an invitation to some assassin.

If a man thus returned to power can ride in safety from the Executive Mansion to the Capitol, to be inaugurated, we are fitted for the slavery that will follow the inauguration. We do not believe the people of the United States are of this servile sort. We do not believe that they are prepared, without a blow, to part with their hard-earned, bloodstained possessions. . . . If there is law for fraud, there is reason for violence. And to that we make our last appeal.[6]

Oddly the author of this fiery editorial, Donn Piatt, formerly of Cincinnati, lawyer and poet as well as editor of *The Capital*, had been a friend of Hayes in the beloved Literary Club of Cincinnati. Piatt was promptly indicted for inciting sedition and rebellion, and arrested.

Later Hayes used his Presidential influence to quash the case and even entertained Piatt at the Mansion, along with other members of the Literary Club. But no one was certain on inauguration day that some reader of *The Capital* would not act on Piatt's idea. Indeed, the day before, police held a man, later placed in an insane asylum, who had confided to a government employee that he had been "directed by God" to end Hayes's life at the inaugural ceremony.[7]

3

Until the last there was talk that die-hard Tilden supporters might yet persuade Tilden to consider staging a coup and have himself inaugurated. There was not the slightest basis to believe that Tilden lent himself to any such undertaking. But the chatter had received some apparent reinforcement on the preceding Saturday, when the Democratic majority of the House, in a show of pique after the vote was completed, passed a resolution that said Tilden had been "elected."

This resolution was meaningless as a legal matter, but it provided cause for worry. "They may make the resolution the basis of some revolutionary proceeding," said so sober a man as Garfield.[8]

There was excited comment because perhaps a majority of the Democratic Congessmen boycotted the inaugural. Senator Joseph E. McDonald of Indiana refused to serve on the committee of arrangements. And the two Democratic Justices on the electoral commission, Clifford and Field, were not with the other Supreme Court Justices on the platform.[9]

Adding to the excitement was a more serious House action. As a final thrust, the Democratic majority insisted on attaching to the army appropriation bill a provision that the army not be used to support governments in any state, specifically mentioning Louisiana, unless approved by Congress. A penalty of five to ten years of hard labor for anyone who violated this provision, including the President, was a part of the bill. Of course, the Senate refused to agree. But the Democratic House did not back down. So the session ended without providing any funds for the army.[10]

Nervousness had extended all the way up to usually stolid Grant. He and others were especially concerned over an interregnum that perhaps prevailed because March 4, the Constitutional date for the changeover of Presidents, was Sunday. There was a good deal said in newspapers about a supposed necessity for Hayes to take the oath of office privately on March 4, to make certain that the nation did not pass even one day without a President. There were those who seriously argued that in the event of an attempted coup or other commotion the Republic might fall, if there were no "Constitutional President" sworn in as of March 4.

4

Hayes did not wholly share the vague fears. Matthews had urged that he leave Columbus for Washington "twenty-four hours in advance of any knowledge of the fact," for reasons of safety.[11] Sherman wanted him to come a week before the inauguration, so as to be available for meetings with political leaders.

But Hayes did not wish to enter Washington until he was officially the President-elect, and he disliked making a secret trip. Such an entrance was contrary to the faith he had, and which he intended to express, that the country as a whole would accept the verdict of the electoral commission.

At Kenyon, in December 1840, he had written a paper on the subject, "Is Political Excitement Beneficial?" His youthful answer was: "I do not deny that in the whirl of excitement that tremendous engine for good or evil, the Press, is too often prostituted to the vile and despicable work of slander & petty malice. But after all that has been said, there is nothing dangerous or terrific in the noisy din of wordy warfare. It is the very opposite of the silence & dismal gloom of Tyranny & despotism."[12] This was still his view.

The "wordy warfare," including headlines that called him "His Fraudulency" and "Rutherfraud B. Hayes," disturbed but did not dismay him. As for Donn Piatt, Hayes could only smile, as he had back in the 1850s when Piatt had challenged a Cincinnati critic to a duel for having published devastating reviews of a play he wrote.

He had expected that the count would be completed before March 1, the original date he had set for leaving Columbus. He kept that schedule, and so was on his way to Washington without knowing for sure whether or not the lawsuit was completed. The trip, with Lucy, Scott, Fanny, Webb, Mrs. John G. Mitchell (Sister Fanny's daughter Laura) and a group of friends and political associates, was made quite openly. At the Columbus station there were several thousand persons to bid him farewell and he was serenaded by a band.

He made a talk, good-humoredly referring to the situation in Congress by saying that "perhaps" he would "be back immediately." His most serious remarks showed that the Southern question was uppermost in his mind. Recalling that it was from Columbus that he had gone off to war in 1861 to participate in the use of force to preserve the union, he added: "But there was something that force could not do. We would have our union be a union of hearts, and we would have our Constitution obeyed, not merely because of force that compels obedience, but . . . because the people love the principles of the Constitution." [13] In substance he gave there a synopsis of the main theme of his inaugural message. He made similar talks at various station stops.

About dawn March 2 he was awakened near Harrisburg, Pennsylvania, to be handed a telegram which told him that he had been declared elected. A group in the private car lent by Tom Scott broke into cheers. It was, his friends felt, an historic moment. Whatever Hayes thought, his words were, "Boys, boys . . . you'll waken the passengers." [14]

5

His entry into Washington was so far from being secret—just as he wished it—that 2,000 persons were at the railroad station to cheer as the train pulled in shortly after 9:00 A.M. The two Shermans met him. In an open carriage he rode with them to Senator Sherman's home, his quarters until the inauguration. A short time later he went to the Executive Mansion to pay his respects to Grant. He and Grant exchanged only commonplace remarks. But it was then that Hayes betrayed, by his manner, his most marked emotional reaction of the whole period since the election—an excessive show of cordiality, excessive for him. [15]

Later he went to the Capitol and there held an impromptu reception in the office of the president of the Senate. He obviously enjoyed the expressions of astonishment by members of Congress that he was showing himself so openly. Indeed, his calm manner and the cordiality with which Democratic leaders greeted him acted more than anything else as a sedative on the capital jitters.

6

Grant and Secretary of State Fish, however, were still concerned about the interregnum. They persuaded Hayes to go through with a secret oath-taking ceremony on the evening of Saturday, March 3. It occurred in the Red Room of the Mansion, just before a dinner given by the Grants for the Hayeses. Chief Justice Waite administered this advance oath in the presence of Grant, Fish and Ulysses Grant, Jr. "I did not altogether approve, but acquiesced," Hayes commented on this extraordinary event.[16] So in a sense Hayes was already President when, on March 5, Sardis' friend "Mott" Waite again swore him in at the formal ceremony and he gave his inaugural address.

After the inauguration there was a "grand reception" at the Executive Mansion, only then starting to be called, unofficially, the White House. No one enjoyed more than Hayes this splendid affair—a brilliant gathering of Justices, uniformed officers, Congressmen, decorated foreign diplomats, and their ladies—unless it was Lucy, or the children, or Laura Mitchell, to whom Hayes was especially attentive, out of deference to his sister Fanny's memory.

Indeed, in a personal sense, as distinguished from the political, the first few days in the Mansion were excitingly pleasurable, even for Hayes, who did not often show excitement. He was especially delighted with Lucy's pleasure in being now "the first lady of the land," with the compliments paid to her, even by unfriendly newspapers, for her graciousness—just as when she was first lady of Ohio.

It was pleasing to him also, as a father, to note the enjoyment that the blue-eyed girl Fanny took from being the President's daughter, and the boy Scott received from romping in the corridors of the Mansion. He took pride in the efficiency with which Webb continued to assist him as unofficial secretary. The two other sons, Birchard and Rutherford, interrupted college to participate in the first days at the Mansion. So the inauguration was also a pleasant family reunion.

There was special gratification for him, too, in being able, as President, to welcome friends whose presence recalled milestones in his life—for example, J. L. M. Curry, the Harvard roommate, now a professor of theology in Virginia after having served in the Confederate Army; Ralph Buckland, the Lower Sandusky days partner; John Herron, with whom he had started his law practice in Cincinnati; Dr. and Mrs. John Davis, also of Cincinnati, close friends since his marriage, Mrs. Davis having been a chum of Lucy's at the female seminary; Ainsworth Spofford, an old Literary Club fellow, then Librarian of the Library of Congress; and such Kenyon classmates as Matthews, R. T. "Old Trow" Trowbridge, now a Congressman from

Birmingham, Michigan, and, of course, Guy Bryan, on hand especially to help out on the Southern question.

Rogers was there too, though not as a guest but as his official Presidential Secretary. From an efficiency standpoint the choice of Rogers for this post was not a good one. He often made errors that caused embarrassment, politically and otherwise. He was responsible for such blunders as that when Mark Twain came to see Hayes, who would have been eager to see him. Twain was turned away because Rogers or an aide confused him with George F. Train, the eccentric.

Twain had come armed with a letter from William Dean Howells, but even this did not impress Rogers. As Twain later jocularly told Howells of the incident:

I called at the White House, and got admission to Col. Rodgers [sic], because I wanted to inquire what was the right hour to go and infest the President. It was my luck to strike the place in the dead waste and middle of the day, the very busiest time. I perceived that Mr. Rodgers [sic] took me for George Francis Train and had made up his mind not to let me get at the President; so at the end of a half hour I took my letter of introduction from the table and went away. It was a great pity all round, and a great loss to the nation, for I was brim full of the Eastern question. . . .

Rogers was also inept in handling newspaper reporters, one of his most important duties.[17] And this caused unnecessary trouble for Hayes during his Presidency.

For all his affection for Rogers Hayes himself later characterized him as a man "easily duped; trusts all men who profess friendship. . . . He seems to lack a sense of duty and responsibility."[18] But Rogers' loyalty to Hayes made up for such defects. At least, Hayes thought so. "Rogers thinks well of almost anything I do," Hayes later said, and there would be many times when that alone would be important to him.[19]

7

In the press from then on he would nearly always be portrayed as a man of grim austerity. His pictures, mainly because of the beard, now fuller and with more gray in it, usually confirmed that impression. Moreover, as President he did take on a manner of more than usual solemnity—as if he felt called on to play a role.

But one of his numerous cousins, Horatio Smith Noyes, brother of John Humphrey Noyes, found him to be beaming and even sprightly when he and a group of New Englanders called at the Mansion two days after the inauguration. Hayes was "in his shirt sleeves—no coat or vest on," Noyes recalled. Noyes asked if he could pay his respects then to Lucy. "No! Unless you wish to see a lady a good deal more undressed than I am!" Hayes laughed, explaining that his wife was dressing for a reception to the diplomatic corps to be given that afternoon—as he had begun to do himself when his visitors arrived.[20]

Later Hayes often was seen about the Mansion or its grounds wearing worn clothes and his old army service boots. In the mornings it was his habit to go about the corridors in his slippers and robe to knock on the doors himself to wake up the children or guests. There were almost always guests, frequently young people, often cousins, so many that son Rutherford later said, though with some exaggeration, that the Mansion at times was so crowded he and his brothers had to sleep in bathtubs.[21]

Some of this informality was perhaps consciously excessive, perhaps as compensation for a guilt both he and Lucy seemed to feel—that the "elevation" to the Presidency might "turn" their heads.[22] In particular, Hayes seemed to wish to impress on his cousin Noyes that he had not changed because he was President. He invited Noyes to stay for lunch and for the diplomatic reception and showed him about his private rooms. "Let's look in here, this is pretty fine, isn't it?" he said of a room used for a library. At lunch he talked animatedly of his father's family, especially of "good old Grandmother Chloe Smith." [23] It was evident that he took immense satisfaction from the fact that he, descendant of Chloe Smith Hayes, wife of the blacksmith and tavern-keeper at Brattleboro, Vermont, was the President of the United States.

CHAPTER LXII

The Nationalist

1

He had no intention of being, or trying to be, a President of heroic mold. That would have been foreign to his nature and also to his concept of his role. Moreover, he mirrored faithfully the trend of the time. America then was weary of governmental excitements, especially since the electoral dispute. Reaction from the war and its aftermath definitely had set in. Steadiness was what was wanted. The nation was in transition from the Civil War period to the modern industrial era. New problems were arising, including the problem of labor and capital, so-called. There was no clear public opinion on how to deal with these. In the meantime, what was indicated was a kind of caretaker regime. This Hayes was singularly equipped to provide.

Two things the nation wanted, apparently. It wanted the festering Southern problem quieted. It wanted the excesses charged, rightly or wrongly, to the Grant administrations—graft, "cronyism," nepotism, amorality, executive irresponsibility, Congressional arrogance— replaced by something that some called purity and others called reform. These things Hayes intended to achieve.

Toward those goals he set almost exclusively his course. In his inaugural address he outlined his program. Problems not stated in his inaugural he largely ignored, or he was satisfied merely to define. Thus he was often a disappointment to those who hoped for a Jefferson or a Jackson or a Lincoln. But if he had tried to be like them, as they had been portrayed, he would have been both out of character and out of tune with his times. He did neither, and stepped willingly into the niche among Presidents that was suited to him—halfway between those rated as great and those rated as only fair—in a phrase, the middle ground, which might be called also the most truly indigenous American ground, which he personified in almost all matters personal and political.

2

In the main, his inaugural address, which charted his course, was affirmation of the major points in his Letter of Acceptance. But it was significant that whereas in the letter he had given first importance to the issue of civil-service reform, this place in his inaugural was awarded to the Southern question. "Permanent pacification of the country is now the one subject in our public affairs which all thoughtful and patriotic citizens regard as of supreme importance," he said.

He did not say definitely then how he proposed to achieve this goal. He carefully refrained from mentioning in any specific way the subject of bayonet rule. But he gave a clear hint of what his policy would be by saying that the Southern states did not yet fully enjoy "the inestimable blessings of wise, honest, and peaceful self-government." He added: "Whatever difference of opinion may exist as to the cause of this condition of things, the fact is clear that, in the progress of events, the time has come when such government is the imperative necessity required by all the varied interests, public and private, of those states."

If anything, these statements meant that federal troops would be withdrawn by him from Louisiana and South Carolina. They made it official too, by implication, that he was for granting the Southerners' demands for white rule. However, he took great pains to insist that this policy did not mean abandoning the Negro. For he of course knew, if the country did not, of the pledges by the Southern leaders in connection with the electoral-dispute settlement.

The greater part of his remarks on the Southern question was a lecture on the theme that self-government in the Southern states ought to be accompanied by "complete protection of all its citizens in the free enjoyment of all their constitutional rights," as had been promised (though he did not say so) to Matthews and Sherman by the Southern leaders. He also said: "That a moral obligation rests upon the National government to employ its constitutional power and influence to establish the rights of the people it has emancipated, and to protect them in the enjoyment of those rights when they are infringed or assailed, is also generally admitted."

3

This last, of course, was wishful thinking. Leaders of the South did not really admit any such thing, and Hayes was to find himself engaged in a memorable conflict over precisely this idea.

He did not intend to use force to back up the "moral obligation" of the national government. "There is to be an end to all that, except in emergencies which I can't think of as possible again," he had written to Schurz a month before.[1]

But he hoped to make clear that, though standing for pacification, he was not turning his back on his views, reinforced by his war career, that the Southern states, like all the other states, were part of a nation, not of a confederacy. He hoped that the making of this point would act as pressure on the Southerners to keep their pledges of fair and equal treatment of the Negroes. Indeed, more than any President up to then he talked in his inaugural, as well as later, of the United States in the terms of their being a *nation*—a union, true, but a union that formed a nation also. He was, in fact, the first "nationalist" in the White House.

4

He hoped, too, that he could dull the criticism which he knew would be made against him by leaders of his party that he was giving up doctrine considered basic to the Republican Party. He was loyal to the old doctrine as a philosophical matter, though as a practical matter he was for giving the South a chance to show, like a "gentleman," that it could voluntarily work out a satisfactory adjustment of its race problem.

He defended the legitimacy of the use of force in the states to support national ends. But his pronounced instinct for reconciliation caused him to view settlement of the race issue in the South as a matter for the slower, though more permanent (he felt) process of education.

This led him, it should be noted, to recommend that the federal government give financial support to the public-school systems of the various states. "Universal suffrage should rest upon universal education," he said in his inaugural. "To this end, liberal and permanent provision should be made for the support of free schools by the State governments, and, if need be, supplemented by legitimate aid from national authority." Sixty years later this kind of recommendation would bring the charge of socialism against anyone who made it. But in 1877 Hayes made it as the spokesman of Republican conservatism.

5

His remarks concerning the South were undoubtedly disappointing to the men connected with the Texas and Pacific railroad. About two weeks before the inauguration General Dodge, in Washington, wrote to Tom Scott, "When Hayes gets here you and I want to see him, but more especially do we want our Southern friends to submit to him something that he can put into his inaugural that will give us standing. He is ready to do it, unless somebody coaxes him out of it. He has a clear understanding that he shall do so."

Dodge added that efforts to have the subsidy passed by Congress during the settlement of the election dispute had failed because "the Democrats had no heart in the matter and to a certain extent they got this inspiration from Tilden. There is no question about this, and the way to give the Republicans faith in it is to have it come from Headquarters."[2]

As a minimum, Dodge, William Henry Smith and General Boynton expected Hayes to use at least the key words, internal improvements. But Hayes shied from using even those words. He did say: "In the important work of restoring the South it is not the political situation alone that merits attention. The material development of that section of the country has been arrested by the social and political revolution through which it has passed, and now needs and deserves the considerate care of the National Government, within the just limits prescribed by the Constitution and wise public economy."

But these comments did not commit Hayes to anything definite. The fact was, even these vague sentiments were missing from the draft copy of the address he had brought with him to Washington. William Henry Smith and Stanley Matthews had to persuade him to include them after he reached Washington. "The omission from the original draft must have been fairly accidental," Smith later told Boynton.[3]

It may be guessed that Smith and Matthews told Hayes that failure to make at least an oblique reference to the Texas and Pacific matter would embarrass them, his friends. Such an appeal to his strong sense of loyalty to friends would have been an important one to him—that, in addition to observations that grumbling was already heard among certain Republicans who felt ignored, as many were, in the picking of his cabinet. This made support by Democrats from the South all the more desirable. Thus he finally agreed to put in so much but no more, that could cover the Texas and Pacific matter.

6

Coming at the very start of his Presidency, this matter brought into focus the ambivalence that colored much of his conduct in the office, as was true in his career before. It was an ambivalence that reflected, to a large extent, mixed motives and concepts—his Sophialike fear of being soiled by politics, his Fannylike urge for fame and power, his Sardislike practical streak, and his own promptings toward the idealistic. The net result was that he often appeared to go in different directions at the same time. He gave the impression often of being uncertain or unclear of objectives, though he was clear enough and certain enough when he knew precisely what he wanted.

There was another reason, too, for an apparent ambivalence. His education and predilection for Whiggery conditioned him to consider the Presidential office as subservient to the Congressional power. It had been a basic principle of Whiggery that the President should scarcely do more than execute faithfully the acts passed by Congress. Strong Presidents were frowned on by the Whigs, perhaps because they had formed their party mainly in opposition to Jackson.

Hayes thought he believed in that doctrine. To an extent he did. But events, as well as his personality and his policies, conspired to force him to show at times a wholly un-Whiggish strength, which perhaps surprised him more than anyone else. It was either that or see himself dominated by a Congressional oligarchy, as had happened to Grant.

So even against his wishes, at times, a fact that made him seem more uncertain than he was, he became a champion of Presidential power and dignity, and as such deserved rank among the Chief Executives who built up, rather than depreciated, the office.[4]

7

If he showed himself somewhat on the defensive in stating his Southern policy, obviously seeking to sell his views to his own party, he was not so with reference to civil-service reform. He did not retreat in his inaugural from the promise in his Letter of Acceptance that reform there should be "thorough, radical and complete." He renewed his pledge that Senators and Representatives would no longer be supreme in the selection of officeholders from their districts.

He admitted his indebtedness to his party. "The President of the United States of necessity owes his election to office to the suffrage and zealous labors of a political party." But then he stated what he wished to be considered his credo: "But he [the President] should strive to be always mindful of the fact that *he serves his party best who serves his country best.*" He was proud of that sentence, with its Lincolnian simplicity. It came to him one night, he later said, while walking with friends in Columbus.[5]

"Stalwart" politicians scoffed. But Hayes had the satisfaction of knowing that his statement became part of the political literature of the nation.

8

In a way, his inaugural address was almost as remarkable for what it did not say as for what it said. He made no reference at all to the tariff question. He ignored the issue of sectarian influence in the public-school question, which involved the Catholic issue.

He did reiterate his previously expressed views on behalf of sound money. "The only safe paper currency is one which rests upon a coin basis, and is at all times promptly convertible into coin. . . . I adhere to the views heretofore expressed by me in favor of congressional legislation in behalf of an early resumption of specie payment." But even on this explosive topic he spoke so briefly as to give the impression that he was leaning backward to avoid ruffling the feathers of the Greenbackers, who were strong and getting stronger in both parties.

Indeed, in keeping with his character the whole tenor of his inaugural address was designedly "reasonable." It reflected his desire that the political passion stirred by the election dispute should disappear and that he be accepted as he envisioned himself—a President who would unite the country, who would restore respect for the government, who would lead his own party on the path of correct principles, who would strive toward the ideal of nonpartisanship, though he would be loyal to party also. There was much in this last goal that was contradictory, but he obviously felt that the contradiction could be overcome.

He discussed at some length the election dispute. He conceded that "for the present, opinion will widely vary as to the wisdom of the several conclusions" reached by the electoral commission. But, he said, this was to be "anticipated in every instance where matters of

dispute are made the subject of arbitration under the forms of law."
He admitted that "good men differ as to the facts and the law," but
observed that it was "an occasion for general rejoicing" that the dispute was settled.

Upon one point there is entire unanimity in public sentiment, that
conflicting claims to the Presidency must be amicably and peaceably
adjusted, and that when so adjusted the general acquiescence of the
Nation ought surely to follow. It has been reserved for a Government
of the people, where the right of suffrage is universal, to give to the
world the first example in history of a great Nation, in the midst of a
struggle of opposing parties for power, hushing its party tumults, to
yield the issue of the contest to adjustment according to forms of law.

"Appropriate and well-timed," said the New York *Times* of these
remarks in particular.[6]

<h1 style="text-align:center">9</h1>

He did not reiterate in his inaugural his "inflexible purpose" not to
seek a second term. Instead, he recommended "an amendment to the
Constitution prescribing a term of six years for the Presidential office,
and forbidding re-election."

This proposal, probably first urged in 1871 by Medill when he was
a member of the civil-service commission named by Grant, implied
that Hayes was reaffirming the statement in his Letter of Acceptance.
But the politically minded were bound to speculate on whether or not
this actually did leave open what he would do. This speculation was
all to his advantage. For the renunciation of an ambition for re-
election obviously gave him a weaker hold on his party than he might
have had. The possibility that he might run again after all gave him
some added political strength. This, as he soon discovered, he desperately needed.

CHAPTER LXIII

START

1

For his cabinet he picked a group of seven men who, in the aggregate, faithfully reflected his personality and his political views. It was a cabinet that was political, but not glaringly so. It was reformist, but not radically so.

Naturally it included Senator Sherman, as deep-dyed and practical a politician as any of the machine leaders who had dominated the Republican Party under Grant. Sherman was appointed Secretary of the Treasury. But the cabinet also included Carl Schurz, who had led the Liberal Republican revolt of 1872. Schurz still symbolized, perhaps more than any other figure of the time, the reformer in politics. He was named Secretary of the Interior.

Sherman and Schurz were most often consulted by Hayes. If they were merged, as in a composite photograph, the result would be something quite like Hayes himself as President—practical and visionary, sometimes shrewd and sometimes naïve, often all these things at one and the same time.

For Secretary of State he selected the urbane but verbose Evarts, who occupied middle ground politically between Sherman and Schurz. On the surface the Evarts appointment seemed to have no more significance in a political sense than that a highly regarded public figure had been selected, one especially acceptable to important commercial interests. Yet it represented some other interesting implications.

Because Evarts had been in Johnson's cabinet as Attorney General, and had defended Johnson in the impeachment case, his appointment showed that Hayes, at least, was minded to show that the passion-stirring period of reconstruction was indeed history, part of the past to be considered dead and buried. To an extent, by naming Evarts, Hayes was atoning for having endorsed the impeachment of Johnson.

Another implication lay in the fact that Evarts, a New Yorker, with his selection considered recognition of his state, was not a "stalwart" in the New York party organization. At times Evarts had been associated with the so-called silk-stocking Republican elements in New York who opposed the "organization" leadership under Senator Conkling, who himself, as noted, perhaps wanted to be Secretary of State.

In appointing Evarts, Hayes did not even consult Conkling. Thus, at the outset, he paved the way for conflict with the Senator from New York. Hayes later wrote: "After I went to Washington and after the delivery of the inaugural, he [Conkling] was profuse in his admiration of my opinions and course—*this to me personally*—until the announcement of my Cabinet, when he became hostile, never again calling on me. We never spoke with each other afterwards." [1]

2

He also later said:

If the boss system is to go down, as now [1884] seems probable, I can say that I struck the first and most difficult blows. It is based on Congressional patronage and Senatorial prerogative, or courtesy. This was fully entrenched at Washington when I was inaugurated in 1877. . . . Any reform was at the expense of the power of the Senator and Representative. The first and principal step was the appointment of members of the Cabinet.

This belonged, according to the prevailing system, to the leaders of the party in the Senate. A Cabinet of independent men was organized. The Cabinet, it was claimed by champions of the boss system, should be formed not unfriendly to the system. The announcement of the names of Mr. Evarts and Mr. Schurz, both independent men, both opposed by the bosses, opened the war. . . . [2]

Hayes also showed bold independence of Blaine. Along with Hannibal Hamlin of Maine, Lincoln's first-term Vice-President, Senator Blaine had called on Hayes at Senator Sherman's home to urge that Congressman William P. Frye of Maine be placed in the cabinet, presumably as Postmaster General. "Hamlin much vexed and grieved when I told him I couldn't appoint Fry [sic]," Hayes noted in his diary. "Blaine seemed to claim it as a condition of good relations with me." [3]

Likewise, Hayes spurned the request of Senator Cameron, the long-time boss of Pennsylvania Republicanism, that his son J. Donald be retained as Secretary of War. [4] Zach Chandler was ignored altogether. For these and other acts of independence Hayes would win applause—but much venomous criticism and opposition also.

3

He was not, however, always consistent—something that infuriated many politicos. He went far out of his way to please Indiana's Senator Morton. Indeed, he told Morton's brother-in-law, W. R. Holloway of Indianapolis, who came to him with a list of Hoosiers acceptable to Morton as cabinet appointees, that he "wanted Morton to name a member of his cabinet." [5] Hayes's real choice from Indiana was Benjamin Harrison (later President), but he did not select Harrison because of Morton's opposition. He considered John M. Harlan for Attorney General, but dropped him because Morton again objected, though later Hayes placed Harlan on the Supreme Court.[6]

To please Morton, he named Richard W. Thompson of Indiana for Secretary of the Navy, not considering it a liability that Thompson, once a conspicuous Whig orator, had been an avowed Know-Nothing and as late as 1876 had published a bitterly injudicious attack on the Catholic church, or that Thompson's financial and political ethics often had been publicly challenged. Even Grant had refrained from appointing him to his cabinet after Secretary of State Fish raised a question as to Thompson's connection with an alleged land fraud.[7]

Hayes made the Thompson appointment in an almost whimsical way. As told by Morton's biographer:

When Holloway came to the name of Colonel R. W. Thompson, of Terre Haute, Hayes inquired [his] age. Holloway answered that he was in his sixties, and Hayes replied that this was the very prime of life; that he remembered a speech made by Thompson during the forties, and had never forgotten the sweetness and bell-like tones of his voice. Holloway replied that his voice was still as clear as ever, and that he was good for a three hours' speech at any time. They next passed on to the name of John W. Foster, then minister to Mexico. Hayes said he would like to make up his cabinet at once, and asked how soon Mr. Foster could come to Washington. It was learned that he could not reach that city until after the 4th of March. Thompson was appointed Secretary of the Navy.[8]

4

This appointment was certainly not in accord with Hayes's aim for a cabinet of independent men. For in 1877 Thompson was a mere puppet of Morton, as much a Senatorial oligarch as Cameron, Conkling or Blaine. But Hayes still admired Morton. He was grateful for

"The Cinderella of the Republican Party and Her Haughty Sisters"

Puck thus presented Blaine and Conkling walking out on Hayes in October 1880.

Puck on Civil-Service Reform

Hayes, Schurz and Evarts ride toward it; Sherman is undecided; Field, Blaine and Charles Dana hold back.

Morton's unquestioned zeal in working for his election and for his having championed the Hayes position for settling the electoral dispute.

Then, too, Hayes was displaying here some practical political sagacity. Morton was considered the outstanding champion, after Thad Stevens' death, of the reconstruction policy, a leader in the Senate who stoutly defended the Republican regimes in the South and their protection by federal intervention. In case of controversy within the party over a new Southern policy, it would be well to have Morton at his side.

In addition, Morton was a strong enough man, personally as well as politically, to be more than a match for Conkling and Blaine in speeches or in Senatorial strategy. Hayes needed such a champion on the floor of the Senate and in the party councils. So he wooed Morton —and it was greatly unfortunate for him politically, as well as personally, that Morton, on whom he depended for so much needed support in handling the party leaders, died within six months of the inauguration, an occurrence similar to what happened to a later Republican President, Dwight D. Eisenhower, in the death of Senator Robert Taft, grandson of Alphonso Taft. Morton's passing was a loss in political support from which Hayes never recovered.

Nor were other appointments so free from practical political considerations as Hayes and his admirers liked to imagine. It would be asserted at the time, and repeated by historians, that George W. McCrary, Iowa Congressman, was appointed Secretary of War simply because he had sponsored the House draft of the electoral-commission bill. But McCrary was "sponsored" by General Dodge and the railroad interests that he represented, those of Jay Gould as well as Tom Scott.[9] So this appointment was an apparent step in the direction, it seemed, of fulfilling the commitments in connection with the Texas and Pacific subsidy.

For Attorney General, Hayes selected a Massachusetts judge, Charles A. Devens, distinguished mainly as an after-dinner speaker, the chief consideration being that he was acceptable to the Massachusetts Senator George F. Hoar, whose law partner he had been.[10] Thus, here too Hayes catered to Senatorial influence.

5

Next to that of Schurz, his most striking appointment was his choice for Postmaster General. To this post, usually reserved for the political manager of the administration party, he named a Southern Democrat who had been a Confederate colonel, David M. Key of Tennessee, a retiring Senator. Hayes liked to refer to this appointment in romantic terms, as purely a "hands across the chasm" gesture toward the South, to show his friendly feelings toward the former Rebels. In his diary he recalled:

My task was to wipe out the color line, to abolish sectionalism, to end the war and bring peace. To do this, I was ready to resort to unusual measures and to risk my own standing and reputation with my party and the country. For the first time in our history a gentleman who had opposed the election of the President was by that President invited into his Cabinet. Judge Key, a Confederate soldier and a Democrat who had supported Tilden against me, was made Postmaster-General and one of my constitutional advisers.[11]

This was all true. But it was also true that the appointment of Key was in line with the negotiations for winning Southern Democrats to his support in the electoral dispute and also to rebuild the Republican Party in the South along the lines of the old Whig Party. The Southerners had asked for a post in his cabinet, and they had received it in Key, a friend of Kellar, the Memphis newspaper editor, and the choice of the group with whom Kellar had been working.[12]

6

"If elected, the firmest adherence to principle against all opposition and temptations is my purpose. I shall show a *grit* that will astonish those who predict weakness," Hayes wrote in his diary back in September.[13] He knew quite well that his cabinet choices did not in all respects come up to this ideal—the Thompson appointment, for example. But if he felt qualms, they were greatly eased by the attitude taken toward his cabinet choices by "stalwarts" of his own party in the Senate.

Some "stalwarts" talked as if they intended to block confirmation of the whole cabinet on the ground that it was too independent, not only of them personally but of party considerations. "Hayes has passed the Republican party to its worst enemies!" cried Zach Chandler.[14]

By tradition, Senatorial courtesy called for confirmation of present or former Senators without reference to committees. Sherman was still a Senator. Schurz and Key were former Senators. But in an atmosphere of obvious sullenness their names were ordered sent to committees along with the others. Blaine and Conkling were especially prominent in the making of motions to that end.[15]

Cameron was the most direct in voicing Old Guard objections to what he sensed, correctly, was the purpose of Hayes—to reform the party and also to appease the South. "A Republican President should appoint Republicans!" he growled. He scorned Schurz as a "literary fellow." The aging Cameron also objected that a majority, if not all, of the men selected by Hayes for the cabinet obviously were such as would approve a pacification of the South. To Cameron, this was treason to the party. "There is no merit or excuse for the Southern policy adopted by Hayes," he said.[16]

7

Actually it was a stroke of luck for Hayes that the "stalwarts" did oppose his cabinet. For most of the Republican newspapers, and many Democratic ones, went to Hayes's support, and for once full attention was centered on his aims as President rather than on how he had come to be President.

"*Press & people* all with the President," William Henry Smith happily advised Webb Hayes on the basis of a survey of the papers served by the Western Associated Press.[17] Mass meetings on the theme "Stand by the President" were held in various large cities, notably New York, St. Louis, Memphis and Philadelphia. For the most part, the sponsors were independent-minded citizens whose regard Hayes especially coveted. From Cambridge, Henry Wadsworth Longfellow joined James Russell Lowell and others of Boston in writing to him: "The course of the President is what we expected and heartily approve." [18]

This was all welcome relief from being attacked, or even defended, in connection with his "right" to be President, a subject about which he was more sensitive than he admitted. Moreover, the "stalwarts" quickly backed down, and by March 10 all the Hayes choices were confirmed. The "stalwarts" had intended to humiliate him, to put him in his place. But the net result was to get him off to a good start.

CHAPTER LXIV

"HEALER OF STRIFE"

1

HE PREPARED then for the action that was to bring him more praise and more denunciation—both exaggerated at the time and in conventional history texts afterward—than anything else associated with his administration. As the matter usually is put, this was to pull the troops out of the South. But it was exaggeration to describe the action in that way. The South had not been occupied since 1871. Only in the two states of South Carolina and Louisiana were federal troops still performing, in effect, political duty. Only a small contingent in each case guarded the last two Republican "governors" of the South, Chamberlain in South Carolina and Packard in Louisiana.

Hayes's role was to ring down the curtain on the last of such scenes. He almost did not have even this to do, in view of Grant's apparent intention to fulfill his pledge on March 2 to Major Burke and other Louisianians. But when Grant did send a telegram to New Orleans to tell General Augur to withdraw protection from the Packard regime, Secretary of War "Don" Cameron, just before succeeding his father as Senator, went to the telegraph office and stopped the retiring President's order. It had to go through him, he said, and anyway, he wished to hold up the action until the Louisiana Democrats showed good faith on the matter of the Senators. Then, too, General Sherman sent orders to General Augur to "go slow." [1] All the facts about this side play are covered over with confusion, probably intentional on Grant's part. But the upshot was that in the end there was no definitive action by Grant and thus the decision on both Louisiana and South Carolina was left to Hayes.

2

He knew at the outset what he would do. "My policy is trust, peace, and to put aside the bayonet. I do not think the wise policy is to decide contested elections in the States by the use of the national army," he wrote in his diary on March 14, reiterating what he had written confidentially to Schurz back in February.

The most direct way of achieving his purpose would have been to issue an order immediately that the army was to play no further role

420

in the affairs of South Carolina and Louisiana. A day or two before inauguration, in a talk with Lamar of Mississippi, one of the Southern leaders who had opposed the filibuster in the House and who then was in the Senate, he indicated that such would be his course. So Lamar had urged—and understood.[2] But Hayes did not take the direct course.

This was in part a reflection of prudence. To have simply withdrawn the troops, without being reasonably sure that there would be no violence, would have been irresponsible. Two kinds of violence were feared. One was in connection with the ousting of the Republican governors. The other was vengeance against Republicans in general.

A way of guarding against violence was to persuade Chamberlain and Packard to accept the inevitable and not put up any resistance to the White League and Red Shirts taking over. Stanley Matthews, as will be recalled, made such an approach to Packard back in February but had met with a rebuff. On March 4 Matthews sent a similar unofficial request to Chamberlain.[3] Adding weight to this request was an accompanying note to Chamberlain by Evarts, which, while noncommittal in its precise words, showed that he, about to be made Secretary of State, approved the suggestion that Chamberlain abdicate.[4]

Chamberlain's response revealed that he could not be so easily persuaded.

I desire to aid and relieve President Hayes, but this is a life and death struggle, and I know that I should consign myself to infamy in the eyes of all Republicans here who know the situation by fearful experience, if I were to accept any terms or do any act which could result in the monstrous conspiracy against law and humanity which the Democracy of this state embodies and represents. There are better ways than this to conciliate and pacify the South. . . . Neither you nor any man moved by a sense of justice can understand the situation here and be willing, for any political advantage or freedom from embarrassment, to abandon the Republicans to the fate that awaits them whenever Hampton becomes the undisputed governor of this state. . . .[5]

Chamberlain's letter certainly emphasized the desirability of caution. However political it was its implied warning that the Democrats in South Carolina under Hampton might conduct a reign of terror against the Republicans in revenge for real or fancied reconstruction grievances could not be ignored.

3

Hayes also had to face squarely the fact that letting Democrats take over in South Carolina and Louisiana was bound to be opposed by leaders of his party, who had no faith in the theory that the act would benefit the party. Blaine opened an attack in advance of any action, when the Senate debated Kellogg's right to be seated as a Senator from Louisiana. Democrats, of course, challenged Kellogg's right. Temporarily the issue was laid on the table, pending further investigation, with some Republicans co-operating in thus carrying out the understanding agreed on by Sherman, Matthews and the others with the Louisiana Democrats.

But Blaine argued for the immediate seating of Kellogg, in the course of which he said:

I know there has been a good deal said, here and there, in the corridors of the Capitol, round and about in by places and high places of late, that some arrangement has been made by which Packard was not to be recognized or upheld; that he was to be allowed to slide and Nicholls was to be accepted as Governor of Louisiana. I want to know who had the authority to make any such arrangement.

I deny it. . . . I shall find myself grievously disappointed, wounded and humiliated if my denial is not vindicated by the policy of the administration. . . . I hope a Republican Senate will say at this point that there shall be no authority in this land large enough or adventurous enough to compromise the honor of the great Republican party. . . .

Blaine went further, jabbing Hayes with an especially sharp point: "If Packard is not the legal governor of Louisiana, Hayes has no title to the office of President." [6]

This was something that could be argued. Hayes believed it was not true, and there were facts to support his conviction. But it was also something on which he was sensitive. Zach Chandler had made the same point at Hayes's first cabinet meeting, with Grant's cabinet officers holding over until Hayes's nominees were confirmed. Hayes showed some heat then in rebuking Chandler. [7] For Blaine to repeat such a statement in the Senate was, in effect, a declaration of war on

Hayes, if not also the first gun fired by Blaine in a campaign to get in 1880 what he had lost to Hayes in 1876, the Presidential nomination of the party.

4

Hayes was also disturbed by Blaine's references to "arrangements," Blaine's way of bringing up the matter of the bargaining for support of the Southern Democrats. And he was disturbed that his Southern policy laid him open to the charge that he was disinterested in the welfare of the Negroes. William Lloyd Garrison quickly confirmed his anticipation of this by writing a strong letter to Blaine, one that Blaine promptly publicized, congratulating him for "defending the validity of Senator Kellogg's election and the legitimacy of the claim of Governor Packard of Louisiana and Governor Chamberlain of South Carolina to the recognition and respect of the general government." The Garrison letter contained such phrases as "betrayal of the blacks," "cowardly compromise with the despotic and rebellious spirit of the South," and "sacrificing principle to expediency." "Conciliation," he wrote, "is truckling to the South as of yore." [8]

In answer, partly at least, to such attacks Hayes just then made an interesting appointment, naming a celebrated Negro, Frederick Douglass, to be United States Marshal of the District of Columbia. This appointment, he told a delegation of Negro ministers, "should be accepted as an indication of a purpose to advance the equal rights of the people of the entire country." [9]

The Douglass appointment was accompanied by some compromise. For, whereas it had been the custom, though not among legally defined duties, for the Marshal of the District to act as official greeter at formal White House social functions, Douglass was "relieved" of this duty. It was taken over by Hayes's son Webb. This was a concession to what the New York Times called "timid people." [10]

But the uproar of protest against the appointment of the Negro from lawyers of the district, most of them Southerners, made the appointment serve well the purpose intended. In his diary Hayes wrote: " . . . If a liberal policy towards late Rebels is adopted, the ultra Republicans are opposed to it; if the colored people are honored, the extremists of the other wing cry out. I suspect I am right in both cases." [11] Most Americans then, when not overheated by politics, probably agreed with Hayes in that assessment of his position.

5

The Blaine attack had the effect, however, of throwing him into a temporary state of ambivalence on the Louisiana and South Carolina matter. Some imaginary indecision as well as prudence marked his conduct. Thus, though he knew what he intended to do in the end, he suddenly is found acting as though he were approaching the problem as something still to be debated. In his diary as late as March 16 he set down some curious entries:

Different plans for Louisiana and South Carolina are offered: 1. A new election. 2. Lawful action of Legislatures. 3. Acknowledge Packard and Chamberlain, and leave them to their own state remedies. 4. Withdraw troops and leave events to take care of themselves. *Here I am too crowded with business to give thought to these questions. Let me get a few outside opinions. . . .*[12]

Probably he himself could not explain why he felt it necessary to indicate that he was so undecided, why, in particular, he let his diary give the impression that he might acknowledge Packard and Chamberlain, when there was no possibility that he would do so. Oddly, on the same day he talked with newspaper correspondents in a way that led them to report definitely that the troops would be withdrawn in a matter of days.

6

He might have carried out the withdrawal promptly after all had there not appeared in the New York *Times* a powerful editorial that urged that he go slow. Up to then the *Times* had been giving him support on a policy of conciliation and had defended him against the Blaine attacks. But the new *Times* line was:

If the first step in the Southern policy of President Hayes be, as stated in our Washington dispatches, the immediate withdrawal of United States troops from South Carolina and Louisiana, he is on the point of making a serious blunder. No one will dispute that the withdrawal of the troops is a necessary part of any plan that may be devised for the restoration of order and stable government in these states, but such an order should follow, not precede . . . some plan of conference and settlement.

The troops cannot be withdrawn at the present juncture without the implied admission that they were sent in the first instance for a totally indefensible purpose, and retained without any obvious necessity. Such an opinion is certainly not that of the vast majority of the Republican party, and it will be nothing short of a national misfortune should the President fail to carry the majority along with him. . . .[13]

Hayes then consulted his cabinet. It was decided that deference had to be shown to the *Times* editorial viewpoint. A strategy was adopted to meet the points raised by the newspaper. "Louisiana troubles discussed," Hayes summarized a cabinet meeting on March 20. "All but Devens seemed indisposed to use force to uphold Packard's government and he is not decidedly for it. All finally agreed to send a commission to Louisiana." [14]

In the case of South Carolina the strategy was not to create a commission but to invite the rival governors, Chamberlain and Hampton, to Washington for conferences.

7

These, of course, were devices intended to mollify Republican critics. They achieved this purpose, but only to have Democratic critics open up. Southern Democrats in particular began to assert with great heat that Hayes was betraying them, that he planned to stand by the carpetbag regimes after all.

John Young Brown of Kentucky decided in anger that the time had come to make use of the meaningless statements which he and Senator Gordon had extracted from Matthews and Foster at Wormley's Hotel during the filibuster. He released them to the press.

In an interview in Watterson's Louisville *Courier-Journal,* one copied in leading newspapers elsewhere, Brown said:

Passionate men are heaping invective upon the heads of those Democrats who voted to stand by the Electoral bills. . . . I have full faith in the fulfillment of the assurances contained in the letters of Messrs. Foster and Matthews. They are honorable men. I cannot believe that they would attempt deliberate deception. . . . It is impossible that the President, under all the circumstances, and in view of his own utterances, and the promises of his friends, can refuse at once to make Louisiana and South Carolina as free as Ohio, and have the flag fly over states, not provinces, over free men, not subjects. . . . If not done, the whole responsibility for the consequences, whatever they may be, will rest upon President Hayes.[15]

Pacification was not proceeding in a pacific atmosphere. A crack in the Republican-Southern Democrat alliance was developing.

But pacification did proceed.

8

Governor Chamberlain came to Washington March 27. Wade Hampton came two days later. Chamberlain learned quickly that he could not expect to win recognition. He grasped at a straw. He asked that the South Carolina dispute also be referred to a commission. But serious consideration was not given to his proposal.

The real objection was that Hampton would not accept it.[16] Indeed, Hampton came to Washington in a mood that Republican newspapers called arrogant. In speeches en route he indicated that he spurned conferring with Hayes. He would merely make one demand—that the troops be withdrawn. "I am going there to demand our rights, nothing less and, so help me God, to take nothing less," he said in one speech. In another he said: "We will not submit our case to the arbitration of any commission or compromise of any sort." [17]

To Hayes himself, in accepting the invitation to Washington, Hampton was similarly arrogant. The invitation had said that Hayes wanted Hampton's views on the best way for removing the impediments to establishment of one government in the state. Hampton said he accepted "through motives of proper courtesy . . . though I cannot hope by doing so to throw additional light on questions which have already been so ably and thoroughly presented and the solution of which is so obvious and simple—that is, withdrawal of the federal troops." [18]

Hayes, however, did not let himself show any sense of affront. Having decided that the troops would be withdrawn, he felt his main objective now was to get Hampton on record as endorsing the views expressed by him in his Letter of Acceptance and in his inaugural, in which he had qualified his program of pacification with emphasis on the necessity of protecting the Constitutional rights of the Negroes.

In this he succeeded. For, just before leaving Washington, Hampton signed a letter which said:

. . . If the Federal troops are withdrawn from the State House, there shall be on my part, or on that of my friends, no resort to violence to assert our claims. . . . I shall use all my authority to repress the use or the exhibition of force in the settlement of all disputed questions, and this authority shall be exercised in such a manner that peace shall be preserved.

We only desire the establishment in our state of a government which will secure *to every citizen, the lowest as well as the highest, black as well as white, full and equal protection in the enjoyment of all his rights under the Constitution of the United States.* . . . With the recognition of the perfect equality of every citizen before the law, with a just and impartial administration of the laws, with a practical, secure exercise of the right of suffrage, with a system of public education which will open the sources of knowledge to all classes, we may hope to see our state soon take the position to which she is entitled.[19]

Not even William Lloyd Garrison could find fault with such pledges, which the Hampton legislature formally endorsed—if they could be relied on. "Time will tell," Hayes commented later.[20]

9

On April 3, 1877, Hayes sent to Secretary of War McCrary a carefully worded letter. It concerned the nineteen enlisted men and two officers of the U. S. Infantry "stationed by my predecessor in the State House at Columbia, South Carolina."

Finding them in that place, I have thought proper to delay a decision of the question of their removal until I could consider and determine whether the condition of affairs in that State is now such as either to require or justify the continued military occupation of the State House. In my opinion there does not now exist in that State such domestic violence as is contemplated by the Constitution as the ground upon which the military power of the National Government may be invoked for the defense of the State.

There are, it is true, grave and serious disputes as to the rights of certain claimants to the chief executive office of that State. But these are to be settled and determined, not by the Executive of the United States, but by such orderly and peaceable methods as may be provided by the constitution and laws of the State. I feel assured that no resort to violence is contemplated in any quarter. . . . Under these circumstances and in this confidence, I now deem it proper to take action in accordance with the principles announced when I entered upon the duties of the Presidency.

You are, therefore, directed to see that the proper orders are issued for the removal of said troops from the State House to their previous place of encampment.

R. B. Hayes

McCrary then advised General Sherman, who in turn advised General Ruger, in command in South Carolina, that the soldiers should leave the State House at 12:00 noon on April 10.[21] On April 9 Chamberlain informed Hampton that he would turn over the offices of governor the next day to him or his representative. Promptly at noon on the tenth the soldiers departed—and Hampton became undisputed governor.

South Carolina was "redeemed" amid a chorus of praise for Hayes —from Southern Democratic papers. Said Hampton: "President Hayes is a good and benevolent man, and not only so, a truly great man." Moderate Republicans approved, moderately, while "stalwarts" were either silent or fumed, though Chamberlain issued a statement which, while bitter, said, "The motives and purposes of [Hayes] . . . are unquestionably honorable and patriotic." [22]

10

Meanwhile the commission to settle the Louisiana problem was at work in New Orleans. Its purpose obviously was to bring about the end of the Packard regime in a way that would spare Hayes as much criticism within his own party as possible, and to make the agreed result seem to follow a fresh investigation unrelated to any arrangements.·

One of the five members was an ex-Whig turned Democrat, John C. Brown, former governor of Tennessee. The four others were Republicans who had been carefully selected for party prestige and connections: Harlan, who had been Bristow's manager at the 1876 convention; General Joseph R. Hawley of Connecticut, who had presided at the 1868 convention that nominated Grant; Wayne MacVeagh of Pennsylvania, a son-in-law of Cameron; Justice Charles B. Lawrence of the Illinois Supreme Court. If such men contrived the downfall of the Republican regime in Louisiana, or co-operated in that result, it could not be said that it had all been arranged as part of the negotiations in connections with the election dispute, for none of these men was in those negotiations. Such, at least, was the hope.

Secretary of State Evarts prepared for the commission a letter of instruction that was a model of political finesse. It seemed to imply that the commission was to gather facts, on which Hayes would make a decision "as to the time, manner and conditions which should be observed in putting an end" to "the apparent intervention of the military power of the United States in the controversies which, unhappily, divide the opinions and disturb the harmony of the people of" Louisiana. But the Commissioners were specifically told not to determine who was elected. Evarts wrote:

It will be readily understood that the service desired of and entrusted to this commission does not include any examination into or report upon the facts of the recent State election, or of the canvass of the votes cast at such election. So far as attention to these subjects may be necessary the President cannot but feel that the reports of the committees of the two Houses of Congress, and other public information at hand, will dispense with and should preclude any original exploration by the commission of that field of inquiry.

A careful reading of the document shows that the commissioners were expected to achieve a result that would permit Hayes to side-step a direct choice between Packard and Nicholls. They were to bring about a single legislature. The result then, in Evarts' words, would be that "the rest of the problem could gradually be worked out by the prevalent authority which the legislative power, when undisputed, is quite competent to exert in composing conflict in the co-ordinate branches of the Government." [23]

11

In both Louisiana legislatures there were members who were unchallenged. As described later by the commission, the situation was: "The Nicholls legislature had a quorum in the Senate upon either the Nicholls or Packard theory of law, and a quorum in the House on the Nicholls, but not on the Packard theory. The Packard legislature had a quorum in the House on its own theory, but . . . not in the Senate." [24] An objective approach would have been to form a single legislature by bringing together, from the two legislatures, the unchallenged members from each. This kind of body could then have passed on the qualifications of the contesting claimants. Indeed, in a display of fairness, the commission did make this proposal. It was acceptable to the Republicans but was rejected by the Democrats. [25]

The Democratic strategy was to cause enough members of the Packard legislature, including Negroes, to switch allegiance to the Nicholls legislature so that the Packard legislature would be disintegrated. Then the single legislature would be Democratic. A powerful argument to promote desertions from Packard ran: That Packard could not expect to be sustained by the Hayes administration, that the final result in Louisiana was forecast by the result in South Carolina, that if the Packard legislators needed to fill out the Nicholls legislature quorum wanted to remain as legislators, it was in their interest to make the switch.

This argument was buttressed by the fate of appeals by Packard to Hayes. These asked that the instructions to the commission be changed. Hayes did not answer.[26]

An incentive to desertion also was a promise by the Nicholls forces to pay the Packard men eight dollars a day for the time they served in the Packard legislature, plus mileage—a total of $30,000. There were reports, though never wholly verified, that the Louisiana State Lottery Company provided funds for this as well as for even more substantial financial "persuasion." This aspect concerning desertions could be exaggerated. But there can be no doubt that the commission aided the Democratic strategy.

12

By April 19 enough Packard men had indicated they would transfer to the Nicholls legislature to give it a quorum in both houses "on the Packard theory of the law." On the day before, Nicholls addressed to the commission a letter in which he committed himself to a joint resolution already adopted by his legislature, which said:

. . . We hereby solemnly declare that it is and will be the purpose of the government of Louisiana, represented by Francis T. Nicholls as its executive head—

First, to accept in good faith the thirteenth, fourteenth, and fifteenth amendments to the Constitution of the United States in letter and spirit.

Second. The enforcement of the laws rigidly and impartially, to the end that violence and crime shall be suppressed and promptly punished, and that peace and order prevail, and that the humblest laborer upon the soil of Louisiana, throughout every parish of the State, of either color, shall receive full and equal protection of the laws in person, property, political rights, and privileges.

Third. To the promotion of kindly relations between the white and colored citizens of the State upon the basis of justice and mutual confidence.

Fourth. The education of all classes of the people being essential to the preservation of free institutions, we do declare our solemn purpose to maintain a system of public education by an equal and uniform taxation upon property . . . and which shall secure the education of the children of white and colored citizens with equal advantages.

Fifth. Desirous of healing the dissensions that have disturbed the State for years past, and anxious that the citizens of all political parties may be free from the feverish anxieties of political strife and join hands in honestly restoring the prosperity of Louisiana, the Nicholls government will discountenance any attempted persecution, from any quarter, of individuals for past political conduct.

These pledges were, of course, precisely those that had been agreed to privately by Major Burke in his negotiations with Matthews. They now had been repeated openly and officially. Thus, like Governor Hampton, Governor Nicholls of Louisiana had promised the political and social conditions which Hayes had said should accompany self-government. Thus, too, the stage was set to dispose of what remained of the Packard legislature.

13

The Evarts instructions had indicated that there would be no order for withdrawal of the troops from the Packard Statehouse until after the commission had returned to Washington and made its report. But on April 20 the commission sent to Hayes the following telegraphed message: "In view of the purpose of the President to withdraw the troops to the barracks whenever it can be done without any outbreak of violence, the commission are unanimously of the opinion that the immediate announcement of the date when such withdrawal is to take place will be better for the peace of the people than to delay such announcement. We believe there is no danger of such outbreak." [27]

Hayes acted the same day. He did not set a definite date for withdrawal of the troops—a technical matter—but did send to Secretary McCrary a letter concerning Louisiana almost identical with the one that ended the military intervention in South Carolina.[28] Announcement of this order was followed on the same day by the anticipated result. The Packard legislature committed suicide. Its caucus adopted a resolution "to the effect that it was useless to prolong the contest and advising all members on the rolls of the Nicholls legislature to go and take their seats." [29]

At the same time the caucus advised "Governor" Packard also to give up the contest, at least "for the time being, trusting to the future to vindicate the righteousness of your cause." [30]

On April 24 General Augur ended the assignment of his troops at the Packard Statehouse. The next day Packard, in a statement addressed "To the Republicans of Louisiana," announced that "the aid and countenance of the national government has been withdrawn from the Republicans of Louisiana, and that a government, revolutionary in form, is practically on the point of usurping control of affairs in this state." He blamed both Grant and Hayes. Then he attacked the commission which, he said, "by direct action" caused the "disintegration" of his legislature. He concluded: "I waive none of my legal rights, but yield only to superior force . . . for the present." [81]

14

Everyone, including Packard, knew, however, that he was yielding not merely "for the present" but permanently. Moreover, he had yielded not so much to "superior force," though that was a factor, nor even just to immediate political realities, which also were factors, but essentially to the historical facts that the Civil War period in American history was definitely ended, and that Hayes, in the role of "healer of strife," as Dr. Oliver Wendell Holmes called him,[32] had executed the national will.

The Negroes? In their behalf Hayes and his representatives had insisted on getting the most solemn pledges from the recognized spokesmen of the South that the freedmen's rights under the Thirteenth, Fourteenth and Fifteenth Amendments would be respected; also that equal public education would be provided for them. Hayes did get those precise pledges—a sort of contract, so to speak—backed, presumably, by the chivalry and high honor that he, at Kenyon, had come to associate with and expect from Southern gentlemen. Later it served the purposes of Southern politicians, as well as their apologists, to center attention only on those aspects of the "bargain" which made it appear that the exclusive consideration on their part was to let him be counted in as President.

The pledges by Hampton and Nicholls, as well as by their respective legislatures, would be forgotten. Certain Republican leaders, for reasons of their own, co-operated in this forgetfulness. But the record was there.

CHAPTER LXV

Broken Pledges

1

THE PRACTICAL results for his party that Hayes hoped for from the new Southern policy did not materialize. He had been confident that Southern Democratic members would allow the Republicans to organize the House. So certain of this was he that he had urged Garfield not to be a candidate for John Sherman's seat in the Senate, telling him that he would undoubtedly be elected Speaker of a Republican House. Garfield acquiesced.[1] With Hayes's support Stanley Matthews won the Sherman vacancy in a contest with Alphonso Taft. But the following October 1877, when Congress convened in a special session called by Hayes to have funds appropriated for the army, the Southern Democrats, ignoring the understanding, went along with their Northern colleagues in organizing the House, and the House remained in Democratic control.

And this was after Hayes and members of his cabinet had made a good-will tour of several Southern states, one trumpeted by Wade Hampton, to urge co-operation between the sections on the basis of his pacification policy. It was a tour which he felt was "altogether happy and successful." It convinced him that "there are thousands of intelligent people in the South who are not Democrats and who would like to unite with the conservative Republicans of the North."[2] But failure of the Southern Democrats to let the Republicans organize the House was a straw in the wind pointing to failure as a whole of the grand political plan for a "new" Republican Party in the South.

In a burst of optimism, when Southern politicians and newspapers were showering him with praise for withdrawal of the troops (also for appointing Southern Democrats to federal jobs), Hayes had said he was certain the "pacification policy" would "secure North Carolina, with a fair chance in Maryland, Virginia, Tennessee, and Arkansas" and that he was "not without hopes of Louisiana, South Carolina and Florida."[3] That is, these states might be won by the Republicans in elections ahead. But in the Congressional elections of 1878, the first test, every Southern State went overwhelmingly against the Republicans and for white-supremacy Democrats, though in some cases other party names, such as "Readjusters" or "Conservatives," disguised the Democratic victories.

Hayes had to admit that there had emerged precisely what he had hoped his policies would prevent, a "solid" Democratic South.[4] An immediate result was that the Republicans lost control of the Senate also.

2

These elections, moreover, contradicted the rosy assurances Hayes gave the country in December 1877 in his first annual message, to the effect that Negroes would be permitted to vote freely throughout the South, that there would be no intimidation, no violence, and that a general spirit of "concord" prevailed. For violence occurred, especially in Louisiana, where in political clashes, some between whites and blacks, thirty or forty persons were killed.[5] There were incidents in South Carolina also. Hampton, who was re-elected governor, apparently tried personally to keep his promises. But the same could not be said of all his followers. In some areas in South Carolina, as well as in Louisiana, not a single Republican vote was counted.

As a man who had urged that the South "be trusted," Hayes found himself making a sorry admission in his diary: "In South Carolina and Louisiana, and perhaps in some of the other cotton states, grave charges are made. . . . By state legislation, by frauds, by intimidation, and by violence of the most atrocious character, colored citizens have been deprived of the right of suffrage . . . and of the protection to which the people of those states have been solemnly pledged." [6]

If all, or even a part, of this were true, he faced a dilemma. He wished to be known as having reconciled the North and South. In July 1877 he wrote to Guy Bryan: "We are now getting old, and it is, I assure you, a happiness to think that I have done, and am doing, something to make this people indeed one people." [7] But if he were to act aggressively to call the South to account, the old sectional division was bound to revive, he felt, and so he followed a policy largely of "watch and wait."

He decided to scold the South and threaten action. In his first message to Congress after the 1878 elections he said:

It becomes the duty of the Executive and Judicial Departments of the Government, each within its province, to inquire into and punish

violations of the laws of the United States which have occurred. . . .
Whatever authority rests with me to this end I shall not hesitate to put
forth. . . . No means within my power will be spared to obtain a full
and fair investigation of the alleged crimes, and to secure the conviction and just punishment of the guilty.[8]

This had a good ring. But he did not carry out an aggressive program
of prosecutions. He still hoped that the South would accept the amendments voluntarily. As President and as titular head of his party, he felt
compelled to voice threats of using force. But his personal conviction
still was that the real solution lay in education. The Southerners knew
this, and took advantage of their knowledge.

3

Also, pending the working of that long-term process, his hope was
that the native Southern whites would divide into two parties. With
each party bidding for the votes of the Negroes, this, he felt, would
assure that Negro rights would be respected for political reasons if for
no other. But as time would show, the 1878 elections were a forecast
of a one-party system in the South which excluded Negroes from
participation in politics.

The unanimity of mass white opinion in the South was that the
Republican Party stood for Negro rule. Thus few white citizens of
standing dared affiliate with it. Despite their economic affinity for
Republican economic doctrines, the Whiggish Southerners remained
in the Democratic Party. This brought much struggle within the
Democratic Party, as conservatives battled "radicals" for control. But
on the racial issue, the conservatives and radicals closed ranks. The
Whig alliance, to be constantly attempted again and again in various
forms in later years, under Theodore Roosevelt, William Howard Taft,
Herbert Hoover and Dwight D. Eisenhower, did not come to pass.

True, certain Southerners in Congress supported Hayes at times.
Often they were conspicuously friendly when leaders of his own party
fought him bitterly. But the hope that he would be able to end the
sectional division of party life and see Southerners like Guy Bryan
and Northerners like himself united in one party, for emotional as
well as practical reasons, turned out to be fanciful.

Not even a fairly generous program of internal improvements notably through appropriation of federal funds for Southern river and
harbor development, nor the appointment of Democrats as post-

masters, district attorneys, marshals and judges, had any effect. The jobs and the federal largess were accepted. But the recipients remained Democrats—with some becoming more actively anti-Republican than otherwise to prove that they had not been "corrupted."

To be sure, the South did not get so much financial help as its leaders wished, not nearly so much as Boynton, Kellar and Smith had indicated the South could expect after resolution of the election dispute in Hayes's favor. So the theory that Southern whites could be lured into the Republican Party by economic means was not fully tried.

The South received a great deal under Hayes, so much that Northern newspapers protested against "looting of the treasury for the former rebels." But it did not get so much as the Southern leaders felt was coming to them. Hayes was too economy-minded—and also too wary of being involved in scandal.

4

The Texas and Pacific subsidy? Its final fate illustrated Hayes's frame of mind. Just after the troops were withdrawn in Louisiana, he talked with newspapermen and others as if he would back the subsidy. On the basis of "concurrent and direct sources," Watterson's paper reported that "the President, in conversation lately has expressed himself in very decided terms in favor of . . . such government aid as may be appropriate to secure the completion of the Texas & Pacific Railway." The paper added that Hayes's views would be "carried into his executive policy." [9] Guy Bryan, who had been a guest at the White House while the troops issue was being decided, told the press when he returned to Texas that he, as close friend of the President, was sure Hayes would give "hearty support" to the railroad project.[10]

In March 1877 Garfield wrote in his diary: "The President believes we can organize the next House and is willing to favor internal improvements in the South, including the Pacific Railroad if that will bring Southern support to the Administration to make it worthwhile." [11] But even before the Southern Democrats backed away from the arrangement concerning the House, Hayes had begun to look for a graceful way of retreating to where he wished to stand anyway—against the subsidy.

His out came as a result of renewed rivalry between Scott's Texas and Pacific and Huntington's Southern Pacific in laying tracks in the

Southwest Indian territory. It was Huntington's idea to extend the Southern Pacific eastward from California to Fort Yuma, Arizona Territory, into the area to be served by the Texas and Pacific, thus showing that without a subsidy a Southern connection with the Pacific coast could be accomplished. He started to build a bridge across the Colorado River for moving trains into Arizona.

Although the completed Texas and Pacific tracks then were still 1,200 miles away in the east, Scott also obtained permission from the War Department, under Secretary McCrary, to build in the Fort Yuma area. There were clashes between railroad construction crews and also much political wirepulling by the rival systems, with the result that McCrary in September used his authority to order both companies to cease operations in the government territory until both sides could be heard. But Huntington ignored the order and continued laying track.

5

On October 4, 1877, Medill's Chicago *Tribune* carried an interesting editorial.

It is very distressing to the Texas & Pacific people to know that every day brings more and more conclusive verification of the danger that a railroad may be built across the Southern portion of the continent before they can muster up sufficient force to put their subsidy scheme through Congress. The Southern Pacific R. R., asking no guarantee or bonds, but paying cash for the work as it goes along, is steadily pushing Eastward. . . . Let it alone and it will complete the entire system. . . . This would be giving the South what it clamors for, but is not what the subsidy grabbers clamor for.

In a letter on October 10, 1877, Huntington himself told an associate, David D. Colton, the rest of the story:

I went to Washington night before last and returned last night. I think I have the bridge question settled for the present. I found it harder to do than I expected. The Secretary of War told me that they had it up at two cabinet meetings and had concluded not to do anything as Congress would come to gather next week, but I got him out of that idea in about 20 minutes. I then saw three others of the cabinet; then went and saw the President.

He was a little cross at first; said we had defied the government, but I soon got him out of that belief. I said to him that we were very much in earnest about building the S. P. I said to him that I had written out [to associates], after we were given the right to go on and complete the bridge after once being stopped, that they had better push the work night and day, as we had been stopped once before without any reason known to us and that we might be again, and that I guessed the boys very likely quit work and went to supper, and the military quit at the same time and got their supper and went to bed, supposing the workmen would do the same, but instead of going to bed, [they] went back and laid track across the bridge, so as to be sure and have it so trains would cross before they received any order to quit.

The President laughed heartily at that and said he guessed we meant business. He then said, "What do you propose to do if we were to let you run over the bridge?" I said, "Push the road right on through Arizona." He said, "Will you do that? If you will, that will suit me first rate." Now, I think you had better spend a little more money building east, and have it telegraphed as often as you can. It will do us much good here.[12]

6

That interview foreshadowed Hayes's final attitude—to keep hands off. Matthews, usually considered his spokesman, plumped for the subsidy in the Senate, or professed to. But Hayes gave no help. In the following December he gave to the New York *Tribune* an interview which showed what, for him, amounted to hostility toward the Texas and Pacific subsidy. Scott was asking too much, he said. He was "in grave doubt" that a subsidy should be granted at all. He mentioned the Crédit Mobilier scandal. He said he did not want to make possible any such operations. Besides, with Huntington in mind he felt that the South would eventually get its line without government help.[13]

Later it came out that Jay Gould was in the picture, behind Scott. In 1880 Gould publicly took over Scott's interest. In the end, with Gould and Huntington working together, the system that the South wanted was constructed jointly by Gould's Texas and Pacific and Huntington's Southern Pacific.[14] But there was no federal subsidy "grab." Hayes had kept his skirts clean. The Scott lobby failed again, and finally.

To the Southern Democrats in the Boynton-Smith-Kellar negotiations, this, of course, was a betrayal. They felt as outraged as the Hayes Republicans did over their own failure to redeem their pledge on organizing the House.

7

These were not the only broken pledges—on either side. For example, the Louisiana Democrats felt double-crossed when a renewed move was made by Northern Republicans to seat Kellogg in the Senate as a result of his "election" by the nonexistent Packard legislature. Kellogg was seated. In reprisal, the Nicholls legislature then elected two U. S. Senators, both Democrats, which set off much heated controversy over their seating.

Then, too, the Louisiana Democrats had violated, in spirit if not technically, the pledge that there would be no persecution of the ousted Republicans. For in June 1877 the Democrats at New Orleans obtained the indictment of J. Madison Wells and the other members of the now abolished Republican returning board on charges of having "falsely and feloniously published as true" a "certain altered, false, forged, and counterfeited public record." The "record" was the report of the result of the 1876 election in one of the Louisiana parishes, Vernon. Strong evidence showed that the report had been altered so as to count 178 votes for the Hayes electors, though in fact there were only two such votes, and that the members of the returning board knew of the alteration when they accepted the report as valid.[15]

This case subjected Hayes to considerable embarrassment. It brought into the limelight once more painfully ugly phases of the maneuverings by which the returning board had certified the election of the Republican electors in 1876. The matter was also embarrassing in his relations with his party leaders. At the time of the settlement of the troops issue the point most feelingly made against his policy in the party circles, even by those who conceded that withdrawal was inevitable, was that Republicans in Louisiana and South Carolina would be persecuted once the Democrats obtained power. His answer was to point to the assurances given him.

8

The action against the former returning-board members weakened that answer. It placed him more than ever on the defensive with already antagonistic party chieftains, such as Conkling and Blaine, as well as with more friendly ones. Garfield wrote to a friend: "The policy of the President has turned out to be a give-away from the beginning. He has *nolled* suits, discontinued prosecutions, offered conciliation everywhere in the South, while they have spent their time in whetting their knives for any Republican they could find." [16]

The grumbling within his party intensified after one of the defendants, General Thomas C. Anderson (whom Sherman had praised with Wells), was found guilty in February 1878 and sentenced to two years of hard labor in prison, though the jury had recommended mercy. J. Madison Wells escaped prosecution, as was said, by "taking to the bayous."

Hayes was disturbed along with his critics. He wrote in his diary after the Anderson verdict:

I put it as a simple question of good faith, of honor, on the part of Louisiana. Suppose all the facts proved against Anderson to have existed, but suppose the Returning Board had counted the state for Tilden; would there have been any prosecution? Nobody believes there would. Is it not a clear case within the resolutions of the Nicholls Legislature and the letter of Governor Nicholls? Believing the affirmative, I rely upon—I trust—the honor of Governor Nicholls.[17]

9

He took steps to prod Nicholls' "honor." Some years later he mentioned that General Winfield Scott Hancock, Democratic candidate for President in 1880, aided him "especially" in "the embarrassing and exasperating" Louisiana prosecution. It may be inferred that Hancock intervened with Nicholls.[18] In any event, a month later the Nicholls-appointed Louisiana Supreme Court set aside the conviction on the technical point that General Anderson could not have been guilty of publishing a forged "public" document because the report of the canvass was not a "public" document. The cases against the others were then dropped too.

Hayes tried to view this outcome as a victory for his Southern policy. "The favorable fact," he observed, "is that the court followed the best public opinion of Louisiana in opposition to the Bourbons. The ruffian class, the implacables, and the press were for the severest punishment—determined to persecute the members of the board to the bitter end. For the first time the better classes have overruled the violent. Pacification begins to tell." [19]

So much satisfaction on his part from the outcome of so relatively minor a case reflected an overeagerness to see some immediate concrete success come out of pacification. He was aware that much of his prestige, certainly in the collective judgment of his party, and in the judgment of history, depended on the outcome of his Southern policy. So he was forced to grab at straws.

But however optimistically he viewed developments, he could not help seeing that his hopes for pacification were far from becoming reality, especially those concerning the Negroes. He continued to have hope. But he was never to see anything remotely approaching complete vindication of his hopes.

Instead, he was to have denunciation and scorn heaped on him, mostly from his own party leaders, though none of them stood definitely for any positive alternative to reverse what had been done. The most positive action would have been to restore bayonet rule, to have federal troops once again supervising elections in the South and backing up Negroes in their civil rights.

But this approach was over, and everyone, including Hayes's critics, knew it. He might have used other, less positive methods, such as political pressure, employment of civilian federal officers, and the like. This he failed to do, at least aggressively. Rather, he continued, naïvely, to rely on Southern promises.

CHAPTER LXVI

LANDMARKS

1

BY HISTORIANS his administration was to be cited mainly for the Southern policy, whatever opinion was held as to the results. However, his administration did produce some additional landmarks.

In his various messages to Congress he made recommendations which entitled him to credit for helping to form important national policy in various other fields, though few were carried out while he was in office. He urged the building of a big navy. He called for subsidies for merchant ships. In general he supported a program that eventually established the United States for the first time as a real factor in world trade, a world power in the modern sense, especially in the Pacific and in Latin American areas.[1]

At a crucial time, when French interests marshaled by the French promoter-engineer, Ferdinand DeLesseps, were moving to take over, it was Hayes who helped shape the final American course on the Panama Canal. In a message to Congress in March 1880 he said: "The policy of this country is a canal under American control."

This view should prevail, he made plain, even if a private company backed largely by non-American capital were to construct the canal.

The United States cannot consent to the surrender of this control to any European power or any combination of European powers. The capital invested by corporations or citizens of other countries in such an enterprise must in a great degree look for protection to one or more of the great powers of the world. No European power can intervene for such protection without adopting measures on this continent which the United States would deem wholly inadmissible.[2]

He recommended legislation for protecting forests against depredation and for controlling the use of other public lands, thus enunciating views, especially those championed by Secretary Schurz, which eventually led to the federal conservation program.[3]

Again backing Schurz, he recommended legislation for a more enlightened policy toward Indians, frankly admitting that in many cases

442

the blame for Indian uprisings rested on the government, which had broken its treaty obligations. While he authorized vigorous action by the army to suppress such uprisings, and though he sympathized with the western advance—which meant that the Indians were pressed by the white population into smaller and smaller territory—he extended a hand of paternal friendship to the Indians, calling for a program by which they were to be encouraged to own land as individuals, and to have their children educated, with government help, for agricultural and other pursuits. Thus would they become merged into "the great body of American citizenship." [4] Seventy-five years later this was still the professed government policy on American Indians.

2

He faced an explosive Mexican problem. This involved raids into Texas by Mexicans and also by Indians who had previously lived in the United States. Under Grant repeated demands had been made on the various Mexican governments that they halt the raids, but to little avail. Porfirio Diaz was dictator of Mexico when the problem fell to Hayes, but, "strong man" though he was, Diaz too failed to suppress the border depredations.

As early as 1870 the Grant administration had threatened to send United States soldiers in pursuit of the raiders into Mexico, but this aggressive policy was not carried out.[5] Grant went only so far as to delay recognition of the Diaz government.

Hayes adopted a stiffer stand than Grant. He respected the Mexican territorial integrity, he said. But in June 1877 he issued orders that United States troops stationed on the border "put an end to the invasion of our territory by lawless bands . . . even if the effectual punishment of the outlaws should make the crossing of the border by our troops . . . necessary." [6]

At the same time he announced a new doctrine on recognition of governments established by revolution: They not only had to show that they had popular approval— the *de facto* principle—but they also had to be able to fulfill their international obligations. He applied this doctrine against the Diaz regime.

The "hot-pursuit" order was indignantly protested by Mexican leaders. Diaz' minister of foreign relations said it disregarded "the rules of international law and the practices of civilized nations . . . treated the Mexicans as savages." Diaz' minister of war sent troops to the

border with orders to "repel any invasions of Mexican territory." [7]
However, when the Mexican commander and the United States commander met at the border, the result was not a clash, despite much talk of war, but an agreement for joint action against marauders.

3

Hayes's strong Mexican policy was denounced almost as hotly in the United States as in Mexico. He found himself accused of seeking to provoke a war with Mexico without consent of Congress, and of planning to have the United States acquire more territory from Mexico. Usually Hayes did not answer criticism directly, but he promptly denied these charges through the press. It all sounded like 1846-47 over again, this time with himself the butt of the same type of accusations he, the young Whig, had made against President Polk.

Blaine took the lead in attacking him. At a July Fourth celebration in Connecticut Blaine devoted much of a widely heralded speech to viewing the Mexican policy with alarm. He implied, too, that the Mexican order was really connected with Hayes's Southern policy, that Hayes was in a "conspiracy" with Southern Democrats to enhance their power by adding to the territory of the South, at Mexico's expense—the same charge that young Rutherford B. Hayes had made against Polk during the Mexican War in 1847. [8]

Blaine had the support of important United States business interests, to whom the Diaz regime had granted commercial concessions in Mexico. In view of this Hayes did yield to pressure for a softer policy by extending recognition to the Diaz government, on getting assurances that it would act energetically against bandits. But he continued the "hot-pursuit" order for almost three years, withdrawing it only when he was able to report that the border raids had "almost wholly ceased."

He counted the vigorous Mexican policy one of the "successes" of his administration. [9] It was not a characteristic success. Temperamentally he was inclined to favor more moderate approaches. He clearly preferred that his administration be marked by quiet times. The Southern crisis was enough. He had not wanted a Mexican crisis, or any other. However, he was not able to escape other crises, especially some resulting from the continuing depression.

4

In July 1877 there occurred the first labor crisis of a national character in the nation's history. For some time railroad workers in particular had been protesting against gradual reductions in pay, reductions which brought the wages of many of them below $1.50 a day. Then came a decision by a number of the railroads for a horizontal cut of ten per cent.

Grievance committees representing employees who belonged to the Brotherhood of Locomotive Engineers filed protests. The result was that members of the committees were discharged. Baltimore and Ohio Railroad men at Martinsburg, West Virginia, struck and began stopping trains. The management attempted to operate with nonstrikers. The strikers interfered. Rioting followed, and the West Virginia state militia was called out to maintain order and protect railroad property. The strikers resisted orders of the militia.

Soon the strike had spread to near-by Maryland, with similar disorder and similar defiance of state militia. In Baltimore alone, in connection with subsequent clashes, nine strikers and bystanders were killed.

This touched off what amounted to an angry general railroad strike, though not called by any union and without any preconceived plan, with nearly all the major railroads in the East, Middle West and even on the California coast involved. Soon the governors of half a dozen states had called out the militia. But in many instances the railroad workers, joined in various communities by men of other trades, especially those among the unemployed, refused orders to disperse. So there was fighting.

Pittsburgh was the scene of a pitched battle. There was much destruction of railroad property and numerous casualties as a result. In Chicago, where the police broke up a gathering of strikers, nineteen men were killed. Sympathy strikes occurred. In Columbus workers invaded factories to force shutdowns. Alarmists began talking and writing as if America were on the verge of "revolution"—as in the time of Shays' Rebellion.

Up to then federal troops had never been used in America in connection with labor disturbances involving privately owned industry, although in 1834 President Jackson had used troops to break a strike by canal workers near Williamsport, Maryland.[10] Up to then there had never been a national labor crisis. But the railroad strikes of 1877 seemed national, with the various governors apparently unable or unwilling to cope with the occurrences in their jurisdiction. The governors of four states—West Virginia, Maryland, Pennsylvania and Illinois—appealed to Hayes to send federal troops. Thus the crisis was shifted by the states to the federal government.

5

It was then, if ever, that the nation—and Hayes—faced a basic break with past doctrines. He decided the problem on the basis of what he had come to believe had happened to America since the war. America had become a nation in fact. He complied with the request of the governors in each case, used federal troops to protect private property and to maintain order in a struggle between labor and management, and thus set a precedent.

By sympathizers with labor it was said that he used federal soldiers to break the railroad strikes of 1877 eagerly and callously, which was not true. He did act promptly, on the assurance of the governors that they were unable to suppress the "domestic violence." Governor Hartranft of Pennsylvania went so far as to tell him by telegraph, "The whole country will soon be in anarchy and revolution unless you can save it by prompt action." [11] This was doubtful, but who could be sure?

Hayes raised the matter at a cabinet meeting. It was decided that it was his Constitutional duty to act on the governors' requests. He raised the point then that if railroad workers were to be subjected to governmental force, perhaps the railroads should be subjected to governmental supervision in their labor policies.[12] He carefully ordered that the federal troops were not to resort to gunfire unless forced to do so. These orders were observed. But the mere presence of the army, of course, was enough to cause the strikers and their allies to give up any further resistance.

He felt none of the bitterness toward strikers that marked many who praised his action. He did not consider the explosion a forerunner of revolution. On August 5, 1877, he wrote in his diary: "The strikes have been put down by *force*; but now for the *real* remedy. Can't something [be] done by education of the strikers, by judicious control of the capitalists, by wise general policy to end or diminish the evil? The railroad strikers, as a rule, are good men, sober, intelligent, and industrious."

He did not make any public recommendations along the lines of his comments in his diary. Later—when he was long out of the Presidency—he concluded that the real remedy lay in a fairer distribution between owners and employees of the profits of industry, which is all that the strikers had wanted.[13] But his thinking showed the course that American thought was taking toward wider federal government intervention in the affairs of the citizenry. Nor did State-rights Democrats raise objections at the time to the new use of federal power. Two of the governors concerned, in fact, were Southerners.

6

Out in the Far West this unrest over unemployment and low wages was characterized by violent anti-Chinese agitation. Even before the depression there had been a widespread demand for restricting Chinese immigration, or cutting it off altogether.[14] The depression made the issue acute, Caucasian workers becoming so resentful over the idea that the Orientals were taking their jobs and forcing down wage standards by working for "coolie wages" that they engaged in mob actions which resulted in the murder of many Chinese.

The problem became the liveliest of political issues in California, as well as in Nevada and other Western states. Sand-lot orators, notably Denis Kearney of San Francisco, used it to stir discontented labor into the formation of a formidable workingmen's party, described by conservatives as revolutionary because its leaders attacked capitalists in general and in particular the railroad and mine magnates who had been the largest employers of Chinese.

In February 1879 this explosive problem also became one for Hayes. For Congress passed a bill which, in effect, was a unilateral denunciation of a treaty that covered immigration as well as commercial relations with the Chinese rulers. The bill specifically was tantamount to ending the flow of Chinese into the United States, though the Burlingame Treaty, which the United States had initiated, provided that Chinese were to be treated on the same basis as subjects of "most favored nations." It also called for abrogation of two articles of the treaty, one that recognized "the inherent and inalienable right of man to change his home and allegiance," and another that provided that Chinese subjects in the United States, like United States citizens in China, shall "enjoy the same privileges, immunities, or exemptions in respect to travel or residence as may be . . . enjoyed by citizens or subjects of the most favored nation."

Hayes favored restricting Chinese immigration. Before the bill reached him, he wrote in his diary: "I am satisfied the present Chinese labor invasion (it is not in any proper sense immigration—women and children do not come) is pernicious and should be discouraged. Our experience in dealing with weaker races—the Negroes and Indians, for example—is not encouraging." But, he added, "I suspect that this bill is inconsistent with our treaty obligations. . . . If it violates the National faith, I must decline to approve it." [15]

He decided that the bill did violate the national faith. He said, "We should deal with China in this matter precisely as we expect and wish other nations to deal with us." He noted that abrogation of parts of the treaty could be interpreted in China as abrogation of the whole treaty, thus "our citizens, who as missionaries and in commercial pursuits are domiciled in China, would be left without treaty protection." [16] He vetoed the bill on those lines.

7

Praise and abuse for this veto were both extravagant, mainly because the issue had become so mixed with politics and also with emotional attitudes about capital and labor. Henry Ward Beecher, as vigorous in the 1870s in attacking labor unions as in the 1860s he had been in promoting antislavery agitation, applauded the veto as a blow against socialism and class legislation destructive of the capitalist system. In urging the veto, Beecher wrote to Hayes: "You are aware of the progress of socialism among our laboring population, especially our foreign people. You have seen already the threatening complications arising out of labor questions. This California craze is another carbuncle." Beecher, of course, was much over-heated.

Later Beecher told Hayes, "We need *Cheap* labor in New States, just as we need *Machines*." A plentiful supply of "cheap labor," i.e., the Chinese, not only would encourage capitalists to take risks, but would be a good antidote for labor unrest, he said. [17]

Hayes did not accept Beecher's odd thesis. He was pictured by extremists of the other side as an oppressor of labor because he did veto the Chinese exclusion bill. He was burned in effigy in one Far Western community. But he could not go along with Beecher, and those for whom Beecher was eloquent spokesman. He had other reasons. He wrote in his diary: "No doubt a population without women—without wives and mothers—that can't assimilate with us, that underbids our laborers, must be hateful. It should be made certain by proper methods that such an invasion cannot permanently override our people. It cannot safely be admitted into the bosom of our American society." [18]

So he followed up his veto by the use of "proper methods." He caused the State Department to begin negotiations immediately with the Chinese government for treaty revision by normal procedure.[19] In 1880, owing mainly to James B. Angell, president of the University of Michigan, who was persuaded to become minister to China to work out a solution, a new treaty with China was signed.[20]

Ratified in 1881, this provided that the United States might "regulate, limit, or suspend, but not absolutely prohibit" the immigration of Chinese into its territory. An exclusion act in accord with the new treaty went into effect in 1882, after Hayes had retired from office. The problem was—and remained—a perplexing one, involving a complex of considerations that ruled out a solution that could satisfy all viewpoints.

In his handling of it, avoiding taking any extremist position, using abstract principles to guide him on a practical course, which usually reflected the middle-ground view of the practical, nondoctrinaire America of his period, Hayes, of course, was again being true to his nature. And being so, he reflected also what probably was the true American view.

CHAPTER LXVII

Un-Whiggish Old Whig

1

By the Chinese exclusion veto, as well as other vetoes, together with policies already mentioned and actions ahead, he showed also how far he had strayed from the basic Whig notions about the Presidential office.

Indeed, without fully realizing it, he who had been so loyal and fervent a Whig proved as zealous for the Presidential power, and as generous in its use, as almost any Jacksonian Democrat could have wished. Moreover, just before the labor crisis he himself produced a crisis in his relations with his party, and with Congress, that in its fullest meaning projected him into the position of shedding Whig Presidential doctrine altogether. He stood at last as a frank champion of executive authority.

This crisis developed from an order in line with his Letter of Acceptance and inaugural promises on civil-service reform. It was sweeping, perhaps naïvely so, calling for the divorcing of officeholding in the federal government from politics. Not only were officers not to be required to perform partisan political services, they were expressly *forbidden* to do so—in effect, the substance of the Hatch Act of a later period.

Also, the practice of assessing officers and employees for contributions to party treasuries was forbidden—this in line with a pledge he had made to Schurz during his election campaign: "I need hardly assure you that if ever I have charge of an Administration this whole assessment business will go up, 'hook, line, and sinker.' " [1]

2

The order followed an investigation by a committee appointed by Secretary Sherman of the largest patronage office in the federal service, the New York Customhouse. This customhouse had long been cited as one example of the spoils system at its worst. Through it flowed two thirds of all imports into the country, the revenues collected forming a major source of the total income of the federal government. [2] Headed by John Jay, grandson of the first Chief Justice, the com-

450

mittee had presented to Sherman a report confirming what everyone knew: The more than 1,000 employees of the office had been appointed mainly for political reasons, specifically in the interest of the dominant faction—headed by Senator Conkling—of the New York Republican Party. Twenty per cent of the employees were superfluous. Businesslike methods were absent, opening the way to bribe taking and other forms of corruption. Undoubtedly, too, New York merchants were granted favors denied merchants from other cities, notably Chicago.

After reading this report in May 1877, Hayes sent to Sherman a letter in which he was even more specific than the Jay committee in stating how the reform of the office should be attained.

It is my wish that the collection of the revenues should be free from partisan control. . . . Party leaders should have no more influence in appointments than other equally respectable citizens. No assessments for political purposes, on officers or subordinates, should be allowed. No useless officer or employe should be retained. *No officer should be required, or permitted, to take part in the management of political organizations, caucuses, conventions, or election campaigns.* Their right to vote, and to express their views on public questions, either orally or through the press, is not denied, provided it does not interfere with the discharge of their official duties.[3]

A month later, on June 22, he followed this with Executive Order No. 1. In it he quoted from his letter and advised *all* department heads that it constituted a "rule, applicable to every department of the civil service."

3

He hoped to avoid open warfare between himself and party leaders on the issue he had now raised. He hoped that men who held both a federal job and a party post would voluntarily resign from one or the other. In many cases this happened. But in other cases the officeholders had to be prodded by the threat of removal. In many other cases his rule was defied, and he was subjected to much newspaper criticism because he did not summarily remove from office all who failed to resign from one of their two positions.

He finally decided that the reasonable course was to take the criticism and follow the policy of letting violators remain in office, especially in the cases of "small fellows," until their terms expired, then refusing to reappoint them.[4]

He followed this line even with the postmaster at Camden, New Jersey, who was so abusive of him in public that it appeared a matter of honor that he should be discharged. Hayes planned to discharge him. But he learned that

. . . the man had been a good soldier, was poor, and greatly needed the place. He therefore sent for him, told him what he had heard, and pointed out to him the impropriety and indecency of his course. The man confessed that it was true, said he was intoxicated . . . greatly regretted it, etc. [Hayes] gave him some good advice, told him to go back to his office and that he would be allowed to hold it to the end of his term, for all of which the poor fellow was grateful.[5]

4

At first, he was inclined to be lenient even with the heads of the New York Customhouse and to permit the incumbents themselves to reform the office. To reform leaders this was backing away from a fight. Then Hayes found himself attacked not only by the organization politicians but also by the independents. He saw that he had to make a choice between his desire to be conciliatory and fair, as he viewed it, and his desire to strike an unmistakable blow for reform. Prodded by additional reports from the Jay committee, which cited specific instances of irregularities in the operation of the customhouse, he decided for the latter course.

This meant replacing two of Conkling's principal political lieutenants, Chester A. Arthur, the collector, and Alonzo B. Cornell, the naval officer, as well as George H. Sharpe, the surveyor. Sharpe's term was about to expire anyway, and he voluntarily agreed to withdraw an application for reappointment. So the issue turned on Arthur and Cornell.

Though his mind was made up to replace Arthur and Cornell, Hayes still wished no explosive incident. The two men were quietly urged to resign voluntarily, both being told that other positions would be offered them. "The President was quite willing to base his request for their resignation, not upon the ground that they were guilty of the offenses charged, but that new officers could probably deal with the reorganization of the custom-house with more freedom and success than the incumbents," Sherman recalled.[6]

5

But both men declined. Arthur was incensed because he *had* acted to introduce reforms. So the stage was set for the explosion that Hayes did not want. Moreover, Cornell was chairman of the Republican State Committee and had publicly announced that he had no intention of conforming to the Hayes Executive Order No. 1, which he held to be a restriction on his "personal and political rights."

Two weeks after the resignations were asked, Cornell called to order a convention of the New York Republicans which Conkling converted into an anti-Hayes demonstration. "Boss" Platt denounced Hayes's supporters in the convention, led by Curtis, the *Harper's Weekly* editor, as "political pecksniffs and tricksters" bent on getting offices for themselves and wrecking the party.[7]

Conkling referred to Curtis as a "man milliner." He paid his respects to Hayes's general program: "When Dr. Johnson defined patriotism as the last refuge of a scoundrel, he was unconscious of the then undeveloped capabilities and uses of the word 'Reform'." Parties "are not built up by deportment, or by ladies' magazines, or gush," he said.[8] Then, too, the convention refused by a large majority to adopt a resolution presented by Curtis saying that "the lawful title of Rutherford B. Hayes to the Presidency is as clear and perfect as that of George Washington." [9]

Of course, rejection of this was intended as an act of supreme contempt for Hayes. It was also understood by everyone that the convention was Conkling's challenge for a test of strength between himself and Hayes—and also of a test of Hayes's basic civil-service policy that appointments to office should be removed from the control of Senators and Representatives. For confirmation by the Senate was needed to install permanent successors to Arthur, Cornell and Sharpe. On that issue Conkling courted a battle. It was a battle that involved not only reform but the old struggle between President and Congress.

6

Amended provisions of the Tenure of Office Act that had been enacted against President Johnson permitted a President to make removals of officers whose appointments required confirmation by the Senate, if Congress was not in session. If Congress was in session, the removals could not be made without Senate approval. Congress was not in session at the time of the New York convention. It was not to meet for almost a month.

Had Hayes wished to retaliate in kind, he could have ousted Cornell and Arthur at once and replaced them immediately with others. Curtis and other reform leaders hoped that he would do that, thus promptly disposing of Arthur and Cornell. Again Hayes chose a lenient course. He delayed acting until after Congress had convened on October 15.

On October 19, however, he sent to the Senate the nominations of new customhouse appointees—Theodore Roosevelt, Sr., to replace Arthur; L. Bradford Prince to replace Cornell; and General E. A. Merritt to replace Sharpe. These nominations were deemed excellent from every point of view—except that of Conkling and his machine followers. Both Roosevelt and Prince were highly esteemed wealthy businessmen. Merritt formerly was the surveyor, but had been removed for purely political reasons back in 1870 by President Grant, with Conkling approving his removal.[10] So he could be counted on to favor nonpolitical administration, as could Roosevelt especially.

The appointment of Roosevelt (whose son, then a student at Harvard, was to become a civil-service enthusiast) showed also that Hayes, though he had not answered the Conkling attacks, could hit back vigorously. For Conkling considered Roosevelt a bitter enemy. At the 1876 Republican convention he headed a delegation of citizens in support of Bristow, with the special purpose of preventing the nomination of Conkling.[11] Indeed, the Roosevelt appointment was a declaration of war on Conkling.

7

Conkling did not have a hard time to line up formidable Senate opposition to the confirmations. His Republican colleagues were virtually unanimous in opposing the Hayes policy of ignoring their "right" to control patronage. There was resentment also that Democrats in Southern states were being appointed to offices. That they should be slighted, while Democrats obtained jobs from a Republican administration, was to many of the Republican Senators an unbearable inconsistency on Hayes's part.

They found fault, too, with Hayes's manner of dealing with Senators. Some complained that if they called on him to protest an appointment on which they had not been consulted, his response was to take from a desk drawer a copy of the Republican platform of 1876 and ask them to read its pledges on civil-service reform. "He thinks he is George Washington!" Senator Henry M. Teller of Colorado exclaimed derisively when Hayes reminded him that, on appointments, he was serious about going back to the standards of "the Founding Fathers."

The Republican Senatorial caucus sent a committee, headed by Senator Edmunds, the majority leader, to advise Hayes, in effect, to mend his ways or forfeit the co-operation of the Republicans in the Senate. He answered that he wished to co-operate, but it was his duty to abide by his pledges for reform. "We must all co-operate in the interest of the country," he said. "We must not forget that I am President of the whole country, not of any party."

Edmunds reported back to his colleagues that Hayes's views were "more suggestive of a political dreamer than of the sober sense of a statesman." On the question of "senatorial courtesy" on appointments, Edmunds said, Hayes's attitude was one of "substantial defiance." [12]

It was no wonder then that the New York appointments were smothered in committee for the duration of the special session, a defeat for Hayes. For Edmunds, who later came around to Hayes's views, was one of the most respected of Republican Senators.

When Congress met in regular session in the following December, Hayes resubmitted the nominations. An open floor fight was now staged. "The Senatorial usurpation is now the question," Hayes wrote to William Henry Smith, then the new collector of customs at Chicago. "The immediate result is in doubt." [13] Actually there was no doubt that Conkling would win another victory. When Hayes compiled a list of "sincere friends of the reform," he was able to list only four Senators, two Democrats and two Republicans, one of whom was Matthews. [14]

On a showdown vote General Merritt was confirmed, but Roosevelt and Prince were rejected, thirty-one to twenty-five. Of the twenty-five who voted to sustain the nominations, only six were Republicans, the others were Southern Democrats. "In the language of the press, 'Senator Conkling has won a great victory over the Administration.' . . . But the end is not yet. I am right, and shall not give up the contest," Hayes said in his diary. [15]

He did not give up. After Congress adjourned in June 1878 he dropped his attitude of leniency toward Arthur and Cornell, and removed them summarily from their offices. This was open defiance of Congress, non-Whiggery with a vengeance. So the issue was joined between Hayes and Conkling personally, but also between the Chief Executive and Congress.

8

In its personal aspects this collision was softened somewhat by the fact that Roosevelt had died a few months before. This opened the way for some interim appointments less obnoxious to the Conkling machine. General Merritt was promoted from surveyor to collector. The businessman Prince was dropped, and Cornell's deputy, S. W. Burt, who actually had performed the duties of naval officer, was named to Cornell's post. That he did not choose as successors pronounced enemies of Conkling was Hayes's way of meeting the charge that he was motivated by personal animus. But he did not avoid a bitter reaction even so. "Persecution!", "Treachery!", "Defiance of the Senate!" were some of the outbursts against him as the stage was set for another bitter fight on confirmation at the next session of Congress.

A majority of the Republicans once again voted against confirmation. "Senatorial courtesy, the Senatorial prerogative, and the fear of Conkling's vengeance . . . control them," Hayes commented.[16] However, this time instead of merely six, Hayes won thirteen Republicans to his banner. With Democratic aid Merritt was confirmed by a vote of thirty-three to twenty-five, and Burt, thirty-one to nineteen.[17] So at the last Hayes had won a victory over Conkling for reform, and for the right of a President to make appointments without unconstitutional interference from legislators—though it took Democratic Senators to win the victory.

There were some ironic sequels. In the following fall Cornell was nominated as the Republican candidate for governor and was elected, with Secretary Sherman campaigning for him and Hayes announcing that he, too, was for him as a matter of party loyalty.[18] In 1880 the ousted Arthur was nominated by the party for Vice-President. More ironically, in 1881 Arthur became President. And it would be Arthur, as President, who would advocate and put through legislation for civil-service reform that Hayes had recommended but could not get passed by the Congress.

But Hayes conducted no crusade. It was not his objective to overthrow the party organizations. He merely wanted them to conform to principles which, he felt, would strengthen them.

He would have obtained a better press then and later had he followed up the New York Customhouse victory by ordering wholesale discharges there of job holders because they owed allegiance to the machine. But he preferred the quieter way of not making removals except on the basis of regulations applied as fairly to followers of Conkling as to others. In the same quiet way he did not press hard for legislation to reform the civil service. Thus he failed to win reform support, except temporarily, while he incurred the enmity of spoils politicians who followed Conkling.

To General Merritt, the new collector, he said: "Let no man be put out merely because he is a friend of the late collector, and no man be put in merely because he is our friend." He also said: "Neither my recommendation nor that of the Secretary of the Treasury, nor the recommendation of any member of Congress, or other influential person, should be specially regarded. Let appointments and removals be made on business principles and fixed rules." [19]

9

During the Grant administration an effort had been begun to have some federal employees, in subordinate positions such as clerks, hired on the basis of examinations. This was under a law enacted in 1871, which authorized the President to adopt voluntarily regulations governing federal employment and to establish a civil-service commission to secure their enforcement. Rules were adopted. But Congress failed to provide the means for enforcing the system. It failed also to appropriate for expenses of the civil-service commission. Moreover, no provision was made by Congress to protect employees in the tenure of their positions. So what there was of a merit system was mild.

By the time Hayes took office even the mild, voluntary system was all but nonexistent. Hayes did approve a return to the voluntary system of examinations in some offices, especially in the Department of Interior under Schurz and in the New York Post Office. After the victory over Conkling the examination system was also applied to the New York Customhouse. Thereafter, employees were hired and promoted on substantially a competitive basis. Later the examination system was followed in post offices of various other large cities and also in other customhouses. [20]

All this was a start toward reform, but it was not the "thorough, radical and complete" reformation promised in the Letter of Acceptance. Hayes admitted this.[21] He also admitted that he had made some "bad" appointments of his own, for example, the reappointment of a notorious spoilsman as postmaster at St. Louis, who, as Curtis complained, was "the shining example of 'the thing to be reformed.' "[22]

There were other lapses. He had announced that applications for jobs made to him personally, or to members of the family, would receive no attention, that the requests must be sent to department heads.[23] This rule was violated, the pressure coming most frequently from ex-soldiers, some in his old regiment, which Hayes could not resist for sentimental reasons. Many such applicants were "taken care of."

Garfield complained: "If nobody is to be appointed because he is your friend or my friend, then nobody should be appointed because he is any other man's friend. The President himself should exercise the same self denial as other officials. . . ."[24]

In *The Nation* Godkin wrote: "He has shown no more hesitation than Conkling or Blaine would have done in providing for nearly everyone, good, bad and indifferent, by means of office."[25]

There was exaggeration in Godkin's remarks and pique in Garfield's complaint. Nor did they give Hayes credit for adhering strictly to one rule, that there be no nepotism, a practice by Grant that had aroused so much resentment. Lucy's brother, Dr. Joe Webb, wanted to be minister to Germany. He rounded up many influential endorsers, besides Lucy. But Hayes refused, appointing first Bayard Taylor, the writer, to the post, then on Taylor's death, President Andrew White of Cornell University. A grandson of Hayes's uncle, Austin Birchard, wanted a clerkship, even "raised his voice" against Hayes during an interview with him in the White House on getting a no, but Hayes stuck by the refusal, though it pained him.

And it was so with many other cousins. But there was substance to the criticisms, enough to turn a number of civil-service reformers against Hayes. He conceded afterward that he made many mistakes in appointments. Nor were all to be excused because, he said, he was under so much pressure as a result of the Southern problem, the labor troubles, the Mexican border crisis, the Chinese immigration problem and all the other problems that seemed to develop all at once.

He was criticized also, and properly, for not having vigorously pressed on Congress demands for legislation to place his civil-service

reform principles on the statute books. He did ask Congress to appropriate funds for the civil-service commission. He also asked that it
enact into law the substance of Executive Order No. 1—that Congressmen should not dictate appointments—and that it provide for a general
system of examinations as well as protect employees against political
removals. But Congress ignored him, and he seemed content merely
to let the record show that he had made the requests.

So it remained for other administrations to achieve general and lasting civil-service reforms. Yet among Presidents he was nonetheless
a pioneer in the cause, even if, like pioneers in many fields, he merely
started what others would finish.

George William Curtis, often his severest critic, felt that one service
alone entitled Hayes to recognition as having "done more for a reform of the civil service upon sound principles than any other President in history up to then. That service," Curtis wrote toward the
end of Hayes's term, "consists in introducing in the two chief offices
of their kind in the country, a system of appointment of proved merit
and without personal favor or influence, and in sustaining the system
for nearly two years against the most contemptuous and rancorous
and insidious hostility." Hayes had shown, continued the crusad-
ing *Harper's Weekly* editor, that civil-service reform was "perfectly
practicable." [26] But to do so he practically had to abandon whiggery altogether.

10

He was even more pronouncedly un-Whiggish when "sound-
money" issues came up. Congress was unquestionably in favor of a
"cheap-money" program as a cure for the depression. It even threatened to reopen the question of resumption of specie payments, a matter supposedly settled. Only Presidential intervention could have
saved even that much of a sound-money program, and intervention
on such a matter meant again abandoning the Whig doctrine that
Congress alone should decide such issues.

Under a law adopted in 1874 resumption was to begin January 1,
1879. After that date the Treasury was committed to redeeming with
gold, on demand, the greenbacks issued to finance the war, and also to
pay off in gold most bonds issued during the war by the government.
Inasmuch as the war greenbacks had been worth, at some periods,
even less than twenty-five cents on the dollar and the $100 bonds had

sold for less than $35, resumption meant paying them off not only at full value but at more than full value. But Hayes and his party were, of course, committed to resumption.

In November 1877 the House of Representatives in special session reflected popular feeling by passing two cheap-money bills with Republicans acting with the Democrats. One of these bills, in effect, would have impeded the pledged resumption of specie payments and perhaps upset the resumption program altogether. The other called for free coinage of silver. Both measures were pending, awaiting action by the Senate, when the special session was merged into the regular session of the Forty-fifth Congress in December. In his message to the Congress Hayes firmly opposed both.

In later years, when he noted the opposition of financial interests to pensions for war veterans on the grounds of economy, he was not so sure about the general justice of the resumption program as an abstract matter. Thus in 1889, as a private citizen, in reply to a minister in Evanston, Illinois, who criticized him for making that point, he wrote:

The rich, the well-to-do, and those who depend mainly on them, are strangely blind as a class, to what is due—in short, to justice to the Union soldier. Bonds for money lent the Government in paper, worth thirty-five to sixty-five cents on the dollar, are paid in gold at their face, with gold interest at highly remunerative rates. *That* national obligation, I, with you and the rich people, insisted upon, because it was just. But the men paid twenty to thirty cents a day for life and uncounted sacrifices are said to make a "raid on the Treasury" if they ask that promises be kept.[27]

But as President, elected on a sound-money platform, he made it plain that he intended to carry out the resumption law and he called on Congress to adopt no legislation that would hamper him.[28]

11

The legislation that would have impeded resumption was finally stopped in the Senate. But it took some extraordinary exercise of Presidential power and maneuvering to do it. Hayes later said that he was not able to be so aggressive in pushing his civil-service program as he wished because concessions had to be made by him there in order to win the battle for resumption. He recalled:

It is simply true that a two-thirds vote in both houses of Congress were ready and anxious to repeal the Resumption Act and to launch the country on the dangerous sea of unlimited and irredeemable paper currency. This could not be prevented merely by a veto. The veto would have been pushed aside by Congress. The only salvation was in Congress and in the committees on finance. Action must be prevented. *It was prevented,* and by the influence of the Administration with unfriendly Senators and Representatives. . . . There was nothing questionable done. The *truth* brought home to a few minds did it.[29]

The "truth," of course, was buttressed by such appointments as the St. Louis postmaster, which subjected Hayes to such bitter criticism from editors Curtis and Godkin.

Resumption was carried out. There were outstanding $382,000,000 in United States notes and the Treasury had on hand only $140,-000,000 worth of gold coins for redeeming them on January 2, 1879.[30] Fear had been widely expressed that there would be such a great demand for gold, a veritable run, that the gold fund could not meet it, meaning ruin to the government credit.

This was a tense time for Hayes—an acid test for his money policy. But after the first day of resumption had passed, he received cheerful news. At the New York bank designated to redeem the notes only $135,000 worth were presented. Indeed, some $400,000,000 worth of gold actually had been *brought in* to be exchanged for notes. As Sherman had predicted, when the government announced it would pay out coin, "nobody wanted it."[31] In his diary Hayes commented at the time, "A great event, if it sticks, as I believe it will." It did.

12

The silver issue did not have a similarly happy ending for Hayes. True, "Silver Dick" Bland's bill was finally much watered down, emerging as the milder Bland-Allison bill. The unlimited and free coinage provisions were removed. Instead, the revised bill placed rigid limits on the amount of silver to be coined—not less than $2,000,000 per month, nor more than $4,000,000. The seigniorage was to go not to the silver owners but to the government.

Even so, there was tremendous sentiment behind the bill, not only among Greenbackers and Democrats but also among Republicans who, by conviction or for political reasons, favored it as a step toward relief for debtors. Needless to say, Senators and Representatives from the silver-mining states—more than one of whom owned mines or stock in mines—were enthusiastic. The key aspect of the bill was that it provided that silver, when exchanged for certificates, could be used to pay private and public debts, including duties and taxes.

The bill passed both houses by large majorities. Of the Ohio delegation of Republicans in the House Garfield was almost alone in voting against the measure. Even Matthews deserted Hayes on the issue, went so far "wrong," from Hayes's view, as to sponsor a Senate resolution to permit paying off government bonds in silver.[32] McKinley, destined to be elected President eighteen years later over the free-silver advocate, William Jennings Bryan, also deserted in the House.[33]

His own party leaders brought tremendous pressure on Hayes not to veto the Bland-Allison bill. Even Sherman felt that Hayes should not stand against it. A veto, Sherman felt, might so inflame Congress as to cause it to adopt legislation that would impede resumption. Besides, Sherman had his eye on the next Presidential election, envisioning himself as a candidate.

So stanch and conservative a Republican spokesman as Joseph Medill opposed a veto. Like his Chicago *Tribune,* he was for silver anyway, a heresy which would seem odd, some years later, for the *Tribune* and Medill, in view of their stand in the time of Bryan and John Peter Altgeld. But to Hayes, Medill put his argument against Presidential intervention on grounds similar to Sherman's. If Hayes did veto the silver legislation, wrote Medill, and the veto were sustained, "the country will be convulsed with excitement and indignation, and wild, desperate men will get control of popular feeling and make mischief. Ultra measures will be forced through Congress, and repeal of the Resumption Act will be attached to vital appropriation bills. Vast and incalculable injuries may result from thwarting the popular will. . . ."

Besides, Medill did not think it "immoral" to redeem in silver bonds which the "contract" gave the government the option of paying in gold or silver. "The American people are not educated up to any higher standard of morality than to pay their debts according to contract."[34] Even Medill's wife wrote to Lucy, urging that she persuade Hayes to sign the bill.[35]

Halstead also counseled against a veto. It would be, he said, "the greatest possible mistake. On the side of silver are the laws, the morals, and the interests of the nation." Perhaps most surprising of all, Will Platt, whose business acumen or soundness Hayes could not deny, wrote a letter on the side of silver, saying that restoration of silver as legal tender was more important than resumption.[36] Of course, these persons represented then the thinking of the West, the debtor area.

Hayes also was a "western man." But on this question all his New England heritage (except that of the Austins of Shays' Rebellion) came out strong. Despite the assurances of Sherman, even despite the fact that a banker like August Belmont feared that a veto would be more disturbing than otherwise to financial stability,[37] Hayes could not get it out of his head that to approve coining even a relatively few depreciated dollars was wrong.

"I shall veto the bill," he said in his diary, even before it was passed. He wrote that he had given the matter "anxious reflection." He realized "it will probably become a law notwithstanding." But he could not "consent to a measure which stains our national credit," or one that "is a violation of the national faith." [38]

He discussed the matter thoroughly with his cabinet. Secretary McCrary preferred no veto but finally approved "with doubts," though frankly saying that he hoped a veto would be overridden, as otherwise he feared the Democrats, "with their worst elements in advance," would come into power. Sherman, reluctantly, approved a veto. Secretaries Evarts, Key, Devens and Schurz approved "decidedly." [39]

Secretary Thompson, whose biographer refers to him as "the Persistent Whig," not only stood out against a veto but put up an argument that shook Hayes, at least temporarily. Thompson pointed out that he, like Hayes, was "an old Whig." He "believed the old Whig doctrine was sound . . . [that] there be no veto on grounds of expediency or policy. There must be a violation of the Constitution, or haste, or mistake. Here was a measure, long discussed, the people almost unanimously for it, two-thirds of each House for it; the measure a wise one, and demanded very earnestly by the country." [40]

13

In short, was Hayes still a Whig, or not? Hayes did not answer that question directly. Probably he could not. But he answered indirectly when he overruled Thompson's Whig arguments and decided that his duty in the national interest, as he saw it, as well as his campaign pledges, required that he, as President, place his judgment above that of Congress.

Moreover, he saw more clearly than many credited with more political sense that the Republican Party was in need of just such a unifying appeal: an uncompromising stand on "honest money" to hold the allegiance of its principal supporters, no matter how popular the silver issue was then, even among conservatives. So on February 28, 1878, he sent a veto message to the House.

As expected, both houses overrode his veto by more than two-thirds majority, in the House the vote being 196 to 73, in the Senate, 46 to 19. This was a stinging defeat for him personally. But he took immense satisfaction then from showing that he could stand his ground, ground that confirmed his place as one of the true founders of modern Republicanism, which, for a generation and more, was to make sound money a major tenet.

CHAPTER LXVIII

"Revolution"?

1

It would take a long time, however, before he would be remembered by his own party as a President deserving distinction in the party roll of honored founders, this neglect being a carry-over of the attitude of dominant leaders toward him while he was President. "I am not liked as a President, by the politicians in office, in the press, or in Congress," he wrote in his diary on the day his silver veto message was read in the House of Representatives.[1]

Referring to his standing in his own party, no truer statement appears in his diary. Indeed, so hostile were Republican Congressmen, their antagonism for the most part stemming from the fact that they were no longer overlords of federal job holders in their districts, that for six months Garfield postponed the calling of a House Republican caucus, except for electing officers.[2] The Congressmen, he feared, would adopt resolutions of such bitterness that the country would conclude the party was hopelessly split. Hayes, he said, is "almost without a friend."

While most of the abuse of Hayes came from Republicans, the Democrats were not quiescent. In the summer of 1877 the Democratic New York *Sun* began to run a series of articles purporting to reveal new facts to support the claim that Louisiana was assigned to Hayes in the 1876 election through fraud. Presumably with the idea that Hayes would be ousted from office by quo warranto proceedings in the courts, the *Sun* clamored for reopening of the election controversy by Congress. Most of the *Sun* "revelations" in the beginning were a rehash of what already had been investigated by several Congressional committees. But soon it became apparent that the *Sun* possessed some interesting, if true, new material.

This material related especially to two large Louisiana parishes, East and West Feliciana, the votes of which had been discarded by the returning board, along with those of several other parishes, on the testimony of election supervisors that intimidation had occurred. The *Sun*, it came out, had documents purporting to prove that the Feliciana supervisors in fact had reported no intimidation but were "induced" by leading Republicans to testify otherwise.

What made this material sensational at the outset was the claim that a "confession" of fraud had been made in a notarized statement by the supervisors themselves. Their purpose, apparently, was to use this confession later for political blackmail.[3] Moreover, the East Feliciana supervisor, "Scamp" Anderson, had himself, out of pique for not having obtained the kind of appointment he desired from the Hayes administration, supplied the *Sun* with this incriminating material.

Later the story took on a broader aspect. It was claimed that Anderson and D. A. Weber, the other supervisor (who was mysteriously murdered in March 1877), had decided to repudiate their affidavits—or at least threatened to—but were induced not to do so by John Sherman. It was also asserted in this connection that Sherman, after talking with them, had put in writing a promise that the supervisors would be "provided for." Sherman was surprisingly slow to deny these allegations, apparently deciding not to lend dignity to the exposures. Obviously, if the alleged role of Sherman were a fact, the fraud story involved the integrity of the highest-level Republican national leadership—and Hayes's official family.

2

Coincidentally with this sensation, in March 1878 a story of similar nature emanated from Florida. There S. B. McLin, a member of the Florida returning board in 1876, also made a "confession." This was to the effect that he had been "influenced" by "partisan zeal," and also by promises of being "rewarded," to render decisions in favor of the Hayes electors which, he now said, were not justified. He asserted that he was now convinced that certain precincts should not have been thrown out, and that others were improperly counted for Hayes. McLin named former Governor Noyes, appointed by Hayes minister to France, as one who had made promises to him.[4]

McLin had been "rewarded." At least an effort was made to do so. He was appointed Associate Justice of the Supreme Court of New Mexico Territory. But he lost this post when Senator S. B. Conover, who belonged to a different Florida Republican faction, blocked confirmation. McLin did not get another job,[5] and he was obviously angry with Hayes personally. In his confession he spoke of Hayes as guilty of "willful and cowardly desertion of the very men who had contributed so largely to his election," and said: "My contempt for the pitiable littleness of the man is beyond my power of expression."

But despite his transparent pique, the Democrats considered McLin's statement a telling blow against the Republicans and Hayes, especially as it cited confessions of ballot-box stuffing by several Republican precinct inspectors, and included the flat statement: "The conclusion . . . is irresistible that Mr. Tilden was entitled to the electoral vote of Florida, and not Mr. Hayes." [6]

3

Aged Montgomery Blair, who had been Postmaster General in Lincoln's cabinet but since 1872 was a Democrat, in the meantime had been busy as a member of the Maryland legislature in promoting agitation to have Hayes's right to continue in office challenged in the Supreme Court. Blair succeeded in getting the Maryland legislature to instruct the state attorney general of Maryland to file a bill in the Supreme Court, subject to approval by Congress, calling for the court to review the decisions of the electoral commission by which Hayes was declared elected.[7] The Maryland resolution to that end was then presented to the House by a Democrat from that state, whereupon there was a rash of predictions that it was the first step in a plan to oust Hayes from the Presidency.

On the basis of the Maryland resolution, and also of the "confessions" of Anderson and McLin, Representative Clarkson N. Potter, New York Democrat, friend and next-door neighbor of Tilden, presented to the House a resolution calling for a new investigation of the 1876 elections in Louisiana and Florida. The Potter resolution cited in particular the charges against Sherman and Noyes, asserting that their conduct called for investigation—in effect, as Hayes noted, charging them with "crookedness." [8] The resolution was adopted and there came into being the Potter investigation.

Whether or not there was serious intent behind this investigation to pave the way for ousting Hayes by court proceedings or impeachment will never be known. That such was the case, insofar as the responsible Democratic leadership was concerned, seems doubtful, though Senator Hill of Georgia later said that "some portion" of the party did have that in mind.[9]

The more reasonable purpose was merely to make a record for election-campaign purposes. Yet Speaker Randall, in ruling that the Potter resolution could be considered as a "question of privilege," used language with an ominous ring. "A higher privilege than the one here involved and broadly and directly presented as to the rightful occupancy of the Chief Executive chair, and the connection of high government officials with the frauds alleged, the Chair is unable to conceive."

Leading Republicans immediately adopted the view that Speaker Randall's words disclosed an intention to oust Hayes, which, they said, was tantamount to revolution. Senator Hoar of Massachusetts took this so seriously that he spoke of the need for possibly organizing "military companies" to "prepare for trouble." [10]

The Republican Congressional committee issued an address to the country. It said that the Potter investigation was sought in order "to lay the foundation for a *revolutionary* expulsion of the President from his office." Republican newspapers followed this with solemn warnings that the Democrats were "playing into the hands of communists and labor agitators," that "civil war and rebellion" were being courted. Thurlow Weed of New York, a respected elder statesman, was widely quoted as saying, "The people may have to call on U. S. Grant to take over as dictator, if revolution breaks out." [11]

All this caused businessmen all over the country to deluge Democratic Congressmen with demands that they specifically disavow any intention to revive the kind of crisis that the nation faced just after the 1876 election.

Hayes himself unwittingly, perhaps, added to the excitement. On May 30, 1878, two days before the Potter committee was to hold its first hearing, he was at Gettysburg for a Decoration Day observance. Some friends at a reception there brought up the Potter matter. John Herron's brother mentioned to Hayes that there was an "understanding in some circles" that after the Potter committee issued a report, Hayes was to be "put out of the Executive Office."

"Who is to take my place?" Hayes asked.

"Mr. Tilden."

"Mr. Tilden will be arrested and shot. He cannot attempt to take possession of the White House without a fight. That means civil war, and in that event we shall whip them badly." [12]

4

He was only half serious—and apparently did not know that George Alfred Townsend, newspaper writer known as "Gath," was standing behind some palms where he was able to hear these and other remarks. For the Philadelphia *Times*, Townsend wrote what purported to be an interview with Hayes, constructing the story on what he had heard. He quoted Hayes:

Such schemes cannot be carried out without war. I swore to preserve the Constitution of the United States, and will deliver the Executive Office in its integrity to my successor. They can impeach me in the House of Representatives and try me in the Senate. There is no other way in which I will recognize any attempt of Congress to remove me. But I do not believe that the United States Senate has fallen to that point where high-class Democrats like Bayard and Thurman, Gordon and Hill, will agree to make the Senate a vehicle for carrying out the revolutionary edict of a party caucus by a conviction or impeachment. . . . I should defend my office and the independence of the Executive against any intruder.[18]

Immediately other newspapermen wanted to know if "Gath's" "stolen interview," as it was called, was authentic. Rogers was requested to ask Hayes. He came back to the newspapers with the answer that Hayes neither denied nor confirmed it.

Two weeks later, bowing to public opinion against a remote possibility of a new Presidential crisis, the Democratic House found it expedient to declare, by formal resolution, that "no subsequent Congress, and neither house, has jurisdiction" to revise the action of the Forty-fourth Congress in the electoral dispute and that "any attempt by either house to annul or disregard such action or the title to office arising therefrom would be revolutionary and is disapproved by this House." This was a decided victory from Hayes's personal standpoint. It scotched permanently annoying gossip and threats that he might be confronted with an ouster attempt. But the investigation that Potter asked for went on. The results were embarrassing enough.

5

Naturally the Potter committee was heavily weighted with Democrats. Moreover, one of the minority Republicans was even more antagonistic toward Hayes than the Democrats. This was Butler, who had been one of the managers of the impeachment case against Andrew Johnson. Then a Greenbacker and about to change to a Democrat, Butler showed that he relished using all his exceptional talents as a prosecutor to "get" Hayes, who was told later that both Butler and Conkling had secretly engineered the Potter investigation, or at least had egged the Democrats on, promising to provide help from Republican sources for smearing him.

This may have been true. Both resented Hayes's appointment policies. On one occasion, after being turned down on a local postmaster appointment, Butler voiced a protest that could have been interpreted as a threat.[14] Conkling, of course, still fumed over the customhouse controversy.

Butler, despite the backdown by the House Democrats, possibly would have enjoyed seeing Hayes ousted. At one of the hearings, in speaking of the overthrow of Governor Packard in Louisiana, he tossed at Garfield this question: "If a legislative body has the right, after a governor has been duly elected and declared and counted in and inaugurated, to turn him out, do you know any reason why Congress has not an equal right to turn out a President under the same circumstances?"[15]

6

Before the investigation got under way Hayes wrote in his diary that it would "do no more than raise a dust, throw dirt and the like." He was not, however, so unconcerned as that comment indicated. By way of self-assurance he also wrote: "I neither knew nor suspected fraud on our side. The danger was fraud by our adversaries."[16]

However true that may have been at the time, his year as President must have forced him to suspect that there was more than mere partisanship behind allegations of irregularity, if not downright fraud on "our side." The type of appointments urged on him from Louisiana alone, including "Scamp" Anderson, whom Matthews seemed to have recommended for a consulship on a Pacific island, must have caused him to wonder—also to note that most such recommendations were endorsed by Sherman.

It may be, as Sherman said, that loyal Republicans were being "taken care of" only for normal political reasons. It may be that Sherman was getting jobs for numerous Louisiana Republicans merely by way of preparing to win support for his ambition to secure the Republican nomination for President in 1880. Or it may be, as the Democrats alleged, that Sherman had been rewarding rascals for having committed rascality in the 1876 election. Hayes could have been as much in the dark as anyone as to Sherman's real reasons. But he could not have been wholly unaware of the possibilities.

One consolation, however, he did have—that he, personally, was not involved in any of the 1876 skullduggery. The Democrats knew this. Miss Austine Snead, whose newspaper columns signed "Miss Grundy" were then popular, had a talk about this with Congressman Blackburn, who had made the "Black Friday" speech at the close of the electoral-vote count and who was on the Potter committee. If Hayes was found guilty of wrongdoing, she would lose her "faith in human nature," Miss Snead said. "You can keep your faith in human nature," Blackburn responded promptly, but for her ears alone. "We do not expect to connect Hayes with anything wrong. We do expect to show that Republican leaders and managers were guilty, and to collect material to be used against them in the next election." [17]

7

Even so, the Potter hearings were an ordeal for Hayes. For they permitted Democratic newspapers to emphasize over a period of many months that top leaders of the Republican Party—Sherman, Garfield, Matthews, Noyes and others of their stature who had been to Louisiana and Florida to assure a fair count—at the least had not been averse to looking the other way when irregularities were obvious.

Sherman did not come off well at all. When he was shown the text of the letter that Anderson claimed he had written, Sherman, in his first appearance before the committee, only went so far as to say, "I do not believe I ever wrote that letter." [18] Later he disavowed the letter without qualification. But this was after Anderson had exposed himself as an inveterate liar and political blackmailer, as willing to sell out to the Democrats (one of his offers was to Major Burke) as to swear falsely for the Republicans and any faction thereof.

It was also after an obviously neurotic woman, one Agnes Jenks, a close associate of Anderson, testified that she had acted as his messenger to ask Sherman for such a letter but decided not to ask him, thinking a man of his standing should not be so treated. She indicated that she herself had written the supposedly incriminating letter, without Sherman's knowledge.[19] So bizarre as to give the whole matter the aspect of farce, her story did seem to clear Sherman. He insisted that it did.[20] And perhaps it did.

Most citizens probably concluded that it was safer, and saner, to accept Sherman's word against that of Anderson, whom the Democratic majority of the committee, after expecting him to be a star witness, in their report conceded was a liar and an "adventurer and rascal." [21] But Sherman's first, hesitant reaction was odd—and left a lingering bad impression.

This was all the worse for Hayes because Sherman was acknowledged to be his most intimate political adviser. Schurz and the other members of his cabinet would drop in occasionally, for musicales and the like. But it was with Sherman that Hayes every Sunday took a two or three-hour drive about Washington "to talk over affairs and visit the finest drives and scenes."

8

Butler saw to it that the committee gave much attention to the dealings between Hayes's friends and the Southern Democrats, though curiously he did not bring up the Texas and Pacific matter. He apparently hoped to establish facts about a bargain which, in his view, amounted to a confession that Hayes knew he did not carry the disputed states. All the various conferences, especially those at Wormley's Hotel, were given a full airing. "I am after President Hayes," Butler said bluntly while interrogating Major Burke.[22] But Butler could squeeze no more than innuendoes out of the testimony. The testimony on this phase did tend to corroborate the charge that there had been bargaining with Hayes's knowledge, if not participation.

But the Potter committee itself had produced so much evidence as to the bad character of the carpetbaggers in the disputed states that much of the public reaction was contrary to what Butler expected. Even "stalwart" Republicans were forced to conclude that if Hayes abandoned the Southern Republican regimes, it was a good thing that he did, exclusive of the question of Negro rights, if such rascals in those regimes were Republicans.

Probably the worst blow that Hayes personally received from the investigation was the showing that dozens of Louisiana carpetbaggers and scalawags, men with disgraceful records, were given positions in his administration, mainly in the customhouse and other divisions of the Treasury Department under Sherman. Or they were allowed to retain federal jobs that they had garnered under Grant. In short, with respect to appointments he had not carried the policy of abandonment far enough.

The record also showed that Louisiana politicians connected with fraud charges seemed curiously exempt from the standards of the civil-service reform program. This laid Hayes open to the charge that men who were indisputably involved in political practices which he was the foremost in condemning had been rewarded by his administration. How much of this was connected with the election itself, or how much was done to persuade Packard men to accept the settlement which led to the disintegration of the Packard legislature, it would be impossible to say.

That there was much to such charges was undeniable, and these added up to a blot on Hayes's record. But nothing was brought out, not even by the astute Butler, that impeached Hayes's title to the office or on which ouster proceedings could have been securely based, had such been contemplated by any besides embittered Montgomery Blair, crafty Butler, or sulking Roscoe Conkling.

CHAPTER LXIX

BOOMERANG IN CIPHERS

1

FOR ALL the political campaign fodder that it manufactured against Hayes and his party, and despite all the discomfort that it caused him, the Potter investigation turned out in the end a boomerang for the Democrats and especially for Tilden. For Republican strategists succeeded in converting the final phase of the investigation into a devastating exposure of dealings by close associates of Tilden which added up to an intention to "save" Florida and South Carolina for Tilden through outright bribery. This concerned the chapter of the 1876 election usually denominated as "the Cipher Dispatches," probably the most striking example in American history of a pot calling a kettle black.

Back in January 1877, while the electoral-commission bill was debated, William E. Chandler had written to Hayes: "You needn't be alarmed for fear there is anything behind about the conduct of the Florida canvassers or that there are any injurious telegrams or letters. The Democrats will get them all in due time and more than they want!" [1]

This turned out to be an accurate prediction. In particular Chandler referred to a large batch of original telegrams, many of them in cipher, sent by and to Tilden's nephew, Colonel Pelton, already involved in the Oregon imbroglio. These were among thousands sent by both Democrats and Republicans and subpoenaed from the Western Union Telegraph Company by Senate and House committees for the investigations held immediately after the election. All of the telegrams were supposed to have been returned to the telegraph company and destroyed. But some farsighted Senate committee clerk, a Republican, had contrived to hold back the Democratic batch. In due time these were given to Chandler, who picked out several hundred that looked interesting and gave them to Whitelaw Reid of the New York *Tribune*.

2

For the most part these were messages sent in November and December 1876 between Pelton and Manton Marble, who had been an

474

editor of the Democratic New York *World,* and Smith M. Weed, a lawyer associated with the Democratic Party. Marble had been in Florida and Weed in South Carolina, in Tilden's interest, while the returning boards were doing their work.

At first the *Tribune* published a few of the messages in cipher, inviting readers to try their hands at decoding them. Presumably the *Tribune* did not know how to read them. But in October 1878—just in time to influence the Congressional elections—the *Tribune* announced that it had broken the code. It published some 400 of the telegrams with translations. An example was a message sent from Florida to Pelton, at Tilden's residence. Translated, it read:

HAVE JUST RECEIVED A PROPOSITION TO HAND OVER AT ANY HOUR REQUIRED TILDEN DECISION OF BOARD AND CERTIFICATE OF GOVERNOR FOR 200,000 [DOLLARS].

MARBLE

To which Pelton replied: DISPATCH HERE. PROPOSITION TOO HIGH.[2]

Similar telegrams indicated that Pelton was in communication with another agent, an adventurer named Woolley, who had telegraphed that he could deliver the decision for $50,000, and that Pelton agreed to raise this sum but did not act quickly enough.[3] Even more interesting, and apparently more incriminating, were telegrams relating to Weed's activities in South Carolina. These showed that on November 18, 1876, Weed telegraphed to an associate of Pelton's that "the majority of the board" in South Carolina had been "secured" for $80,000, and requested that Pelton go to Baltimore to close the transaction.

Pelton did go to Baltimore to meet Weed there, after asking Edward Cooper, brother-in-law of Hewitt and treasurer of the Democratic National Committee, to provide the money.[4] Cooper declined and advised Tilden, who had a message sent to Pelton, ordering him to return home.

Tilden later testified that he "reprimanded" Pelton and said he would have nothing to do with such negotiations. Yet, as the Republicans would stress, it was after this that Pelton, still from Tilden's home, carried on the Florida negotiations. In neither case was a transaction actually completed. But the inference was clear that Pelton and others close to Tilden or the Democratic National Committee, of which Pelton was secretary, were negotiating, though perhaps with third-party adventurers not actually able to "deliver."

A question that everyone asked was whether or not Tilden knew about the great numbers of these telegrams that came to his home, some addressed there to his private secretary, as well as to his nephew. It was never asserted that Tilden was a party to such negotiations. But it was asked whether he permitted them to go on.

3

Tilden gave an answer in a "card" in the New York *Herald*. He said that he had "no knowledge of the existence of these telegrams, nor any information about them, except what has been derived from or since the publications of the 'Tribune.' " He also wrote:

I will add that no offer to give the certificates of any returning board or State canvassers of any State to the Democratic electors in consideration of any office or money or property; no negotiation of that nature in behalf of any member of such board or with any such member or to influence the action of any elector . . . by such motives,—was ever entertained, considered, or tolerated by me or by anybody within my influence by my consent, or with my knowledge or acquiescence. No such contemplated transaction would at any time have come within the range of my power without that power being instantly exerted to crush it out.[5]

The Republicans, however, kept up the commotion. Tilden's statement was ex parte—and not under oath. Was he really so naïve, he, among the nation's shrewdest corporation lawyers? Whitelaw Reid wrote to Chandler the day Tilden's card appeared: "We can hardly estimate the real force of these cipher revelations. . . . They have certainly ended the fraud cry here [against Hayes], have placed Tilden's whole crowd on the defensive . . . while, no matter whether Tilden's card is believed or not, they have made an effective end of any political future he may have had." [6]

4

On January 21, 1879, the Republicans in the House shamed the Democrats into permitting passage of a resolution directing the Potter committee to include an inquiry into the cipher telegrams and their significance. Then the activity of the Potter committee changed from harassing Hayes to an ordeal for the Democrats.

Pelton admitted frankly on the witness stand that "propositions to

sell the returning boards were made to me and I did assent to them." [7]
But he insisted that his uncle was not a party to his activity. Smith
Weed's defense was to quote what, he testified, he had said to Tilden
a week after South Carolina was declared for Hayes. "I said to him
that I looked upon it as paying money for the recovery of stolen property, or as a ransom to a robber, and that it was justifiable to pay these
thieves, who had us in their power, for doing what every man knew to
be right." [8]

Manton Marble, who, as an editor, had made a point of attacking
Hayes personally and the Republicans generally as lacking in "political morality," tried to squirm out of his predicament by insisting that
his telegrams did not mean he was acting as a medium for bribery.
Rather, they were "danger signals" as to what the Republicans were
up to, he insisted.[9] But he was far from successful in getting his
curious explanation accepted.

Tilden took the stand by his own courageous request. He repeated
substantially what he had written to the *Herald.* "I swear positively
that I never saw any of those telegrams, either in cipher or in translation; the contents of no one of them, nor the purport of any one of
them, was communicated to me in any manner whatever," he said.

No evidence was presented to contradict Tilden. Yet, like Sherman
in the Anderson letter matter, he did not come off well. Known as
a man who kept an especially close watch on all details of his affairs,
Tilden's answers placed him in the light of showing a remarkable
disinterest in the activities of his nephew and the others with whom
he had close relations and who had been helping to try to elect him
President. He testified, for example, that after Pelton came back from
Baltimore on his angry orders, he did not bother to ask Pelton for any
details of the transaction his nephew had planned. "I did not think
it was necessary," he said.[10]

5

Harper's Editor Curtis, though a Republican partisan, expressed
a reaction that was general among Democrats as well as Republicans.

It is evident from all the testimony that when Mr. Tilden learned
of Pelton's visit to Baltimore to conclude the bargain, he called him
back and reproved him. But there is no evidence or pretense that he
took care to deprive such a dangerous fellow of further opportunities
of mischief. In fact, with the exception of a scolding, Pelton occupied
the same position as before, and actually continued the attempt to buy

a vote. . . . His [Tilden's] conduct was that of a man who knew that such things, if brought to his knowledge, "would not do." But there is no sign of that mighty indignation with which his card last October declared that he should "crush out" any intimation of contemplated fraud. . . . It is, of course, impossible to know what Mr. Tilden, as a shrewd and experienced politician, suspected, and what he chose not to know. But that his political conscience is very sensitive is probably not generally supposed.[11]

The implications of such observations may have been too harsh on Tilden. But they were inevitable, just as it was inevitable that Hayes should be charged with at least suspecting skullduggery in his behalf in Louisiana. One immediate result was that the fraud issue became noticeably less attractive to Democrats as a weapon to be used against Hayes. Many Democrats were willing to forget it altogether, knowing that for a politically effective answer the Republicans had only to use one word: "cipher."

6

Hayes refrained from public comment about Tilden's sad predicament. In a little notebook, in which he made occasional jottings, he did note that the Potter investigation was one of the "most fortunate" occurrences in his administration, in that it "took the stigma of crookedness off his election and showed the crookedness of Tilden efforts."

It certainly deflated the importance in the public mind of the majority report of the Potter committee, which, after summarizing all the charges of deception, bribery and forgery that had been made against the Republicans, concluded: "Samuel J. Tilden and Thomas A. Hendricks were, and Rutherford B. Hayes and William A. Wheeler were not, the real choice of a majority of the electors duly appointed by the several states and of the persons who exercised and were entitled to the right of suffrage at the last general election in the United States." The cipher boomerang also deflated an even more barbed separate report filed by General Butler.[12] He still wanted Hayes ousted. But few people paid him any attention.

Sherman was fairly correct in writing to Noyes in Paris: "The report of the Potter committee . . . was received in silence and was scarcely printed or noticed in the newspapers of the United States two days after its presentation to the House."[13] The Hayes luck had operated again.

CHAPTER LXX

A Period of "Ups"

1

Before the House formally repudiated the idea that the Potter matter might be followed by ouster proceedings, Colonel Ingersoll cracked a joke that came close to describing accurately the lukewarm, if not cold, feeling that most Republican leaders then had for Hayes. "Suppose a half dozen Democrats go up to the White House armed with old flintlocks, and turn Hayes out. Who is to prevent it?" [1]

Even the party press obliquely deprecated him, or was out-and-out denunciatory. A much quoted remark by Evarts—"The Administration is not well edited"—was understatement. Indeed, up to then Hayes could feel certain of being referred to cordially in only two areas of the world—in England, because of his sound-money views, and in the tiny republic of Paraguay, because in 1878 he had acted as arbiter in a boundary dispute between Paraguay and Argentina and had awarded the disputed area, the Chaco, to Paraguay. A town in Paraguay was named "Villa Hayes."

To be sure, Hayes had the highly articulate and even fervent support of one element in the country—the crusaders for temperance. To them, the really important question in national affairs, or so they gave the impression of believing, was whether or not wine and other alcoholic beverages should be served at the White House.

"What a thrill of joy it would send to millions of hearts in this land and other lands could it be announced that no intoxicating liquors would find a place in the Presidential Mansion during the administration of its present occupant. . . . As an historical fact it would be worthy to stand by the side of Lincoln's Proclamation of Emancipation, and I am not sure but some day it would outshine it." So President Frederick Merrick of the Ohio Wesleyan University at Delaware had written to Lucy on the day that Hayes was inaugurated.

Dr. Merrick knew quite well that liquor was not served in the Hayes household in Ohio, that Lucy was true to the total-abstinence views of her youth. In fact, that liquor would have no part in the private life of the Hayes family in the White House was assumed.

The real question was: What would Hayes do about the so-called state dinners and formal receptions?

At the outset Hayes and Lucy themselves did not seem to be quite sure. At their first official dinner, held six weeks after Hayes took office at the request of the State Department in honor of a son of the Czar of Russia, a wine punch was served, according to the official record.[2] Probably stronger alcoholic drinks were served unofficially. It was the position of the State Department that "a dinner without wine would be an annoyance, if not an affront" to the Grand Duke, that good relations with Russia, with whom a commercial treaty was being negotiated, required the wine. Matthews was prevailed on to endorse this argument with Hayes—and Hayes yielded.[3]

But later it was made known that even at such affairs in the future wine would not be served. The result was praise unstinted for Hayes in the not inconsiderable Protestant religious press of the nation. Naturally this was true also in the publications of various temperance societies, notably the W.C.T.U., though Lucy, contrary to common report, was not a member.[4]

2

There was also a good deal of ridicule. Even Garfield, the lay preacher in the Disciples church, privately joined those who sneered, noting in his diary (January 8, 1880) that he attended "a State dinner at the President's wet down with coffee and cold water." Much nonsense was said and printed on both sides about the decision. Lucy was dubbed "Lemonade Lucy" by the "wets." It was asserted that she had laid down the law to Hayes, and in the so-called circles of fashion she was made the butt of numerous jokes in that regard. One widely circulated story, blamed by Hayes on a disappointed office seeker, was that parsimony, not the temperance principle, caused the Hayeses to omit wine from their table, though their expenditures on entertainment of guests (which came from Hayes's personal budget) were especially high.

All this was annoying to Hayes. He especially resented derisive comments about Lucy. He prepared a statement later which indicated that it was he, not Lucy, who initiated the White House abstinence program. "It seemed to me that the example of excluding liquors from the White House would be wise and useful, and would be approved by good people generally. I knew it would be particularly gratifying to Mrs. Hayes to have it done." He also stopped his own casual drinking, becoming, after the furor developed, a total-abstinence man himself—for the first time.[5]

He was not altogether happy even about the praise from the temperance advocates. Nor did he like to be portrayed as a Puritanical bluenose intent on forcing others to conform to certain moral standards. His only purpose, he said, was to set a good example. He was exceedingly conscious that it was his duty to do so as President, though he also admitted that he had in mind that it was good politics to keep the temperance people in the Republican ranks rather than to have them join a Prohibition Party.[6] In later years he said: "In avoiding the appearance of evil, I am not sure but I have sometimes unnecessarily deprived myself and others of innocent enjoyments."[7] But at the time he certainly welcomed the political support of the earnest temperance advocates. Until the Potter investigation this was almost the only support of any consequence he had.

But the Potter investigation, accompanied as it was until the end by the bitterest kind of abuse of Republican leadership in general, caused most Republican leaders to decide that the time had come to close ranks. In defending their party against the accusation that it had been, as a whole, an instrument of fraud, they also took to defending Hayes.

Then, too, the Potter attack, so obviously in line with Abram Hewitt's declaration during the electoral dispute that the Democrats planned to make the fraud issue the basis of their election campaign in 1880, brought home to Republicans as nothing else could the fact that the 1880 campaign was really under way already. Whether or not they liked Hayes or his policies, the practical politicians, except for a few like Conkling, understood that self-preservation demanded they cease tearing down their own President.

3

He was helped by the Democrats also toward the end of his term in another way. For, while the Potter investigation was still on, the Democratic leadership in both houses embarked on a course that reopened the Southern question. This was through an effort to bring about practical annulment of the federal election laws—and also repeal of the so-called jurors' test-oath law (which kept former Rebels from serving on federal juries) by the strategy of attaching riders to two main appropriation bills, one for the army and the other for the executive, judicial and legislative departments.

These riders originated in the Democratic House in February 1879. They were designed to coerce the still Republican-controlled Senate into accepting the Democrats' objective of taking from the federal government the ability to enforce remaining wartime and reconstruction statutes. The statutes authorized the use of the army to maintain the peace at the polls when Congressmen were being elected (but not to interfere in the manner of conducting the elections). They also authorized use of marshals to exercise supervisory authority at such elections, guard against fraud and see that all qualified citizens, including the Negroes especially, cast votes without discrimination and free from intimidation.

The Senate refused to agree to the riders. The House stood firm, and the Forty-fifth Congress adjourned on March 4—the day after the Potter report was filed—without the appropriation bills being passed. Hayes hit back on the same day by issuing a proclamation calling the Forty-sixth Congress into a special session two weeks hence. "Now the question will come to me," he commented.[8]

4

Toward the end of April, when the Democrats also controlled the Senate, he was presented with an army appropriation bill, passed by both chambers, with the objectionable riders. This bill not only repealed the provision in the election laws permitting use of the Army to keep the peace at the polls, but also forbade federal marshals to use civilian means to enforce election laws. Hayes promptly vetoed the bill, objecting mainly to the device of incorporating into the army bill legislation pertaining to civil officers. "It makes a vital change in the election laws of the country, which is in no way connected with the use of the Army," he said.[9]

Congress came back the following month with an army appropriation bill which omitted the objectionable rider concerning civil officers, thus meeting Hayes's objections to an attempt to force acceptance of irrelevant legislation. But the new bill included, in effect, the provision that the army was not to be used at any place where an election was being held unless requested by the state "where such force is to be used."

Hayes promptly vetoed this also. "What is this," he asked, "but the substitution of the discretion of the State governments for the discretion of the Government of the United States as to the performance of its own duties? In my judgment, this is an abandonment of its obligations by the National government—a subordination of National authority, and an intrusion of State supervision over National duties, which amounts, in spirit and tendency, to State supremacy." [10]

5

Then the Congress came back with an appropriation bill for the judicial department that forbade the employment of marshals in connection with elections. Standing firm, Hayes again used his veto power. Before this tug of war between the White House and Congress was over, Hayes had sent in six vetoes—"pistol shots," Whitelaw Reid called them.[11]

The upshot was a degree of compromise. But in the main Hayes scored a victory. The jurors' test-oath law was repealed, but only the most implacable of Republicans objected to this. Hayes himself did not object and had indicated that a separate bill to that effect would have had his cordial approval.

The army appropriation bill, as finally passed, did include the provision that the federal military were not to be used at the polls as "a police force." But this phraseology was held to be so innocuous as not to change anything, especially, as Hayes pointed out, since previous legislation specifically forbade any officer of the army or navy to interfere "in any manner" with "the freedom of any election in any State" and also (by an act adopted in 1878) made it unlawful to use the army as a posse comitatus except as "expressly authorized by the Constitution or by act of Congress." [12]

Appropriations for the executive and legislative functions were passed without riders. Also, provision was made for the judicial department, though appropriations for payment of marshals was omitted. The pay for the marshals was covered in a separate bill, which provided that none of the money was to be used in elections without a special act of Congress. But this (which did not prevent the use of marshals, who could serve without pay on the assumption that a later Congress would reimburse them) was almost all that the Democratic House and Senate achieved of the program that originally called for voting no appropriations at all unless the election laws were repealed or rendered wholly ineffective.

6

A great deal was said by Hayes in his veto messages and in the debates in Congress to the effect that the controversy concerned primarily the propriety of rider legislation. Much also was said of the claim, held to be revolutionary, that the House could withhold appropriations as a means of obtaining "redress of grievances," in accord with the British parliamentary system.[13]

But the real issue plainly was whether or not the federal government was to be deprived of any means of enforcing the Fifteenth Amendment in the South, with respect to the right of Negroes to vote. It would be charged then and later, by Southerners, that Hayes was inconsistent in his position. He had gone back on his Southern policy, these said. Hill of Georgia, usually friendly toward Hayes, was especially bitter in voicing that charge.[14]

He hadn't, of course. What he had done was resist again encroachment by Congress on Presidential power, and also maintain the right of the federal government to use federal power to enforce federal laws, whether or not he chose to exercise that right. But the charges against him that he had abandoned his pacification of the South, as well as the strength he had shown by his "pistol shots," reacted in his favor with his own party. The overdrawn impression that he was partial to the South, at the expense of his party, had played into the hands of party enemies like Conkling and Butler, as well as Blaine, permitting them to cover up their real objections to him by assailing him as a traitor to Republican principles. His "pistol shots" made it possible for him to stand clear and unchallenged as a loyal Republican, yet without Southerners being able to deny his fairness toward their section.

So, for one of the few periods of his administration since its start, he was able to read praise of himself in his party's press as a whole. "There is a growing impression among Republicans that Mr. Hayes is a remarkably cool hand; patient, wary, not capable of getting scared, a shrewd and long-headed politician, and a far wiser and safer party leader than the irate senators who have vainly battled against him so often." So the usually critical New York *Herald* commented concerning the outcome of his struggle with Congress. "The President has the courtesy of a Chesterfield and the firmness of a Jackson," said the

New York *Tribune* of the way his veto messages defended national sovereignty without, however, waving "the bloody shirt."

In his diary he wrote, "I am now experiencing one of the *'ups'* of political life." [15]

An unexpected upsurge in his popularity was brought about, too, by unmistakable signs, first showing up in 1879 and becoming stronger in 1880, that the long economic depression at last was lifting.[16] There was less unemployment. Farm prices went up. A principal cause for this return of better times probably was a general crop failure in Europe, which brought heavier than normal demand for American produce. But the resumption of specie payments was given much of the credit. It apparently had not hurt. So Hayes's stock rose, even among the working-class folk.

CHAPTER LXXI

BYSTANDER'S VINDICATION

1

NORMALLY it might have been expected that these pleasant circumstances would lead to a movement for Hayes to be the Republican candidate in 1880 to succeed himself, despite his declaration in 1876 that he would not be a candidate for a second term.

He had clearly enhanced the prospects of the party to win in 1880, despite the increased electoral vote potential of the solid Democratic South. His reform program, for all its shortcomings, had undoubtedly won back for the party the allegiance of many independents. This meant that the loss of New York in particular, which, by itself, had made necessary the retention of some Southern states in 1876, could reasonably be expected not to be repeated in 1880.

But the party chieftains still did not want any more of Hayes in office. He had given the party the new respectability that it needed. But they wanted someone more co-operative politically and less obsessed, from their view, with the value of even moderate nonpartisanship. They preferred that he be forgotten. So none of them attempted to persuade him or any part of the public that it was his duty to lead the party again, though of course his declaration against being a candidate for a second term obviously could have been neutralized by a draft movement.

With the power of his office Hayes himself might have produced some kind of a draft movement despite the leaders, had he wished it. There were a number of friends who hoped that he would—and some were ready to launch a boom.

William Henry Smith was among these. In March 1879, in a letter addressed to Webb Hayes but obviously meant for Webb's father's eyes, Smith wrote: "Events are fast leading Republicans to an intelligent apprehension of what the present Administration has done for the party & country, and we shall in all human probability have again in 1880—Hayes & Wheeler." Indeed, Smith, still a potent behind-the-scenes political manipulator, began promoting that ticket again.[1] "It would be a long story to tell of the numbers who took an interest in the second-term talk for you," Rogers told Hayes.[2]

2

There were those who believed Hayes was a party to this talk. Among these was Boynton. "Hayes & his friends are nearly ready to burst with the idea of a second term," he wrote to Bristow.[3] Boynton was writing out of spite. The newspaperman who had been so prominent in the 1876 negotiations had several grievances by then against Hayes —that the Texas and Pacific subsidy had not been supported, that Harlan, instead of Bristow, had been appointed by Hayes to the Supreme Court, and that numerous suggestions for appointments by Boynton himself had not been followed.

Even Sherman was not sure that Hayes meant what he had said about not seeking a second term. On June 5, as Sherman knew, Hayes had written to a Philadelphia newspaper publisher, who had raised the subject with him, "I cannot conceive of a case in which I would consider it." [4] Yet about two weeks later Sherman requested of Hayes a special interview in which he asked him point-blank "whether, under certain circumstances, he would not in spite of his declination, become a candidate for re-election." Sherman had an urgent personal reason for getting a definite answer. He was on the verge of announcing publicly his own candidacy. "He [Hayes] was very explicit—that he would not be a candidate under any circumstances," Sherman reported.[5]

Nonetheless, Hayes would have liked to see a spontaneous movement develop among the people for him to have a second term, with the result of having the people make known that desire to the politicians. This view is supported by the numerous trips that he took from the beginning of his term, more than any one of his predecessors had taken, causing the Chicago *Times* to dub him "Rutherford, the Rover," [6] and by his penchant for accepting invitations to many county and state fairs where he shook thousands of hands.

The spontaneous movement did not develop. Yet the disappointment that he naturally felt was not from frustration of a desire to serve a second term. What he hoped for—quite humanly and also in keeping with his character—was a chance to *refuse* in some dramatic way a "call" to continue in office; in short, the glory of underscoring, after he had been President, his pre-election statement that he would serve but one term and not seek another.

3

The fact was that by the time his term was half over he had really had enough of the Presidential office, especially as by then he had accomplished all that the political system would permit of his personal program. Actually his strong streak of ambition had been satisfied the moment he attained the office. He had really wanted not so much to *be* President as to *have been* President.

He still enjoyed more than he liked to admit the social side of the office, the deference that was shown to him, and all that. He also enjoyed the power to confer offices on friends or others whom he especially esteemed. For example, one candidate for an office was none other than an old hero, John C. Frémont. By the time of Hayes's term the glamorous Frémont had come on lean days. In 1878, when friends asked for a suitable place for the then-graying explorer, who once had been worth millions, Hayes did not think there was a position open that he would accept. But Jessie Benton Frémont, the explorer's "Immortal Wife," made a confession to Lucy. Frémont was in such bad financial straits that he would take anything for an income. So Hayes named Frémont territorial governor of Arizona, salary $2,000 *a year*. There was keenly nostalgic pleasure for him in this act, which Frémont in part repaid with interviews in which he defended Hayes against sullen Republicans, saying, "President Hayes means well—the trouble is, the people are not acquainted with him." [7]

There were, to be sure, other such pleasures for Hayes in the Presidency. He was also keenly conscious of the drawbacks. In the same June of 1879, when so much interest was being shown in his true second-term intentions, he placed in his diary some interesting comments: "Lucy and I have had a few minutes' talk on this laborious, anxious, slavish life. It has many attractions and enjoyments, but she agrees so heartily with me as I say: 'Well, I am heartily tired of this life of bondage, responsibility, and toil. I wish it was at an end. . . .'" [8]

The responsibility and those phases of his Presidency which caused him to use the word "anxious" were real, burdensome and often distasteful. He did not like the constant necessity of making decisions on controversial matters—for example, the case of Fitz John Porter, the general who was court-martialed during the war for alleged cowardice in connection with the disaster at Bull Run, a highly charged matter which one student, Otto Eisenschiml, has called an "American Dreyfus affair."

Hayes established a board of inquiry to review this controversy, with the idea of perhaps removing the stigma from Porter. He approved, he said, clemency for Porter. But the case was so loaded with personal and political emotions that in the end he evaded a decision and decided to let Congress determine the issue.[9] Nor did he like choosing (when the choice was really his) between this and that man for an important post, or making the inevitable compromises which he, like all Presidents, had to make.

4

But what made him most painfully anxious was the same fear that he had when governor. In his diary toward the end of his term he wrote of "the ever-present danger of scandals and crimes among those we are compelled to trust."[10] Indeed, this fear was so strong in him that it, perhaps more than any other consideration, made him accept with such equanimity—surprising to nearly everyone and incredible to many—the fact that he was so conspicuously left out of the politicians' calculations for 1880.

As a matter of fact, a scandal was brewing—a carry-over situation from Grant's time—in the Post Office Department in connection with so-called "star route" mail contracts. A Congressional committee began an investigation in 1879, in particular in regard to the activities of Assistant Postmaster Generals Thomas J. Brady and James Tyner, who were part of Senator Morton's legacy to the administration. Hayes had asked Postmaster General Key to be alert. Also, he directed that "hereafter no contract should be made or altered involving any considerable expense or liability unless it was submitted to the Postmaster-general and by him brought before the President and the Cabinet."

But this order was not observed. Neither Key, who not long afterward resigned for a lifetime post as a federal judge, nor Hayes was vigilant enough in view of the craftiness of the ring involved. "All agree that Key was honest, but too inexperienced and confiding," Hayes said.[11]

The same could be said of Hayes himself. In any event corruption went on—with a dismaying exposure occurring a few months after Hayes left office.

5

When his party went through the quadrennial procedure of selecting its next standard-bearers, he, the President, ostensibly the head of the party, conducted himself as scarcely more than a bystander. He seemed not to have any affirmative choice for his successor. Sherman said he had told him that "as far as he could properly, without any unseemly interference," he would "favor" the Sherman candidacy.[12] But those qualifications were so broad as to make the implied support of Sherman mean almost nothing. He did very little or nothing for Sherman, though the Secretary's nomination would have been interpreted as a clear endorsement of his own administration.

Some time before his interview with Sherman he talked with Garfield in a way that led Garfield to believe that Hayes was thinking favorably of *him* for the nomination.[13] Probably he was being merely amiable toward both Ohioans, as well as careful not to take sides in an undercover rivalry between Sherman and Garfield, the latter already shaping up for designation as favorite-son choice of Ohio. Most important, as Sherman's comment suggested, Hayes felt that it was improper for him as the President to interfere.

He did deviate, to an extent, from his policy of noninterference in connection with a formidable boom for Grant for a third term. Grant's nomination, of course, would have been an out-and-out repudiation of much that Hayes symbolized. Moreover, as it later turned out, one of the principal promoters of the Grant boom, if not the principal one, was none other than Conkling. So Hayes had good reasons for opposing the movement behind Grant.

But he was careful not to reveal his true feelings at the time, not even in his diary. Commenting on the undoubted fact that in December 1879 Grant was "the popular favorite," he wrote: "But many thoughtful men dislike a departure from Washington's precedent— dislike the third term; and many more fear a return to the unfortunate methods and men of General Grant's former Administrations." [14] These were his own feelings, though he couldn't bring himself to oppose Grant openly.

He was so concerned that he personally tried to persuade Grant to withdraw, and arranged to meet Grant in Philadelphia for a private talk the day after Christmas 1879. He left no record of what he or Grant said at the meeting. He was even cautious in writing about it to Lucy, who was much interested in the outcome. "My Darling: We had a quiet nice time last night. A most agreeable talk with General Grant for two hours alone. He looks well and is in excellent spirits. . . ." [15]

6

His mission failed. Grant did not repudiate the boom. When the Republican national convention opened in Chicago in June 1880, Grant had more pledged votes than anyone else. Worse yet from Hayes's standpoint, the Grant campaign was being managed by three Senators—the "triumvirs," as the anti-Grant press called them—who represented bitter-end antipathy for him—Conkling, "Don" Cameron and John A. Logan of Illinois. A victory for Grant would have meant, in such circumstances, a colossal personal defeat for Hayes.

The next leading candidate was Blaine, who, oddly enough, despite the Mulligan Letters exposure of 1876, was at first the hope of most of the reform elements for stopping Grant. The nomination of Blaine would not have been much more pleasing to Hayes than that of Grant, though he was prepared to be satisfied with him in preference to a victory for Conkling and his allies.

Had Conkling and his associates succeeded in their strategy of trying to get the convention to adopt the unit rule, by which all the votes of a state would be cast for the choice of the majority of its delegates, in all probability they would have put over Grant. But they were defeated.

On learning this in Washington, Hayes was so pleased that he allowed himself to record in his diary some of his true feelings: "It now seems impossible to nominate Grant. Blaine's chances are good. It may be Sherman or a fourth—either Edmunds or Windom [Senator from Minnesota]. . . . The immediately valuable result is the condemnation of the machine as organized by Conkling and Cameron. . . ."

Out of his old sense of loyalty to Grant, the man, he added: "I greatly regret that Grant, our first soldier and a man of many sterling qualities, should be so humiliated and degraded as he has been by his unprincipled supporters." But he did not succeed in concealing his elation.[16]

7

Until the final outcome (and not wholly then), the reports from the convention did not contain much else to please Hayes. It was painfully obvious that he was no hero to any of the delegates, that he was to be studiously denied the degree of praise normally given by a Republican convention to a Republican President in office. William Henry Smith later reported to him: "The good people in attendance on the convention were very free in expressing the opinion that if the Republican convention were wise it would renominate you, despite your refusal." [17] But "good people," apparently, were decidedly in the minority on the convention floor.

The platform adopted did contain an endorsement of Hayes. It stated that "the purity and patriotism which characterized" his "earlier career" had "continued to inspire him in his career as Chief Executive." It predicted that "history will accord to his Administration the honors which are due to an efficient, just and courteous discharge of the public business, and will honor his interpositions between the people and proposed partisan laws." This was obviously less than wholehearted endorsement.

The report of the platform committee, when presented to the convention, had no reference to civil-service reform. The oversight was corrected from the floor and a mild endorsement of civil-service reform, "in principle," was adopted. This was a victory for Hayes, but one considerably diluted by the attitude of patent disinterest by the majority of the delegates.

8

Nothing so underlined Hayes's bystander role as the nomination itself. Garfield emerged as the choice for President and, of all persons, Chester Arthur—the Conkling man removed by Hayes from the New York Customhouse—for Vice-President.

Hayes was as surprised as any average citizen who depended only on the newspapers. He wrote in his diary:

General Garfield's nomination at Chicago was the best that was possible. It is altogether good. The convention accomplished a great deal of good. . . . The defeat of the rule-or-ruin Senators, who usurped the power of the people; the defeat of a third term against so great a chieftain as Grant. There is much personal gratification in it: The defeat of those who have been bitter against me; the success of one who has uniformly been friendly; Ohio to the front also and again; the endorsement of civil service reform. . . .

But the nomination of Arthur was hard for him to view with any personal gratification. He was politician enough to appreciate its practical desirability, by way of appeasing the defeated "stalwarts," in particular the Conkling machine in New York. But it was all too plain that in choosing Arthur the convention had shown contemptuous disregard for Hayes. Yet his desire to view the result of the convention optimistically finally enabled him to rationalize even that action. "The sop thrown to Conkling in the nomination of Arthur only serves to emphasize the completeness of his defeat," he wrote. "He was so crushed that it was from sheer sympathy that this bone was thrown to him." [18]

9

He was more pleased probably with the outcome of the Democratic national convention held at Cincinnati later in the same month. For the Democrats quite willingly acquiesced when Tilden sent to it a letter "renouncing renomination for the Presidency." Tilden gave as his reason the state of his health. Yet the impression remained that the revelation of the cipher dispatches was a factor in his decision.[19] The Democratic convention not only did not nominate Tilden, it passed up all other Democrats who had been prominently associated with the fraud issue. It selected General Hancock for its Presidential candidate.

To Hayes, Hancock's nomination was a "yielding" by the Democrats of the "fraud issue," a "conclusive reply to the 'fraud cry'." [20] He considered Hancock's conduct after settlement of the 1876 dispute especially significant in this regard. For when other prominent Democrats had announced they would not recognize Hayes as entitled to the Presidency, and boycotted the inaugural ceremonies, Hancock had made it a point to stand by Hayes.[21]

10

He was keenly interested in seeing Garfield emerge from the campaign as the victor, largely because he was basically loyal to the party.

But he took no overt part in the campaigning. That summer and fall he had an unusually full schedule of public appearances, but carefully refrained from converting these into obvious vote-seeking appeals. In August 1880 he was the principal speaker at a great Ohio soldiers' reunion at Columbus, the one at which General Sherman, sharing in the speaking, made his celebrated "War is hell" utterance.

This might have been seized as an occasion for him to urge the soldiers to rally behind the party of the Union. Instead, he delivered one of his strongest pleas for a program of national aid to the public-school system, especially in the South. "To perpetuate the Union and to abolish slavery were the work of the war. To educate the uneducated is the appropriate work of peace." He would deal with the problem, he said, on the public-works principle.

Wherever a public improvement is of national importance, and local and private enterprise are inadequate . . . the General Government should undertake it. . . . Wherever in the United States the local systems of popular education are inadequate, they should be supplemented by the General Government, by devoting to the purpose . . . the public lands, or if necessary, appropriations from the Treasury of the United States.[22]

On September 1, 1880, after attending a reunion of the Twenty-third Regiment at Canton, Ohio, where he made a similar talk, he began a trip of two months that took him to California and the Pacific Northwest—the first President to visit the western coast while in office. Such a journey, through so many western states and territories, had political value to the Republican cause. But the topics of his numerous speeches were all studiedly nonpolitical.

Only after the transcontinental trip ended with his arrival in Fremont on the day before the election did he permit himself to make a direct appeal for Garfield. It was "too late now to enter upon a political discussion," he told the Republicans of the county—his neighbors, who gathered at Spiegel Grove to serenade him. But he felt free to say that Garfield should be elected in the interest of "national unity, in the supremacy of the General government," and for the preservation of "this prosperity which we are now enjoying."

Garfield won, but the victory was not impressive in terms of the popular vote. It was by a plurality of only about 10,000 votes. Nor did the North remain solid, though the South did, despite Hayes's continued hope that it might be broken. The electoral-vote result, however, was conclusive, 215 to 155. So Hayes had the satisfaction of feeling that the record, for all the snide predictions of the Conklingites, showed that his administration had helped to keep his party in power and that, in the most concrete way possible, he had won vindication for his policies.

CHAPTER LXXII

Out of It

1

ELINOR HOWELLS, while a guest at the White House with her husband, William Dean Howells, in May 1880, remarked to Hayes, "Well, you will soon be out of it." "Yes," he replied, "out of a scrape, out of a scrape." [1]

But after the election of Garfield he still had four months more of the responsibility, of the continuing scramble for jobs (though of course nothing like what Garfield was then experiencing) and, to use his word, the "embarrassments" connected inevitably with the office. One "embarrassment" involved his cabinet. For Secretary of the Navy Thompson accepted, at a salary of $25,000 a year, the presidency of an American subsidiary of the DeLesseps canal company, and, oddly, believed he could hold that post and also remain in the cabinet. Hayes acted promptly, accepting Thompson's resignation before the Secretary resigned. But it was a painful episode.

He was distressed also by the reaction of General Sherman when he recommended the rank of captain-general for General Grant and made some other army promotions that Sherman did not approve. Sherman went into a high dudgeon. [2] The loss of friendship that resulted (only temporary, however) emphasized sharply the disagreeable side of the power of his office to change the fortunes of men—and how willingly he would relinquish that power.

2

An angry controversy over an Indian matter threatened to place even Schurz and the Interior Department under a cloud. This involved the peaceful Poncas, who had been transferred from their ancestral land in the Dakota Territory in 1877 to the Indian Territory in the Southwest in accord with an act of Congress but in violation of a treaty. The transfer was attended by much hardship for this small tribe, especially as Congress had failed to provide funds to help them to build new homes. Many died from malaria in the Southwest.

Some of the "best people" of Boston in particular took up the cause.

Mass meetings were held, bitter tracts were written, with Helen Hunt Jackson especially active. Charges of inhumanity and of favoritism to railroads, allegedly interested in the Poncas' land, were soon given much prominence in the press and also in Congress.

Schurz, who admitted that the Indians had been "grievously wronged," blamed Congress, asserting that his department had had no choice but to obey the law, though it was unjust. He pointed to requests by his department for remedial legislation. But the friends of the Poncas countered that it had been the duty of Schurz to hold up the transfer until Congress had taken proper action.

Hayes at first suspected a political attack on Schurz. "I suppose General Schurz has been most shamefully treated in this affair, but I may be mistaken," he wrote to Senator Hoar, who had told him that "the country" would be "satisfied" only by Hayes's action to redress the wrong to the Poncas, but not that of "any lesser authority," meaning Schurz.[3]

Hayes did not wish to show lack of confidence in Schurz. But finally he took the matter over personally and appointed a special committee that worked out a solution, which the Poncas accepted.[4] His assumption of the responsibility and his positive action helped quiet the storm. But it had been especially worrisome and was further underscoring of the fact that his peace of mind and reputation depended on factors over which he had only tenuous control. It was no wonder that on January 2, 1881, though elated over success of a New Year's reception the day before, which won for him and Lucy much praise as hosts, he put in his diary: "We long for home and freedom more and more as the time draws nearer."

3

Toward the end of that January he sent to the Senate one of his most important and interesting, from a personal standpoint, appointments—the nomination of Stanley Matthews as Associate Justice of the Supreme Court. His two previous Supreme Court appointments, Justice Harlan and Justice William B. Woods, had been made from strong political motives. The Harlan appointment, though largely reward for the Kentuckian's role in the 1876 convention and on the Louisiana settlement commission, was a splendid one, certainly from the standpoint of those who still championed respect for Negro rights. For Justice Harlan stood almost alone in dissenting from decisions that whittled away the force of the "freedom amendments" to the Constitution with regard to the Negroes. In particular, Harlan dissented from the decision in the case of *Plessy v. Ferguson* (1896), which upheld the "separate but equal" doctrine by which segregation of Negroes, especially in the public schools, was to be deemed lawful until 1954. In this regard the Woods appointment was a less shining one. Though from Newark, Ohio, Justice Woods had become known as a "Southerner of Southerners," and he was placed on the court by Hayes apparently as appeasement of the South, if not as part of the understandings reached in 1877.

But the appointment of Matthews, the friend since the Kenyon days, was largely personal. Probably that explained in some part the bitterness which this last significant appointment generated among key Senators. By blocking the appointment they would be able to administer to Hayes a last personal thrust of special sharpness, though they placed their objections to Matthews on other grounds.

4

There then occurred one of the ugliest tempests of Hayes's entire term. Republican newspapers joined Democratic ones in assailing the choice of Matthews. The New York *Times* asserted that the appointment was "reward" for Matthews' role in the election dispute "bargain." To the *Sun,* Matthews was "the burglar's accomplice" in connection with the "steal." His prosecution of the man in Cincinnati who had befriended a runaway slave was "exposed" again.

But the most serious and telling objection was that Matthews had been, probably still was, an attorney for Jay Gould. "Mr. Jay Gould has been appointed to the United States Supreme Court," said the Detroit *Free Press.* It was pointed out in this connection that in the Senate Matthews had vigorously opposed the Pacific Railroad Refunding Act, which provided stricter arrangements by which the Union Pacific Railroad, in which Gould was the leading shareholder, was to repay government-granted loans. This act, involving millions of dollars, was destined to be challenged before the Supreme Court, and the implication was that Matthews, on the court, would champion Gould's interest.[5]

The uproar in the press and in the Senate continued until the end of Hayes's term, for the Judiciary Committee refused to act on the appointment, allowing it to lapse. Matthews later did get the post—

confirmed by one vote—after Garfield resubmitted the nomination. "I held Garfield to it," Hayes said later.[6] But the episode meant that his term closed with a rebuff, mainly from his own party.

5

However, there was much connected with the last days in the White House that made them pleasant, enabling him to write in his diary two days before he relinquished the office to Garfield: "My closing days are full of satisfaction." At the last reception over which he and Lucy presided, one for the diplomatic corps, there was an outpouring of cordiality.

Wonder of wonders, in view of his stand in the 1875 election for governor as well as in 1876, he went out with even the good will of Catholic leaders. For in the fall of 1880 he had made a point of naming a Catholic priest as an army chaplain for federal troops in the West, the first so appointed. Bishop Gilmour of Cleveland, he who had provoked such a storm over the Geghan Act in Ohio, was among those who congratulated him for an act which the bishop hoped meant the beginning of "fair play" for the Catholic church—even, he might have added, from a Protestant Republican adminstration.[7]

Hayes was delighted with expressions of regard now paid to him and Lucy, not only by political leaders but also by ordinary citizens who came to bid them farewell. On March 2, 1881, he wrote in his diary: "I have shaken hands with five hundred today. Many clergymen congratulate me. The burden of the talk on all sides is a clean, honest, independent and successful Administration." Alexander Stephens, Vice-President of the Confederacy, then a Congressman from Georgia, called to pay him a tribute that was especially pleasing in connection with Hayes's desire to be recalled as a symbol of reunion. "Mr. Stephens . . . says he never saw an Administration go out so well spoken of."

Much of the praise, of course, that he then heard from politicians was voiced in a spirit of "bygones are bygones," though probably just as sincere as much of the criticism heretofore.

Yet he had a right to believe that, on the whole, true feelings were being expressed. Pertinent is the judgment that Abram Hewitt finally expressed—though not until long after Hayes was dead, and his term nearly forgotten. Hewitt remained harsh in his opinion of the 1876 election, saying Hayes "was not elected to the office and his conduct in securing it was that of a traitor." But with Hayes's sound-money and Southern policies in mind especially, Hewitt then went on to say:

Nevertheless, I think his administration was creditable to all concerned and was far better than four years of unrest which we should undoubtedly have had if Tilden had occupied the office of President. Sometimes we are disposed to doubt the guiding will of Providence in the history of mankind, but looking over the ground I feel that there never was in the history of the world an occasion where the interposition of a Higher Power was more manifest and more productive of good to the welfare of an entire country.[8]

And Hewitt had been chairman of the Democratic National Committee in 1876!

6

In January 1881 Hayes wrote to Guy Bryan: "Nobody ever left the Presidency with less regret, less disappointment, fewer heartburnings, or more general content with the result of his term (in his own heart, I mean) than I do." [9]

His demeanor during the inauguration ceremonies for Garfield on Friday, March 4, 1881, underscored those expressions. George W. Julian, the old Indiana politician, one of the Lincoln Republicans turned Democrat who was always a sharp critic of Hayes, preserved in a letter to his wife the contrast between Hayes, the President who was then shedding the burdens of the office, and Garfield, who was assuming them: "Hayes looked as sweet & lamblike as possible, but Garfield's face looked worn." [10]

That night, after looking on at the parading and other festivities for Garfield, Hayes and Lucy left the White House for John Sherman's home, thus ending the Washington period of their lives where they had begun it. The next evening with the children and a party of Ohio friends, escorted by a Cleveland military troop, they boarded a train for Fremont—and home.

BOOK TEN

The "Nihilist"

"Abolish plutocracy if you would abolish poverty."

—RBH in his diary,
February 16, 1890

CHAPTER LXXIII

PRIVATE CITIZEN AGAIN

1

"WE WISH to get as completely back into private life as we can; to keep out of public observation enough to show the truth that we have no hankering after the pleasures we have left," he wrote to Guy Bryan six weeks after their return to Fremont.

On the night of his return he had made a talk to the neighbors who gathered at the grove to welcome him back, during which he brought up the question, "What is to become of the man—what is he to do—who, having been Chief Magistrate of the Republic, retires at the end of his official term to private life?"

Perhaps he remembered a statement attributed to President Pierce who, answering the same question, quipped, "There is nothing left . . . but to get drunk." Hayes's own answer was: "Let him, like every other good American citizen, be willing and prompt to bear his part in every useful work that will promote the welfare, the happiness, and the progress of his family, his town, his state and his country. With this disposition, he will have enough work to do." And this was how he earnestly conducted himself for the next twelve years.

One of the first things he did was rejoin the Odd Fellows in Fremont, and later he accepted election as the "noble grand" of the chapter. He fulfilled the duties of that office as seriously as though he were presiding over a cabinet session. He joined the local post of the G. A. R., and was as comradely with the former privates, still mostly "humble folk," who mainly made up the organization, as he had been accustomed to being with distinguished generals. When a new savings bank was organized—capital $50,000—he became a director and devoted to its affairs the conscientious attention that the financial policies of the national treasury had received from him, as was the case also with his directorship of Sardis' bank.

He spent countless hours on the affairs of the Birchard Library, and contributed funds of his own at a time when he had to borrow heavily in order not to sacrifice his real-estate holdings. He was one of the founders of a Fremont board of trade, organized mainly to attract new industries to the community.[1] Of course, his own property in Fremont stood to increase in value through the success of such a project. But his main motive was to shoulder the responsibility of a public-spirited citizen. He was a member of the county-fair association, the local "pioneer" society, and similar groups—indeed, he identified himself with the Fremont civic life as completely as had been true of his uncle.

2

To the end he refrained from joining a church. Strong pleas had been made to him before and after he assumed the Presidency by clergymen with whom he was on the closest of terms, not only for his own sake but for the example it would represent. "I wish you were a professing Christian," Bishop G. T. Bedell of the Episcopal Diocese of Ohio, a valued friend, had written to him in February 1877. "While I am sure that in your private thoughts you bow submissively to God . . . is there not the highest of all reasons that your allegiance should be openly made known?" [2] But, as had been the case with him at Kenyon, he could not, or would not, make a formal profession of faith.

Yet while with seemingly studied emphasis he described himself as a "non-church member, a non-professor of religion," [3] he nevertheless was active in the religious life of Fremont. He was a vice-president of the county Bible Society, supported the holding of revivals—even against ardent church members who opposed them—and was a trustee of the Methodist church, Lucy's church, in Fremont. He was not merely a perfunctory trustee out of loyalty to Lucy, but notably interested. He was especially active soon after his return to Fremont in co-operating to have the frame church building on Birchard Avenue replaced by one of brick, pledging to pay one-fourth of the cost himself. When this was practically destroyed by fire a few years later, he promptly pledged the same share of the cost of its replacement.[4]

He was so much a part of the church that he let himself become deeply involved in a near schism, a familiar kind of tragicomedy, over the removal of the pastor, D.D. Mather, a man of about his own age, who had been accused of an improper interest in women parishioners. Hayes defended the pastor, whom he considered "a pure and good man, an excellent preacher, and a true and devoted Christian." The charges, he felt, were "idle" and "absurd gossip" about "imprudent but not in the least licentious conduct." Mather's removal was to him a "cruel injustice." The congregation divided into sides, with Hayes substantially the leader of the pro-Mather faction. "I will not remain in a congregation so divided," he wrote in his diary.

As a member of a Mather committee, he sent to the bishop of the area, Randolph Foster, one of the most strongly worded letters he ever wrote.

The injustice to our pastor is so plain . . . that not to repair it . . . would be criminal. It would be permanently disastrous . . . to the church and to Methodism in Fremont. . . . The work of calumny and misrepresentation ought not to stand. The good name of a clergyman who has been clear in his office, and the reputation of a pure Christian woman, in humble circumstances, and a member of the church in good standing, require that what has been done shall be undone.[5]

Then he called on the bishop in Cleveland, and, among other arguments, made one that was perhaps especially potent in connection with his position as leading guarantor for the building of the new church building. "One thing, sir, is certain," he told the bishop. "Unless Dr. Mather is returned, not another brick shall be put on that church to complete it." [6] The minister was reinstated.

This incident, in the fall of 1883, illustrated more sharply than anything else could that President Hayes had made by then an almost complete transition to Private Citizen R. B. Hayes of Fremont.

3

He did not, however, limit his activity to the affairs of Fremont. One link with the outside world that he had at the time he returned to Fremont was membership on the board of trustees of the Peabody Education Fund, to which he had been elected when he was President. This fund, with an ultimate endowment of almost $3,500,000, had for its purpose the promotion of education in the South.

Although the trustees met but once a year in New York, Hayes devoted a good deal of attention to the affairs of this fund. In 1882 a similar fund for the cause of education in the South, but specifically for Negroes, was established by a Connecticut manufacturer, John F. Slater. Hayes became its first president.

He took special satisfaction out of the work of both funds because it enabled him to play a personal role in furthering his concept that the ultimate solution of the racial question in the South lay in education. One may suspect that some of his zeal was by way of penance for the failure of the South to do as much for education of the Negroes as it had promised him, and as he, in turn, had in effect promised would be done. Incidentally, one young Negro for whom he used his personal influence to get a fellowship from the Slater Fund (even against the rules) turned out to be the later distinguished historian and writer, Dr. W. E. B. Du Bois.[7] And this Negro leader became a leading spirit in the National Association for the Advancement of Colored People, a project of which was to persuade the Supreme Court to reverse the "separate but equal" doctrine that sanctioned segregation in schools of the South. So, if the 1954 decision of the court achieved its purpose, Hayes indirectly had done more than he realized for the final attainment of full educational opportunities for the Negroes along the line of the pledges made to him in 1877.

"My reflections lead me to the idea," Hayes wrote in his diary in April 1883, "that the practical good thing for me to try to give the public is general education. With my family affairs, my place, my town, and this as an object, I can always be agreeably and usefully employed. I am averse to writing for the public; I am out of official life; but it seems to me that I can accomplish something in this direction." In this connection he was grateful for his election as a trustee of Western Reserve University in Cleveland, of Ohio Wesleyan University in the old town of Delaware, and of the fledgling Ohio State University at Columbus.

His special interest in education, aside from its relation to the Negro problem, became the promotion of the manual-training movement. Indeed, concerning the concept that everyone, the children of the rich as well as of the poor, should be taught how to use tools skillfully, he came closer to being a crusader than on any other subject during his entire life. "I preach the gospel of work," he said. "I believe in skilled labor as a part of education," [8] precisely the kind of education he himself did not get. Practicing what he preached, he had his youngest son, Scott, attend a manual-training school in Toledo before he went on to Cornell.

About the same time he embraced another interest—prison reform and crime prevention. In 1883 he accepted the presidency of the National Prison Association and held that post for nearly ten years, presiding over the sessions of the little band of social reformers that were held each year in various parts of the country. "We prefer to give special attention to the unpopular questions—to those that need friends," he once explained when asked why he bothered with such a seemingly inconsequential group.[9] He linked this interest with the manual-training idea. A way to reduce crime was to teach all persons to know and respect the value of work. A way to reform men convicted of crime was the same. These were favorite ideas of his and he plumped for them indefatigably.

4

He occupied himself greatly, too, with activities of the ex-soldiers. He never failed to be present at reunions of his regiment, usually with Lucy, who was a special favorite of the "old comrades." The annual encampments of the G. A. R., for the state and for the nation, found him in faithful attendance, requiring speeches, which he prepared with care. When an organization for officers, the Military Order of the Loyal Legion, modeled after the Society of the Cincinnati of the American Revolution, was formed, he was chosen head of the Ohio commandery and later of the national commandery. It pleased him to be singled out for these offices. They involved much correspondence— and the inevitable speeches. But these were burdens that he undertook cheerfully.

Not until the very end did he become a man who lived in the past —indeed, he was singularly free from that then. But he dearly loved talking over with men who had shared his own experiences the episodes of the Civil War fighting. The Loyal Legion meetings frequently took him to Cincinnati, where he enjoyed visits also with the old friends there, the Herrons, the Forces and the Davises.

He attended meetings again of the Literary Club, though these did not give him the same pleasure as of old. "The Legion has taken the place of the club . . . in my affections," he wrote in 1885 to his daughter Fanny, then at a private school for girls at Farmington, Connecticut. "In the club I meet only Herron, Mallon, and Force of the old set. The chairs are all well filled with nice and interesting young fellows, but they are of recent times, and 'knew not Joseph.' The military circles are interested in the same things with myself, so we *endure,* if not enjoy, each other."

5

As for politics, he was interested. But he did not attempt to play any role, not even that of an elder statesman. He did not attend any conventions. In his diary and in letters to friends, such as William Henry Smith and Guy Bryan, he expressed his opinions freely on political questions, but not in public. He had surprisingly little association with political leaders, even those with whom he had been closely connected while he was President. When the Peabody or Slater fund activity took him to New York, he would arrange to see Schurz, especially, who continued active in politics. But such visits were purely social.

Almost the only occasions that placed him again prominently in the public eye in association with political leaders were funerals, starting with that of Garfield in September 1881. Grant died in 1885, Arthur in 1886. So he helped to bury three who had been President before scarcely more than five years had passed since he had himself left the White House.

Certain newspaper wits took to printing items, some cruel, poking fun over the relative obscurity of his life and the fact that the politicians, including some who had been helped by him, generally "knew not Joseph" any more. One of the most pungent of these was Eugene Field, who probably did not know that through the Smith line he and Hayes were at least third cousins. In his famous column "Sharps and Flats" in the Chicago *Daily News*, Field printed a supposed side light on the unveiling of a monument to Garfield, which Hayes had helped to finance. Of Hayes, Field said: "He carried a black velvet bag on one arm and on one side of the bag was embroidered the legend 'R.B.H. from Lucy.' Nobody knew him; nobody recognized him; nobody spoke to him—except a policeman, and he told him to keep off the grass." [10]

Of course, this never happened, but the item illustrated how quickly he had slipped from public life, how quickly, even in his own lifetime, he was largely forgotten.

CHAPTER LXXIV

SOPHIA'S VICTORY

1

OTHER deaths in this period did accent the fact that his era was passing. Wheeler, his Vice-President, died. Tilden died. Hancock died. Hendricks died, not long after he at last had been elected Vice-President in 1884, with Grover Cleveland.

In the winter of 1888 death touched Hayes's own family circle for the first time since the death of the little boy, Manning, in 1874. His eldest son, Birchard, practicing law in Toledo, had on December 30, 1886, thirty-fourth anniversary of Hayes's and Lucy's wedding, married Mary Sherman of Norwalk. Their first child, a son born in October 1887, was named Rutherford—another Ruddy Hayes. A second boy, called Sherman Otis, was born about a year later. From these grandchildren—a new generation!—Hayes and Lucy received much pleasure. There was much visiting back and forth between Spiegel Grove and Toledo. But in November 1888 the new Rutherford died of the croup at his home in Toledo. So there was a sad trip to the cemetery near Spiegel Grove.

In March 1889 Justice Matthews died. This was an event that evoked recollections of nearly every important phase of his life since his youth. Except for Guy Bryan, there were now no more friends of the Kenyon days. "You are the last!" he wrote to Bryan on the day he went to Glendale, Cincinnati suburb, to help bury Matthews.

2

Then in the following June came the blow that shook him more than anything else since the death of the beloved sister. On June 17, 1889, he had left Spiegel Grove for Columbus, where he attended some meetings in connection with Ohio State University. Lucy apparently was in the best of health.

In the previous April she, like himself, had especially enjoyed a return to the national spotlight in connection with ceremonies in New York for the one-hundredth anniversary of the inauguration of President Washington. He had been on the program to give the toast to the Presidency. Thus they had mingled again with the nation's great, including the new President, Benjamin Harrison, and the recently retired—temporarily as it turned out—Cleveland.

But when he returned to Fremont from Columbus on June 22, accompanied by his niece Laura, he received shattering news from his son Rutherford at the little railroad station. While sitting in their bedroom sewing that day, Lucy had suffered some kind of stroke. A maid noticed that she was "looking fixedly at her needle," spoke to her and received no response. She had lost the ability to speak.[1]

When Hayes reached her side, after she had been placed in bed and a doctor had attended her, she "seemed" to know him, he related. "In her old manner, she pressed my hand and tried to smile, or smiled!" he said. But she never recovered speech and soon was in a coma. She lived on for two days more, with Hayes constantly beside her. "It was pathetic to see [him] lie on the bed beside her, holding her hand and often leaning over to kiss her brow," a cousin recalled.[2] Early in the morning of June 25, 1889, Lucy's brown eyes were closed forever.

3

It was interesting that he, who as a youth had been skeptical of his mother's views on death—that it was "no bad thing"—now wrote in his diary quite as his mother used to write and speak. Even before Lucy had passed away, but in the last hours when he knew there was no hope, he wrote:

. . . Lucy . . . is so sweet and lovely, as she lies unconsciously breathing away her precious life, that I feel a strange gratitude and happiness as I meditate on all the circumstances of this solemn transition we are waiting for. Would I change it? Oh, yes, how gladly would we all welcome the least indication of the restoration of the darling head of the home circle.
But we cannot, we must not, repine. Lucy Hayes is approaching the beautiful and happy ending of a beautiful, honored and happy life. . . . Without pain, without the usual suffering, she has been permitted to come to the gates of the great change which leads to the life where pain and suffering are unknown. . . . Who knows what the future might have brought to her? It is indeed hard—hard indeed —to part with her, but could I or should I call her back? Rather let me try to realize the truth of the great mystery. . . .[3]

As did his mother after each of the deaths that marked her life, starting with Daniel Austin, he told himself that he would one day be re-
united with Lucy and that it was right and necessary to bow to God's
will.

I believe in the moral government of the universe. I trust and have
faith in the power, wisdom and goodness of the Divine Eternal. Death
must be good for its victims. The living behind must grieve, and for
a time seem to lose. But for those who depart the transition must be
good and cannot be bad. What is universal, what is alloted to all
God's highest creatures, is surely to promote their welfare and happiness. It is not to be feared—to be approached with dread.

And: "She is in Heaven. She is where all the best of earth have
gone." [4]

4

Again like his mother, who all her life filled her diary and letters
with recollections of Ruddy Hayes, he filled numerous pages of his
diary now with thoughts about Lucy, setting down descriptions of all
of her appealing characteristics, frequently repeating, "I think of Lucy
as the Golden Rule incarnate," and reviewing in detail the events of
their long life together. He was greatly interested in having a biography of Lucy written. He hoped that Howells would do one. [5]

In part the recollections of Lucy were set down by him for that purpose. But in large part, too, this preoccupation meant that he was his
mother's son, receiving the same melancholy pleasure that she received from dwelling on life with those who were gone.

It is interesting, too, that among his first thoughts about future
activity after Lucy died were those that concerned a desire to visit
Vermont. "I long for kindred—for my own blood. I must visit the old
home while this cloud is over me," he wrote a cousin, Mrs. Mary
Hayes Bigelow, widowed daughter of Russell Hayes, his father's long-
dead brother. [6]

The old home was the former Hayes Tavern in Brattleboro, restored by Mrs. Bigelow as a summer residence. He had kindred at
Spiegel Grove and near by. His daughter, Fanny, past twenty-one,
and his sons, Scott and Rutherford—the latter cashier at the savings
bank—were then living at home. Webb was in business in Cleveland,
an officer of the Thompson-Houston Electric Company. But the

away-from-home sons were close enough, especially Birchard in Toledo, for regular week-end visits. So his longing for kindred was a
kind of mystical yearning, such as his mother might have felt, for the
apparent security of the ancestral environment, a link with the long
past of his people. •

5

In the following October, accompanied by Daughter Fanny, who
from then on often would go with him on the trips that Lucy would
have made with him, he attended a Peabody Fund meeting and also
a conference at Lake Mohonk, New York, on problems of the Negroes
and Indians, the Mohonk conferences having been added to his hob-
bies. Then he went on to Vermont, and visited with the kindred,
especially with a daughter of his mother's brother, Austin, in Newfane, and the cousin at the old tavern. A newspaper in New York
printed a long story to the effect that his visit to his cousin, Mrs.
Bigelow, meant that he and she intended to be married. This was
nonsense to be repeated even by a biographer. He could no more have
taken a second wife than his mother had been able to take a second
husband.

He spent considerable time in the old graveyards, in particular the
one where the first Rutherford Hayes and Chloe were buried, and in
going over old family records, and talking over the family history.[7]
This steeping of himself in associations with his family origins was
good for him. He went on to attend a meeting of the Slater Fund in
New York and of the Loyal Legion in Philadelphia with an obviously
lighter spirit.

It was noticeable too that in his speeches, of which he still would
make many before the soldier groups, at the prison reform and educational meetings, there was now a marked ethical, almost religious
tone. In almost all of them he laid emphasis on the golden rule as a
way of solving social and personal problems. He became, in fact,
something of a preacher, just as his mother had wished him to be. So
his life from then on, in this respect, was a kind of victory for Sophia,
with her legacy, like those of the others, now coming into clearer view.

Yet he did not become otherworldly or reclusive, any more than had
his mother. He enjoyed being with others and was almost always
genial. In many ways he was more active than ever, physically and
mentally. He did much more reading for pleasure, as well as for self-

improvement, than ever·before. With Mrs. Herron, whose son-in-law, William Howard Taft, Hayes considered "a fine young fellow," he carried on a pleasant correspondence concerning literature.

They agreed to engage in a Chautauqua course together, reading the same books and exchanging comments. They wrote each other letters reminiscent of those he used to exchange with his sister Fanny about books. They started, at his suggestion, with Emerson, "my ancient favorite." "He deals wisely, I think, with the deep questions—with God, the soul, our present and future well-being." [8]

6

A few years back he had begun to express ideas about labor, capital, plutocracy and monopoly that must have seemed shocking to some wealthy men who had supported him as President and hailed his policies for their conservatism. In a Toledo talk in March 1886 he said that "free government cannot long endure if property is largely in a few hands and large masses of people are unable to earn homes, education, and a support in old age." [9]

It was then that he started to do some extensive reading, for the first time, in this field, making up at last for the gaps left by his Kenyon and Harvard education. He was impressed by Henry George's *Progress and Poverty* for the way the book described, he noted in his diary, "the rottenness of the present system." [10] He did not think the country was ready for George's remedy, the single tax on land. But he began to feel that changes in laws regulating corporations were needed and also some to limit inheritances.

Even earlier he had said in his diary: "We ought not to allow a permanent aristocracy of inherited wealth to grow up in our country." He thought that perhaps no one should get by inheritance more than $500,000—that the balance should go to the State.[11] By 1888 he was writing: "Vast accumulations of wealth in a few hands are hostile to labor. Their tendency is to break down fair competition, to build up monopoly, to corrupt politics, to bribe conventions, legislative bodies, courts and juries, to debauch society; and churches are not beyond the reach of their baneful influence." [12]

7

As time went on he became not less interested in such matters but more interested. Indeed, his mind seemed to be more resilient than ever. Curiously, perhaps under the influence of Howells, who was then busy stirring interest of Americans in the writings of Tolstoi, as well as beginning to produce novels of his own with strong social viewpoints, he began to consider himself a nihilist. After reading one of Howells' novels, *Annie Kilburn,* he approvingly wrote in his diary:

It opens the democratic side of the coming questions. I do not find a ready word for the doctrine of true equality of rights. Its foes call it nihilism, communism, socialism, and the like, Howells would perhaps call it justice. It is the doctrine of the Declaration of Independence, and of the Sermon on the Mount. But what is a proper and *favorable* word or phrase to designate it? [13]

He finally decided on nihilism, saying in 1890:

I use it to mean all opinions tending to show the wrong and evils of the money-piling tendency of our country, which is changing laws, government, and morals and giving all power to the rich and bringing in pauperism and its attendant crimes and wretchedness like a flood. Lincoln was for a government of the people. The new tendency is "a government of the rich, by the rich, and for the rich," The man who sees this and is opposed to it, I call a "nihilist." [14]

Mark Twain's books became favorites, especially as he considered some of them not merely humorous but, like Howells', "nihilistic." [15]

He took a kind of pride in possessing his own "nihilistic" views, and began incorporating some of them, though cautiously, even into speeches to the Loyal Legion.[16] In his talks on crime he now emphasized that the problem was not merely personal but social, one that grew largely out of poverty. "Abolish plutocracy if you would abolish poverty," he would say.

In Boston he gave a talk to the National Prison Congress which he described as "a little communistic in its tendency, the 'privileged class' will say." But he had a defense—he had done no more, he said, than to quote "such high authorities" as the revered Whig, the political hero of his youth—Daniel Webster! [17]

8

There was stuff here to be pondered. For a seemingly surprising fact was this—between the 1840s, when he was a student at Harvard and disciple of Story and worshiper of Webster, and the 1880s, when he was an ex-President of the United States, he, Rutherford B. Hayes, American of Americans, a founder of the Republican Party, had not only departed from Whiggery as it was understood (perhaps incorrectly), but also laid himself open to being called socialistic, along with Howells and Mark Twain.

But perhaps, after all, this was not surprising. A new stirring was manifest in the land, and Hayes and his people had been involved in every great stirring. This new one was reminiscent of the stirring to abolish slavery, with a new kind of "abolitionism" being preached— abolition of poverty.

Nor was this being done, as some publicists professed to believe, only by a few poor foreigners, mainly German immigrants, who called themselves not nihilists but anarchists, philosophical or otherwise, and became involved in the shocking Haymarket bomb episode in Chicago in May 1886. Many of the "best people" were enlisted, or enlisting, in a new crusade, one against poverty and against certain obvious crudities of the "new capitalism" that had developed after the war, crudities that Hayes, Howells, Mark Twain and others lumped as plutocracy.

Not all of the "best people," to be sure, were in the crusade. Many were against it, or unconcerned. Medill's *Tribune* in Chicago, Reid's *Tribune* in New York, also Dana's *Sun* and other Democratic as well as Republican journals represented the thinking of many who considered strikers "tramps" or hopelessly evil folk, to be exterminated ruthlessly. John Hay, one of Lincoln's secretaries, later Secretary of State, came out, though anonymously, with a novel, *The Breadwinners*, which seemed to imply that labor agitation menaced the stability of America and the agitators should be treated as enemies of the State.

Hay's novel was widely praised—Henry Adams, his intimate friend, especially liked it. But so also were Howells' novels. Indeed, large numbers of the former Abolitionists and early Republicans were concerned now about "industrial slavery." Wendell Phillips was one, though not Henry Ward Beecher, who about this time would suggest that a man who complained of not being able to support his family on one dollar a day, was not "fit to live." [18]

Also concerned was former U. S. Senator Lyman Trumbull of Illinois, founder of the Anti-Nebraska Party, who received his nomination for Senator in place of Lincoln and authored the Thirteenth Amendment. Trumbull's concern over plutocracy was so great that it switched him, elder statesman of the Republican Party, over to the

Populists, making him even more "radical" than Democratic Governor John Peter Altgeld of Illinois, a new type of leader, the "eagle forgotten" who in 1893 was to pardon three unhanged members of the Haymarket anarchist group—with the ardent approval of Howells especially.

A number of founding Republicans saw a disturbing likeness between the intensity of the emotional hatred for anarchists and socialists and the hatred in the 1850s for the Abolitionists. For example, the Illinois Republican "war governor," Richard J. Oglesby, an intimate of Lincoln, saw, or thought he saw, an important point about the Haymarket case. If the interpretation of conspiracy, a form of "guilt by association" concept that had been used to justify the hanging of the Haymarket anarchists, had been applied also, he said, in the case of John Brown, all of the Abolitionists in America and most of the Republican Party leaders might also have been hanged, he, Hayes and Lincoln included.[19]

9

These early Republicans, indeed, were intensely disturbed about the kind of America they saw in the 1880s and early 1890s. Actually this new America was the one that had been churning its way up since the days of Hayes's ancestors in the old valley, an inevitable product of the industrial revolution that had brought most of Hayes's people from England in the first instance.

They recognized the wonderfully good things about the new America. The new America was a land of freedom, certainly in law, for all, blacks as well as whites. It was big, and rich, despite the baffling amount of poverty that Henry George and Hayes especially noted. It was strong. Soon it would be strong enough to do what England had failed to accomplish in the War of Jenkins' Ear—knock Spain entirely out of the Western Hemisphere, with Hayes's son Webb showing up as a victorious soldier, along with Theodore Roosevelt's son, Theodore, Junior, on the same island of Cuba on which Daniel Austin had been held so ignominiously as a prisoner of Spain.

Hayes himself was one of the architects of this new America, indirectly at first, and later directly, as President. Oddly it was the Fourteenth Amendment, the second "freedom amendment" to the Constitution, passed with his help, that was blamed by many legal students for the ability of plutocracy to run rampant, as charged. For when the Supreme Court in a case in which Conkling appeared as counsel held that the clause, "Nor shall any State deprive any person of life, liberty, or property without due process of law, nor deny to any person under its jurisdiction the equal protection of the laws," applied to corporations as well as to Negroes and other citizens, the states for a long time afterward were helpless, it was thought, to exercise such control over corporations that even conservatives deemed wise. In short, due process in this theory became a tool of double purpose, one that cut some shackles and put on others, both in the name of freedom. It would be years before the courts and Congress would be able to get around that unexpected interpretation even partially.[20]

The "divine war" and Northern victory had speeded up the process of industrialization, just as the Southern leaders feared. Indeed, the Southern leaders had warned against many of the harsh aspects that industrialization brought, including the so-called wage slavery of free workingmen in factories. In the light of the numerous strikes, especially on the railroads, and the festering labor question in general in the 1880s, the old Southerners had some reason to feel that their warnings had been grimly justified. The North had brought all this on itself and the whole nation, they felt. Some believed it was all deserved retribution for having upset the old ways, including slavery.

10

But Hayes, as well as many fellow Republicans, no more condoned the uglier results of the new industrialization than did the ante-bellum Southerners, or the underpaid Northern workers, most of these representing a new wave of immigration from Europe. He was frankly dismayed.

Also dismayed was David Davis, the Lincoln appointee to the Supreme Court, who had resigned in time to avoid acting on the electoral commission. For in 1881 Davis wrote to a Kansas friend that the "growth of monopolies" made it appear to him that "free institutions are to be doomed to be substituted by an oligarchy resting upon the bases of money and of corporate power." [21] And he perhaps more than any other individual had helped Lincoln become elected President in 1860.

Hayes was not sure that the remedy was Tolstoian or Howellsian socialism. But he bent that way, though ambivalently and cautiously, as usual. In this, too, he was being typical of his time and of his social group; not typical of the new capitalists, to be sure, but of the old class of genteel, educated Americans who, like the old landed Tories of England, did not like plutocracy, or commercialism, as Emerson called it, much more than out-and-out socialists did.

Naturally, he was not "ultra" on this, any more than he was "ultra" on the past Abolitionism. Besides, the socialism that he studied, at least sympathetically, was not the European type which Karl Marx, not so long ago a part-time correspondent for the New York *Tribune*, expounded. Hayes and the others equated the doctrines they studied, or pushed, with old-fashioned American ideas of democracy—a word he began to use more and more—Jeffersonian ideas such as those held by the nearly hanged Austin ancestor involved in Shays' Rebellion in Massachusetts, near "ye Great River" of the old valley.

11

Had he lived on, he might have played a role in the shaping of one more division, even schism, in the modern Republican Party, one related to the Liberal Republican split of 1872. This new division was to be one between a new breed of "stalwarts" and a new breed of "liberals," a split on economic and social outlook to become sharply manifest by 1912 in the Bull Moose movement led by the son of the Roosevelt named by Hayes as Arthur's successor in the New York Customhouse fight with Conkling. It was to continue within the party for at least another four decades, breaking out violently again in the 1920s under Robert M. LaFollette, Sr., James Couzens, George W. Norris and other so-called Progressives, and still again in the 1950s under President Eisenhower. Where Lincoln, the patron saint of the party, might have stood in this split was something for the party leaders to wonder about, perhaps. But Hayes's position would have been clearly predictable.

However, there was no role for him in this new party development. The time for his passing had come to him, as it had come to Daniel Austin back in 1804.

CHAPTER LXXV

"Shoving On to the End!"

1

In APRIL 1890 he made one of his few purely pleasure trips, going with daughter Fanny to Bermuda for a two-week visit with his sister's daughter, Emily, and her husband, General Russell Hastings, who had a flower-bulb plantation there. In the following June he was in Kansas for the Loyal Legion. In a letter to William Henry Smith in September 1890 he indicated the pace he was keeping: "I go to West Virginia reunion next week at Parkersburg; to National Prison Congress, Cincinnati, the week after; and the following week Peabody in New York; 13th and 16th of October, Indianapolis and St. Louis, Loyal Legion."

About that time he began feeling some symptoms of vertigo. One night he felt so uncomfortable that, as he conscientiously noted in his diary, he took a "small" glass of sauterne, though he "paid" for this lapse from teetotalism by being wakeful half the night, finally getting up to set down more recollections of Lucy.[1] But it did not occur to him to relax.

In November 1891, just after he had turned sixty-nine, he embarked on a tour of the South with son Rutherford and his old Harvard classmate, J.L.M. Curry, whom he had made general agent of both the Peabody and Slater funds. His purpose was to see for himself the condition of Southern schools and what use was being made of the fund's appropriations. In less than three weeks he covered much of the states of South Carolina, Georgia, Alabama, Mississippi, Louisiana and Tennessee, making many talks on the old theme that education, liberally supported, would solve the peculiar problems of the South.

It was like an election campaign tour, and he received the same kind of exhilaration from it that he had in the days when he was running for Congress or governor. There was no doubt that he was especially pleased that political leaders treated him with particular deference as a "friend of the South." [2] To a friend shortly after he was back home he wrote: "Busy as ever—busier! Shoving on to the end! The

519

trip South gratified me. The corner seems to be turned. Reaction, 'second sober thought,' seems to be on my side." [3]

2

He referred in that last sentence to favorable notices in the press about himself and even his administration. "An abundance of friendly comment comes to me these days. The stream of abuse has gone by," he noted in his diary. He was especially delighted that, in his absence, on motion of a *Democrat* and with the approval of a board on which a majority were Democrats, a new building at Ohio State University was to be called Hayes Hall.[4]

In January 1892 he presided at a ceremony which, though pleasant, was one more forceful reminder that he was of another generation. This was the inauguration of McKinley as governor of Ohio. McKinley—already being mentioned for President—had been his young aide in the war!

No wonder in his diary from then on he set down more frequent comments about feelings of old age. He hoped, he wrote, that he would live at least until he was seventy.

Such thoughts led him to note with great satisfaction the way his sons had showed that they could make their way. Birchard was doing quite well with his law practice in Toledo, and in 1890 had had another son, called Webb Cook II. Hayes received much pleasure from the new little boy and his elder brother. In Cleveland Webb Cook I, Hayes's own son, was showing himself to be a good business-man; also Rutherford, in the bank. Young Scott went to Cincinnati in January 1892 to start a business career, working with the Thompson-Houston Electric Company there, with which Webb had been associated in Cleveland.

Hayes was glad none of the sons was interested in a political career. He discouraged any such interest—again like his mother.[5]

3

In the following September, the month before his seventieth birth-day, he debated whether he should march in the parade of a mam-moth soldiers' reunion in Washington, or ride in a carriage, or be just a reviewer. He decided to march—as he had back in 1865, during the great end-of-the-war parade. Perhaps what really showed that he was aging in spirit was his intense gratitude for the applause of approval that his marching provoked.[6]

But he still shoved on. The attendance at funerals, the speeches, the conferences, the trustee meetings, continued as though to keep himself so busy that he would have no time to reflect on his loneliness. There was no doubt that he was a lonely figure, for all the pleasure he received from his daughter and his sons and associates, lonely for Lucy, lonely for the many departed comrades.

Once again he seemed like the boy Rud Hayes, for whom "all the folks were gone." "Poor, dear man!" a young girl cousin, who adored him, said of him.[7]

He accepted more responsibilities, such as the presidency of the Ohio Archaeological and Historical Society. In October 1892 he took Fanny and Rutherford to the dedication of the Columbian Exposition in Chicago. Cries of "Hayes! Hayes!" from the people in the crowd there who recognized him gave him a thrill.

4

He began this new year, 1893, however, with an unusual weariness of spirit, for him. His beard was as white as the snow that covered Spiegel Grove. On Sunday, January 8, he drove in a sleigh to the cemetery to visit Lucy's grave. "My feeling was one of longing to be quietly resting in a grave by her side," he wrote that evening in his diary.

The next day he went to Columbus for a board meeting of Ohio State University. He remained there two days, visiting Billy Rogers among others. He called on Governor McKinley. He talked with the secretary of the university board, Alexis Cope, about the choice of a director of manual training, the courses in this to be given at Hayes Hall, and offered to interview a candidate for the post in Cleveland.

When he started for the depot to get his train for Cleveland, Cope went along to carry his bag, although Hayes "protested that the weather was very cold," and that the younger man "must not think of going." But Cope insisted. "He took my arm [Cope recalled] and we walked to the station together. Arriving there, we found his train a half hour late. He proposed that we take a cup of coffee, so we climbed onto the high stools in the luncheon room and had our coffee." He "seemed to be nervously depressed and anxious for companionship," Cope recalled. He talked "of his early life . . . of his father's death . . ." of Sardis.[8]

5

In Cleveland he went to the Linus Austin home on Prospect Street. This was a kind of second home to him, though the cousin, Linus, had been dead several years. Mrs. Austin was attached to him, and Webb lived there. The next day, though there was a deep snow and the temperature was near zero, he went about his duties on foot and by streetcar—hunting up the manual-training instructor and visiting Western Reserve University. With Webb he went to the station on Saturday, January 14, to get a train for Fremont. At the station he was attacked by a severe pain in the chest, one that reminded him, he said later, of the wound at South Mountain.

Some brandy relieved him. Webb suggested that he return to the Austin home, but he insisted on taking the train for Fremont, Webb going along. "I would rather die at Spiegel Grove than to live any-where else," he said.

At the Grove he was immediately put to bed. His physician was optimistic at first, feeling that complete rest would restore his "over-worked heart." "This is almost impossible," Webb wrote on January 16 to Mrs. Austin. "Father has not been confined to his bed since he was badly wounded at South Mountain . . . and he does not recognize the necessity and is very restless."

At times he spoke of plans for the future, of another trip to the South, this one to include another visit to Texas to see Guy Bryan. Yet, he seemed to know that it would not happen so. "I know I am going where Lucy is," he said.

At eleven o'clock on the night of January 17, 1893, he died. Of moving significance was the fact that Grover Cleveland attended the funeral at snow-covered Spiegel Grove—Sardis' grove of buckeye trees. That was something that would have gratified Hayes especially. For Cleveland was then the undisputed titular head of the Democratic Party of the United States. He had made the journey to Spiegel Grove in his roles both as former President, the first Democrat elected to the office since Buchanan, and as the Democratic President-elect to take office in March 1893. By this gracious and statesmanlike act—"He was coming to see me, but he is dead and I will go to him"[9]—Cleveland made it clear that the Democrats had officially called to an end the once bitter propaganda that Hayes had not been "entitled" to the office in that hectic term, 1877-1881, which by then seemed so long ago—almost as long ago as the dispute over Jefferson's title to the office in Daniel Austin's time.

Cleveland's standing beside the coffin put an end, so far as any human act could, to the unhappy dispute over the 1876 election. So there was more peace for Hayes at the last than anyone could have imagined.

Fittingly, by his own previous arrangement, there was placed over his—and Lucy's—grave a simple monument made of granite brought from Dummerston—the town in the Green Mountains from which his mother and father had come to settle in the "far distant land" of Ohio.

NOTES

CHAPTER I

Lonely Little Boy

[1] RBH, "Recollections of My Sister Fanny," 1856, MSS. in Hayes Memorial Library (HML), reproduced in part in *Diary and Letters of Rutherford Birchard Hayes,* ed. by Charles R. Williams, I, 4-12.

[2] Sophia Hayes to Roger Birchard, May 14, 1826.

[3] Sophia Hayes to Sardis Birchard, March 27, 1847.

[4] Sophia Hayes to Dyar Bancroft, September 26, 1824.

[5] RBH, "Recollections, etc." *op. cit.,* 5.

[6] *Ibid.*

[7] RBH to Fanny Hayes Platt, June 4, 1854.

[8] RBH *Diary* (Williams), IV, 170; Sophia Hayes Diary, HML, October 6, 1863.

[9] RBH *Diary* (Williams), III, 556.

[10] Sophia Hayes to Dyar Bancroft, September 26, 1824.

CHAPTER II

The Endless Search

[1] Sophia Hayes to Austin and Roger Birchard, September 3, 1825.

[2] RBH *Diary* (Williams), IV, 134, 590.

[3] *Ibid.,* I, 4; IV, 170; and *History of Delaware,* 503.

[4] Sophia Hayes to Roger Birchard, May 14, 1826.

[5] *Ibid.*

[6] Sophia Hayes Diary, December 30, 1863; Henry Crocker, *History of the Baptists in Vermont,* 211, 429.

[7] Sophia Hayes to Roger Birchard, May 14, 1826; Henry Bushnell, "History of Granville," in Henry Howe, *Historical Collections of Ohio,* (1907), II, 79-80.

[8] Sophia Hayes to Roger Birchard, May 14, 1826.

[9] RBH, "Recollections," *op. cit.,* 7; RBH to Fanny Hayes, February 5, 1839, in *Diary* (Williams), I, 29.

[10] RBH, "Recollections," *op. cit.,* 5.

[11] RBH *Diary* (Williams), I, 515.

[12] William Dean Howells, *Sketch of the Life and Character of Rutherford B. Hayes,* 6-9; see also Mildred Howells, *Life in Letters of William Dean Howells,* I, 222-223.

[13] RBH, "Recollections," *op. cit.*

[14] RBH *Diary* (Williams), IV, 590; V, 46.

CHAPTER III

Sardis

[1] RBH Diary, MSS., 4, 94a; U.S. passport issued to Sardis Birchard, September 29, 1840.

[2] Rutherford Hayes, Jr., to Austin Birchard, 1820-1821, HML. J. Fletcher Brennan, ed., *A Biographical Encyclopedia and Portrait Gallery of Distinguished Men* [of Ohio], probably the best single account of Sardis Birchard, edited by RBH himself. Also Horace S. Knapp, *History of the Maumee Valley*.

[3] RBH Diary, MSS., 4, August 1, 1851.

[4] *Ibid.*, 4, 95a.

[5] Sophia Hayes to Dyar Bancroft, September 26, 1824.

[6] RBH *Diary* (Williams), III, 161-162; also Knapp, *op. cit.*, 518.

[7] Sophia Hayes to Sardis Birchard, May 9, 1835.

[8] Sophia Hayes to Austin Birchard, May 11, 1821.

[9] Henry Howe, *op. cit.*, I, 483; II, 885ff.

[10] Knapp, *op. cit.*, 518.

[11] Marquis James, *Andrew Jackson, The Border Captain*, 337.

[12] RBH *Diary* (Williams), III, 165-166.

[13] *Ibid.*

[14] RBH, "Recollections," *op. cit.*, 4; RBH, Address, June 24, 1876, in Russell H. Conwell, *Life and Public Services of Gov. Rutherford B. Hayes,* 196; RBH to C. W. Torrey, February 10, 1882; Delaware Court of Common Pleas, entry of April 22, 1834.

[15] RBH Diary, MSS., 4, 97.

[16] Sophia Hayes to Austin and Roger Birchard, September 3, 1825; July 21, 1827.

[17] Sophia Hayes to Austin Birchard, May 11, 1821.

CHAPTER IV

The Scorching Fire

[1] Sophia Hayes to Austin and Roger Birchard, September 3, 1825; July 21, 1827; her diary, March 2, 1864

[2] Sophia Hayes to Austin and Roger Birchard, September 3, 1825; July 21, 1827.

[3] RBH to Fanny Hayes Platt, August 8, 1847, in *Diary* (Williams), I, 212.

[4] Sophia Hayes to Austin and Roger Birchard, July 21, 1827; to Sardis Birchard, March 4, 1858; also her diary, October 23, 1863.

[5] Sophia Hayes to RBH, July 20, 1839.

[6] Sophia Hayes to Sardis Birchard, July 31, 1849.

[7] Organization minutes of Branch Bible Society Auxiliary, written down by Sophia Hayes; also account book 1835.

[8] Deeds, etc., 1823-1828, Sophia Hayes Papers, HML.

[9] Sandusky *Gazette*, April 24, 1822.

[10] *History of Delaware*, 343.

[11] Wilbur H. Siebert Papers on the Underground Railroad, III, Ohio Archaeological and Historical Society, Columbus, Ohio.

[12] Letters of Fanny Hayes Platt to RBH, her brother, contain good analyses, especially February 3, March 3, 1849.

[13] Sophia Hayes to Emily Trowbridge Hayes, August 13, 1852.

[14] Sophia Hayes Diary, July 16, 1864; RBH *Diary* (Williams), III, 212; also Conwell, *op. cit.*, 43-45, who interviewed Arcena Smith in 1876.

[15] *Ibid.*

[16] Sophia Hayes to RBH, March 1856.

¹⁷ Sophia Hayes to RBH, July 20, 1855; *ibid.,* to Austin and Roger Birchard, July 21, 1827.

CHAPTER V

Progenitor

¹ RBH *Diary* (Williams), III, 217.

² Hezekiah Spencer Sheldon, *Documentary History of Suffield in the Colony and Province of the Massachusetts Bay, in New England, 1660-1749;* RBH *Diary* (Williams), I, 561.

³ See for references to Shays men in the area the "History of the Wilmington Reunion," 47, 49-51; Hamilton Childs, *Gazetteer and Business Directory of Windham County, Vermont, 1724-1884;* John Stetson Barry, *History of Massachusetts,* 227-229; Josiah G. Holland, *History of Western Massachusetts,* I, 285. Also David M. Ludlum, *Social Ferment in Vermont, 1791-1850;* Chilton Williamson, *Vermont in Quandary, 1763-1825;* Lewis D. Stilwell, *Migration from Vermont;* also Timothy Dwight, *Travels in New England and New York, 1796-1815.*

⁴ The Austin Family of Suffield," MSS. in the Connecticut Historical Society; RBH, Genealogical Memorandum on the Austins, HML; Frances M. Caulkins, *History of Norwich,* 436; William Chauncey Fowler, *History of Durham, Connecticut,* 211ff., 288; Eugene C. Barker, *The Life of Stephen F. Austin, Founder of Texas,* 1-3.

⁵ RBH, Genealogical Memorandum, HML; also Sophia B. Wasson to RBH March 8, 1870; *Records of the Congregational Church in Suffield;* RBH *Diary* (Williams), I, 561.

⁶ See Ludlum, *op. cit.;* also Crocker *op. cit.;* and Russell Streeter, *Mirror of Calvinistic Fanaticism, or Jedediah Birchard & Co.*

⁷ *Colonial Records of Connecticut, 1735-43,* VIII, 295ff., 316, 324, 461; Sylvester Judd, *History of Hadley,* 342; also John Tate Lanning, "The American Colonies in the Preliminaries of the War of Jenkins' Ear," *Georgia Historical Quarterly,* XI, No. 2 (June 1927), 131ff. Also RBH *Diary* (Williams), III, 217, quoting Daniel Austin, a grandson; and *The Adventures of Roderick Random,* Oxford edition (1930), 233.

⁸ Lanning, *op. cit.,* 199, the Austin descendant at Cuba later (1898) was Webb C. Hayes, I.

⁹ RBH *Diary* (Williams), III, 217.

¹⁰ *Records of the Congregational Church in Suffield,* 55, 125; RBH, Genealogical Memorandum, *op. cit.*

¹¹ *Connecticut Historical Society, Collections,* IX; the French-Indian War Rolls, 1755-1757, I, 245. Also *Collections of Massachusetts Historical Society,* VII, first series, I, 245; "History of the Wilmington Reunion," 21-24.

¹² Suffield, Connecticut, town records; Jesse Fowler Smith to author, April 19, 1951.

¹³ Oliver S. Phelps and Andrew T. Servin, *The Phelps Family in America and Their English Ancestors,* I, 118, 204; also Noah A. Phelps, *History of Symsbury, Granby and Canton,* 94-95.

¹⁴ *Record of Connecticut Men in the War of the Revolution,* 549, 575.

¹⁵ Sophia Birchard Hayes to RBH, November 8, 1863.

¹⁶ See George Richards Minot, *The History of the Insurrections in Massachusetts in the Year 1786 and the Rebellion Consequent Thereon;* also Hol

land, *op. cit.*; Ralph Volney Harlow, *Samuel Adams, Promoter of the American Revolution*; Chard Powers Smith, *The Housatonic, Puritan River*, 192ff.; Edward Bellamy, *The Duke of Stockbridge*, a fact-based novel; A. Burnham, *History of Brattleboro, Vermont*, 91-92.

[17] Massachusetts *Centinel*, April 11, 1787.

[18] *Record of Service of Connecticut Men in the War of the Revolution*, 511-513, 647; *Massachusetts Soldiers and Sailors of the Revolutionary War*, 360; "The Austin Family of Suffield," *op. cit.*; the town records of Suffield.

[19] *Indictment and Finding in the Matter of Nathaniel Austin, et al.*, 1787 volume, 58, Supreme Judicial Court, Boston.

[20] *Ibid.*; see also Holland, *op. cit.*, I, 284; Massachusetts *Independent Chronicle and Advertiser*, May 10, 1787.

[21] "Warrant of Reprieve for Peter Wilcox and Nathaniel Austin to Caleb Hyde, Esq., Sheriff of Berkshire County, by John Hancock, Governor and Commander in Chief," in *ibid.*, June 28, 1787; also Joseph Parker Warren, "The Shays Rebellion," Ph.D. thesis, in Harvard University Library, 1902, II, 30ff.

[22] Oliver Phelps and Servin, *op. cit.*, 189-190.

[23] *Records of the Congregational Church in Suffield*; Childs, *op. cit.*, 304 (95).

CHAPTER VI

Young Sophia

[1] Dwight, *op. cit.*, IV, 457.

[2] RBH *Diary* (Williams), I, 568.

[3] Sophia Hayes to RBH, June 2, 1839.

[4] Sophia Hayes Diary, September 12, 1846.

[5] Mary Birchard, Fayetteville, Vermont, to RBH, February 1, 1871; also Rev. K. B. Glidden, Mansfield Centre, Connecticut, to RBH, November 14, 1882; RBH *Diary* (Williams), I, 561; III, 139.

[6] RBH, "Notes on Conversation with Uncle Austin Birchard, in Wilmington, July 14, 1871," HML.

CHAPTER VII

Young Ruddy and the Clan of Hayes

[1] RBH Diary, MSS., 4, 94a-95; also John Humphrey Noyes, "Memoir of John Noyes," *The Dartmouth*, September 3, 1877, 55.

[2] Conwell, *op. cit.*, 30-31. Conwell interviewed, among others, Clarissa Hayes Moody, a sister.

[3] RBH Scrapbook 6, 57, HML.

[4] John Humphrey Noyes, "Memoir," *op. cit.*, September 20, 1877, 38, and September 27, 54.

[5] Janette Elliott Keeler, a granddaughter, Reminiscences, MSS., HML.

[6] Genealogy section in Judd, *op. cit.*

[7] Janette Elliott Keeler, *op. cit.*, 17; H. S. Noyes to RBH, January 14 1871; RBH, Genealogical Book, 70; RBH Diary, MSS., 93a.

[8] Charles Wells Hayes, *George Hayes of Windsor and His Descendants*

[9] Benjamin Trumbull, *A Complete History of Connecticut*, I, 483; James L Kingsley, "A Sketch of the History of Yale College in Connecticut," *American Quarterly Register*, VIII. 14-15; John L. Sibley, *Harvard Graduates*, III, 236

[10] Henry R. Stiles, *History of Ancient Wethersfield*, I, 139-140.

[11] *Ibid.*, 158-163; also *Colonial Records of Connecticut*, L, 319; Alonzo B. Chapin, *Glastenbury for Two Hundred Years*, 13; and John Farmer, "Memoirs of Ministers Who Have Been Graduated at Harvard College," *American Quarterly Register*, VII.

[12] Holland, *op. cit.*, II; also Judd, *op. cit.*, 190, 164, 169, 170.

[13] "Humble Petition of the Inhabitants of the Town of Hadley, to the General Court of Massachusetts, April 25, 1665," in Judd, *op. cit.*, 81-82.

[14] Ezra Stiles, *A History of Three of the Judges of King Charles I*; Edward E. Atwater, *History of the Colony of New Haven to Its Absorption into Connecticut*, 435-443; Farmer, *op. cit.* In 1676, presumably before the Falls Fight, one of the regicides, Goffe, supposedly came out of the Russell cellar one Sabbath day to save the town of Hadley from an Indian attack, an incident which Sir Walter Scott tells in his novel, *Peveril of the Peak*, and which James Fenimore Cooper also used in *Wept of Wish-ton-Wish*, and on which Nathaniel Hawthorne based the hero of his short story, "The Gray Champion."

[15] Henry Howe to RBH, April 29, 1879.

[16] W. R. Trowbridge, *The Trowbridge Family*.

[17] Charles Wells Hayes, *George Hayes of Windsor*, *op. cit.*, 19.

[18] Chloe Smith Hayes Diary, MSS., October 3, 1840, 2-4; also Hayes Bigelow Papers, Brattleboro.

[19] Chloe Smith Hayes Diary; E. B. O'Callaghan, *The Documentary History of the State of New York*, IV, 981; B. B. Hall, *History of Eastern Vermont*, II, 339, 723.

[20] O'Callaghan, *op. cit.*, IV, 764-765. See also Hall, *op. cit.*, 937.

[21] *Collections of Vermont Historical Society*, II, 197.

[22] Petition to Governor Chittenden, in *ibid.*, 406.

[23] Chloe Smith Hayes to Fanny Hayes, September 10, 1817.

CHAPTER VIII

The Connecticut Yankee

[1] Richard L. Pease, "The Burchards of Edgarton, Martha's Vineyard, Massachusetts," memorandum MSS. prepared for President R. B. Hayes, 1878, in HML, Scrapbook 17; C. J. Hoadley, "The Birchard Family," a memorandum prepared for Governor R. B. Hayes, 1873, MSS. in HML; Caulkins, *History of Norwich*, *op. cit.*, 61, 73, 165-167; Samuel G. Drake, *Result of Some Researches Among the British Archives for Information Relative to the Founders of New England*, 42.

[2] The approximate dating of Roger Birchard's birth is fixed from the fact that on his death, August 22, 1805, he was "47 years & 8 mos." old, RBH Diary, 4, 97a; also 10, 69a; R. W. Storrs, town clerk, to C. L. Beckwith, April 16, 1879, HML.

[3] Rev. K. B. Glidden to RBH, December 18, 1876; the marriage took place January 25, 1758, according to R. W. Storrs to C. L. Beckwith, grandson of Elias, April 16, 1879, HML. Also correspondence between RBH and Bradley M. Sears, town clerk, December 28, 1870, and Charles J. Hoadley, Connecticut State Librarian, December 24, 1870; also Rev. K. B. Glidden to RBH, November 14, 1882; RBH Diary, MSS., 10, 70; RBH *Diary* (Williams), III, 58.

⁴ RBH to Mary Birchard, February 5, 1871.

⁵ Henry Reed Stiles, *Bundling, Its Origin, Process and Decline in America* (Albany, 1869), 107; also his *History and Genealogies of Ancient Windsor, Connecticut*, I.

⁶ *Record of Service of Connecticut Men in I, The War of the Revolution; II, War of 1812; III, Mexican War,* Compiled by Authority of the General Assembly, Hartford, 1889, 54, 103, 566; also K. B. Glidden, "Centennial Discourse," First Congregational Church, Mansfield Centre, July 1876, Willimantic, Connecticut, 25.

⁷ Glidden, *op. cit.*, 23-25

⁸ *Record of Service of Connecticut Men, op. cit.*, 53, 58.

⁹ RBH, "Notes on Conversation," *op. cit.*, HML; *Record of Service of Connecticut Men, op. cit.*, 152, 638.

¹⁰ RBH *Diary* (Williams), I, 561, and "Notes on Conversation," *op. cit.*

¹¹ Town of Wilmington Records, Book I, 2, 39.

¹² RBH, Genealogical Book, 80; RBH Diary, MSS., 4, 98, quoting Sardis Birchard.

CHAPTER IX

Love in the Green Mountains

¹ Town of Wilmington Records, Book I, 115, entry of March 3, 1809.

² Brattleboro *Reporter*, May 3, 1806.

³ RBH *Diary* (Williams), III, 154; also deed from Lewis Joy to Drusilla Joy, April 19, 1810, HML.

⁴ David L. Mansfield, *History of the Town of Dummerston, Vt.*, 159.

⁵ RBH Diary, MSS., 4, 94a.

⁶ RBH *Diary* (Williams), I, 568.

⁷ Rutherford Hayes, Jr., to Sophia Birchard, May 30, 1813.

⁸ Sophia B. Wasson to RBH, March 8, 1870; RBH, memorandum dated June 18, 1871, HML.

⁹ Rutherford Hayes, Jr., to Sophia Birchard, May 10, 1812.

¹⁰ RBH Diary, MSS., 97a, quoting Sardis Birchard.

¹¹ RBH *Diary* (Williams), IV, 640; Certificate of Marriage, Town of Wilmington Records, Book I, 1813; Chloe Smith Hayes Diary, August 17, 1824.

CHAPTER X

War and Peace

¹ Rutherford Hayes, Jr., to Sophia Birchard, letters, 1811-1813.

² John Humphrey Noyes, "Memoir," *op. cit.*

³ Brattleboro *Reporter*, November 28, 1812, and January 9, 1813; see also S. G. Goodrich (Peter Parley), *Recollections of a Lifetime*, I, 447-451.

⁴ Brattleboro *Reporter*, January 23, 1813; also Mary Rogers Cabot, *Annals of Brattleboro, 1681-1895*, 329; and Harlow H. Ballard, "A Forgotten Fraternity," *Collections of the Berkshire Historical and Genealogical Society*, 1913; Certificates of W. B. Membership, Hayes Bigelow Papers, *op. cit.*

⁵ MSS. report of W. B. Society meeting at Newfane, December 13, 1814, in Vermont Historical Society.

⁶ Sophia Hayes to RBH, November 2, 1845.

⁷ Chloe Smith Hayes to Sophia Hayes, August 1, 1841.

8 Fanny Hayes Platt to her brother, RBH, July 10, 1849.

9 Chloe Smith Hayes to Sophia Hayes, August 1, 1841.

10 John Humphrey Noyes, "Memoir," *op. cit.*, September 27, October 4, 1877, 55.

11 *Ibid.*, October 4, 1877; excerpt from letters of John Noyes to Polly Hayes Noyes, April 6, 1816.

12 George W. Noyes, ed., *John Humphrey Noyes, The Putney Community*, 80; also Chloe Smith Hayes Diary, *op. cit.*

13 Brattleboro *Reporter*, January 28, 1814; Mansfield, *op. cit.*, 161; RBH Diary, MSS., 4, 94a.

14 Cabot, *op. cit.*, 325.

CHAPTER XI

To the Far-Distant Land

1 The *Portfolio*, January 1817, 57.

2 Charles Wells Hayes, *George Hayes of Windsor, op. cit.*

3 Chloe Smith Hayes Diary.

4 Barrows Mussey, "Yankee Chills, Ohio Fever," *New England Quarterly*, XXII (December 1949), 435ff.; also S. L. Vigilante, "Eighteen-Hundred-and Froze-to-Death: The Cold Summer of 1816 and Westward Migration from New England," *Bulletin of the New York Public Library*, LII (September 1948), 454-457; and Mansfield, *op. cit.*, 114.

5 Goodrich, *op. cit.*, II, 79.

6 Mansfield, *op. cit.*, 45ff.; O. L. Baskin, *History of Delaware County and Ohio*, 318.

7 M. H. Moore, "Ex-President Hayes—His Family in Vermont," Dubuque (Iowa) *Telegraph-Herald*, July 5, 1902.

8 Dummerston Township Records, I, 2, entry of deed from Rutherford Hayes, Jr., to John Noyes, June 11, 1817.

9 John Humphrey Noyes, "Memoir," *op. cit.*, October 4, 1877, 71.

10 Chloe Smith Hayes Diary, February 28, 1825; also Cabot, *op. cit.*, 203; and Vermont *Phoenix*, August 12, 1892.

11 RBH Diary, MSS., 4, 93-95.

12 Harlan Hatcher, *The Western Reserve*, 121.

13 Knapp, *op. cit.*, 532.

14 Ellery Bascom, Lower Sandusky, Ohio, July 1, 1834, first minister of the Presbyterian church there, original in Chicago Theological Seminary library; quoted in Colin Goodykoontz, *Home Missions of the American Frontier*, 191.

15 RBH Diary, MSS., 4, 94-95.

16 "Release of Mortgage, John Worline to Sophia Hayes," February 15, 1838, filed in Delaware, Ohio, County Recorder's Office, February 16, 1838, v. 16, 461; also v. 3, 871, original in HML.

17 *Ibid.*, also RBH Diary, MSS., 4, 94-95; *History of Delaware*, 382.

18 "The Hayes Memorial," article in RBH *Diary* (Williams), V, 456.

19 Chloe Smith Hayes Diary, February 28, 1825; William D. Howells, *op. cit.*, 10.

20 John Humphrey Noyes, "Memoir," *op. cit.*, September 27, 1877.

21 Sophia Hayes to Austin Birchard, May 11, 1821.

22 Inventory of the Estate of Rutherford Hayes, Jr., in HML.

23 RBH Diary, MSS., 4, 95.

[24] Conwell, *op. cit.*, 190. Also Sophia Hayes to Austin Birchard, May 11, 1821; G. Hollbrook to Sophia Hayes, November 11, 1828; Rutherford Hayes, Jr., to Russell Hayes, September 15, 1820.

[25] Sophia Hayes to Sardis Birchard, December 5, 1850.

[26] Rutherford Hayes, Jr., to Russell Hayes, September 16, 1820.

[27] Session Records of the United Congregations of the Presbyterian Church of Radnor, Liberty and Delaware, 1819-1835, in the First Presbyterian Church of Delaware, courtesy of Dr. Louis E. Campbell, minister, October 23, 1950.

[28] Sophia Hayes to Sardis Birchard, December 5, 1850.

CHAPTER XII

The Mother's Boy

[1] RBH *Diary* (Williams), IV, 590; III, 212; also *History of Delaware*, 332, 340. The present city of Delaware, seat of Ohio Wesleyan University, up to now has not been certain precisely where its most distinguished native was born. A memorial boulder, erected in the 1920s at a gasoline station, is in the wrong place. See "The Birthplace of President Hayes: A Study in Oral Tradition," by C. E. Van Sickle and James T. May, in *Ohio State Archaeological and Historical Quarterly*, v. 61, No. 2 (April 1952), 167.

[2] Session Records of the United Congregations of the Presbyterian Church of Radnor, Liberty and Delaware, *op. cit.*

[3] Conwell, *op. cit.*, 44-45; Sophia Hayes Diary, October 4, 1866.

[4] Webb C. Hayes I, Memorandum prepared for W. O. Stoddard with cooperation of RBH, in HML.

[5] RBH, "Recollections," *op. cit.*, 5-6.

[6] RBH *Diary* (Williams), V, 63; also II, 437-439. J. A. Howells, the Ashtabula (Ohio) *Sentinel*, January 22, 1893.

[7] RBH to Lucy Hayes, February 14, 1862.

[8] Copybooks, HML; William O. Stoddard, *Hayes, Garfield, Arthur*, 9.

[9] Conwell, *op. cit.*, 47; see also RBH to Clark Waggoner, *Diary* (Williams), III, 636.

[10] Sardis Birchard to Austin Birchard, April 22, 1827; Austin Birchard to Sophia Hayes, August 2, 1829

[11] Sardis Birchard to Roger Birchard from New York City, December 7, 8, 1826; also Brennan, *op. cit.*; and RBH, "Recollections," *op. cit.*, 7-8.

[12] *Ibid.*, 8.

[13] Sardis Birchard to Austin Birchard from New York, April 22, 1827.

[14] Sophia Hayes to Roger Birchard, September 20, 1820.

[15] Sophia Hayes to Austin and Roger Birchard, July 27, 1827.

[16] Sardis Birchard to Austin Birchard, April 22, 1827; RBH *Diary* (Williams), III, 161; Brennan, *op. cit.*; Sophia Hayes to Austin and Roger Birchard, November 4, 1830.

[17] RBH, "Recollections," *op. cit.*, 8.

[18] Letters of proposal to Sophia Hayes, 1824-1830, HML; also Sophia Hayes to Dyar Bancroft, September 26, 1824.

[19] Letter to "Mrs. Sophia Hayes," with salutation, "Madam," date and signature erased by her, but preserved in her papers, HML. Probably 1829.

[20] Copy made and kept by Sophia Hayes, dated Delaware, April 27, 1830, HML. She kept four written proposals from as many suitors, destroying the signature in each case.

²¹ *History of Delaware*, 494.
²² Austin Birchard to Sophia Hayes, September 28, 1822.
²³ Rutherford Hayes, Sr., to Sophia Hayes, May 25, 1824.
²⁴ Chloe Smith Hayes Diary, February 28, 1825.
²⁵ Sophia Hayes to Dyar Bancroft, September 26, 1824.
²⁶ Joseph Fessenden of Brattleboro to Sophia Hayes, August 19, 1822.
²⁷ Hatcher, *op. cit.*, 117; see also Samuel Rezneck, "The Depression of 1819-1822, A Social History," *American Historical Review*, XXXIX (October 1933), 28-47, 33, 35.
²⁸ Sophia Hayes to Dyar Bancroft, September 26, 1824.
²⁹ Chloe Smith Hayes, August 12, 17, 26, 1824.
³⁰ Sophia Hayes to Sardis Birchard, April 25, 1839.
³¹ RBH, "Recollections," *op. cit.*, 4.
³² Sophia Hayes to Dyar Bancroft, September 16, 1824.

CHAPTER XIII

Legacies

¹ RBH, "Recollections," *op. cit.*, 4.
² RBH to Sophia Hayes, October 23, 1853.
³ Sophia Hayes to RBH, December 31, 1849; January 22, 1865.
⁴ RBH *Diary* (Williams), I, 420.
⁵ Sophia Hayes to RBH, January 22, 1865.
⁶ RBH Diary, MSS., 4, 93a; also see J. Q. Howard, *The Life, Public Services and Select Speeches of Rutherford B. Hayes*, 13.
⁷ RBH *Diary* (Williams), III, 209; *History of Delaware*, 233.
⁸ Sophia Hayes Diary, September 4, 1863; *History of Delaware*, 396; also Cyrus Platt, "History of St. Peter's Episcopal Church, Delaware, Ohio," 5.
⁹ RBH *Diary* (Williams), III, 226.
¹⁰ RBH Diary, MSS., 4, 94a.
¹¹ RBH *Diary* (Williams), I, 61, 64, 90-91.
¹² June 23, July 9, 1839.

CHAPTER XIV

The Beloved Sister

¹ RBH to Guy Bryan, July 23, 1856.
² RBH, "Recollections," *op. cit.*, 7; also Sophia Hayes to RBH, November 1, 1838, April 30, 1939.
³ RBH, "Recollections," *op. cit.*, 7.
⁴ *Ibid.*, 11.
⁵ *Ibid.*
⁶ *Ibid.*
⁷ *Ibid.*; also W. D. Howells, *op. cit.*, 12.
⁸ Letters of Fanny Hayes Platt to RBH, HML, especially May 26, 1839; January 19, 1840; March 2, 1840; June 15, 1847.
⁹ Fanny Hayes Platt to RBH, July 20, 1852; February 3, 1849; RBH to Samuel Rheem, December 22, 1883, in *Diary* (Williams), IV, 134-135; *History of Delaware*, 327.
¹⁰ October 3, 1847.
¹¹ Fanny Hayes Platt to RBH, July 20, 1852.

¹² Fanny Hayes Platt to RBH, July 20, 1852; March 26, 1852; RBH *Diary* (Williams), I, 385.

¹³ Henry Trowbridge to RBH, March 28, 1870.

¹⁴ RBH to Clark Waggoner, January 7, 1881.

¹⁵ Sophia Hayes to RBH, October 6, 1838; February 14, 1841; Fanny Hayes to RBH, May 26, 1839.

CHAPTER XV

The Secret Burden

¹ RBH to Sardis Birchard, December 9, 1837; RBH *Diary* (Williams), I, 161.

² Sophia Hayes to Sardis Birchard, October 6, 1838.

³ RBH to Sophia Hayes, July 7, 1838.

⁴ A. R. Spofford, "R. B. Hayes, Beloved Son of Memory," 1893, MSS. of Cincinnati Literary Club talk, HML; also RBH to M. F. Force, April 18, 1871.

⁵ Janette Elliott Keeler, *op. cit.*, 11, 77; Lucy E. Keeler, "Recollections of My Mother," 1905, MSS. in HML.

⁶ RBH *Diary* (Williams), I, 47.

⁷ Address of General Roeliff Brinkerhoff, National Prison Association Congress, 1893, reproduced in RBH *Diary* (Williams), V, 195; also in Proceedings, 17; also RBH *Diary* (Williams), V, 111.

⁸ *Ibid.*; Brinkerhoff address, *op. cit.*; also Lucy Elliot Keeler Journal, IV, February 16, 1891, HML.

⁹ RBH, Genealogical Book, 71a, entry of April 18, 1872; also RBH *Diary* (Williams), V, 111.

¹⁰ August 10, 1845.

¹¹ June 11, 1851.

¹² Fanny Hayes Platt to RBH, December 1, 1845; also September 16, 1849.

CHAPTER XVI

The Ancestral Valley Beckons

¹ William Lang, *History of Seneca County, Ohio*, 133ff.; Knapp, *op. cit.*, 520-521.

² *Ibid.*, 520; also Fremont *Journal*, January 30, 1874; R. Dickinson, Jr., to Sardis Birchard, December 20, 1836; February 3, 15, 1838; March 15, 1840.

³ Sardis Birchard to Austin Birchard, April 22, 1827; also Knapp, *op. cit.*, 521.

⁴ William P. Dixon to Sardis Birchard, February 20, 1835. Agreement between Dixon and Sardis Birchard, June 20, 1835, HML; also Dixon to Sardis Birchard, October 9, November 17, 19, 1835; December 15, 1835; February 27, 1836.

⁵ *Ibid.*, August 24, 1835; August 26, 1836.

⁶ *Ibid.*, December 19, 1836; April 25, 1835; April 6, 1837; October 16, 1837; also February 3, 1837; November 3, 1839; July 7, August 24, 1840; January 23, 1842; July 22, 1843.

⁷ Lang, *op. cit.*, 133.

⁸ "Ebenezer Lane," *Ohio State Bar Association Proceedings*, I-IV.

⁹ Webb C. Hayes I, Memorandum for W. O. Stoddard, *op. cit.*; Lucy Elliot

Keeler Journal, December 30, 1890, quoting RBH; RBH *Diary* (Williams), III, 304; *History of Delaware*, 367.

[10] Sophia Hayes to Sardis Birchard, May 17, 1837; June 27, 1837.

[11] *Ibid.*, February 26, 1836.

[12] Sophia Hayes to Fanny Hayes, June 7, 1837.

[13] J. M. Barker, *History of Ohio Methodism*, 407; also *The Firelands Pioneer*, II, 46; VI, 66; *ibid.* (new series), 14-19, p. 1394; J. H. Pitezel, "History of the Methodist Episcopal Church of Norwalk, Ohio, and the Norwalk Seminary."

[14] Sophia Hayes to Sardis Birchard, March 26, 1836; May 1836.

[15] RBH to Sardis Birchard, June 21, 1836.

[16] *Ibid.*, September 20, October 13, 1836.

[17] Sophia Hayes to Sardis Birchard, July 1836.

[18] *Ibid.*, January 11, 1837.

[19] *Ibid.*, May 1, 1837.

[20] RBH to Sardis Birchard, September 18, 1838; RBH *Diary* (Williams), I, 16; Isaac Webb circular, March 24, 1840. The building burned down in 1929, when it was known as East Hall of Wesleyan University. The *Wesleyan University Alumnus*, May 1929.

[21] RBH to Sardis Birchard, December 9, 1837.

[22] RBH, Translation Book, Middletown, 3; also Stoddard, *op. cit.*, 13.

[23] RBH to Harriet Moody, February 24, 1838.

[24] RBH *Diary* (Williams), V, 61; RBH, Middletown Account Book, 1838, HML; "Workus" to RBH, March 1839.

[25] RBH to Sardis Birchard, April 28, 1838.

[26] Sophia Hayes to Sardis Birchard, August 12, 1838; February 20, 1838.

[27] See John Humphrey Noyes, *History of American Socialisms* (copy in Sardis Birchard's library, HML, inscribed February 5, 1870, presented "by the author to Sophia Hayes"). Also, his *The Way of Holiness*, 1838, in HML; Charles Nordhoff, *The Communistic Societies of the United States*; W. H. Dixon, *New America*; Allan Eastlake, *The Oneida Community*; Pierrepont B. Noyes, *My Father's House*; S. Newhouse (ed. by J. H. Noyes and T. L. Pitt), *The Trapper's Guide*; John B. Ellis, *Free Love and Its Votaries*, or *American Socialism Unmasked*.

[28] Sardis Birchard to Austin Birchard, February 6, 1835.

[29] See Slason Thompson, *Life of Eugene Field*, I, chapter II, "His Father's First Love Affair," 13ff.; also *History of Newfane*, 156-157; Childs, *op. cit.*, 266; and Cabot, *op. cit.*, 751.

[30] Sophia Hayes to Sardis Birchard, August 6, 1838.

[31] Isaac Webb to Sardis Birchard, September 29, 1838.

[32] RBH, "Recollections," *op. cit.*, 12.

[33] October 6, 1838.

[34] RBH, 1839 Account Book, HML.

CHAPTER XVII

Son of Kenyon

[1] Sophia Hayes to RBH, June 2, 1839.

[2] RBH to Fanny Hayes, February 5, 1839.

[3] Fanny Hayes to Sardis Birchard, April 25, 1839.

[4] Cornelius Walker, *Life and Correspondence of William Sparrow D. D.*

[5] Cleveland *Leader*, December 27, 1892; William B. Bodine, *The Kenyon Book*, 229.

[6] RBH to Manly D. Covell, January 6, 1838; *ibid.* to Fanny Hayes Platt, November 22, 1846; RBH *Diary* (Williams), I, 357; RBH to Lucy Webb Hayes, July 5, 1860.

[7] Fanny Hayes to RBH, May 26, 1839.

[8] *Ibid.*, January 19, 1840.

[9] *Ibid.*, May 26, 1839.

[10] *Ibid.*, July 22, 1839.

[11] RBH to Fanny Hayes, August 1839.

[12] Bodine, *op. cit.*, 363.

[13] Sardis Birchard to RBH, January 15, 1842.

[14] Sophia Hayes to Sardis Birchard, March 8, 1834.

[15] Fanny Hayes Platt to RBH, January 19, 1840.

[16] RBH *Diary* (Williams), I, 64.

[17] RBH to Fanny Hayes, February 5, 1839.

[18] *Ibid.*; Fanny Hayes to RBH, January 20, 1839; Sophia Hayes to Sardis Birchard, N.D., 1838.

[19] William Jennings Bryan, ed., *The World's Famous Orations*, 38ff., 63.

CHAPTER XVIII

Young Whig

[1] RBH Diary, MSS., April 10, 1892.

[2] George W. Noyes, *The Religious Experiences of John Humphrey Noyes*, 58, 172, 227; Robert Allerton Parker, *A Yankee Saint: John Humphrey Noyes and the Oneida Community*, 48-50; *William Lloyd Garrison, 1805-1879. The Story of His Life Told by His Children*, II, 151-166.

[3] Henry Howe, *op. cit.*, 511.

[4] Barker, *op. cit.*, 22.

[5] RBH *Diary* (Williams), I, 61-62, 187.

[6] Sophia Hayes to Sardis Birchard, N.D., 1839, "by Mrs. Sprague."

[7] Sardis Birchard to Austin Birchard, April 1, 1839.

[8] RBH to Sardis Birchard, June 6, 1838.

[9] RBH *Diary* (Williams), I, 47.

[10] Testimony of Colonel William Roberts in U. S. House of Representatives, Potter Committee Investigation, Misc. Doc. No. 31, 45th Congress, 3rd Session, I, 880.

[11] Minutes Book, Philomathesian Society, 1832-1848, Kenyon College Library, excerpts compiled by Wyman Parker.

[12] RBH, "The Boston Port Bill," MSS., February 26, 1841, HML

CHAPTER XIX

"Statesman of Reunion"

[1] George Franklin Smythe, *Kenyon College, Its First Century*, 323-324; see also "History, Statistics, Library, and Honorary Members of the Philomathesian Society of Kenyon College," 1853, a pamphlet, 6.

[2] RBH to Guy Bryan, July 4, 1877, reproduced in "The Hayes-Bryan Correspondence," *Southwestern Historical Quarterly*, XXVI, 1922-1923, 243, E. W. Winkler, ed.

[3] Guy Bryan to RBH, March 28, 1840.

[4] Bodine, *op. cit.*, 206.

[5] Guy Bryan, September 12, 1842; March 3, 1842.

[6] Conwell, *op. cit.*, 55; RBH *Diary* (Williams), IV, 458.

[7] *Ibid.*, I, 70; Guy Bryan, quoted in Cleveland *Leader*, January 22, 1893; also Bodine, *op. cit.*, 364.

[8] RBH, Kenyon Papers, 1840, HML.

[9] Lorin Andrews to RBH, May 26, 1840.

[10] RBH to Guy Bryan, April 10, 1892.

CHAPTER XX

Fanny, Alas!

[1] *Lathrop's Columbus Directory*, 1862; Alfred E. Lee, *History of the City of Columbus*; G. Louis Platt, *The Platt Lineage*, 211-215; Columbus *Times*, August 8, 1882; Fanny Hayes Platt to RBH, April 8, 1848.

[2] Fanny Hayes Platt to RBH, October 19, 1851.

[3] Fanny Hayes Platt to Sardis Birchard, July 8, 1849; see also her letter to RBH, on back of a letter to him from Sophia Hayes, September 1849, in bound book of letters by Fanny Hayes Platt, HML.

[4] Helen Kelley Collins to RBH, October 27, 1856.

[5] RBH to Fanny Hayes Platt, December 1, 1839.

[6] Fanny Hayes Platt to RBH, October 19, 1851.

[7] Fanny Hayes Platt to Sardis Birchard, February 1, 1840.

[8] Fanny Hayes Platt to RBH, April 7, 1850.

[9] January 13, 1849.

[10] RBH to Sardis Birchard, February 11, 1855.

[11] Fanny Hayes Platt to RBH, July 9, 1841.

[12] November 7, 1839.

[13] Sophia Hayes to Sardis Birchard, August 31, 1840. See also *ibid.*, April 13, 1847.

[14] Fanny Hayes Platt to RBH, July 9, 1841; February 27, 1842.

[15] W. A. Platt to RBH, April 17, 1842, and to Sardis Birchard, April 20, 1842.

[16] William A. Platt to RBH, April 22, 1842.

[17] Sophia Hayes to RBH, April 30, 1842.

[18] RBH to William A. Platt, April 25, 1842.

[19] RBH to Sardis Birchard, October 29, 1842.

[20] Sardis Birchard to Sophia Hayes, July 12, 1842; Sophia Hayes to Austin Birchard, July 17, 1842.

[21] Ed S. Barkdull, "Hayes at Kenyon," Cleveland *Leader*, January 22, 1893.

[22] Sardis Birchard to Austin Birchard, July 25, 1841.

CHAPTER XXI

Happy Interlude

[1] *Columbus Business Directory*, 1843-1844.

[2] Sophia Hayes to Sardis Birchard, September 19, 1841.

[3] Fanny Hayes Platt to Sardis Birchard, December 28, 1842.

[4] November 26, 1842.

[5] October 29, 1842.

[6] Sardis Birchard to Austin Birchard, August 21, 1843; November 14, 1842.
[7] Fanny Hayes Platt to RBH, September 24, 1843.
[8] RBH *Diary* (Williams), I, 162.

CHAPTER XXII

Son of Harvard

[1] RBH to Sophia Hayes, August 27, 1843; *Harvard Law School Book of Entrances, 1839-64,* II; also Harvard Law School Faculty, *Centennial History of the Harvard Law School, 1817-1897,* 11.
[2] RBH *Diary* (Williams), I, 343.
[3] May 26, 1844.
[4] December 17, 1843.
[5] RBH *Diary* (Williams), 129, 162.
[6] Harvard Law School Alumni Roll, in Charles Warren, *History of the Harvard Law School,* III, 26-40.
[7] RBH *Diary* (Williams), I, 137.
[8] Chloe Smith Hayes to Sophia Hayes, February 1844.
[9] *Ibid.,* October 9, 1846.
[10] Sophia Hayes to Sardis Birchard, August 4, 1846.
[11] September 4, 1846.
[12] RBH *Diary* (Williams), I, 137.
[13] *Ibid.,* I, 385.
[14] Harvard Law School Faculty, *op. cit.,* 259.
[15] RBH *Diary* (Williams), I, 131.
[16] William Buckley, *History of Methodism,* II, 79ff., 113, 130.
[17] RBH *Diary* (Williams), I, 130.
[18] Fanny Hayes Platt to RBH, February 25, 1844.
[19] RBH *Diary* (Williams), I, 159.
[20] *Ibid.,* I, 162.

CHAPTER XXIII

False Start

[1] Sophia Hayes to Sardis Birchard, March 31, 1845; Sardis Birchard to Austin Birchard, April 4, 1845.
[2] Fanny Hayes Platt to RBH, April 3, 1847.
[3] *Ibid.,* January 19, 1840.
[4] Ephraim W. Bond to RBH, January 30, 1849.
[5] RBH *Diary* (Williams), I, 163; to W. G. Lane, April 12, August 11, 1845, July 11, 1846, originals in Yale University Library.
[6] RBH *Diary* (Williams), I, 548.
[7] RBH to Janette Elliott, August 20, 1846.
[8] April 20, 1845.
[9] RBH Account Book, Lower Sandusky, April 1845; RBH to Fanny Hayes Platt, April 16, July 9, 1848; RBH *Diary* (Williams), I, 280-281; IV, 260; RBH to W. G. Lane, September 22, 1845, in Yale University Library.
[10] RBH to Sardis Birchard, April 18, 1850; RBH to Ebenezer Lane, January 19, 1847, in Chicago Historical Society; RBH to Sardis Birchard, May 13, 29, October 30, 1850. The land case is cited as *Lessee of Thomas E. Boswell v. Rudolphus Dickinson, Sardis Birchard, et al.,* decided in the Supreme

Court of the United States, Justice McLean for the majority, December term, 1849, "Stanberry, Hayes, Lane & Son, for Defendants—Argument for Defendants, by Hayes, Lane & Son."

[11] See Illinois Central Papers, Newberry Library, Chicago, especially Lane to W. H. Osborn, August 14, 1857, and to Lincoln, July 30, 1856.

[12] Fanny Hayes Platt to RBH, June 29, 1845; RBH *Diary* (Williams), I, 166-167.

[13] RBH to Fanny Hayes Platt, March 22, 1847; also "Centenary History, First Presbyterian Church, Fremont, Ohio," a pamphlet, 1933, 28.

[14] April 20, 1845.

[15] January 24, 1847.

[16] Lower Sandusky *Telegraph*, May 18, 1847.

[17] Knapp, *op. cit.*, 526-527; RBH *Diary* (Williams), I, 184; III, 56; V, 86; Fremont *Messenger*, September 20, 1883; Fremont *Journal*, September 13, 1867; RBH to Sophia Hayes, December 14, 1846.

[18] RBH to W. G. Lane, April 12, September 13, 1845, originals in Yale University Library; RBH *Diary* (Williams), IV, 131.

[19] Fanny Hayes Platt to RBH, March 4, 1848.

[20] James Bowland, *Pioneer Recollections of the Early Thirties and Forties in Sandusky County, Ohio*, 21-22; RBH to Fanny Hayes Platt, July 9, 1848; Lower Sandusky Telegraph Company Subscription List, 1847, HML.

[21] RBH to W. G. Lane, September 13, 1845.

[22] Henry Howe, *op. cit.*, (1897 ed.), II, 531-532.

[23] July 9, 1848.

[24] RBH to Sophia Hayes, December 14, 1846.

[25] RBH *Diary* (Williams), I, 185.

[26] RBH to Lucy Webb, July 17, 1852.

[27] Fanny Hayes Platt to RBH, September 11, 1845.

[28] RBH to Fanny Hayes Platt, June 1, 1845.

[29] RBH to Sophia Hayes, June 18, 1848.

[30] Fanny Hayes Platt, August 10, 1845.

[31] RBH *Diary* (Williams), I, 184; RBH to Sophia Hayes, August 20, 1845.

[32] *Ibid.*, August 27, 1845; October 12, 1846.

[33] Springfield (Massachusetts) *Republican*, December 6, 1891.

[34] W. C. Hedges to RBH, September 27, 1848.

[35] RBH to W. G. Lane, July 11, 1846, in Yale University Library.

[36] RBH to Fanny Hayes Platt, August 27, 1845; Fanny Hayes Platt to RBH, September 12, 1845.

[37] RBH *Diary* (Williams), I, 280-281.

CHAPTER XXIV

First Love

[1] James Schouler, *Eighty Years of Union*, 319, 341; Allan Nevins, *Ordeal of the Union*, I, 8.

[2] Reginald Charles McGrane, *William Allen, A Study in Western Democracy*, 93ff., 104.

[3] Sophia Hayes to Sardis Birchard, February 1846.

[4] RBH, Kenyon Papers, 1842.

[5] Lower Sandusky *Telegraph*, December 25, 1847.

[6] RBH to W. G. Lane, July 11, October 10, 1846 in Yale University Library.

[7] Fremont *Democratic Messenger,* May 27, 1886.

[8] RBH to Ebenezer Lane, June 8, 1847, original in Chicago Historical Society.

[9] RBH *Diary* (Williams), I, 197.

[10] RBH to W. G. Lane, July 11, 1846.

[11] Judge Ebenezer Lane to W. G. Lane, in Yale University Library collection, quoted by Wolcott G. Lane, son of W. G. Lane, to Anna Nevins, April 18, 1950, HML.

[12] RBH to W. G. Lane, October 10, 1846.

[13] RBH *Diary* (Williams), I, 184.

[14] F. G. P.'s identity had to be worked out by the author from a number of letters and books and, in the end, through a visit to the cemetery in Sandusky, Ohio, where, as Fanny Griswold Perkins Camp, as her tombstone states, she was buried in 1855, victim of consumption. The highly interesting personal letters of RBH to W. G. Lane, in the Yale University Library, make the identification indubitable.

[15] Fanny Hayes Platt to RBH, September 8, 1847, October 24, 1847; RBH to Fanny Hayes Platt, October 4, 1846.

[16] *Ibid.,* August 8, 1847.

[17] Anna L. Nevins, New London, Connecticut, to author, November 2, 1950; the Griswold family genealogy, *Magazine of American History,* II, 329; *The Firelands Pioneer,* VII (June 1884), 58; RBH to Fanny Hayes Platt, December 27, 1846.

[18] *Ibid.*

[19] *Ibid.,* January 6, 1847.

[20] *Ibid.,* October N. D., 1847.

[21] RBH *Diary* (Williams), I, 289

[22] RBH to Fanny Hayes Platt, January 6, 1847.

CHAPTER XXV

Confusion and Decision

[1] RBH to Ebenezer Lane, June 1, 1847, original in Chicago Historical Society; also to Sophia Hayes, May 31, 1847.

[2] RBH to Ebenezer Lane, June 9, 1847.

[3] RBH to Sophia Hayes, May 31, 1847.

[4] *Ibid.,* May 30, 31, 1847; William A. Platt, May 31, 1847; RBH to Sardis Birchard, June 13, 1847; Ebenezer Lane to RBH, June N.D., 1847, in Scrapbooks 6 and 7, HML; RBH to Ebenezer Lane, June 1, 1847.

[5] RBH *Diary* (Williams), I, 204-205.

[6] *Ibid.,* IV, 592.

[7] *Ibid.,* I, 205.

[8] Sophia Hayes to Sardis Birchard, June 19, 1847.

[9] RBH to Sardis Birchard, June 6, June 13, 1847.

[10] June 15, 1847.

[11] RBH *Diary* (Williams), I, 208; RBH to Sardis Birchard, June 13, 1847; also to Fanny Hayes Platt, same date.

[12] Sophia Hayes to Sardis Birchard, June 19, 1847.

[13] RBH to Sardis Birchard, June 19, 1847.

[14] Fanny Hayes Platt to RBH, July 25, 1847; RBH to Fanny Hayes Platt, August 8, 1847.

[15] *Ibid.*; also October 1847.

[16] RBH *Diary* (Williams), I, 215.

[17] RBH to Fanny Hayes Platt, October N.D., 1847; Fanny Hayes Platt to RBH, October 24, 1847.

[18] RBH to Fanny Hayes Platt, August 8, 1847.

[19] *Ibid.*, July 9, 1848.

[20] W. A. Platt to Sardis Birchard, March 24, 1847.

[21] Sophia Hayes to RBH, May 15, 1849.

[22] RBH *Diary* (Williams), I, 475.

[23] Sophia Hayes to RBH, May 15, 1849.

[24] May 16, 1849.

[25] RBH to Henry Howe, January 22, 1889; also to RBH, William Darby August 4, 1849, Ohio Archaeological and Historical Society; and Homer Everett, *History of Sandusky County, Ohio,* 418.

[26] October 1, 1849.

[27] RBH *Diary* (Williams), I, 275-276.

CHAPTER XXVI

Cincinnati Lawyer

[1] RBH to Sardis Birchard, January 4, 1850; M. H. Tilden to J. F. Meline, October 17, 1849.

[2] RBH *Diary* (Williams), I, 277.

[3] RBH to Sardis Birchard, January 4, 1850.

[4] *Ibid.*, February 19, 1850; and W. W. Reilly & Company, *Cincinnati Business Directory.*

[5] RBH to Sardis Birchard, February 19, 1850.

[6] *Ibid.*; also RBH *Diary* (Williams), I, 283.

[7] Fanny Hayes Platt to RBH, March 17, 1850.

[8] RBH *Diary* (Williams), I, 338.

[9] Lewis Alexander Leonard, *Life of Alphonso Taft;* and James Wickes Taylor, *Diary of a Cincinnati Law Clerk,* 11, 55.

[10] Cincinnati *Gazette,* November 27, 1852.

[11] Manning F. Force to RBH, May 18, 1852.

[12] Charles Cist, *Sketches and Statistics of Cincinnati in 1851,* 158-159.

[13] Cincinnati *Enquirer,* April 17, 1851.

[14] RBH *Diary* (Williams), I, 338.

[15] Brief by RBH, for Corwine, Rogers and Hayes, in "Liquor Cases," Ohio Supreme Court, December term, 1854. Copy in RBH bound pamphlets, I, HML; also Cincinnati *Gazette,* June 12, 13, 1854, and January 13, December 6, 8, 1855.

[16] Cincinnati *Gazette,* November 27, 1852; RBH *Diary* (Williams), I, 393; see also Curtis W. Garrison, "President Hayes: The Opponent of Prohibition," *Historical Society of Northwestern Ohio,* July-October 1944, 164ff.

[17] RBH to Fanny Hayes Platt, November 20, 1850.

[18] Literary Club of Cincinnati, Minutes Books, 1849-1861, used by courtesy of Mr. Carl Vitz, Club Librarian and Librarian of the Cincinnati Public Library; RBH to Sardis Birchard, February 19, 1850; Cincinnati *Enquirer,* January 24, 1850; Murat Halstead, "Recollections of President Hayes," *The Independent,* February 9, 1899.

[19] See Moncure Daniel Conway, *Autobiography*; James Albert Green, "The Literary Club and Cincinnati in 1849," a paper read at the club, October 12, 1931, 8; and articles by Green and Joseph W. Sagmaster in *The Literary Club of Cincinnati, 1849-1949*, a centennial book published by the club; RBH *Diary* (Williams), IV, 537.

[20] Cincinnati *Gazette*, October 30, 1852; Minutes of the Literary Club, *op. cit.*; John W. Herron, Patrick Mallon, Aaron F. Perry, Ainsworth R. Spofford, Manning F. Force, "Report of Special Committee of Literary Club of Cincinnati on The Death of Rutherford B. Hayes," original in HML; Manning F. Force, "Reminiscences of Rutherford B. Hayes," MSS. in HML; Spofford, *op. cit.*, RBH *Diary* (Williams), I, 329-330.

[21] RBH *Diary* (Williams), II, 127-128.

[22] RBH to Fanny Hayes Platt, November 7, 1850.

[23] RBH *Diary* (Williams), IV, 351.

[24] RBH to Sardis Birchard, February 19, 1850; Henry Allen and Kate B. Ford, *History of Cincinnati, Ohio*, 139.

[25] RBH to Sardis Birchard, September 14, 1852.

[26] Cincinnati *Gazette*, June 1, 1852.

CHAPTER XXVII

Laurels for Fanny

[1] Ford, *op. cit.*, 312.

[2] RBH *Diary* (Williams), I, 407; Cincinnati *Gazette*, October 18, November 3, 1851, and January 19, 1852.

[3] *Ibid.*; also R. B. Warden, *Life of Salmon P. Chase*.

[4] Cincinnati *Enquirer*, March 27, 1851; Cincinnati *Gazette*, April 23, 25, 28, and May 23, 1852; RBH to Sardis Birchard, May 1, 1852; Cincinnati *Gazette*, May 2, 1852.

[5] *Ibid.*, May 5, 6, June 8, 9, 1852; also RBH *Diary* (Williams), I, 421.

[6] See 5 Ohio State Reports 325; also 19 Ohio 52 (1850).

[7] RBH Memorandum, Scrapbook 7, 75; Cincinnati *Gazette*, November 27, 1852.

[8] W. D. Howells, *op. cit.*, 40.

[9] RBH *Diary* (Williams), I, 425, 474-475.

[10] *Ibid.*

[11] For full accounts of the Nancy Farrer case see J. J. Quinn, "Homicidal Insanity—The Case of Nancy Farrer," *The Western Lancet*, XVI (November 1855), 643ff.; L. R. Johnston, "Moral Insanity and Its Legal Relations," *American Psychological Journal*, I, 4ff.; and A. G. W. Carter, *The Old Court House*, quoting the Cincinnati *Commercial*, July 19, 1878, 440ff.

[12] RBH *Diary* (Williams), III, 170; also RBH Diary, MSS., 4, 39-40.

[13] Fanny Hayes Platt to Sardis Birchard, January 31, 1853.

CHAPTER XXVIII

At Last, A Wife

[1] RBH Diary, MSS., 4, entry of May 18, 1851.

[2] Fanny Hayes Platt to RBH, June 10, 1848.

[3] See RBH *Diary* (Williams), I, 289-290.

[4] Fanny Hayes Platt to RBH, June 10, 1848.

[5] Sophia Hayes to RBH, November 17, 1847. For sketches of Lucy Webb Hayes see Henry Howe, *op. cit.* (1907), II, 541ff.; Mrs. John Davis, "Lucy Webb Hayes, a Memorial Sketch for the Woman's Home Missionary Society"; Margaret Cook Gilmore, in *Che-le-co-the, Glimpses of Yesterday, A Souvenir of the Hundredth Anniversary of the Founding of Chillicothe, Ohio;* also a manuscript by Laura Platt Mitchell in HML.

[6] RBH *Diary* (Williams), IV, 477; Fanny Hayes Platt to RBH, June 10, 1848.

[7] RBH to W. A. Platt, January 14, 1850; RBH to John A. Little, January 20, 1850.

[8] *The Alumna of Wesleyan Female College* (1855), 54.

[9] RBH *Diary* (Williams), IV, 129; Lucy Webb to Maggie Cook, March 11, 1851.

[10] Lucy W. Webb to RBH, August 20, 1851; RBH to Fanny Hayes Platt, July 19, 1847.

[11] Sophia Hayes to RBH, July 20, 1855.

[12] RBH to Fanny Hayes Platt, October 23, 1847.

[13] RBH *Diary* (Williams), I, 361-362, V, 61.

[14] Margaret Scott Cook, *Sketch of the Life of Matthew Scott Cook,* 7; also *Portrait and Biographical Record of the Scioto Valley, Ohio,* 141-142.

[15] RBH *Diary* (Williams), I, 292, 294.

[16] *Ibid.,* I, 342.

[17] *Ibid.,* 366.

[18] *Ibid.,* 364; Sophia Hayes to RBH, November 4, 1851.

[19] RBH to Lucy W. Webb, August 22, 1852.

CHAPTER XXIX

The Contented Man

[1] See Louis J. Bailey, "Caleb Blood Smith," *Indiana Magazine of History,* XXXIX, No. 3 (September 1933), 213ff.

[2] RBH to Sardis Birchard, December 19 and 25, 1853; also RBH to W. K. Rogers, February 2, 1853; Carter, *op. cit.,* 397.

[3] Agreement by Richard M. Corwine, Rutherford B. Hayes and William K. Rogers, signed December 31, 1853, original in HML; RBH to Sardis Birchard, December 19, 1853.

[4] February 9, 1854; see also RBH *Diary* (Williams), II, 6.

[5] C. S. Williams, *Cincinnati Directory, City Guide and Business Mirror for 1858,* 78.

[6] RBH to Sardis Birchard, January 8, 1854; January 22, 1854.

[7] *Ibid.,* March 20, 1856.

[8] RBH to H. S. Noyes, October 19, 1855.

[9] RBH *Diary* (Williams), I, 463.

[10] RBH to Sardis Birchard, December 22, 1850; RBH to W. K. Rogers, February 23, 1857.

[11] RBH *Diary* (Williams), I, 491; Fanny Hayes Platt to Laura Platt, May 6, 1855.

CHAPTER XXX

On Freedom's Road

[1] RBH *Diary* (Williams), I, 470.

[2] *Ibid.,* IV, 129.

[8] See Harold M. Helfman, "The Contested Confirmation of Stanley Matthews to the Supreme Court," *Bulletin of the Historical and Philosophical Society of Ohio*, July 1950.

[4] Levi Coffin, *Reminiscences*, 548.

[5] Cincinnati *Gazette*, August 27, 29, and September 3, 1853; also RBH to Lucy W. Hayes, September 4, 1853.

[6] RBH Memorandum, fragment, HML; also Wilbur H. Siebert, *The Underground Railroad from Slavery to Freedom*, 282.

[7] William Henry Smith, *A Political History of Slavery*, 148.

[8] Siebert, *Underground Railroad*, *op. cit.*, 420.

[9] Wilbur H. Siebert, "Ex-President R. B. Hayes, Spring of 1893, Interview," in Siebert materials, 6, Ohio Archaeological and Historical Society.

[10] See Cincinnati *Commercial Gazette*, February 11, 1894; also *Suppressed Book About Slavery*, 309-310.

[11] April 6, 1855.

[12] Cincinnati *Enquirer*, October 22, 1853; Coffin, *op. cit.*, 548ff., contains good accounts of both the Louis and Rosetta cases. Warden, *op. cit.*, 345, has material on the Rosetta case; also J. T. Trowbridge's campaign biography of Chase, *The Ferry Boy and the Financier*. Contemporary newspaper accounts include the Cincinnati *Gazette*, October 17, 1853, and subsequent issues, concerning the case of Louis, the Cincinnati *Enquirer*, especially October 18, 19, 22, 1853, and the *Liberator*, October 28, 1853. The *Gazette*, April 2, 3, 4, 1855, and the *Columbian* of Columbus, April 4, and 11, 1855, concerning the Rosetta case. See also *Ex Parte, H. H. Robinson, Marshal of the U. S.*, 6th McClean's Reports, Circuit Court of the U. S., April term, 1855.

[13] H. W. Coffin to RBH, March 27, 1877.

CHAPTER XXXI

The New Republican

[1] RBH to Guy Bryan, April 16, 1856.

[2] Ebenezer Lane to Sardis Birchard, June 2, 1856.

[3] See Nevins, *Ordeal of the Union*, II, 227ff.; also Gunnar Myrdal and Associates, *An American Dilemma*, 441ff.

[4] Fremont *Journal*, March 7, 1856; Lucy Elliot Keeler Journal, February 13, 1883, quoting RBH; also RBH to Carl Schurz, September 15, 1876.

[5] Minutes of the Literary Club, *op. cit.*

[6] Halstead, "Recollections of President Hayes," *op. cit.*, 393; also W. H. Smith to T. W. Davenport, July 25, 1876, quoted in Edgar Laughlin Gray, "The Career of William Henry Smith, Politician-Journalist," Ph.D. thesis, Ohio State University, 1950.

[7] RBH to Guy Bryan, April 16, 1856; RBH to R. C. McCormick, October 14, 1876, in *Diary* (Williams), III, 367; and to W. S. Ridgway, October 24, 1876.

[8] Cincinnati *Gazette*, March 6, 1854.

[9] RBH to Sardis Birchard, June 5, 1854.

[10] RBH to Guy Bryan, April 16, 1856.

[11] RBH Memorandum, fragment, HML, prepared for campaign biographies in 1876; also Cincinnati *Gazette*, July 20, 27, 1856; and Joseph P. Smith, ed., *History of the Republican Party in Ohio*, I, 34, 38, 63; also RBH *Diary* (Williams), I, 514; III, 611.

CHAPTER XXXII

Sorrow and Advance

[1] RBH *Diary* (Williams), I, 453.

[2] RBH to Lucy W. Hayes, July 5, 7, 11, 1856; Sardis Birchard to RBH, July 14, 1856; Sophia Hayes to RBH, June 16, 1856; RBH to J. T. Webb, July 5, 1856.

[3] RBH *Diary* (Williams), I, 499; RBH to Russell Hayes, July 19, 1856.

[4] July 4, 1856.

[5] July 23, 1856.

[6] Sophia Hayes to Sardis Birchard, October 14, 1856.

[7] RBH to W. K. Rogers, August 24, 1856.

[8] *Ibid.*, September 28, 1856.

[9] *Ibid.*, August 24, November 25, 1856.

[10] September 28, 1856.

[11] October 30, 1856.

[12] RBH to Sardis Birchard, August 31, 1856.

[13] J. W. Herron to RBH, July 21, 1852.

[14] RBH to Sardis Birchard, August 20, 31, 1856; and to W. K. Rogers, August 31, 1856.

[15] RBH to Sardis Birchard, August 20, 1856.

[16] Cincinnati *Enquirer*, September 15, 1858; also June 27, 1858.

[17] Petitions dated November 30, 1858, in HML.

[18] RBH to Sardis Birchard, November 30, 1858; RBH *Diary* (Williams), II, 6.

[19] *Ibid.*, IV, 619; also Cincinnati *Commercial Gazette*, January 31, 1893.

[20] See Peter Guilday, "Gaetano Bedini, An Episode in the Life of Archbishop John Hughes," *Historical Records and Studies*, United States Catholic Historical Society, XXIII, 1933

[21] Cincinnati *Gazette*, December 28, 29, 31, 1853. For material on Hassaurek and other German leaders see Carl F. Wittke, *We Who Built America, the Saga of the Immigrant*, and also his *Reformers of Revolution, German Forty-eighters in America.*

[22] Cincinnati *Gazette*, January 19, 1854.

[23] Cincinnati *Enquirer*, January 21, 1893, interview with R. M. Bishop; also *Commercial Gazette*, January 31, 1893.

[24] RBH *Diary* (Williams), IV, 619.

CHAPTER XXXIII

Lawyer for Cincinnati

[1] RBH Memorandum dated February 17, 1858; RBH to Sardis Birchard, December 9, 1859.

[2] See *History of Newfane*, 44-46.

[3] RBH to Sophia Hayes, May 30, 1857.

[4] RBH *Diary* (Williams), I, 543, 561.

[5] RBH to Laura Platt, April 20, 1860.

[6] "Mayor's Annual Report, Cincinnati, Year Ending April 10, 1861."

[7] See Law Department Letter Book, January 7, 1858-February 20, 1868, in City Solicitor's Office, Cincinnati.

[8] *Ibid.*, 226.

[9] Cincinnati *Enquirer*, June 16, 20, 1859; also "City Solicitor's Annual Report, February 23, 1860, R. B. Hayes, City Solicitor," 6; RBH to Sardis Birchard, June 11, 1860.

[10] RBH *Diary* (Williams), I, 503.

CHAPTER XXXIV

Lincoln—and the Storm

[1] Joseph P. Smith, *op. cit.*, 114-117.

[2] Paul Angle, *Abraham Lincoln Day Book*, 331.

[3] See Albert J. Beveridge, *Abraham Lincoln, 1809-1858*, II, 460, 708-710; also Charles and Mary Beard, *The Rise of American Civilization*, II, 18-19.

[4] RBH to Sardis Birchard, May 11, 1860.

[5] *Ibid.*, May 23, September 30, 1860; RBH *Diary* (Williams), I, 563-564.

[6] Howard, *op. cit.*, 221.

[7] RBH to A. P. Russell, Secretary of State of Ohio, September 14, 1860.

[8] RBH to Sardis Birchard, February 13, 1861; see Carl Sandburg, *Abraham Lincoln, The War Years*, I, 41ff. concerning Lincoln in Cincinnati.

[9] RBH to Laura Platt, February 13, 1861.

[10] RBH *Diary* (Williams), II, 4.

[11] Carl Sandburg, *Abraham Lincoln, The Prairie Years*, II, 407ff.

[12] RBH to Sardis Birchard, April 2, 1861.

CHAPTER XXXV

At Last, A Soldier

[1] RBH to Sardis Birchard, April 10, 1861.

[2] RBH to William McKinley, November 6, 1866.

[3] RBH to Sardis Birchard, April 19, 1861.

[4] RBH to Guy Bryan, May 8, 1861.

[5] RBH to Sardis Birchard, May 12, 1861.

[6] Literary Club of Cincinnati, Minutes Books, April 17, 1861.

[7] Sophia Hayes to Sarah Wasson, May 20, 1861.

[8] RBH to Sardis Birchard, July 21, 1861.

[9] May 16, 1861.

[10] RBH to Sardis Birchard, April 15, 1861.

[11] RBH *Diary* (Williams), II, 127.

[12] *Ibid.*, 563; also IV, 286-287.

[13] J. T. Webb to Webb C. Hayes I, September 5, 1878.

[14] RBH *Diary* (Williams), V, 96.

[15] June 10, 1861.

[16] RBH to Manning Force, June 12, 1861.

[17] August 25, 1861.

[18] RBH *Diary* (Williams), II, 88.

[19] September 19, 1861.

[20] RBH *Diary* (Williams), IV, 312.

[21] Roeliff Brinkerhoff, "Rutherford Birchard Hayes as a Philanthropist and Friend," in *Proceedings of the Congress of the National Prison Association, June 7-10, 1893*, 33. See also Joseph Warren Keifer, *Slavery and Four Years of War*, II, 106.

[22] November 2, 1861.

CHAPTER XXXVI

Search's End

[1] RBH to Lucy Webb Hayes, May 26, 1862, a recollection by him.
[2] H. F. Devol to Webb C. Hayes I, February 6, 1893.
[3] RBH *Diary* (Williams), II, 282.
[4] *Ibid.*, 528.
[5] Excerpts of diary of E. E. Henry, May 10, 1862, MSS. in HML.
[6] RBH *Diary* (Williams), II, 68.
[7] RBH, Civil War Correspondence, HML.
[8] William McKinley, address, May 16, 1893, copy in HML.
[9] RBH *Diary* (Williams), II, 347, September 7, 1862.
[10] *Ibid.*
[11] *Ibid.*, entry of September 8, 1862; RBH to Sardis Birchard, September 8, 1862.
[12] RBH *Diary* (Williams), II, 355.
[13] *Ibid.*
[14] RBH to Sophia Hayes, December 8, 1862.
[15] RBH *Diary* (Williams), II, 355-357.
[16] Howard, *op. cit.*, 35; RBH *Diary* (Williams), III, 303.
[17] *Ibid*, II, 420; V, 71. For a listing of all engagements in which Hayes's Twenty-third Ohio Volunteers participated see *Roster of Ohio Soldiers, 1861-1866*, III. William F. Fox, *Regimental Losses in the Civil War*, also includes a summary.
[18] RBH *Diary* (Williams), II, 128.

CHAPTER XXXVII

Rewards

[1] RBH *Diary* (Williams), II, 218, 286; RBH to Lucy W. Hayes, July 14, 1862.
[2] RBH to Sardis Birchard, July 30, 1864.
[3] H. F. Devol to Webb C. Hayes I, February 6, 1893.
[4] RBH to W. H. Smith, August 24, 1864; reproduced in facsimile in RBH *Diary* (Williams), II, 496; also Smith to T. W. Davenport, July 25, 1876, in W. H. Smith Collection, Letterpress Copybook, v. 22, 303-309, Ohio State Archaeological and Historical Society.
[5] John G. Nicolay and John Hay, *Abraham Lincoln*, IX, 370; RBH *Diary* (Williams), IV, 506.
[6] October 21, 1864.
[7] See Elbridge D. Hadley, "Cedar Creek—Popular History Refuted," a paper read before the Iowa Commandery, Military Order of the Loyal Legion, for a good discussion of the literature on this episode.
[8] RBH *Diary* (Williams), II, 527.
[9] Sophia Hayes to RBH, November 8, 1863.
[10] Sophia Hayes Diary, August 31, 1866.
[11] RBH *Diary* (Williams), III, 232; IV, 535.
[12] *Ibid.*, II, 173.
[13] Lucy W. Hayes to RBH, April 22, 1862.

[14] Hadley, *op. cit.*
[15] Lucy W. Hayes to RBH, August 30, 1864.
[16] February 14, 1862.

CHAPTER XXXVIII

"Capitalist," Perhaps

[1] RBH *Diary* (Williams), III, 249.
[2] *Ibid.*, 232, 239, 248-249.
[3] *Ibid.*, 229, 251.
[4] Sophia Hayes Diary, March 16, 1866.
[5] RBH Diary, MSS, May 2, 1873.
[6] See Gray, *op. cit.*, 51ff.
[7] See Marion Thompson Wright, "Negro Suffrage in New Jersey, 1776-1875," *Journal of Negro History*, XXXIII, No. 2 (April 1948); also Paul L. Haworth, *Reconstruction and Union*, 30ff.
[8] See William Cochran, biography of J. D. Cox, in manuscript, copy in HML.
[9] Conwell, *op. cit.*, 261.
[10] RBH *Diary* (Williams), III, 8.
[11] *Congressional Globe*, v. 36, 39th Congress, 1st Session, Part 1, 67.
[12] *Ibid.*, 1095.
[13] RBH to Guy Bryan, October 1, 1866; Fremont *Journal*, July 12, 1867.
[14] *Congressional Globe*, v. 37, 39th Congress, 2nd Session, Part 1, 320-321.
[15] *Ibid.*, 747.
[16] *Ibid.*, 1739.
[17] RBH to Russell Hastings, May 20, 1865.
[18] RBH *Diary* (Williams), III, 7, 25; RBH to Lucy Hayes, December 7, 1865.
[19] See, for example, speech at Lebanon, Ohio, August 5, 1867, in Charles R. Williams, *Life of Rutherford Birchard Hayes*, I, 293ff.
[20] RBH *Diary* (Williams), III, 48.
[21] See Minutes of the North Ohio Conference, Methodist Episcopal Church, 1867-1869, as an example.
[22] See Randolph C. Downes, *Lake Port*, III, in Lucas County (Ohio) Historical Series, 226-228, for a good summary of this campaign.
[23] RBH *Diary* (Williams), III, 110; see also Theodore C. Smith, *The Life and Letters of James Abram Garfield*, I, 476; also Matthew Josephson, *The Politicos, 1865-1896*, 188ff.
[24] See William D. Foulke, *The Life of Oliver P. Morton*, II, 103.
[25] RBH *Diary* (Williams), III, 74.

CHAPTER XXXIX

The Good Governor

[1] RBH *Diary* (Williams), III, 269.
[2] October 4, 1870.
[3] *Congressional Globe*, v. 37, 39th Congress, 2nd Session, Part 1, 210.
[4] *Ibid.*, 1st Session, Part 2, 1097.
[5] Cleveland *Leader*, June 7, 1867.
[6] RBH to Lucy W. Hayes, January 10, 1866.

[7] February 2, 1866.

[8] *Congressional Globe*, v. 36, 39th Congress, 1st Session, Part 4, 22, 1723; also article by Ainsworth R. Spofford, Librarian of Congress, a member of the Literary Club of Cincinnati, *Magazine of History*, XXIX, 1893.

[9] RBH to Sardis Birchard, February 2, 1867.

[10] July 9, 1865.

[11] "Proceedings of the Congress of the National Prison Association," June 7, 1893, pamphlet, HML.

[12] RBH, Message to Legislature, January, 1872 text in Howard, *op. cit.*, 121ff.

[13] RBH *Diary* (Williams), III, 127-129; also 1875 campaign leaflet against Hayes, "Facts for the People," in HML.

[14] Murat Halstead, "The War Claims of the South," an address at Cooper Institute, October 25, 1876; also RBH *Diary* (Williams), III, 189.

[15] William Henry Smith to T. W. Davenport, July 25, 1876.

[16] RBH, Message to Legislature, January 1870, in Howard, *op. cit.*, appendix, 95.

[17] Message to Legislature, January 1872.

[18] RBH *Diary* (Williams), IV, 354, 367, 546, 565, 635; also C. R. Williams,, *Life, op. cit.*, II, 382-385.

[19] "Proceedings of the Society of the Army of the Tennessee," Fifth Annual Meeting, Cincinnati, April 6, 1871, 48-50.

[20] Henry Howe, *op. cit.*, (1896), I, 110.

[21] Lucy Elliot Keeler Journal, January 1, 1889.

[22] RBH to E. C. Wines of the Prison Association of New York, December 7, 1869; Roeliff Brinkerhoff, "The Achievements of Ohio in the Care of Her Unfortunate Classes," *Ohio Centennial*, 1903, 501. Also William M. F. Round, "Ex-President Rutherford B. Hayes," *The Charities Review*, February 1893.

[23] See Minutes of the Board of Trustees of Ohio State University, January 19, 1893, reproduced in RBH *Diary* (Williams), V, 196, 203; also RBH to William Henry Smith, November 27, 1887.

[24] Alex Cope, secretary of the university, Minutes, January 19, 1893.

[25] RBH *Diary* (Williams), III, 102.

[26] January 4, 1870.

[27] January 10, 1870.

[28] John Mabry Matthews, *Legislative and Judicial History of the Fifteenth Amendment*, 66; also H. of R. Misc. Doc., No. 42, 41st Congress, 2nd Session, RBH to Speaker of House, January 28, 1870.

CHAPTER XL

"No More Ambition"

[1] RBH to J. Irving Brooks, March 1, 1870.

[2] RBH to James D. Webb, June 3, 1870.

[3] RBH to Charles Nordhoff, March 13, 1871.

[4] March 16, 1871.

[5] RBH to John Hopley, April 29, 1871.

[6] RBH to Joseph A. Joel, May 29, 1871.

[7] RBH to Sardis Birchard, January 9, 1872.

[8] E. P. Oberholtzer in *Jay Cooke, Financier of the Civil War*, II, 165, makes a reference to this.

[9] RBH to Sardis Birchard, January 31, February 20, 1870; Jay Cooke to RBH, February 9, 17, 21, 1870.
[10] Jay Cooke and Company correspondence with RBH.
[11] RBH to Lucy W. Hayes, May 7, 1871.
[12] May 29, 1871.

CHAPTER XLI

Renunciations

[1] January 11, 1872.
[2] RBH to John Hopley, April 29, 1871; also RBH *Diary* (Williams), III, 186; also C. R. Williams, *Life, op. cit.*, I, 363.
[3] December 31, 1871.
[4] RBH to R. H. Stephenson, June 15, 1871.
[5] May 5, 1871.
[6] RBH *Diary* (Williams), III, 146.
[7] RBH to Sardis Birchard, January 3, 1872; also RBH *Diary* (Williams), III, 186.
[8] *Ibid.*
[9] *Ibid.*, 192-193.
[10] *Ibid.*
[11] *Ibid.* See also William Dennison to John Sherman, February 4, 1872, Sherman Papers, Library of Congress.

CHAPTER XLII

Piqued "Stalwart"

[1] RBH *Diary* (Williams), III, 196-197.
[2] RBH to Sardis Birchard, June 30, 1872.
[3] See *Harper's Weekly*, May 18, 1872.
[4] Royal Cortissoz, *Life of Whitelaw Reid*, I, 215.
[5] April 5, 1870.
[6] RBH to David A. Wells, April 6, 1870.
[7] RBH to Sardis Birchard, May 14, 1872.
[8] E. F. Noyes correspondence with Grenville M. Dodge, *i.e.*, April 16, 1872, Dodge Papers, Iowa State Historical Department.
[9] Proceedings of Republican National Convention, 1872, 9; also film copy of diary of Thomas Donaldson, William Henry Smith Papers, HML.
[10] See *Harper's Weekly*, July 27, 1872.
[11] RBH to Sardis Birchard, September 8, 1872.
[12] *Ibid.*, July 24, 1872.
[13] Fremont *Journal*, August 2, 1872.
[14] RBH *Diary* (Williams), III, 208.
[15] August 10, 1872.
[16] November 8, 1872.
[17] RBH *Diary* (Williams), III, 241.
[18] Jacob D. Cox to RBH, 1872 letters, HML.
[19] RBH to John Sherman, April 2, 1873.

CHAPTER XLIII

Farewell to "Stalwartism"

1 McGrane, *op. cit.*, 188ff.
2 Haworth, *Reconstruction and Union, op. cit.*, 54-55.
3 RBH to J. C. Lee, May 6, 1868.
4 See Haworth, *Reconstruction and Union, op. cit.*, 9ff.; but also W. E. B. Du Bois, *Black Reconstruction in America.*
5 January 2, 1875.
6 See Rayford W. Logan, *The Negro in American Life and Thought,* 8-9 and ff.
7 William B. Hesseltine, *Ulysses S. Grant, Politician,* 308ff. and 368ff.
8 *Ibid.*, 342ff.; also J. G. Randall, *The Civil War and Reconstruction,* 849ff. and 868ff.
9 RBH *Diary* (Williams), III, 269, March 28, 1875.
10 Howard, *op. cit.*, 230.
11 RBH to Sardis Birchard, March 7, 1869.
12 Charles R. Lingley, in review of Claude G. Bowers, *The Tragic Era, American Historical Review,* XXXV, 383.
13 See Frances Butler Simkins, *A History of the South,* 283, 295ff.

CHAPTER XLIV

Third-Term Feather

1 Howard Carroll, *Twelve Americans, Their Lives and Times,* 328.
2 RBH *Diary* (Williams), III, 269.
3 Theodore C. Smith, *op. cit.*, 584.
4 April 14, 1875.
5 Oberlin College Prudential Committee Minutes, 1875, courtesy William P. Davis, treasurer, to author, January 12, 1950.
6 RBH *Diary* (Williams), III, 269.
7 *Ibid.*, 274.
8 *Ibid.*, 273, May 31, 1875.
9 William McKinley to RBH, June 8, 1875.
10 RBH *Diary* (Williams), III, 274.
11 See *Harper's Weekly* files for 1875, nearly every issue with such material, especially articles signed by Eugene Lawrence, February 27, March 13, 1875, in particular.
12 McGrane, *op. cit.*, 229; Philip D. Jordan, *Ohio Comes of Age, 1873-1900* (History of the State of Ohio), V, 44-46.
13 McGrane, *op. cit.*, 229; Catholic *Telegraph,* quoted in Fremont *Journal,* June 18, 1875.
14 George F. Houck, *A History of Catholicity in Northern Ohio and in the Diocese of Cleveland,* I, 105.
15 Hesseltine, *op. cit.*, 392.
16 McGrane, *op. cit.*, 231.
17 *John D. Minor, et. al., vs. The Board of Education,* reprinted in "The Bible in the Public Schools," 1870; Stanley Matthews to Rev. W. H. Bebbitt, November 18, 1869, in Historical and Philosophical Society, Cincinnati.

[18] See Allen O. Myers, *Bosses and Boodle in Ohio Politics*, 131-133.

[19] *Ibid.*, 132.

[20] RBH *Diary* (Williams), III, 274.

[21] RBH, Speech at Marion, Ohio, July 31, 1875, in Howard, *op. cit.*, 241, 255.

[22] RBH *Diary* (Williams), III, 274.

[23] James Garfield Diary, June 12, 1875, Library of Congress.

[24] RBH to D. A. Higby, November 3, 1869, in Governor's Letter Book, November 1, 1869, to June 30, 1870, HML.

[25] See John S. Hare, "Allen Thurman," Ohio State University Ph.D. thesis, 1933, 236ff.

[26] Hesseltine, *op. cit.*, 331ff.; Allan Nevins, *Hamilton Fish, The Inner History of the Grant Administration*, 705ff.; also Nevins, *Abram S. Hewitt: With Some Account of Peter Cooper*, 294.

[27] Hare, *op. cit.*, 257-258; Forrest W. Clonts, "The Political Campaign of 1875 in Ohio," *Ohio State Archaeological and Historical Quarterly*, XXXI, 1922, 31.

[28] Howard, *op. cit.*, 256.

[29] Schurz, in *Harper's Weekly*, January 28, 1893.

[30] See Halstead, "Recollections of President Hayes," *op. cit.*, 486.

[31] RBH *Diary* (Williams), III, 295.

[32] Fanny Hayes Platt to Sardis Birchard, November 7, 1839, quoting Austin Birchard.

CHAPTER XLV

The "Passive" Runner

[1] June 27, 1888.

[2] March 21, 1876, in RBH *Diary* (Williams), III, 309.

[3] *Ibid.*, 305, 311.

[4] Webb C. Hayes to Birchard A. Hayes, March 12, 1875.

[5] October 18, 1875.

[6] January 29, 1876.

[7] December 22, 1875.

[8] Alfred R. Conkling, *Life and Letters of Roscoe Conkling*, 451, 497.

[9] H. V. Boynton to Bristow, January 11, 1880, Bristow Papers, Library of Congress.

[10] To Clark Waggoner, November 13, 1875, quoted to RBH; Waggoner to RBH, November 27, 1875.

[11] RBH *Diary* (Williams), III, 309.

[12] Hogg to RBH, March 17, 1876; RBH to Hogg, March 20, 1876. Waite's statement on the Presidency in Ohio Bar Association, Centennial volume, 1888, 187.

[13] Halstead, "Recollections of President Hayes," *op. cit.*, 486.

[14] January 24, 1876, Bristow Papers, Library of Congress.

[15] *Ibid.*

[16] See Cortissoz, *op. cit.*, I, 330ff.

[17] *The Nation*, October 3, 1872.

[18] Clark Waggoner to RBH, May 15, 1876.

[19] John Sherman to State Senator A. M. Burns, January 21, 1876, in John Sherman, *Recollections*, I, 522-523.

20 Theodore C. Smith, *op. cit.*, II, 956.

21 RBH *Diary* (Williams), V, 14; also RBH to John Sherman, June 19, 1876.

22 See "The Letter That Made Hayes President," *Chaperone Magazine*, March 1891, 629, General Sherman to J. M. Dalzell.

23 William Henry Smith to RBH, January 26, 1876.

24 Dalzell to RBH, December 7, 1875; June 19, 1876.

25 W. D. Howells to Charles Dudley Warner, August 23, 1876, in Mildred Howells, *op. cit.*, 226.

CHAPTER XLVI

Secret Maneuvering

1 Halstead, "Recollections of President Hayes," *op. cit.*, 486.

2 Smith to RBH, August 1877, in William Henry Smith Letter Book, v. 23, 257-269, Ohio State Archaeological and Historical Society Collection; also Garfield Diary, April 2, 1875.

3 RBH *Diary* (Williams), III, 320, May 19, 1876.

4 Bristow to General Wilson, June 11, 1876, Bristow Papers, Library of Congress; Hesseltine, *op. cit.*, 401-402.

5 Smith's part in the Blaine matter as told here is based on letters in the William Henry Smith Collection in the Indiana State Library, a correspondence beginning in February 1876, between Smith and H. V. Boynton, Joseph Medill, Murat Halstead, Richard Smith and W. R. Holloway. In particular see Smith to Boynton, April 30, 1876.

6 May 9, 1876.

7 May 17, 1876, Allison Papers, Iowa State Historical Library.

8 Smith to RBH, June 12, 1876.

CHAPTER XLVII

"Hour of Triumph"

1 See Foulke, *op. cit.*, II, 387.

2 RBH *Diary* (Williams), III, 326; also see Jordan, *Ohio Comes of Age, op. cit.*, 51ff.

3 RBH to John Sherman, May 19, 1876.

4 Jordan, *Ohio Comes of Age, op. cit.*, 53.

5 See Nevins, *Hamilton Fish, op. cit.*, 826.

6 RBH to James G. Blaine, June 12, 1876.

7 RBH to Ralph Buckland, June 14, 1876.

8 Foulke, *op. cit.*, II, 399n.

9 See Josephson, *The Politicos, op. cit.*, 214ff.

10 It has been frequently asserted that the convention was forced to adjourn because anti-Blaine elements disrupted the gas system of the convention hall. Some Hayes supporters have taken credit for the disruption. But this seems to be apocryphal. It may be that an argument used for voting for adjournment was that the hall could not be properly lighted. But contemporary newspaper accounts show that the motion to adjourn was put and voted on without any such dramatics.

See New York *Times*, June 16, 1876. Cf. David S. Muzzey, *James G.*

Blaine, 111; Paul L. Haworth, *The Hayes-Tilden Disputed Presidential Election of 1876*, 22, citing A. K. McClure, *Our Presidents and How We Make Them*; and Ben: Perley Poore, *Life of U. S. Grant*, 225.

[11] June 14, 1876.

[12] See Jacob Dolson Cox, "The Hayes Administration," *The Atlantic Monthly*, June 1893, 822, for a good analysis of this situation. See also Henry Adams, *Letters*, and Mrs. Henry Adams, *Letters*.

[13] See Harlan to Bristow, June 19, 1876, Bristow Papers, Library of Congress.

[14] William Henry Smith to RBH, January 26, 1876.

[15] RBH *Diary* (Williams), III, 326.

[16] *Ibid.*

[17] W. K. Rogers, in *The Kenyon Collegian*, XX, No. 3 (1893), 42.

CHAPTER XLVIII

"Too Good a Man"

[1] RBH *Diary* (Williams), IV, 590.

[2] Guy Bryan to RBH, December 30, 1876, with enclosure of letter to Senator S. B. Maxey, originals in Guy M. Bryan Collection, University of Texas Library, Austin.

[3] R. B. Warden to RBH, June 16, 1876.

[4] John A. Little to RBH, April 11, 1848.

[5] RBH *Diary* (Williams), III, 328, June 23, 1876.

[6] See Claude G. Bowers, *The Tragic Era*, 489.

[7] Dixon Wecter, *Sam Clemens of Hannibal*, 271.

[8] See Mark D. Hirsch, "Samuel J. Tilden: The Story of a Lost Opportunity," *American Historical Review*, LVI, No. 4 (July 1951), 788ff.; also Alexander C. Flick, *Samuel Jones Tilden, A Study in Political Sagacity*; and also John Bigelow, *The Life of Samuel J. Tilden*.

[9] RBH *Diary* (Williams), III, 362.

[10] *Ibid.*, 333.

[11] See Nevins, *Abram S. Hewitt, op. cit.*, 288ff.; RBH *Diary* (Williams), III, 360; also Benjamin Harrison to RBH, October 16, 1876.

[12] Testimony, "Presidential Election Investigation, 1878-79," House of Representatives Misc. Doc. No. 31, 45th Congress, 3rd Session, IV, 91, henceforth to be cited as Potter Investigation Testimony.

[13] The 1876 election story is developed most fully in thousands of printed pages of testimony taken by various House and Senate investigating committees and published as reports to the 43rd, 44th and 45th Congresses. The best single document, in five volumes, is the Potter Investigation Testimony, cited in note above.

Though it must be read with care, as partisan, the factual case against Southern Democratic intimidation of the Negroes is in "Message from the President" (Grant), Senate Exec. Doc. No. 2, 44th Congress, 2nd Session, consisting mainly of affidavits.

For alleged Democratic efforts to win electoral votes by bribery see "Electoral Vote of Certain States—Testimony Before the Sub-committee of the Committee on Privileges and Elections," Senate Misc. Doc. No. 44, 44th Congress, 2nd Session; also Potter Investigation Testimony, IV, "The Cipher Dispatches" and questioning of Tilden.

Basic, too, is "Proceedings of the Electoral Commission, Count of the Presidential Vote, 1877."

Other pertinent documents are: House Report No. 261, 43rd Congress, 2nd Session, concerning alleged frauds in Louisiana; House Misc. Doc. No. 13, 44th Congress, 2nd Session, "Proceedings and Debates of Congress Relating to Counting the Electoral Votes for President and Vice President of the United States"; House Misc. Doc. No. 34, 44th Congress, 2nd Session, "Testimony Taken by the Select Committee on the Recent Election in the State of Louisiana"; House Report No. 140, 45th Congress, 3rd Session, "Investigation of Alleged Electoral Frauds in the Late Presidential Election" (Potter Committee *Report*); Senate Report No. 611, 44th Congress, 2nd Session, "Report of the Senate Committee on Privileges and Elections With Testimony and Evidence on the Election in the State of Florida in 1876"; Senate Report No. 678, 44th Congress, 2nd Session, "Electoral Vote of Oregon"; Senate Report No. 701, 44th Congress, 2nd Session, "Election in Louisiana in 1876."

Paul L. Haworth's *The Hayes-Tilden Disputed Presidential Election of 1876* is, and probably will remain, the best summary of the election, factual and perhaps as unbiased as is possible. Haworth had the co-operation of Webb C. Hayes I, son of President Hayes. A. M. Gibson, *A Political Crime*, is the "official" Tilden summary, written by a participant in some of the secret maneuvering for Tilden. For Tilden's side see also his "official" biography, John Bigelow, *The Life of Samuel J. Tilden*, but to be corrected by Alexander C. Flick, *Samuel Jones Tilden, A Study in Political Sagacity*, and by Mark D. Hirsch, "Samuel J. Tilden: The Story of a Lost Opportunity," in *American Historical Review*.

For illumination on maneuverings by political leaders on both sides see Leon Burr Richardson, *William E. Chandler, Republican*, for the Republican side, and Allan Nevins, *Abram S. Hewitt*; Allan Nevins, ed., *Selected Writings of Abram S. Hewitt*; and Henry Watterson, "The Hayes-Tilden Contest for the Presidency," in the *Century*, for the Democratic side, all to be read with the proper allowances. Also see Elmer Davis, *History of the New York Times, 1851-1921*.

Claude G. Bowers, *The Tragic Era*, is a tour de force concerning the Southern and Democratic viewpoint on reconstruction and its overthrow. So also is Matthew Josephson, *The Politicos*, concerning reconstruction and the over-all national picture, in particular the machinations of the 1876 election. But these are balanced by James G. Randall, *The Civil War and Reconstruction*; and by such newer studies as Francis Butler Simkins, *A History of the South*; W. E. B. Du Bois, *Black Reconstruction in America*; C. Vann Woodward, *Origins of the New South* and also *Reunion and Reaction, The Compromise of 1877 and the End of Reconstruction*; Rayford W. Logan, *The Negro in American Life and Thought, The Nadir, 1877-1901*; Paul H. Buck, *The Road to Reunion*; E. Merton Coulter, *The South During Reconstruction*; Arthur M. Schlesinger, Sr., *New Viewpoints in American History*; Avery O. Craven, *The Coming of the Civil War*; Wirt A. Cate, *Lucius Q. C. Lamar*; William B. Hesseltine, *Ulysses S. Grant, Politician*; and Gunnar Myrdal and Associates, *An American Dilemma*—by no means a complete list.

In addition, the story is filled in by contemporary newspapers, the *Congressional Globe* and *Congressional Record*, and letters or diaries, such as those of John Sherman, William T. Sherman, James A. Garfield, Grenville M. Dodge, William Henry Smith, William E. Chandler, Benjamin H. Bristow, David

Davis, Stanley Matthews, Henry Watterson, John M. Palmer, Carl Schurz, William M. Evarts, Hamilton Fish, Thomas A. Donaldson, W. B. Allison, Whitelaw Reid, Salmon P. Chase, Alphonso Taft, Benjamin H. Hill, Lucius Q. C. Lamar, Wade Hampton, John M. Harlan and, of course, R. B. Hayes—published and unpublished.

14 See Josephson, *The Politicos, op. cit.*

15 Foulke, *op. cit.*, II, 380-381.

16 Simkins, *A History of the South, op. cit.*, 315; also Logan, *op. cit.*, 9ff.

17 Simkins, *A History of the South, op. cit.*, 289, 314.

18 House Report No. 140, *op. cit.*, I, 97 (Potter Committee Report).

19 See Potter Investigation Testimony, 1ff., also the Report; also RBH *Diary* (Williams), III, 484-485.

20 *Ibid.*, I, 74, November 7, 1841.

21 Potter Investigation Testimony, V.

22 RBH *Diary* III, 370.

CHAPTER XLIX

The Supposed Defeat

1 New York *Times*, June 17, 1876.

2 Matthews to RBH, June 24, 1876.

3 W. H. Painter to RBH, July 10, 1876.

4 Chicago *Tribune*, February 19, 1885.

5 Richardson, *op. cit.*, 180.

6 RBH *Diary* (Williams), III, 333.

7 See Nevins, *Hamilton Fish, op. cit.*, 838ff.

8 Ben: Perley Poore, *op. cit.*, 228.

9 *Ibid.*, 228-229.

10 RBH, *Letters and Messages Together with Letter of Acceptance and Inaugural Address*, 5-6.

11 In Bristow Papers, July 16, 1876.

12 RBH to Grant, July 14, 1876, in *Diary* (Williams), III, 334.

13 Schurz address in Cincinnati, 1876.

14 See Henry Adams, *Letters*, and Mrs. Henry Adams, *Letters*.

15 Charles Nordhoff to RBH, July 10, 1876; J. D. Cox, "The Hayes Administration," *op. cit.*, 823.

16 W. D. Howells to RBH, July 13, 1876.

17 Gail Hamilton (Mary A. Dodge), *Biography of James G. Blaine*, 422.

18 Flick, *op. cit.*, 276-277.

19 RBH *Diary* (Williams), III, 357.

20 RBH to W. S. Ridgway, October 24, 1876, in *Diary* (Williams), III, 370-371; see also William Henry Smith Letter Book, *op. cit.*, 323-325.

21 RBH *Diary* (Williams), III, 357.

22 Smith to RBH, October 5, 1876.

23 RBH to R. C. McCormick, October 14, 1876.

24 See RBH *Diary* (Williams), IV, 396; cf. Conkling, *op. cit.*, 511.

25 RBH to Schurz, August 25, September 15, 1876.

26 RBH *Diary* (Williams), III, 345.

27 Adlai E. Stevenson, *Something of Men I Have Known*, 34.

28 Flick, *op. cit.*, 303.

29 Halstead address, "The War Claims of the South," *op. cit.*, 37.

[30] Theodore C. Smith, *op. cit.*, I, 613.
[31] Dana to RBH, November 10, 1876.
[32] RBH *Diary* (Williams), III, 374-375.

CHAPTER L

The Claim of Victory

[1] New York *Herald*, November 9, 1876.
[2] New York *Times*, November 8, 1876, 6:30 edition.
[3] Sworn testimony by W. F. Chandler appears in Potter Investigation Testimony, 527.
[4] The fullest telling of this story, by John Reid, is in the New York *Times*, June 15, 1887; see Haworth, *The Hayes-Tilden Disputed Election*, *op. cit.*, 45ff., for a good summation; also Elmer Davis, *op. cit.*; see also Potter Investigation Testimony.
[5] Original in HML.
[6] Potter Investigation Testimony, I, 705; also New York *Times* and New York *Herald*, November 7, 1876.
[7] Hewitt, "Secret History of the Election, 1876-77," in Nevins, *Writings of Hewitt, op. cit.*, 163.
[8] In Senate Exec. Doc. No. 2, *op. cit.*, 31.
[9] Hewitt testimony, Senate Misc. Doc. No. 44, *op. cit.*, 489.
[10] Nevins, *Abram S. Hewitt, op. cit.*, 326-327.
[11] *Ibid.*, 329; also "Proceedings of the Electoral Commission," *op. cit.*, 22.

CHAPTER LI

Serene Man

[1] RBH to R. C. McCormick, secretary of the National Committee, October 14, 1876; RBH *Diary* (Williams), III, 372.
[2] New York *Times*, November 11, 1876.
[3] RBH *Diary* (Williams), III, 378.
[4] *Ibid.*
[5] Quoted in *ibid.*, 379.
[6] November 26, 1876, in Lew Wallace, *Autobiography*, 901; see also Irving McKee, *"Ben Hur" Wallace*, 133ff.
[7] RBH *Diary* (Williams), V, 54.
[8] Matthews to RBH, November 9, 1876.
[9] November 14, 1876.

CHAPTER LII

"I Have No Doubt"

[1] See Senate Misc. Doc. No. 44, *op. cit.*
[2] *Ibid.*, 489, 495.
[3] *Ibid.*, 448.
[4] *Ibid.*, 90, 284, 346.
[5] *Ibid.*, 502.
[6] *Ibid.*, 248, 271. The later developments are also in the Potter Investigation Testimony, IV.

[7] W. G. Eliot, Jr., to Watt P. Marchman, September 20, 1948, citing a letter of February 21, 1877.
[8] See Gibson, *op. cit.*, 214-215.
[9] *Ibid.*, 220.
[10] See Potter Investigation Testimony, I, 1410, 1418.
[11] *Ibid.*, 1417.
[12] "Secret History," in Nevins, *Writings of Hewitt, op. cit.*, 179.
[13] Potter Investigation Testimony, 1417ff.
[14] This is based on a reading of the Potter Investigation Testimony and other transcripts of testimony taken by Congressional committees. See Note 13, Chapter XLVIII, this volume.
[15] November 29, 1876, in John Sherman Papers, Library of Congress.
[16] Theodore C. Smith, *op. cit.*, I, 618.
[17] John Sherman, *op. cit.*, I, 558-559.
[18] Theodore C. Smith, *op. cit.*, I, 622.
[19] Potter Investigation Testimony, I, 725.
[20] *Ibid.*, 719.
[21] November 27, 1876.
[22] RBH *Diary* (Williams), III, 384.

CHAPTER LIII

Impasse

[1] Guy Bryan to RBH, December 30, 1876.
[2] *Ibid.*, December 10, 1876.
[3] RBH to John Sherman, January 21, 1877.
[4] See Flick, *op. cit.*, 352ff.
[5] RBH to Samuel Shallabarger, December 29, 1876.

CHAPTER LIV

Danger

[1] Henry George, Jr., *The Life of Henry George*, 272.
[2] Watterson, "The Hayes-Tilden Contest," *op. cit.*, 17.
[3] See Woodward, *Reunion and Reaction, op. cit.*, 110-112; and Flick, *op. cit.*, 360-361.
[4] Senate Misc. Doc. No. 44, *op. cit.*, 407.
[5] *Ibid.*, 411.
[6] L. C. Weir to RBH, February 7, 1877; see also Flick, *op. cit.*, 361.
[7] Nevins, *Writings of Hewitt, op. cit.*, 163-164.
[8] Watterson to the editor of *Century*, June 1913, 286.
[9] Tyler to Taft, November 27, 1876, copy in John Sherman Papers.
[10] January 3, 1877, Smith Papers, Indiana State Library.
[11] Chester H. Krum to Babcock, December 21, 1876, Babcock Papers, Newberry Library, Chicago.
[12] H. C. Leighton to W. B. Allison, December 18, 1876, Allison Papers, Iowa State Historical Library.
[13] Lloyd Lewis, *Sherman, Fighting Prophet*, 623.
[14] Stanley Matthews to RBH, December 15, 1876.

CHAPTER LV

"Fishing"

[1] See Woodward, *Reunion and Reaction, op. cit.*; for this and other works, Professor Woodward should be credited with being the first historian to see realities behind appearances in the election dispute of 1876.

[2] Stanley Matthews to RBH, December 15, 1876.

[3] Quay to RBH, January 20, 1877; also RBH *Diary* (Williams), III, 391.

[4] Cortissoz, *op. cit.*, I, 360.

[5] Sherman to RBH, December 12, 1876.

[6] RBH *Diary* (Williams), III, 390-391.

[7] See Theodore C. Smith, *op. cit.*, I, 626.

[8] George Thomas Palmer, *A Conscientious Turncoat, The Story of John M. Palmer*, 247-248.

[9] Benjamin H. Hill, Jr., *Senator Benjamin H. Hill of Georgia, His Life, Speeches and Writings*, 479.

[10] Theodore C. Smith, *op. cit.*, I, 624.

[11] Garfield to RBH, December 12, 1876; see Theodore C. Smith, *op. cit.*, I, 624-625; and Woodward, *Reunion and Reaction, op. cit.*, 22.

[12] Kasson to RBH, December 17, 1876.

[13] RBH to Guy Bryan, October 24, 1876, "The Hayes-Bryan Correspondence," *op. cit.*, (April 1923), 310; also RBH *Diary* (Williams), III, 286, July 27, 1875.

CHAPTER LVI

The Unwanted Compromise

[1] Woodward, *Reunion and Reaction, op. cit.*, 129. This book gives a ae-tailed and pertinent analysis of the connection between the Texas and Pacific Railroad and the 1876 election, though its interpretation may be too sharp. See also S. G. Reed, *A History of the Texas Railroads*.

[2] Allan Nevins, *John D. Rockefeller*, I, 317ff.

[3] Josephson, *The Politicos, op. cit.*, 210-211.

[4] Woodward, *Reunion and Reaction, op. cit.*, 135-136.

[5] *Ibid.*, 102.

[6] February 2, 1877.

[7] RBH to Garfield, December 16, 1876.

[8] Sherman to RBH, December 9, 1876; RBH to Sherman, December 17, 1876.

[9] December 31, 1876.

[10] Comly to RBH, January 8, 1877.

[11] Potter Investigation Testimony, I, 879.

[12] RBH *Diary* (Williams), III, 382-383.

[13] Potter Investigation Testimony, I, 879.

[14] RBH *Diary* (Williams), III, 383.

[15] Potter Investigation Testimony, I, 900.

[16] Comly to RBH, January 8, 1877, cited in Woodward, *Reunion and Reaction, op. cit.*, 117.

[17] H. V. Boynton to W. H. Smith, December 20, 1876, Smith Collection, Indiana State Historical Library.

[18] See Grenville M. Dodge to Boynton, April 2, 1876, Dodge Papers, Iowa State Historical Museum.

[19] Dodge's letters in the Iowa Library are illuminating as to his connections. See also Jacob R. Perkins, *Trails, Rails and War, The Life of General G. M. Dodge.*

[20] December 20, 1876, in Smith Papers; also in Woodward, *Reunion and Reaction, op. cit.,* 66.

[21] Gray, *op. cit.,* 119-125; also W. H. Smith to RBH, December 22, 1876.

[22] December 18, 1876, in Smith Papers; also in Woodward, *Reunion and Reaction, op. cit.,* 31.

[23] RBH to W. H. Smith, December 24, 1876.

[24] *Ibid.,* January 3, 1877.

[25] Smith to RBH, January 5, 1877.

[26] Boynton to Smith, January 14, 1877, in Smith Papers, quoted by Woodward, *Reunion and Reaction, op. cit.,* 119.

[27] Nevins, *Writings of Hewitt, op. cit.,* 385; also Stanley Matthews to RBH, December 15, 1876, who described a meeting of the wealthiest citizens of New York City, equally divided as to party, to bring about a "satisfactory settlement."

[28] Nevins, *Writings of Hewitt, op. cit.,* 366.

[29] *Ibid.,* 385.

[30] RBH *Diary* (Williams), III, 404-410.

[31] Foulke, *op. cit.,* I, 444.

[32] Hesseltine, *op. cit.,* 419.

[33] Chicago *Tribune,* January 27, 1877.

[34] *Congressional Record,* January 26, 1877.

CHAPTER LVII

The "Fifth Justice"

[1] Chicago *Tribune,* January 19, 30, 1877.

[2] Nevins, *Writings of Hewitt, op. cit.,* 385.

[3] January 29, 1877.

[4] Nevins, *Writings of Hewitt, op. cit.,* 385.

[5] J. W. Fell to John M. Palmer, January 15, 1877, copy with comments in library of Illinois Historical Survey, University of Illinois.

[6] Statement by James E. Harvey, March 17, 1887, close friend of Davis, in Davis Papers, courtesy of Willard L. King.

[7] January 30, 1877.

[8] RBH *Diary* (Williams), III, 411.

[9] January 25, 1877, in HML.

[10] Nevins, *Writings of Hewitt, op. cit.,* 172.

CHAPTER LVIII

Decision

[1] "Proceedings of the Electoral Commission," *op. cit.,* 11ff.

[2] *Ibid.,* 105, 107.

[3] *Ibid.,* 91, 95.

[4] *Ibid.,* 138.

[5] RBH *Diary* (Williams), III, 413-414.

[6] "Proceedings of the Electoral Commission," *op. cit.*, 172.

[7] Nevins, *Writings of Hewitt, op. cit.*, 172.

[8] Bigelow, *Tilden, op. cit.*, I, 95; Hewitt to Joseph M. Rogers, February 24, 1902, in Nevins, *Writings of Hewitt, op. cit.*, 397.

[9] Nevins, *Abram S. Hewitt, op. cit.*, 373; also Woodward, *Reunion and Reaction, op. cit.*, 159ff.

[10] *Ibid.*, for a good summary of this.

[11] "Proceedings of the Electoral Commission," *op. cit.*, 196, 202-203.

[12] RBH *Diary* (Williams), III, 414.

[13] "Proceedings of the Electoral Commission," *op. cit.*, 261.

[14] *Ibid.*, 424.

[15] Hampton to Hayes, December 23, 1876; RBH *Diary* (Williams), III, 396.

[16] "Proceedings of the Electoral Commission," *op. cit.*, 662, 668.

[17] *Ibid.*, 699.

[18] *Ibid.*, 555ff.

[19] *Ibid.*, 559.

[20] *Ibid.*, 581.

[21] *Ibid.*, 639.

[22] RBH *Diary* (Williams), IV, 370, February 10, 1888.

[23] "Proceedings of the Electoral Commission," *op. cit.*, 641.

[24] *Ibid.*, 702.

CHAPTER LIX

Filibuster

[1] Woodward, *Reunion and Reaction, op. cit.*, 177-178.

[2] Boynton to William Henry Smith, February 18, 1877.

[3] Potter Investigation Testimony, III, 631-632.

[4] *Ibid.*, 632.

[5] *Ibid.*, 614.

[6] *Ibid.*, 595ff.

[7] *Ibid.*, 534-535, also 980.

[8] *Ibid.*, I, 1008.

[9] *Ibid.*, 967-968, 975.

[10] Charles Foster to RBH, February 21, 1877.

[11] *Ibid.*

[12] *Ibid.*

[13] Nevins, *Abram S. Hewitt, op. cit.*, 348-352; Flick, *op. cit.*, 357-358.

CHAPTER LX

Re-enter Grant, Re-enter Sherman, Finis Filibuster

[1] See Haworth, *The Hayes-Tilden Disputed Election, op. cit.*, 273.

[2] Burke to Nicholls, February 27, 1877, in Potter Investigation Testimony, III, 618.

[3] Potter Investigation Testimony, III, 618.

[4] *Ibid.*, 617; also I, 991-992.

[5] Young to W. E. Horne, February 23, 1877, in *ibid.*

[6] Nevins, *Hamilton Fish, op. cit.*, 854.

[7] Potter Investigation Testimony, III, 598.

[8] *Ibid.*

[9] *Ibid.*, 618.
[10] *Ibid.*, 620.
[11] *Ibid.*, 595, 618.
[12] Theodore C. Smith, *op. cit.*, I, 644.
[13] Potter Investigation Testimony, III, 595, testimony of Ellis.
[14] *Ibid.*, 622, 625.
[15] See statement by Alphonso Taft, May 9, 1888, in William Howard Taft Papers, Library of Congress.
[16] Potter Investigation Testimony, III, 33.
[17] Foster interview in Fostoria (Ohio) *Review*, March 29, 1877.
[18] Potter Investigation Testimony, III, 624.
[19] *Ibid.*
[20] Dodge to Boynton, April 2, 1877, in William Henry Smith Papers.
[21] Potter Investigation Testimony, I, 990.
[22] *Ibid.*, III, 624.
[23] "Proceedings of the Electoral Commission," *op. cit.*, 712.
[24] Nevins, *Writings of Hewitt, op. cit.*, 176.
[25] *Ibid.*
[26] Potter Investigation Testimony, I, 537.
[27] *Ibid.*, III, 625.
[28] *Congressional Record*, 44th Congress, 2nd Session (March 1, 1877), 2046-2047; also Potter Investigation Testimony, I, 989.
[29] "Proceedings of the Electoral Commission," *op. cit.*, 719.
[30] Theodore C. Smith, *op. cit.*, II, 900.
[31] Flick, *op. cit.*, 395.
[32] "Proceedings Relating to Counting the Electoral Votes," *op. cit.*, 728.

CHAPTER LXI

Number Nineteen

[1] Chicago *Tribune*, March 6, 1877.
[2] Ben: Perley Poore, *op. cit.*, 237.
[3] *Ibid.*, 235.
[4] C. R. Williams, *Life, op. cit.*, II, 1-2.
[5] Halstead to Bristow, November 26, 1876, Bristow Papers, Library of Congress.
[6] *The Capital*, February 18, 1877.
[7] *Ibid.*, July 31, 1881.
[8] Theodore C. Smith, *op. cit.*, I, 646.
[9] Ben: Perley Poore, *op. cit.*, 235.
[10] Theodore C. Smith, *op. cit.*; and Woodward, *Reunion and Reaction, op. cit.*, 203.
[11] Matthews to RBH, February 19, 1877.
[12] RBH, Kenyon Papers, HML.
[13] Chicago *Tribune*, March 2, 1877.
[14] James Dalzell to Webb C. Hayes, September 24, 1922.
[15] Chicago *Tribune*, March 3, 1877.
[16] RBH *Diary* (Williams), III, 426.
[17] William Henry Smith to RBH, October 3, 1877; Mark Twain (S. L. Clemens) to W. D. Howells, May 1, 1877, in Mark Twain's *Letters*, A. B. Paine, ed., I, 293.

[18] RBH *Diary* (Williams), IV, 619.
[19] *Ibid.*, III, 619.
[20] Horatio S. Noyes Diary, courtesy of Mrs. Wallace Goldsmith, Ossining, New York.
[21] *Literary Digest,* February 5, 1927.
[22] RBH *Diary* (Williams), III, 508.
[23] Horatio S. Noyes Diary.

CHAPTER LXII

The Nationalist

[1] February 4, 1877.
[2] February 20, 1877, in G. M. Dodge Letter Book, 1876-1878, Iowa State Department of History.
[3] April 7, 1877, William Henry Smith Papers, Letter Book, Ohio State Archaeological and Historical Society.
[4] See W. E. Binkley, *The Powers of the President,* especially 107, 186ff.
[5] RBH *Diary* (Williams), III, 618.
[6] March 6, 1877.

CHAPTER LXIII

Start

[1] RBH *Diary* (Williams), IV, 385.
[2] *Ibid.*, 149-150.
[3] *Ibid.*, III, 426.
[4] *Ibid.*
[5] Foulke, *op. cit.,* II, 479.
[6] William Henry Smith, report of conversation with RBH in 1890, in RBH *Diary* (Williams), III, 426-427 and C. R. Williams, *Life, op. cit.,* II, 23n.
[7] Nevins, *Hamilton Fish, op. cit.;* Charles Roll, *Colonel Dick Thompson, The Persistent Whig;* also *Dictionary of American Biography.*
[8] Foulke, *op. cit.,* II, 480.
[9] Grenville M. Dodge to RBH, February 17, 1877, and to Jay Gould, same date, Dodge Papers, Iowa State Library.
[10] See John W. Burgess, *The Administration of President Hayes,* 64-65.
[11] RBH *Diary* (Williams), III, 595.
[12] See Woodward, *Reunion and Reaction, op. cit.,* 169ff.
[13] RBH *Diary* (Williams), III, 363.
[14] Josephson, *The Politicos, op. cit.,* 237.
[15] New York *Times,* March 8, 1877.
[16] *Ibid.*, March 9, 1877.
[17] March 9, 1877.
[18] C. R. Williams, *Life, op. cit.,* II, 29.

CHAPTER LXIV

"Healer of Strife"

[1] Potter Investigation Testimony, I, 1012; III, 577, 627-630.
[2] Cate, *op. cit.,* 289.
[3] New York *Times,* March 11, 1877.

⁴ *Ibid.*
⁵ Chamberlain to Matthews, March 7, 1877, in New York *Times,* March 26, 1877.
⁶ New York *Times,* March 7, 1877.
⁷ Nevins, *Hamilton Fish, op. cit.,* 858.
⁸ New York *Times,* March 12, 1877.
⁹ March 15, 1877.
¹⁰ March 14, 1877.
¹¹ RBH *Diary* (Williams), III, 427.
¹² *Ibid.,* 428.
¹³ New York *Times,* March 17, 1877.
¹⁴ RBH *Diary* (Williams), III, 428.
¹⁵ Reprinted in New York *Times,* March 28, 1877.
¹⁶ *Ibid.,* April 1, 1877.
¹⁷ *Ibid.,* March 29, 1877.
¹⁸ Hampton to RBH, March 26, 1877, published in New York *Times,* March 27, 1877.
¹⁹ Hampton to RBH, March 31, 1877, published in New York *Times,* April 4, 1877.
²⁰ RBH *Diary* (Williams), III, 430.
²¹ New York *Times,* April 4, 1877.
²² *Ibid.,* April 10, 11, 1877.
²³ Text of Evarts' instructions in RBH, *Letters and Messages, op. cit.,* 19ff.
²⁴ Report of the Louisiana Commission to RBH, April 24, in RBH, *Letters and Messages, op. cit.,* 30.
²⁵ S. B. Packard to RBH, April 16, 1877, in Potter Investigation Testimony.
²⁶ Potter Investigation Testimony, III, 25-28.
²⁷ See House Exec. Doc. No. 97, 45th Congress, 2nd Session.
²⁸ RBH, *Letters and Messages, op. cit.,* 25.
²⁹ New York *Tribune,* April 22, 1877.
³⁰ Potter Investigation Testimony, III, 10.
³¹ *Ibid.,* 11-12.
³² In C. R. Williams, *Life, op. cit.,* II, 241.

CHAPTER LXV

Broken Pledges

¹ Theodore C. Smith, *op. cit.,* I, 647.
² RBH *Diary* (Williams), III, 450; see also Logan, *op. cit.,* 21ff.
³ RBH to W. D. Bickham, May 3, 1877.
⁴ RBH *Diary* (Williams), III, 508.
⁵ Woodward, *Origins, op. cit.,* 57.
⁶ RBH *Diary* (Williams), III, 510.
⁷ July 4, 1877, in "Hayes-Bryan Correspondence," *op. cit.,* 243.
⁸ RBH Message, December 2, 1878, in *Letters and Messages, op. cit.,* 121.
⁹ April 26, 1877, cited in Woodward, *Reunion and Reaction, op. cit.,* 224.
¹⁰ *Ibid.,* citing "The Hayes-Bryan Correspondence," *op. cit.,* XXVII (1923-1924), 70.
¹¹ Theodore C. Smith, *op. cit.,* I, 647ff.
¹² Huntington to D. D. Colton, October 10, 1877, published in Chicago *Tribune,* December 27, 1883.

NOTES

565

[13] New York *Tribune*, December 19, 1877, cited by Woodward, *Reunion and Reaction, op. cit.*, 234.

[14] See Reed, *op. cit.*, 544ff.

[15] "Trial of Thomas C. Anderson for Publishing Forged Election Returns," reported by T. Wharton Collings, 1878, 121ff.

[16] Theodore C. Smith, *op. cit.*, II, 665.

[17] RBH *Diary* (Williams), III, 459.

[18] *Ibid.*, IV, 280.

[19] *Ibid.*, III, 470-471.

CHAPTER LXVI

Landmarks

[1] See especially Message to Congress, December 6, 1880, in RBH, *Letters and Messages, op. cit.*, 314.

[2] RBH Message to House of Representatives, March 8, 1880, in *ibid.*, 291.

[3] *Ibid.*, 280, December 1, 1879.

[4] *Ibid.*, December 6, 1880.

[5] See Nevins, *Hamilton Fish, op. cit.*, 916ff.

[6] RBH Message to Congress, December 3, 1877, in *Letters and Messages, op. cit.*, 91.

[7] Charles C. Tansill, *The Foreign Policy of Thomas F. Bayard*, quoting John W. Foster to William M. Evarts, June 20, 22, 1877; also House Exec. Doc. No. 13, 45th Congress, 1st Session, I, November 12, 1877.

[8] *Harper's Weekly*, July 26, 1877.

[9] RBH, Message of December 6, 1880, *Letters and Messages, op. cit.*, 270; RBH *Diary* (Williams), III, 467.

[10] Richard B. Morris, "Andrew Jackson, Strikebreaker," *American Historical Review*, LV, No. 1 (October 1949), 54ff.

[11] J. F. Hartranft to RBH, July 23, 1877.

[12] George F. Howe, "President Hayes's Notes of Four Cabinet Meetings, *American Historical Review*, XXXVII, No. 1 (October 1931); also Frederick W. Seward, *Reminiscences of a Wartime Statesman and Diplomat, 1830-1915*, 441.

[13] See RBH *Diary* (Williams), IV, 282, 637.

[14] See Allan Nevins, *The Emergence of Modern America*, 150ff.

[15] RBH *Diary* (Williams), III, 522.

[16] *Ibid.*, 523-524.

[17] February 26, March 4, 1879, originals in HML; Lionel Crocker, *History and Criticism of American Public Address*, 276.

[18] RBH *Diary* (Williams), III, 526.

[19] RBH, *Letters and Messages, op. cit.*, 270.

[20] See Wilfred B. Shaw, chapter on Angell, *Michigan and the Cleveland Era, Sketches of University of Michigan Staff Members and Alumni Who Served in the Cleveland Administrations*, edited by Earl D. Basbt and Lewis G. Vander Velde.

CHAPTER LXVII

Un-Whiggish Old Whig

[1] Executive Order No. 1, June 22, 1877, in RBH, *Letters and Messages, op. cit.*; RBH to Schurz, September 15, 1876.

[2] See R. Wheatley, "The New York Customhouse," *Harper's New Monthly,* June 1884, 38ff.

[3] RBH to Sherman, May 26, 1877.

[4] William Henry Smith, conversation with RBH, in RBH *Diary* (Williams), III, 474.

[5] *Ibid.,* 475.

[6] John Sherman, *op. cit.,* II, 677, 681.

[7] T. C. Platt, *Autobiography,* 88.

[8] Conkling, *op. cit.,* 538ff.

[9] *Ibid.,* 537.

[10] Hesseltine, *op. cit.,* 212.

[11] Venila Levina Shores, *The Hayes-Conkling Controversy,* 247.

[12] Elmer Ellis, *Henry Moore Teller;* Selig F. Adler, "George F. Edmunds," Ph.D. thesis, Ohio State University, 1936, 173.

[13] December 8, 1877.

[14] RBH *Diary* (Williams), III, 448.

[15] *Ibid.,* 454.

[16] *Ibid.,* 514.

[17] John Sherman, *op. cit.,* II, 684.

[18] *Ibid.,* 747-748; RBH *Diary* (Williams), III, 577.

[19] RBH to E. A. Merritt, February 4, 1879, in *Letters and Messages, op. cit.,* 151.

[20] RBH Message to Congress, December 1, 1879, in *ibid.,* 265-266.

[21] RBH *Diary* (Williams), III, 450.

[22] *Harper's Weekly,* December 8, 1877.

[23] RBH *Diary* (Williams), III, 429.

[24] Theodore C. Smith, *op. cit.,* II, 654.

[25] September 11, 1879.

[26] *Harper's Weekly,* February 26, 1881.

[27] RBH to Rev. R. M. Hatfield, March 22, 1889.

[28] RBH Message to Congress, December 3, 1877, in *Letters and Messages, op. cit.,* 77-80.

[29] RBH *Diary* (Williams), V, 6.

[30] John Sherman, *op. cit.,* I, 507; II, 701.

[31] *Ibid.,* 702.

[32] See Helfman, *op. cit.,* 151; also RBH *Diary* (Williams), IV, 459.

[33] C. S. Olcott, *Life of McKinley,* 197.

[34] Medill to RBH, February 25, 27, 1878.

[35] C. R. Williams, *Life, op. cit.,* II, 123.

[36] December 10, 1877.

[37] RBH *Diary* (Williams), III, 461.

[38] *Ibid.,* 459-461.

[39] *Ibid.,* 461.

[40] *Ibid.*

CHAPTER LXVIII

"Revolution?"

[1] RBH *Diary* (Williams), III, 463.

[2] Theodore C. Smith, *op. cit.,* II, 659.

[3] Potter Investigation Testimony, I, 8.

[4] *Ibid.*, II, 98-99.
[5] Richardson, *op. cit.*, 195.
[6] Potter Investigation Testimony, II, 99.
[7] William E. Smith, *The Francis Preston Blair Family in Politics*, II, 486.
[8] RBH *Diary* (Williams), III, 482.
[9] Benjamin H. Hill, Jr., *op. cit.*, 591.
[10] Theodore C. Smith, *op. cit.*, II, 666.
[11] New York *Illustrated Graphic*, May 28, 1878, which summarizes much newspaper comment.
[12] William Henry Smith, in notes of conversation with RBH in 1883, in RBH *Diary* (Williams), III, 484.
[13] C. R. Williams, *Life, op. cit.*, II, 155.
[14] RBH *Diary* (Williams), III, 491, 536.
[15] Potter Investigation Testimony, I, 806.
[16] RBH *Diary* (Williams), III, 482.
[17] *Ibid.*, IV, 235.
[18] Potter Investigation Testimony, I, 17.
[19] *Ibid.*, 357ff.
[20] John Sherman, *op. cit.*, II, 656.
[21] Potter Committee Report, *op. cit.*, March 3, 1879, 30.
[22] Potter Investigation Testimony, I, 1015.

CHAPTER LXIX

Boomerang in Ciphers

[1] January 18, 1877.
[2] Potter Investigation Testimony, IV, 176-177.
[3] *Ibid.*, 178ff.
[4] *Ibid.*, 184.
[5] October 16, 1878. For full text, see Bigelow, *Tilden, op. cit.*, II, 175ff.
[6] Quoted by Richardson, *op. cit.*, 232.
[7] Potter Investigation Testimony, IV, 214.
[8] *Ibid.*, 235.
[9] *Ibid.*, 266ff.
[10] *Ibid.*, 276.
[11] *Harper's Weekly*, March 1, 1879.
[12] Potter Committee Report, 95-118.
[13] John Sherman, *op. cit.*, II, 657.

CHAPTER LXX

A Period of "Ups"

[1] Thomas Donaldson Diary, June 9, 1878, copy in HML.
[2] Garrison, "President Hayes: The Opponent of Prohibition," *op. cit.*, 171ff.; and contemporary newspaper accounts.
[3] Force, "Reminiscences," MSS., *op. cit.*
[4] Frances Hayes, interview.
[5] RBH *Diary* (Williams), III, 644-645; see also Bess Furman, *White House Profile*, 218ff.
[6] RBH, "Memorandum for Garfield," January 17, 1881, in *Diary* (Williams), III, 639.

[7] Brinkerhoff, in "Hayes as a Philanthropist," *op. cit.,* 15.
[8] RBH *Diary* (Williams), III, 528.
[9] RBH Message, April 29, 1879, in *Letters and Messages, op. cit.,* 186.
[10] RBH Message, May 12, 1879, in *ibid.,* 199.
[11] Cortissoz, *op. cit.,* x.
[12] RBH, *Letters and Messages, op. cit.,* 182-183.
[13] See Burgess, *op. cit.,* 114ff.; and C. R. Williams, *Life, op. cit.,* II, 170ff.
[14] Benjamin H. Hill, Jr., *op. cit.,* 602, speech in the Senate, May 10, 1879; see also Hamilton J. Eckenrode, *Rutherford B. Hayes, Statesman of Reunion,* 161.
[15] RBH *Diary* (Williams), III, 564.
[16] *New York Daily Graphic,* November 8, 1879.

CHAPTER LXXI

Bystander's Vindication

[1] Smith to Webb C. Hayes, March 31, 1879; also February 17, 1880.
[2] RBH *Diary* (Williams), IV, 351.
[3] June 10, 1879, in Bristow Papers.
[4] RBH to L. Clarke Davis, June 5, 1879.
[5] John Sherman to John B. Henderson, June 23, 1879, in *Recollections, op. cit.,* II, 731.
[6] September 6, 1878.
[7] Lucy E. Keeler Journal, quoting RBH; also Allan Nevins, *Frémont, The West's Greatest Adventurer,* 689; Irving Stone, *Immortal Wife,* 493; Chicago *Inter-Ocean,* September 5, 1878, quoting Frémont.
[8] RBH *Diary* (Williams), III, 557.
[9] See Otto Eisenschiml, *The Celebrated Case of Fitz John Porter,* 212ff.; RBH *Diary* (Williams), III, 583, 630.
[10] *Ibid.,* 637.
[11] *Ibid.,* IV, 10-12.
[12] John Sherman, *op. cit.,* II, 731.
[13] Theodore C. Smith, *op. cit.,* II, 945.
[14] RBH *Diary* (Williams), III, 582.
[15] In *ibid.,* III, 583; see also Bascom N. Timmons, ed., *Charles G. Dawes, A Journal of the McKinley Years,* 9.
[16] RBH *Diary* (Williams), III, 600.
[17] June 15, 1880.
[18] RBH *Diary* (Williams), III, 600-601.
[19] Bigelow, *Tilden, op. cit.,* II, 270.
[20] RBH *Diary* (Williams), IV, 298; also RBH to W. E. Chandler, September 29, 1885.
[21] RBH *Diary* (Williams), IV, 298.
[22] RBH, *Letters and Messages, op. cit.,* 305-306.

CHAPTER LXXII

Out of It

[1] Howells to Webb C. Hayes, August 23, 1919.
[2] See RBH *Diary* (Williams), III, 640.
[3] RBH to George F. Hoar, November 24, 1880.

[4] RBH, *Letters and Messages, op. cit.*, 351.
[5] Helfman, *op. cit.*
[6] RBH *Diary* (Williams), IV, 459.
[7] R. Gilmour to RBH, October 8, 1880.
[8] Nevins, *Writings of Hewitt, op. cit.*, 381.
[9] January 1, 1881.
[10] March 4, 1881, original in Indiana State Library.

CHAPTER LXXIII

Private Citizen Again

[1] Fremont *Messenger*, September 20, 1883.
[2] February 7, 1877.
[3] RBH *Diary* (Williams), IV, 168.
[4] *Ibid.*, 111, 195.
[5] September 28, 1883.
[6] Clipping in RBH Diary, MSS., October 1, 1883; also Fremont *Journal*, October 5, 1883.
[7] RBH *Diary* (Williams), V, 74-75.
[8] *Ibid.*, IV, 245.
[9] *Ibid.*, V, 133.
[10] Slason Thompson, *op. cit.*, 221-223.

CHAPTER LXXIV

Sophia's Victory

[1] Lucy E. Keeler Journal, June 22, 1889; also RBH *Diary* (Williams), IV, 471.
[2] Lucy E. Keeler Journal, June 23, 1889.
[3] RBH *Diary* (Williams), IV, 473-474.
[4] *Ibid.*, 491, 595.
[5] RBH to Howells, September 14, 1889.
[6] July 5, 1889, in Hayes Bigelow Papers.
[7] Lucy E. Keeler Journal, October, 1889; RBH *Diary* (Williams), IV, 515.
[8] RBH to Mrs. John Herron, October 29, 1889; RBH *Diary* (Williams), IV, 296.
[9] *Ibid.*, 277.
[10] *Ibid.*, 354.
[11] *Ibid.*, 261-262.
[12] *Ibid.*, 367.
[13] *Ibid.*, 435.
[14] *Ibid.*, 556.
[15] *Ibid.;* also 546.
[16] *Ibid.*, 565, 635.
[17] *Ibid.*, 397.
[18] Paxton Hibben, *Henry Ward Beecher, An American Portrait*, 288.
[19] See the author's *Eagle Forgotten; The Life of John Peter Altgeld*, 110.
[20] Charles and Mary Beard, *op. cit.*, II, 113.
[21] David Davis to John Norton, April 8, 1881, in Chicago *Times*, April 13, 1881.

CHAPTER LXXV

"Shoving On to the End!"

[1] RBH *Diary* (Williams), IV, 629-632.
[2] Edwin Alderman, *J. L. M. Curry; A Biography*, 338.
[3] RBH to Henry C. Corbin, December 14, 1891.
[4] RBH *Diary* (Williams), V, 35.
[5] RBH to John DeWitt, March 29, 1890.
[6] RBH *Diary* (Williams), V, 106.
[7] Lucy E. Keeler Journal, HML.
[8] Memorial Meeting, Board of Trustees, Ohio State University, January 19, 1893, in RBH *Diary* (Williams), V, 202.
[9] Allan Nevins, *Grover Cleveland*, 563.

SELECTED BIBLIOGRAPHY

Collections of Letters, Manuscripts and Journals
(HML refers to Hayes Memorial Library at Fremont, Ohio.)

Allison, W. B., Papers, Iowa State Historical Department, Des Moines.

"The Austin Family of Suffield," a Memorandum, Connecticut Historical Society.

Babcock, General Orville, Papers, Newberry Library, Chicago.

Bigelow, Hayes, Papers, Brattleboro, Vermont.

Bigelow, Russell A., Diary, owned by Hayes Bigelow, Brattleboro, Vermont.

Birchard, Sardis, Letters, HML.

————, Memorandum Book, Lower Sandusky, Ohio, begun October 11, 1832, HML.

Bristow, Benjamin, Papers, Library of Congress.

Camp, J. A., Papers, in Collection of Regional History, Cornell University Library.

Cochran, William, MSS. biography of J. D. Cox, copy in HML.

"A Complete Record of the Proceedings of R. Dickinson, Executor of George Grant, Dec'd, August 21, 1843," HML.

Dodge, Grenville M., Papers, Iowa State Historical Department, Des Moines.

Donaldson, Thomas, Diary, copy in HML.

Force, Manning L., "Reminiscences of Rutherford B. Hayes," MSS. in HML.

Garfield, James, Diary and Letters, Library of Congress.

Hayes, Chloe Smith, Diary, owned by Hayes Bigelow, Brattleboro, Vermont; copy in HML.

Hayes, Fanny, Letters to RBH, in bound volume, HML.

Hayes, Russell, Diary, owned by Hayes Bigelow, Brattleboro, Vermont.

Hayes, Rutherford, Sr., "History of My Ancestors," HML.

Hayes, Rutherford B., Genealogical Book, HML.

————, Letters as Governor, Governor's Letter Books, Ohio State Archaeological and Historical Society, Columbus, Ohio.

————, Letters, Diaries and General Papers, HML.

————, Papers, Kenyon College, Gambier, Ohio.

————, "Recollections of My Sister Fanny," 1856, HML.

————, Scrapbook Clippings, HML.

Hayes, Sophia, Letters, Papers, Diary, HML.

Hayes, Webb C. I, Journal, 1877-1881, HML.

Herron, John W., Patrick Mallon, Aaron F. Perry, Ainsworth R. Spofford, Manning F. Force, "Report of Special Committee of Literary Club of Cincinnati on The Death of Rutherford B. Hayes," HML.

Hoadley, C. J., "The Birchard Family," 1873, HML.

Illinois Central Papers, Newberry Library, Chicago.

Keeler, Janette Elliott, Reminiscences, HML.

Keeler, Lucy Elliot, Journal (with many conversations with Hayes), HML.

————, "Recollections of My Mother," 1905, HML.

Lane, Ebenezer, Letters, Chicago Historical Society.
Lane, W. G., Letters, Yale University Library.
Law Department Letter Books, City Solicitor's Office, Cincinnati.
Literary Club of Cincinnati, Minutes Books, 1849-1861, courtesy of Carl Vitz.
Matthews, Stanley, Letters, a collection in Historical and Philosophical Society, Cincinnati.
Mitchell, Laura Platt, MSS. on Lucy Hayes, HML.
Morton, Oliver P., Materials, Indiana Historical Society, Indianapolis.
————, Papers, Henry County Historical Society, Newcastle, Indiana.
Noyes, Horatio S., Diary, owned by Mrs. Wallace Goldsmith, Ossining, New York.
Oberlin College Prudential Committee Minutes, 1875.
Pease, Richard L., "The Burchards of Edgarton, Martha's Vineyard, Massachusetts," a Memorandum, HML.
Philomathesian Society, Minutes Book, 1832-1848, Kenyon College Library.
Session Records of the United Congregations of the Presbyterian Church of Radnor, Liberty and Delaware, 1819-1835.
Sherman, John, Papers, Library of Congress.
Siebert, Wilbur H., Papers on the Underground Railroad, Ohio Archaeological and Historical Society.
Smith, Samuel, Account Book, Brainbridge, New York.
Smith, William Henry, Letter Books, Ohio State Archaeological and Historical Society.
————, Papers in the William Henry Smith Memorial Library, Indiana Historical Society, Indianapolis.
Spofford, Ainsworth R., "R. B. Hayes, Beloved Son of Memory," 1893, Cincinnati Literary Club talk, MSS. in HML.
Taft, William Howard, Papers, Library of Congress.
Town of Wilmington Records.
Vermont Historical Society, Collections, Montpelier.
Western Reserve Historical Society, Manuscript Collections, Cleveland.

Published Books

Abbot, Abiel, *History of Andover from Its Settlement to 1829*, Andover, 1829.
Adams, Henry, *The Education of Henry Adams*, Boston, 1918.
Adams, James Truslow, *The Founding of New England*, Boston, 1921.
Alderman, Edwin, *J. L. M. Curry; A Biography*, New York, 1911.
Alexander, D. S., *A Political History of the State of New York, 1774-1882*, 3 vols., New York, 1906-1909.
Alumna of Wesleyan Female College, Cincinnati.
Annals of Cleveland, 1818-1876, W. P. A. Digest and Index of the Newspaper Record of Events and Opinions, 59 vols., Cleveland, 1937-1938.
Appletons' Annual Cyclopedia, New York.
Atwater, Edward E., *History of the Colony of New Haven to Its Absorption into Connecticut*, New Haven, 1881.
Bancroft, George, *History of the United States*, 10 vols., Boston, 1834-1874.
Barker, Eugene C., *The Life of Stephen F. Austin, Founder of Texas*, Nashville, 1925.
Barker, J. M., *History of Ohio Methodism*, Cincinnati, 1898.

Barnard, Harry, *Eagle Forgotten, The Life of John Peter Altgeld*, Indianapolis, 1938.

Barnes, W. H., *History of the Thirty-ninth Congress of the United States*, New York, 1868.

Barrows, Chester L., *William E. Evarts, Lawyer, Diplomat, Statesman*, Chapel Hill, 1941.

Barry, John Stetson, *History of Massachusetts*, 3 vols., Boston, 1855-1857.

Barton, W. E., *The Life of Clara Barton*, 2 vols., Boston, 1922.

Baskin, O. L., *History of Delaware County and Ohio*, Chicago, 1880.

Bassett, John Spencer, *Makers of a New Nation*, New Haven, 1928.

Bates, Ernest Sutherland, *The Story of Congress, 1789-1935*, New York, 1936.

Beale, Howard K., *The Critical Year, A Study of Andrew Johnson and Reconstruction*, New York, 1930.

Beard, Charles and Mary, *The Rise of American Civilization*, New York, 1937.

Bemis, Samuel Flagg, *John Quincy Adams and the Foundations of American Foreign Policy*, New York, 1949.

Beveridge, Albert J., *Abraham Lincoln, 1809-1858*, 2 vols., Boston, 1928.

Bigelow, John, *The Life of Samuel J. Tilden*, 2 vols., New York, 1895.

————, *Retrospections of an Active Life*, 5 vols., New York, 1909.

Billington, R. A., *Westward Expansion, A History of the American Frontier*, New York, 1949.

Binkley, W. E., *The Powers of the President*, New York, 1937.

————, *President and Congress*, Garden City, New York, 1947.

Blackwell, A. S., *Lucy Stone*, Boston, 1930.

Blaine, J. G., *Twenty Years of Congress: From Lincoln to Garfield*, 2 vols., Norwich, Connecticut, 1884-1886.

Bowers, Claude G., *The Tragic Era*, Boston, 1929.

Bowland, James, *Pioneer Recollections of the Early Thirties and Forties in Sandusky County, Ohio*, Fremont, Ohio, 1903.

Brennan, J. Fletcher, ed., *A Biographical Encyclopedia and Portrait Gallery of Distinguished Men* [of Ohio], 2 vols., Cincinnati, 1880.

Brinkerhoff, Roeliff, *Recollections of a Lifetime*, Cincinnati, 1900.

Buck, Paul H., *The Road to Reunion, 1865-1900*, Boston, 1937.

Buck, Solon J., *The Granger Movement, 1870-1880*, Cambridge, 1913.

Burgess, John W., *The Administration of President Hayes*, New York, 1916.

Butterfield, Consul W., *History of Seneca County, Ohio*, Sandusky, 1848.

Cabot, Mary Rogers, *Annals of Brattleboro, 1681-1895*, Brattleboro, 1921-1922.

Cargill, Oscar, *Intellectual America; Ideas on the March*, New York, 1941.

Carpenter, W. H., and T. S. Arthur, *The History of Vermont*, Philadelphia, 1853.

Carroll, Howard, *Twelve Americans, Their Lives and Times*, New York, 1880.

Carter, A. G. W., *The Old Court House; Reminiscences*, Cincinnati, 1880.

Cary, Edward, *George William Curtis*, Boston, 1894.

Catalogue of Harvard University, 1844-1845, Cambridge.

Cate, Wirt A., *Lucius Q. C. Lamar, Secession and Reunion*, Chapel Hill, 1935.

Cater, Harold Dean, ed., *Henry Adams and His Friends, A Collection of His Unpublished Letters, etc.*, Boston, 1947.

Caulkins, Frances M., *History of New London, Connecticut, 1612-1852,* New London, 1852.

————, *History of Norwich, Connecticut, from Its Possession by the Indians to the year 1866.* Hartford, 1866.

Chamberlain, William Henry, *Sketches of War History, 1861-1865,* v. 4; Papers read before Ohio Military Order of the Loyal Legion of the United States, Cincinnati, 1887.

Chapin, Alonzo B., *Glastenbury for Two Hundred Years,* Hartford, 1853.

Chapman, Frederick W., *The Trowbridge Family,* New Haven, 1872.

Che-le-co-the, Glimpses of Yesterday, Chillicothe, Ohio, 1896.

Chidsey, D. B., *The Gentleman from New York: A Life of Roscoe Conkling,* New Haven, 1935.

Childs, Hamilton, *Gazetteer and Business Directory of Windham County, Vermont, 1724-1884.*

Cist, Charles, *Sketches and Statistics of Cincinnati in 1851,* Cincinnati, 1851.

Clapp, Margaret, *Forgotten First Citizen: John Bigelow,* Boston, 1947.

Cleaves, Freeman, *Old Tippecanoe, William Henry Harrison,* New York, 1939.

Clemenceau, Georges, *American Reconstruction, 1865-1870,* New York, 1928.

Coffin, Levi, *Reminiscences,* Cincinnati, 1876.

Coleman, Charles H., *The Election of 1868,* New York, 1933.

Commager, Henry Steele, *Documents of American History,* New York, 1940.

Commons, J. R., et al., *History of Labour in the United States,* 4 vols., New York, 1918-1935.

Conkling, Alfred R., *The Life and Letters of Roscoe Conkling,* New York, 1889.

Conway, Moncure Daniel, *Autobiography,* 2 vols., Boston, 1904.

Conwell, Russell H., *Life and Public Services of Gov. Rutherford B. Hayes,* Boston, 1876.

Cook, Margaret Scott, *Sketch of the Life of Matthew Scott Cook,* Chillicothe, Ohio, 1883.

Cooke, D. G., *William Dean Howells, A Critical Study,* New York, 1922.

Cortissoz, Royal, *Life of Whitelaw Reid,* 2 vols., New York, 1921.

Coulter, E. Merton, *Georgia, A Short History,* Chapel Hill, 1947.

————, *The South During Reconstruction, 1865-1877,* Baton Rouge, 1947.

Cox, Jacob Dolson, *Military Reminiscences of the Civil War,* New York, 1900.

Cox, James M., *Journey Through My Years,* New York, 1946.

Craven, Avery O., *The Coming of the Civil War,* New York, 1942.

Crocker, Henry, *History of the Baptists in Vermont,* Bellows Falls, Vermont, 1913.

Curti, Merle E., *The Growth of American Thought,* New York, London, 1943.

Davis, Elmer, *History of the New York Times, 1851-1921,* New York, 1921.

Davis, Mrs. John, *In Memoriam, Lucy Webb Hayes,* Cincinnati, 1890.

Davis, W. W., *The Civil War and Reconstruction in Florida,* New York, 1913.

de Chambrun, C. L., *Cincinnati, Story of the Queen City,* New York, 1939.

Depew, C. M., *My Memories of Eighty Years,* New York, 1922.

Destler, Chester McA., *American Radicalism, 1865-1901*, New London, 1946.

Dewey, D. R., *Financial History of the United States*, New York, 1903.

Dickerman, E. D., *Dickerman Genealogy*, New Haven, 1922.

Dictionary of American Biography.

Dodge, G. M., *How We Built the Union Pacific Railway*, New York, 1910.

Dorr, Rheta Louise, *Susan B. Anthony*, New York, 1928.

Downes, Randolph C., *Canal Days*, Toledo, 1949.

———, *Lake Port*, Toledo, 1951.

Du Bois, W. E. B., *Black Reconstruction in America*, New York, 1935.

———, *Dusk of Dawn*, New York, 1940.

Dunning, William A., *Reconstruction, Political and Economic*, New York, 1907.

Dwight, Timothy, *Travels in New England and New York, 1796-1815*, 4 vols., New Haven, 1821-1822.

Eastman, Hubbard, *Noyesism Unveiled*, Brattleboro, 1849.

Eckenrode, Hamilton J., *Rutherford B. Hayes, Statesman of Reunion*, New York, 1930.

Eisenschiml, Otto, *The Celebrated Case of Fitz John Porter*, Indianapolis, 1950.

Elliott, Samuel, *Extracts from "Ruricus," Journals and Letters*, Clifford Hayes Smith, ed., Brattleboro, 1928.

Ellis, Elmer, *Henry Moore Teller, Defender of the West*, Caldwell, Idaho, 1941.

Evarts, Sherman, ed., *William Maxwell Evarts, Arguments and Speeches*, 3 vols., New York, 1919.

Everett, Homer, *History of Sandusky County, Ohio*, Cleveland, 1882.

Field, David Dudley, *Speeches, Arguments and Miscellaneous Papers*, New York, 1884.

Finley, Isaac J., *Pioneer Record and Reminiscences of the Early Settlers and Settlement of Ross County, Ohio*, Cincinnati, 1871.

Fish, C. R., *Civil Service and the Patronage*, Cambridge, 1904.

Fleming, Walter F., *The Civil War and Reconstruction in Alabama*, New York, 1905.

———, *Documentary History of Reconstruction*, 2 vols., Cleveland, 1906.

Flick, Alexander C., with G. S. Lobrano, *Samuel Jones Tilden; A Study in Political Sagacity*, New York, 1939.

Foraker, Mrs. J. B., *I Would Live It Again*, New York, 1932.

Ford, Henry Allen and Kate B., comp., *History of Cincinnati, Ohio*, Cleveland, 1881.

Foulke, William D., *Life of Oliver P. Morton*, 2 vols., Indianapolis, 1889.

Fowler, William Chauncey, *History of Durham, Connecticut*, Hartford, 1866.

Fuess, C. M., *Carl Schurz, Reformer*, New York, 1932.

Furman, Bess, *White House Profile; A Social History of the White House, Its Occupants and Its Festivities*, Indianapolis, 1951.

Gabriel, Ralph Henry, *The Course of American Democratic Thought*, New York, 1940.

Galbreath, Charles B., *History of Ohio*, New York, 1925.

Garraty, John A., *Henry Cabot Lodge*, New York, 1953.

George, Henry, Jr., *The Life of Henry George*, New York, 1900.

Gibson, A. M., *A Political Crime*, New York, 1885.

Gillett, F. H., *George Frisbie Hoar*, Boston, 1934.

Goodrich, S. G. (Peter Parley), *Recollections of a Lifetime*, New York, 1857.

Goodykoontz, Colin, *Home Missions on the American Frontier*, Caldwell, 1939.

Gosnell, Harold F., *Boss Platt and His New York Machine*, Chicago, 1924.

Goss, Charles Frederick, ed., *Cincinnati, The Queen City*, Cincinnati, 1912.

Grant, U. S., *Personal Memoirs*, New York, 1885-1886.

Green, James Albert, *The Literary Club of Cincinnati in 1849*, Cincinnati, 1949.

Greve, C. T., *Centennial History of Cincinnati*, 2 vols., Chicago, 1904.

Hacker, Louis M., *The Triumph of American Capitalism*, New York, 1940.

———, *The United States Since 1865*, New York, 1939.

Hall, B. H., *History of Eastern Vermont from Its Earliest Settlement to the Close of the Eighteenth Century*, New York, 1858.

Halstead, Murat, *The Illustrious Life of William McKinley*, Chicago, 1901.

———, *Life of Jay Gould*, Philadelphia, 1892.

Hamilton, Gail (Mary A. Dodge), *Biography of James G. Blaine*, Norwich, Connecticut, 1895.

Hamilton, J. G. de R., *Reconstruction in North Carolina*, New York, 1914.

Haney, L. H., *A Congressional History of Railways to 1887*, 2 vols., Madison, 1908-1910.

Harlow, Alvin F., *The Serene Cincinnatians*, New York, 1950.

Harlow, Ralph Volney, *Samuel Adams, Promoter of the American Revolution*, New York, 1923.

Hart, A. B., *Salmon Portland Chase*, Boston, 1899.

Harvard Law School Book of Entrances, Cambridge, 1839-1864.

Harvard Law School Faculty, *The Centennial History of Harvard Law School, 1817-1897*, Cambridge

Hatch, Louis C., and Earl Shoup, *A History of the Vice Presidency of the United States*, New York, 1943.

Hatcher, Harlan, *The Western Reserve*, Indianapolis, 1949.

Haworth, Paul L., *The Hayes-Tilden Disputed Presidential Election of 1876*, Cleveland, 1906.

———, *Reconstruction and Union*, New York, 1912.

Hayes, Charles Wells, *A Long Journey, The Story of Daniel Hayes*, Portland, Maine, 1876.

———, *George Hayes of Windsor and His Descendants*, Buffalo, 1884.

Hayes, Rutherford B., *Letters and Messages, Together with Letter of Acceptance and Inaugural Address*, Washington, 1881.

Hemenway, Abby Maria, *The Vermont Historical Gazetteer*, 5 vols., 1868-1891.

Henry, Robert Selph, *The Story of Reconstruction*, Indianapolis, 1938.

Hesseltine, William B., *Ulysses S. Grant, Politician*, New York, 1935.

Hibben, Paxton, *Henry Ward Beecher, An American Portrait*, New York, 1927.

Hicks, J. D., *The American Nation; A History of the United States from 1865 to the Present*, Boston, 1941.

Hill, Benjamin, Jr., *Senator Benjamin H. Hill of Georgia, His Life, Speeches and Writings*, Atlanta, 1891.

Hill, Norman N., Jr., comp., *History of Knox County, Ohio*, Mt. Vernon, Ohio, 1881.

———, *History of Licking County, Ohio*, Newark, Ohio, 1881.

Hirsch, Mark D., *William C. Whitney, Modern Warwick*, New York, 1948.

History of Berkshire County, Massachusetts, New York, 1885.

History of Seneca County, Ohio, 1886.

Hoar, George F., *Autobiography of Seventy Years*, New York, 1903.

Hofstadter, Richard, *The American Political Tradition and the Men Who Made It*, New York, 1948.

———, *Social Darwinism in American Thought, 1860-1915*, Philadelphia, 1944.

Holbrook, Stewart H., *The Yankee Exodus: An Account of Migration from New England*, New York, 1950.

Holcombe, Arthur N., *The Middle Classes in American Politics*, Cambridge, 1940.

Holland, Josiah G., *History of Western Massachusetts*, 2 vols., Springfield, Massachusetts, 1855.

Houck, George F., *A History of Catholicity in Northern Ohio and in the Diocese of Cleveland*, Cleveland, 1896.

Howard, J. Q., *The Life, Public Services and Select Speeches of Rutherford B. Hayes*, Cincinnati, 1876.

Howe, G. F., *Chester A. Arthur*, New York, 1934.

Howe, Henry, *Historical Collections of Ohio*, Cincinnati, 1869, 1897, 1907.

Howells, Mildred, *Life in Letters of William Dean Howells*, 2 vols., New York, 1928.

Howells, William Dean, *Sketch of the Life and Character of Rutherford B. Hayes*, New York, Boston, 1876.

Hudson, W. C., *Random Recollections of an Old Political Reporter*, New York, 1911.

Hunt, Thomas, *The Life of William H. Hunt*, Brattleboro, 1922.

Hyman, Sidney, *The American President*, New York, 1954.

James, Marquis, *Andrew Jackson, The Border Captain* and *Portrait of a President*, 2 vols., Indianapolis, 1933-1937.

Jarrell, Hampton M., *Wade Hampton and the Negro, The Road Not Taken*, Columbia, S. C., 1949.

Jordan, Philip D., *The National Road*, Indianapolis, 1948.

———, *Ohio Comes of Age, 1873-1900*, Columbus, 1941.

Josephson, Matthew, *The Politicos, 1865-1896*, New York, 1938.

———, *The Robber Barons*, New York, 1934.

Judd, Sylvester, *History of Hadley*, Northampton, 1863.

Kazin, Alfred, *On Native Grounds*, New York, 1942.

Keifer, Joseph Warren, *Slavery and Four Years of War*, New York, 1900.

Kennedy, J. H., *History of the City of Cleveland*, Cleveland, 1896.

Key, V. O., Jr., *Southern Politics in State and Nation*, New York, 1949.

King, Willard L., *Melville Weston Fuller*, New York, 1950.

Kinsley, Philip, *The Chicago Tribune, Its First Hundred Years*, 3 vols., New York, 1943-1946.

Knapp, Horace S., *History of the Maumee Valley*, Toledo, 1872.

Krock, Arthur F., *Editorials of Henry Watterson*, New York, 1923.

Lang, William, *History of Seneca County, Ohio*, Springfield, Ohio, 1880.

Larson, Henrietta M., *Jay Cooke, Private Banker*, Cambridge, 1936.

Lee, Alfred E., *History of the City of Columbus*, 2 vols., New York, 1892.

Leonard, Lewis Alexander, *Life of Alphonso Taft*, New York, 1920.

Lewis, Lloyd, *Captain Sam Grant*, Boston, 1950.

————, *Sherman, Fighting Prophet*, New York, 1932.

Logan, Rayford W., *The Negro in American Life and Thought, The Nadir, 1877-1901*, New York, 1954.

Lonn, Ella, *Reconstruction in Louisiana After 1868*, New York, 1918.

Lorant, Stephen, *The Presidency*, New York, 1951.

Ludlum, David M., *Social Ferment in Vermont, 1791-1850*, New York, 1939.

Lynch, D. T., *The Wild Seventies*, New York, 1941.

Madison, Charles A., *Critics and Crusaders*, New York, 1947.

Mansfield, David L., *The History of the Town of Dummerston, Vt.*, Ludlow, Vermont, 1884.

Marcosson, Isaac F., *"Marse Henry," a Biography of Henry Watterson*, New York, 1951.

Mather, Cotton, *Magnalia Christi Americana*, Hartford, 1855.

Mathews, John Mabry, *Legislative and Judicial History of the Fifteenth Amendment*, Baltimore, 1909.

Mayes, Edward, *Lucius Q. C. Lamar*, Nashville, 1896.

Mayo, Bernard, *Henry Clay*, Boston, 1937.

McClure, A. K., *Our Presidents and How We Make Them*, New York, London, 1900.

McClure, S. S., *My Autobiography*, New York, 1914.

McCulloch, Hugh, *Men and Measures*, New York, 1888.

McGrane, Reginald Charles, *William Allen, A Study in Western Democracy*, Columbus, 1925.

McKee, Irving, *"Ben Hur" Wallace*, Berkeley, 1947.

McPherson, Edward A., *A Political History of the United States During Reconstruction*, Washington, 1875.

Mearns, David C., ed., *The Lincoln Papers*, Garden City, New York, 1948.

Meek, Basil, ed., *Twentieth Century History of Sandusky County, Ohio*, Chicago, 1909.

Merriam, G. S., *The Life and Times of Samuel Bowles*, 2 vols., New York, 1885.

Minnigerode, Meade, *The Fabulous Forties, 1840-50*, New York, 1924.

Minot, George Richards, *The History of the Insurrections in Massachusetts in the Year 1786 and the Rebellion Consequent Thereon*, Boston, 1788.

Mott, Frank L., *A History of American Magazines*, New York, 1938.

Muzzey, David S., *James G. Blaine*, New York, 1934.

Myers, Allen O., *Bosses and Boodle in Ohio Politics*, Cincinnati, 1895.

Myers, Gustavus, *History of the Great American Fortunes*, Chicago, 1911.

Myrdal, Gunnar, and Associates, *An American Dilemma*, 2 vols., New York, 1944.

The National Cyclopedia of American Biography.

Nevins, Allan, *Abram S. Hewitt: With Some Account of Peter Cooper*, New York, 1935.

————, *The Emergence of Modern America*, New York, 1927.

————, *Frémont, The West's Greatest Adventurer*, 2 vols., New York, 1928.

————, *Grover Cleveland, A Study in Courage*, New York, 1932.

———, Hamilton Fish, The Inner History of the Grant Administration, New York, 1936.

———, John D. Rockefeller, New York, 1940.

———, Ordeal of the Union, New York, 1947.

———, ed., Selected Writings of Abram S. Hewitt, New York, 1937.

Nichols, Roy Franklin, The Disruption of American Democracy, New York, 1948.

Nicolay, John G., and John Hay, Abraham Lincoln, 10 vols., New York, 1890.

Nordhoff, Charles, The Communistic Societies of the United States, New York, 1875.

———, The Cotton States in the Spring and Summer of 1875, New York, 1876.

Noyes, Alexander Dana, Forty Years of American Finance, New York, 1907.

Noyes, George Wallingford, ed., The Religious Experiences of John Humphrey Noyes, New York, 1923.

———, ed., John Humphrey Noyes, The Putney Community, Oneida, New York, 1931.

Noyes, John Humphrey, History of American Socialisms, Philadelphia, 1870.

Noyes, Pierrepont Burt, My Father's House; An Oneida Boyhood, New York, 1937.

Nye, Russel Blaine, George Bancroft, the Brahmin Rebel, New York, 1944.

Oberholtzer, E. P., A History of the United States Since the Civil War, 5 vols., New York, 1917-1937.

———, Jay Cooke, Financier of the Civil War, 2 vols., Philadelphia, 1907.

O'Callaghan, E. B., ed., Documentary History of the State of New York, 4 vols., Albany, 1849-1851.

Ohio Early State and Local History, Tiffin, 1915.

Olcott, C. S., The Life of William McKinley, 2 vols., Boston, 1916.

Osgood, H. L., The American Colonies in the 17th Century, 3 vols., New York, 1904-1907.

———, The American Colonies in the Eighteenth Century, 4 vols., New York, 1924-1925.

Palmer, George Thomas, A Conscientious Turncoat, The Story of John M. Palmer, New Haven, 1941.

Parker, Robert Allerton, A Yankee Saint: John Humphrey Noyes and the Oneida Community, New York, 1935.

Parrington, Vernon Louis, Main Currents in American Thought, New York, 1927-1930.

Peck, H. T., Twenty Years of the Republic, 1885-1905, New York, 1906.

Perkins, Jacob R., Trails, Rails and War, The Life of General G. M. Dodge, Indianapolis, 1929.

Phelps, Mary M., Kate Chase, Dominant Daughter, New York, 1935.

Phelps, Noah A., History of Symsbury, Granby and Canton, from 1642 to 1845, Hartford, 1845.

Phelps, Oliver Seymour, and Andrew T. Servin, The Phelps Family in America and Their English Ancestors, 2 vols., Pittsfield, Massachusetts, 1899.

Platt, G. Louis, The Platt Lineage, New York, 1891.

Platt, T. C., Autobiography, New York, 1910.

Poore, Ben: Perley, Life of U. S. Grant, Philadelphia, New York, 1885.

Portrait and Biographical Record of the Scioto Valley, Ohio, Cincinnati, 1894.

Pringle, H. F., *The Life and Times of William Howard Taft*, 2 vols., New York, 1939.

———, *Theodore Roosevelt*, New York, 1931.

Randall, E. O., and D. J. Ryan, *History of Ohio*, 5 vols., New York, 1912.

Randall, J. G., *The Civil War and Reconstruction*, New York, 1937.

———, *Lincoln the President*, New York, 1945.

Reavis, L. U., *The Texas and Pacific Railway*, New York, 1878.

Record of Service of Connecticut Men in I, The War of the Revolution; II, War of 1812; III, Mexican War, comp. by authority of the General Assembly, Hartford, 1889.

Reed, S. G., *A History of the Texas Railroads*, Houston, 1941.

Reid, Whitelaw, *After the War: A Southern Tour*, Cincinnati, 1866.

———, *Ohio in the War*, 2 vols., Columbus, 1893.

Rhodes, J. F., *History of the United States from the Compromise of 1850*, 7 vols., New York, 1893-1906.

Richardson, Leon Burr, *William E. Chandler, Republican*, New York, 1940.

Rodabaugh, James H. and Mary Jane, *Nursing in Ohio, A History*, Columbus, 1951.

Rogers, Cameron, *Colonel Bob Ingersoll*, Garden City, New York, 1927.

Roll, Charles, *Colonel Dick Thompson, The Persistent Whig*, Indianapolis, 1948.

Rose, W. G., *Cleveland, The Making of a City*, Cleveland, 1950.

Roseboom, Eugene H., *The Civil War Era, 1850-1873*, Columbus, 1941.

Roseboom, Eugene H., and Francis Weisenburger, *History of Ohio* (ed. by J. H. Rodabaugh), Columbus, 1953.

Ross, E. D., *Liberal Republican Movement*, 1919.

Roster of Ohio Soldiers, 1861-1866.

Rusk, Ralph L., *The Life of Ralph Waldo Emerson*, New York, 1949.

Russell, A. P., *Thomas Corwin*, Cincinnati, 1881.

Russell, Charles E., *Blaine of Maine, His Life and Times*, New York, 1931.

Sabine, Lorenzo, *Biographical Sketches of Loyalists*, 2 vols., Boston, 1847.

Salamanca, Lucy, *Fortress of Freedom: The Story of the Library of Congress*, Philadelphia, 1942.

Sandburg, Carl, *Abraham Lincoln*, 6 vols., New York, 1926-1939.

Savage, James, *Genealogies of New England*, 4 vols., Boston, 1860-1862.

Schlesinger, Arthur M., *New Viewpoints in American History*, New York, 1926.

———, *Paths to the Present*, New York, 1949.

Schlesinger, Arthur M., Jr., *The Age of Jackson*, Boston, 1945.

Schouler, James, *History of the United States of America under the Constitution*, 6 vols., New York, 1880-1899.

———, *History of the United States*, 2 vols., New York, 1894-1913.

———, *Eighty Years of Union*, New York, 1913.

Schuckers, J. W., *The Life and Public Services of Salmon P. Chase*, New York, 1874.

Schurz, Carl, *Reminiscences*, 3 vols., New York, 1907-1908.

Seward, Frederick W., *Reminscences of a Wartime Statesman and Diplomat, 1830-1915*, New York, 1916.

Sheldon, Hezekiah Spencer, *Documentary History of Suffield in the Colony and Province of the Massachusetts Bay, in New England, 1660-1749.*

Sherman, John, *Recollections*, 2 vols., Chicago, New York, 1895.
Sherman, W. T., *Home Letters*, M. A. DeW. Howe, ed., New York, 1909.
Shores, Venila Levina, *The Hayes-Conkling Controversy*, New York, 1919.
Sibley, John Langdon, *Harvard Graduates*, 8 vols., Cambridge, 1873.
Siebert, Wilbur H., *The Underground Railroad from Slavery to Freedom*, New York, 1898.
Simkins, Francis Butler, *A History of the South*, New York, 1953.
Simkins, Francis Butler, and Robert H. Woody, *South Carolina During Reconstruction*, Chapel Hill, 1932.
Slade, William, ed., *Vermont State Papers*, Middlebury, 1823.
Smith, Chard Powers, *The Housatonic, Puritan River*, New York, 1946.
Smith, Joseph P., ed., *History of the Republican Party in Ohio*, 2 vols., Chicago, 1898.
Smith, Laura Chase, *Life of Philander Chase*, New York, 1903.
Smith, Theodore C., *The Life and Letters of James Abram Garfield*, 2 vols., New Haven, 1925.
Smith, William E., *The Francis Preston Blair Family in Politics*, New York, 1933.
Smith, William Henry, *A Political History of Slavery*, New York, 1903.
Smythe, George Franklin, *Kenyon College, Its First Century*, New Haven, 1924.
Spiller, R. E., et al., *Literary History of the United States*, 3 vols., New York, 1948.
Stanwood, Edward, *A History of the Presidency*, 2 vols., Boston, 1921.
Stevenson, Adlai E., *Something of Men I Have Known*, Chicago, 1909.
Stiles, Ezra, *A History of Three of the Judges of King Charles I*, New Haven, 1794.
Stiles, Henry Reed, *History of Ancient Wethersfield*.
———, *History and Genealogies of Ancient Windsor, Connecticut*, Albany, 1863.
Stilwell, Lewis D., *Migration from Vermont*, Montpelier, 1948.
Stoddard, William O., *Hayes, Garfield, Arthur*, New York, 1889.
Stone, Irving, *They Also Ran*, New York, 1951.
Storey, Moorfield, with E. W. Emerson, *Ebenezer Rockwood Hoar*, Boston, 1911.
Stryker, L. P., *Andrew Johnson, A Study in Courage*, New York, 1929.
Suppressed Book About Slavery, New York, 1864.
Swisher, C. B., *Stephen J. Field*, Washington, 1930.
Taft, Mrs. William Howard, *Recollections of Full Years*, New York, 1914.
Tansill, Charles C., *The Congressional Career of Thomas Francis Bayard, 1868-1885*, Washington, 1946.
———, *The Foreign Policy of Thomas F. Bayard*, Washington, 1940.
Tarbell, Ida, *The Nationalizing of Business, 1878-1898*, New York, 1936.
Taylor, Walter F., *The Economic Novel in America*, Chapel Hill, 1942.
Thompson C. Mildred, *Reconstruction in Georgia, Economic, Social, Political, 1866-1872*, New York, 1915.
Thompson, Slason, *Life of Eugene Field*, New York, 1927.
Thorndike, Rachel Sherman, *The Sherman Letters*, New York, 1894.
Timmons, Bascom N., ed., *Charles G. Dawes, A Journal of the McKinley Years*, New York, 1953.

Tourgee, Albion Winegar, *A Fool's Errand*, New York, 1879.

Trowbridge, J. T., *The South*, Boston, 1866.

Trowbridge, F. B., *The Trowbridge Genealogy*, New Haven, 1908.

Trumbull, Benjamin, *A Complete History of Connecticut*, 2 vols., New London, 1898.

Turner, O., *Pioneer History of the Holland Purchase of Western New York*, Buffalo, 1849.

Twain, Mark, *Letters*, A. B. Paine, ed., 2 vols., New York, 1917.

Van Deusen, G. G., *Life of Henry Clay*, Boston, 1937.

Villard, Oswald Garrison, *John Brown*, New York, 1943.

Von Abele, Rudolph, *Alexander H. Stephens*, New York, 1946.

Walker, Cornelius, *Life and Correspondence of William Sparrow D.D..* Philadephia, 1876.

Warden, R. B., *Life of Salmon P. Chase*, Cincinnati, 1874.

Warren, Charles, *The Supreme Court in United States History*, 2 vols., Boston, 1937.

Watterson, Henry, *"Marse Henry": An Autobiography*, 2 vols., New York, 1919.

Wecter, Dixon, *Sam Clemens of Hannibal*, Boston, 1952.

Weisenburger, F. B., *John McLean, A Politician on the U. S. Supreme Court*, Columbus, 1937.

Welker, Martin, *Farm Life in Central Ohio Sixty Years Ago,* Wooster, Ohio, 1892.

Welles, Gideon, *Diary*, 3 vols., Boston, 1911.

Western Reserve Historical Society, *Tracts*, Cleveland.

White, Andrew D., *Autobiography*, 2 vols., New York, 1905.

White, Horace, *The Life of Lyman Trumbull*, Boston, 1913.

William Lloyd Garrison, 1805-1879, The Story of His Life Told by His Children, 4 vols., New York, 1885-1889.

Williams, Charles R., ed., *Diary and Letters of Rutherford Birchard Hayes*, 5 vols., Columbus, 1922-1926.

————, *The Life of Rutherford Birchard Hayes*, 2 vols., Boston, 1914.

Williams, C. S., *Cincinnati Directory, City Guide and Business Mirror for 1858*, Cincinnati, 1858.

Williamson, Chilton, *Vermont in Quandary, 1763-1825*, Montpelier, 1949.

Wilson, Henry, *History of the Rise and Fall of the Slave Power in America*, 3 vols., Boston, 1872-1877.

Wilson, Robert Forrest, *Crusader in Crinoline, The Life of Harriet Beecher Stowe*, Philadelphia, 1941.

Wister, Owen, *Ulysses S. Grant and the Seven Ages of Washington*, New York, 1928.

Wittke, Carl F., ed., *History of the State of Ohio*, 6 vols., Columbus, 1941-1944.

————, *Reformers of Revolution, German Forty-eighters in America*, 1952.

————, *We Who Built America, the Saga of the Immigrant*, New York, 1939.

Woodward, C. Vann, *Origins of the New South*, Boston, 1951.

————, *Reunion and Reaction, The Compromise of 1877 and the End of Reconstruction*, Boston, 1951.

————, *Tom Watson, Agrarian Rebel*, New York, 1938.

Articles and Pamphlets
(*OSAHQ refers to Ohio State Archaeological and Historical Quarterly*)

Pamphlets

"Birchard Library, 1874-1949," Fremont, 1949.

Bond, Frank Stuart, "Texas and Pacific Railway," Argument, January 29, 1878, House of Representatives, Washington, D. C., 1878.

Brinkerhoff, Roeliff, "Rutherford Birchard Hayes as a Philanthropist and Friend," Proceedings of the Congress of the National Prison Association in Chicago, June 7, 1893.

Chandler, William E., "Letters of Mr. William E. Chandler Relative to the So-called Southern Policy of President Hayes, Together With a Letter to Mr. Chandler of Mr. William Lloyd Garrison," Concord, 1878.

Davis, Mrs. John, "Lucy Webb Hayes, A Memorial Sketch for the Woman's Home Missionary Society," Cincinnati, 1889.

Field, David Dudley, "The Vote that Made the President," New York, 1877.

Garfield, James A., "Counting the Electoral Vote," Speech, January 25, 1877, Washington, 1877.

Gladden, Washington, "The Great Commoner of Ohio—Discourse in Memory of Rutherford Birchard Hayes," First Congregational Church, Columbus, Ohio, January 22, 1893.

Glidden, K. B., "Centennial Discourse," First Congregational Church, Mansfield Centre, Willimantic, Connecticut, July 1876.

Green, James A., "The Literary Club and Cincinnati in 1849," Paper read October 12, 1931, Cincinnati.

Grout, Lewis, "A discourse on the early history of the Congregational Church in West Brattleboro, Vermont," Brattleboro, 1877.

Hadley, Elbridge D., "Cedar Creek—Popular History Refuted," A paper read before the Military Order of the Loyal Legion of the United States, Des Moines, 1898.

Halstead, Murat, "The War Claims of the South," An address at Cooper Institute, October 25, 1876.

"History of the Wilmington Reunion, 1876," Brattleboro, Vermont, 1876.

Holy, T. C., et al., "Survey of the Ohio Soldiers' and Sailors' Orphans' Home," Ohio State University, 1938.

Johnston, John W., "The True Southern Pacific Railroad vs. Texas Pacific Railroad," Speech in Senate, June 5, 1878, Washington, 1878.

Johnston, William, "Speeches on Life of Rutherford B. Hayes," Lebanon, Ohio, 1876.

Keeler, Lucy E., "Centenary celebration of the birth of Rutherford Birchard Hayes, at Spiegel Grove, Fremont, O., October 4, 1922," Columbus, 1923.

Lamar, Lucius Q. C., "The Texas Pacific Railroad," Speech in Senate, May 22, 1878, Washington, 1878.

Literary Club of Cincinnati, "Literary Club of Cincinnati, 1849-1949," Cincinnati, 1949.

Marchman, Watt P., "The Hayes Memorial, The Library and Museum, Spiegel Grove, the Hayes Homestead," Columbus, 1950.

"Mayor's Annual Report, Cincinnati, Year Ending April 10, 1861," Cincinnati, 1861.

Metzmann, Gustav, "Cincinnati and Ohio, Their Early Railroads," New York, 1948.

Military Order of the Loyal Legion, "Proceedings."

Newton, A., "Sketch of the Life and Character of Ebenezer Lane, LL. D.," Norwalk, Ohio, N.D.

"Peabody Fund Reports."

Pitezel, J. H., "History of the Methodist Episcopal Church of Norwalk, Ohio, and the Norwalk Seminary," Norwalk, Ohio, 1888.

Platt, Cyrus, "History of St. Peter's Protestant Episcopal Church, Delaware, Ohio," 1880.

Scott, Thomas A., "The Texas and Pacific Railway," Argument in Senate, February 7, 1878, Washington, 1878.

"Slater Fund Reports."

Throckmorton, James W., "Texas and Pacific Railway," Speech in House, March 1, 1877, Washington, 1877.

Wines, Frederick Howard, "Memorial address in honor of General Rutherford B. Hayes, Chicago, June 12, 1893," Chicago, 1893.

Articles

Bailey, Louis J., "Caleb Blood Smith," *Indiana Magazine of History*, XXXIX, No. 3 (September 1933).

Barber, George, "One of Ohio's Six Presidents and His Religious Convictions," *Zion's Herald*, August 18, 1920

Barkdull, Ed S., "Hayes at Kenyon," Cleveland *Leader*, January 22, 1893.

Brown, Wenzell, "Hayes, The Forgotten President," *American Mercury*, February 1949.

Clonts, Forrest W., "The Political Campaign of 1875 in Ohio," *OSAHQ*, XXXI, 1922.

Cox, Jacob Dolson, "The Hayes Administration," *The Atlantic Monthly*, June 1893.

———, "Why the Men of '61 Fought for the Union," *The Atlantic Monthly*, March 1892.

"Ebenezer Lane," *Ohio State Bar Association Proceedings*, I-IV.

Farmer, John, "Memoirs of Ministers Who Have Been Graduated at Harvard College," *American Quarterly Register*.

Farnum, George R., "Rutherford B. Hayes in War and Peace," *American Bar Association Journal*, August 1943.

Garrison, Curtis W., "Conversations with Hayes: A Biographer's Notes," *Mississippi Valley Historical Review*, XXV, No. 3 (December 1938).

———, "President Hayes: The Opponent of Prohibition," *Historical Society of Northwestern Ohio*, July-October 1944.

———, "A President's Library," *OSAHQ*, v. 48, No. 2 (April 1939).

Granger, M. M., "Hayes, The Lawyer," *Kenyon Collegian*, XX, No. 3, 1893.

Guilday, Peter, "Gaetano Bedini, An Episode in the Life of Archbishop John Hughes," *Historical Records and Studies*, United States Catholic Historical Society, XXIII, 1933.

Halstead, Murat, "Recollections and Letters of President Hayes," *The Independent*, LI, February 9, 16, 1899.

Hampton, William J., "The Religion of Rutherford Birchard Hayes," *National Republican*, XXI, No. 7 (November 1933).

Hayes, Rutherford Platt, "The Age of Innocence in the White House," *Literary Digest*, February 5, 1929

Helfman, Harold M., "The Contested Confirmation of Stanley Matthews to the Supreme Court," *Bulletin of the Historical and Philosophical Society of Ohio*, July 1950.

Hirsch, Mark D., "Samuel J. Tilden: The Story of a Lost Opportunity," *American Historical Review*, LVI, No. 4 (July 1951).

House, Albert V., Jr., "President Hayes' Selection of David M. Key for Postmaster General," *Journal of Southern History*, IV, 1938.

Howe, George Frederick, "President Hayes's Notes of Four Cabinet Meetings," *American Historical Review*, XXXVII, No. 1 (October 1931).

"Industry Reviving Everywhere," [End of the Depression of 1873], New York *Daily Graphic*, November 8, 1879.

Johnson, Rossiter, "Turning Points in the Civil War," *Annual Report of the American Historical Association*, 1894.

Johnston, L. R., "Moral Insanity and Its Legal Relations," *American Psychological Journal*, I.

Keller, Kathryn Miller, "Just Before the World Came to an End: The Story of Thomas L. Hawkins," *Northwest Ohio Quarterly*, April 1948.

Lanning, John Tate, "The American Colonies in the Preliminaries of the War of Jenkins' Ear," *Georgia Historical Quarterly*, XI, No. 2 (June 1927).

"The Letter That Made Hayes President," *Chaperone Magazine*, March 1891.

McGrane, R. C., "Ohio and the Greenback Movement," *Mississippi Valley Historical Review*, XI, 1924-1925

Moore, M. H., "Ex-President Hayes—His Family in Vermont," Dubuque (Iowa) *Telegraph-Herald*, July 5, 1902.

Morris, Richard B., "Andrew Jackson, Strikebreaker," *American Historical Review*, LV, No. 1 (October 1949).

Mussey, Burrows, "Yankee Chills, Ohio Fever," *New England Quarterly*, XXII (December 1949).

Nichols, J. P., "Sherman and Silver Drive of 1877-78," *OSAHQ*, XLVI, 1937.

Northrup, Milton H., "A Grave Crisis in American History, The Inner History of the Origins and Formation of the Electoral Commission of 1877," *Century*, LXII, 1901.

Noyes, Edward, "The Ohio G. A. R. and Politics from 1866-90," *OSAHQ*, LV, 1946.

Noyes, John Humphrey, "Memoir of John Noyes," *The Dartmouth*, September 3, 20, 27, October 4, 1877.

Parker, Wyman W., "The College Reading of a President," *Library Quarterly*, XXI, No. 2 (April 1951).

———, "President Hayes's Graduation Speeches," *OSAHQ*, LXIII, No. 2 (April 1954).

Parry, George M., "A Century of Cabinet Ministers," *Magazine of History*, XXIII.

Quinn, J. J., "Homicidal Insanity—The Case of Nancy Farrer," *The Western Lancet*, XVI (November 1855).

Reeve, James K., "The Homes of Hayes and Garfield," *The American Garden*, v. 12, No. 4 (April 1891).

Rezneck, Samuel, "The Depression of 1819-1822, A Social History," *The American Historical Review*, XXXIX (October 1933).

Richardson, Lyon Norman, "What Rutherford B. Hayes Liked in Emerson," *American Literature*, v. 17, No. 1 (March 1945).

Rodabaugh, James H., "The Negro in Ohio," *Journal of Negro History*, XXXI, 1946.

Round, William M. F., "Ex-President Rutherford B. Hayes," *The Charities Review*, February 1893.

Roseboom, Eugene H., "Salmon P. Chase and the Know Nothings," *Mississippi Valley Historical Review*, XXV, No. 3 (December 1938).

Smith, Martha Votey, "The Hayes House," *The Vermonter*, 1924.

"The Tafts of Cincinnati," *Life* Magazine, May 26, 1952.

Trowbridge, Thomas R., Jr., "Ancient Houses of New Haven," *Papers of the New Haven Colony Historical Society*.

Van Sickle, C. E., and James T. May, "The Birthplace of President Hayes: A Study in Oral Tradition," *OSAHQ*, v. 61, No. 2 (April 1952).

Vigilante, S. L., "Eighteen-Hundred-and-Froze-to-Death: The Cold Summer of 1816 and Westward Migration from New England," *Bulletin of the New York Public Library*, LII (September 1948).

Watterson, Henry, "The Hayes-Tilden Contest for the Presidency," *Century*, May 1913.

Wheatley, R., "The New York Customhouse," *Harper's New Monthly*, June 1884.

Winkler, E. W., ed., "The Hayes-Bryan Correspondence," *Southwestern Historical Quarterly*, XXV-XXX, 1920-1926.

Wright, Marion Thompson, "Negro Suffrage in New Jersey, 1776-1875," *Journal of Negro History*, XXXIII, No. 2 (April 1948).

Government Documents and Legal Reports

"The Bible in the Public Schools," Robert Clarke & Co., Cincinnati, 1870.

Ex Parte H. H. Robinson, Marshal of the U. S., 6th McClean's Reports, Circuit Court of the U. S., April term, 1855.

Hayes, Rutherford B., Brief for Corwine, Rogers and Hayes in "Liquor Cases," Ohio Supreme Court, December term, 1854, in HML.

——, "City Solicitor's Annual Report, February 23, 1860, R. B. Hayes, City Solicitor," presented to the City Council, Cincinnati.

House Misc. Doc. No. 13, 44th Congress, 2nd Session, "Proceedings and Debates of Congress Relating to Counting the Electoral Votes for President and Vice President of the United States."

House Misc. Doc. No. 31, 45th Congress, 3rd Session, "Presidential Election Investigation, 1878-79," 4 vols. (Potter Investigation Testimony).

House Misc. Doc. No. 34, 44th Congress, 2nd Session, "Testimony Taken by the Select Committee on the Recent Election in the State of Louisiana."

House Report No. 140, 45th Congress, 3rd Session, "Investigation of Alleged Electoral Frauds in the Late Presidential Election" (Potter Committee *Report*).

House Report No. 261, 43rd Congress, 2nd Session.

Indictment and Finding in the Matter of Nathaniel Austin, et al. (Shays' Rebellion). At the Supreme Judicial Court Begun and Holden at Great Barrington within and for the County of Berkshire on the Third Tuesday of March in the Year of Our Lord, 1787, 1787 volume, 58ff., Supreme Judicial Court, Boston.

"Proceedings of the Electoral Commission, Count of the Presidential Vote, 1877," Washington, 1877.

Senate Exec. Doc. No. 2, 44th Congress, 2nd Session, "Message from the President" (Grant).

Senate Misc. Doc. No. 44, 44th Congress, 2nd Session, "Electoral Vote of Certain States—Testimony Before the Sub-committee of the Committee on Privileges and Elections."

Senate Report No. 611, 44th Congress, 2nd Session, "Report of the Senate Committee on Privileges and Elections With Testimony and Evidence on the Election in the State of Florida in 1876."

Senate Report No. 678, 44th Congress, 2nd Session, "Electoral Vote of Oregon."

Senate Report No. 701, 44th Congress, 2nd Session, "Election in Louisiana in 1876."

"Trial of Thomas C. Anderson for Publishing Forged Election Returns," reported by T. Wharton Collins, 1878.

United States Supreme Court, "In Memoriam Stanley Matthews." Proceedings of the bench and bar of the Supreme Court of the U. S., Washington, 1889.

Unpublished Treatises

Adler, Selig F., "George F. Edmunds," Doctor's thesis, Ohio State University, 1936.

Cropko, Sister Mary Cornoth, "Religious Issues in Ohio Politics, 1875," Master's thesis, Xavier University, 1953.

Gray, Edgar Laughlin, "The Career of William Henry Smith, Politician-Journalist," Doctor's thesis, Ohio State University, 1950.

Gunn, Stanley F., "Oliver Cowdery, Second Elder of the Church," Master's thesis, Brigham Young University, 1943.

Hare, John S., "Allen Thurman," Doctor's thesis, Ohio State University, 1933.

Krebs, Frank John, "Hayes and the South," Doctor's thesis, Ohio State University, 1950.

Palmer, Upton S., "An Historical and Critical Study of the Speeches of Rutherford B. Hayes," Doctor's thesis, University of Michigan, 1950.

Warren, Joseph Parker, "The Shays Rebellion," Doctor's thesis, Harvard University, 1902.

Newspapers and Magazines

The Atlantic Monthly
Brattleboro Reformer
Brattleboro Reporter
Century
Chicago Daily News
Chicago Inter-Ocean
Chicago Times

Chicago *Tribune*
Cincinnati *Enquirer*
Cincinnati *Gazette*
Cincinnati *Leader*
Cleveland *Plain Dealer*
Columbus *Dispatch*
Congressional Globe
Congressional Record
Delaware (Ohio) *Gazette*
Fostoria (Ohio) *Review*
Fremont *Democratic Messenger*
Fremont *Journal*
Fremont *News*
Fremont *News-Messenger*
Harper's New Monthly
Harper's Weekly
The *Independent*
The *Liberator*
Louisville *Courier-Journal*
Lower Sandusky *Telegraph*
Massachusetts *Centinel*
Massachusetts *Independent Chronicle and Advertiser*
The Nation
New Orleans *Item*
New Orleans *Times*
New York *Herald*
New York *Illustrated Graphic*
New York *Sun*
New York *Times*
New York *Tribune*
Ohio State *Journal*
The *Portfolio*
Toledo *Blade*
Vermont *Phoenix* (Brattleboro)
Washington *Capital*
Windsor (Vermont) *Washingtonian*

ACKNOWLEDGMENTS

Except for those which are ex parte, as my lawyer friends say, or "think pieces," as my former newspaper colleagues put it, all biographies represent a putting together of material previously set down by others. In a work like this the author, indeed, often is no more than a collator, though responsible for what he picks and how he collates.

In acknowledging this, it is a problem to know where to begin and where to stop, not only in the matter of literary works from which I have profited or quoted, but also other assistance more personal. I am indebted, for example, to Cotton Mather, among others, for the writing he did two and a half centuries ago that helped to give insight, I think, into the minds of the early members of the Hayes-Smith-Austin-Birchard clan. And also I am indebted, though not equally, to my wife, Ruth, of the Eisenstat-Loeffler clan, for much help that sustained me and kept me at this task, including wise, wifely discussion of problems which needed a woman's understanding as well as skepticism. If not for the compiler of *The Records of the Congregational Church of Suffield, Connecticut,* as another example, I could not have found out precisely when the Old Captain, Daniel Austin, great-great-grandfather of Hayes became and then left off being a "visible saint," a detail, but one of the many that helped me to re-create, to an extent, the life of this Connecticut River Valley ancestor who to me became important as a symbol of Haye's forebears as well as of the America of the past that Hayes linked with his own time and our own. Then too, without my friends, Alfred and Esther Solomon, I would not have been able to interpret such, and more important, details with whatever psychological correctness has been managed. Even my son, Davey, now six, born precisely as this new life of Hayes was coming into being, helped in his fashion, as did Buddy and Judy, and Karen, in their fashion, and Regina and Joseph Eisenstat.

It goes without saying that this biography owes debts to the earlier biographers of Hayes—Charles R. Williams, son-in-law of Hayes's friend, William Henry Smith; and H. J. Eckenrode, with his helper, Pocahontas Wright; and also, for their "campaign" lives, William Dean Howells, Russell Conwell and J. Q. Howard. Their viewpoints are not, in many cases, mine. But I considered theirs and used them profitably, if, in some cases, with caution. In the reference notes and in the bibliography are cited their and many other published works, though not all, that I have used. To list all might make a book in itself.

Hayes's was a prolific period for reminiscences, diaries, biographies, letters— and Congressional reports. Especially was this true of the Civil War time and its aftermath, including reconstruction. So many of the leading actors had so much to say, to explain, as well as to explain away, that I make no claim to having used or digested it all. But I think that the main ones, as of now, are represented.

I feel a special debt, however, to certain authors for material about Hayes specifically, or for background illumination. This list should include Charles Wells Hayes for his genealogical treatise on the Hayes clan; and, importantly, among newer historical and biographical writings, C. Vann Woodward, especially for his *Reunion and Reaction* and his *Origins of the New South;*

Francis Butler Simkins for his *A History of the South;* Alexander Flick for his *Tilden;* Leon Burr Richardson, for his *William E. Chandler;* William B. Hesseltine for his *Grant;* Arthur M. Schlesinger, Sr., for his various works; Carl Wittke for the six-volume *History of Ohio* which he edited, and the various authors represented therein, especially Francis Weisenburger and Philip Jordan; Richard McGrane for his *William Allen;* Arthur N. Holcombe for his *The Middle Classes in American Politics;* W. E. Binkley for his studies on the Presidency; Claude G. Bowers for his *The Tragic Era;* W. E. B. DuBois for his *Black Reconstruction* and his more personal works on the Negro problem; Gunnar Myrdal, Ralph Bunche and others for *An American Dilemma;* Matthew Josephson especially for his *The Politicos* and *The Robber Barons;* Carl Sandburg (naturally) for the Lincolnian background; as well as Avery O. Craven and James G. Randall for Civil War and Reconstruction studies; and Richard Hofstadter for what I deem a classic in over-all historical interpretation, *The American Political Tradition and Those Who Made It.* Everyone in nearly every field of American history is sooner or later indebted to Allan Nevins, and I am no exception, especially for his biographies that pertain to Hayes and the Hayes period. I owe also a special debt for general enlightenment on the period to Charles A. and Mary Beard, for their *Rise of American Civilization,* and to Vernon L. Parrington for his *Main Currents of American Thought,* this perceptive study corrected, I think, by the writings of Alfred Kazin, Merle Curti, Ralph H. Gabriel, Louis M. Hacker and Oscar Cargill.

It was my fortune to have had some talks with RBH's daughter, Frances (Fanny) Hayes, a few months before she died in 1950. She was eighty-three years old when I saw her at her home in Maine, but her faculties were still keen and from her I received some good and sharp impressions about her father, also some good anecdotes. One I probably should have included but did not. This was that one of the first things RBH did on finally getting out of uniform, after four years of fighting in the Civil War, was "to go on a toot" in Cincinnati. That in itself, she felt (and I agreed), gives a very different picture of him from what is usually presented.

To R. B. Hayes himself I owe the greatest debt of all. From the time he was a boy he saved almost all letters written to him, and his sons collected many that he wrote, especially to his mother, his sister and his uncle. He also kept a diary from youth, and it was from it and his letters, as well as letters of his family, that I was able to reconstruct his personal life. Counting his letters, his mother's, his sister's, his uncle's, his wife's and his children's, as well as diaries of some of them, this collection of personal material is more complete, I think, than exists for any other comparable American. The collection is such as to make possible as intimate a portrait of a prominent American, on a documentable basis, as might be imagined, an aspect that peculiarly attracted me as biographer. Especially am I indebted to RBH for having saved in a bound volume some 200 letters written to nim by his beloved sister, these having showed up, thanks to her grandson, Grant Mitcnell, almost miraculously, I felt, after having been "lost," precisely at the time when I became convinced that his sister and his relationsnip to her formed a major key to his character and career.

This brings me to a large indebtedness I owe to the Hayes Memorial Library at Fremont, Ohio, for its co-operation without any reservations. This co-operation made it possible for me to use conveniently all of the Hayes papers.

as well as other materials. Naturally, too, I am indebted to the late Colonel Webb C. Hayes I, second son of RBH, who, with his wife, established the Library in memory of President and Mrs. Hayes. There at Spiegel Grove is a great collection, not only of Hayes material, but other material on the period, and I recommend the library to other students. The director, Watt P. Marchman, who has built up the collection considerably in recent years, was especially helpful to me. He was indefatigable in hunting up items that I wanted, and co-operated in other ways, always with the spirit of objectivity that all researchers must appreciate. Historians in the Hayes period generally will always owe a large debt to Watt Marchman for his expert work at the Hayes Library.

I am indebted, too, for personal aid from James H. Rodabaugh, editor and head of the division of history and science of the Ohio Historical Society, formerly known as the Ohio Archaeological and Historical Society, at Columbus.

A number of historians, writers and librarians around the country, as well as various other individuals, were uniformly courteous and helpful in assisting me to round up specific items, or answering questions, and I am glad to express thanks for such help from:

Leslie H. Adams, Wilmington, Vt.; Fanny K. Ahrens, Cleveland; Paul M. Angle, Chicago; John W. Apperson, Memphis; Earl Ash, Amsden, O.; Ruth Ballinger, Hayes Memorial Library, Fremont, O.; Ronald Barnard; Ewing C. Baskette, Illinois State Library; Judge A. V. Baumann, Fremont, O.; Mr. and Mrs. Hayes Bigelow, Brattleboro, Vt.; Katherine E. Brand, Library of Congress; Corrine Braswell, Memphis; Francis Breese, Missouri Historical Society, St. Louis; Clarence C. Brigham, American Antiquarian Society, Worcester, Mass.; Mrs. D. W. Brown, Romulus, N. Y.; Dr. Homer C. Bryant, Burlington, Vt.; A. T. Burch, Chicago; Alexina P. Burgess, Kent Memorial Library, Suffield, Conn.; Dr. Lewis E. Campbell, Delaware, O.; Wirt A. Cate, Nashville; C. M. Coffin, Gambier, O.; Jacob D. Cox, Cleveland; James M. Cox, Dayton; Alfred C. Coxe, New York; Edward J. Cronin, Boston; Norma Cuthbert, Henry E. Huntington Library, San Marino, Calif.;

George Daley, Brattleboro, Vt.; Jonathan Daniels, Raleigh, N. C.; Hal C. DeRan, Fremont, O.; Mrs. Frank C. DeWitt, Brattleboro, Vt.; Harrison S. Dimitt, Harvard Law School, Cambridge, Mass.; Shirley Dodds, Newberry Library, Chicago; Sally Dortch, Raleigh, N. C.; John Foster Dulles, Washington, D. C.; Rena Durkan, Amherst College, Amherst, Mass.; Florence Dyckman, Newberry Library, Chicago; Louis Filler, Antioch College, Yellow Springs, O.; Roy G. Fitzgerald, Dayton Public Library, Dayton; Clara E. Follette, Vermont Historical Society, Montpelier; William N. Foster, Conroe, Tex.; Julian S. Fowler, Oberlin College Library, Oberlin, O.; Elsa St. John Frisbie, Hill-Stead Museum, Farmington, Conn.; Rutherford Fullerton, Laguna Beach, Calif.; Mrs. George H. Gassett, East Putney, Vt.; Dr. Frank Glassman, Chicago; Mrs. Wallace Goldsmith, Ossining, N. Y.; Colin B. Goodykoontz, University of Colorado, Boulder; Roland Gray, Boston; James A. Green, Cincinnati; Hallie M. Grimes, Birchard Library, Fremont, O.;

Frederick Hale, Lake Wales, Fla.; Elna Hall, Simsbury Free Library, Simsbury, Conn.; William L. Halstead, Ann Arbor, Mich.; Ralph V. Harlow, Westbrook, Conn.; George N. Harman, Rutland, Vt.; Mrs. Paul V. Harper, Libertyville, Ill.; Elizabeth Hatfield, Public Library, Centerville, Ind.; Miss Hawkins, Geneva Public Library, Geneva, N. Y.; John B. Heffernan, U. S. Navy, Washington, D. C.; J. D. Hicks, University of California, Berkeley;

Edith C. Holmes, Town Clerk, Sheffield, Mass.; John Mead Howells, New York; Mildred Howells, Tryon, N. C.; Edward A. Hoyt, Montpelier, Vt.; Mary H. Humphrey, Simsbury, Conn.; Ethel L. Hutchins, Public Library, Cincinnati; Albert O. Jacobs, Denver; Edna L. Jacobson, New York State Library, Albany; James R. Joy, Methodist Historical Society, New York; Alfred Kamin, Chicago; S. R. Kamm, Wheaton College, Wheaton, Ill.; David Karno, Chicago; Annette Karr, Collection of Regional History, Cornell University, Ithaca, N. Y.; Evah Kincheloe, Hammond Library, Chicago; Willard L. King, Chicago; Sebastian Kletzky, Pueblo, Colo.;

Wolcott G. Lane, Old Lyme, Conn.; John Tate Lanning, Duke University, Durham, N. C.; Henrietta M. Larson, Harvard University, Cambridge, Mass.; Dr. Sidney Case McCammon, Cincinnati; Rev. John McCullen, Fremont, O.; Arthur J. McLoughlin, Albany, N. Y.; Katherine Oakman MacVeagh, Santa Barbara, Calif.; Helen Taft Manning, Bryn Mawr College, Bryn Mawr, Pa.; Rev. Lloyd E. Marble, Wilmington, Vt.; T. S. Matthews, New York; Arthur E. Meyerhoff, Chicago; W. G. Meyers, Cuyahoga Falls, O.; Ballinger Mills, Galveston, Tex.; Bertram B. Moss, Chicago; Barrows Mussey, Duesseldorf, West Germany; Anna L. Nevins, New London, Conn.; Pierrepont B. Noyes, Oneida, N. Y.; Mary L. Pappas, Dalton Free Public Library, Dalton, Mass.; Wyman W. Parker, University of Cincinnati Librarian; Margaret Pierson, Indiana State Library, Indianapolis; Robert S. Platt, Chicago; Warren C. Platt, Cleveland; Harry E. Pratt, Illinois State Historical Library, Springfield;

Paul North Rice, New York Public Library; Stephen T. Riley, Massachusetts Historical Society, Boston; W. S. Rosecrans, Los Angeles; Gertrude Clark Ryon, Fairport, N. Y.; Rev. Charles Sanford, Wilmington, Vt.; Beatrice Schneiderman, Chicago; Karl Schriftgiesser, Londonderry, Vt.; Lucy M. Schulze, Mason Library, Great Barrington, Mass.; A. Hadley Shumway, Brattleboro, Vt.; Wilbur H. Siebert, Ohio State University, Columbus; Emma E. Sihler, Public Library, Adrian, Mich.; Barbara D. Simison, Yale University Library, New Haven; Mary B. Slade, Thetford, Vt.; Jesse F. Smith, Suffield Academy, Suffield, Conn.; William E. Smith, Miami University, Oxford, O.; Richard Snyder, Yellow Springs, O.; Edmund D. Soper, Leonard Theological College, Jubbulpore, C. P., India; Alfred Spencer, Bath, N. Y.; Katherine Garford Thomas, Elyria, O.;

Robert Thompson, Dallas, Tex.; Burt Tolhurst, Fremont, O.; Ronald Tree, New York; Elaine D. Trehub, Harvard University, Cambridge, Mass.; Charlotte Tripp, Davenport Library, Bath, N. Y.; Amelia Tschumy, Fremont, O.; Frederic F. Van de Water, Brattleboro, Vt.; Carl Vitz, Public Library, Cincinnati; Mary Wadsworth, Fremont, O.; Margery F. Waterman, Connecticut Historical Society, Hartford; Margaret H. Wick, Hudson, O.; Grace B. Wilcox, Library Association, Stockbridge, Mass.; Virginia R. Wing, Cleveland; Erwin C. Zepp, Ohio Historical Society, Columbus.

It goes without saying, though I wish to say it, that I am indebted also for much expert counsel and other services on the part of the staff of The Bobbs-Merrill Company. I gratefully acknowledge special debt in this regard to that amiable as well as firm and able editor, Harrison G. Platt, and of course, in common with so many authors, to that grand figure of publishing, who for fifty years has meant so much in the literary growth of Middle America especially, David Laurance Chambers.

Of course, for results of all this help I alone am responsible.

H.B.

INDEX

Abbott, Josiah G., 366
Abolitionism, 34
Adams, Charles Francis, 257, 258
Adams, Henry, 515
Adams, John Quincy, 24, 30, 34, 136
Agassiz, Louis, 135, 177
Allen, Ethan, 43, 46, 53, 134, 194
Allen, Sen. William, 128, 149, 262, 270, 273, 275, 281, 311
Allison, Sen. William D., 287, 344
Altgeld, John Peter, 462, 516
Ambos, Peter, 128
American Hotel, 128
American Party, *see* Know-Nothing Party
Anderson, Dick, 328
Anderson, James E. ("Scamp"), 305, 466, 470-471
Anderson, Col. T. C., 334, 440
Andrews, Lorin, 120
Angell, James B., 449
Annie Kilburn, Howells, 514
An-Se-Queg, 97
Anti-Masonic Party, 194
Anti-Nebraska Party, 193, 515
Arthur, Chester A., 8, 452, 455, 456, 492, 508
Ashley, James, 237
Athens, Ohio, 113
Atkinson, N. H., 50
Atlantic and Great Western Railroad, 257, 299
Atlantic Monthly, 310
Augur, Gen. C. C., 393, 420, 432
Austin, Abigail, 32, 41, 49, 53, 153
Austin, Daniel, 28, 32, 41-47, 48, 53, 65, 83, 114, 131, 159, 399, 511, 516, 518, 523
Austin, Linus, 24, 46, 522
Austin, Mrs. Linus, 522
Austin, Moses, 42
Austin, Nathaniel, 45, 46

Austin, Richard, 42
Austin, Sallena, 46
Austin, Stephen, 42, 114

Babcock, Gen. Orville, 344
Backus, Mrs. ———, 144
Backus, Rev. ———, 144
Bacon, Francis, 204
Baldwin, Henry, 34
Ball, Flamen, 173
Baltimore and Ohio R.R. strike, 445
Bancroft, Dyar, 78, 79
Bancroft, Sally Hayes, 78, 298
Bank of Norwalk, Ohio, 153
Banning, Henry B., 259
Barnum, P. T., 170
Barnum, Sen. William, 318
Battle of Breed's Hill (Bunker Hill), 57
Bayard, Thomas F., 339, 366, 469
Bedell, Bishop G. T., 504
Bedini, Cardinal, 202
Beecher, Henry Ward, 135, 204, 369, 448-449, 515
Beecher, Dr. Lyman, 34
Belknap, William Worth, 298
Bellepoint, Ohio, 77
Belmont, August, 313, 462
Ben Hur, Wallace, 326
Benjamin, Park, 169
Bennett, Steve, 29
Bigelow, Mary Hayes, 511, 512
Birchard, Arabella, 32, 49, 61
Birchard, Austin, 49, 58, 61, 77, 512
Birchard, Cynthia, 33, 58; *See also* Taylor, Cynthia
Birchard, Drusilla, 41, 43, 48, 56, 58, 77
Birchard, Elias, 57
Birchard, Jedediah, 43
Birchard, John, 158

593

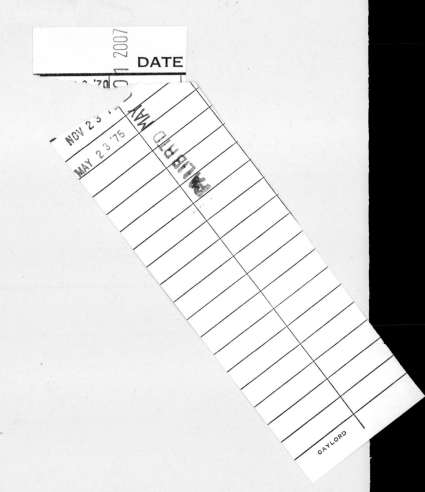